THE NARROW CORRIDOR

Also by Daron Acemoglu and James A. Robinson

Why Nations Fail

Economic Origins of Dictatorship and Democracy

THE NARROW CORRIDOR

States, Societies, and
the Fate of Liberty

DARON ACEMOGLU
AND JAMES A. ROBINSON

PENGUIN PRESS
NEW YORK
2019

PENGUIN PRESS
An imprint of Penguin Random House LLC
penguinrandomhouse.com

Page 542 constitutes an extension of this copyright page.
Picture research by Toby Greenberg
Maps prepared by Carlos Molina and Jose Ignacio Velarde Morales

LIBRARY OF CONGRESS CATALOGING-IN-PUBLICATION DATA
Names: Acemoglu, Daron, author. | Robinson, James A., 1960– author.
Title: The narrow corridor: states, societies, and the fate of liberty /
Daron Acemoglu and James A. Robinson.
Description: New York : Penguin Press, 2019. | Includes bibliographical references and index.
Identifiers: LCCN 2019009146 (print) | LCCN 2019981140 (ebook) |
ISBN 9780735224384 (hardcover) | ISBN 9780735224391 (ebook) |
ISBN 9781984879189 (international/export)
Subjects: LCSH: Liberty. | State, The. | Power (Social sciences)—Political aspects. |
Direct democracy. | Decentralization in government. | Executive power. |
Violence—Political aspects.
Classification: LCC JC585 .A188 2019 (print) | LCC JC585 (ebook) | DDC 320.01/1—dc23
LC record available at https://lccn.loc.gov/2019009146
LC ebook record available at https://lccn.loc.gov/2019981140

Printed in the United States of America
1   3   5   7   9   10   8   6   4   2

Designed by Daniel Lagin

To Arda and Aras, even if this is much less than I owe you.   —DA

Para Adrián y Tulio. Para mí el pasado, para ustedes el futuro.   —JR

CONTENTS

Liberty

This book is about liberty, and how and why human societies have achieved or failed to achieve it. It is also about the consequences of this, especially for prosperity. Our definition follows the English philosopher John Locke, who argued that people have liberty when they have

> perfect freedom to order their actions and dispose of their possessions
> and persons, as they think fit . . . without asking leave, or depending
> upon the will of any other man.

Liberty in this sense is a basic aspiration of all human beings. Locke emphasized that

> no one ought to harm another in his life, health, liberty, or possessions.

Yet it is clear that liberty has been rare in history and is rare today. Every year millions of people in the Middle East, Africa, Asia, and Central America flee their homes and risk life and limb in the process, not because they are seeking higher incomes or greater material comfort, but because they are trying to protect themselves and their families from violence and fear.

Philosophers have proposed many definitions of liberty. But at the most fundamental level, as Locke recognized, liberty must start with people being free from violence, intimidation, and other demeaning acts. People must be able to make free choices about their lives and have the means to carry them out without the menace of unreasonable punishment or draconian social sanctions.

All the Evil in the World

In January 2011 in the Hareeqa market in the old city of Damascus, Syria, a spontaneous protest took place against the despotic regime of Bashar al-Assad. Soon afterward in the southern city of Daraa some children wrote "The people want the fall of the government" on a wall. They were arrested and tortured. A crowd gathered to demand their release, and two people were killed by the police. A mass demonstration erupted that soon spread throughout the country. A lot of the people, it turned out, did want the government to fall. A civil war soon broke out. The state, its military, and its security forces duly disappeared from much of the country. But instead of liberty, Syrians ended up with civil war and uncontrolled violence.

Adam, a media organizer in Latakia, reflected on what happened next:

We thought we'd get a present, and what we got was all the evil in the world.

Husayn, a playwright from Aleppo, summed it up:

We never expected that these dark groups would come into Syria—the ones that have taken over the game now.

Foremost among these "dark groups" was the so-called Islamic State, or what was then known as ISIS, which aimed to create a new "Islamic caliphate." In 2014, ISIS took control of the major Syrian city of Raqqa. On the other side of the border in Iraq, they captured the cities of Fallujah, Ramadi, and the historic city of Mosul with its 1.5 million inhabitants. ISIS and many other armed groups filled the stateless void left by the collapse of the Syrian and Iraqi governments with unimaginable cruelty. Beatings, beheadings, and mutilations became commonplace. Abu Firas, a fighter with the Free Syrian Army, described the "new normal" in Syria:

It's been so long since I heard that someone died from natural causes. In the beginning, one or two people would get killed. Then twenty. Then fifty. Then it became normal. If we lost fifty people, we thought, "Thank God, it's only fifty!" I can't sleep without the sound of bombs or bullets. It's like something is missing.

Amin, a physical therapist from Aleppo, remembered:

One of the other guys called his girlfriend and said "Sweetheart, I'm out of minutes on my phone. I'll call you back on Amin's phone." After a while she called asking about him, and I told her he'd been killed. She cried and my friends said, "Why did you tell her that?" I said, "Because that's what happened. It's normal. He died." . . . I'd open my phone and look at my contacts and only one or two were still alive. They told us, "If someone dies, don't delete his number. Just change his name to Martyr." . . . So I'd open my contact list and it was all Martyr, Martyr, Martyr.

The collapse of the Syrian state created a humanitarian disaster of enormous proportions. Out of a population of about 18 million before the war, as many as 500,000 Syrians are estimated to have lost their lives. Over 6 million have been internally displaced and 5 million have fled the country and are currently living as refugees.

The Gilgamesh Problem

The calamity unleashed by the collapse of the Syrian state is not surprising. Philosophers and social scientists have long maintained that you need a state to resolve conflicts, enforce laws, and contain violence. As Locke puts it:

Where there is no law there is no freedom.

Yet Syrians had started protesting to gain some freedoms from Assad's autocratic regime. As Adam ruefully recalled:

Ironically, we went out in demonstrations to eradicate corruption and criminal behavior and evil and hurting people. And we've ended up with results that hurt many more people.

Syrians like Adam were grappling with a problem so endemic to human society that it is a theme of one of the oldest surviving pieces of written text, the 4,200-year-old Sumerian tablets that record the Epic of Gilgamesh. Gilgamesh was the king of Uruk, perhaps the world's first city, situated on a now dried-up channel of the Euphrates River in the south of modern-day Iraq. The epic tells us that Gilgamesh created a remarkable city, flourishing with commerce and public services for its inhabitants:

> See how its ramparts gleam like copper in the sun. Climb the stone staircase . . . walk on the wall of Uruk, follow its course around the city, inspect its mighty foundations, examine its brickwork, how masterfully it is built, observe the land it encloses . . . the glorious palaces and temples, the shops and marketplaces, the houses, the public squares.

But there was a hitch:

> Who is like Gilgamesh? . . . The city is his possession, he struts through it, arrogant, his head raised high, trampling its citizens like a wild bull. He is king, he does whatever he wants, takes the son from his father and crushes him, takes the girl from her mother and uses her . . . no one dares to oppose him.

Gilgamesh was out of control. A bit like Assad in Syria. In despair the people "cried out to heaven" to Anu, the god of the sky and the chief deity in the Sumerian pantheon of gods. They pleaded:

> Heavenly father, Gilgamesh . . . has exceeded all bounds. The people suffer from his tyranny . . . Is this how you want your king to rule? Should a shepherd savage his own flock?

Anu paid attention and asked Aruru, mother of creation, to

> create a double for Gilgamesh, his second self, a man who equals his strength and courage, a man who equals his stormy heart. Create a new hero, let them balance each other perfectly, so that Uruk has peace.

Anu thus came up with a solution to what we'll call the "Gilgamesh problem"— controlling the authority and the power of a state so that you get the good things and not the bad. Anu's was the doppelgänger solution, similar to what people today call "checks and balances." Gilgamesh's double Enkidu would contain him. James Madison, one of the founding fathers of the U.S. system of government, would have sympathized. He would argue 4,000 years later that constitutions must be designed so that "ambition must be made to counteract ambition."

Gilgamesh's first encounter with his double came when he was about to ravish a new bride. Enkidu blocked the doorway. They fought. Although Gilgamesh ultimately prevailed, his unrivaled, despotic power was gone. The seeds of liberty in Uruk?

Unfortunately not. Checks and balances parachuted from above don't work in general, and they didn't in Uruk. Soon Gilgamesh and Enkidu started to conspire. As the epic records it:

> They embraced and kissed. They held hands like brothers. They walked
> side by side. They became true friends.

They subsequently colluded to kill the monster Humbaba, the guardian of the great cedar forest of Lebanon. When the gods sent the Bull of Heaven to punish them, they combined forces to kill it. The prospect for liberty vanished along with the checks and balances.

If not from a state hemmed in by doppelgängers and checks and balances, where does liberty come from? Not from Assad's regime. Clearly not from the anarchy that followed the collapse of the Syrian state.

Our answer is simple: Liberty needs the state and the laws. But it is not given by the state or the elites controlling it. It is taken by regular people, by society. Society needs to control the state so that it protects and promotes people's liberty rather than quashing it like Assad did in Syria before 2011. Liberty needs a mobilized society that participates in politics, protests when it's necessary, and votes the government out of power when it can.

The Narrow Corridor to Liberty

Our argument in this book is that for liberty to emerge and flourish, both state and society must be strong. A strong state is needed to control violence, enforce laws, and provide public services that are critical for a life in which people are empowered to make and pursue their choices. A strong, mobilized society is needed to control and shackle the strong state. Doppelgänger solutions and checks and balances don't solve the Gilgamesh problem because, without society's vigilance, constitutions and guarantees are not worth much more than the parchment they are written on.

Squeezed between the fear and repression wrought by despotic states and the violence and lawlessness that emerge in their absence is a narrow corridor to liberty. It is in this corridor that the state and society balance each other out. This balance is not about a revolutionary moment. It's a constant, day-in, day-out struggle between the two. This struggle brings benefits. In the corridor the state and society do not just compete, they also cooperate. This cooperation engenders greater capacity for the state to deliver the things that society wants and foments greater societal mobilization to monitor this capacity.

What makes this a corridor, not a door, is that achieving liberty is a process; you have to travel a long way in the corridor before violence is brought under control, laws are written and enforced, and the state starts providing services to its citizens. It is a process because the state and its elites must learn to live with the shackles society puts on them and different segments of society have to learn to work together despite their differences.

What makes this corridor narrow is that this is no easy feat. How can you contain a state that has a huge bureaucracy, a powerful military, and the freedom to decide what the law is? How can you ensure that as the state is called on to take on more responsibilities in a complex world, it will remain tame and under control? How can you keep society working together rather than turning against itself, riven with divisions? How do you prevent all of this from flipping into a zero-sum contest? Not easy at all, and that's why the corridor is narrow, and societies enter and depart from it with far-reaching consequences.

You can't engineer any of this. Not that very many leaders, left to their own devices, would really try to engineer liberty. When the state and its elites are too powerful and society is meek, why would leaders grant people rights and liberty? And if they did, could you trust them to stick to their word?

You can see the origins of liberty in the history of women's liberation from the days of Gilgamesh right down to our own. How did society move from a situation where, as the epic has it, "every girl's hymen . . . belonged to him," to one where women have rights (well, in some places anyway)? Could it be that these rights were granted by men? The United Arab Emirates, for instance, has a Gender Balance Council formed in 2015 by Sheikh Mohammed bin Rashid Al Maktoum, vice president and prime minister of the country and ruler of Dubai. It gives out gender equality awards every year for things like the "best government entity supporting gender balance," "best federal authority supporting gender balance," and "best gender balance initiative." The awards for 2018, given out by Sheikh Maktoum himself, all have one thing in common—every one went to a man! The problem with the United Arab Emirates' solution was that it was engineered by Sheikh Maktoum and imposed on society, without society's participation.

Contrast this with the more successful history of women's rights, for example, in Britain, where women's rights were not given but taken. Women formed a social movement and became known as the suffragettes. The suffragettes emerged out of the British Women's Social and Political Union, a women-only movement founded in 1903. They didn't wait for men to give them prizes for "best gender balance initiative." They mobilized. They engaged in direct action and civil disobedience. They bombed the summer house of the then chancellor of the exchequer and later prime minister, David Lloyd George. They chained themselves to railings outside the Houses of Parliament. They refused to pay their taxes and when they were sent to prison, they went on hunger strikes and had to be force-fed.

Emily Davison was a prominent member of the suffragette movement. On June 4, 1913, at the famous Epsom Derby horse race, Davison ran onto the track in front of Anmer, a horse belonging to King George V. Davison, according to some reports holding the purple, white, and green flag of the suffragettes, was hit by Anmer. The horse fell and crushed her, as the photograph included in the photo insert shows. Four days later Davison died from her injuries. Five years later women could vote in parliamentary elections. Women didn't get rights in Britain because of magnanimous grants by some (male) leaders. Gaining rights was a consequence of their organization and empowerment.

The story of women's liberation isn't unique or exceptional. Liberty almost always depends on society's mobilization and ability to hold its own against the state and its elites.

Chapter 1

HOW DOES HISTORY END?

A Coming Anarchy?

In 1989, Francis Fukuyama predicted the "end of history," with all countries converging to the political and economic institutions of the United States, what he called "an unabashed victory of economic and political liberalism." Just five years later Robert Kaplan painted a radically different picture of the future in his article "The Coming Anarchy." To illustrate the nature of this chaotic lawlessness and violence, he felt compelled to begin in West Africa:

> West Africa is becoming the symbol of [anarchy] . . . Disease, overpopulation, unprovoked crime, scarcity of resources, refugee migrations, the increasing erosion of nation-states and international borders, and the empowerment of private armies, security firms, and international drug cartels are now most tellingly demonstrated through a West African prism. West Africa provides an appropriate introduction to the issues, often extremely unpleasant to discuss, that will soon confront our civilization. To remap the political earth the way it will be a few decades hence . . . I find I must begin with West Africa.

In a 2018 article, "Why Technology Favors Tyranny," Yuval Noah Harari made yet another prediction about the future, arguing that advances in artificial intelligence are heralding the rise of "digital dictatorships," where governments will be able to monitor, control, and even dictate the way we interact, communicate, and think.

So history might still end, but in a very different way than Fukuyama had imagined. But how? The triumph of Fukuyama's vision of democracy, anarchy, or digital dictatorship? The Chinese state's increasing control over the Internet, the media, and the lives of ordinary Chinese might suggest that we are heading toward digital dictatorship, while the recent history of the Middle East and Africa reminds us that a future of anarchy is not so far-fetched.

But we need a systematic way to think about all of this. As Kaplan suggested, let's begin in Africa.

The Article 15 State

If you keep going east along the West African coast, the Gulf of Guinea eventually turns south and heads to Central Africa. Sailing past Equatorial Guinea, Gabon, and Pointe-Noire in Congo-Brazzaville, you arrive at the mouth of the river Congo, the entry point to the Democratic Republic of the Congo, a country that is often thought to be the epitome of anarchy. The Congolese have a joke: there have been six constitutions since the country gained its independence from Belgium in 1960, but they all have the same Article 15. The nineteenth-century French prime minister Charles-Maurice Talleyrand said that constitutions should be "short and obscure." Article 15 fulfills his dictum. It is short and obscure; it says simply *Débrouillez-vous* (Fend for yourself).

It's usual to think of a constitution as a document that lays out the responsibilities, duties, and rights of citizens and states. States are supposed to resolve conflicts among their citizens, protect them, and provide key public services such as education, healthcare, and infrastructure that individuals are not able to adequately provide on their own. A constitution isn't supposed to say *Débrouillez-vous*.

The reference to "Article 15" is a joke. There isn't such a clause in the Congolese Constitution. But it's apt. The Congolese have been fending for themselves at least since independence in 1960 (and things were even worse before). Their state has repeatedly failed to do any of the things it is supposed to do and is absent from vast swaths of the country. Courts, roads, health clinics, and schools are moribund in most of the country. Murder, theft, extortion, and intimidation are commonplace. During the Great War of Africa that raged in the Congo between 1998 and 2003, the lives of most Congolese, already wretched, turned into a veritable hell.

Possibly five million people perished; they were murdered, died of disease, or starved to death.

Even during times of peace the Congolese state has failed to uphold the actual clauses of the constitution. Article 16 states:

> All persons have the right to life, physical integrity and to the free development of their personality, while respecting the law, public order, the rights of others and public morality.

But much of the Kivu region, in the east of the country, is still controlled by rebel groups and warlords who plunder, harass, and murder civilians while looting the country's mineral wealth.

What about the real Article 15 in the Congolese Constitution? It begins, "The public authorities are responsible for the elimination of sexual violence . . ." Yet in 2010 an official of the United Nations described the country as the "rape capital of the world."

The Congolese are on their own. *Débrouillez-vous.*

A Journey Through Dominance

This adage is not apposite just for the Congolese. If you retrace the Gulf of Guinea, you arrive at the place that seemed to best sum up Kaplan's bleak vision of the future, Lagos, the business capital of Nigeria. Kaplan described it as a city "whose crime, pollution, and overcrowding make it the cliché par excellence of Third World urban dysfunction."

In 1994, as Kaplan wrote, Nigeria was under the control of the military with General Sani Abacha as president. Abacha did not think that his job was to impartially resolve conflicts or protect Nigerians. He focused on killing his opponents and expropriating the country's natural wealth. Estimates of how much he stole start at around $3.5 billion and go higher.

The previous year the Nobel Prize–winning writer Wole Soyinka returned to Lagos, crossing the land border from Cotonou, the capital of neighboring Benin (which is shown on Map 1). He recalled, "The approach to the Nigeria-Cotonou border told the story at first glance. For miles we cruised past a long line of vehicles parked along the road right up to the border, unable or unwilling to cross." People who ventured across "returned within an hour of their venture either with damaged

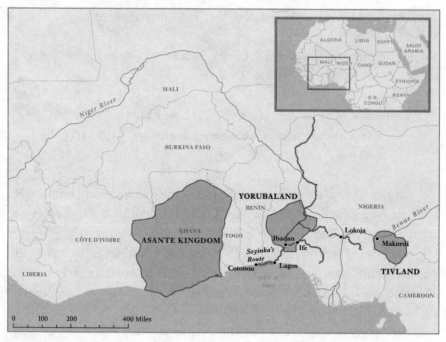

Map 1. West Africa: The Historic Asante Kingdom, Yorubaland and Tivland, and Wole Soyinka's Route from Cotonou to Lagos

vehicles or with depleted pockets, having been forced to pay a toll for getting even as far as the first roadblock."

Undeterred, Soyinka crossed into Nigeria to find somebody to take him to the capital, only to be told, *"Oga* Wole, *eko o da o"* (Master Wole, Lagos is not good). A taxi driver came forward pointing to his bandaged head with his bandaged hand. He proceeded to narrate the reception he had received; a bloodthirsty gang had pursued him even as he drove his car in reverse at full speed.

> *Oga* . . . Dose rioters break my windshield even as I dey already reversing
> back. Na God save me self . . . *Eko ti daru* [Lagos is in chaos].

Finally, Soyinka found a taxi to take him to Lagos, though the reluctant driver opined, "The road is ba-a-ad. Very bad." As Soyinka put it, "And thus began the most nightmarish journey of my existence." He continued:

> The roadblocks were made up of empty petroleum barrels, discarded
> tires and wheel hubs, vending kiosks, blocks of wood and tree trunks,

huge stones . . . The freelance hoodlums had taken over . . . At some roadblocks there was a going fee; you paid it and were allowed to pass—but that safe conduct lasted only until the next barrier. Sometimes the fee was a gallon or more of fuel siphoned from your car, and then you were permitted to proceed—until the next barrier . . . Some vehicles had clearly run a gauntlet of missiles, cudgels, and even fists; others could have arrived directly from the film set of *Jurassic Park*—one could have sworn there were abnormal teeth marks in the bodywork.

As he approached Lagos, the situation grew worse.

Normally the journey into the heart of Lagos would take two hours. Now it was already five hours later, and we had covered only some fifty kilometers. I became increasingly anxious. The tension in the air became palpable as we moved nearer to Lagos. The roadblocks became more frequent; so did the sight of damaged vehicles and, worst of all, corpses.

Corpses are not an unusual sight in Lagos. When a senior policeman went missing, the police searched the waters under a bridge for his body. They stopped looking after six hours and twenty-three corpses, none of them the one they were seeking.

While the Nigerian military looted the country, Lagosians had to do a lot of fending for themselves. The city was crime ridden and the international airport was so dysfunctional that foreign countries banned their airlines from flying there. Gangs called "area boys" preyed on businessmen, shaking them down for money and even murdering them. The area boys weren't the only hazard people had to avoid. In addition to the odd corpse, the streets were covered in trash and rats. A BBC reporter commented in 1999 that "the city is . . . disappearing under a mountain of rubbish." There was no publicly provided electricity or running water. To get light you had to buy your own generator. Or candles.

The nightmarish existence of Lagosians wasn't just that they lived in rat-infested, trash-strewn streets and saw corpses on the sidewalk. They lived in continual fear. Living in downtown Lagos with the area boys wasn't fun. Even if they decided to spare you today, they might come after you tomorrow—especially if you had the audacity to complain about what they were doing to your city or didn't show them the subservience they demanded. This fear, insecurity, and uncertainty may be as debilitating as actual violence because, to use a term introduced by political philosopher Philip Pettit, it puts you under the "dominance" of another group of human beings.

In his book *Republicanism: A Theory of Freedom and Government*, Pettit argues that the fundamental tenet of a fulfilling, decent life is non-dominance—freedom from dominance, fear, and extreme insecurity. It is unacceptable, according to Pettit, when one has to

> live at the mercy of another, having to live in a manner that leaves you vulnerable to some ill that the other is in a position arbitrarily to impose.

Such dominance is experienced when

> the wife . . . finds herself in a position where her husband can beat her at will, and without any possibility of redress; by the employee who dare not raise a complaint against an employer, and who is vulnerable to any of a range of abuses . . . that the employer may choose to perpetrate; by the debtor who has to depend on the grace of the moneylender, or the bank official, for avoiding utter destitution and ruin.

Pettit recognizes that the threat of violence or abuses can be as bad as actual violence and abuses. To be sure, you can avoid the violence by following some other person's wishes or orders. But the price is doing something you don't want to do and being subject to that threat day in and day out. (As economists would put it, the violence might be "off the equilibrium path," but that doesn't mean that it doesn't affect your behavior or have consequences that are almost as bad as suffering actual violence.) As Pettit sees it, such people

> live in the shadow of the other's presence, even if no arm is raised against them. They live in uncertainty about the other's reactions and in need of keeping a weather eye open for the other's moods. They find themselves . . . unable to look the other in the eye, and where they may even be forced to fawn or toady or flatter in the attempt to ingratiate themselves.

But dominance doesn't just originate from brute force or threats of violence. Any relation of unequal power, whether enforced by threats or by other social means, such as customs, will create a form of dominance, because it amounts to being subject to arbitrary sway: being subject to the potentially capricious will or the potentially idiosyncratic judgement of another.

We refine Locke's notion and define liberty as the absence of dominance, because one who is dominated cannot make free choices. Liberty, or in Pettit's words, non-dominance, means

emancipation from any such subordination, liberation from any such dependency. It requires the capacity to stand eye to eye with your fellow citizens, in a shared awareness that none of you has a power of arbitrary interference over another.

Critically, liberty requires not just the abstract notion that you are free to choose your actions, but also the ability to exercise that freedom. This ability is absent when a person, group, or organization has the power to coerce you, threaten you, or use the weight of social relations to subjugate you. It cannot be present when conflicts are resolved by actual force or its threat. But equally, it doesn't exist when conflicts are resolved by unequal power relations imposed by entrenched customs. To flourish, liberty needs the end of dominance, whatever its source.

In Lagos liberty was nowhere to be seen. Conflict was resolved in favor of the stronger, the better-armed party. There was violence, theft, and murder. Infrastructure was crumbling at every turn. Dominance was all around. This was not a coming anarchy. It was already there.

Warre and the Leviathan

Lagos in the 1990s may seem an aberration to most of us living in security and comfort. But it isn't. For most of human existence, insecurity and dominance have been facts of life. For most of history, even after the emergence of agriculture and settled life about ten thousand years ago, humans lived in "stateless" societies. Some of these societies resemble a few surviving hunter-gatherer groups in the remote regions of the Amazon and Africa (sometimes also called "small-scale societies"). But others, such as the Pashtuns, an ethnic group of about 50 million people who occupy much of southern and eastern Afghanistan and northwestern Pakistan, are far larger and engaged in farming and herding. Archaeological and anthropological evidence shows that many of these societies were locked in an even more traumatic existence than the inhabitants of Lagos suffered daily in the 1990s.

The most telling historical evidence comes from deaths in warfare and murder, which archaeologists have estimated from disfigured or damaged skeletal remains; some anthropologists have observed this firsthand in surviving stateless societies. In 1978, the anthropologist Carol Ember systematically documented that there were very high rates of warfare in hunter-gatherer societies—a shock to her profession's image of "peaceful savages." She found frequent warfare, with a war at least every other year in two-thirds of the societies she studied. Only 10 percent of them had no warfare. Steven Pinker, building on research by Lawrence Keeley, compiled evidence from twenty-seven stateless societies studied by anthropologists over the past two hundred years, and estimated a rate of death caused by violence of over 500 per 100,000 people—over 100 times the current homicide rate in the United States, 5 per 100,000, or over 1,000 times that in Norway, about 0.5 per 100,000. Archaeological evidence from premodern societies is consistent with this level of violence.

We should pause to take in the significance of these numbers. With a death rate of over 500 per 100,000, or 0.5 percent, a typical inhabitant of this society has about a 25 percent likelihood of being killed within a period of fifty years—so a quarter of the people you know will be violently killed during their lifetimes. It is hard for us to imagine the unpredictability and fear that such brazen social violence would imply.

Though a lot of this death and carnage was due to warring between rival tribes or groups, it wasn't just warfare and intergroup conflict that brought incessant violence. The Gebusi of New Guinea, for example, have even higher murder rates—almost 700 per 100,000 in the precontact period of the 1940s and 1950s—mostly taking place during peaceful, regular times (if times during which almost 1 in 100 of the population gets murdered each year can be called peaceful!). The reason appears to be related to the belief that every death is caused by witchcraft, which triggers a hunt for the parties responsible for even nonviolent deaths.

It's not just murder that makes the lives of stateless societies precarious. Life expectancy at birth in stateless societies was very low, varying between twenty-one and thirty-seven years. Similarly short lifespans and violent deaths were not unusual for our progenitors before the past two hundred years. Thus many of our ancestors, just like the inhabitants of Lagos, lived in what the famous political philosopher Thomas Hobbes described in his book *Leviathan* as

> continuall feare, and danger of violent death; And the life of man, solitary, poore, nasty, brutish, and short.

This was what Hobbes, writing during another nightmarish period, the English Civil War of the 1640s, described as a condition of "Warre," or what Kaplan would have called "anarchy"—a situation of war of all against all, "of every man, against every man."

Hobbes's brilliant depiction of Warre made it clear why life under this condition would be worse than bleak. Hobbes started with some basic assumptions about human nature and argued that conflicts would be endemic in any human interaction. "If any two men desire the same thing, which nevertheless they cannot both enjoy, they become enemies; and . . . endeavor to destroy, or subdue one an other." A world without a way to resolve these conflicts was not going to be a happy one because

> from hence it comes to passe, that where an Invader hath no more to fear, than an other mans single power; if one plant, sow, build, or possesse a convenient Seat, others may probably be expected to come prepared with forces united, to dispossess and deprive him, not only of the fruit of his labour, but also of his life, or liberty.

Remarkably, Hobbes anticipated Pettit's argument on dominance, noting that just the threat of violence can be pernicious, even if you can avoid actual violence by staying home after dark, by restricting your movements and your interactions. Warre, according to Hobbes, "consisteth not in actuall fighting; but in the known disposition thereto, during all the time there is no assurance to the contrary." So the prospect of Warre also had huge consequences for people's lives. For example, "when taking a journey, he arms himself, and seeks to go well accompanied; when going to sleep, he locks his dores; when even in his house he locks his chests." All of this was familiar to Wole Soyinka, who never moved anywhere in Lagos without a Glock pistol strapped to his side for protection.

Hobbes also recognized that humans desire some basic amenities and economic opportunities. He wrote, "The Passions that encline men to Peace, are Feare of Death; Desire of such things as are necessary to commodious living; and a Hope by their Industry to obtain them." But these things would not come naturally in the state of Warre. Indeed, economic incentives would be destroyed.

> In such condition there is no place for industry, because the fruit thereof is uncertain, and consequently no culture of the earth, no navigation nor use of the commodities that may be imported by sea, no commodious

building, no instruments of moving and removing such things as require much force, no knowledge of the face of the earth.

Naturally, people would look for a way out of anarchy, a way to impose "restraint upon themselves" and get "themselves out from the miserable condition of Warre, which is necessarily consequent . . . to the natural Passions of men." Hobbes had already anticipated how this could happen when he introduced the notion of Warre, since he observed that Warre emerges when "men live without a common Power to keep them all in awe." Hobbes dubbed this common Power the "great LEVIATHAN called a COMMON-WEALTH or STATE," three words he used interchangeably. The solution to Warre was thus to create the sort of centralized authority that the Congolese, the Nigerians, or the members of anarchic, stateless societies did not have. Hobbes used the image of the Leviathan, the great sea monster described in the Bible's Book of Job, to stress that this state needed to be powerful. The frontispiece of his book, shown in the photo insert, featured an etching of the Leviathan with a quotation from Job:

There is no power on earth to be compared to him. (Job 41:24)

Point taken.

Hobbes understood that the all-powerful Leviathan would be feared. But better to fear one powerful Leviathan than to fear everybody. The Leviathan would stop the war of all against all, ensure people do not "endeavor to destroy, or subdue one an other," clean up the trash and the area boys, and get the electricity going.

Sounds great, but how exactly do you get a Leviathan? Hobbes proposed two routes. The first he called a "Common-wealth by Institution . . . when a Multitude of men do Agree, and Covenant, every one, with every one" to create such a state and delegate power and authority to it, or as he put it, "to submit their Wills, every one to his Will, and their Judgments, to his Judgment." So a sort of grand social contract ("Covenant") would accede to the creation of a Leviathan. The second he called a "Common-wealth by Acquisition," which "is acquired by force," since Hobbes recognized that in a state of Warre somebody might emerge who would "subdueth his enemies to his will." The important thing was that "the Rights, and Consequences of Sovereignty, are the same in both." However society got a Leviathan, Hobbes believed, the consequences would be the same—the end of Warre.

This conclusion might sound surprising, but Hobbes's logic is revealed by his discussion of the three alternative ways to govern a state: through monarchy, aristocracy, or democracy. Though these appear to be very different decision-making institutions, Hobbes argued that "the difference between these three kindes of Common-wealth consisteth not in the difference of Power; but in the difference of Convenience." On balance, a monarchy was more likely to be convenient and had practical advantages, but the main point is that a Leviathan, however governed, would do what a Leviathan does. It would stop Warre, abolish "continuall feare, and danger of violent death," and guarantee that the life of men (and hopefully women too) was no longer "solitary, poore, nasty, brutish, and short." In essence, Hobbes maintained that any state would have the objective of the "conservation of Peace and Justice," and that this was "the end for which all Common-wealths are Instituted." So might, or at any rate sufficiently overwhelming might, makes right, however it came about.

The influence of Hobbes's masterpiece on modern social science can hardly be exaggerated. In theorizing about states and constitutions, we follow Hobbes and start with what problems they solve, how they constrain behavior, and how they reallocate power in society. We look for clues about how society works not in God-given laws, but in basic human motivations and how we can shape them. But even more profound is his influence on how we perceive states today. We respect them and their representatives, regardless of whether they are monarchies, aristocracies, or democracies. Even after a military coup or civil war, representatives of the new government, flying in their official jets, take their seats in the United Nations, and the international community looks to them to enforce laws, resolve conflicts, and protect their citizens. It confers on them official respect. Just as Hobbes envisaged, whatever their origins and path to power, rulers epitomize the Leviathan, and they have legitimacy.

Hobbes was right that avoiding Warre is a critical priority for humans. He was also correct in anticipating that once states formed and began monopolizing the means of violence and enforcing their laws, killings declined. The Leviathan controlled the Warre of "every man, against every man." Under Western and Northern European states, murder rates today are only 1 per 100,000 or less; public services are effective, efficient, and plentiful; and people have come as close to liberty as at any time in human history.

But there was also much that Hobbes didn't get right. For one, it turns out that stateless societies are quite capable of controlling violence and putting a lid on conflict, though as we'll see this doesn't bring much liberty. For another, he was too optimistic about the liberty that states would bring. Indeed, Hobbes was wrong on one defining issue (and so is the international community, we might add): might does not make right, and it certainly does not make for liberty. Life under the yoke of the state can be nasty, brutish, and short too.

Let us start with this latter point.

Shock and Awe

It wasn't simply that the Nigerian state didn't want to prevent the anarchy in Lagos or that the state in the Democratic Republic of Congo decided it would be best not to enforce laws and let rebels kill people. They lacked the capacity to do these things. The capacity of a state is its ability to achieve its objectives. These objectives often include enforcing laws, resolving conflicts, regulating and taxing economic activity, and providing infrastructure or other public services. They may also include waging wars. The capacity of the state depends partly on how its institutions are organized, but even more critically, it depends on its bureaucracy. You need bureaucrats and state employees to be present so that they can implement the state's plans, and you need these bureaucrats to have the means and motivation to carry out their mission. The first person to spell this vision out was the German sociologist Max Weber, who was inspired by the Prussian bureaucracy, which formed the backbone of the German state in the nineteenth and twentieth centuries.

In 1938, the German bureaucracy had a problem. The governing National Socialist German Workers' (Nazi) Party had decided to expel all Jews from Austria, which had recently been annexed by Germany. But a bureaucratic bottleneck quickly emerged. Things had to be done properly, so each Jew had to assemble a number of papers and documents to be able to leave. This took an inordinate amount of time. The man who occupied desk IV-B-4 in the SS (Schutzstaffel, a Nazi paramilitary organization), Adolf Eichmann, was put in charge. Eichmann came up with the idea for what the World Bank would nowadays call a "one-stop shop." He developed an assembly line system that integrated all the offices concerned—the Ministry of Finance, the income tax people, the police, and the Jewish leaders. He also sent Jewish functionaries abroad to solicit funds from Jewish organizations so that the Jews could buy the visas needed for emigration. As Hannah Arendt put it in her book *Eichmann in Jerusalem*:

At one end you put in a Jew who still has some property, a factory, or a shop, or a bank account, and he goes through the building from counter to counter, from office to office, and comes out at the other end without any money, without any rights, with only a passport on which it says: "You must leave the country within a fortnight. Otherwise you will go to a concentration camp."

As a result of the one-stop shop, 45,000 Jews left Austria in eight months. Eichmann was promoted to the rank of *Obersturmbannführer* (lieutenant colonel), and moved on to become the transport coordinator for the Final Solution, which involved solving many similar bureaucratic bottlenecks to facilitate mass murder.

Here was a powerful, capable state at work, a bureaucratic Leviathan. But it was using this capacity not for solving conflicts or stopping Warre, but for harassing and dispossessing and then murdering Jews. The German Third Reich, building on the tradition of Prussian bureaucracy and its professional military, certainly counts as a Leviathan by Hobbes's definition. Just as Hobbes wanted, Germans, at least a good portion of them, did "submit their Wills, every one to his Will, and their Judgments, to his Judgment." Indeed, the German philosopher Martin Heidegger told students, "The Führer alone is the present and future German reality and its law." The German state also generated awe in the population, not just among Hitler's supporters. Not many wanted to cross it or break its laws.

Awe turned into fear, with the SA (Sturmabteilung, brown-shirted paramilitaries), SS, and Gestapo roaming the streets. Germans spent their nights in cold sweats, waiting for the hard knocks on their doors and the jackboots in their living rooms that would take them to some basement for interrogation or draft them to go to the Eastern front to face almost certain death. The German Leviathan was feared much more than the anarchy in Nigeria or the Congo. And for good reason. It imprisoned, tortured, and killed huge numbers of Germans—social democrats, Communists, political opponents, homosexuals, and Jehovah's Witnesses. It murdered 6 million Jews, many of whom were German citizens, and 200,000 Roma; according to some estimates, the number of Slavs it murdered in Poland and Russia exceeded 10 million.

What Germans and citizens of the territories Germany occupied suffered under Hitler's reign wasn't Hobbes's Warre. It was the war of the state against its citizens. It was dominance and murder. Not the sort of thing Hobbes was hoping for from his Leviathan.

Reeducation Through Labor

Fear of the all-powerful state is not confined to abhorrent exceptions such as the Nazi state. It is much more common than that. In the 1950s, China was still the darling of many Europeans on the left, Maoist thought was de rigueur in French cafés, and Chairman Mao's *Little Red Book* was a choice item in trendy booksellers. After all, here was the Chinese Communist Party that had thrown off the yoke of Japanese colonialism and Western imperialism and was busy building a capable state and socialist society out of the ashes.

On November 11, 1959, the secretary of the Communist Party in Guangshan County, Zhang Fuhong, was attacked. A man called Ma Longshan took the lead and started to kick him. Others set on him with fists and feet. He was beaten bloody and his hair ripped out in patches, his uniform was torn to threads, and he was left barely able to walk. By November 15, after repeated further attacks, he could only lie on the floor while he was kicked and punched and the rest of his hair torn out. By the time he was dragged home he had lost control of his bodily functions and could no longer eat or drink. The next day he was attacked again, and when he asked for water, it was refused. On November 19, he died.

This harrowing depiction is painted by Yang Jisheng in his book *Tombstone*. He recalls how earlier that year he was urgently called home from boarding school because his father was starving. Upon reaching home in Wanli, he noticed that

> the elm tree in front of our house had been reduced to a barkless trunk, and even its roots had been dug up and stripped, leaving only a ragged hole in the earth. The pond was dry; neighbors said it had been drained to dredge for rank-tasting mollusks that had never been eaten in the past. There was no sound of dogs barking, no chickens running about . . . Wanli was like a ghost town. Upon entering our home, I found utter destitution; there was not a grain of rice, nothing edible whatso-ever, and not even water in the vat . . . My father was half-reclined on his bed, his eyes sunken and lifeless, his face gaunt, the skin creased and flaccid . . . I boiled congee from the rice I'd brought . . . but he was no longer able to swallow. Three days later he departed this world.

Yang Jisheng's father died in the great famine that struck China in the later 1950s, when possibly 45 million people starved to death. Yang shows how starvation was a prolonged agony. The grain was gone, the wild herbs had all been eaten, even the bark had been stripped from the trees, and bird droppings, rats, and cotton batting were all used to fill stomachs. In the kaolin clay fields, starving people chewed on the clay as they dug it. The corpses of the dead, famine victims seeking refuge from other villages, even one's own family members, became food for the desperate.

Cannibalism was widespread.

The Chinese lived through a nightmare in this period. But, just as in the Third Reich, it was not brought on the people by the absence of a Leviathan. It was planned and executed by the state. Zhang Fuhong was beaten to death by his comrades in the Communist Party, and Ma Longshan was the county party secretary. Zhang's alleged crime was "right deviationism" and being a "degenerate element." That meant he attempted to instigate some solutions to the mounting famine. Even mentioning the famine in China could cause you to be labeled "a negator of the Great Harvest" and to be subjected to "struggle," a euphemism for being beaten to death.

In Huaidian People's Commune, another part of the same county, 12,134 people, a third of the population, died between September 1959 and June 1960. Most starved to death, but not all; 3,528 people were beaten by cadres of the Communist Party, 636 of those died, 141 were left permanently disabled, and 14 committed suicide.

The reason so many people perished in Huaidian is simple. In the autumn of 1959, the grain harvest brought in 5.955 million kilos, which was not unusually low. But the Communist Party had decided to procure 6 million kilos from the farmers. So all the grain from Huaidian went to the cities and the party. The farmers ate bark and mollusks, and starved.

These experiences were part of the "Great Leap Forward," the "modernization" program launched by Chairman Mao Zedong in 1958 with the aim of using the Chinese state's capacity to dramatically transform the country from a rural, agrarian society into a modern urban and industrial one. This program required heavy taxes on peasants in order to subsidize industry and invest in machinery. The result was not just a human disaster, but also an economic tragedy of major proportions, all planned and implemented by the Leviathan. Yang's disturbing book brilliantly illustrates how the Leviathan, which had "the power to deprive an individual of everything," implemented the measures, such as requisitioning the entire grain production from Huaidian commune, and how they were enforced by "struggle" and violence. One technique was to centralize cooking and eating into a "communal kitchen" run by the state so that "anyone who proved disobedient could be deprived of food." Consequently, "villagers lost control of their own survival." Anyone who opposed the system was "crushed," and the consequence was to turn everyone into either "despot or slave." To stay alive, people had to allow others to "trample upon the things they most cherished and flatter things they had always most despised" and demonstrate their loyalty to the system by engaging in "virtuoso pandering and deceit"—dominance pure and simple.

Hobbes argued that life was "solitary, poore, nasty, brutish, and short" when "men live without a common Power to keep them all in awe." Yet Yang's description shows that even though all "stood in awe and terror before Mao," this led to the creation rather than the abatement of a nasty, brutish, and short life for most.

Another tool of governance the Communist Party created was the "Reeducation Through Labor" system. The first document to use this phrase was the "Directives for a Complete Purge of Hidden Counter-revolutionaries," published in 1955. By the next year the reeducation system had been born and camps set up throughout the country. These camps perfected various types of "struggle." Luo Hongshan, for example, was sentenced to three years of reeducation through labor. He recalled:

> We woke up at 4 or 5 every morning and went to work at 6:30 am . . . laboring straight until 7 or 8 in the evening. When it was too dark to see, we would stop. We really had no notion of time. Beatings were common, and some detainees were beaten to death. I know of 7 or 8 detainees on the number 1 middle work unit who were beaten to death. And this doesn't count those who hung themselves or committed suicide because they couldn't bear the abuse . . . They used iron clubs, wooden bats, pick handles, leather belts . . . They broke six of my ribs, and today I am covered with scars from head to foot . . . All kinds of torture—"taking a plane," "riding a motorcycle" . . . "standing on tiptoe at midnight" (these were all names for types of punishment)—were common. They would make us eat shit and drink urine and call it eating fried dough sticks and drinking wine. They were really inhuman.

Luo was not arrested during the Great Leap Forward, but in March 2001, when China was already a respected member of the international community and an economic powerhouse. Indeed, the Reeducation Through Labor system was expanded after 1979 by Deng Xiaoping, the engineer of China's legendary economic growth over the last four decades, who saw it as a useful complement to his "economic reform" program. In 2012 there were around 350 reeducation camps with 160,000 detainees. A person can be committed to such a camp for up to four years without any legal process. The reeducation camps are just one part of an extensive gulag of detention centers and various illegal "black jails" dotting the Chinese countryside and are complemented by an expanded "community corrections system," which has grown rapidly in recent years. In May 2014 the system was "correcting" 709,000 people.

The struggle continues. In October 2013 Premier Xi Jinping decided to praise the "Fengqiao experience," and urged Communist Party cadres to follow its example. The phrase refers to a district in Zhejiang Province that implemented Mao Zedong's "Four Clean-ups" political campaign in 1963 without actually arresting anyone, but rather by inducing people to publicly monitor, report on, and help to "reeducate" their neighbors. It was a prelude to China's Cultural Revolution, in which hundreds of thousands and perhaps millions of innocent Chinese would be murdered (the exact numbers are unknown and undisclosed).

The Chinese Leviathan, just like the Leviathan in the Third Reich, has the capacity to resolve conflicts and get things done. But it uses its capacity not to promote liberty but for naked repression and dominance. It ends Warre, but only to replace it with a different nightmare.

The Janus-Faced Leviathan

The first crack in Hobbes's thesis is the idea that the Leviathan has a single face. But in reality, the state is Janus-faced. One face resembles what Hobbes imagined: it prevents Warre, it protects its subjects, it resolves conflicts fairly, it provides public services, amenities, and economic opportunities; it lays the foundations for economic prosperity. The other is despotic and fearsome: it silences its citizens, it is impervious to their wishes. It dominates them, it imprisons them, maims them, and murders them. It steals the fruits of their labor or helps others do so.

Some societies, like the Germans under the Third Reich or the Chinese under the Communist Party, see the fearsome face of the Leviathan. They suffer dominance, but this time at the hand of the state and those controlling the state's power. We say that such societies live with a Despotic Leviathan. The defining characteristic of the Despotic Leviathan isn't that it represses and murders its citizens, but that it provides no means for society and the regular people to have a say in how its power and capacity are used. It isn't that China's state is despotic because it sends its citizens to reeducation camps. It sends people to camps because it can, and it can because it is despotic, unrestrained by—and unaccountable to—society.

Hence we are back to the Gilgamesh problem from the Preface. The Despotic Leviathan creates a powerful state but then uses it to dominate society, sometimes with naked repression. What's the alternative? Before answering this question, let's return to the other problem with Hobbes's account—his presumption that statelessness means violence.

The Cage of Norms

Though the human past is replete with instances of Warre, there are plenty of stateless societies (living under the "Absent Leviathan") that managed to control violence. These range from the Mbuti Pygmies of the Congo rain forest to several large agricultural societies in West Africa, such as the Akan people of modern Ghana and Côte d'Ivoire. In Ghana the British administrator Brodie Cruickshank reported in the 1850s that

> the paths and thoroughfares of the country became as safe for the trans-
> mission of merchandize, and as free from interruption of any descrip-
> tion, as the best frequented roads of the most highly civilized countries
> in Europe.

As Hobbes would have expected, the absence of Warre led to flourishing commerce. Cruickshank observed, "There was not a nook or corner of the land to which the enterprize of some sanguine trader had not led him. Every village had its festoons of Manchester cottons and China silks, hung upon the walls of the houses, or round the trees in the market-place, to attract the attention and excite the cupidity of the villagers."

You couldn't have such bustling enterprise in a society that was incapable of resolving conflicts and ensuring some type of justice. Indeed, as the French trader Joseph-Marie Bonnat observed later in the nineteenth century:

> It is to the exercise of justice, in the small villages, that the first hours
> of the day are devoted.

How did the Akan people exercise justice? They used (social) norms—customs, traditions, rituals, and patterns of acceptable and expected behavior—that had evolved over generations.

Bonnat described how people gathered around for consultation. The elders are "accompanied by those in the village who are not working," and they "go and sit under the most shady tree, the slaves following their master and carrying the chair on which he is to sit. The company, which always includes a large part of the inhabitants, goes to listen to the debate and takes the part of one of the litigants. On most occasions the matter is arranged amicably, the guilty person paying the costs; this consists usually of palm wine which is distributed to those present. If the matter is serious, the penalty consists of a sheep and also of a specified quantity of gold dust."

The community listened and used its norms to decide who was guilty. The same norms then ensured that the guilty desisted, paid up, or undertook another form of restitution. Though Hobbes saw the all-powerful Leviathan as the fountainhead of justice, most societies aren't that different from the Akan. Norms determine what is right and wrong in the eyes of others, what types of behaviors are shunned and discouraged, and when individuals and families will be ostracized and cut off from the support of others. Norms also play a vital role in bonding people and coordinating their actions so that they can exercise force against other communities and those committing serious crimes in their own community.

Although norms play an important role even under the auspices of a Despotic Leviathan (could the Third Reich have survived if all Germans thought that it lacked all legitimacy, stopped cooperating with it, and organized against it?), they are critical when the Leviathan is absent because they provide the only way for society to avoid Warre.

The problem for liberty, however, is multifaceted. The same norms that have evolved to coordinate action, resolve conflicts, and generate a shared understanding of justice also create a cage, imposing a different but no less disempowering sort of dominance on people. This too is true in every society, but in societies without centralized authority and relying exclusively on norms, the cage becomes tighter, more stifling.

We can understand how the cage of norms emerges and how it restricts liberty by staying in the Akan country and studying the account of another British official, Captain Robert Rattray. In 1924 Rattray became the first head of the Anthropological Department of Asante, one of the largest Akan groups, and part of the British colony of the Gold Coast, now Ghana. His job was to undertake a study of Asante society, politics, and religion. He transcribed an Asante proverb thus:

When a chicken separates itself from the rest, a hawk will get it.

For Rattray this proverb captured a critical aspect of the organization of Asante society—that it was molded by immense insecurity and potential violence. Though the Asante eventually developed one of the most powerful states in precolonial Africa, this state was founded on basic social structures dating from an era before centralized political authority emerged. Without effective state institutions, how could you avoid "a hawk"? Norms had evolved to reduce vulnerability to violence and exposure to those who could carry it out, providing some protection against hawks. But at the same time, they imposed their cage; you would have to surrender your freedom and stand with the other chickens.

Even in stateless societies some people were more influential than others, had more wealth, better connections, more authority. In Africa these people were often the chiefs, or sometimes the most senior people in a kinship group, the elders. If you wanted to avoid the hawks, you needed their protection and you needed numbers to defend yourself, so you attached yourself to a kin group or lineage. In return, you accepted their dominance over you, and this is what became the status quo, enshrined in Akan norms. As Rattray put it, you accepted "voluntary servitude."

> A condition of voluntary servitude was, in a very literal sense, the heritage of every Ashanti; it formed indeed the essential basis of his social system. In West Africa it was the masterless man and woman who ran the immanent danger of having what we should term "their freedom" turned into involuntary bondage of a much more drastic nature.

By involuntary bondage of a "much more drastic nature," Rattray meant slavery. So if you tried to free yourself from the chains of voluntary servitude, most likely you would be captured by hawks, in this instance slavers, and sold into slavery.

Indeed, a lot of the Warre in Africa was rooted in different groups trying to capture and sell others into slavery. Many vivid accounts describe the experience of Africans who were caught up in this trade. One, the story of Goi, was translated into English by a missionary, Dugald Campbell. Toward the end of the nineteenth century, Goi lived in the south of what is now the Democratic Republic of the

Congo, in the lands of a Chief Chikwiva from the Luba people. His father died when he was young and he grew up with his mother, sister, and brother. One day

> a war party appeared, and came yelling along the path shouting their war cries. They attacked the village and killed several women. They caught young women, chased and captured us boys, and tied us all together. We were driven to the capital and sold to the slave traders, who nailed wooden shackles on our feet.

From there Goi was taken to the coast, "Dragged thus from my house and from my mother, whom I never saw again, we were driven along the 'red road' to the sea." The road was "red" because of all the blood spilled along it. By this time Goi was so weak and emaciated from starvation and constant violence that he was almost worthless.

> Reduced to a skeleton, a mere shadow, and unable to travel, I was carried round the villages and offered for sale. No one was willing to give a goat or a hen for me . . . Finally one of the missionaries named "Monare" paid a coloured handkerchief for me, worth about fivepence, and I was free. So at any rate they told me, but I did not believe it, for I could not understand what freedom meant, and I thought I was now a slave of the white men. I did not want to be free, for I would only be caught and sold again.

The threat from slavers and the cage of norms conspired to create a spectrum of unfreedom. At one end of the spectrum was the extreme of slavery experienced by Goi. At the other end were obligations and duties you had to accept in order to avoid the hawks. This meant that belonging to a kinship group or society protected you, but didn't make you free from dominance. If you were a woman, you could be traded for bridewealth and exchanged in a marriage, not to mention the more general subjugation and abuse that was the lot of women in a patriarchal society dominated by chiefs, elders, and men generally.

Within this spectrum of unfreedom were many different types of relationships. One of those, fraught with dominance, can be seen from the story of Bwanikwa, also written down by Campbell. Bwanikwa too was a Luba and her father had a dozen wives. The head wife was a daughter of an important local chief, Katumba. Bwanikwa recalled how the head wife had just died. According to Luban custom he [her father] was mulcted for death dues. He was ordered to pay three slaves, as compensation for his wife's death . . . my father could raise only two.

One of his four daughters had to be handed over to make a third, and I was chosen . . . When he handed me over to my master, he said to him as we parted: "Be kind to my little daughter; do not sell her to anyone else, and I will come and redeem her." As my father was unable to redeem me, I was left in slavery.

Bwanikwa's status was that of a pawn or a pledge, another relationship of subjugation common in Africa. Pawning someone meant giving them to another person for a specific purpose. Often this was payment for some sort of loan, debt, or obligation. But in Bwanikwa's case it was because her father couldn't find an extra slave. If he'd found the slave, he could have redeemed Bwanikwa. A pawn was different from a slave; there was no automatic sale, and the expectation was that the situation was temporary. But as Bwankiwa realized, it could merge into slavery. F. B. Spilsbury, a visitor to Sierra Leone in 1805 and 1806, explained:

If a king or any other person goes to a factory, or a slave ship, and procures articles which he is not at that time able to pay for, he sends his wife, sister, or child as a pawn, putting a tally round their necks; the child then runs among the slaves until exchanged.

A related condition was that of a ward. People would send their children as wards to a more powerful family to be brought up in their household. It was a way of keeping them safe, even if they knew this would often involve permanent separation and even if it meant plunging them into a relationship of subservience to their caretakers.

These stories show that people were routinely treated as objects to be pawned and pledged. They often ended up in relationships of dominance. You had to obey the chief, the elders, your caretakers, and, if you were a woman, your husband. You had to follow the customs of your society closely. If you recall Pettit's definition of being dominated—as living "in the shadow of the other's presence . . . in need of keeping a weather eye open for the other's moods . . . forced to fawn or toady or flatter in the attempt to ingratiate themselves"—you'll see this fits it very well.

How did these subservient social statuses emerge? How were they justified?

The answer is, again, norms; these relationships evolved as customs accepted by society and supported by beliefs of what was proper and right. People could be pawned and wards had to relinquish their freedom; wives had to obey their husbands; people had to tightly follow their prescribed social roles. Why? Because everybody else expected them to. But at a deeper level, these norms were not completely arbitrary. Though norms are not chosen by anybody and evolve over time from practices and collective beliefs, they are more likely to become widely accepted if they also play a useful role in society, or at least for some people in society. Akan society consented to norms restricting freedoms and the unequal power relations they implied because they reduced people's vulnerability to Warre. If you were a ward or pawn of an important person, the hawks were less likely to mess with you, and maybe less likely to capture you and enslave you. Another Asante proverb Rattray wrote down summarized their situation even more succinctly: "If you have not a master, a beast will catch you."

To be free was to be a chicken among the hawks, a prey for the beast. Better to settle for voluntary servitude and give away your liberty.

———

The cage of norms isn't just about preventing Warre. Once traditions and customs become so deeply ingrained, they start regulating many aspects of people's lives. It's then inevitable that they will start favoring those with a little more say in society at the expense of others. Even when norms have evolved over centuries, they get interpreted and enforced by these more powerful individuals. Why shouldn't they tilt the board in their favor and cement their power in the community or the household a little more?

With the exception of a few matriarchal groups, the norms of many stateless societies in Africa have created a hierarchy with men on top and women at the bottom. This is even more visible in the surviving customs in the Middle East and some parts of Asia, for example, among the Pashtuns, whom we mentioned earlier. Pashtun lives are tightly regulated by their ancestral customs, called the Pashtunwali. The Pashtunwali system of law and governance puts a lot of emphasis on generosity and hospitality. But it also creates a stifling cage of norms. One aspect of this is the sanctioning of revenge for a whole host of acts. One of the most common compilations of the Pashtunwali starts by noting that

> a Pashtun believes and acts in accordance with the principles of . . . an
> eye for an eye, a tooth for a tooth and blood for blood. He wipes out insult

with insult regardless of cost or consequence and vindicates his honor
by wiping out disgrace with suitable action.

Warre is always around the corner, even if there is a lot of generosity and
hospitality aimed at preventing it. This has predictable consequences for everybody's liberty. But the weight falls more heavily on women. Pashtun norms not
only make women subservient to their fathers, brothers, and husbands; they also
restrict their every action. Adult women do not work and mostly stay inside. If they
go outside, they go covered from head to toe with a burka and must be in the
company of a male relative. Punishments for extramarital relations are draconian.
The subjugation of women is another facet of the illiberty created by the cage of
norms.

Beyond Hobbes

All in all, we are seeing a rather different picture from the one Hobbes painted.
The problem in societies where the Leviathan is absent isn't just uncontrolled violence of "every man, against every man." Equally critical is the cage of norms,
which creates a rigid set of expectations and a panoply of unequal social relations
producing a different but no lighter form of dominance.

Perhaps centralized, powerful states can help us achieve liberty? But we have
seen that such states are likely to act despotically, repress their citizens, and stamp
out liberty rather than promote it.

Are we then doomed to choose between one type of dominance over another?
Trapped in either Warre or the cage of norms or under the yoke of a despotic state?
Though there is nothing automatic about the emergence of liberty, and it hasn't
been easy to achieve in human history, there is room for liberty in human affairs
and this critically depends on the emergence of states and state institutions. Yet
these must be very different from what Hobbes imagined—not the all-powerful,
unrestrained sea monster, but a shackled state. We need a state that has the capacity to enforce laws, control violence, resolve conflicts, and provide public services
but is still tamed and controlled by an assertive, well-organized society.

Shackling the Texans

The U.S. state of Wyoming was created by the Pacific Railroad Act of 1862, which
called for the construction of a railroad to connect the eastern and western United

States. The Union Pacific was built west from the Missouri River to link up with the Central Pacific heading east from Sacramento, California. In 1867 it reached what was to become the state of Wyoming, at that time merely a county of the Dakota Territory. By July 1867, settlers were already arriving and General Grenville M. Dodge, chief engineer of the Union Pacific, began the survey for a city at Cheyenne, which would become the capital of the state. It was to be four miles square with well-organized blocks, alleys, and streets. The Union Pacific, the beneficiary of a huge land grant from the government as an incentive to get the railroad constructed, started selling off the lots three days after Dodge surveyed them. The first went for $150. By August 7, though Cheyenne was mostly a city of tents, a mass meeting in a local store chose a committee to write a city charter. On September 19 the first newspaper of the town, a triweekly tabloid called the *Cheyenne Leader*, was launched. By December the newspaper was advising its readers to carry guns at night for self-protection because of "frequent occurrences of garroting." On October 13 of the next year, the editor asserted:

> Pistols are almost as numerous as men. It is no longer thought to be an affair of any importance to take the life of a fellow being.

At this point Cheyenne resorted to vigilante justice to solve the problems endemic to the American frontier. In January 1868 three men were arrested for theft but released on bail. The next morning they were found tied together with a sign that read "$900 stole . . . $500 Recovered . . . Next case goes up a tree. Beware of Vigilance Committee." The next day vigilantes caught and hanged three "ruffians."

In the rural cattle areas, things were much worse. As Edward W. Smith of Evanston told the United States Public Land Commission in 1879, "Away from settlements the shotgun is the only law." As the cattle spread, conflicts between ranchers and homesteaders grew, and the reaction of the cattlemen led to the Johnson County Range War. On Tuesday, April 5, 1892, a special six-car train sped north from Cheyenne, carrying twenty-five Texas gunmen along with another twenty-four locals who had joined them. The men had a "Dead List of seventy men" they intended to kill.

We don't have information about the homicide rate in Cheyenne in the 1890s, though data for the mining town of Benton, California, suggests that there it may have reached an incredible high of 24,000 per 100,000! More likely it was closer to 83 per 100,000, the rate during the California gold rush, or 100 per 100,000, the rate in Dodge City, Kansas, in the days of Wyatt Earp.

This sounds as bad as Lagos when Soyinka was trying to make it there with his Glock pistol at the ready. But things turned out quite differently in Wyoming (actually, they turned out rather differently from what Kaplan expected in Lagos too, as we'll explain in Chapter 14). The anarchy, fear, and violence were contained. Indeed, the Texans were soon holed up at the TA Ranch surrounded by lawmen from the town of Buffalo who were warned of their arrival. After three days of siege, the cavalry came, ordered in by President William Henry Harrison, and shackled all of the Texans and their collaborators. Today Wyoming largely enjoys freedom from fear, violence, and dominance. It has one of the lowest homicide rates in the United States, about 1.9 per 100,000.

Wyoming has a pretty good record when it comes to helping people break free from the cage of norms too. Take the subjugation of women. Even during the worst of times, women in Wyoming did not face the same restrictions as those in Pashtun areas of Afghanistan and Pakistan or many parts of Africa. But as every-where else in the world, women in the first half of the nineteenth century had very limited power and no say in public affairs, and had to put up with myriad con-straints on their behavior, both because of their unequal status in marriage and because of the norms and customs of their societies. That started to change as women got the right to vote. The first place in the world to grant female suffrage was Wyoming in 1869, earning it the nickname the Equality State. This wasn't because Wyoming's customs and norms favored women compared to other parts of the world. Rather, the state's legislature granted them voting rights, partly to make it more attractive for women to move to this new state, partly to ensure that there would be enough voters to meet the population requirement for statehood, and partly because once African Americans began gaining full citizenship and voting rights, it seemed less acceptable to leave women out of this process. We'll see in the next chapter that there are many reasons why the cage of norms often starts breaking down once a state capable of shackling the hoodlums and enforc-ing laws is in place.

The Shackled Leviathan

The Leviathan that got the Warre under control and started to break the cage of norms in Wyoming is a different kind of beast from the ones we have discussed so far. It wasn't absent except in the very early days. It had the capacity to shackle the Texans. Since then it has massively expanded this capacity and can now resolve myriad conflicts fairly, enforce a complex set of laws, and provide public services that its citizens demand and enjoy. It has a large, effective bureaucracy (even if it is at times bloated and inefficient) and a huge amount of information about what its citizens are up to. It has the strongest military in the world. But it doesn't use this military power and its information to repress and exploit its citizens (for the most part). It responds to its citizens' wishes and needs, and it can also intervene to loosen the cage of norms for everybody, particularly for its most disadvantaged citizens. It is a state that creates liberty.

It is accountable to society not just because it is bound by the U.S. Constitution and by the Bill of Rights, which emphatically exalts the rights of the citizens, but more important because it is shackled by people who will complain, demonstrate, and even rise up if it oversteps its bounds. Its presidents and legislators are elected, and they are often kicked out of office when the society they are ruling over doesn't like what they are doing. Its bureaucrats are subject to review and oversight. It is powerful, but coexists with and listens to a society that is vigilant and willing to get involved in politics and contest power. It is what we'll call a Shackled Leviathan. In the same way that the Leviathan can shackle the Texan gunmen, so that they cannot do harm to ordinary citizens, it can itself be shackled by common people, by norms, and by institutions—in short by society.

It is not that the Shackled Leviathan isn't Janus-faced. It is, and repression and dominance are as much in its DNA as they are in the DNA of the Despotic Leviathan. But the shackles prevent it from rearing its fearsome face. How those shackles emerge, and why only some societies have managed to develop them, is the major theme of our book.

Diversity, Not the End of History

Liberty has been rare in human history. Many societies have not developed any centralized authority capable of enforcing laws, resolving conflicts peacefully, and protecting the weak against the strong. Instead they have often imposed a cage of norms on people, with similarly dire consequences for liberty. Wherever the Leviathan has shown up, the lot of liberty has hardly improved. Even though it has enforced laws and kept the peace in some domains, the Leviathan has often been despotic, thus unresponsive to society, and has done little to further the liberty of its citizens. Only shackled states have used their power to protect liberty. The Shackled Leviathan has been distinctive in another sense too—in creating broad-based economic opportunities and incentives and promoting a sustained rise in economic prosperity. But this Shackled Leviathan has arrived on the scene only late in history, and its rise has been contested and contentious.

We are now seeing the beginnings of an answer to the question we started with. It isn't that we are heading toward the end of history with the inexorable rise of liberty. It isn't that anarchy will spread around the world uncontrollably. It isn't even that all countries around the world will succumb to dictatorships, whether digital or just of the good old-fashioned sort. These are all possibilities, and this diversity, rather than convergence to one of these outcomes, is the norm. Nevertheless, there is also a glimmer of hope, because humans are capable of constructing a Shackled Leviathan, which can resolve conflicts, refrain from despotism, and promote liberty by loosening the cage of norms. Indeed, a lot of human progress depends on societies' ability to build such a state. But building and defending—and controlling—a Shackled Leviathan takes effort, and is always a work in progress, often fraught with danger and instability.

Brief Outline of the Rest of the Book

In this chapter, we introduced the tripartite distinction between the Absent, Despotic, and Shackled Leviathans. In the next chapter, we present the heart of our theory, which concerns the evolution of state-society relations over time. We explain why the emergence of powerful states is often resisted (because people are afraid of despotism) and how societies use their norms, not just to mitigate the possibility of Warre, as we saw in Asante, but also to counter and control state power. We focus on how the Shackled Leviathan emerges in a narrow corridor where society's involvement in politics creates a balance of power with the state, and illustrate this possibility with the early history of the Greek city-state Athens and the founding of the U.S. Republic. We also draw out some of the implications of our theory, emphasizing how different historical configurations lead to the Absent, Despotic, and Shackled Leviathans. We further show that in our theory it is the Shackled Leviathan, not the despotic sort, that develops the most and the deepest state capacity.

In Chapter 3 we explain why Absent Leviathans may be unstable and yield to political hierarchy in the face of the "will to power"—the desires of some actors to reshape society and accumulate greater political and economic power. We'll see how these transitions away from stateless societies are a mixed bag for liberty. On the one hand, they bring order and may relax the cage of norms (especially when it is in their way). On the other hand, they introduce unrestrained despotism. Chapter 4 examines the consequences of the Absent and Despotic Leviathans for the economic and social lives of citizens. It explains why economic prosperity is more likely to emerge under the Despotic Leviathan than under either the anarchic conditions of Hobbesian Warre or in the cramped space created by the cage of norms. But we'll also see that prosperity created by the Despotic Leviathan is both limited and rife with inequities.

Chapter 5 contrasts the workings of the economy under the Absent and Despotic Leviathans to life in the corridor. We'll see that the Shackled Leviathan creates very different types of economic incentives and opportunities and permits a much greater degree of experimentation and social mobility. We focus on the Italian communes and the ancient Zapotec civilization in the Americas to communicate these ideas and also to highlight that there is nothing uniquely European about Shackled Leviathans. This last point notwithstanding, it is of course the case that most examples of the Shackled Leviathan we have come from Europe. Why is this so?

Chapter 6 explains why several European countries have managed to build broadly participatory societies with capable but still shackled states. Our answer focuses on the factors that led much of Europe toward the corridor during the early Middle Ages as Germanic tribes, especially the Franks, came to invade the lands dominated by the Western Roman Empire after its collapse. We argue that the marriage of the bottom-up, participatory institutions and norms of Germanic tribes and the centralizing bureaucratic and legal traditions of the Roman Empire forged a unique balance of power between state and society, enabling the rise of the Shackled Leviathan. Underscoring the importance of this marriage, very different types of states emerged in parts of Europe where either the Roman tradition or the bottom-up politics of Germanic tribes were absent (such as Iceland or Byzantium). We then trace the path of liberty and the Shackled Leviathan, which had considerable ups and downs and veered out of the corridor on several occasions.

Chapter 7 contrasts the European experience with Chinese history. Despite historic similarities, the early development of a powerful state in China completely removed societal mobilization and political participation. Without these countervailing forces, the Chinese development path closely follows that of the Despotic Leviathan. We trace the economic consequences of this type of state-society relationship both in Chinese history and today, and discuss whether the Shackled Leviathan can emerge in China anytime soon.

Chapter 8 moves to India. Unlike China, India does have a long history of popular participation and accountability. But liberty has been no more successful in taking root in India. We argue this is because of the powerful cage of norms in India, as epitomized by its caste system. Caste relations have not only inhibited liberty but also made it impossible for society to effectively contest power and monitor the state. The caste system has produced a society fragmented against itself and a state that lacks capacity, which is nonetheless unaccountable as the fragmented society remains immobilized and powerless.

Chapter 9 returns to the European experience, but this time to study why some parts of Europe and not others found their way into and stayed in the corridor. In the process of answering this question, we develop another one of the central ideas of the book: the conditional nature of how structural factors influence state-society relationships. We emphasize that the impact of various structural factors, such as economic conditions, demographic shocks, and war, on the development of the state and the economy depend on the prevailing balance between state and society. There are thus no unambiguous conclusions to be drawn about structural factors. We illustrate these ideas by discussing why, starting with similar conditions and facing similar international problems, Switzerland developed a Shackled Leviathan, while Prussia fell under the dominance of the Despotic Leviathan. We contrast these cases with Montenegro, where the state did not play much of a role in either conflict resolution or in organizing economic activity. We apply the same ideas to explain why Costa Rica and Guatemala diverged sharply in the face of nineteenth-century economic globalization, and why the Soviet Union's collapse led to a diverse set of political paths.

Chapter 10 returns to the development of the American Leviathan. We emphasize that, although the U.S. managed to build a Shackled Leviathan, this was based on a Faustian bargain—the Federalists accepted a Constitution that kept the federal state weak both to appease a society that was concerned about the threat of despotism and to reassure Southern slaveholders who were worried about losing their slaves and assets. This compromise worked, and the U.S. is still in the corridor. But it also led to an unbalanced development of the American Leviathan which, even as it has become a veritable international sea monster, still has only limited capacity in several important domains. This is most visible in the inability or unwillingness of the American Leviathan to protect its citizens from violence. This unbalanced development also led to the American Leviathan's patchy record in structuring economic policy to ensure equitable gains from economic growth. We'll see how uneven state development has caused a distorted evolution of the power and capabilities of society, and paradoxically how it created room for the state's power to evolve in unmonitored and unaccountable ways in some domains (such as national security).

Chapter 11 shows that states in many developing countries may act as despots but lack the capacity of the Despotic Leviathan. We explain how these "Paper" Leviathans have come about and why they make so little attempt to build capacity. Our answer is that this is mostly because they are afraid of mobilizing society and thereby destabilizing their control over it. One origin of these Paper Leviathans lies in the indirect rule of colonial powers, which set up modern-looking administrative structures but at the same time empowered local elites to rule with few constraints and little participation from society.

Chapter 12 turns to the Middle East. Though state builders will often loosen the cage of norms as it limits their ability to mold society, there are circumstances under which despotic states may find it beneficial to strengthen or even to refashion the cage. We explain how this tendency has characterized Middle Eastern politics, the historical and social circumstances that have made it an attractive strategy for would-be despots, and the implications of this development path for liberty, violence, and instability.

Chapter 13 discusses how the Shackled Leviathan may get out of control when the race between state and society turns "zero-sum," with each side trying to undercut and destroy the other for survival. We emphasize how this outcome is more likely when institutions are not up to the task of impartially resolving conflicts and lose the trust of some segments of the public. We look at the collapse of the Weimar Republic in Germany, Chilean democracy in the 1970s, and the Italian communes to illustrate these dynamics and identify the structural factors making this type of zero-sum competition more likely. Finally we link these forces to the rise of modern-day populist movements.

Chapter 14 discusses how societies move into the corridor and whether anything can be done to facilitate such a move. We emphasize several important structural factors, focusing on what makes the corridor wider and thus easier to move into. We explain the role of broad coalitions in such transitions and discuss a number of cases of successful transitions as well as some failed ones.

In Chapter 15 we turn to the challenges facing nations in the corridor. Our main argument is that as the world changes, the state must expand and take on new responsibilities, but this in turn requires society to become more capable and vigilant, lest it find itself spinning out of the corridor. New coalitions are critical for the state to gain greater capacity while keeping its shackles—a possibility illustrated by

Sweden's response to the economic and social exigencies created by the Great Depression and how this led to the emergence of social democracy. It is no different today when we are facing many new challenges, ranging from inequality, joblessness, and slow economic growth to complex security threats. We need the state to develop additional capabilities and shoulder fresh responsibilities, but only if we can find new ways of keeping it shackled, mobilizing society and protecting our liberties.

Chapter 2

THE RED QUEEN

The Six Labors of Theseus

By around 1200 BCE, the Bronze Age civilizations that had dominated the Greek world for the previous millennium had started collapsing and were making way for the so-called Greek Dark Ages. Bronze Age Greek societies were run by chiefs or kings living in centralized palaces and bureaucratic administrations that used a writing system called Linear B, collected taxes, and regulated economic activity. All this disappeared during the Dark Ages. The chaos of this new era is the subject of the legends of Theseus, the mythical ruler of Athens. One of the best accounts of his exploits was written by the Greek scholar Plutarch, who spent much of his life as one of the two priests of the Oracle of Delphi.

Theseus, the illegitimate son of the king of Athens, Aegeus, was raised in Troezen in the northeastern Peloponnese. To claim his rightful throne, Theseus had to travel back to Athens by land or sea. He chose land, but Plutarch notes:

> It was difficult to make the journey to Athens by land, since no part of
> it was clear nor yet without peril from robbers or miscreants.

During the trip Theseus had to battle a series of bandits. The first he encountered, Periphetes, stalked the road to Athens, robbing and killing people with a bronze club. Plutarch recounts how Theseus wrestled with Periphetes and used

Periphetes's own club against him. Theseus then managed to avoid other sticky ends, including being tied between two pine trees and gnawed by an enormous wild pig, the Crommyonian Sow; thrown off a cliff into the sea; and wrestled to death. He finally bested Procrustes, the Stretcher, who notoriously cut off people's limbs to make them fit onto his bed. Theseus's quest to claim his kingship in Athens vividly illustrates the lawlessness of Greece at the time, without any state institutions to keep order. As Plutarch has it:

> Thus Theseus . . . went on his way chastising the wicked, who were visited with the same violence from him, which they were visiting on others, and suffered justice after the manner of their own injustice.

Theseus's strategy was therefore very much "an eye for an eye, a tooth for a tooth." Athens was living Mahatma Gandhi's "an eye for an eye makes the whole world blind."

Athenian kings didn't last long, however. By the end of the Dark Ages the city was ruled by a group of Archons, or chief magistrates, who represented its rich families. These elites competed endlessly for power, a process which sometimes led to coups such as the one by Cylon in 632 BCE. Elites recognized that they needed to develop more orderly ways of dealing with conflicts in the city. But it was to be a slow, treacherous road, with unexpected twists and turns.

The first attempt was a decade after Cylon, in 621 BCE, when a legislator named Draco was charged with producing the first written Athenian laws. The fact it took so long to write them down had a lot to do with the disappearance of the Linear B script of Bronze Age Greeks during the Dark Ages. Writing had to be reinvented with a completely different script borrowed from the Phoenicians. Draco's constitution, as the Greek philosopher Aristotle called it in his *Athenian Constitutions*, consisted of a series of written laws, only one of which survives. We do know that the punishment for breaking these laws was typically death (hence the modern expression "draconian"). The one surviving fragment of Draco's laws, which pertains to homicide, reveals that these laws corresponded to something rather different from what we mean today by "constitution," largely because they were dealing with a society trapped in endemic lawlessness, blood feuds, and violence. The fragment states:

> And if anyone kills anybody not from forethought, he shall be exiled.
> There shall be reconciliation, if there are a father or brother or sons,
> to be granted by all, or the objector shall prevail. If these do not exist,

then as far as cousinhood and cousin, if they are all willing to grant reconciliation, or the objector shall prevail. . . .

There shall be a proclamation against the killer in the agora by those as far as cousinhood and cousin; there shall join in the prosecution cousins and cousins' sons and brothers-in-law and fathers-in-law and phratry members.

This fragment is concerned with involuntary homicide. Someone who commits such an act should go to exile and await justice. If the extended kin of the person murdered unanimously decide to grant reconciliation, it ends there, but if they don't, the extended family "shall join in the prosecution" of the killer. The term "phratry" refers to extended kin groups. As we'll see, however, the influence of the phratry would soon diminish.

All of this looks similar to what we see in other societies living with the Absent Leviathan. In fact, there are many similarities between Draco's law and other codifications of informal laws without centralized authority, like the Albanian *Kanun*. The *Kanun*, attributed to Lekë Dukagjini in the fifteenth century, was a collection of norms that governed behavior in the Albanian mountains (and wasn't written down until the early twentieth century). Without a centralized state, Albanian rules and norms were enforced, just like Draco's homicide law, by extended families and clans. The *Kanun* heavily featured blood feuds in retaliation for transgressions. This is vividly illustrated by the first clause dealing with murder, which starts with blood feuds.

Ambush involves taking up a position in covert in the mountains or plains of Albania and lying in wait for an enemy in the blood feud or someone else who is intended to be killed. (To waylay, to lie in ambush, to set a trap for someone.)

It was an initial principle of the *Kanun* that "blood follows the finger," meaning that

according to the old Kanun of the mountains of Albania, only the murderer incurs the blood-feud, i.e. the person who pulls the trigger and fires the gun or uses some other weapon against another person.

The later *Kanun* extends the blood feud to all males in the murderer's family, even an infant in the cradle; cousins and close nephews incur the blood feud during the twenty-four hours following the murder. Culpability then spreads to extended kinfolk. With respect to accidental murders, the *Kanun* states, "In this type of killing, the murderer must leave and remain concealed until the affair is clarified." Exactly as in Draco's law, except that nobody even tried to write down, clarify, or regulate what these norms were in Albania until the twentieth century.

Solon's Shackles

Less than thirty years after Draco wrote his laws, Athens started the process of building a Shackled Leviathan. The problem of controlling routine conflicts and the power struggles among elites was ongoing. To this was now added conflict between elites and citizens over the direction of society. Aristotle observed that around the time of Draco there was "an extended period of discord between the upper classes and the citizens." In the words of Plutarch, there was a

> long-standing political dispute, with people forming as many different
> political parties as there were different kinds of terrain in the country.
> There were the Men of the Hills, who were the most democratic party,
> the Men of the Plain, who were the most oligarchic, and thirdly the Men
> of the Coast, who favored an intermediate, mixed kind of system.

In essence, the disagreement was over the balance of power between elites and regular people, and whether the state would be controlled democratically or oligarchically (meaning by the handful of richest and most powerful families). Solon, a trader and widely respected military commander, played the defining role in charting Athens's course.

In 594 BCE, Solon was made Archon for a year. As Plutarch put it, "The rich found him acceptable because of his wealth, and the poor because of his integrity." The post of Archon had been monopolized by elites, but Solon likely assumed the role through popular pressure, as the struggle between the elites and the citizens tilted a little in favor of the latter. He turned out to be quite a reformer, transforming Athenian institutions in order to constrain the elites' and the state's power over the citizens, while at the same time increasing the capacity of the state to resolve conflicts. In a surviving fragment of his writings, Solon observed that his institutional design was intended to create a balance of power between the rich and the poor.

> To the people I gave as much privilege as was sufficient for them, nei-
> ther reducing nor exceeding what was their due. Those who had power
> and were enviable for their wealth I took good care not to injure. I stood
> casting my strong shield around both parties and allowed neither to
> triumph unjustly.

Solon's reforms attempted to strengthen the people against the elites while at the same time assuring the elites that their interests would not be radically threatened.

When Solon became Archon the basic political institutions of Athens con-sisted of two assemblies, the Ekklesia, which was open to all male citizens, and the Areopagus, which was the main executive and judicial institution. The Areop-agus was composed of former Archons and was under elite control. Many Athe-nians were getting poorer during this period and had been excluded even from the Ekklesia, because they were trapped in debt peonage and servitude and had lost their rights as citizens. Aristotle noted that "all loans were made on the secu-rity of the person of the debtor until the time of Solon." This was the Athenian version of the cage of norms, with people turning into perpetually indebted, un-free pawns as a result of their worsening economic conditions. Solon understood that political balance in Athens would require regular citizens to participate in politics, but this wasn't possible when they were in a position of servitude, and certainly not when they were losing their citizenship. In Aristotle's words, "The mass of the people . . . had virtually no share in any aspect of government." So to ensure greater participation Solon canceled all contracts of debt peonage and passed a law that banned borrowing by using one's own person as security. He also made it illegal to enserf an Athenian. There was to be no more pawning. At a stroke Solon broke Athenians free from this part of their cage of norms.

But banning debt peonage wasn't enough when people were economically subservient to the elite. Greater liberty was necessary to make Athenians more active citizens so that they could get even more liberty. To this end, Solon sought to improve their access to economic opportunities. He implemented a land reform by uprooting the boundary markers of fields. These markers recorded the obliga-tion of the tenants farming the land to pay a sixth of their produce. By eliminat-ing them Solon in effect freed the tenants from the landowners, giving them the land they owned, and turning Attica, the region surrounding Athens, into a land of small farmers. Solon also eliminated restrictions on movement within Attica.

These measures greatly extended the citizenry that could participate in the Ekkle-sia. The existing balance of power was reconfigured in one fell swoop.

Solon also revamped the process of selecting the Archons and increased their number to nine, in part to improve political representation. But he had to keep the elites happy too, and for this he divided the population into four classes based on their incomes from land, and only men from the top two classes could become Archons (chosen by lot from a list of people nominated by the four traditional "tribes" of Athens). After serving as Archon, which he could do only once, and for a year, a man could still serve in the Areopagus. Thus the elites would continue to control the Archonship and the Areopagus, but now there were clear rules that opened up the Areopagus to a greater subset of (elite) society and helped to balance different interests. Solon also created a new council of 400, the Boule, which was to serve as the main executive council, and he redefined the role of the Areopagus to be largely judicial. As with the Archons, the four traditional tribes of Athens were equally represented in the Boule.

Having established a balance between elites and citizens, Solon started the process of state building. The critical step was judicial reform. Solon first abol-ished all but one of Draco's laws. The laws he promulgated were very different. One fragment records that

> Draco's law about homicide the *anagrapheis* ["writers up"] of the laws shall write up on a stone *stele*, taking it over from the *basileus* and the secre-tary of the council, and shall place in front of the Stoa. The *poletai* shall make the contract in accordance with the law; the *hellenotamiai* shall pro-vide the money.

Even in the one law that Solon kept, he replaced the role of the *basileus* with the *poletai* and the *hellenotamiai*. The word *basileus*, typical of the Homeric epics the *Iliad* and the *Odyssey*, translates as something like "big man," which was a type of Dark Age chief. Odysseus, whose exploits during his ten-year voyage after the Trojan War are recounted in the *Odyssey*, was a *basileus*. The *poletai* and the *hel-lenotamiai*, on the other hand, were magistrates or state officials. So Solon intro-duced a radical change—bureaucratized state institutions to enforce the law.

The most distinctive feature of this process was that the more Solon managed to strengthen regular Athenians politically, the further he went in building state institutions. And the more these institutions took shape, the further he went in establishing popular control over them. Thus once the Ekklesia was re-empowered, it featured greater popular participation. In order to achieve this objective, his reforms didn't just introduce greater representation in assemblies and political institutions, they also brought about changes in institutions and norms, such as the end of pawning, which changed the nature of society and made it more capable of acting collectively and controlling the elites and the state.

Aristotle agreed that empowering regular Athenians was the most important aspect of Solon's reforms and singled out the end of pawning, improved means of resolving conflicts, and access to justice. He remarked:

> These three seem to be the features of Solon's constitution which most favored the people: first and greatest, forbidding loans on security of a person's body; second, the possibility of a volunteer seeking justice for one who was wronged; third, and they say that this particularly strengthened the people, appeal to the court.

Here Aristotle is emphasizing the presence of some type of "equality before the law," where laws applied to everybody and common citizens could turn to the courts to seek justice. Though political representation in the Boule and membership of the Areopagus excluded the poorest, anyone could bring a lawsuit and have it heard, and the same laws applied to elites and ordinary citizens alike.

One of the most interesting ways in which Solon institutionalized popular control over the elites was via his Hubris Law. A surviving fragment states:

> If anybody commits *hubris* against a child (and surely one who hires commits hubris) or man or woman, whether free of slave, or if anybody commits anything unlawful against any of these, it has created *graphai* [public suits] *hubreos*.

This law thus created the crime of *graphai hubreos* in response to an act of hubris, behavior aimed at humiliation and intimidation. Remarkably, people could be charged with hubris against slaves, who were protected as well, and people were occasionally executed for repeated violations of the law. The Hubris Law enabled Athenians not only to control the elites, but also to enjoy liberty from the dominance of powerful individuals.

By banning debt peonage and ending the status of unfree pawns, Solon started simultaneously undermining the elites' dominance over ordinary citizens and preparing conditions for democratic politics. But there was much more to the power of the elites in Athens at this time. They had become significantly richer, and any increase in the capacity of the state, unless matched by a similar empowerment of society, might increase their political dominance by giving them additional tools for repression and control. So it was vital to strengthen the hands of regular citizens against the elite. This is what the Hubris Law helped achieve by codifying and intensifying existing norms.

Solon's Hubris Law reveals a more general aspect of life in the corridor—the delicate balance for creating liberty requires institutional reforms to work with and build on existing norms, while at the same time modifying and even obliterating aspects of those norms that are holding liberty back. No easy feat to be sure, but Solon's reforms broke considerable ground on both objectives. In the period before Draco, the rules and laws that governed people's lives were not written down and were enforced by families and kinship groups, most often using social ostracism and exclusion. Solon managed to build on these norms by codifying and strengthening them as in his Hubris Law, but in the process he also changed these norms, so that hubristic behavior became far less acceptable in Athenian society. We'll see many examples of this complex dance between institutional change and norms, and how failing to strike the right balance between them may damage the prospects of liberty. Solon struck the right balance.

The Red Queen Effect

How Solon limited the elites' control over the state and dominance over regular citizens on the one hand and increased the capacity of the state on the other is not a peculiar feature of an ancient civilization. It is the essence of the Shackled Leviathan. The Leviathan can build greater capacity and become much stronger when society is willing to cooperate with it, but this cooperation requires people to trust that they can control the sea monster. Solon built this trust.

But it's not just trust and cooperation. Liberty and ultimately state capacity depend on the balance of power between state and society. If the state and the elites become too powerful, we end up with the Despotic Leviathan. If they fall behind, we get the Absent Leviathan. So we need both state and society running together and neither getting the upper hand. This is not unlike the Red Queen effect described by Lewis Carroll in *Through the Looking-Glass, and What Alice*

Found There. In the book, Alice meets and runs a race with the Red Queen. "Alice never could quite make out, in thinking it over afterwards, how it was that they began," but she noticed that even though they both appeared to be running hard, "the trees and the other things round them never seemed to change their places at all: however fast they went they never seemed to pass anything." Finally, when the Red Queen called a halt,

> Alice looked around her in great surprise. "Why I do believe we've been under this tree the whole time! Everything's just as it was!"
>
> "Of course it is," said the Queen, "what would you have it?"
>
> "Well in our country," said Alice, still panting a little, "you'd generally get somewhere else—if you ran very fast for a long time, as we've been doing."
>
> "A slow sort of country!" said the Queen. "Now, *here*, you see, it takes all the running *you* can do, to keep in the same place."

The Red Queen effect refers to a situation where you have to keep on running just to maintain your position, like the state and society running fast to maintain the balance between them. In Carroll's book all that running was wasteful. Not so in the struggle of society against the Leviathan. If society slacks off and does not run fast enough to keep up with the state's growing power, the Shackled Leviathan can quickly turn into a despotic one. We need society's competition to keep the Leviathan in check, and the more powerful and capable the Leviathan is, the more powerful and vigilant society must become. We need the Leviathan to keep on running too, both to expand its capacity in the face of new and formidable challenges and to maintain its autonomy, which is critical not only for resolving disputes and impartially enforcing laws but also for breaking down the cage of norms. This all sounds quite messy (all that running!), and that, we'll see, is often the case. Even though it's messy, we depend on the Red Queen for human progress and for liberty. But the Red Queen herself creates lots of swings in the balance of power between state and society, as one party and then the other pulls ahead.

The way Solon managed to activate the Red Queen effect illustrates these broader issues. His reforms not only set up the institutional basis for popular participation in politics, but also helped relax the cage of norms that both directly restricted liberty and prevented the sort of political participation that is necessary in the corridor. The Athenian cage wasn't as stifling as in many other societies we'll see, such as the Tiv later in this chapter. Nevertheless, it was still oppressive enough to block the path of the Red Queen. By breaking down part of that cage, Solon started to fundamentally change society and forge a different type of politics capable of supporting a budding Shackled Leviathan.

How to Ostracize If You Must

Solon was Archon for a mere (busy!) year after which he went into exile for ten years in order to avoid the temptation to fiddle with his laws. He opined that his laws should not be changed for a hundred years. It didn't quite work out like that. Instead, a repeated contest between elites and society ensued.

Solon had tried to move Athens toward a more capable state and institutionalize popular control while keeping the elites happy, or happy enough. But how happy is happy enough? Conflict soon broke out and led to a series of tyrants, in effect dictators, holding power sometimes with force, sometimes with popular support. Yet Solon's reforms were popular and had gained legitimacy so that all Athenians, even eager tyrants, had to at least pay homage to them, and in the process, they often deepened them.

Peisistratos, the first tyrant to follow Solon, is famous for the cunning ways in which he overthrew Athenian political institutions. On one occasion he deliberately wounded himself and duped the citizens into allowing him armed bodyguards for protection, which he then used to take control of Athens. On another occasion, having been deposed, he rode back into Athens in a chariot with a stately woman dressed as Athena and fooled people into thinking he had been chosen by the god herself to rule Athens. Once in power, however, Peisistratos didn't totally repudiate Solon's legacy, but instead continued to increase the state's capacity. He undertook monumental constructions in Athens and launched a series of measures to integrate Athens with the countryside in Attica. These innovations included rural circuit judges, a system of roads centered on Athens, and processions linking Athens with rural sanctuaries, as well as the Great Panathenaea festival. The religious festivals were a direct descendant of some of Solon's other measures because he had tried to restrict private elite festivals in favor of more communal public ones. Peisistratos also coined the first Athenian money.

This is the Red Queen in action. Solon started this dynamic path in earnest, and Peisistratos followed along it, even if the process involved wild gyrations. Tyrants, when they rose to power, gave the upper hand to the state and the elites. Yet they couldn't dominate society and the demos ("the people"), and they also vied for its support. Though Peisistratos was succeeded by his sons Hippias and Hipparchus and then by Isagoras backed by the rival city-state of Sparta, the demos struck back. In 508 BCE a massive popular uprising swept Cleisthenes into power. The reforms Cleisthenes implemented were again aimed at strengthening both state and society, but he went further in the three objectives that Solon had tried to achieve over eight decades earlier—strengthening the hand of society against the elites, increasing the state's capacity, and loosening the cage of norms.

Let's start with state building. Cleisthenes developed an elaborate fiscal system, which levied a poll tax on metics (resident foreigners); direct taxes on the wealthy, who had to pay for festivals or outfitting warships; a variety of customs, tolls, and charges, particularly at the port of Piraeus; and taxes on the silver mines of Attica. During his Archonship, the state began to provide an array of public services, not just security and coinage, but also infrastructure in the form of walls, roads, bridges, prisons, and relief for orphans and the handicapped. Equally remarkable was the emergence of a type of state bureaucracy. Aristotle claims that in the days of Aristides, around 480–470 BCE, there were 700 men working for the state in Attica and 700 abroad, and in addition 500 guards in the docks and 50 on the Acropolis.

This state was also far more democratically controlled than the one that Solon had set up. To achieve this democratic control, Cleisthenes recognized that he had to further weaken the cage of norms and move away from the tribal basis of political power. So in a daring move, he abolished the four tribes that had populated Solon's Boule of 400 and replaced them with a new Boule of 500 composed of people chosen by lot from 10 new tribes named after Athenian heros. Each tribe had 50 representatives in the Boule. Each of the tribes was divided into three smaller units, called trittyes ("thirds" of tribes), and each of these was further subdivided into regional political units, called demes. There were 139 demes scattered throughout Attica (as shown in Map 2). The creation of the regional units in itself was a significant step in the process of state building, almost completely polishing off what was left of the preexisting kin-based identities. Aristotle summarized the effects of this reform by noting that Cleisthenes "made fellow demesmen of those living in each deme so they would not reveal the new citizens by using a man's father's name, but would use his deme in addressing him."

To further increase the political power of Athenian citizens against the elites, Cleisthenes also lifted the class restrictions on membership of institutions that had existed during Solon's days. Membership of the Boule was now open to all

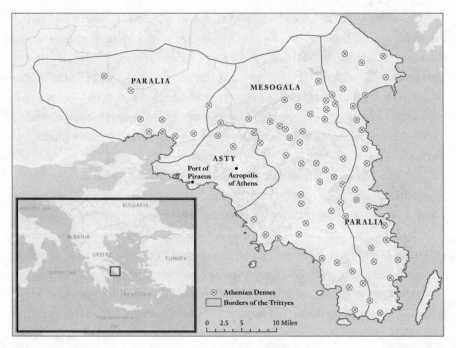

Map 2. The Athenian Demes

male citizens over the age of thirty, and because each could serve for only a year and at most twice in his lifetime, most Athenian men served at some point in their lives. The Boule's president was randomly chosen and served for twenty-four hours, allowing most Athenian citizens to be in charge at some point. Aristotle summed all of this up by stating:

> The people had taken control of affairs.

The Boule had authority over expenditures and there was a series of boards of magistrates that implemented policy. Though these boards were chosen by lot and served annually, they were aided by professional slaves acting as state functionaries.

Cleisthenes followed in Solon's footsteps in building on and institutionalizing existing norms that were helpful for strengthening the political power of Athenian citizens while also battling the cage of norms. Most notably, he formalized the institution of ostracism as a means of restraining the political dominance of powerful individuals. According to this new law, every year the assembly could take a vote on whether or not to ostracize someone. If at least 6,000 people voted and at least half of them were in favor of an ostracism, then each citizen got to write the name of a person whom they wanted ostracized on a shard of pottery (called an "ostrakon," and hence the term ostracism). The person whose name was written on the most shards was ostracized—banished from Athens for ten years. Aristotle notes about the law that "it had been passed by a suspicion of those in power." Like Solon's Hubris Law, it was a tool using and transforming the norms of society for disciplining elites. Even Themistocles, the genius behind the Athenian victory at Salamis over the Persians and probably the most powerful man in Athens in his day, was ostracized sometime around 476 BCE, when people began to worry that he was getting too powerful and because he wanted to focus on Sparta, and not Persia, as the real enemy. (An ostrakon with Themistocles's name is shown in the photo insert.) Ostracism was used sparingly, and only fifteen people were ostracized over the 180-year period when the institution was in full force, but just the threat of ostracism was a powerful way for citizens to discipline elites.

The evolution of the Athenian Constitution did not stop with Cleisthenes, who wrote, according to Aristotle, what turned out to be only the sixth of the eleven Athenian constitutions (did we mention that the Red Queen effect could be messy?). In the process, Athens steadily moved toward both greater empowerment of citizens and a stronger state. True to the nature of the Red Queen, none of this happened without a protracted struggle, with elites pushing in one direction and society in the other.

During this period, Athens gradually (and with lots of back-and-forth) built one of the world's first Shackled Leviathans, a powerful, capable state effectively controlled by its citizens. Athenians had the Red Queen effect to thank for this achievement. The state could not dominate society, but society could not dominate the state either; progress by each was met with resistance and innovation by the other, and society's shackles enabled the state to expand its remit and capacity into new areas. In the process, society cooperated too, enabling a further deepening of the state's capacity as it remained under popular control. Critical in all of this was the way the Red Queen eroded the cage of norms. To shackle a Leviathan, society needs to cooperate, organize collectively, and take up political participation. That's hard to do if it's divided among itself into pawns and their masters, phratries, tribes, or kinship groups. The reforms of Solon and Cleisthenes gradually eliminated these competing identities and made room for a broader axis of cooperation. This is a feature we'll see time and time again in the creation of Shackled Leviathans.

The Missing Rights

The story of how the American Leviathan became shackled, which we started in the previous chapter, has many parallels to the Athenian case. The U.S. Constitution, brought into existence by the founding fathers, men such as George Washington, James Madison, and Alexander Hamilton, is widely considered a brilliant piece of institutional design, introducing checks and balances and gifting freedom to future generations of Americans. Though there is some truth in this, it's only part of the story. The bigger part is about the empowerment of the people and how this constrained and modified American institutions and unleashed a powerful Red Queen effect.

Let's take the issue of rights. We owe the protection of rights to the founding fathers and their Constitution, don't we? Yes and no. The Constitution, which replaced the first laws of the new nation, the Articles of Confederation adopted in 1777–1778, does enshrine certain basic rights, but these were not in the much-lauded document written during the summer of 1787 in Philadelphia. The founding fathers absentmindedly overlooked a gamut of basic rights that we now think of as essential to American institutions and society. These ended up in the Constitution, but only later in the form of the Bill of Rights, a list of twelve amendments to the Constitution, ten of which were passed by the first Congress and were ratified by state legislatures. They included the sixth article of the Bill of Rights:

> The right of the People to be secure in their persons, houses, papers and effects, against unreasonable searches and seizures, shall not be violated, and no warrants shall issue, but upon probable cause supported by oath or affirmation, and particularly describing the place to be searched, and the persons or things to be seized.

The eighth article stated:

> In all criminal prosecutions, the accused shall enjoy the right to a speedy and public trial, by an impartial jury of the State and district

wherein the crime shall have been committed, which district shall have been previously ascertained by law, and to be informed of the nature and cause of the accusation; to be confronted with the witnesses against him; to have compulsory process for obtaining witnesses in his favor, and to have the Assistance of Counsel for his defence.

All of these rights seem pretty basic. So how come the founding fathers overlooked them? The reason is quite simple, and helps us understand the origins of the U.S. Leviathan's shackles—and why these shackles do not emerge automatically or easily.

Madison, Hamilton, and their collaborators, known as the Federalists, didn't want to replace the Articles of Confederation because they wanted to strengthen people's rights. Rather, the Constitution they drafted was designed to control the types of policies being adopted by state legislatures, which the Federalists saw as dangerously subversive. State legislatures, for example, could print their own money, tax trade, forgive debts, and refuse to fund the national debt. Worse, there was also quite a bit of disorder and popular mobilization, with people from all walks of life having caught the idea that they could govern themselves, organize, protest, and get elected to legislatures to push their interests. In this context, the Constitution was designed to tackle two distinct problems at the same time. The first was to build the federal state in order to coordinate laws, defense, and economic policy across the states. The second was to put the genie of the powerful democratic instinct that the War of Independence against the British had unleashed back into the bottle. The Constitution would achieve both of these objectives by centralizing political power, putting the central government in charge of fiscal policy, and reining in the hurly-burly of popular politics and the autonomous powers of the states.

The Federalists were what we call "state builders." Though Hobbes did allow for two paths to a Leviathan, via Covenant or Acquisition, in practice state building is often spearheaded by some state builders—individuals or groups, like Solon, Cleisthenes, or the Federalists, with the determination and a plan to create centralized authority—who found a proto-state or increase the power of a nascent state. The Federalists had a vision to build a Leviathan that Hobbes would have appreciated (but the Articles of Confederation didn't allow).

The Federalists were also well aware of what we called the Gilgamesh problem; they understood that there were risks in giving the federal state too much power. For one, it might be so powerful that it would start to prey on society, showing its fearsome face. In a famous passage of the Federalist Papers, a series of pamphlets he wrote with Hamilton and John Jay in order to urge people to ratify the Constitution, Madison noted:

> In framing a government which is to be administered by men over men,
> the great difficulty lies in this: you must first enable the government to
> control the governed; and in the next place oblige it to control itself.

Though it is Madison's statement on the need for the government to control itself that receives most attention today, his initial emphasis, the critical importance of a government "to control the governed," highlights the second objective of the Federalists—the need to limit the involvement of the common people in politics. Many readers at the time recognized this and were alarmed by it, particularly since the document that was written in Philadelphia lacked any explicit statement of people's rights. They had a point. As Madison put it in a private letter to Thomas Jefferson shortly after the Constitution was drafted in 1787:

> Divide et impera, the reprobated axiom of tyranny, is under certain
> qualifications, the only policy, by which a republic can be administered
> on just principles.

Divide et impera—divide and rule—was the strategy to control democracy. Madison emphasized "the necessity . . . of enlarging the bounds of the general government [and] of circumscribing more effectively the State governments." The "general government," which means the federal government, was made less democratic through such devices as the indirect election of senators and the president. The need to circumscribe "more effectively the State governments" was rooted in the social turmoil of the 1780s, including revolts and uprisings by farmers and debtors, which Madison thought could jeopardize the whole project of American independence. In fact, an important reason that the Federalists favored the Constitution was that it would provide the federal government with the tax revenues to field a standing army. One consequence of this would be "to ensure domestic tranquility," as the prologue of the Constitution put it. Indeed, the first action of George Washington's federally funded army after the Constitution was ratified was to march west from the capital to suppress an anti-tax uprising, the Whiskey Rebellion.

Madison and the Federalists' state-building project generated a great deal of dissent in American society. People feared what a more powerful state, and the politicians controlling it, could do without the protections offered by a Bill of Rights. Even in the United States, the fearsome face of the Leviathan lurked not far beneath the surface. Several state conventions refused to ratify the Constitution without explicit protection for individual rights. Madison himself was forced to admit the need for a Bill of Rights to persuade his own state of Virginia's convention to endorse the Constitution. He subsequently ran for Congress in Virginia on a pro–Bill of Rights ticket and defended the need for it in Congress in August 1789 on the grounds that it was needed to "conciliate the minds of the people." (But we'll see a little later in this chapter and again in Chapter 10 that there were other, more sinister considerations too, and Madison and his collaborators ended up endorsing slavery to make the Constitution acceptable to Southern elites. This would ensure that the Bill of Rights neither protected slaves nor applied against abuses by state governments.)

The transition from the Articles of Confederation to the Constitution reveals the vital ingredients necessary for a Shackled Leviathan to emerge. First there must be a set of individuals or groups in society, our state builders, to push for a powerful state, which will work to put a stop to the Warre "of every man, against every man," help resolve conflicts in society, protect people from dominance, and provide public services (and perhaps look after their own interest a little too). The role of this group of state builders—their vision, their ability to form the right coalitions to support their endeavor and their sheer power—is pivotal. The Federalists played this role in the founding of the U.S. federal state. They intended to build a veritable Leviathan, and understood that it was vital for the security, unity, and economic success of the new country that it should have a much mightier central state with the power to tax, the monopoly right to print money, and the ability to set a federal trade policy. Moreover, the Federalists were powerful enough to attempt such a state-building project; they already had considerable authority, as well-established politicians themselves. They also drew power from their alliance with George Washington and other respected leaders of the War of Independence. They were highly adept at influencing public opinion too, through the media and their brilliantly argued pamphlets, the Federalist Papers.

The second pillar of the Shackled Leviathan, societal mobilization, is even more critical because it is the essence of the Red Queen effect. By societal mobilization we mean the involvement of society at large (in particular non-elites) in politics, which can take both noninstitutionalized forms, such as revolts, protests, petitions, and general pressure on elites via associations or the media, and institutionalized forms through elections or assemblies. Noninstitutionalized and institutionalized powers are synergistic and support each other.

Despotism flows from the inability of society to influence the state's policies and actions. Though a constitution may specify democratic elections or consultation, such a decree is insufficient to make the Leviathan responsive, accountable, and shackled unless society is mobilized and becomes actively engaged in politics. So the reach of a constitution depends on ordinary people's ability to defend it and demand what was promised to them, if necessary via noninstitutional means. Constitutional provisions in turn matter both because they grant greater predictability and consistency to society's power and because they enshrine the right of society to remain engaged in politics.

Society's power is based on people's ability to solve their "collective action" problem to get engaged in politics, block changes they oppose, and impose their wishes on major social and political decisions. The collective action problem refers to the fact that even when it may be in the interest of a group of people to organize to engage in political action, each member of the group may "free-ride" and go about his or her business without exerting the needed effort to protect the group's interests, or may even remain unaware of what's going on. Noninstitutionalized means of exercising power are unpredictable because they do not provide a reliable way of solving the collective action problem, while institutionalized power can be more systematic and predictable. Constitutions can thus enable society to exercise its power in a more consistent manner. It was critical that in the years leading to the drafting of the Constitution, U.S. society had both sources of power.

Its noninstitutionalized power was rooted in the popular struggle during the war against the British. Thomas Jefferson captured the essence of this mobilization when he wrote in 1787:

> God forbid we should ever be 20 years without such a rebellion . . . What country can preserve its liberties if their rulers are not warned from time to time that their people preserve the spirit of resistance? Let them take arms.

Thanks to the Articles of Confederation, American society had institutional means of preventing the Federalists' state-building project as well, for example, by refusing to ratify the Constitution in state legislatures. These institutional constraints did not end with ratification, since according to the Constitution, the legislature continued to be a potent restraint on the executive and on federal power.

The degree of popular mobilization and the extent to which society was well organized had already played a central role in the War of Independence, which had been fueled by ordinary people's resentment of British policies. These were the same features of American society that attracted the attention of a young French intellectual touring the country half a century later, Alexis de Tocqueville. In his masterpiece, *Democracy in America*, Tocqueville commented that

> in no country of the world has the principal of association been more successfully used, or more unsparingly applied to a greater multitude of different objects, than in America.

Indeed, it was a "nation of joiners," and Tocqueville marveled at "the extreme skill with which the inhabitants . . . succeed in proposing a common object to the exertions of a great many men, and in getting them voluntarily to pursue it." This tradition of robust popular mobilization empowered U.S. society to have a say in what type of Leviathan would be built. And even if Hamilton, Madison, and their allies wanted to build a more despotic state, society would not comply. So the Federalists were persuaded to introduce the Bill of Rights and other checks on their power to make their state-building project palatable to those who would have to "submit their Wills" to the Leviathan. They weren't too keen about all of this; Hamilton decried this "excess of democracy," and proposed that the president and Senate serve for life, which is understandable since the Federalists thought they would control the Leviathan.

Not only did this critical second pillar initially prevent the American state from embarking on a despotic path, but the balance of power it engendered ensured that the state remained shackled even as it became more powerful over time (and we'll see later that in some respects they may have been too successful, constraining the capabilities of the state in the next two centuries, especially when it came to the role of the state to provide protection and equal opportunities for all of its citizens). The American state in 1789 was far less powerful than, and almost rudimentary in comparison to, our modern state. It had a tiny bureaucracy and provided only a few public services. It did not even dream of regulating monopolies or providing a social safety net, and it did not view all of its citizens, certainly not slaves or women, as equals, so loosening the cage of norms entrapping many Americans at the time was definitely not high on its priority list. Today, we expect so much more from the state in terms of conflict resolution, regulation, a social safety net, provision of public services, and protections of individual freedom against all sorts of threats. That these can be provided is a consequence of the Red Queen. If all U.S. society at the time could manage was to set in stone hard limits on what the state should do, we would not get many of the benefits (and to be sure also not suffer some of the intransigencies) of our current state. Instead, the American state did evolve over the last 230 years and changed its capabilities and role in society. In the process, it became more responsive to the wishes and needs of its citizens. The reason why it could achieve this growth was because the shackles on its ankles meant that society could, with some caution, trust that even with a further increase in its power, it would not become completely unaccountable and display its fearsome face. Its shackled nature also meant that society could contemplate cooperating with the state. Yet in the same way that U.S. society at the end of the eighteenth century did not fully trust Madison and Hamilton without guarantees, society generally does not fully trust those striving to increase the state's capacity and reach. It will allow them to do so only as it increases its own capability to control the state.

The subsequent development of state-society relations in the nineteenth-century United States played out in the same messy, unpredictable way that is the hallmark of the Red Queen, as we saw in the Athenian case. As the centralized state became more powerful and more involved in people's lives, society tried to reassert its control. As society became more mobilized, the elites and state institutions reacted and attempted to wrest back control. Though we see this dynamic in many aspects of U.S. politics, the biggest fault line was the tension between the Northern and Southern states over slavery, which forced many distasteful compromises in the Constitution. This tension erupted into one of the deadliest conflicts of the nineteenth century after seven Southern states (out of the thirty-four states at the time) declared their secession, forming the Confederate States of America, after the inauguration of Abraham Lincoln in 1861. The secession was not recognized by the government, and the Civil War erupted on April 12, 1861, between the Union and the Confederacy. In the four years it lasted, the war destroyed much of the transport system, infrastructure, and economy of the South, and cost as many as 750,000 lives. The end of the war led to a powerful swing in the balance of power against the elites, especially Southern elites, as the slaves were freed (with the Thirteenth Amendment), their civil rights were recognized (with the Fourteenth Amendment), and their voting rights were recognized (with the Fifteenth Amendment). But this wasn't the end of the series of reactions. The Reconstruction Era, lasting until 1877, empowered the freed slaves and incorporated them into the economic and political system (and they participated with gusto, voting in great numbers and getting elected into legislatures). Yet the Redemption period that followed after Northern troops left the South disenfranchised them again, locked them into low-wage agriculture, and made them subject to a gamut of formal and informal repressive practices, including murders and lynchings at the hands of local law enforcement officers and the Ku Klux Klan. The pendulum did not swing back against the elites and in favor of the most disadvantaged segment of Southern society until after the civil rights movement got going in the mid-1950s. (And of course we are nowhere near the end of history as far as the evolution of American liberty is concerned.)

Though the standard narrative paints a picture in which the U.S. Constitution protects our rights, there was nothing pretty about the way those rights came to be protected for most Americans—and we owe these rights as much to society's mobilization as to the document drafted in Philadelphia in 1787. That's just in the nature of the Red Queen.

Chiefs? What Chiefs?

So the Red Queen effect isn't pretty, and as we'll see later in the book, all that running is rife with danger. But when it works, it creates conditions for the type of liberty that Athenians and Americans have enjoyed. But then, why do many societies remain with the Absent Leviathan? Why not attempt to create centralized authority and shackle it? Why not unleash the Red Queen effect?

Social scientists have typically linked the failure of centralized authority to emerge to the absence of some key conditions that made it worthwhile to have a state, such as high population density, established agriculture, or trade. It has also been argued that some societies didn't have the requisite know-how to create states. According to this view, building state institutions is primarily an "engineering" problem of bringing in the right expertise and institutional blueprints. Though these aspects all play a role in some contexts, another factor is often more important—the desire to avoid the fearsome face of the Leviathan. If you fear the Leviathan, you will prevent the accumulation of power and resist the social and political hierarchy that is necessary to launch it.

We can see a clear instance of this fear blocking the rise of the Leviathan in Nigeria's history. Away from Lagos and the coastal lagoons, you enter Yorubaland, the home of the Yoruba people. The A1 heads north first to Ibadan, and then if you swing east on the A122, you pass Ife, the traditional spiritual home of Yoruba chiefs, and then reach Lokoja via the A123 (which can be seen on Map 1 in the previous chapter). Lokoja, located at the confluence of the Niger and Benue Rivers, was made the first capital of colonial Nigeria by Sir Frederick Lugard in 1914. It is supposedly here that his wife-to-be, Flora Shaw, coined the name for the country-to-be. Heading farther east, the A233 dips below the Benue. By the time you reach Makurdi, back on the river, you are firmly in Tivland.

The Tiv are an ethnic group, organized around kin relations, who were state-less when Nigeria was colonized. They nevertheless formed a coherent group with a well-defined, large, and even expanding territory and a distinct language, cul-ture, and history. We know quite a bit about the Tiv thanks to the anthropologist couple Paul and Laura Bohannan, who studied them from the mid-1940s onward. Their and others' accounts make it very clear that the same problem as in Athens—preventing powerful individuals from becoming too dominant and bossing around everybody else—was a major concern for Tiv society. But the way the Tiv dealt with this problem was very different. It was by means of norms that made them suspi-cious of power and willing to take action against those building their power. These norms then prevented the emergence of any political hierarchy. Consequently, though the Tiv did have chiefs, these chiefs had little uncontested authority over others; their main role was mediation and arbitration in resolving conflict and supporting cooperation of the sort we saw with Asante elders in the previous chapter. There was no possibility for a ruler or a big man establishing enough authority to impose his will.

To understand how the Tiv contained political hierarchy, let us return to Lord Lugard. Lugard wanted to perfect what came to be known as "indirect rule," a method of running colonies with the help of local notables and indigenous political authorities. But how could you run a country in this way when there weren't any such authorities? When Lugard demanded to be taken to their chiefs, the Tiv responded, "Chiefs? What chiefs?" The system of indirect rule had already developed in Southern Nigeria during the 1890s as British authority spread. Here administrators created "warrant chiefs," so called because the Brit-ish gave warrants to powerful indigenous families whom they made chief. After 1914 Lugard wanted something even more ambitious. He argued, "If there are no chiefs . . . the first condition for progress in a very loosely knit community such as the I[g]bos or the . . . [Tiv] is to create units of some size under progres-sive chiefs."

But just who were these "progressive chiefs"? Lugard and colonial officials got to decide. Lugard wanted progressive chiefs to enforce order, collect taxes, and organize labor to build roads and railways in Tivland. If the Tiv didn't have real chiefs, he would create them. And so he did after 1914, imposing a new version of the warrant chief system on the Tiv.

Yet the Tiv hadn't signed up for that, and they weren't too pleased with Lugard's plan. Trouble quickly brewed. Things exploded in 1929 in nearby Igboland, home of another stateless society, the "loosely knit community" of the Igbos. By the summer of 1939, most social and economic activity had come to a standstill in Tivland. The trouble came from a cult called Nyambua, which can be viewed as the Tiv's revenge against Lugard, now a baron, enjoying his peaceful retirement in England, and his warrant chiefs. The head of the cult was a man called Kokwa, who sold charms to provide protection from *mbatsav*, or "witches." *Mbatsav* is derived from the word *tsav*, which means "power" in the Tiv language, particularly power over others. Tsav is a substance that grows on the heart of a person and can be examined after death by cutting open the chest. If you have it, you can make others do what you want, and kill them using fetishes. Crucially, although some people naturally have tsav, it can be increased by cannibalism. As Paul Bohannan put it:

> A diet of human flesh makes the tsav, and of course the power, grow large. Therefore the most powerful men, no matter how much they are respected or liked, are never fully trusted. They are men of tsav—and who knows?

The people with tsav belong to an organization—the Mbatsav. *Mbatsav* has two meanings: powerful people (it is the plural of *tsav*); and, as we saw, a group of witches. These witches could engage in nefarious activities, for example robbing graves or eating corpses. This is an interesting double meaning. Imagine if in English the word "politicians" simultaneously meant "people who contest for or control elected government offices" and "a group of witches organized for nefarious purposes." (Not a bad idea, actually.)

People initiated into the Nyambua cult were given a leather wand and a fly whisk. The whisk allowed one to smell out tsav created by cannibalism. A photograph taken by Paul Bohannan of a Tiv diviner with a fly whisk is included in the photo insert. In 1939 the whisks were pointed toward the warrant chiefs accused of being witches, an accusation that stripped them of any authority and power that they got from the British. Were the Tiv fighting back against the British? Yes and no. Looking deeper you can see that the movement was not simply anti-British; it was anti-authority. As a Tiv elder, Akiga, told the colonial official Rupert East at the time:

> When the land has become spoilt owing to so much senseless murder [by tsav] the Tiv have taken strong measures to overcome the mbatsav. These big movements have taken place over a period extending from the days of the ancestors into modern times . . .

In fact, religious cults like Nyambua were part of a set of norms that had evolved to protect the Tiv status quo, which meant preventing anybody from becoming too powerful. In the 1930s, the warrant chiefs were the ones getting dangerously powerful, but in the past others had similarly become too big for their boots. Bohannan pointed out how

> men who had acquired too much power . . . were whittled down by means of witchcraft accusations . . . Nyambua was one of a regular series of movements to which Tiv political action, with its distrust of power, gives rise so that the greater political institution—the one based on the lineage system and a principle of egalitarianism—can be preserved.

What's really significant here, and brings to mind Athenians' preoccupation with hubris and ostracizing powerful individuals, is the phrase "distrust of power." We have so far talked of the power or the capacity of the state. But the state itself is controlled by a set of agents, which includes rulers, politicians, bureaucrats, and other politically influential actors—what might be called the "political elite." You cannot have the Leviathan without having a political hierarchy, without somebody— the political elite, a ruler, or a state builder—exercising power over others, giving orders, deciding who is right and who is wrong in disputes. Distrust of power breeds fear of this political hierarchy. The Tiv norms didn't just regulate and control conflict; they also severely restricted social and political hierarchy. Since curbing political hierarchy means curbing the power of the state, some of these norms, including witchcraft accusations, simultaneously stopped state building in its tracks.

A Slippery Slope

The Tiv society was terrified of the fearsome face of the Leviathan and the dominance that it might bring once it got off the ground. It also had powerful norms preventing the emergence of political hierarchy, so the Tiv ended up living with the Absent Leviathan. But there is a puzzle. If society was so powerful and the state and its elites so weak, why were the Tiv terrified of the Leviathan? Why couldn't they activate the Red Queen effect and benefit from the dynamics that would bring a Shackled Leviathan? Why couldn't they develop the same sorts of solutions for controlling political hierarchy that Solon and Cleisthenes and other Greek institutional innovators or the American founding fathers devised?

The answer is related to the nature of the norms guarding against the emergence of political hierarchy. But it also highlights that it is difficult to build the conditions for a Shackled Leviathan and there are limitations to the different types of societal power. In contrast to general societal mobilization and the institutionalized forms of political power, Tiv norms relying on rituals, witchcraft practices, and general beliefs against hierarchy could not be easily "scaled up"; they were not the sort of institutions and norms that would be useful once one group within society became sufficiently powerful and exercised authority over the rest. So the Tiv had the capability to nip the emergence of political inequality in the bud, but not necessarily the capacity to control the process of state building once it was under way. This made any state-building attempt a bit of a slippery slope for the Tiv—once you go down that path, you might slip and end up somewhere you did not intend.

To understand this better, it is useful to contrast the social tools available to the Tiv for controlling political hierarchy to those at the disposal of Athenians and Americans while they were engaged in their state-building efforts.

Americans had at least two robust weapons in their arsenal for combating an overeager Leviathan. First, they had institutionalized power for controlling the Leviathan, since state legislatures were influential and could not easily be cast aside, and the federal state would be subject to electoral and judicial controls. Second, American society was mobilized in a way that Tiv society certainly wasn't. America, in many ways, was a society of smallholders, nurturing not just economic but also political aspirations. It had norms making it unwilling to accept despotic authority and ready to erupt into a rebellion (as the British discovered). As a result, even if they were apprehensive about a centralized state acquiring much greater powers than might have appeared advisable a decade before, Americans still thought that they could prevent the state from turning into a Despotic Leviathan.

Athenians had similar weapons and used them to the same effect. Athens had come out of the Dark Ages with a society intent on reining in the dominance of the elites and their privileges. Its economic structure facilitated societal mobilization. After Solon's reforms, Athens had become a smallholder society, like the thirteen American colonies, with all of the mobilization that this engendered. Critically, Greek society around this time also became more assertive thanks to changes in military technology. While during the Bronze Age the metal of choice for weapons was bronze, by the eighth century BCE, iron had supplanted it. Bronze weapons were expensive and hence the natural monopoly of the elite. Iron weapons, on the other hand, were much cheaper and "democratized warfare," in the words of the archaeologist V. Gordon Childe. In particular, they led to the famous hoplites, the heavily armed Greek citizen-soldiers, who could fight not just other city-states and the Persians but also overeager elites. The balance of power thus tilted further in favor of Athenian society against the elite. All of this mobilization was institutionalized by Solon, Cleisthenes, and other leaders after them, making it much harder for elites to usurp power and quickly reassert their dominance. As a consequence, Athenians, worried though they were like the Tiv about elites becoming too strong and dominant, nonetheless believed that they could rein them in with their ostracism law, iron armor, and assemblies. They weren't completely wrong.

This wasn't so for the Tiv. The power of Tiv society emanated from their norms directed against any type of political hierarchy. Such norms are a powerful way of preserving the stateless status quo because they help solve the collective action problem and induce people to organize in order to cut down to size individuals attempting to become dominant and excessively powerful. They are not, however, that good for organizing collective action for other purposes, such as shackling a Leviathan once it gets going. This is partly because the Tiv, like many other stateless societies, were organized into a series of family lineages grouped together into larger clans. Though the Athenians did have phratries, these were more fluid and less based on powerful geneological ties, and Cleisthenes severely undercut their role in politics. In contrast, the lowest level of aggregation of Tiv society was an extended family community known as a *tar*, and if anyone had authority in a tar, it was male elders. This was a society organized vertically through the kinship system where people's roles in life were closely regulated and prescribed. There was little chance for people to freely form and join any sort of association that could help them mobilize and monitor political power. In addition, beliefs that any inequality had its roots in witchcraft would start crumbling as soon as hierarchy emerged and gained respect. Kin relations would not provide a platform on which society could deliberate and participate in collective decisions.

What's worse, in a kin-based society political hierarchy is most likely to take the form of one clan's dominance over the others, paving the way for a type of Leviathan that would ultimately crush all opposition. A slippery slope indeed. Better to keep the Leviathan absent.

Staying Illegible

Many historical and a few surviving stateless societies look like the Tiv. Not only do they live without a state or much political hierarchy, but they diligently guard against the emergence of hierarchy using whatever tools they have available. Often these are norms and beliefs, just like witchcraft, that have evolved over many generations. But does this have any relevance to modern nations? All 195 countries that exist today have states and laws, and courts and security forces enforcing those laws. Could the Absent Leviathan of stateless societies have any relevance to them? The answer turns out to be yes. Though states do exist, they can be extremely weak, leaving large swaths of their countries in the same situation as stateless societies, governed by their norms like the Tiv, or frequently plunging into violence like the Gebusi of Papua New Guinea. More strikingly, despite their modern façade, some states may refrain from setting up basic institutions, acting like the Absent Leviathan in all but name, and for the same reason as the Tiv—because they fear the slippery slope. The modern state of Lebanon is one example.

The U.S. Constitution specifies that the representation in the House of Representatives should be proportional to the population of each state. To determine these populations, within three years of the ratification of the Constitution a census had to be held and it had to be updated every ten years. The first census was launched in 1790 and has since been repeated assiduously every decade. There are many reasons why censuses are a good idea, apart from being the basis for a fair distribution of representation in the legislature. They help the government know where its people are, where they come from, how they are living, how educated they are, and perhaps what their income or wealth is. This is important for the state to provide services and raise revenues and taxes. In the words of the political scientist James Scott, censuses help make society "legible" to the state— they provide the information to understand, regulate, tax, and if necessary coerce society. These activities seem so essential to the existence and function of a state that every state should want to make society legible. The people should also want some degree of legibility, since otherwise they won't receive any services or be properly represented. You can by now see the flaws in this argument. What if society doesn't trust the state? What if it is worried about legibility being misused? What if it fears the slippery slope? This is exactly what the Lebanese are concerned about.

Lebanon was part of the Ottoman Empire until World War I and then briefly a French colony until it became independent in 1943. Since independence Lebanon has never held a census. There was one in 1932, which became the basis for a National Pact agreed in 1943, but nothing since then. The 1932 census found that Christians made up 51 percent of the population with a slight edge over the Shia, Sunni, and Druze Muslim communities in Lebanon (which are shown in Map 3). The pact recognized this configuration by dividing power between the various groups. For example, the president always had to be a Maronite Christian, while the prime minister would be a Sunni Muslim and the speaker of parliament a Shia Muslim. The division didn't stop there. The deputy speaker and the deputy prime minister always had to be Greek Orthodox Christians, while the chief of the general staff of the armed forces would be a Druze Muslim. Representation in

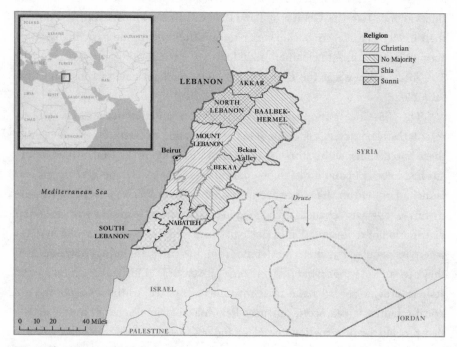

Map 3. The Communities of Lebanon

parliament was frozen in a ratio of six to five in favor of Christians to Muslims; within this ratio the different communities were represented according to their population share in the 1932 census.

Predictably, this pact resulted in an incredibly weak state. Power in the country resides not in the state, but in the individual communities, just as you would expect under the Absent Leviathan. The state does not provide public services such as healthcare or electricity, but the communities do. The state does not control violence or law enforcement either. Hezbollah, a Shia Muslim group, has its own private army, as do the many armed clans in the Bekaa Valley. Each community has its own television station and football team. In Beirut, for example, Al-Ahed is a Shia team, while Al-Ansar is Sunni. The Safa Sporting Club is Druze, while Racing Beirut is Orthodox Christian and Hikmeh is Maronite Christian.

The intense power sharing in the Lebanese state allows every community to monitor what the others are doing. This gives each group a veto over anything anybody else wants, and leads to terrible gridlock in the government. The gridlock has obvious consequences, such as an inability to make decisions. This matters for public services. In July 2015 the main landfill in the country at Naameh shut down. The government didn't have an alternative and the trash began to mount in Beirut. Rather than spring into action, the government did nothing. The trash continued to pile up. A picture of the mounting trash in Beirut is included in the photo insert.

In fact, doing nothing was the government's normal state. Parliament has not voted on a budget for almost ten years, letting the cabinet write its own. After the prime minister Najib Mikati resigned in 2013, it took politicians a year to agree on a new government. No big rush, since between the parliamentary election of June 2009 and 2014, as the landfill filled up, the 128 members of parliament met twenty-one times, about four times a year. In 2013, lawmakers met only twice and passed two laws. One of the laws was to extend their mandate for another eighteen months so they could stay in power. This strategy was used year after year and new elections were held only in May 2018. In the meantime, Lebanon was facing one of its most existential threats, as one million refugees from the civil war in neighboring Syria, equivalent to almost 20 percent of Lebanon's population, poured into the country. Thus a parliament, elected for four years and refraining from taking any action on vital problems facing the country, ended up "sitting" for nine years. Sitting is all relative, of course. After parliamentarians managed to pass a law to plan the 2018 elections, a competition was held by a media outlet for the best tweets to commemorate the event. One of the submissions was "WELL DONE

GENTLEMEN, YOU'VE COMPLETED YOUR ONE HOUR OF WORK. You can now return to your permanent vacations." No big rush to deal with the trash.

The situation got so bad that people began to organize and protest, and a movement calling itself YouStink emerged, using the trash problem as a trigger to call for more profound change in the system. But suspicion is the order of the day in Lebanon. An organization, any organization, is immediately suspected of being the tool of one of the other communities attempting to increase its power. As a despairing Facebook post from the movement on August 25, 2015 put it:

> Since the beginning of the #YouStink movement, we have tried to bite our tongues concerning the accusations that fell upon us as a movement . . . Our movement, since its outset, has been accused of being a partisan of Al-Mustaqbal (Future Movement) and working against the rights of the Christians (on the Tayyar website). We were then accused of being partisans of the 8th of March bloc and working against the Al-Mustaqbal (according to both El-Machnouk Ministers and the Government). As for the movement's members themselves, they have been accused of being bribed, partisans of Walid Jumblat, foreign embassies, the Amal Movement, Hezbollah . . . No one has remained safe from these accusations which main purpose was and is to distort and refute the idea of having an independent non-sectarian alternative.

This post illustrates something we often see under an Absent Leviathan: a society divided against itself, unable to act collectively, and in fact deeply suspicious of anybody and any group attempting to influence politics.

The behavior of the parliament reflects the fact that the communities do not want it to do anything. As Ghassan Moukheiber, a Christian lawmaker from central Lebanon, put it:

> They don't like the institutions such as the parliament meeting too often and competing with them in running the country.

The Lebanese state is not weak because its people have not worked out the right engineering design. In fact, the country has one of the most educated populations in the Middle East, with a fairly modern university system. Many Lebanese study abroad in some of the world's best academic institutions. It isn't that they don't know how to build a capable state. Rather, the state is weak by design because the communities fear the slippery slope. Parliamentarians know they are not supposed to do much, so what is the incentive to show up? They can vote to delay elections because nobody really cares who is elected. Sometimes, as with the trash problem, this has terrible social consequences, but even then it's hard to make something happen. Nobody wants to give power to parliament, they don't trust it, and they don't like social activism either. You never know whom you can trust.

Lebanon is not a stateless society. It's a modern state of six million people with a seat in the United Nations and ambassadors all over the world. But just as with the Tiv, power is elsewhere. Lebanon has an Absent Leviathan.

Between 1975 and 1989 Lebanon was plunged into a vicious civil war between its different communities, after being destabilized by an influx of Palestinian refugees from Jordan. The Taif Agreement of 1989, which ended the conflict, brought one adjustment to the National Pact, moving to a 50–50 split between Christians and Muslims in parliament and increasing the representation of Shias. But it also weakened presidential power.

Did the 50–50 split represent the communities better than the six-to-five division adopted in the 1943 pact? Probably, but nobody really knows the populations of different communities, and nobody wants to know. Society wants to remain illegible to a state it fears might be captured by others, and to ensure against the possibility, it makes sure the Leviathan continues to slumber. The trash piles up.

The Narrow Corridor

This book is about liberty. Liberty depends on the different types of Leviathans and their evolution—whether a society will live without an effective state, put up with a despotic one, or manage to forge a balance of power that opens the way for the emergence of a Shackled Leviathan and the gradual flourishing of liberty.

In contrast to Hobbes's vision of society submitting its will to the Leviathan, which much of social science and the modern world order take for granted, it is fundamental to our theory that Leviathans are not always welcomed with open arms and their path is a rocky one, to say the least. In many instances society will resist their ascendancy and will do so successfully, just like the Tiv did and the Lebanese still do. The result of this resistance is illiberty.

When this resistance crumbles, we may end up with a Despotic Leviathan, which looks a lot like the sea monster that Hobbes imagined. But this Leviathan, though it prevents Warre, does not necessarily make its subjects' lives much richer than the "nasty, brutish, and short" existence that people eke out under the Absent Leviathan. Nor do its subjects really "submit their wills" to the Leviathan—any more than East Europeans chanting the "Internationale" in the streets before the collapse of the Berlin Wall really submitted their wills to Soviet Russia. The implications for citizens are different in some ways, but still there is no liberty.

A very different type of Leviathan, a shackled one, emerges when there is a balance between its power and society's capacity to control it. This is the Leviathan that can resolve conflicts fairly, provide public services and economic opportunities, and prevent dominance, laying down the basic foundations of liberty. This is the Leviathan that people, believing that they can control it, trust and cooperate with and allow to increase its capacity. This is the Leviathan that also promotes liberty by breaking down the various cages of norms tightly regulating behavior in society. But in a fundamental sense this is not a Hobbesian Leviathan. Its defining feature is its shackles: it does not have Hobbes's sea monster's dominance over society; it does not have the capability to ignore or silence people when they try to influence political decision making. It stands not above but alongside society.

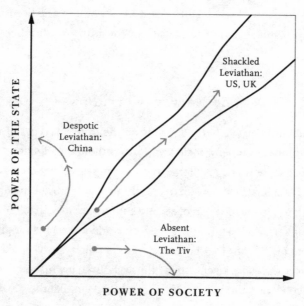

Figure 1. The Evolution of Despotic, Shackled, and Absent Leviathans

Figure 1 on the previous page summarizes these ideas and the forces shaping the evolution of different types of states in our theory. To focus on its main outlines, we simplify matters and reduce everything to two variables. The first is how powerful a society is in terms of its norms, practices, and institutions, especially when it comes to acting collectively, coordinating its actions, and constraining political hierarchy. This variable, shown on the horizontal axis, thus combines society's general mobilization, its institutional power, and its ability to control hierarchy via norms, as among the Tiv. The second is the power of the state. This variable is shown on the vertical axis and similarly combines several aspects including the power of political and economic elites and the capacity and power of state institutions. Of course, ignoring conflicts within society is a huge simplification, and so is ignoring conflicts within the elite and between the elite and state institutions. Nevertheless, these simplifications enable us to highlight several important ingredients and novel implications of our theory. Later in the book, we'll go beyond these simplifications and discuss the richer tableau that emerges without them.

Think of most premodern polities starting somewhere near the bottom left, without powerful states or societies. The arrows that emanate from this bottom left trace the divergent development paths of state, society, and their relations over time. One typical path shown in the figure, approximating our discussion of the Tiv or Lebanon, begins where society is more powerful than the state and can stymie the emergence of powerful centralized state institutions. This results in a situation where the Leviathan is largely absent because initially the state and elites are too weak relative to society's norms against political hierarchy. The fear of the slippery slope implies that, when possible, society will try to cripple the power of elites and undercut political hierarchy, so the power of state-like entities declines further, and the Absent Leviathan gets established even more firmly. The greater power of society relative to the state also explains why the cage of norms is so potent in this case—with no institutional ways of resolving and regulating conflicts, norms take on all sorts of functions, but in the process also create their own social inequities and various forms of stifling restrictions on individuals.

On the other side, starting with greater initial levels of state and elite power than societal power, we see an arrow approximating our initial discussion of the Chinese case where the configuration favors the emergence of the Despotic Leviathan. Here the arrows travel toward yet higher levels of state power. In the meantime, the power of society gets eroded as society finds itself no match for the state. This tendency is exacerbated as the Despotic Leviathan works to emasculate society so that it remains unshackled. In consequence, over time the Despotic

Leviathan becomes overwhelmingly powerful relative to a meek society, and a change in the balance of power ultimately leading the Leviathan to be shackled becomes less likely.

But the figure also shows that we can have capable states matched by capable societies. This happens in the narrow corridor in the middle, where we see the emergence of the Shackled Leviathan. It is precisely in this corridor that the Red Queen effect is operative, and the struggle of state and society contributes to the strengthening of both and can, somewhat miraculously, help maintain the balance between the two.

In fact, the Red Queen—the race between state and society—does more than render both of them more capable. It also reconfigures the nature of institutions and makes the Leviathan more accountable and responsive to citizens. In the process, it transforms people's lives too, not just because it removes the dominance of states and elites over them, but also because it relaxes and even breaks down the cage of norms, advancing individual liberty and enabling more effective popular participation in politics. Consequently, it is only in this corridor that true liberty, unencumbered by political, economic, and social dominances, emerges and evolves. Outside the corridor, liberty is curbed either by the absence of the Leviathan or by its despotism.

Yet it is important to recognize the precarious nature of the Red Queen effect. In all of that reaction and counterreaction, one party may pull ahead of the other, yanking both out of the corridor. The Red Queen effect also requires that the competition between state and society, between elites and non-elites, isn't completely zero-sum, with each side trying to destroy and dispossess the other. So in all of that competition, some room for compromise, an understanding that there will be a counterreaction after every reaction, is critical. We'll see in Chapter 13 that a process of polarization can sometimes turn the Red Queen effect into a zero-sum affair, making the process much more likely to spin out of control.

Another noteworthy feature of this figure is that at the bottom left corner, where both state and society are very weak, there is no corridor. This represents an important aspect of our discussion of the Tiv. Recall that the Tiv did not have norms and institutions capable of controlling political hierarchy once it emerged, and this was the reason why they were so keen to stamp out any whiff of political hierarchy; the choice wasn't between a Shackled and Absent Leviathan, but between despotism and no state at all. This is a general feature that applies to many cases where both state and society are weak, and highlights that moving into the corridor is feasible only after both parties in the struggle have built some rudimentary capabilities and after some basic institutional prerequisites for a balance of power are in place.

The Proof of the Pudding

A theory is most useful when it offers new ways of thinking about the world. Let's consider a few insights that follow from the theory we have just presented. We started in Chapter 1 with the question of where the world is heading. An idyllic version of Western democracy with no rivals? Anarchy? Or a digital dictatorship? From the vantage point of our theory, each one of these looks like one of the paths described in Figure 1. But what our theory clarifies is that there should be no presumption that all countries will follow the same path. We should expect not convergence but diversity. What's more, it's not as if countries can seamlessly transition from one path to the other. There is a lot of "path dependence." Once you are in the orbit of the Despotic Leviathan, the state and elites controlling state institutions become stronger and society and the norms meant to keep the state in check become even weaker. Take China. Many policy makers and commentators have continued to predict that as it grows richer and more integrated into the global economic order, China will become more like a Western democracy. But the path of the Despotic Leviathan in Figure 1 doesn't converge toward the corridor as time goes by. We'll see in Chapter 7 that there is a lot of history shaping the dominance of the Chinese state over society and these relationships are reproduced by the specific actions that leaders and elites take in order to impair society so that it cannot challenge and constrain the state. This history makes a transition into the corridor much harder.

Nonetheless, that history matters doesn't mean that history is destiny. This brings out a second important implication of our theory. There is a lot of agency—meaning that actions by leaders, elites, and political entrepreneurs can facilitate collective action and form new coalitions to reshape the society's trajectory. That's why path dependence coexists with occasional transitions from one type of path to another. This coexistence is particularly true for societies in the corridor because the balance between state and society is fragile and can easily break if society ceases to be vigilant or the state lets its capabilities atrophy.

A third, related implication is about the nature of liberty. In contrast to a vision emphasizing the virtues and relentless rise of Western institutions or constitutional designs, in our theory liberty emerges from a messy process, one that cannot be easily designed. Liberty cannot be engineered and its fate cannot be ensured by a clever system of checks and balances. It takes society's mobilization, vigilance, and assertiveness to make it work. We need all that running!

Recall from the Preface that the strategy of restraining Gilgamesh with checks and balances, via his doppelgänger Enkidu, didn't work in Uruk. It's no different in most other settings, including in the U.S., even if the checks and balances introduced by the Constitution are often emphasized as the mainstay of American liberty. In 1787 James Madison and his collaborators descended on Philadelphia and seized the agenda of the constitutional assembly with the Virginia Plan, which became the basis for the Constitution. But the institutional architecture of the new country turned out to be different from the Virginia Plan because society (or some portion of it) didn't fully trust the Federalists and wanted to have greater protections for their liberty. As we saw, Madison had to concede the Bill of Rights. It was society's involvement and assertiveness that secured the protection of rights in the founding of the U.S. Republic.

A fourth implication of our theory is that there are many doorways into the corridor and quite a variety of societies inside. Think of all the ways a country can enter the corridor. Indeed, creating the conditions for liberty is a multifaceted process, involving the control of conflict and violence, the breaking down of the cage of norms, and the shackling of the power and despotism of state institutions. This is why liberty doesn't emerge the moment a nation enters the corridor, but evolves gradually over time. Some will travel a long time in the corridor without fully controlling violence, some will make only limited progress in loosening the cage of norms, and for others combating despotism and making the state listen to society will be a work in progress. The historical conditions and coalitions that determine how a society gets into the corridor also influence what particular compromises are made in the corridor—often with major and long-lasting consequences.

The U.S. Constitution illustrates this point too. The Bill of Rights wasn't the only concession that was necessary for ratification. The issue of states' rights was a litmus test for Southern elites hell-bent on protecting slavery and their assets. To this end, the founders agreed that the Bill of Rights would apply only to federal legislation, not to state legislation. This "principle" gave free rein to all sorts of abuses at the state level, especially against black Americans. The Constitution itself enshrined this gross violation of the liberty of a large fraction of the population with the clause that agreed to count slaves as three-fifths of a free person when determining a state's representation in Congress. Discrimination was not just woven into the very fabric of the Constitution; it was also forged by the deep-rooted norms in many parts of the country. The way in which the United States moved into and traveled in the corridor meant that the federal government did not attempt to weaken these norms and their institutional foundations in the South. So intense discrimination and dominance against black Americans lived on well after the Civil War and the end of slavery in 1865.

One of the many egregious manifestations of these discriminatory norms was the existence of "sundown towns," towns where black people (and sometimes Mexicans and Jews) were not allowed after sunset. America is the country of the car, where people get their kicks "on Route 66." But not everyone could get their kicks. In 1930, in 44 of the 89 counties that Route 66 wound through, there were "sundown towns." What happened if you wanted to eat or maybe go to the toilet and the restaurants and bathrooms were only for whites? Even Coca-Cola machines had "White Customers Only" printed on them. Imagine the quandary of a black driver. The situation was so bad that in 1936 Victor Green, an African American postal worker in Harlem, New York, felt compelled to publish *The Negro Motorist Green-Book*, providing detailed instructions to black motorists about where they were allowed after dark or where they could go to the toilet (the last edition is dated 1966). So the U.S. experience exhibits the profound implications of how a society gets into the corridor. We'll see in Chapter 10 that these have consequences not just for the extent of liberty but also for many policy and social choices, with far-reaching global significance.

A surprising, fifth implication of our theory concerns the development of state capacity. In Figure 1 the arrow inside the corridor is heading toward higher levels of state capacity than the Despotic Leviathan is achieving. This is because it is the contest between state and society that underpins greater state capacity. This notion runs counter to many arguments accepted in social science and policy debates, especially on the critical role of strong leaders, that contend that complete control of security and powerful armed forces are necessary for building state capacity. It is this belief that makes many argue that China may be a good role model for other developing (and perhaps even developed) countries because the lack of challenges to the dominance of the Communist Party enables its state to have such great capacity. But look deeper, and you will see that the Chinese Leviathan, despotic though it is, possesses less capacity than a Shackled Leviathan like the U.S. or Scandinavian states. This is because China doesn't have a robust society to push it, cooperate with it, or contest its power. Without this balance of power between state and society, the Red Queen effect doesn't come into play and the Leviathan ends up with less capacity.

To see the limitations of Chinese state capacity, you need to look no further than the education system. Education is a priority for many states, and not just because a nation would be more successful with an educated workforce. It is also because education is an effective way of inculcating the right sort of beliefs among citizens. So you would expect that a state with significant capacity would be able to provide affordable, high-quality, and meritocratic education and mobilize its public servants to work for that objective. But the reality is rather different. In the Chinese education system, everything is up for sale, including front-row seats near the blackboard or a post as class monitor.

When Zhao Hua went to enroll her daughter in a Beijing elementary school, she was met by officials from the district education committee who already had a list showing how much each family had to pay. The officials didn't hang out at the school, but at a bank where Zhao had to deposit $4,800 to get the enrollment. The schools are free, so these "fees" are illegal and the government has banned them five times since 2005 (and it is telling that they had to be banned five times). In another elite Beijing high school, students receive an extra point for each $4,800 their parents contribute to the school. If you want to get your child into a top school, such as the one associated with the prestigious Renmin University in Beijing, the bribe could be as much as $130,000. Teachers also expect gifts—lots of gifts. Chinese news media report that many teachers now expect to be given designer watches, expensive teas, gift cards, and even vacations. More aggressive teachers welcome debit cards attached to bank accounts that can be replenished throughout the year. In an interview with *The New York Times*, a Beijing businesswoman summed it up: "If you don't give a nice present and the other parents do, you're afraid the teacher will pay less attention to your kid."

How can public servants be so venal? Isn't China the home of the world's first meritocratic state bureaucracy? Yes and no. As we'll see in Chapter 7, there is a long history of a complex, capable bureaucracy in China, but there is an equally long history of pervasive corruption in which many positions are given to the politically connected or auctioned off to the highest bidder. That history continues today. A 2015 survey of 3,671 Communist Party officials found that two-thirds of them thought that "political loyalty," not merit, was the most important criterion for getting a government job. Once you've surrounded yourself with loyalists, you can get down to the business of shaking down businesspeople and citizens. You can also create compliant subordinates by selling government jobs. The political scientist Minxin Pei analyzed a sample of 50 court cases of Communist Party officials who had been found guilty of corruption between 2001 and 2013. On average, each had sold 41 positions for money. At the bottom of the pile were county bosses, like Zhang Guiyi and Xu Shexin of Wuhe County in Anhui Province.

Zhang sold 11 positions for an average price of 12,000 yuan, a measly $1,500. Xu sold 58 positions at over $2,000 each on average. But higher up the food chain, for example in the prefectures, jobs were sold for a lot more, with some officials managing to get over $60,000 per position. In Pei's sample the average corrupt official made about $170,000 from selling posts.

People like Zhang and Xu are just small fry. When railway minister Liu Zhijun was arrested in 2011, his charges included having 350 apartments in his name and over $100 million in cash. This is largely because China's high-speed rail system had presented an unrivaled opportunity for graft. But so do most other aspects of Chinese economic expansion. Though Liu fell from grace, most don't. In 2012, 160 of China's wealthiest 1,000 people were members of the Communist Party Congress. Their net worth was $221 billion, about twenty times that of the top 660 officials in all three branches of the government of the United States, a country whose income per capita is over seven times that of China. All of this shouldn't be completely surprising. Controlling corruption, whether in the bureaucracy or in the education system, requires cooperation from society. The state needs to trust that people will report to it truthfully, and the people need to trust state institutions to the extent that they put their neck on the line by sharing their information. That doesn't happen under the stern gaze of the Despotic Leviathan.

You might think this is mostly a problem of corruption. Could it be that corruption is tolerated in China despite high state capacity? That interpretation is contradicted not only by the persistent (and only mildly successful) attempts by the Chinese state to rein in corruption, but also by the fact that even beyond corruption, routine state functions do not come easily to the Chinese Leviathan. As we mentioned when discussing Lebanon, making society legible appears to be a primary goal of any self-respecting state. This is doubly true for making the economy legible. Indeed, given the critical role that economic growth plays in the Communist Party's ability to justify its dominant position in China, understanding and accurately measuring economic activity must be a key objective. But legibility, just like controlling corruption, requires cooperation from society. When cooperation is withheld, problems creep in; will businesses seek shelter in the informal, unregistered sector? Will individuals withhold their information from a state they do not trust? Will bureaucrats manipulate data to get ahead? The answer to all three questions is yes, especially in China. That is why nobody seems to trust national income statistics in China, not even the premier Li Keqiang, who in 2007, before he was promoted to this post, described the country's national income numbers as "man-made and unreliable." He suggested eschewing official statistics and looking at electricity consumption, the volume of rail cargo, and bank lending as better gauges of how the economy is doing. So much for the capacity of the Chinese state to make its economy legible.

Shackling the Leviathan: Trust and Verify

The Shackled Leviathan sounds exactly like the sort of state we should all dream of, and one we can trust. But if it is indeed to be a Shackled Leviathan, this trust must have limits. After all, the Leviathan, shackled or not, is Janus-faced, and despotism is in its DNA.

This means that living with the Leviathan is hard work, particularly because there is a natural tendency for it to become more powerful over time. The Leviathan is not itself an agent; when we are talking of the Leviathan, we are typically referring to political elites, such as rulers, politicians, or leaders controlling it, and sometimes to economic elites with a disproportionate influence on it. The majority of these elites, as well as many of those working for the Leviathan, have an interest in expanding the Leviathan's power. Think of the bureaucrats who are tirelessly working to provide you with public services or to regulate economic activity so that you do not get dominated by a monopoly or by predatory lending practices. Why wouldn't they want their own power and authority expanded? Think of the politicians who are steering the Leviathan. Why wouldn't they wish their own sea monster to become even more capable and dominant? What's more, the more complex our lives become, the more we need conflict resolution, regulation, public services, and protection for our liberties. And yet, the more capable the Leviathan becomes, the harder it is to control. So the more powerful society—meaning the common people, all of us and our organizations and associations—must become in order to control it. This is the Red Queen effect in action.

But there is more to the Red Queen. As we have seen, cooperation with a powerful society can greatly increase the capacity of the state. Once the Leviathan is shackled, society may choose to give it a long leash and allow it to increase its reach so that the state uses its capacity for things that its citizens want and need. It is a strategy of "trust and verify"—trust the state to acquire more powers but at the same time increase your own control over it. When it works, as it has to some degree in the United States and Western Europe, the outcome is an ongoing process of both state and society becoming more powerful, and expanding in a balanced way, so that neither dominates the other. When this fine balance works, the Shackled Leviathan not only ends Warre but also becomes an instrument for the political and social development of society, for the blossoming of civic engagement, institutions, and capabilities, for the dismantling of the cage of norms, and for economic prosperity. But only if we manage to keep it shackled. Only if we succeed in preventing the messy Red Queen effect from getting out of control. No easy feat.

Before we turn to the Shackled Leviathan, it is useful to understand how and why states emerge, how they deal with conflicts in society, and how they transform economic conditions of societies under the Absent Leviathan. That's where we start in the next chapter.

Chapter 3

WILL TO POWER

The Rise of a Prophet

Muhammad was born in Mecca around 570 CE into a merchant family. Brought up by his uncle, he grew up in the vibrant trading hub that Mecca was in this period. The origins of the city seem to have been tied to the Kaaba, the dense black granite cube that was a sacred place for pre-Islamic local gods and later became the holiest shrine of Islam. During part of the year people came to Mecca on pilgrimage, which turned out to be a great opportunity to engage in commerce. The nascent trading community of the town soon spread far and wide to intermediate more broadly between the Arabian Peninsula and Damascus and the Byzantine and Persian Empires.

But the people who settled Mecca and the neighboring town of Medina, 250 miles to the north (see Map 4), were desert nomads, new to sedentary life. Their societies lacked states and centralized authorities, and like many other stateless societies, they were organized around kinship groups known as clans. Muhammad's clan was the Hashim, part of the Quraysh tribe. Adjusting to life in the new town around the Kaaba wasn't easy. The clans were used to migrating with their flocks of camels and goats across hundreds of miles of open desert. There were the potential disputes about access to a water hole or good pasture for the flocks, or any of myriad daily conflicts. But these were usually handled by the norms and

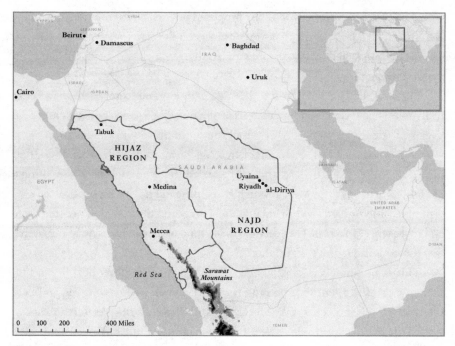

Map 4. The Arabian Peninsula: The Origins of Islam and the Saudi State, and the Historic City of Uruk

traditions of the nomadic tribes, and when that didn't work, especially for conflict between different groups, they could just go their own separate ways in the sparsely populated peninsula. When this strategy couldn't solve the disputes, there was retaliation and feud. The basic principle was an eye for an eye, but in some cases it had evolved into a hundred camels for an eye.

Life was more complicated around the Kaaba, and not just because of more frequent and varied conflicts that arose when people from different clans settled in the town. The new economic opportunities arising from the pilgrimage and the subsequent spread of trade fostered individualism and generated novel conflicts at the same time as they started to slightly relax the cage of norms and erode previous solidarities and bonds of community that had dominated life in the desert.

It was in this social context that a prophet emerged. At around the age of forty, Muhammad began to have visions and received revelations that he eventually identified as coming from the Angel Gabriel. These revelations, which formed the beginning of what would come to be the Quran, the holy book of Muslims, were in the form of aphorisms exhorting people to recognize a new monotheistic religion with Allah as the one true God. They proposed not just a new religion, but a new community and new norms that would transcend the clans, such as the Hashim. They also criticized many of the new individualistic behaviors and the focus on making money.

Muhammad began to preach this new religion and exhort others to swear fealty to this new God. His first converts were his wife Khadija and his close relatives and friends. By 613 he was preaching more broadly in the town. But this wasn't welcomed by everybody. Other trading clans resented the attacks on their behavior and religious beliefs, and they worried that Muhammad was making a bid for political power in Mecca, which at the time did not have a centralized government. Muhammad's following gradually grew and the situation became more and more tense. In 622 he fled, along with a group of his followers, to Medina; this was the famous Hegira ("emigration").

This emigration was precipitated not just by the mounting hostility to Muhammad in Mecca, but by a petition from citizens of Medina to come and help them solve their problems. Like Mecca, Medina was suffering the birth pangs of settled life. Unlike Mecca, however, it was not a trading hub but an oasis specializing in highly productive agriculture. Different parts of the oasis had been settled by different clans from two tribes, the Aws and the Khazraj. There were also three Jewish clans. The clans had built small forts as their strongholds, and engaged in incessant conflict that had culminated in 618 in the battle of Bu'ath. Life was starting to resemble Warre.

Some of the Medinans came up with the idea that Muhammad, as a neutral outsider and with the authority of his new religion, could be the arbiter for disputes and would bring peace and order to the town. In June 622, seventy-five of them went to Mecca to request that he move to Medina; they pledged themselves to protect him and the new religion. Muhammad agreed. The agreement between him and the Medinans is recorded in a document known as the Constitution of Medina. This declares that "wherever there is anything about which you differ, it is to be referred to God and to Muhammad." In effect Muhammad was to take on the role of judge in disputes between individuals and clans. But how could he do that if he did not have the power to enforce his laws and make others do what he commanded? Yet the reference to God in the Constitution of Medina made it clear that Muhammad didn't come just as an individual; he came as a prophet, and part of the package was that the Medinans had to accept his teachings and revelations. Indeed, the Constitution of Medina started thus:

In the name of God, the Merciful, the Compassionate!

This is a writing of Muhammad the prophet between the believers and Muslims of Quraysh and Yathrib and those who follow them and are attached to them and who crusade along with them. They are a single community distinct from other people.

This ought to have signaled to the Medinans (the people from Yathrib) that they were perhaps getting more than they bargained for with the new constitution. The constitution didn't just make Muhammad a judge. It recognized a new sort of society, based not on kin and clan, but on religion and the nascent centralized authority of a prophet. This was the end of statelessness.

Muhammad didn't at first have any official position or executive power, but from this modest platform he soon got moving. His approach ought to have been evident from the opening paragraph above, which says "who crusade along with them." Crusade? By 623, the year after the Hegira, Muhammad started to organize raids on Meccan trade caravans with the people he had brought with him from Mecca, known as the Emigrants. Engaging in such raids was not unusual among the tribes of Arabia, but they began to take on a new connotation. Instead of just being raids of one tribe on another, they were raids by Muslims against unbelievers. By 624 the raids began to include not just the Emigrants, but also the Helpers, the name for Medinans who had converted to Islam. By March of that year the Emigrants and Helpers together defeated a large Meccan force sent out against them at the battle of Badr.

Badr and the subsequent battle of Uhud increased Muhammad's prestige and control over Medina. He proceeded to remove clans that had proved disloyal, particularly the Jews, and he started to use his religious authority to reform local society, changing both marriage and inheritance practices.

Muhammad might have been brought in with a limited mandate to resolve disputes, but he was building a new state over which the preexisting clans would have little control. Over time his power grew. One reason for this was that nomadic tribes in the desert heard of his success and came to Medina to swear their loyalty to him. Another reason stemmed from the fact that part of the benefit of the raids which the Emigrants carried out was booty. Muhammad himself received one-fifth of this. He also stipulated that they make contributions (actually taxes), which had to be paid to the "community of God," and in addition imposed taxes for protection on Jews and Christians. Growing power and wealth are evident in the number of horses that Muhammad was able to field as cavalry in different raids. At the battle of Badr in 624 he had two horses. By the year 630 he could put 10,000 horses into the field.

Muhammad capitalized on his growing authority in 628 when he led a large mission of Emigrants and Helpers to Mecca purportedly to engage in pilgrimage. Understandably anxious, the Meccans forced them to stop short of the town and negotiated a deal whereby the Meccans would vacate the town the following year so that Muhammad and his followers could come on pilgrimage. While they waited for the deal to be struck, Muhammad gathered all his people under a tree and made them pledge themselves to him. This pledge, known as the Pledge of Good Pleasure, was one more step in the establishment of the state in Medina. As Hobbes imagined, the Leviathan needs people to submit to its will. This is what the people of Medina did, agreeing to do whatever Muhammad commanded. Though he still had no formal legislative or executive office, he was in effect the ruler of a new state.

His great authority is illustrated by an event that occurred in 630, just two years before he died. Muhammad was set on expanding the scope of his state and converting more people to the new religion. To achieve this objective, he decided to send a military force against the town of Tabuk in the north, and he insisted that all Muslims from Medina take part in this raid as a religious duty. He was now commander in chief.

———

The story of Muhammad's creation of the new Islamic state encapsulates some of the key ideas of this chapter. Prior to his emergence as a prophet, there were no real states in Arabia, just tribes. Even more urbanized areas, like Mecca and Medina, didn't really have centralized government. This created a lot of problems, not least violence and insecurity. When they lived in the vast wilderness of the Arabian Desert, there was plenty of room for all the tribes, but in the cramped oasis of Medina or around the sacred Kaaba in Mecca, they had to figure out how to live with one another. The creation of more centralized authority was one obvious way out. But how to do that without ceding control to another clan or tribe?

Then came Muhammad and his revelations from the Angel Gabriel, and the Medinans saw in his teachings a solution to their predicament. They brought him in to resolve conflicts between the clans and tribes. He succeeded in bringing peace, clearly a great service to the people living in Medina. But it didn't stop there. Though Muhammad and the Emigrants might have been a small minority to start with, they grew in number and became more powerful and wealthier as people joined them and agreed to contribute to their finances. This was the birth of political hierarchy in Arabia. By 628, with the Pledge of Good Pleasure, Muhammad's authority in Medina was unassailable. Two years later in the attack on Tabuk, he ordered the entire oasis to march north.

The Medinans had come a long way in eight years. They had acceded to a more centralized authority to help resolve their conflicts, but in doing so they had started the process of state formation and got onto the slippery slope. They never got off it. Muhammad was engaged in a state-building project; part of his objective was to centralize authority in his and his followers' hands, and in the process transform not just conflict resolution but the overall organization of society, its norms, its customs. He succeeded brilliantly. In less than a decade, he created the seeds of a powerful Islamic state, a giant pan–Middle Eastern empire and a new impressive civilization.

What's Your Edge?

The birth of Islam is an example of what anthropologists call "pristine state formation"—the building of political hierarchy and some type of centralized authority where none existed before. It also illustrates the critical issues and difficulties associated with this.

The most important one, which we already highlighted in the previous chapter, is the slippery slope. The reason why centralized authority doesn't arise easily in many stateless societies is because these societies have developed norms and practices not just to control conflict, but also to prevent anybody from getting too strong. Once an individual or group manages to increase their power sufficiently to be able to adjudicate conflicts and provide security against major threats, it is difficult to stop them from getting even more power and start telling others what to do in every sphere of their lives. This is exactly what happened in Medina. The Medinans thought they could set up a system to redress some of the defects of not having a state, without submitting wholesale to the authority of a state or a charismatic, powerful leader. They failed. Several other societies starting off without centralized authority have similarly failed, sliding down the slippery slope toward a dominating Leviathan.

So why do the norms and the other controls that such societies have developed sometimes fail to rein in state builders? To start with, there is what the German philosopher Friedrich Nietzsche dubbed the "will to power"—the desire of men (and sometimes women) and groups to increase their power and authority over others, even if the norms are against it. For this reason, even in the most harmonious-looking stateless societies, there will be upstart individuals wishing to acquire more power, more wealth, and greater ability to dominate others. There will also be individuals and groups wishing to obtain more power because they have a vision of reorganizing society in a different manner. Many of these upstarts will be prevented from achieving their objectives by the prevailing norms and the actions of others in their societies, and yet some will succeed.

Would-be state builders are more likely to succeed and emasculate the norms meant to restrain them if they have an "edge"—something special, making it possible for them to overcome the barriers in their way. For Muhammad, the edge came from religion. He had a religious ideology that gave him a legitimate authority in his conflict resolution role and also afforded him great influence over his followers, which he used to found a new community. Once unleashed, this religious ideology created an unstoppable drive toward more centralized authority.

Another powerful edge is organizational, emanating from the ability of a leader to forge new coalitions or more effective organizations to exercise greater command or military force, a possibility illustrated by the formation of the Zulu state in Southern Africa, which we turn to next. Yet another possibility, which we discuss a little later in this chapter, is a technological edge, exemplified by the successful state-building project of King Kamehameha of Hawaii, which heavily relied on his use of guns, a military technology his enemies did not have access to. In all of these cases, personal charisma and other sources of legitimacy, for example, resulting from lineage, past exemplary or heroic behavior, or simply a force of personality, help as well.

A final important feature of many examples of pristine state formation illustrated by Muhammad's rise is the reorganization of society following the emergence of political hierarchy. As we saw in the previous chapter, societies without centralized authority are typically organized by a complex of norms that regulate and control conflict—and in fact every aspect of people's lives. Once the process of state formation is under way, state builders have an incentive to destroy these norms or at the very least transform them to serve their own objectives. This is not necessarily because they want to relax the cage of norms and unleash liberty, but because the norms that restrain and limit political hierarchy are standing in their way to greater power. In Muhammad's case, an important target was to supplant the kin-based relations prevailing in Medina and Mecca, which he could successfully do because his religious teachings elevated a new community over kin. For Shaka, as we'll next see, the target was the authority of witch doctors.

The Horns of the Buffalo

In his memoirs, British officer Horace Smith-Dorrien recalled the events of
January 22, 1879:

> At about 12 a.m. the Zulus . . . again showed in large numbers, coming
> down into the plain over the hills with great boldness, and our guns and
> rifles were pretty busy for some time . . . It was difficult to see exactly
> what was going on, but firing was heavy. It was evident now that the
> Zulus were in great force, for they could be seen extending (i.e. throwing
> out their horns) away across the plain to the south-east, apparently work-
> ing towards the right rear of the camp.

Smith-Dorrien was a member of an expeditionary force under Frederic The-
siger, Lord Chelmsford, that was sent into Zululand, now part of the province of
KwaZulu-Natal in South Africa (which is shown in Map 5). Chelmsford's force was
the vanguard of an expanding colonial empire whose aim was to eliminate the
independent Zulu state, then ruled by King Cetshwayo. The king's response to the
British invasion was simple. He told his army:

> March slowly, attack at dawn and eat up the red soldiers.

That's what they did on January 22. Chelmsford made the mistake of dividing
his force, leaving about 1,300 soldiers, mostly members of the 24th Regiment of
Foot, and two artillery pieces camped at the feet of the rock of Isandlwana. Over-
confident and underprepared, the red soldiers faced an army of 20,000 Zulu warriors who in the previous sixty years had cut out and consolidated a huge state in
Southern Africa. So large was the Zulu state that it had already sent shock waves
through the region, into modern-day Botswana, Lesotho, Mozambique, Swazi-
land, Zambia, and Zimbabwe (see Map 5).

Smith-Dorrien recorded:

> The advancing Zulus' line . . . was a marvellous sight, line upon line of
> men in slightly extended order, one behind the other, firing as they came
> along, for a few of them had firearms, bearing all before them. The rocket
> battery, apparently then only a mile to our front, was firing, and suddenly
> it ceased, and presently we saw the remnants of Durnford's force, mostly

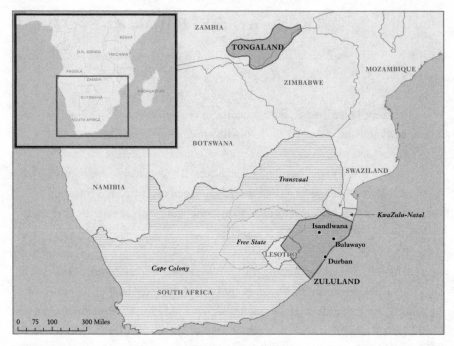

Map 5. Southern Africa: The Lands of the Zulu and the Tonga, and the Four South African Colonies

mounted Basutos, galloping back to the right of our position. What had actually happened I don't think we ever shall know accurately. The ground was intersected with "dongas," and in them Russell with his rocket battery was caught, and none escaped to tell the tale. I heard later that Durnford, who was a gallant leader, actually reached the camp and fell there fighting.

By the end of the day the British force had been wiped out. Smith-Dorrien escaped because of his dark blue officer's uniform. The Zulu soldiers had been told not to kill people in black because they were civilians, possibly priests. Just a few others lived to tell the tale and witness the greatest military defeat suffered by the British in their colonization of Africa.

In watching, apparently quite calmly, the advance of the Zulu army, Smith-Dorrien witnessed one of the great tactical innovations that had helped empower the Zulu state, the "horns of the buffalo." This was a military formation created by Shaka Zulu, the founder of the state, where the army formed into four main components: the chest of the buffalo at the center, the loins behind it, and two horns on either side that encircled the enemy. Smith-Dorrien also saw some of Shaka's other innovations in action—the disciplined regiments that were formed when Shaka took traditional ritual associations and militarized them, and the *iklwa*, a short stabbing spear with which Shaka had replaced the previous weapon of choice, the *assegai*, a javelin.

The Wrong Doer Who Knows No Law

Shaka was born around 1787, the illegitimate son of the then Zulu chief. At that time the Zulu formed a small chieftaincy among many others spread out over southern South Africa. Something of an outcast because of her illegitimate child, Shaka's mother took refuge with a neighboring people, the Mthethwa. In 1800 the Mthethwa had a new chief, named Dingiswayo. Dingiswayo anticipated some of Shaka's subsequent reforms and began a highly successful military and territorial expansion, conquering about thirty surrounding groups, including the Zulu. The young Shaka, called into the Mthethwa army, became one of its most effective warriors, soon known for his bravery and unscrupulousness. Dingiswayo tried to behave magnanimously toward defeated enemies; not so Shaka, who was typically in favor of massacring them all. His behavior won him the moniker "the wrong doer who knows no law." Shaka made his way up through the ranks until eventually he was promoted to be head of the army. In 1816, when Shaka's father died, Dingiswayo made sure that Shaka became the new chief of the Zulu.

Shaka immediately set about reorganizing Zulu society and those that he conquered into a new type of social system. He first called up all of the adult males and separated them into four regiments, which would form his first buffalo's chest, loins, and horns. Probably only about 400 men appeared at this juncture. He started to train them in the use of the *iklwa*, the spear that he had blacksmiths forge, and a new type of battle shield. He made them throw away their sandals and walk barefoot, which allowed them to move faster. Then with his first serious military force ready for action, he began to conquer surrounding areas. First were the eLangeni, who quickly succumbed and were incorporated into his rule. Next came the Butelezi, who put up a fight and were massacred. Within one year Shaka's army grew to 2,000 men. By the next year Dingiswayo was killed and Shaka made himself king of the Mthethwa. His ruthless tactics subdued one tribe after another, incorporating many into the expanding Zulu state. As one oral history records:

> The Butelezi, amaQungebe, Imbuyeni, amaCunu, Majola, Xulu, Sika-kane, are all tribes which were quite close . . . Tshaka attacked and killed off these tribes; he crept up on them in the night. Tribes further off were the amaMbata, Gasa, Kumalo, Hlubi, Qwabe, Dube, Langeni, Tembu, Zungu, Makoba.

The phrase "killed off" had different meanings in different contexts. In some cases, like the Butelezi, it seems to literally describe what happened. But in others the tribe was simply incorporated into the expanding Zulu state. Still others stayed more distant but declared themselves tributaries to the Zulus and paid "taxes" in cattle and young women. By 1819 Shaka had expanded the Zulu territory from about 100 square miles to 11,500, and his army stood at 20,000.

Shaka built a new capital at Bulawayo (marked on Map 5), and we have a firsthand description of it from 1824, when a party of English traders from Port Natal, now Durban, visited it. One of them, Henry Flynn, left a written record:

> On entering the great cattle kraal we found drawn up within about 80,000 natives in their war attire . . . Shaka then raised the stick in his hand and after striking with it right and left and springing out from amidst the chiefs, the whole mass broke from their position and formed up into regiments. Portions of these rushed to the river and the surrounding hills, whilst the remainder, forming themselves into a circle, commenced dancing with Shaka in their midst. It was an exciting scene, surprising to us, who could not have imagined that a nation termed "savages" could be so well disciplined. Regiments of girls, headed by officers of their own sex then entered the center of the arena to the number of 8,000 to 10,000 each holding a slight staff in her hand. They joined in the dance, which continued for about two hours.

Shaka also started the process of transforming existing norms. Instead of being based on kinship and clan, Shaka's state was based on two new axes. One was age. In many parts of Africa and elsewhere, when boys and girls come of age, they are initiated into the secret lore of the society, a process that typically goes along with circumcision and scarification. It involves staying for long periods in the wilderness and various types of ordeals. In some African societies these initiations became so institutionalized that when a cohort of boys, and sometimes even girls, was initiated, they became inducted into a group known as an "age set" (or "age grade") to which they would belong for their entire life.

In many parts of East Africa, whole peoples became organized not around kinship or a state, but around a sequence of these age grades. The grades undertook different functions as their members grew older, for example young men would be warriors, protecting the people or cattle. As they got older and a new cohort came along, they would transition into marriage and economic activities such as farming. Among the Zulu and other related peoples in Southern Africa these social structures were already present, even if in a rudimentary form. Shaka took them and militarized them. He turned age grades into military regiments and got them to live together in separate barracks. He also started recruiting the youth of the peoples he conquered. These regiments provided a way of breaking down the ties of family and integrating people into the new state. The role of the age sets in creating a new Zulu identity is revealed by an interchange at the annual harvest festival of Umkosi. At this time it was permissible for anyone to ask any question of the chief, and one impertinent soldier asked Shaka, "Why are outsiders promoted over the heads of Zulus?" To which Shaka supposedly retorted, "Any man who joins the Zulu army becomes a Zulu. Thereafter his promotion is purely a question of merit, irrespective of the road he came by."

The other new axis was geographic. Shaka divided the territory into counties and either left existing chiefs in place, though making it clear they now served at his pleasure, or appointed loyal soldiers of his army as governors.

In the process, Shaka centralized many functions into his own hands. Previously the harvest festival of Umkosi had been celebrated widely in the region, with individual chiefs conducting the ceremony. Now only Shaka presided over the annual rites. He also created a centralized court. Although chiefs could adjudicate disputes and solve local problems, ultimate appeal could be made to Shaka in Bulawayo.

A primary way in which Shaka maintained his system was tribute and its distribution among his supporters. As he conquered or subdued surrounding peoples, he forcibly demanded huge numbers of cows and women. He endowed his regiments with cattle in reward for their services and organized women into age regiments as well, and segregated them, forbidding the men to marry or have sexual relations with them until he allowed it.

Of course this was a state that was not bureaucratized in the way modern states are. Though Shaka had advisers, the state was run by the army and his appointed chiefs, and in the absence of writing, laws and rules were oral. Bureaucratized or unbureaucratized, Shaka's state-building project had to break parts of the cage of norms that were inhibiting the emergence of political hierarchy and Shaka's authority. A pillar of these norms, just as with the Tiv's norms we saw in Chapter 2, was the complex of supernatural beliefs often used for grinding down anyone getting too big for their boots.

In a famous incident, not long after he became chief of the Zulus, Shaka had to deal with some evil omens. A hammerhead crane flew over Shaka's kraal; then a porcupine wandered into it; then a crow perched on a fence and began to utter human words. These omens necessitated summoning a team of witch doctors, headed by a woman called Nobela, who indicated the identity of witches by hitting them with the gnu tails the team carried. Not so different from the fly whisk of the Tiv. The parallels with the Tiv didn't stop there. The Zulus were lined up and Nobela and her associates began "smelling out" the witches who had brought on the evil omens. They picked on prosperous people. One had grown rich through frugality. Another had put cattle manure on his lands as fertilizer, producing a bountiful harvest much greater than his neighbors'. Yet another was a fine stock breeder who had picked the best bulls and taken great care of his stock and as a result had seen a prodigious expansion of his herds. But taking down the rich was not enough. Nobela was after the politically powerful too. She started by "smelling" two of Shaka's trusted lieutenants, Mdlaka and Mgobozi. Anticipating this move, Shaka told them to stand next to him and claim sanctuary if they were accused of being witches. According to eyewitness accounts:

> With a hideous cackle, imitating the hyena's demoniacal laugh all five
> jumped up simultaneously. With lightening speed Nobela struck right
> and left with her gnu-tail and jumped over Mdlaka's and Mgobozi's
> shoulders, while each of her immediate assistants also struck the man
> in front of her and vaulted high over his head.

But Shaka wasn't putting up with this. After all, he was the most powerful person in Zululand, intent on exercising his naked will to power; he might be the next one to be smelled out. He granted Mdlaka and Mgobozi sanctuary and charged Nobela with falsely accusing them of being witches, decreeing that two of the witch doctors must die in compensation. He made them throw divining bones to identify which two should be chosen. This led to panic between the witch doctors, who appealed to Shaka to protect them. He agreed on the stipulation that they "cheat me no more, for on that day you will fail to find sanctuary anywhere." From that day on, any "smelling out" had to be confirmed by Shaka. He broke the witch doctors' power. He also banished every rainmaker. It was all part of creating a state. Any part of the cage of norms that stood in his way had to be taken apart.

The longevity of the institutions that Shaka built is best illustrated by the current population of the Zulus. Starting from a clan of possibly 2,000 people in 1816, there are now between 10 and 11 million people who identify themselves as Zulu in South Africa (out of a population of 57 million) and they dominate the province of KwaZulu-Natal. The "Zulu" had originally been the descendants of a single man, but are now a massive society including millions of people who are completely unrelated genetically to the original Zulu.

The Red-Mouthed Gun

For thousands of years, people spread out from Asia onto the great swath of Polynesian islands. Among the last to be colonized was the Hawaiian archipelago, probably in about 800 CE. Though all the Polynesian islands started with the same culture, religion, language, technology, and political and economic institutions, they gradually diverged as different innovations arose and stuck. Ancestral Polynesian societies, as reconstructed by archaeologists and historical ethnographers, were not that different from the types of kinship-based societies that we saw in pre-Shaka Zululand; they were small-scale chieftaincies organized around kinship, and as usual their suite of norms had evolved to manage conflict and stop would-be strongmen.

By the time the first outsider, Captain James Cook, stumbled on the Hawaiian Islands in January 1778, this traditional system had already started to break down. The islands were by now organized around three competing proto-states, already beyond the stage of pristine state formation. Even though land was not held as private property and its use and control rights were vested in kin groups and lineages, chiefs had already laid claim to all the land. The people who grew the staple crops of taro and sago had access to the land only because the chiefs gave it to them in exchange for tribute and labor services. The historian David Malo, one of the first Hawaiians to receive a Western education and become literate early in the nineteenth century, recorded:

The condition of the common people was that of subjection to the chiefs, compelled to do their heavy tasks, burdened and oppressed, some even to death. The life of the people was one of patient endurance, of yielding to the chiefs to purchase their favor . . . It was from the common people, however, that the chiefs received their food and their apparel for men and women, also their houses and many other things. When the chiefs went forth to war some of the commoners also went out to fight on the same side with them . . . It was the *makaainanas* also who did all the work on the land; yet all they produced from the soil belonged to the chiefs; and the power to expel a man from the land and rob him of his possessions lay with the chief.

The *makaainanas* were the ordinary people, the vast mass of society.

The three proto-states in Hawaii at this time were in Oʻahu, Maui, and the "big island" of Hawaii itself ruled by chief Kalaniʻōpuʻu (see Map 6). Cook first visited the island of Kauaʻi, part of Oʻahu. He returned later in the year for more exploration and mapping with his two ships, the *Discovery* and the *Resolution*. He landed on Maui, then moved farther east and met Kalaniʻōpuʻu, who was then

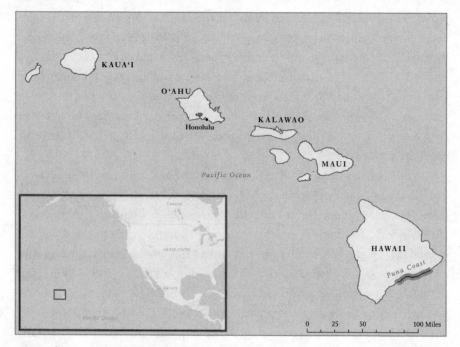

Map 6. The Hawaiian Islands and the Puna Coast

engaged in a battle to take control of Maui. Kalaniʻōpuʻu came aboard Cook's ship with his nephew Kamehameha, one of the leaders of his army. Cook then set sail for Hawaii and anchored on the western side of the island. There he was again visited by Kalaniʻōpuʻu and Kamehameha, who saw for the first time something marvelous—the power of firearms. In the photo insert we reproduce a painting by John Webber, an artist who accompanied Captain Cook, showing the arrival of Kalaniʻōpuʻu in his war boats. These were on display on February 14, when Cook was killed after leading a shore party trying to recover a cutter, a small boat, which had been stolen from his flagship the previous night.

After the departure of the *Discovery* and the *Resolution*, the aging Kalaniʻōpuʻu decided to bequeath his kingdom to one of his sons, but he put Kamehameha in charge of the God of War, which was a significant honor. The two young men quickly fell out. They met in battle in 1782 and Kamehameha won. In the succession struggle that ensued, one of Kalaniʻōpuʻu's brothers declared an independent polity on the eastern side of Hawaii, while another one of Kalaniʻōpuʻu's sons declared independence for the south. It was now a three-way fight for who would control the big island.

The outcome would be determined by an edge that Kamehameha acquired. He'd seen the power of gunpowder weapons. From this point onward, all Hawaiian chiefs tried to acquire such weapons via trade. But having them was one thing, knowing how to use them was another. Help arrived for Kamehameha first in the shape of Isaac Davis. Davis was a sailor on the schooner *Fair American*, which visited Hawaii in early 1790. It became becalmed off the western coast and was attacked by a local chief who harbored resentments against a previous ship. Only Davis survived the attack, and he was taken under Kamehameha's protection. Meanwhile another ship, the *Eleanor*, was dropping anchor in the same place where Cook had died. The boatswain was an Englishman called John Young. He came ashore and was detained by Kamehameha's men. Both Davis and Young were treated royally and became trusted advisers. Even better, they knew how to maintain and use firearms. Kamehameha now had his edge.

With Davis and Young in charge of his firearms, Kamehameha invaded Maui, and then successfully defended Hawaii against several attacks, in the process scoring a famous victory called "the red-mouthed gun," a name used by the locals to express their awe at the fire and smoke that issued from the new gunpowder weapons. Kamehameha quickly established uncontested control over Hawaii. He then spent the next several years consolidating his rule and developing the institutions of his new state. In 1795 he sailed with Davis and Young and a giant war fleet, overwhelming Maui and finally capturing Oʻahu. The westernmost island of Kauaʻi, which had escaped capture thanks to rough seas and diseases stopping Kamehameha's army, was at last subdued in 1810, completing the unification of all of Hawaii for the first time. Kamehameha proceeded to create a new set of political institutions to govern this massive state of far-flung islands. He appointed governors to each island, and Young was made governor of the big island itself.

Breaking Taboos

Muhammad and Shaka had to break parts of the cage of norms in their societies since many of these norms limited the emergence and exercise of political authority. Muhammad, for example, fought against kin-based relations while Shaka transformed both kin relations and supernatural beliefs in order to weaken sources of competing power. Kamehameha and his followers would similarly have to break down the norms that stood in their way.

Central to Polynesian society's norms were regulations of *tapu*, or taboos, as they came to be known in English after their first documentation by Captain Cook. Tapu was a common institution throughout Polynesia, and in Hawaii it had evolved into *kapu*. In English, "taboo" means something forbidden, off limits. In Polynesia, in the words of Edward Handy, the first great modern ethnographer of Hawaii,

> in its fundamental meaning tapu [kapu] as a word was used primarily as an adjective and as such signified that which was physically dangerous, hence restricted, forbidden, set apart, to be avoided, because: (a) divine, therefore requiring isolation for its own sake from both the common and the corrupt; (b) corrupt, hence dangerous to the common and the divine, therefore requiring isolation from both for their sakes.

In essence, tapu meant a prohibition or restriction. These were everywhere in Polynesian society. Tapu was so important because it was supposed to protect *mana*. Mana was the manifestation of supernatural power in the human world. Handy says:

> Mana was exhibited in persons, in power, strength, prestige, reputation, skill, dynamic personality, intelligence; in things, in efficacy, in "luck"; that is, in accomplishment.

But how did you protect mana, exactly? Notable among the many restrictions was the "eating taboo," which dictated that men and women could not eat together; their foods had to be cooked in separate ovens and some foods were prohibited to women (such as pork and certain kinds of fish, and bananas). It wasn't just eating that was controlled. So were clothing and many other aspects of life. Most famous was the "prostrating taboo," which required that ordinary people immediately strip off their upper body garments and lie prostrate on the ground in the presence of a chief. The nineteenth-century Hawaiian historian Kepelino recorded:

> As to the prostrating tapu of the chief, when the chief wished to go forth the announcer went ahead proclaiming the tapu of the chief, thus: "Tapu! Lie down!" Then everyone prostrated himself on the way by which the chief was passing and the tapu chiefs who followed him, all dressed with great splendor in feather cloaks and helmets.

Just as our earlier discussion of the cage of norms suggested, the prevailing norms did not necessarily treat everyone equally because they were shaped in part by existing power relations in Polynesian society. Chiefs had a lot more mana than ordinary people—hence all the prostration. In Hawaii it was this power of chiefs that also transformed tapu into kapu. Chiefs were not just protecting the gods and their mana; they came to be regarded as direct descendants of the gods, and kapu was about enshrining this dominance. At its root, mana is not so different from the tsav of the Tiv. Remember that tsav, like mana, helped explain different outcomes in life—why it was that some people were more successful than others or behaved in a different way. But with tsav, someone who was very successful could be so because they were intrinsically talented or simply because they were a witch. With mana, instead, success came from being chosen by the gods. Despite this enormous difference, the whole kapu system was still hedged about by myriad regulations and restrictions limiting what the elites could do. Although political hierarchy had already started to form in Hawaii, it was still far from what it would become under Kamehameha.

The erosion of norms limiting political hierarchy started under Kamehameha. He had named his son Liholiho as his successor, and upon taking over the newly created kingship of Hawaii following his father's death in 1819, Liholiho, crowned as King Kamehameha II, decided to abolish the kapu system. He felt confident of his power to do something no previous chief had done. So he dissolved the prohibition against eating altogether. Soon after being crowned king, he organized a feast. As a contemporary recalled it:

> After the guests were seated, and had begun to eat, the king took two or three turns round each table, as if to see what passed at each; and then suddenly, and without any previous warning to any but those in the secret, seated himself in a vacant chair at the women's table, and began to eat voraciously, but was evidently much perturbed. The guests, astonished at this act, clapped their hands, and cried out "*Ai Noa*,—the eating tabu is broken."

A Time of Troubles

We have so far focused on the emergence of political hierarchy where none, or very little of it, existed before. How the will to power breaks down the resistance against it and may move a society along the slippery slope is not confined to the distant past. The will to power and its consequences can also be seen in contemporary cases where state institutions are present but unable to exercise control over society, such as in Georgia in the early 1990s.

In the late 1980s the Soviet Union was collapsing. Moves were afoot to establish independence in many Soviet republics, including Estonia, Latvia, and Lithuania as well as Georgia. Georgia's first genuine free multiparty elections took place in 1990. A coalition called "Round Table—Free Georgia" got two-thirds of the vote against the Georgian Communists. In May 1991 the country declared itself independent of the Soviet Union, and Zviad Gamsakhurdia, the leader of the Round Table, was elected president with 85 percent of the vote. He took over a country riven by fractures and contesting visions, and without any real consensus about how it should be run. Many minority groups were concerned about being dominated by ethnic Georgians and started to talk about secession. By January 1992, Gamsakhurdia had fled the country, and the capital, Tbilisi, was mostly in the hands of two warlords, Dzhaba Ioseliani, head of a paramilitary group called the Mkhedrioni, and Tengiz Kitovani, head of the National Guard. At one point in just Tbilisi there were as many as twelve other militias and armed groups (with colorful names like the White Eagles and Forest Brotherhood). Georgia had a state at this point (well, sort of), but things weren't so far from the condition of Warre.

Tengiz Segura, a former prime minister dismissed by Gamsakhurdia, managed to have himself reinstated in the job. Gamsakhurdia formed another armed group, the Zviadists. Without an effective state, the capital experienced a wave of violence, looting, crime, and rape. The state lost control of the regions of South Ossetia and Abkhazia, which declared themselves independent, and other places, like Adjara and Samtskhe-Javaketi, remained completely autonomous. A civil war began. Georgians call it the Time of Troubles.

By the spring of 1993 the warlords were trying to find a way out of the chaos. Ioseliani and Kitovani had taken over what was left of the Georgian state, but conflict was rife and they weren't making any progress in bringing order. Just as important, they needed a respectable face to show to the international community to gain legitimacy and access to foreign aid and resources. They hit on the plan to make Eduard Shevardnadze president. Shevardnadze, a native of Georgia, had been Mikhail Gorbachev's minister of foreign affairs for six years until resigning in December 1990. By 1992 Shevardnadze had become speaker of the Georgian parliament. It was obvious that with his many contacts and immense international experience, he'd be the ideal face for the new nation. The idea of the warlords was simple. Shevardnadze would be the head of state and they would be behind the scenes pulling the strings. They made him Interim Chairman of the State Council, initially a four-person body including Ioseliani and Kitovani that acted only on consensus. They thus had a veto over Shevardnadze's actions. He made Kitovani minister of defense and Ioseliani head of the Emergency Reaction Corps, an autonomous part of the armed forces. One of Ioseliani's cronies became minister of the interior, and Shevardnadze appeared regularly in public with all of them. But then the slippery slope kicked in.

The statute that created the State Council allowed new members to be admitted if two-thirds of the existing members supported it. Shevardnadze started advocating the expansion of the council, which looked innocuous enough. Soon it evolved into a much larger body of warlords and political elites, which Shevardnadze found easier to manage. He then started to promote individuals from the militia to positions within the state apparatus in an attempt to shift their loyalty from Kitovani and Ioseliani to himself. He created a web of new military units with overlapping powers and jurisdictions: the Border Guards, the Special Emergency Response Corps, the Tbilisi Rescue Corps, the Government Guard, the Internal Troops of the Ministry of Internal Affairs, the Special Alpha Unit, and the CIA-trained Presidential Guard. By 1995 the Ministry of the Interior had 30,000 people working for it, many appointed from the former militias. This went along with a huge amount of corruption and impunity as the former militia members were given carte blanche to engage in unofficial taxation and bribe extraction.

Shevardnadze's hand was strengthened by exactly the thing he'd been put in power to do—make the regime respectable internationally so that aid and assistance would come. It did, and it came via Shevardnadze. To be really respectable you had to have a market economy, which meant privatization and regulation, all of which could be manipulated by Shevardnadze to reward his growing cadre of loyalists. In effect, Shevardnadze engaged in an immensely sophisticated high-stakes version of "divide and rule." By September 1994 he was powerful enough to use the Mkhedrioni to arrest Kitovani, and the following year, he turned them against their own leader, Ioseliani. Shevardnadze was finally able to use a failed assassination attempt against himself as the pretext to pass a new constitution to solidify his previously mostly informal powers. The Georgian state had reemerged, and the warlords who had counted on controlling the process were swept down the slippery slope.

Why You Cannot Shackle the Will to Power

We have seen several examples of the will to power obliterating the norms meant to keep the Leviathan down. Muhammad and Shevardnadze were brought in as outsiders to resolve inherent conflicts. They played this role brilliantly, bringing better order, peace, and a firmer hand to resolve disputes. But they also turned out to be much harder to control than their initial allies had bargained for. Shaka successfully exploited his accession to the chiefdom of the Zulu to jump-start the creation of a much more powerful army and expand the power of the state and his own authority, in the process emasculating the norms meant to restrain such state-building efforts. Kamehameha managed to use gunpowder technology to subdue his rivals and build a unified and powerful state in Hawaii, unlike anything the island had experienced before.

In none of these cases, and in few of the countless others where societies previously living under the Absent Leviathan have seen the emergence of political hierarchy, do we observe a transition to a Shackled Leviathan. Nor was the point of breaking the cage of norms to create liberty; it was to eliminate barriers to greater political hierarchy. An exception is of course Dark Age Athens, which as we saw in Chapter 2 managed to build the capacity of its state to resolve conflict, control feuds, and provide public services while at the same time increasing society's control over it and transforming the prevailing norms. So why couldn't these other societies achieve the same thing? The answer relates to the nature of the norms and institutions in place when a society starts its process of state building. In many cases, stateless societies succumb to the will to power of a charismatic leader with an edge. What motivates many of these leaders is not a desire to create a Shackled Leviathan, to promote liberty, or to redress the imbalance between the powers of the elite and citizens, but to increase their own power and domination over society. Solon in Athens, looked at from this vantage point, was an exception because he came to power to rein in the excessive influence of rich families and elites, so building shackles on the Leviathan was part of his mandate. Not so with our other state builders.

But perhaps even more fundamentally, what set apart Athenian society at the time of Solon was that it had already developed some formal institutions that regulated the distribution of political power and the resolution of conflict. Though imperfect, these institutions provided a foundation on which Solon and then Cleisthenes and others could build to introduce greater popular participation in politics and strengthen existing norms curbing social and political hierarchy. This is how they managed to enact the hubris and ostracism laws, meant to prevent powerful individuals getting too big for their britches (and at the same time they were also able to weaken aspects of existing norms that prevented the development of the Shackled Leviathan). No such institutions existed for the Tiv, in Medina and Mecca, among the Zulu, or in Hawaii at the time of Kamehameha. Instead, stacking the cards against the Shackled Leviathan, their methods of preventing would-be strongmen from ascending to power were complex sets of norms, such as witchcraft, kin-based relations, or the kapu system, that regulated conflict and held back political hierarchy. But once the will to power pierced through these norms, not much of them was left to act as an effective counterweight to the power of the newly emerging state. State builders were also quick to reconfigure norms for their own agenda, as we have seen. Going back to Figure 1 in Chapter 2, summarizing our conceptual framework, we can see this situation as corresponding to the bottom left where both state and society are weak to start with. Without the norms and institutions of society capable of restraining the process of state building once it's in motion, there is no corridor. Hence, in the face of the will to power, there is nowhere else for society to go but toward the Despotic Leviathan.

But this wasn't all bad. The aspiring Leviathan in some of the cases we discussed improved conflict resolution, brought order, and sometimes even destroyed the most pernicious aspects of the cage of norms—even if it also created more hierarchy and replaced the potential for fear and violence in a stateless society with the dominance of its newly forming Despotic Leviathan. Its economic consequences weren't bad either, because they improved the allocation of resources and made a primitive type of economic growth possible, as we'll see in the next chapter, by studying the nature of the economy under the Absent Leviathan and its cage of norms and contrasting it to the emerging economy under the Despotic Leviathan.

Chapter 4

ECONOMICS OUTSIDE THE CORRIDOR

The Ghost in the Granary

In 1972, the anthropologist Elizabeth Colson was in the midst of her fieldwork among the Gwembe Tonga, a people of southern Zambia who had been stateless prior to the conquest of the region by the British (see Map 5 in the previous chapter). She was at a homestead collecting information when a woman entered and asked the resident housewife for grain. Both women were members of the same clan, but they lived quite far apart and only knew each other vaguely. In response to the request the housewife went to her granary and filled the visitor's basket until it was overflowing and the visitor departed satisfied.

This type of generous sharing of food within clans, kin, or other types of groups is common among many stateless societies. It is interpreted by most anthropologists and many economists as a sign of deep-rooted customs and norms of cooperation and reciprocity. It also has a clear economic logic: today you help somebody from your clan, and tomorrow when you need it, they will help you. This is exactly how Colson initially interpreted this ostentatious generosity.

It was only later, when she observed a young man in the village receiving a disturbing letter from home, that Colson came to understand that the reality was rather different. She recorded in her field notes, "One evening, lights had been seen about his granary and his wives and brother had later found evidence that ghosts had urinated over the grain, an act which Tonga believe ghosts carry out only if sent by a sorcerer." The likely aim of the sorcerer was to kill the man and his family. He lamented that "his ambition of the previous year—which had led him to work early and late in the large field he had planted—was now bringing him only a harvest of hate." The same housewife, who was present, immediately grasped what was going on. Colson went on: "She thought someone must have visited his homestead and seen all the granaries, and she asked if he could remember anyone having stood to gaze at them or asking for food or making any comment about all that food." The housewife concluded:

> It is not safe to deny them. You saw me give grain to that woman who came the other day. How could I refuse when she asked me for grain? Perhaps she would do nothing, but I could not tell. The only thing to do is to give.

Not giving risked sorcery and violence. It was fear, fear from retribution and violence that would follow if she broke the norm, not some abstract notion of generosity, that made her give.

This type of threat was endemic in Tonga society and was even embodied in the structure of its clans. The neighboring Plateau Tonga, for example, have fourteen clans, each of which has associated "totems"—animals that shouldn't be eaten. The totems of the Bayamba clan are the hyena, rhinoceros, pig, ant, and fish. Members of this clan cannot eat any of these animals. The Batenda clan has the elephant, sheep, and hippopotamus as its totems. Other forbidden animals include leopard (the Bansaka clan), frog (Bafumu clan), and even the white vulture (Bantanga clan). The origins of these food prohibitions, according to Tonga legend, is that long ago some groups of people were eating leopard, and other people became envious of the plentiful food they had and cursed them, making them subsequently allergic to the specific food. The descendants of the cursed people became the clan.

So the norms of hospitality and generosity among the Tonga had emerged and were obeyed not so much because of some moral imperative or because people saw economic benefits stemming from them, but because they feared violence and sorcery, not to mention the social ostracism and other less violent retributions that would be exacted on those deviating from the norms. They lived in a society without a state, so there were no police or government officials who could protect them or resolve disputes. Nevertheless, because of the norms preventing and containing conflict, they didn't suffer endemic violence. The visitor came, the housewife was generous, and any potential conflict was avoided.

No Place for Industry

Hobbes thought that without centralized authority societies would find themselves in a condition of Warre. He also anticipated, as we saw in Chapter 1, that Warre would destroy economic incentives, writing "in such condition there is no place for industry, because the fruit thereof is uncertain." Or put in the language of modern economics, conflict and uncertainty mean that individuals do not have secure property rights on the fruits of their investments and on what they produce, gather, or hunt, and this discourages economic activity.

To get a sense of the economic consequences of Warre, let's return briefly to the Democratic Republic of Congo. At the start of Chapter 1 we mentioned that the east of the country, particularly the Kivus, is plagued by militias and armed groups. Indeed, in the Kivus, Warre isn't just between individuals, as Hobbes often seems to suggest, but between groups. One of these in eastern Congo is the RCD-Goma, based in the city of Goma. This group was a splinter faction of the Congolese Rally for Democracy (in French, Rassemblement Congolais pour la Démocratie, hence the abbreviation RCD), and had its roots in the First and Second Congo Wars, sometimes called the Great War of Africa, between 1996 and 2003. When a peace agreement was finally signed, the RCD-Goma, along with many others, kept fighting and terrorizing local residents. In December 2004, RCD-Goma units approached the town of Nyabiondo in North Kivu. The town was protected by members of another militia, the Mai-Mai. The RCD attacked on December 19. Mai-Mai fighters who were caught were tied up and burned alive. Initially civilian casualties were low, as under the cover of early-morning mist people managed to flee to the fields and forest. But the RCD hunted them down. Within a few days 191 people had been murdered in cold blood. Willy, aged just fifteen, told a researcher from Amnesty International:

> The soldiers came in vehicles and on foot, killing and pillaging. Some were in uniform but others wore civilian clothes . . . The population fled straight to the forest. I was in a group of fifteen, with my mother, neighbours and other relatives. The soldiers found us and made us lie on the ground, where we were beaten with rifle butts. Baroki, the [local chief]

was with us. The soldiers came and took him away, I saw that. Then I
saw his body afterwards, a week later, on 25 December. He had taken a
bullet in the head. He had been tied up and whipped. The body lay on
the ground.

Girls as young as eight were raped and 25,000 people were ultimately displaced. Their belongings were destroyed and their houses burned to the ground.
Nyabiondo was systematically looted with even the tiles being stolen from rooftops.

This is Warre with obvious and wrenching human consequences. The economic consequences are just as evident. The economy of the Kivus is devastated
and the same is true for much of the rest of the Congo. The result is abject poverty.
Income per capita in the Congo is about 40 percent of the level it was in 1960 when
the country became independent. At about $400, less than 1 percent of the U.S. level,
it's as poor as any country in the world. Life expectancy is twenty years less than it
is in the United States. In the Democratic Republic of the Congo, Hobbes was right.
The life of men is indeed "poore, nasty, brutish, and short." It is even worse for women.

Yet the Tonga don't look anything like the Kivus or like the type of stateless,
warring peoples Hobbes portrayed. They resemble the kind of society that would
support claims that we are a "cooperative species," with norms that support cooperation, hospitality, and generosity. But as we have already seen in Chapter 1,
the price that people pay for this is often being locked into the cage of norms. Yet
now we come to understand that the cage constrains not only their social choices,
but also their economic lives.

This is clear for the young man who had worked hard only to see his granaries attacked by ghosts and sorcerers, because people were jealous of his success.
The adverse effects of these norms for economic incentives are not confined to such
attacks. They also impede property rights, even if this takes a less obvious form
than that which Hobbes anticipated would plague the economy of stateless societies. Suppose, for example, you invest and increase your production. With secure
property rights, you would get to enjoy the greater output you produce, and you
may do what you please with it. If you really enjoy being generous, that's part of
the reward. But in Tonga society, as in many other economies shaped by the cage
of norms, you give that output away not because you enjoy it, but because you are
afraid of the social retribution, and even the violence, you may suffer if you fall
afoul of the norms. That effectively means you again do not have secure property
rights, since the additional income you generate will be taken away from you, even
if the taking looks voluntary, couched in customs of generosity. The consequence

would be little different from what Hobbes observed; there would be "no place for industry."

The obvious way that this manifested itself in Tonga society was in the constant presence of hunger. Hunger and begging. Colson noted how close people lived to the edge:

> When a household has exhausted its own food supplies or is near to doing so, it attempts first to obtain food from kinsmen or friends who live nearby. Children and disabled people are sent to kinsmen in areas which still have food. Men go out to work to leave more food for those who must stay at home, but they take little comfort in the thought that they will be fed while at home there will be hunger. When local supplies are exhausted, people walk many miles to tap kinsmen living at a distance. Often they go to the Plateau where their appearance is looked upon with much the same enthusiasm as the settling of a swarm of locusts.

The founding father of economics, Adam Smith, emphasized the propensity of humans to "truck, barter and exchange." In Tongaland, begging was more prevalent than trucking, bartering, or exchanging. Colson pointed out how "the Valley had no middlemen or markets to organize internal trade. It also had no universally accepted medium of exchange." There was trade of sorts, but

> much of the exchange is obligatory, consequent upon institutionalized relationships existing between the parties to the transaction: one has the right to receive and the other the obligation to give.

The result was a society trapped into subsistence agriculture, vulnerable to every sort of economic setback and adversity. Technology was stagnant and backward. Precolonial Tonga society did not use the wheel, either for pottery or transport. Farming, the economic mainstay in the area, was unproductive, not because the land was infertile, but because it was worked using digging sticks rather than plows.

As we have already seen, the origins of the Tonga cage of norms is not unrelated to Hobbes's observations. Part of the reason why such norms have developed in many places is that egalitarianism has a clear political logic. Norms of egalitarianism maintain the status quo. When such norms are weak or nonexistent, hierarchy emerges, the slippery slope kicks in, and statelessness ends. The surviving stateless societies thus tend to be those where norms of egalitarianism are strong and ingrained. These norms also help control conflict. If conflict risks erupting into violence and feuds, it's better to follow a closely scripted economic playbook. With new economic activities, new opportunities, and new inequalities, there will be new conflicts, which are much harder for existing norms to handle. Better not to risk tipping into Warre. Better to stay with the status quo.

The Caged Economy

This is of course very familiar from the Tiv. As you'll recall from Chapter 2, the Tiv developed a set of norms to make sure they never got onto the slippery slope. Anyone who tried to accumulate power to start exerting authority over others was put back in his place by witchcraft accusations. It turns out that their norms and the cage they created also did the same economically, effectively forging a "caged" economy.

The Tiv were a society based on kin and descent. As we have seen, the Tiv word for a territory occupied by the descendants of a single ancestor is *tar*, and within a tar it was the elders who exercised what little authority there was in traditional Tiv society. They allocated sufficient land to people within the tar to provide a livelihood for their family. Sufficient, but not much more than that. As anthropologists Paul and Laura Bohannan noted, if a man "wants to plant many more yams than his wives and children need, so that he can sell them to get more money and goods than others in the compound, he is likely to be refused."

There was also no market in Tivland where labor could be bought and sold, and no land or capital markets either. The labor of the family or the tar was the only thing available for agricultural production. Both men and women farmed, but they each farmed specific crops and only women grew the main staple, yams. Husbands were required to provide land for their wives to farm, but had no automatic claim on what they produced. There were markets for some of these produced goods, but the Bohannans remarked:

> Perhaps the most characteristic feature of the Tiv market is that it is extraordinarily constrained and shows little tendency to invade the other institutions of society.

Indeed, the Tiv didn't have free markets, they had markets that were caged—structured not to facilitate trade but to avoid the slippery slope.

Perhaps the most obvious instance of this is with respect to notions of the exchange of goods, which was strictly limited. The economy was separated into different spheres. One could trade within a sphere but not across spheres. The most flexible sphere was the market for foodstuffs and subsistence goods that included chickens, goats, sheep, household utensils, and other craft products (mortars, grindstones, calabashes, pots, and baskets). Raw materials used to produce any of these items would also be included here. These were traded on local markets that opened periodically, and prices were flexible and subject to haggling. Trading in such markets had already adapted to the availability of money. Nevertheless, this sphere remained completely separate from prestige goods, which could not be exchanged in a market. Prestige goods included cattle, horses, a special type of white cloth known as *tugundu*, medicines, magical items, and brass rods. Formerly slaves were also included in this category of goods. Money was not used in this sphere, but there were equivalences between different goods. For example, historically the price of slaves was quoted in cows and brass rods, the price of cattle in terms of brass rods and *tugundu* cloth.

Akiga, the Tiv elder we encountered in Chapter 2, mentions some specific ways in which various prestige items could be traded: "You could buy one iron bar for a *tugundu* cloth. In those days five *tugundu* cloths were equivalent to a bull. A cow was worth ten *tugundu*. One brass rod was worth about the same as one *tugundu* cloth; thus five brass rods were worth a bull."

To the extent that something like modern-looking exchange happened, the terms of trade were strictly fixed and unchanging. Although these prestige items might be exchanged in this way, this did not mean they were bought or sold, or as the Bohannans put it, "Tiv will not buy cows or horses in a market."

How do you acquire prestige goods then? Moving from subsistence goods to prestige goods was a process that the Bohannans dubbed "conversion." The Tiv recognized that acquiring subsistence goods could be the fruit of hard work, but not so for prestige goods. It took "more than hard work—it takes a 'strong heart.'" Conversion upward may be possible when someone who has to get rid of his existing prestige goods is therefore willing to convert down. But "they try to keep a man from making conversions," because such a man "is both feared and respected. If he is strong enough to resist excessive demands of his kinsmen . . . he is feared as a man of special, potentially evil, talents (tsav)."

There we have it, back to tsav! The Tiv norms caged the economy, eradicated factor markets, and made the lineage the main agent of production. In return, they achieved a balance between the different kin groups, avoided the slippery slope, and made their status quo much more enduring.

Like the enforced generosity of the Tonga, the caged economy of the Tiv had obvious adverse consequences. Markets are critical for an efficient organization of the economy and for prosperity. But they weren't permitted to function among the Tiv. To the extent that trade happened, relative prices were often fixed. The result in Tivland, just as for the Tonga, was dire poverty. The institutions of Tiv society created little incentive for capital accumulation, other than in the form of simple instruments such as digging sticks and devices for processing food. Indeed, even saving could lead one to be accused of having the wrong sort of tsav, so the fear of retribution made accumulation too dangerous. As a result, at the time of the conquest of Tivland by the British, people were living at close to subsistence levels of income with life expectancy of around thirty years.

Ibn Khaldun and the Cycle of Despotism

Our discussion of the Tonga and the Tiv suggests that Hobbes's analysis of the economic consequences of statelessness wasn't exactly right. These societies weren't mired in continual violence and conflict destroying all economic incentives, even if the Kivus in the Congo remind us that there are plenty of examples of societies without centralized authority locked into such conflicts. All the same, Hobbes's conclusion turned out to be not completely off the mark, because the norms that these societies fashioned to control conflict ended up creating highly distorted incentives.

Was Hobbes also right that the Despotic Leviathan would be better for economic incentives because it would create security, predictability, and order? Hobbes was partly—and only partly—right, here too, and there is no better place to start understanding the double-edged nature of the economy that the Despotic Leviathan creates than the work of the great Arab scholar Ibn Khaldun. Born in Tunis in 1332 CE, Khaldun traced his ancestry back to Muhammad via Yemen. Khaldun had a remarkable life which included meeting the Mongol conqueror Tamerlane. His most renowned scholarly work was the *Kitab al-Ibar*, or "Book of Lessons," whose first volume, known as the *Muqaddimah*, or "Introduction," is particularly useful for understanding the economic consequences of a despotic state.

Khaldun's "Introduction" is rich in ideas. In addition to tracing the economic consequences of the emergence of a state in the Arabian Peninsula, it presents a theory of the dynamics of political institutions based on what he viewed as two fundamental conflicts in society. The first is between the desert, with its nomadic life, and sedentary urbanized society. The second is between the rulers and the ruled. Khaldun argued that the odds are stacked in favor of the desert people in the first conflict due to the type of society that the harshness and marginal nature of desert life creates. Their society was characterized by what he called *asabiyyah*, which translates as social solidarity or group feeling. Asabiyyah should be a familiar concept by now. It was part of the cage of norms of a stateless society, but Khaldun brings in a new angle on these norms. From our perspective so far, asabiyyah was something that helped regulate conflicts and preserve the political equality in nomadic societies. Khaldun pointed out that it also makes such a society very good at subjugating neighboring sedentary peoples.

We saw in the previous chapter how Islam provided an edge to Muhammad in his state-building efforts. The Bedouin tribes that Muhammad relied on in this process had a lot of asabiyyah, and this gave him and his followers a second edge to expand the Islamic Empire into a massive empire. In Khaldun's account, this edge was created not only by the economic hardship of the desert, but also by the dense networks of kinship that had evolved to provide mutual help in the tough desert landscape. The desert was always destined to overcome the sedentary world and form new states and dynasties.

Khaldun, however, argued that though asabiyyah helped the desert people to conquer "civilized lands" and set themselves up in power, the intrinsic dynamics of such authority inevitably led to the decay of asabiyyah and the ultimate collapse of a state that groups like the Bedouin founded. Then the whole cycle started over again with a new group from the desert replacing the collapsing state. In Khaldun's words:

> The duration of the life of a dynasty does not as a rule extend beyond three generations. The first generation retains the desert qualities, desert toughness, and desert savagery . . . the strength of group feeling continues to be preserved among them . . . the second generation changes from the desert attitude to sedentary culture . . . from a state in which everybody shared in the glory to one in which one man claims all the glory for himself . . . People become used to lowliness and obedience . . . The third generation . . . has completely forgotten the period of desert life . . . They have lost . . . group feeling, because they are dominated by force . . . When someone comes and demands something from them, they cannot repel him.

Khaldun's analysis also insightfully illustrates the role of conflict between the ruler and the ruled. After coming in from the desert, "one man claims all the glory for himself," while the majority of people "become used to lowliness and obedience." Khaldun gave a new dynasty about 120 years.

———

Before delving into these political dynamics and their economic consequences in more detail, it's worth picking up the history where we left off in the previous chapter and following what happened after the death of Muhammad. The Arab conquests set in motion by Muhammad were initially sustained by four leaders, known as the Caliphs, who derived their authority from their close personal relationships with him. These were Abu Bakr, Umar, Uthman, and Ali, Muhammad's cousin and son-in-law, who was assassinated in 661. Ali's murder came at the end of a period of contention over how the newly emerging state was to be governed. Uthman had tried aggressively to increase central control over the nascent state and had been murdered by rebellious soldiers. Ali's succession was contested by Muawiya, Uthman's cousin and the governor of Syria. This led to a protracted civil war, which ended with Ali's death and Muawiya's being declared caliph. He founded the Umayyad dynasty, which ruled for almost one hundred years until it was replaced in 750 by the Abbasid dynasty, named after Abbas, an uncle of Muhammad. By the time Umayyad rule emerged, Iran, Iraq, Syria, and Egypt had been conquered, and the annexation of North Africa, which was finally completed by 711, was well under way. By the middle of the eighth century, much of Spain was conquered and large swaths of inner Asia were added to the empire.

In the conquered lands, the Umayyads initially superimposed the rule of the Arab warrior class on top of the preexisting institutions of the Byzantine (in Syria, Palestine, Israel, Egypt) and Sassanid (in Iraq and Iran) Empires that they had replaced. It was only when Caliph Abd al-Malik assumed power in 685 that the Umayyads began to build a more distinct state structure based in their new capital in Damascus. But the Umayyads were never able to construct a truly effective centralized state, and neither were their successors, the Abbasids. Though their armies had proved to be hugely effective and occupied a large area, transforming this occupation into a real system of government and gaining the loyalty of the occupied people turned out to be a lot harder. The Umayyads and Abbasids then ended up relying more and more on local elites to govern the provinces of their empire, raise taxes, and keep order. To buy the support of these elites, they engaged in "tax farming," wherein they sold the right to raise taxes for a fixed sum of money. Once you had the right to tax granted to you by Damascus, and subsequently Baghdad when the Abbasids came to power, you had carte blanche to levy whatever taxes you wanted on local communities. This seems to have been a recipe for punitively high rates of taxation and the accumulation of land by elites since they took over the lands of people who could not afford to pay the taxes they levied. This political structure of empire was ultimately self-defeating. Local elites demanded to be named as hereditary governors and recruited their own armies to provide order. Soon Baghdad had no control over them. The empire came apart at the seams and finally collapsed in 945.

None of this was surprising to Khaldun. He was a firm believer in the will to power, noting that

> human beings need someone to act as a restraining influence and mediator in every social organization, in order to keep the members from fighting with each other. That person must, by necessity, have superiority over the others in the matter of group feeling. If not, his power to exercise a restraining influence could not materialize.

Once such a person was recognized, as Muhammad had been in Medina, he became a leader, and "leadership means being a chieftain, and the leader is obeyed, but he has no power to force others to accept his rulings." But Khaldun understood that the mere existence of such a leader was likely to move society swiftly along the slippery slope. Indeed, "When a person sharing in the group feeling had reached the rank of chieftain and commands obedience, and when he then finds the way open toward superiority and the use of force, he follows that way." Thus, because group feeling was not endowed equally on all people, it tended to inexorably lead to royal authority, which "means superiority and power by rule of force."

However, once in power the rulers of the new dynasty "will not need much group feeling to maintain their power. It is as if obedience to the government were a divinely revealed book that cannot be changed or opposed." So, in line with his generational theory, Khaldun argued that the rulers of a dynasty started to distance themselves from those who had helped them into power and to forge relationships with new groups within their empire. This was an intrinsic part of creating an empire once you had conquered new lands. These lands were already occupied and often controlled by local elites and notables, so new dynasties had to come to some sort of agreement with them and obtain their loyalty or face constant rebellion. As the dynasty changed its nature and asabiyyah eroded, despotism emerged, or in

Khaldun's words, "With the disappearance of Arab group feeling and the annihi-lation of the Arab race and complete destruction of Arabism the Caliphate lost its identity. The form of government remained royal authority pure and simple." The consequences of this were simple too:

> The restraining influence of religion had weakened. The restraining influence of government and group was needed. . . .
>
> Royal authority requires superiority and force . . . The decisions of the ruler will therefore, as a rule, deviate from what is right. They will be ruinous to the worldly affairs of the people under his control, since, as a rule, he forces them to execute his intentions and desires, which it may be beyond their ability to do. . . . Disobedience makes itself notice-able and leads to trouble and bloodshed.

Here Khaldun hints at some of the economic implications of the creation of a new dynasty. Early on with the power of group feeling and the "restraining influ-ence of religion," prosperity was a potential. But later, when "royal authority" con-solidated itself, economic policies would be "ruinous to the worldly affairs of the people." Nowhere were the economic implications of Khaldun's generational theory more evident than in his discussion of taxation, which we turn to next.

Ibn Khaldun Discovers the Laffer Curve

> It should be known that at the beginning of the dynasty, taxation yields a large revenue from small assessments. At the end of the dynasty, taxa-tion yields a small revenue from large assessments.

With this statement Khaldun anticipated Reaganomics, the economic doctrines that were promulgated by the American president Ronald Reagan in the early 1980s. One of the plinths of Reaganomics was first sketched out on a napkin in the Two Continents Restaurant in Washington, D.C., by the economist Arthur Laffer. Laffer was trying to explain to Republican rising stars Donald Rumsfeld and Dick Cheney and the journalist Jude Wanniski what he regarded as a basic principle of fiscal policy: the hump-shaped relationship between the tax rate levied by the government and the amount of tax revenues. When tax rates are low, an increase in the rate tends to increase tax revenues for the simple reason that the government takes a greater share of everyone's incomes. However, as the tax rate starts to get too high, it chokes off incentives to work hard, exert effort, and invest because the gains created by all these activities are being taken away by the government. As a result, when tax rates get punitively high, not only economic activity but even tax revenues start falling. This is clear to see in the extreme cases where the tax rate approaches 100 percent, so that the government takes everything and very little incentive is left to generate income; despite the very high tax rates, there won't be any tax revenues. Wanniski named this hump-shaped relationship the Laffer curve in honor of the man who had sketched it out. The exciting implication for Rumsfeld and Cheney was the prospect that you could reduce tax rates while increasing tax revenues as people responded to the more powerful incentives created by lower taxes—the biggest win-win situation of all time, which quickly came to be incorporated into President Reagan's economic policy.

Needless to say, in a world where real tax rates are quite a bit lower than 100 percent, such as in the United States when Reagan became president, whether or not tax cuts actually increase tax revenues is open to doubt.

Khaldun's analysis of the economic dynamics created in the Middle East was on firmer empirical grounds, and his idea of the Laffer curve was somewhat different from the one that Laffer explained to Rumsfeld and Cheney. It was based on his generational theory. To start with, a new dynasty, since it still has asabiyyah, "imposes only the taxes as are stipulated by religious law, such as charity taxes, the land tax, and the poll tax." This had beneficial effects on the economy because "when tax assessments and imposts upon the subjects are low, the latter have the energy and desire to do things. Cultural enterprises grow and increase . . . When cultural enterprises grow . . . the tax revenue, which is the sum total of the individual assessments increases."

Here Khaldun points out that low taxes stimulate economic activity, what he calls "cultural enterprises," and this leads, as in the Laffer curve, to buoyant tax returns. The evidence suggests that this is exactly what happened in the wake of the Arab conquests. The Umayyads brought together a large area under one language, one religion, and one system of government, with a common legal system that flowed from Muhammad's teachings. The first and most obvious economic impact of this megastate was an expansion of trade and mercantile activities. Muhammad, after all, had started life as a trader. The geographer al-Muqaddasi compiled a tenth-century list of the items exchanged between Baghdad and Khorasan-Transoxania, in what is now northeastern Iran. The list starts with "11 different items of clothing and garments, including veils and turbans, all made of expensive cloth, sometime silk, sometime plain cloth as well as bracelets, clothing of hair of superior yarn, iron" from Naysabur, and "cloth, silk brocade of inferior quality, taffeta, raisins, syrup, steel, pistachios and confections" from Harat, and goes on for pages until "silver-coloured fabrics [simgun], and Samarqandi stuffs, large copper vessels, artistic goblets, tents, stirrups, bridle-heads and straps" from Samarqand. This trade was accompanied by a vast amount of travel, the most powerful image of which was perhaps the annual pilgrimage to Mecca, the hadj, which brought hundreds of thousands of believers together from all across the empire, and provided a huge opportunity not just for piety, but also for trading.

Another piece of evidence for the economic benefits of the rise of the Caliph- ate was an agricultural revolution. This was to some extent a consequence of the rise in trade, which created a much larger market than had existed before. The Arab conquests were followed by the diffusion throughout the region of a variety of crops that had previously not been grown there. These included rice, sorghum, hard wheat, sugar cane, cotton, watermelons, eggplants, spinach, artichokes, sour oranges, lemons, limes, bananas, plantains, mangos, and coconut palms. Many of these plants, indigenous to the tropics, were not easy to grow in the cooler and drier regions into which they were now sown, and necessitated a major reorganiza- tion of agriculture. Previously, the growing season had been in the winter, with crops harvested in the spring. During the hot summer months, the land lay fallow. But the new crops came from tropical areas and thrived in the summers, so pro- duction was restructured and intensified. Before the Arab conquests of the Middle East, Byzantine practice was to crop the ground once every two years. Now two crops a year were grown, for example, winter wheat followed by summer sorghum, cotton, or rice. All of these innovations were documented in Arab farming manu- als that helped to spread best practices throughout the empire.

This intensification of production required fertilizer and irrigation too. Vari- ous types of irrigation were already in place in the areas that the Arabs conquered, but those of the Byzantine and Persian Sassanid Empires were often in advanced states of decay. The Arabs repaired these and built a profusion of new public infra- structure, including new kinds of dams, underground canals that tapped ground- water and brought it over long distances, and a variety of wheels for lifting water out of rivers, canals, wells, and storage basins. This infrastructural investment was not based on new technology but involved the adoption and deployment of existing technological know-how. Nevertheless, it greatly increased the productive capacity of the economy.

The state that emerged from Muhammad's political leadership played a decisive role in building and sustaining these renovated irrigation systems. It also encouraged private individuals to make complementary investments. This was not just because of the relative political stability that emerged with the Caliphate. It was also because Medina was an oasis and Muhammad, in his role as the resolver of disputes, had had to deal with conflicts over water and irrigation and had outlined a series of precedents that formed the basis of a legal system that facilitated investments. Particularly significant was the fact that instead of vesting them collectively in tribes or clans, these rulings individualized water rights. This improved incentives and eased disputes between individuals. Other laws directly encouraged production, including one that gave outright private ownership of a piece of land brought into cultivation for the first time and restricted taxation on such land to one-tenth of its output.

But these early benefits soon evaporated along with the buoyant tax revenues that they generated. Khaldun is indeed clear that these early economic advances could not be sustained.

> When the dynasty continues in power and their rulers follow each other in succession . . . the Bedouin qualities of moderation and restraint disappear. Royal authority with its tyranny, and sedentary culture . . . make their appearance . . . individual imposts and assessments upon the subjects, agricultural laborers, farmers, and all the other taxpayers, increase . . . Customs duties are placed upon articles of commerce and levied at the city gates. . . . Eventually, the taxes weigh heavily upon the subjects and overburden them . . . The result is that the interest of the subjects in cultural enterprises disappears, since when they compare expenditures and taxes with their income and gain and see the little profit they make, they lose all hope. Therefore, many of them refrain from all cultural activity. The result is that the total tax revenue goes down.

With tax revenues falling, "the ruler must invent new kinds of taxes. He levies them on commerce. He imposes taxes of a certain amount on prices realized in the markets and on the various imported goods at the city gates . . . Business falls off . . . This situation becomes more and more aggravated, until the dynasty disintegrates. Much of this sort happened in the Eastern cities during the later days of the Abbasid and Ubaydid-Fatimid dynasties." (The Fatimid dynasty is a third caliphate—taking its name from Muhammad's daughter Fatima—which ruled North Africa from the early tenth to late twelfth centuries.)

Existing evidence supports Khaldun's account. While the tax rate on land seems to have risen inexorably after the Arab conquests, revenues fell. Revenues from Iraq, for example, decreased from 12.8 million dinars after the conquest to 8.3 million dinars at the end of the Umayyad dynasty, to 5 million by 819 and just over 3 million by 870. The data from Egypt and Mesopotamia tell the same story.

One common response was that the ruler "himself may engage in commerce and agriculture, from desire to increase [his] revenues." But Khaldun saw that this could be very harmful to the people in the society because "when the ruler, who has so much more money than they, competes with them, scarcely a single one of them will any longer be able to obtain the things he wants, and everybody will be worried and unhappy. Furthermore, the ruler can appropriate much of the agricultural products and the available merchandise . . . He can do it by force, or by buying things up at the cheapest possible price. Further, there may be no one who would dare bid against him. Thus, he will be able to force the seller to lower his price." On the other hand, when the ruler is selling, he forces everyone to pay high prices. Competition from the ruler thus generates a situation where "the farmer gives up agriculture and the merchant goes out of business."

As the Umayyad and Abbasid states disintegrated, the impact of tax farming and their inability to construct effective bureaucratic management also led to a deterioration of infrastructure, and a fall in investment since farmers were at the mercy of local elites. Indeed, land seems to have been abandoned by ordinary farmers who saw no way to make ends meet and instead moved to towns and cities. The entry of elites into the economy had exactly the impact Khaldun identified.

Khaldun explicitly noted how his theory explained the collapse of the Abbasids:

> The group feeling of the Arabs had been destroyed by the time of the reign of al-Mutasim and his son al-Wathiq. They tried to maintain their hold over the government thereafter with the help of Persian, Turkish, Daylam, Saljuq, and other clients. Then the Persians (non-Arabs) and clients gained power over the provinces of the realm. The influence of the dynasty grew smaller, and no longer extended beyond the environs of Baghdad.

Janus-Faced Despotic Growth

Khaldun's theory is a brilliant illustration of the impact of despotic state formation on the economy—not because the type of cycle that Khaldun hypothesized with the bad following the good is some "historical law," but because it highlights both the good and the bad that an economy under despotism will always embody.

A state can provide many benefits in terms of increased order, security, and peace. It can enforce laws, bringing clarity and predictability to conflicts that inevitably emerge in the process of economic transactions. It helps markets and trade expand. The state, and the state builders controlling it, may also find it in their interest to enforce property rights for the same reasons as the Laffer curve: without property rights and predictability of the state's policies, it's as if everyone is facing close to 100 percent tax rates and will lack incentives to produce, work, trade, and invest—and the result would be little tax revenue for the state. Not a desirable outcome. So it's better to keep taxes low. When that happens, economic activity can potentially flourish, with all the benefits that this brings to society as well as to the Despotic Leviathan. The same logic underlies the reason why state builders might find it in their interest to provide public services, infrastructure, and even education to increase productivity and economic activity.

All of this implies that the Despotic Leviathan may create better economic opportunities and incentives than Warre or the cage of norms. It may even organize society, structure laws, and make investments so as to directly stimulate economic growth. This is the essence of what we call "despotic growth."

The history of the Islamic state illustrates this type of growth clearly. Compared to the warring clans that had previously dominated Medina, Muhammad's ability to resolve disputes and enforce his laws spurred economic activity. Property rights became more secure for the Medinans as Muhammad's state prevented disputes from escalating and after his unification of the Arabian tribes put a stop to raids. The same factors also facilitated trade. As we have just seen, this proto-state organized new public infrastructure investments, including dams, underground canals, and other irrigation facilities. Agricultural productivity increased greatly as a result. All in all a far cry from where Medina was heading before Muhammad's arrival.

Yet in the same way that the Leviathan is Janus-faced, so is despotic growth, and Khaldun understood this very perceptively as well. He recognized that the despotic state, lacking any popular control or mechanisms of accountability, is bound to concentrate more and more political power in its hands. With more power comes greater monopolization of economic benefits, greater temptation to violate the property rights that it was meant to protect, and a creeping slide along the Laffer curve toward the place where the tax rates and the risks of expropriation are so high that not only citizens' livelihoods but even the state's tax revenues start to suffer. Khaldun in fact saw this stage, where the state turns against society, as inevitable. This not only meant that the fruits of despotic growth would ultimately dry out, but also that the anticipation of the fearsome face of the Leviathan would undercut the benefits it generates even sooner than that. In Khaldun's poetic language, this meant:

> Like the silkworm that spins and then, in turn
> Finds its end amidst the threads itself has spun.

A second reason why despotic growth will be limited is equally fundamental. As we emphasized in our previous book, *Why Nations Fail*, sustained economic growth necessitates not just secure property rights, trade, and investment, but more critically, innovation and continual productivity improvements. These are much harder to usher in under the stern gaze of the Despotic Leviathan. Innovation needs creativity and creativity needs liberty—individuals to act fearlessly, experiment, and chart their own paths with their own ideas, even if this is not what others would like to see. This is hard to sustain under despotism. Opportunities aren't open to everybody when one group dominates the rest of society, nor is there much tolerance for different paths and experiments in a society without liberty.

Indeed, these are the reasons why we argued in our earlier book that "extractive growth," a close cousin of what we are calling despotic growth here, is limited and is highly unlikely to become the basis of sustained, long-term prosperity. We illustrated this limited nature of extractive growth with several examples, the simplest being the rise and fall of the Soviet growth miracle. The Soviets could organize the economy to pour resources and huge investments into manufacturing and subsequently into the space race and military technologies. Yet they could not generate sufficient innovation and productivity improvements to keep their economy from stagnating and then collapsing. This example underscores the fact that extractive growth results when a ruler who is constrained neither by institutions nor society finds it in his interest to support growth. But even when this is the case, the ruler will not be able to organize or command innovation. Nor will he be able to secure a broad-based distribution of opportunities to make best use of the creativity of the people. It's the same with despotic growth called into existence by the Despotic Leviathan, without any popular control, active participation by society, or true liberty.

The Law of the Splintered Paddle

The benefits of despotic growth for state builders were well understood by Kamehameha as he was unifying the Hawaiian islands. The first law he passed after his final conquest was the Law of the Splintered Paddle. This read:

> Oh my people, honor thy gods;
> respect alike [the rights of] men great and humble;
> see to it that our aged, our women and our children
> lie down to sleep by the roadside without fear of harm.
> Disobey and die.

This law has been seen to be so significant in the history of Hawaii that it was incorporated into the 1978 State Constitution, Article IX, Section 10, of which reads:

> **Public safety.** The law of the splintered paddle, mamala-hoe kanawai, decreed by Kamehameha I—Let every elderly person, woman and child lie by the roadside in safety—shall be a unique and living symbol of the State's concern for public safety.
> The State shall have the power to provide for the safety of the people from crimes against persons and property.

The law's original intention was to indicate that the new state would not tolerate unprovoked attacks on people or property. The name of the law referred to an incident in which Kamehameha, as a young warrior, was engaged in a raid on the Puna Coast, on the southeastern side of Hawaii Island (see Map 6 in the previous chapter), and decided to attack some fishermen to take their catch. Jumping out of his canoe onto the shore, Kamehameha got his foot caught in a crevice of lava, and seeing this, one of the fishermen had the courage to come up and hit him with a paddle that splintered on impact. The title of the law indicates that Kamehameha later realized that the attack had been wrong, and he signaled his intention to eliminate such behavior.

He was worried about unprovoked attacks not just against the persons and property of indigenous Hawaiians, but also against foreigners. He realized that the prosperity of his new island kingdom rested on increased commercial relations with the outside world. During the unification of the islands an active trade in the provisioning of foreign ships had developed, yet this was continually threatened by hostile acts. Hawaiians were particularly fond of stealing the anchors of foreign vessels. In the previous chapter we saw that the chain of events that led to the death of Captain Cook had been initiated by the theft of a cutter from Cook's flagship. As early as 1793, Kamehameha had declared to a Mr. Bell, a member of the explorer George Vancouver's expedition to the islands,

> his most solemn determination never to molest or disturb the weakest vessel that comes to Kealakekua, or where he himself is, on the contrary to do everything he can to make their stay among them comfortable.

Kamehameha was serious about this and about galvanizing despotic growth. Soon he managed to overcome the reticence of foreign traders to come to the islands. The potential economic benefits were substantial, and Kamehameha aptly took advantage of them. He monopolized foreign trade by introducing new kapu regulations to stop common people from engaging in trade with foreigners. He cornered the market so successfully that he was able to choose the terms of trade with foreigners, setting high prices for the supplies they needed to provision their ships. Such provisioning was lucrative, but Kamehameha soon realized that there were even better profits in the export of sandalwood. In 1812 he signed a contract with Boston ship captains the Winship brothers and W. H. Davis, under which he had the monopoly of sandalwood exports from Hawaii. The agreement was to last ten years and Kamehameha personally took one quarter of all profits. Ibn Khaldun would have noted that this arrangement wouldn't bring prosperity for long. It didn't, and in exactly the way Khaldun would have anticipated.

A Shark Going Inland

One of the great scholars of historical Hawaii was a Swede, Abraham Fornander, who arrived in the islands in 1838, learned the language, married a Hawaiian woman, and developed a passion for the society. He died in 1887, and his manuscripts were eventually published by the Bishop Museum in the 1920s. Fornander wrote down a chant:

A shark going inland is my chief,

A very strong shark able to devour all land;

A shark of very red gills is the chief,

He has a throat to swallow the island without choking.

The chant compares the chiefs of Hawaii (before Kamehameha's time) to "sharks going inland." It was an apt, and predatory, analogy.

Just like other instances of despotic growth, the creation of a Hawaiian state under Kamehameha soon followed in the ways of the previous chiefs—the shark went inland. This process was summarized by Samuel Kamakau, another one of the first generations of Hawaiians to emerge as historians of their society. Like David Malo, whose evidence we discussed in the previous chapter, Kamakau witnessed firsthand many of the events he recorded, or interviewed people who had. His description mentions the beneficial aspects of Kamehameha's state building but is also blunt on the huge downside:

> The country as a whole benefitted by the uniting of the government under one head, but most of the chiefs and landlords under Kamehameha oppressed the commoners and took away their lands, thus forcing the people who had owned the land to become slaves . . . Taxes were laid upon all holdings whether large or small and were constantly being added to, for there were many landlords and under landlords who demanded tribute . . . The uniting of the land had brought about excessive taxation . . . "Even the smallest patches are taxed" . . . was a familiar saying.

The progress of the shark—or sharks, since the chiefs below Kamehameha and his successors quickly got into the action—is vividly described in a surviving set of documents written in 1846, in the context of King Kamehameha III's attempt to rationalize and redistribute land rights. A board of three people, one Hawaiian and two foreigners, established a set of "principles" by which property rights were to be formalized. These principles noted that "the King, representing the government, having formerly been the sole owner of the soil . . . must be considered to be so still." Of course, as we already saw, it wasn't the case that kings "owned" the land in the Western sense of the word. Nevertheless, the document went on to note:

> When the islands were conquered by Kamehameha I, he followed the example of his predecessors, and divided out the lands among his

principal warrior chiefs, retaining, however, a portion in his hands, to be cultivated or managed by his own immediate servants or attendants. Each principal chief divided his lands, anew, and gave them out to an inferior order of chiefs, or persons of rank, by whom they were subdivided again and again; after passing through the hands of four, five or six persons, from the King down to the lowest class of tenants. All these persons were considered to have rights in the lands, or the productions of them.

All persons . . . owed and paid to the King not only a land tax, which he assessed at pleasure, but also, service which he called for at discretion, on all the grades from the highest down. They also owed and paid some portion of the productions of the land, in addition to the yearly taxes. They owed obedience at all times.

This wording is significant. Not just the *makaainanas*, the ordinary people, owed tribute and labor now, everyone did—"all the grades from the highest down." Also notable is the reference to "service which he called for at discretion." Forced labor was extensively used on the king's lands. F. I. Shemelin of the Russian-American Company, which had frequent interaction with the islands, recorded that "not only does he pay them nothing for their labor, he even declines to feed them." Kamakau recorded that the sandalwood cutters were reduced to eating "herbs and fern trunks."

Forced labor became especially important as the demand for sandalwood expanded in the 1820s after Kamehameha's death. The wood was usually far from people's farms, growing on the slopes of more mountainous areas, and the king and chiefs began to organize massive missions of hundreds and even thousands of coerced men who would have to find, cut, and transport the wood to the coasts, a process which could take weeks. The English missionaries Tyerman and Bennet saw 2,000 men carrying sandalwood to the royal storehouse in Kailua, Hawaii, in 1822. They were neither paid nor fed, instead having to live off the land. Coerced labor and the dislocation that it entailed soon led to a precipitous fall in agricultural output and to persistent near-famine conditions. One contemporary visitor recorded that

the reasons why provisions are so scarce on this island is, that the people, for some months past, have been engaged in cutting sandalwood, and have of course neglected the cultivation of the land.

The behavior of one chief in the north of Oʻahu, known as Cox, is particularly well documented. In the early 1820s he organized long campaigns to wrest sandalwood from the upland forest surrounding the Anahulu River valley in the north of the island. A trader, Gilbert Mathison, witnessed the scale of this undertaking and the intensity of the coercion involved. He wrote:

> Cox had given orders to some hundreds of his people to repair to the woods by an appointed day to cut sandalwood. The whole obeyed, except one man, who had the folly and hardihood to refuse. Upon this his house was set fire to, and burnt to the ground on the very day; still he refused to go. The next process was to seize his possessions and turn his wife and family off the estate.

Mathison's observations about the way Cox ran his territory show how extractive Kamehameha's state became after he died. For example, an American sailor, who had been granted land by Cox, reported that he was afraid of making any sort of improvement on his land because it might attract Cox's attention, who would then appropriate everything for himself. A local reported to the preacher James Ely in 1824 that

> we are sunk in discouragement. We have no inducement to labor, but many things to deter us from it. If we are enterprising, we are marked by the chiefs, and the property we obtain is taken by them. If we feed the heads of swine, or flocks of sheep, goats or fowl they are borne from us at the pleasure of the chiefs. If we sell produce, the money or property received in return is taken from us. The more enterprising, the more we are oppressed.

By the late 1820s the required work for the king increased from one day to three per week as coerced labor services for harvesting sandalwood were intensified. By the 1830s the sandalwood forests were exhausted, but now the king and chiefs started using coerced labor in agriculture. In the 1840s, the missionary William Roberts estimated that, in addition to all the required labor services, the average farmer was passing on a massive two-thirds of all of the output he produced to the king and the different chiefs.

This extractive system culminated in the Great Mahele of 1848, when King Kamehameha III decided on the radical distribution of lands we mentioned above.

The outcome of this was that 24 percent of the islands' lands were taken as private property by the king. A further 36 percent went to the government—again, in effect, to the king. A further 39 percent went to 252 chiefs, leaving less than 1 percent for the rest of the population.

The sharks were well inland at this point, devouring the land.

The Bird That Devours Others

The economic implications of the Zulu state were similar. In the 1820s, the many small chieftaincies of the area that later became KwaZulu-Natal relied on maize, millet, and ranching. There was not a great deal of trade, and the international slave traders had never penetrated into this part of Africa. As in most precolonial African societies, families and sub-lineages had user rights to farm or graze their herds in certain areas. Both cows and crops were privately owned by families. Although the Zulu economy differed in many ways from that of Tivland, where cows were very scarce because of the presence of the tsetse fly, the evidence suggests that it was similarly caged. Cows, for instance, were a prestige good and could only be sold under very specific and unusual circumstances.

In the process of his state-building efforts, Shaka reorganized the economy, breaking parts of the cage of norms that stood in the way. He declared that all the land belonged to him, a very radical departure from the initial status quo. As one oral history records:

> The land of Zululand belongs to Tshaka, he who unified all of it. Tshaka would take a fancy to a man and then, having conquered some chief's land, would say this man might go and build at any spot he [Tshaka] might indicate. Men used to be given land by Tshaka, and a man might be given permission to occupy land even though other people might be living on it at the time.

Not just the land, but also the cattle belonged to Shaka. Nevertheless, this was still quite a simple economy. There was little manufacturing, though Shaka monopolized for himself the production of weapons, specifically spears and shields, which he gave to his troops. The anthropologist Max Gluckman underscored the limited extent to which inequality could manifest itself in such a society by observing:

> There is only so much maize porridge that a Zulu chief can eat.

All the same, state formation under Shaka coincided with a huge increase in inequality, with Shaka, his relatives, and the core Zulu clan members who made up the royal family being the main beneficiaries. Even if he could eat only so much porridge, Shaka could and did monopolize power completely and establish unchallenged dominance over others. He not only managed to assert property rights over land and cows, he used his control over women and marriage to exert social control. He also monopolized the burgeoning trade with Europeans, who were perched on the coast. He ensured that all trade with Europeans went through his hands and cornered valuable supplies of ivory to sell to them.

But it wasn't just extraction under Shaka. Once the warfare that created the Zulu state subsided, Shaka, like Kamehameha, set up a legal system and centralized institutions of conflict resolution that helped his people while also improving economic incentives. Oral history has it that Dingiswayo's initial plan for territorial expansion was precipitated by a desire to stop the constant fighting and conflicts that broke out between small clans and chieftaincies. Indeed, once they were incorporated into Shaka's state, there was a good deal of order, and the pax Shaka certainly protected people from the threat of raiding and attack from surrounding chieftaincies. Crime within the kingdom also appears to have greatly declined. Thefts of cattle that were quite common before Shaka's rise largely disappeared because of the severe punishments that Shaka meted out against lawbreakers.

As in our other examples, order in Zululand bred despotic growth, which benefited society to some degree, but then it greatly benefited Shaka and his entourage too.

The Economics of the Rose Revolution

In the freewheeling days after the collapse of Communism in Georgia, there was a bonanza in the private sector for transport services. For instance, there was a boom in *maschrutkas*, taxi buses that, compared to the previously tightly regulated system, proved hugely attractive and flexible. But the government of Eduard Shevardnadze, whose rise to power we narrated in Chapter 3, soon showed it could regulate too, and in spades.

All maschrutka drivers had to have a medical exam *every day* to make sure they were not drunk and did not have high blood pressure. If a driver did not display his health certificate, he risked losing his license. By the time Shevardnadze was in power there were hundreds, probably thousands, of maschrutkas ferrying people all over the capital city of Tbilisi. Shevardnadze's government was detail-oriented not only when it came to taxi drivers. It decided that all of the stalls of petty street-side traders had to conform to a particular architectural design. Like maschrutka drivers, such traders had to renew their licenses twice a year. These regulations were only the tip of the iceberg. Gas stations, for example, had to be located at a specific distance from the street.

Shevardnadze's state must have accumulated a considerable amount of capacity to implement such measures. In a sense it did, but not in the obvious meaning of the word. In fact, these regulations, and thousands like them, were never intended to be implemented. Nobody really expected maschrutka drivers to have a daily medical exam, and they didn't. But by creating such a rule, the Georgian state immediately created a pretext for prosecuting the entire fleet of maschrutka drivers. To avoid this, the drivers had to pay bribes. So did the petty traders. So did the gas stations.

There is something in Shevardnadze's naked actions to extract resources and bribes from Georgians that is a little different from Khaldun's generational theory, which foresaw that despotism would first fuel some growth and then start intensifying its extraction—a pattern that seems to fit what happened in the Caliphate, in Hawaii, and even in Zululand. Shevardnadze's state skipped the first step and dived right into thievery. Why was that?

To answer this question we have to first recognize that the treatment of the maschrutka drivers was part of a more systematic policy (if it could be called that), one that was dictated not by economics but by a political logic. It was: Remain in power by creating economic disorder.

Shevardnadze behaved in this way in large part because he was in a much weaker position than the other state builders we have encountered in this and the previous chapter. Even after he outsmarted the warlords he was faced with strong regional powers within Georgia. He was grasping on to power rather than building a capable state, and he tried to do this by placating powerful interests by co-opting them with riches (or at the very least with bribes). Corruption in developing countries is common, so maschrutka drivers' bribing state officials isn't that unusual. But what went on in Georgia was a little different from this type of corruption. Shevardnadze set up the system so that the drivers were bound to break the law, and this provided low-hanging fruit for the police. He made lawbreaking inevitable and created a system that encouraged corruption.

The main reason for this was to control society, which was now continually guilty of breaking the law. You could avoid implementation of the law by paying a bribe today, but the state could come after you at any time. Yet this scheme also controlled officials in the state, another potentially powerful group—accepting bribes was illegal, so the state could go after them too if it wanted to.

Shevardnadze combined what we might call this "low corruption" with an equally labyrinthine system of "high corruption." High-ranking elites, members of the parliament, and senior civil servants were sucked into similar schemes. They were also given a stake in Shevardnadze's regime because he shared with them the incomes that flowed into his government, mostly from international donors. But they would only enjoy these incomes if Shevardnadze stayed in power. So they had to hitch their horses to his wagon. Shevardnadze used multiple methods to do this and he had a huge advantage thanks to the country's Communist history: the Georgian government owned most of the productive sectors of the economy. Though there had been token attempts at privatization, this had not really happened prior to his assumption of power. Shevardnadze then immersed himself in Russian-style privatization—selling selected assets for cheap to powerful people or people he wanted to co-opt (we'll see how this privatization worked in Russia in Chapter 9). Often, to seal the deal, he made them ministers in charge of regulating the firms they owned. In this way he managed to create a series of monopolies. Just as the regulations at the bottom were part of his political strategy, so were those at the top. So, for example, the government passed a law prescribing that every car had to carry a specific type of fire extinguisher—one that was imported exclusively by a relative of the minister of the interior.

Shevardnadze's family got in on the action too. While most of the population suffered repeated power cuts, two commercial firms owned by the president's family sold government-produced electricity on the side for a healthy profit of around $30 million a year. There were many regulations of imports and exports, so smuggling was very profitable and happened on a huge scale. In 2003 a parliamentary commission calculated that 90 percent of flour, 40 percent of gasoline, and 40 percent of cigarettes consumed in the country were smuggled. This generated a huge stream of bribes, but since the elites, many in the government, were involved in the illegal trade, it also provided ample ammunition for the state to go after them if it wanted to, just as with the traffic police and the health checks on the maschrutka drivers. The encouragement of illegality was all part of the strategy.

An indication of the extent to which the membership of the cabinet was used as a tool for co-option and corruption is that it was only in 2000, after he had been in power for eight years, that Shevardnadze finally appointed someone from his own political party as a minister. Significantly, that man was Mikheil Saakashvili, who became minister of justice. Saakashvili refused to be co-opted and was quickly fired, but then became one of the leaders of the Rose Revolution of November 2003, which forced Shevardnadze from power.

Shevardnadze's economic impact was decidedly negative. This wasn't simply because all the monopolies and regulations undermined the ability of markets to create incentives and opportunities for productive activity. It was also because Shevardnadze managed everything with a great deal of discretion and unpredictability. The aim of this economic disorder was to keep everyone off balance. You might be a minister today with a nice monopoly, and tomorrow Shevardnadze might change his mind and take it all away. The idea was to make people so dependent on the president that they became totally loyal. This worked so well that Shevardnadze managed to stay in power for a full decade. But the ambiguity and unpredictability created tremendous disincentives for investment. As a direct consequence, economic growth, even in its despotic form, did not materialize in Georgia.

The political strategy Shevardnadze quickly developed and perfected is not a Georgian aberration. As we have seen, despotism means silencing and sidelining society's participation in political, social, and economic decisions, which in turn enables the exercise of despotic power. It doesn't necessarily mean that the despot will be secure in his position, however, because others may be tempted by the political and economic benefits of controlling a powerful, unrestrained state. The threat of losing power may then push the ruler to structure the economy not for efficiency, but for co-opting willing rivals and cutting down unwilling ones. This is what Shevardnadze achieved in such a short time.

With Shevardnadze, we are thus witnessing the worst facet of despotic growth. Nevertheless, it is important to understand the commonalities linking this episode to other instances. The fragility of despotic growth emanates partly from the fact that it will go on only so long as it is in the interest of the ruler and his entourage. The problem in Georgia was that from the get-go, growth was not Shevardnadze's priority. He was too focused on weakening society, creating corruption, and buying off other powerful actors in Georgia, all with predictably awful consequences for prosperity.

Caged and Despotic Economics

The scorecard for the economy outside the corridor is decidedly mixed. If you live without the Leviathan, the situation is dire. For one, you may end up with ceaseless conflict "of every man, against every man" as Hobbes foresaw, with dismal incentives and thus "no place for industry." If your society manages to mobilize its norms and customs to put a lid on conflict and contain violence, then this tends to create a caged economy, constricted by norms and full of distorted economic incentives that do nothing to end poverty.

Despotism may improve on these outcomes, or so thought Hobbes. Compared to Warre or the caged economy, the Despotic Leviathan has clear advantages. Despotic though it may be, the state can prevent fighting, resolve conflicts, impose laws that help economic transactions, invest in public infrastructure, and help generate economic activity. It can even benefit the economy by relaxing the norm-based restrictions on economic activities. The Caliphate shows how it can unleash huge economic potential because of the order it imposes and the productivity-enhancing investments it undertakes or encourages. This is despotic growth at its best. But it is inherently fragile and limited. It is fragile because, as Khaldun anticipated, the Despotic Leviathan will be continually tempted to extract more revenues from society, monopolize more of the valuable resources, and act in more wanton ways. It is also fragile because the power of the state can be used, as Shevardnadze did, to create a hugely inefficient system just to avoid or cripple challenges to the despot's position. It is limited too when it comes to undergirding sustained economic growth, because it does not activate and nurture the most productive aspects of society—its ability to freely function, generate broad-based opportunities and incentives for economic activity, and bring forth investment, experimentation, and innovation. For that, we have to wait for the emergence of liberty and the Shackled Leviathan.

Chapter 5

ALLEGORY OF GOOD
GOVERNMENT

The Frescoes of Piazza del Campo

As you enter the famous shell-shaped Piazza del Campo at the heart of Siena, the Palazzo Pubblico looms above you. Construction started in 1297. It was to house Siena's government, the most powerful body of which was made up of nine consuls. "The Nine" met in a room in the Palazzo, the Sala dei Nove, the Salon of the Nine. The room has windows only on the side that faces the Piazza. On the other walls are three remarkable frescoes, commissioned by the Nine and painted between February 1338 and May 1339 by Ambrogio Lorenzetti. Standing with your back to the light, the first one that comes into focus is the one opposite the windows, the *Allegory of Good Government* (which you can see in the photo insert).

The first detail to catch your eye in this complex work of art is a seated figure to the right who appears to be a ruler or king. He is surrounded by artistic representations of different cardinal virtues: Fortitude, Prudence, and Peace on the left, Temperance, Justice, and Magnanimity on the right. So, a just and magnanimous ruler possibly? It seems odd that the *Allegory of Good Government* would feature a ruler because Siena didn't have one in 1338, and the Nine would have undoubtedly disapproved of such a person. This mystery is solved by noting that the apparent ruler is wearing black and white, the colors of Siena. At his feet are other symbols of Siena, the wolf and twins, an image appropriated from the founding of Rome by the mythical twins Romulus and Remus, suckled as infants by a wolf. Then look up and above the head of the ruler, and you'll see the initials C.S.C.V., for the Latin *Commune Senarum Civitas Virginis*, translated as "The Sienese Commune, the City of the Virgin." Siena had adopted the Virgin Mary as its patron just before the battle of Montaperti in 1260, when they defeated the Florentines. The ruler in fact represents the commune of Siena.

In this fresco we are seeing something very different from the "will to power" and its consequences. Rulers are in the background and the commune, as a representation of society, has come to the foreground. The Sienese also recognized something special about this form of organization as signaled by their emphasis on "good government." What was distinctive about Siena and the communes that sprang up around the same time all over Italy was a much greater level of liberty. This undergirded a very different economy with broad-based incentives and opportunities paving the way for prosperity.

The notion of a commune seems to have emerged gradually in Italy in the late ninth and tenth centuries as citizens from all over northern Italy began to challenge and overthrow the authority of their ruling bishops, ecclesiastical authorities, and lords (see Map 7). In their place they began to create various systems of republican self-government. We do not have a complete picture of these early days, only fragments. In Modena in 891, for instance, we have a record of a "popular conspiracy" against the bishop. We hear of a similar thing in the same decade in Turin and by 924 in Cremona. In 997 in Treviso the bishop acted only "with the consent of all the leading men and judges and the whole people of Treviso." In 1038 the bishop of Brescia made concessions to 154 named men and "the other free men living in Brescia." The preponderance of ecclesiastical evidence here is probably a consequence of the church's better record keeping. Lay authority was almost certainly being challenged as well.

The defining feature of this new form of government was the popular election of consuls to run the city for a given period of time. Pisa in 1085 had twelve such consuls elected by a popular assembly. In Siena we know they were in place a little bit later, in 1125. During this period communes appeared all over northern and central Italy; in Milan in 1097, Genoa in 1099, Pavia in 1112, Bergamo in 1117, and Bologna in 1123. Though they were nominally part of the Holy Roman Empire, the de facto autonomy of these communes was recognized by the Peace of Constance in 1183, signed with the emperor Frederick Barbarossa. The treaty even granted the communes the right to build fortifications, perhaps bowing to the

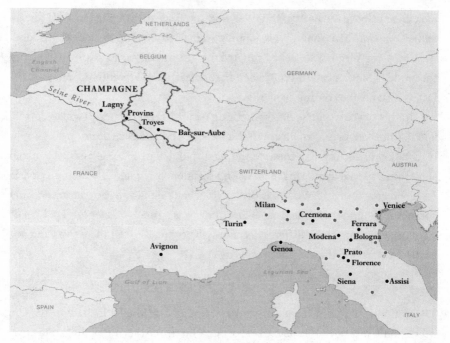

Map 7. The Italian Communes and the Champagne Fairs

inevitable. Barbarossa himself wasn't too happy about this, but understood the implications of what the communes were attempting for liberty. Bishop Otto of Freising, Barbarossa's uncle, wrote about Barbarossa's difficulties in dealing with the communes in *The Deeds of Frederick Barbarossa*, arguing that

> in the governing of their cities . . . and in the conduct of public affairs . . . they are so desirous of liberty that . . . they are governed by the will of consuls rather than rulers . . . And in order to suppress arrogance, the aforesaid consuls are chosen . . . from each of the classes. And lest they should exceed bounds by lust for power, they are changed almost every year. The consequence is that, as practically the entire land is divided amongst the cities . . . scarcely any noble or great man can be found in all the surrounding territory who does not acknowledge the authority of the city.

Bishop Otto also understood the connection between the political autonomy and prosperity of the communes since, he continued, from this it has resulted that they far surpass all other states of the world in riches and in power. They are aided in this not only, as has been said, by their characteristic industry, but also by the absence of their princes [i.e., emperors], who are accustomed to remain on the far side of the Alps.

It's useful to look in detail at what the political institutions of republican Siena looked like at the time of the Nine to get a sense of how communal government worked. The most basic was a popular assembly of all adult male citizens. Though this assembly had atrophied by Lorenzetti's time, it was still in Siena's constitution and seems to have met on special occasions, for example, when the new chief magistrate, the Podestà, took office. By the middle of the fourteenth century the role of this assembly had been taken over by a council known as the "Council of the Bell" because it was summoned by the ringing of a bell. This was made up of 300 male citizens, with 100 elected for one year from each of the three main administrative divisions of Siena, known as *terzi*. The electors for this body were the Nine, the Podestà, and other executive officers of the state including the Chamberlain, the four main treasury officials known as "provisors," and the state-appointed judges. The main functions of the government were carried out by the Podestà and the Nine, and there were other small groups of consuls representing specific organized interests, particularly the powerful merchant guild and old aristocratic families.

The Podestà was an interesting institution, common to most of the Italian communes. The title comes from the Latin word *potestas*, meaning "power." The office had to be filled by someone from outside Siena, so that he could maintain his independence from the different families and factions of the commune. His duties included judicial functions, and calling and presiding over the Council of the Bell. The Podestà didn't act alone; he recruited other officials he would need to fulfill his duties. In 1295, for example, Bernard de Verano came to Siena with seven judges, three knights, two notaries, six squires, and sixty police he brought from his own province. He was initially chosen with a six-month tenure, but by the 1340s the tenure was extended to a year, after which the person was not eligible to act as Podestà again immediately. The next Podestà was selected out of a list of four candidates proposed by the Nine, by a council composed of the Nine, sixty men selected for this purpose, the consuls of the merchant guild, and the knights.

The Podestà was not allowed to receive gifts from citizens or even to eat with them. He could not move more than one day's travel from the city, and each Podestà in turn had to reside in a different *terzo*. When his term was over, the Podestà had to remain in Siena for two weeks while an investigation was conducted of his behavior while in office. This often led to heavy fines on the Podestà.

The Nine had evolved over time, with the form we now recognize emerging after 1292. Between 1236 and 1271 there had been the "Twenty-Four," who were followed by the "Thirty-Six." During the thirteenth century the Sienese had also played with bodies made up of fifteen, nine, eighteen, and six. These numbers always had to be divisible by three because each terzo had to have equal representation. The Nine who commissioned Lorenzetti's frescoes were chosen at a meeting consisting of the previous Nine, the Podestà, the consuls of the merchant guild, and the Capitano del Popolo (another executive position originally intended to represent the Popolo, the people). After serving in the Nine, which was for a two-month period, a person could serve again only after a break of twenty months.

What the Nine were supposed to do is summed up by their oath of office. They had to swear to keep the commune of Siena "in good peace and concord," which sounds very much like a critical aspect of liberty, and also involves the protection of the commune from dominance by the state institutions themselves. Indeed, the oath was quite specific about recognizing that the shackles on the powers of the Leviathan, in this instance represented by the Nine, were crucial for this sort of liberty. Members of the Nine had to make sure

> that law and justice be done and administered to the citizens subject to you and to those persons subject to you without discrimination by your rectors or officials. And that the statutes of your commune and its ordinances be observed for each person who demands it.

But there is more. To some degree anticipating our discussion of the role of the Shackled Leviathan in the origins of economic prosperity, the Nine were charged with economic development:

> You must bring about the increase, growth, and conservation of the city of Siena.

Compared to dozens of other communes in northern and central Italy, there was nothing special about Siena, except the beautiful frescoes that are so telling about what its institutions were trying to achieve. In some, like Siena at the time of the Nine, the original popular impulse that had created the commune had succumbed to an oligarchic system, with rich families playing an oversized role. In others, more powerful popular assemblies acted as effective counterweights against these oligarchic interests. But almost all of these communes had critical features similar to those of Siena. They were republics run by elected consuls or magistrates facing strict limits on their power. Representative bodies, such as popular assemblies and other councils, acted as the shackles on the powers of the state and its executives like the Nine. These bodies were not beholden to any aristocratic or ecclesiastical authority. They were self-governing entities, underpinned by a strong society capable of holding its own against the power of the emerging state, a quality that impressed the traveler Benjamin of Tudela during his passage through Genoa, Lucca, and Pisa around 1165. He noted:

> They possess neither king nor prince to govern them, but only the judges appointed by themselves.

You can see exactly this in the *Allegory of Good Government*. We've noted how the ruler to the right is surrounded by six virtues. Interestingly, the one farthest to the left is Peace, putting her right in the middle of the fresco. As the philosopher Quentin Skinner puts it in his discussion of the frescoes, Peace is "at the heart of our common life." To the left of Peace sits another grand figure, Justice. You can tell because she is holding a scale. From the scale a double rope descends and then passes to the other side of the painting, to the ruler, by way of twenty-four figures representing the Twenty-Four who had previously served as consuls in Siena. The Twenty-Four are given the rope by a seated figure named Concordia—concord—who holds a carpenter's plane in her lap. A plane is used to smooth rough edges and create a level surface, possibly signifying the "rule of law"—the fact that in Siena law was supposed to apply equally to everybody.

It is significant that the Twenty-Four, who represent society, hold the rope but are not held by it. This seems to signify that rule is granted *by* society, not *to* society. Notably, when the double rope gets to the ruler on the other side of the scene, it is knotted around his wrist—the Leviathan is shackled by the rope emanating from Justice.

Indeed, there were various types of "ropes" to keep the Nine under control. In addition to their very limited two months in office, an official called the *maggior sindaco*, who like the Podestà was always from outside Siena, could oppose any proposed constitutional change. To pass a measure that the maggior sindaco had opposed required a supermajority of three quarters of the councillors in favor of it and a quorum of at least two hundred councillors.

It wasn't just laws and institutions, but also norms that were brought to bear to protect the commune from the Nine and other politically powerful individuals. For example, taking a page from the Athenians who came up with the Hubris Law, you could give politicians that were too big for their britches a "bad name"— literally. Take the Milanese Girardo Cagapisto, who was consul fourteen times in Milan between 1141 and 1180. His name begins with the word *caga*, or *caca*, mean- ing "shit." Cagapisto means "shit pesto," as in the Italian pasta sauce. Other ex- amples of politicians whose names include the word "shit" are the brothers Gregorio and Guglielmo Cacainarca, whose family name means "shit in a box." Similarly, the name of the consul Arderico Cagainosa, who held office between 1140 and 1144, is translated as "shit in your pants." Other names of prominent political families include Cacainbasilica, "shit in the church"; Cacarana, "shit a frog"; Cagalenti, or "shit slowly"; and even Cagatosici, which means "toxic shit." Get too powerful or misbehave, and you risked getting a surname featuring Caca.

A few other features of the fresco are noteworthy. At the foot of the ruler, a little to the right, are two kneeling noblemen in armor. They signify the authority of the commune over the aristocracy who too are bound by Justice. Behind them are a group of soldiers carrying lances that may represent the special force that the Nine recruited in 1302 to police the Sienese countryside.

This all sounds very much like liberty from fear (because of Peace), violence (because of Justice), and dominance (because the state and the elite are constrained by laws and popular mandates). At the bottom of the wall are painted words that say as much:

> Wherever this holy virtue [Justice] rules,
> She induces to unity many souls;
> And these, gathered for such a purpose
> A common good (ben comun) for their master undertake;
> Who, in order to govern his state, chooses
> Never to keep his eyes turned
> From the splendor of the faces
> Of the virtues which around him stand.
> For this, with triumph are given to him
> Taxes, tributes, and lordships of lands;

For this, without wars,

Is followed then by every civil result,

Useful, necessary, and pleasurable.

There is a significant wordplay in this statement. The common good is associated with the commune. The political form of the commune serves the common good, because the ruler is tied to Justice and indeed it is the citizens who tie together Justice and the ruler. The fresco thus recognizes that it is the rule by society in the commune that makes the commune serve the common good.

The Effects of Good Government

In Chapter 2 we stressed how powerful states can provide not only protection against violence and dominance but also public services. We see these critical roles of the state in Siena. The people that the Podestà brought with him were there to enforce laws, resolve conflicts, and provide notary and other business services. In addition, the volumes recording communal expenditures for the first six months of 1257 mention some 860 offices held by the Sienese in the city. These include 171 night watchmen, 114 supervisors of tolls and customs, 103 syndics of the districts, and 90 officials in charge of tax assessments. We also find supervisors of weights and measures, supervisors of grain and salt sales, jailers and hangmen, trumpeters, masons whose job it was to maintain public buildings, and custodians of the fountains. There were also six "good men" who oversaw the taverns and prevented swearing, and another six whose tasks included keeping wild donkeys, swine, and lepers out of the city. Spinning wool in the street was not allowed, and the city imposed a host of other regulations. For example, planning permission was required for any new construction within city walls, and the city even ruled that bricks and tiles had to be made in uniform sizes. We see this proliferation of offices and regulations in other communes as well.

The communes got very good at raising taxes too. After all, someone had to pay for all these officials. They used tax revenues to provide public services as well. Some, like the standardization of weights and measures, are implied by the above list of administrative positions, but there were many others, including a fire department, a stable coinage and monetary system, and the construction and maintenance of roads and bridges. In 1292 Siena had a "judge of the roads" who was soon supplemented by three general road commissioners. To make sure that people could travel in peace, a "scourer of the highways" was appointed, though the office was discontinued as the Nine built a much more elaborate system for the provision of rural order. In order to secure the property and human rights of Sienese merchants wherever they were, the city also organized "reprisals" whereby they retaliated against the merchants and citizens of other polities that had been guilty of infractions against any Sienese.

These public services and the support for liberty we see in Siena are unparalleled anywhere outside northern and central Italy during this time. But that wasn't all that the Sienese state promoted. It provided broad-based incentives and economic opportunities as well.

To see that you have to turn your gaze toward the right wall of the Sala dei Nove, where Lorenzetti painted another huge fresco, *The Effects of Good Government* (which is also shown in the photo insert). The fresco depicts a panoramic view of city and country life. On the left, the city is teeming with people. In the foreground, a group of women are dancing, but what is most striking is the flourishing economic activity. To the right of the dancers, a shopkeeper is bargaining over some shoes with a man holding a tethered horse. To the right of them a priest gives a sermon and a woman lays out a stall with jars of olive oil, or maybe wine, for sale. A man passes with a mule loaded with firewood. Others are weaving on a loom and tending a flock of sheep. Two women, one with a basket and the other with a bird, are probably on their way to market. Finally, in the far background, two horses laden with goods pass by. At the top of the fresco a construction crew is busy at work adding to the fine towers that stud the skyline.

The right half of the fresco focuses on the effects of good government in the countryside, where we again witness the distinctive economic implications of the Shackled Leviathan and the liberty it creates. Above the depiction of the countryside, the figure of Security holds a scroll that directly links prosperity to liberty:

> Without fear, let each man freely walk,
> And working let everyone sow,
> While such a commune
> This lady will keep under her rule
> Because she has removed all power from the guilty.

The fresco depicts a scene that is consistent with these sentiments. In the foreground, we see peasants hard at work in front of a bountiful field of wheat. A hunting party exits the city gates on a paved road, while in the other direction merchants are bringing their wares and a pig for sale. In the background other people are sowing, harvesting, and threshing grain. All is peaceful and prosperous amid the well-tended fields and houses.

The message is clear: Among the many benefits of good government is economic prosperity. Is that right or was Lorenzetti just making it up? Was there really a connection between communal government and economic development?

How Saint Francis Got His Name

The life of one of the most famous saints of the Middle Ages, Saint Francis of Assisi, provides some of the answer to this question. Francis, renowned for his love of animals and nature, bequeathed to posterity one of the great images of Christian worship, the Christmas nativity scene. The "of Assisi" bit of his name came from the commune in central Italy where he was born, probably in 1182. The name Francis is a bit more puzzling. When he was born, Francis was called Giovanni di Pietro di Bernardone. So where did Francis come from?

Francis's father, Pietro di Bernardone, a prosperous silk merchant, was in France on business when Giovanni was born. Pietro had married a woman from Provence, Francis's mother, Pica de Bourlemont. Upon his return to Assisi, Pietro took to calling his son Francesco ("the Frenchman"), perhaps as a sign of his love for France.

That love appears to have been related to Pietro's business in France. In 1174, a mere eight years before Francis's birth, Italian merchants had taken part for the first time in the "Champagne fairs" of northern France (see Map 7). These fairs were held six times a year and rotated among four towns in the county of Champagne: Bar-sur-Aube, Lagny, Provins, and Troyes. Each of the fairs usually lasted for six weeks, after which there was a pause that allowed merchants to move to the next town. In consequence, the Champagne fairs turned into a marketplace that was open nearly all year round.

There were several things that were special about Champagne that made it a magnet for trade. One was its location: it became the meeting point for merchants from all over France and then began attracting merchants from the booming cities of Flanders and the Low Countries. The most important advantage of Champagne came from its economic institutions that massively facilitated trade. For one, counts of Champagne recognized a good thing when they saw one. When in 1148 money changers from Vézelay were robbed on their way to the Provins fair, Count Thibault II wrote to the regent of France demanding that the money changers be compensated. "I will not let take place with impunity such an injury, which tends to nothing less than the ruin of my fairs." Count Thibault liked fairs because he could tax them. No merchants, no tax revenue. By the 1170s the local counts had begun appointing special "fair-wardens" with policing, regulatory, and judicial powers at the fairs to create an attractive institutional environment. It was likely this innovation that induced the Italians, Pietro di Bernardone among them, to venture over the Alps to the fairs. But it wasn't just the counts that got involved. Three of the Champagne towns, Provins, Bar-sur-Aube, and Troyes, had privileges as communes themselves, entitling them to operate municipal courts during this period. These courts enforced contracts and mediated trade disputes.

These initial institutional innovations focused on providing basic order and security, and judicial services such as the resolution of disputes. As the Italians got more involved in the fairs, the innovations stretched all the way to Italy. In 1242–1243, a group of Italian merchants on their way to the Champagne fairs were kidnapped and robbed by Piacenzans. This is not what the count of Champagne wanted to see. He wrote to the Piacenzan authorities threatening to ban all merchants from Piacenza from trading in Champagne unless the victims were paid due compensation. After problems of order and dispute were addressed, the local authorities got more ambitious and started to improve the roads and to build a canal between the Seine and Troyes.

The Champagne fairs are one of the most famous examples of the so-called commercial revolution of the Middle Ages. The Italian communes were right at the heart of this. That wasn't a coincidence. The communal system of government created laws and economic institutions that allowed trade and economic activity to take off after the slump that followed the collapse of the Western Roman Empire in the late fifth century. Italy was well placed to benefit from this flourishing. In the east and the south were the Byzantine Empire and the new Muslim states, which we encountered in Chapter 4, supplying Eastern spices and many luxury goods. In the north were England and Flanders. England produced the highest-quality wool, Flanders the most sought-after textiles. The stage was set for a huge system of exchange: wool and cloth for luxuries and spices. Southern Italy—by the mid-twelfth century ruled by Norman kings—and Spain were also well placed, but did not have communal governments. So neither took over the trade the way that communal northern and central Italy did. This had a lot to do with how the communes promoted the institutions necessary for trade.

This is obvious when we look at the financial innovation that was so critical for trade. Here the Italian communes led the way. As their economic activities spread around Europe, they set up bases in all the places they traded. More important, they invented the bill of exchange, which became the prime method to organize medieval commerce. Imagine that a Florentine cloth manufacturer wanted to buy high-quality Norfolk wool in England. He could travel to England with some sacks of Italian ducats, find someone in London to exchange them for pounds, buy the wool, and ship it back. Alternatively he could use a bill of exchange. In the standard terminology, there are four parties to such a bill: the remitter, here the cloth manufacturer; the drawer, which would be the remitter's bank in Florence; the drawee, which would be the corresponding bank of the Florentine bank in England; and the payee, the wool merchant in London whom the cloth manufacturer wanted to buy wool from. In Florence, the remitter would give ducats to the drawer to buy the bill. He would then send the bill to the payee in London, who could take the bill to the drawee and get English pounds for it. Then the payee would ship the wool to Florence. The bill that was bought with ducats in Florence would specify the amount in pounds to be paid in London.

The Florentine bank didn't even need to have a branch in London; it just needed to be able to deal with another bank that did. The presence of the international bank and the bill of exchange massively facilitated international transactions. Implicit in a bill of exchange is a loan. The cloth manufacturer had to wait before getting his wool, and he was in effect lending money to the London wool merchant. This was compensated by the payment of "interest," even if this wasn't always called interest and implemented instead via the use of different exchange rates. For example, say the cloth manufacturer wanted to buy 100 pounds' worth of wool in London and at the exchange rate in Florence this involved a payment of 1,000 ducats. Then a lower exchange rate was used in London to convert the bill into pounds. Innovative Italians soon created a new credit instrument, the "dry exchange," wherein the movement of goods became irrelevant and the use of different exchange rates was specified in advance.

The notion of a dry exchange sounds innocuous. But it was edgy because lending for interest was viewed as usury and was one of the many economic activities discouraged or even banned by the norms, customs, and beliefs of medieval Europeans. Jesus had said in the Gospel of Saint Luke, "Borrow and lend freely, hoping for nothing in return." Church doctrine therefore interpreted the charging of interest on loans as sinful usury. This was a major problem for the development of an effective financial system. It's natural that some people possess capital and wealth and others do not. But these others could be the ones who have the ideas or investment opportunities. A functioning financial system would allow the people with money to extend credit to those with the ideas. Interest is the return that encourages such transactions to take place and compensates the lender for forgoing other opportunities and for the risk of nonpayment. Blocking interest on lending on the basis that it was a sin would stall the development of a financial system. Part of the commercial revolution in Italy was to use innovations like dry exchange to enable lending and credit, but without it risking being condemned as sin and usury. The Church still maintained that it was, but such innovations allowed this one important aspect of the cage of norms to be relaxed, opening the way for significant growth in investment and commerce. It wasn't just the innovative Italians who thought of going around the cage of norms. As life in the corridor evolved, restrictions on social and economic freedoms became harder to sustain. Even the Church began to relax the cage a little. Saint Thomas Aquinas, for example, allowed a debtor to pay "compensation" to a creditor in some circumstances, and this proved to be a flexible justification for interest-like payments. This relaxation of the cage of norms also became a significant source of comparative economic advantage for the Italians, who began to play the role of financial intermediary throughout Europe. The institutional environment of the Italian communes was critical for all of this. Elsewhere, the same activities were not as welcome. In 1394, for example, the king of Aragon was threatening to put on trial all the Italian merchants in Barcelona on the grounds that they were engaging in usury.

Italians led the way with other innovations. They invented mercantile insurance, allowing a third party to take on the risk of trade. They also developed many different contractual forms that facilitated trade. One was the *commenda*, a temporary partnership between two people, one who provided the capital for a trading mission and another who undertook the mission. When the mission was over, the two partners split the proceeds. The commenda was another way in which usury laws could be evaded. Italians also invented long-lived organizational forms that were precursors to the joint stock company, allowing people who were not actively involved in the actual business to put up capital and earn returns in the form of dividends. Also important was a new emphasis on written legal documents defining property rights and the use of notaries. In the 1280s, in cities like Milan or Bologna, there were twenty-five notaries for every thousand inhabitants.

All of this trade needed advanced accounting practices. It's not a coincidence that it was an Italian from Pisa, Leonardo Fibonacci, who revolutionized accounting by adapting the Arabic numerical system in 1202. This made financial calculations much more straightforward. By the middle of the fourteenth century, double-entry bookkeeping appeared in Italy for the first time.

The commercial revolution went along with a great deal of economic growth and stimulated innovation outside the financial sector too. Though we don't have enough evidence to construct national income accounts for this period of history, we can proxy economic development by the extent of urbanization—the fraction of the population living in cities of at least 5,000 people. Urbanization in Western Europe doubled from about 3 percent in 800 at the start of the commercial revolution to 6 percent in 1300. The rise was much more rapid in the places that were heavily involved in this revolution. For Italy in general it increased from 4 to 14 percent over the same period. But this included the south of Italy, which did not experience the flourishing of commerce and communes. The urbanization rate in northern Italy was undoubtedly much higher and has been estimated at 25 percent in Tuscany. Elsewhere, in Flanders and the Low Countries, urbanization increased from about 3 to 12 percent by 1300 and then to a remarkable 23 percent by 1400.

The dynamism of the urban communes is driven home by looking at their relative population size in a wider European context. In 1050 only one of them, Florence, which had a population of just 15,000 people, featured among the thirty largest cities in Europe. By 1200 Florence's population had increased by 400 percent to 60,000 and it had been joined on this list by Bologna, Cremona, Ferrara, Genoa, Pavia, and Venice. By 1330 fully one-third of all of the thirty largest cities in Europe were Italian communes, with the most populous being Venice with 110,000 people, followed by Genoa and Milan, both with 100,000. Siena had a population of 50,000 at this date. Only Paris and Granada, the capital of the highly urbanized Muslim Spain, had larger populations than Venice, Genoa, and Milan.

Another sign of economic growth can be seen in a critical input of economic activity, education, and skills of the workforce. This seems to have increased dramatically in northern Italy during this period. For example, the *New Chronicles*, a fourteenth-century history of Florence written by Giovanni Villani, estimates that in early-fourteenth-century Florence there were about 8,000 to 10,000 boys and girls receiving elementary education and another 550 to 600 in higher education, while another 1,000 to 2,000 attended schools designed to impart commercial skills. If this was the typical situation, then as much as half of Florence's population in this period could have attended some type of formal school. The Florentine Catasto of 1427, a comprehensive survey of the population, suggests that seven out of ten adult males could read and write—a remarkably high number for this era. An estimate for Venice in 1587 suggests that 33 percent of boys were literate.

The spread of literacy and economic development is also illustrated by the data on book production. In the ninth century only 10 percent of the 202,000 books produced in Western Europe were from Italy. By the fourteenth century, Italy was Western Europe's biggest book producer, accounting for 32 percent of the European total of 2,747,000 books. Italy also had more universities than any other part of Western Europe, 39 percent of all European universities by the fourteenth century.

We find broader improvements in technology in this period as well, some of them critical to the commercial revolution, such as improvements in ship design with the spread of the sternpost rudder (whereas before ships were much less effectively steered by oar, as they had been since Roman days). Also produced in Italy were the first pair of spectacles, the first mechanized textile mill, in Lucca, to produce silk cloth, and the mechanical clock of Giovanni de Dondi built in the 1360s, though it is clear from his writings that clocks had existed for quite a while by then.

The First Cat in the Canary Islands

One of the remarkable achievements of the communes was a high rate of social mobility. A famous example is Francesco di Marco Datini. A story from his hometown, the commune of Prato in Tuscany, gives one account of how he first became commercially successful.

> In the days—so the legend runs—when the adventurous traders of Tuscany were sailing to far lands, a merchant of Prato came to a remote island called the Canary Isle; and there the king of the island invited him to dinner.
>
> And the merchant saw the table laid with napkins, and on each of them a club as long as his arm, and he could not fathom its purpose. But having sat down at the table, and the viands having been brought in, the odour thereof brought forth a great abundance of mice, who must perforce be chased away with those clubs, if the guests wished to eat . . . And the next day, having returned at night to his ship, the merchant came back with a cat up his sleeve. And when the viands came, the mice also appeared; and the merchant brought the cat out of his sleeve, and she speedily killed twenty-five or thirty mice, and the others ran away.

"This animal is divine!" cried the king. Whereupon the merchant replied: "Sire, your courtesy to me has been so great that I can only return
it by bestowing on you this cat." The king gratefully accepted the gift,
but before the merchant left the island, he sent for him again and presented him with jewels worth 4,000 *scudi*. And the following year the
merchant came back again to the island, taking with him a tom-cat—
and this time received a further 6,000 *scudi*. The merchant of Prato
came home a rich man; and his name was Francesco di Marco Datini.

It's probably not true that this is how Datini got rich. In fact there is no existing
record that he ever went to the Canary Islands. What we do know is that he was
born the son of a poor taverner, probably in 1335. When he was just thirteen years
old, the Black Death (the bubonic plague) struck Italy, and his mother and father
as well as two of his siblings perished. Only he and his brother Stefano were left,
and there was a little inheritance, a house, a small piece of land, and 47 florins.

About a year after his father's death, Datini moved to Florence, got an appren-
ticeship with a shopkeeper, and began to hear stories about the prosperous city of
Avignon in the south of France. Between 1309 and 1376, the pope lived in Avignon
rather than Rome because of a succession dispute, and the presence of the papal
court created a vibrant market where Italian traders flourished. Most of the luxury
trade and banking were dominated by some six hundred Italian families who lived
in their own quarter of the city. Soon after his fifteenth birthday Datini sold his
little plot of land in Prato to raise some capital and move there. By 1361, at the age
of twenty-six, we find him in partnership with two other Tuscans, Toro di Berto
and Niccolò di Bernardo. Initially he dealt mostly in armor and seems to have done
well selling to both sides of local conflicts. In 1368, for example, his books record
a sale of arms worth 64 livres to Bernard du Guesclin, the French military commander, and in the same year an extensive sale of weapons to the commune of
Fontes, trying to protect itself from the same Guesclin. Before this, in 1363, Datini
had his first shop, bought for 941 gold florins, with another 300 paid for the "customers' goodwill." In 1367 he renewed his partnership with Toro di Berto, each
putting in a capital of 2,500 gold florins, and they now had three shops. In 1376
he began to trade in salt, and launched himself into the money-changing business
as well as trading in silverware and works of art. He opened a wine tavern and a
draper's shop, and started to send his people farther afield, for example to Naples,
to trade. At this point his main shop in Avignon contained Florentine silver
belts and gold wedding rings, leather hides, saddles and mules' harnesses from

Catalonia, household goods from all over Italy, linen from Genoa, fustian from Cremona, and scarlet *zendado*, a special cloth from Lucca. His store in Florence emerged as an active hub of manufacturing by this time and contained white, blue, and undyed woolen cloth; sewing thread and silk curtains and curtain rings; tablecloths, napkins, and large bath towels; and hand-painted coffers and jewel cases used as part of a bride's dowry.

When he returned from Avignon in 1382, he set up a business enterprise based in Prato and Florence with branches in Pisa, Genoa, Barcelona, Valencia, Majorca, and Ibiza. Between these different emporia sailed iron, lead, alum, slaves, and spices from Romania and the Black Sea; English wool from Southampton and London; wheat from Sardinia and Sicily; leather from Tunis and Córdoba; silk from Venice; raisins and figs from Málaga; almonds and dates from Valencia; apples and sardines from Marseille; olive oil from Gaeta; salt from Ibiza; Spanish wool from Majorca; and from Catalonia oranges, olive oil, and wine. His business documents have letters in Latin, French, Italian, English, Flemish, Catalonian, Provençal, Greek, Arabic, and Hebrew. He didn't just trade, he also started a cloth manufacturing business in Florence, buying English and Spanish wool and exporting the finished cloth.

Francesco di Marco Datini made a fortune without any background, connections, or capital, and without the advantage of contacts, monopolies, or government help except for the broad institutional context created by the Italian communes.

There were of course many beholden to the old elite-dominated order who looked upon these developments with dismay. Francesco di Marco Datini represented exactly the sort of upward social mobility that they feared. This was what Emperor Frederick Barbarossa's uncle, Bishop Otto, was railing against when he noted of the Genoese:

> They do not disdain to give the girdle of knighthood or the grades of distinction to young men of inferior status and even some workers of the low mechanical crafts, whom other people bar like the plague from the more respectable and honorable pursuits.

Bishop Otto was complaining about the erosion of hierarchy and the norms that had sustained it. But the relaxation of such norms is critical for economic development because they block "nobodies" with talent, like Datini, from rising to the top. Innovation critically rests on empowering talent like this and allowing many nobodies to chart their own paths and experiment with their own ideas.

Francesco di Marco Datini's isn't the only famous story of upward mobility in this era. One calculation for Pisa in 1369 suggests that of the 106 Florentine companies using the port, 51 of them belonged to "new men." A non-Italian example is that of Godric of Finchale (later Saint Godric). Godric was born around 1065 in Walpole, Norfolk, to poor parents. His biographer Reginald of Durham tells us that his "father was named Ailward, and his mother Edwenna; both of slender rank and wealth." Godric decided against being a "husbandman," the natural thing to have done for a lad slender in rank and wealth in Norfolk. He instead decided to become a merchant. Without capital, he had to work his way up from the bottom, so he started by learning the ways of a "chapman," a peddler, and "he began to follow the chapman's way of life, first learning how to gain in small bargains and things of insignificant price; and thence, while yet a youth, his mind advanced little by little to buy and sell and gain from things of greater expense." Gradually, Saint Godric accumulated enough capital to launch himself on more ambitious business ventures. Reginald tells us that "he began to launch upon bolder courses, and to coast frequently by sea to the foreign lands that lay around him. Thus, sailing often to and fro between Scotland and Britain, he traded in many divers wares and, amid these occupations, learned much worldly wisdom... at length his great labours and cares bore much fruit of worldly gain." After sixteen years of successful trade and mercantile activity Godric decided to give all his wealth away and become a monk.

Returning to Assisi, we noted how Saint Francis's father was a successful merchant in France, but almost certainly still from a modest background. Later in life Saint Francis asked his religious brothers in the Franciscan order, which he had founded, to humiliate him by calling him "worthless peasant-day laborer," to which he replied, "Yes, that is what the son of Pietro di Bernardone needs to hear." Most likely, Pietro had come from the countryside from humble origins to make his fortune in Assisi and then France, in much the same way that Francesco di Marco Datini and Godric had.

The Economy in the Corridor

Compared to the economies of stateless societies and under despotism we saw in the previous chapter, we are witnessing something very different in the Italian communes of the late Middle Ages. We see not only greater security and liberty for the citizens of these communes—not only a state providing public services rather than repressing and bullying its people—but also an entirely different set of economic opportunities and incentives created by the Shackled Leviathan.

Prosperity and economic growth originate from a few basic principles. These include incentives for people to invest, experiment, and innovate. Without a state such incentives are largely absent because either there is no law to adjudicate disputes and no protection for property rights in the midst of conflict, or because the norms that have emerged to fill that stateless void distort economic incentives and discourage economic activity—lest economic opportunities destabilize the very essence of these societies. As a result, the fruits of any investments are likely to be stolen, wasted, or scattered. The Despotic Leviathan could enforce property rights and protect people's investments, but it is often much more interested in imposing high taxes or monopolizing the resources for itself, so economic incentives are often only a little better under his rule than under the Absent Leviathan.

Prosperity and economic growth don't just rest on secure property rights. They critically depend on broad-based economic opportunities. This is the sort of thing that we sometimes take for granted, but it isn't, and it hasn't been, the natural way the economy is organized, as we saw in the previous chapter. Under the Absent Leviathan, the cage of norms often implies that economic opportunities are constricted for everybody. Under the Despotic Leviathan, the ruler and his entourage may have their property rights secure (indeed excessively secure, as they are victorious in any dispute), but not so for regular people. This sort of unequal distribution of economic opportunities isn't enough to undergird economic prosperity either. You need opportunities to be widely and fairly distributed in society, so that whoever has a good idea for an innovation or valuable investment gets a chance to carry it out. This is an important and sometimes overlooked facet of liberty. Recall that dominance can come from the overwhelming economic power some wield against others or from stifling restrictions imposed by norms. Liberty in the economic domain then necessitates the leveling of the playing field and the lifting of these restrictions. This is exactly what we are seeing with social mobility in the Italian communes. Countless men such as Francesco di Marco Datini and Saint Francis's father benefited from these opportunities and the liberty that they created to invest, found businesses, experiment with new ideas, innovate, and rise from their "inferior status" to become rich merchants. This bottom-up experimentation and the social mobility it brings are the economic fruits of liberty.

These opportunities and incentives also need to be upheld by a fair system of conflict resolution and law enforcement (or Justice, as the *Allegory of Good Government* emphasized). This in turn requires that the state and political elites aren't powerful enough to meddle in the administration of justice and attempt to tilt things in their favor (the ropes in the frescoes). Here we see another critical role of the Shackled Leviathan in laying the groundwork for economic prosperity. If the Leviathan weren't shackled, how could we make sure that laws applied to it and to politically powerful people? What is sometimes referred to as the "rule of law" also depends on the shackles on the ankles of the Leviathan. And these shackles don't just come from constitutions and oaths, but as the frescoes emphasize, they are rooted in the ropes that society holds.

Even an abstract commitment to broad-based opportunities and incentives and fair conflict resolution isn't enough in general. If key infrastructure is missing or if only a few people have access to the knowledge and the skills necessary to thrive in business or in work, then opportunities will still be unequally distributed. So public services are vital, not just because they improve the lives of the citizens who gain access to better roads, canals, schools, and benefit from regulation, but also because they underpin broad-based opportunities. This is what the Italian communes achieved, thanks to their ability to found a Shackled Leviathan, and this is what the *Allegory of Good Government* so brilliantly explains.

———

The reader who is familiar with our earlier book *Why Nations Fail* will see strong parallels between what we have just described and the conceptual framework developed in that book. (At least we are not entirely inconsistent with our earlier thinking.) There we referred to institutions that provide broad-based opportunities and incentives for people to invest, innovate, and engage in productivity-enhancing activities as "inclusive economic institutions." We also stressed that these can only survive in the long haul if they are supported by "inclusive political institutions" that prevent the monopolization of political power by a small segment of society while also enabling the state to enforce laws. We emphasized that new innovations, technologies, and organizations, though indispensable for sustained economic growth, will often be resisted because they may destabilize an existing order (what we called "political creative destruction"). The best guarantee that we have to prevent some powerful actors blocking new technologies, and in the process stamping out economic development, is to make sure that nobody, and nothing, is powerful enough to be able to do so.

Looked at from this perspective, our conceptual framework here expands on *Why Nations Fail*. The Shackled Leviathan is not just the culmination of the inclusive political institutions necessary for inclusive economic institutions. It also critically depends on the Red Queen effect—the ability of society to contend with, constrain, and check the state and the political elites. This brings into focus the central role of norms that help society organize, engage in politics, and if necessary rebel against the state and elites. But it isn't just the shackles that are important. So is the ability of the Leviathan to have the power to enforce laws, resolve conflicts, provide public services, and support the economic institutions that create economic opportunities and incentives. Thus equally essential is the capacity of the state so long as it is matched with society's ability to control it.

Another new element here is our emphasis on the relaxation of the cage of norms. This is rooted in our discussion in the previous chapter, which documented how restrictions based on norms, traditions, and customs could dull economic incentives and opportunities, and need to be loosened for economic growth to flourish. This may happen to some degree by itself as people find ways of going around these norms and the most restrictive norms themselves start losing their relevance. But it gets a powerful boost from the Shackled Leviathan, as we already saw in our discussion of Greece in Chapter 2, and this underscores another major role of state capacity—to relax the cage of norms, both to create conditions for liberty and to remove impediments against society's political engagement. Critically, this happens even as other aspects of norms (especially those related to society's organization and willingness to take action against elites) are keeping the Leviathan in check. This observation reiterates the multifaceted interaction between state capacity and norms we saw in the Athenian case in Chapter 2.

The Effects of Bad Government

Now that we've considered the implication of two sides of the Sala dei Nove, let's turn to the left and study the final panel. There we see the *Allegory of Bad Government*, which illustrates the economic consequences of bad government.

This fresco is less well preserved than the others, but the message is clear. It is dominated by a fanged and horned figure called Tyranny (or what we have called despotism). At his feet we see Justice, bound. Flying about, instead of virtues like Magnanimity and Fortitude, we find Vainglory, Treason, Cruelty, Fraud, and Tumult. On the far left we find War with sword upraised. Next to War is Division who, instead of holding a plane, holds a carpenter's saw to cut an object, suggesting that it is division that tears a community apart and brings war. In the background the fresco vividly captures the economic consequences of Tyranny. To the left, the city is desolate. Piles of rocks litter the floor, houses are ill kept with holes in the walls and balconies. A murder is being committed. There is no trade or commerce. The rural consequences of bad government, desolation and poverty in the countryside, are visible too. An army stalks across the abandoned fields. Houses burn and trees are withered. We see a dramatic description of the economic consequences of a Despotic Leviathan, insightfully blamed on bad government.

How Tortillas Were Invented

The Shackled Leviathan and the economic opportunities and incentives it created were not confined to Europe. Another historical example comes from the Valley of Oaxaca in ancient Mexico around 500 BCE. To understand what happened in Oaxaca around this time, let's start with the staple of the Mexican diet today—the tortilla.

The domestication of maize by humans was a key moment in the long-run economic development of the Americas. It occurred in Mexico around 5000 BCE and possibly earlier. There are many ways to eat maize. You can roast it and eat the kernels from the roasted cob, a delicacy available in almost any Mexican city street today. Or you can mash it up into porridge. An alternative, which emerged about 500 BCE in Oaxaca, was to turn maize into tortillas. To do this you have to grind the kernels into flour, mix it with water and salt, and cook it on what Mexicans call a *comal*, a round ceramic plate. A selection of modern *comales* from Oaxaca is shown in the photo insert. We know that the tortillas were invented around 500 BCE because archaeologists discovered that the first comales appeared in the Valley of Oaxaca at that time.

Turning maize into tortillas takes a lot more work than simply roasting the kernels on the cob. But it has the advantage of facilitating the transportation of the maize. Making tortillas keeps only the edible part of the cob, so the rest can be thrown away. Why did the people of the valley, who came to be known as the Zapotec, need to transport maize all of a sudden?

The answer relates to the political history of the valley. Going back to 1000 BCE, the entire valley's population was about 2,000 people and the first truly urban area there, San José Mogote, probably had already reached a population of 1,000. San José soon faced competition from newer urban centers, in particular, Yeguih in the eastern Tlacolula arm of the valley, and San Martín Tilcajete in the southern Valle Grande arm. Some archaeologists have identified these three places as competing chiefdoms, but they had a lot of culture in common. They all used the symbolism of lightning, earthquakes, and the were-jaguar, and they spoke deriva-tives of a language we now call Zapotec. The word seems to come from Nahuatl, the dominant language of central Mexico, meaning "inhabitants of the place of sapote," named after the fruit. In between these three urban centers, where the modern city of Oaxaca stands, was something akin to a no-man's-land. It was here that the mountain Monte Albán, reaching 400 meters above the valley floor, stood.

Monte Albán was a quite desolate place with no natural water sources and it was far from the best farmland in the valley. In 500 BCE it was still uninhabited. Shortly thereafter the three communities of San José Mogote, Yeguih, and San Martín Tilcajete got together and built a city on the mountain that quickly reached a population of 7,000 people. This city was the capital of a new state that came to integrate the whole of the valley into its territory through a hierarchy of settle-ments and administrative centers. Most of the buildings constructed in the early days, during the epoch archaeologists call Monte Albán Early I, are now buried under later construction. Excavations nonetheless show clear evidence of three distinct barrios surrounding the initial central plaza of the city. It seems plausible that people from the three communities migrated to the different barrios. In this period, before cisterns were dug to catch rainwater, all the water for the settlement had to be man-hauled up the mountain, and so did the maize. This is where tor-tillas come in. Though a few agricultural terraces were hewn out of the mountain-side, they weren't nearly enough to grow food for 7,000 people or the 17,000 people who came to inhabit Monte Albán in the Late I epoch. So the food, like the water, had to be lugged up the hill, and tortillas made this easier.

The creation of Monte Albán by the citizens of San José Mogote, Yeguih, and San Martín Tilcajete is another example of pristine state formation, the setting up of a state where none existed before, which we already discussed in Chapter 3. But it was different from the typical pristine state formation. Unlike what Shaka did in Zululand or what we see in the Nile Valley with the emergence of ancient Egyp-tian civilization, this wasn't a charismatic leader or a powerful group of political elites imposing their domination over the rest of society. Rather, it has some no-table similarities to state building in situations such as Athens and the U.S., where society is already strong and capable of restricting what the state and elites can do. Recall, for example, that after the constitutional convention in Philadelphia and the ratification of the Constitution, the federal government had to decide on a capital city. Initially, Congress met in New York, but there was competition be-tween the Northern and Southern states over a permanent site for the capital. Many different options were discussed. New Yorkers wanted it to stay in New York, while the Southerners wanted it closer to the South. The first president, George Washington, favored a compromise, in neutral territory on the Potomac River, just upstream from his house at Mount Vernon. In 1790 he got his way, thanks to a deal forged by James Madison, Alexander Hamilton, and Thomas Jefferson. The Southern states had been blocking legislation that would have allowed the newly created federal state to take over and pay all of the debts accumulated by the states. For Hamilton this was a critical issue in the building of a new state with a centralized fiscal system and the ability to borrow. In exchange for an agreement that the capital be on the Potomac, at a specific location to be determined by Washington, the Southern states agreed to let the federal government take over state debts. Washington, D.C., was then built in neutral, underdeveloped territory, between the two big rival groupings of Northern and Southern states.

Though we don't have any written records of its history, it is likely that what happened in Monte Albán has many parallels to the U.S. experience. Just like Madison and Hamilton, the citizens or at least the elites of San José Mogote, Yeguih, and San Martín Tilcajete may have recognized the benefits of creating a more effective centralized state. This is what the archaeological record suggests happened. After the founding of Monte Albán we find lower conflict and less evidence of burned houses and surface remains of charred pieces of daub or other materials. The evidence indicates that this period of state building led to a significant expansion of trade as well. One archaeological site in the Valle Grande area features a large, open, and accessible platform measuring 55 by 38 meters. It is not a temple and is edged by large rocks. There is evidence of specialization in production: misfired pottery, concentrations of chipped chert and quartzite, a mine for quartz, rocks worn in ways suggesting that they were used for grinding or pounding, and there is a bark beater for making paper. In fact, the platform was almost surely a market.

So what sort of political institutions supported greater peace and economic specialization in Monte Albán? Typically, we learn about the political institutions of long-lost polities from their archaeological record, the names and images of their powerful kings, and their tombs full of valuable goods. And yet for the Zapotec we don't see any of that. We haven't a clue who the early kings were, or even if they had kings or dynasties. If they did, we don't know their names, and there are no elaborate tombs, engravings, or palaces. There seems to have been no personalization of power. The religion of the Zapotec, which plays a central role after the foundation of Monte Albán, was the Cojico cult. Cojico was the Zapotec representation of "lightning-clouds-rain," but this imagery was not captured or co-opted by any individuals. There were no "god kings." That's not so uncommon in pre-Columbian Mexico. The great city of Teotihuacán northeast of Mexico city, which had a population of 200,000 people at its height, similarly did not have named kings, royal tombs, or palaces. When what appear to be elites are depicted in murals, they are always masked; power was not flaunted in Teotihuacán, as if there were laws and norms against the dominance of rulers and elites—as if the Leviathan was tightly shackled. Though we don't know exactly what sort of government either Monte Albán or Teotihuacán had, we do know that at the time of the conquest, there were plenty of states in Mexico that were collectively governed by councils. A well-documented example is the pre-Columbian Tlaxcalan state, which lasted from the middle of the fourteenth century until the Spanish conquest and built sophisticated republican institutions with popular participation. The archaeological evidence makes it likely that the Zapotec were governed in a similar way. So it's reasonable to assume that the state that emerged in Monte Albán was similarly shackled.

We also observe that Monte Albán's institutional arrangements had profound positive economic consequences. We already noted that they seem to have promoted peace and the flourishing of markets, and there is evidence of an important uptick in trade. For one thing, compared to the previous period, people stopped building big storage pits for food, presumably because they could readily buy it in the market and had less need for storage. We also see a marked improvement in the quality of house construction. Before 500 BCE houses tended to be made of wattle and daub, with few houses built of stone and mud brick. Construction of the latter type became the norm after 500 BCE. Most dramatically, we see a large expansion of the population of the valley after the formation of the state. As we saw, around 1000 BCE the valley housed around 2,000 people and it stagnated at this level until the Early I period. With the foundation of Monte Albán and its expansion to 7,000 people, the population of the valley appears to have increased to 14,000. Later Monte Albán's population rose to 17,000 and the population of the entire valley exceeded 50,000. Though Monte Albán grew rapidly, there does not seem to have been a fall in the population of San José Mogote, Yeguih, and San Martín Tilcajete. So while some people may have moved from these places to Monte Albán, their population was soon replenished and the capital city must have benefited from rural-urban migration. There was probably both a marked rise in fertility and a migration of people from outside the valley into the new state as well. Other economic changes included increased production of pottery, the introduction of new types of ceramics, and a notable intensification of agricultural activity.

The cultivated areas expanded and there was investment in irrigation for the first time. All the evidence points to increases in agricultural productivity and consumption.

———

We have witnessed in this chapter something very different from the type of state brought into being by the will to power, and of course also very different from the weak, essentially absent political hierarchy of the stateless societies. We have also seen, as anticipated in Chapter 2, how this early Shackled Leviathan generated much greater levels of liberty and how it brings into existence an entirely different set of economic opportunities and incentives, unleashing powerful forces toward prosperity.

But what are the origins of this very different type of state-society relationship? That's the question we turn to next.

Chapter 6

THE EUROPEAN SCISSORS

Europe Moves into the Corridor

The part of the world that developed the enduring Shackled Leviathans that would shape our recent history was Europe, particularly Western and Northern Europe. The Athenian Shackled Leviathan collapsed as the Macedonian Empire expanded. Similarly the Zapotec state had gone out of the corridor and disappeared by the time the Oaxaca Valley was conquered by the Spanish. As we'll see, the development of a state that was both capable and constrained by society was a gradual, painful historical process in Europe. People who were present at its early stages would not have recognized this as the beginning of a process that would transform their liberty, politics, and economy. But as it evolved, it started bringing liberty, transformed the nature of state institutions, and ushered in a period of prosperity of a sort previously unknown in human society. Why did all of this emerge in Europe?

The answer is not obvious. Going back in history, there was nothing manifest about the rise of Europe. Agriculture originated not in Europe but in the Middle East and the Fertile Crescent and then in China. When it spread to European lands, it did so through the colonizing activities of people moving from the Middle East, reaching Britain around 4000 BCE, over 5,000 years after it had become established in the Levant. Similarly the first towns and cities emerged not in Europe but in the valleys of the Tigris and Euphrates Rivers in modern-day Iraq. The

Gilgamesh problem, as we have seen, arose first in Uruk, not Uxbridge. To all of the great classical empires, Western and Northern Europe were at best marginal. The Romans built a sophisticated civilization centered around the Mediterranean, but had little interest in much of Western and Northern Europe, except when they ventured to areas that are now part of Germany in order to confront the Germanic tribes, which they viewed as barbarians (though they did conquer Gaul, modern-day France, and part of Britain). Only very late in history do we see Europe coming onto the world stage.

All the same, as we discussed in the previous chapter, by the eleventh century, parts of Europe had developed republican governments and were in the middle of a massive economic boom. How did Europe get there? How did these revolutions in government, society, and economy come about and pave the way to an unprecedented rise of liberty and the spectacular technological and economic advances of the eighteenth and nineteenth centuries? What was Europe's advantage?

The answer to these questions lies in a unique series of historical events 1,500 years ago that created a fortuitous balance between the powers of central authority and those of common men (not women, unfortunately). It is this balance that put Europe into the corridor, setting in motion the Red Queen effect in a relentless process of state-society competition. The balance was a consequence of two things. First, the takeover of Europe at the end of the fifth century by democratically organized tribal societies centered on assemblies and norms of consensual decision making. Second, the legacy of critical elements of state institutions and political hierarchy absorbed from the Roman Empire and the Christian church, whose centralizing influence continued even after the fall of the Western Roman Empire at the end of the fifth century. We can think of these two elements as the two blades of a pair of scissors. On its own neither would have put Western Europe onto a new path. But hinge them together and the two blades of the European scissors prepared the scene for the rise of the Shackled Leviathan and the economic incentives and opportunities that it unleashed.

The Assembly Politics of the Long-Haired Kings

To get an inkling of how Europe managed all of this, let's turn to the depiction of an assembly recorded in 882 by Hincmar, the archbishop of Reims in France. Hincmar's book, known as *On the Governance of the Palace*, was written for Carloman II, king of West Francia, on his ascension to the throne. Francia, which was already fragmented by the time Carloman was crowned, was the kingdom created

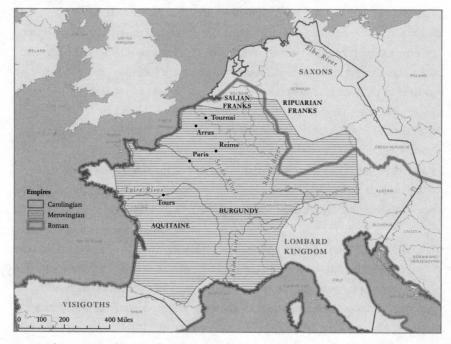

Map 8. The Empires of the Franks: The Merovingian and Carolingian Empires and the Boundaries of the Roman Empire

originally by the Franks, a Germanic tribe that had fought against, and sometimes with, the Romans for nearly two centuries. It became one of the beneficiaries of the collapse of the Western Roman Empire, and then played a defining role in the political developments of post-Roman Europe.

Carloman was part of the Carolingian dynasty that was created by Charles Martel in the early eighth century and greatly expanded by his grandson Charlemagne. By the time of his death in 814, Charlemagne had united into one state France, Belgium, the Netherlands, Germany, Switzerland, Austria, and northern Italy (see Map 8). Hincmar instructed Carloman how to rule over his kingdom by recounting how the kingdom had been run according to Adalhardus, a contemporary of Charlemagne and an eyewitness to how the state functioned then. Remarkably, this rule wasn't going to involve the king exercising his unbridled wishes, but would be based on popular assemblies. As Hincmar noted:

> At that time the custom was followed that no more than two general assemblies were to be held each year. The first assembly determined the status of the entire realm for the remainder of the year. No turn of

events, saving only the greatest crisis which struck the realm at once, could change what had been established. All the important men, both clerics and laymen, attended this general assembly. The important men came to participate in the deliberations, and those of lower station were present in order to hear the decisions and occasionally also to deliberate concerning them, and to confirm them not out of coercion but by their own understanding and agreement.

Participation in the second assembly was broader, but in both assemblies a council of "important persons and senior advisers of the realm" played a key role and "proposed questions to the king and received responses," and

as often as those withdrawn in council wished it, the king would go to them and remain with them for as long as they desired. They then in all friendliness told him how they had found individual matters; they frankly related what they had discussed on one side and the other, in disagreement or argument or friendly rivalry.

The Frankish elites "in council" also could "summon outsiders, as for example . . . when they wanted to pose questions," and the king took this opportunity "to interview persons coming from all parts of the realm, to learn if they brought with them information worthy of consideration." Indeed, before coming to the assembly each participant "was to collect information concerning any relevant matter not only from his own people but from strangers and from both friends and enemies."

What Hincmar describes was the essence of the assembly politics of Germanic tribes, a remarkably participatory form of government. Charlemagne, and later Carloman, had to play by the rules of these assemblies, consult the wishes of a diverse cross section of (male) society, and secure a degree of consensus for their major decisions. Obviously, the number of people who could appear at such an assembly was limited, but Charlemagne deployed messengers to relate the findings to lower-level meetings so that the whole kingdom was informed. This participation is the first blade of the European scissors.

The roots of these assemblies come from the way the Franks were organized. The best description we have comes from Tacitus's book *The Germania*, written in 98 CE. Tacitus was a Roman politician, public servant, and historian, and his book reflected the curiosity that Romans had about the Germans, who had imposed upon them several calamitous military defeats and whose customs and institutions looked so different from theirs. To satisfy this curiosity, Tacitus presented an almost ethnographic account of the organization and culture of the German people. He described their political system in the following way:

> On matters of minor importance only the chiefs debate; on major affairs, the whole community. But even where the commons have the decision, the subject is considered in advance by the chiefs . . . The Assembly is competent also to hear criminal charges, especially those involving the risk of capital punishment . . . These same assemblies elect, among other officials, the magistrates who administer justice in the districts and villages. Each magistrate is assisted by a hundred assessors chosen from the people to advise him and to add weight to his decisions.

One immediately sees the parallel with Hincmar's description right down to the two sorts of assemblies, one where the political elite met and set the agenda and another one with mass participation. The assemblies had other tasks such as presenting young men with a shield and spear and thus publicly making them citizens. In terms of their leaders,

> they choose their kings for their noble birth, their commanders for their valour. The power even of the kings is not absolute or arbitrary.

Julius Caesar, who briefly crossed the Rhine during his conquest of Gaul, also observed that the Germans elected their leaders during wartime at assemblies, but had no leaders in peacetime except chiefs with limited powers. The absence of kings greatly irritated some writers. Gregory of Tours, who wrote his *History of the Franks* in the late sixth century, is our major source of information about the origins and political development of the Franks. Gregory quotes Sulpicius, from a long-lost book, as mentioning "the royal leaders of the Franks," but then adds exasperatedly, "When he says 'regales' or royal leaders, it is not clear if they were kings or if they merely exercised a kingly function." Even more annoying for him, when it finally looks like Sulpicius is talking about a Frankish king, "he forgets to tell us what his name was." Really.

The people who were to become the Franks, though not mentioned explicitly by Tacitus, inherited the popular assemblies as a central part of their political organization. We first hear of them in 250 and 275, when along with the Alamanni and other German tribes they raided the Roman province of Gaul. The Franks seem to have been an amalgamation of other German peoples such as the Bruc-teri, Ampsivarii, Chamavi, and Chattuari who later constructed, or invented, a collective identity. There is little archaeological evidence for their origins, but we know from Roman sources that they were settled around the Rhine in the fourth century and were fighting for the Romans in the early fifth century (see Map 8). Between 400 and 450, the Roman military frontier on the lower Rhine collapsed and the territory became occupied by the Franks. By midcentury, they had spread as far west as Arras and Tournai in France and were still organized in separate kingdoms. The kingdom based in Tournai gained in strength and influence be-tween 450 and 480, first under Chlodio and then his son Merovech, who estab-lished what was to be the Merovingian dynasty, lasting for nearly three hundred years. Chlodio and Merovech are partly mythical figures. Indeed, Merovech is fabled to have been conceived when Chlodio's wife went swimming and encoun-tered a sea monster called the Quinotaur, giving the dynasty supernatural legiti-macy. The Franks emerge into clearer historical focus with the reign of Clovis, Merovech's grandson, who came to the throne in 481. Clovis was the real founder of the Frankish state and he expanded the kingdom to unite nearly all of France by the time of his death in 511.

The Frankish kings had a thing about hair. Long hair. For boys, having long hair was a sign of manhood, so important that cutting a long-haired boy's hair without his parents' consent was considered a crime equivalent to killing him. Gregory records an instance where

> Childebert and Lothar sent Arcadius to the Queen . . . with a pair of scissors in one hand and a naked [unsheathed] sword in the other. When he came into the Queen's presence, he held them out to her. "Your sons, who are our masters, seek your decision, gracious Queen, as to what should be done with the princes. Do you wish them to live with their hair cut short? Or would you prefer to see them killed?" . . . she an-swered: "If they are not to ascend the throne, I would rather see them dead than with their hair cut short."

The assembly politics of the long-haired kings and their powerful, asser-tive societies were the first blade of the scissors that would put Merovingian,

Carolingian, and other related European societies in the corridor. The other blade came from the Roman Empire.

The Other Blade

The Roman Republic was founded in 509 BCE, after the overthrow of King Lucius Tarquinius Superbus. By the second century BCE the republic had to deal with deep conflicts between the rich, aristocratic families and the growing number of Roman citizens. It collapsed for all practical purposes when Julius Caesar declared himself dictator in 49 BCE, though the emergence of its successor state, the Roman Empire, took shape only after a series of civil wars and the accession of Octavian as "Augustus" in 27 BCE.

At this time there was little in the way of an institutionalized state. Rome had been ruled by the Senate and the army, and there were few bureaucrats beyond the slaves and retainers of the elite. Though a more systematic central administration began with Augustus and developed partly to feed the residents of Rome and supply the army, it was not until the second half of the third century that a real bureaucratic administration developed in the empire. The Roman state employed at least 31,000 full-time paid civil servants during the late empire, but this is likely a severe underassessment since it excludes municipal personnel, on whom we have no accurate information. The basic unit of administration was the province, and at the end of the reign of Diocletian in 305 CE there were 114 of these. Each was run by a governor, whose main responsibilities included taxes and justice, and who usually had 100 civil servants working for him. The provinces were grouped together into larger units called dioceses run by a Roman official, *vicarius* (vicar), and above them were four praetorian prefects, one in Gaul (including Britain and Spain), one in Italy (which also covered Africa and the western Balkans), one in Illyricum (Greece, Crete, and the rest of the Balkans) and one in Byzantium in the East. These prefects had very large staffs, of up to 2,000 people. Though civil servants were not recruited on the basis of any examination, the great late Roman legal codes promulgated by emperors Theodosius in 438 and Justinian in 529 mention principles of merit and seniority in promotion.

The best description we have of how this bureaucracy operated comes from the record left by John Lydus ("the Lydian"), who worked for the Eastern praetorian prefect in Byzantium. John came from the town of Philadelphia in Lydia, now the Turkish town of Alaşehir. He was recruited into the civil service by a fellow Philadelphian praetorian prefect, Zoticus. The Eastern prefect was split into two main departments, one administrative and judicial and the other financial. John was assigned to the former, and his book *On the Magistracies of the Roman State* lists the senior officials in this department: *princeps officii, cornicularius, adiutor, commentariensis, ab actis, cura epistularum,* and *regendarius.* Indeed, a law of 384, subsequently amended by the Code of Justinian, sets out a model for this bureaucracy with 443 different positions, divided into eighteen groups listed in order of seniority.

> *Scrinium exceptorum:*
> One official with the rank of *perfectissimus* second class, who is the *primicerius* of the whole *schola.*
> One official with the rank of *perfectissimus* (third class), who is the *primicerius* of the whole *exceptores.*
> Two officials with the rank of *ducenarius,* who are the *tertiocerius* and *quartocerius.*
> One official with the rank of *centenarius,* who is the *primicerius instrumentorum.*
> Two *epistulares.*
> Thirty-six *exceptores* constituting the first grade.

And on and on for another nineteen groups of officials. John started as a middle-ranked *exceptor* in 511.

The bureaucracy ran on, as John put it, a complex set of "customs, forms and language" and members of it wore "distinctive regalia," uniforms of military origin. They had to deal with regulations and procedures and "registers, titles and duties." John was also keen to point out that it had an esprit de corps and an identity that separated it from "ordinary people." Language and writing were particularly important. Only the palatine bureaucrats most closely associated with the emperor were allowed to use the *litterae caelestes* (literally "heavenly writing"), a specific type of script of restricted use, deployed to help stop forgeries because it was so hard to fake. John recounts in detail the various bureaucratic procedures that had to be followed. For instance, everything that came before the prefect's tribunal had to be summarized twice. One was the responsibility of an official known as the *secretarius,* while the other was written by the *personalium,* the most senior judicial official. John was certain that such procedures were critical for a well-functioning government, for example by guarding against fraud or loss. He noted, "And I myself well remember such an occurrence. For although a hearing had been held, the transactions relevant to the case were nowhere to be found. But when the *personalium*, as it is known, had been brought before the magistracy, the case was completely restored."

What John describes is an extensive bureaucracy with well-defined rules, functioning within an elaborate legal system. Of course it was not immune to personal influence, and it didn't work out exactly as the rules specified. John himself got his job not entirely on the basis of merit, but with the help of his Philadelphian contact Zoticus. Moreover, many of the senior positions were reserved for elites, particularly people from the senatorial class, and there was certainly some corruption. For all these faults, the Romans at least had a bureaucratic state with an elaborate structure and territorial organization. This lay institution was paralleled by the hierarchy of the Church, which had already been integrated with the political institutions by the time the Franks came to interact with Rome.

Bringing the Two Blades Together

The early history of the Franks was a struggle to combine the bottom-up political traditions of the Germanic tribes with the state institutions of the Romans. As Clovis ascended to the throne, it wasn't clear how these two blades would come together.

Imposing a stable political hierarchy on Franks was challenging. Gregory recalls how once after a raid Clovis was greatly taken by a particular vessel, a ewer, and asked his men, "I put it to you, my lusty freebooters, that you should agree here and now to grant me that ewer over and above my normal share," to which one of his men replied by cutting the vessel in half with his ax, declaring, "You shall have none of this booty except your fair share!" Clovis eventually got even with this particular soldier, but this episode highlights the egalitarian, non-hierarchic ethos of the war band, which was one of the foundations of the assembly politics of the Franks. It was also a significant impediment to centralizing power.

A major step in the process of state building was the conquest of the last Roman subprovince of Soissons. Clovis took over Roman institutions and seems to have hired Roman administrators. Next, in a skillful move to bring the two blades closer together, Clovis adopted Christianity. He didn't simply convert himself, he converted en masse with his army. From that day on, Clovis could appeal to the ecclesiastical hierarchy, which he commanded for the Merovingians. He then proceeded to declare himself emperor. The setting was a very Roman ceremony in the city of Tours, as described by Gregory:

In Saint Martin's church he stood clad in a purple tunic and the military mantle, and he crowned himself with a diadem. He rode out on his
horse and with his own hand showered gold and silver coins among the
people present . . . From that day he was called Consul or Augustus.

Leaders of Germanic war bands didn't wear purple or call themselves Augustus, but Clovis did. In doing so, he was bringing the blade of the assemblies and
bottom-up norms of Germanic tribes together with the blade of the Roman model
of a centralized state. What emerged was something greater than the sum of its
parts. The blueprint for bureaucratic organization Clovis got from Rome and the
Christian church got embedded in the diametrically different politics and norms
of the Germanic tribes. This combination placed the Merovingians at the entry-
way to the corridor.

Apart from wearing purple, the Roman legacy is also seen in the persistence
of the basic administrative unit, as in Roman times, called the *civitas*, or city, along
with its surrounding areas. The senior Merovingian official in charge of a *civitas*
was called a *comes*, literally "companion," and often translated as "count." This was
a position adapted from the late Roman *comites civitatis* and its duties seem to have
been closely modeled on these—solving legal disputes, administering justice, and
commanding military units. Subordinate officers below the *comes* were called
centenarii, also of Roman origin, and administered a unit called a *centenae*, or a
hundred. The likely origin of the hundred was a German war band comprising a
group of fighters who elected their leader, but, as with Roman territorial institutions, the elected warrior leader became an official in the Frankish state.

One of Clovis's defining acts as emperor was the promulgation of a new legal
code, the Salic Law, and a picture of a surviving Merovingian copy is included in
the photo insert. Clovis was part of the Salian Franks, who distinguished themselves from another group of Franks farther east called Ripuarian. The Salic Law
formalized existing norms and customs that had governed the behavior of the
stateless Franks. These norms included elaborate rules for regulating feuding.
Clovis wanted to codify them and ultimately bring them under the control of his
new centralized state. From this perspective the first clause of the Salic Law is
significant. It read, "If any one be summoned before the Thing by the king's law,
and do not come he shall be sentenced to 600 denarii, which make 15 solidi." Here
"Thing" is the archaic word for the assembly. The first thing Clovis had to do was
to make sure people turned up. In terms of formulating the laws, one of the surviving prologues is particularly telling. It reads:

With God's help it pleased the Franks and their nobility and they agreed that they ought to prohibit all escalations of quarrels for the preservation of enthusiasm for peace amongst themselves . . . Therefore four men, chosen out of many among them, stood out: Their names were Wisogast, Arogast, Salegast and Widogast. They came from the *villae* of Bothem, Salehem and Widohem, beyond the Rhine. Coming together in three legal assemblies, and discussing the origins and cases carefully, they made judgement on each case as follows.

So the Salic Law, though introduced by Clovis, was not his imposition on society. It wasn't even written by him, but by four lawgivers and three assemblies.

The lawgivers, Wisogast, Arogast, Salegast, and Widogast, had to deal with all of the usual problems, which included frequent "quarrels." So "Title XVII. Concerning Wounds" stipulates:

1. If any one have wished to kill another person, and the blow have missed, he on whom it was proved shall be sentenced to 2500 denarii.
2. If any person have wished to strike another with a poisoned arrow, and the arrow have glanced aside, and it shall be proved on him; he shall be sentenced to 2500 denarii.
3. If any person strike another on the head so that the brain appears, and the three bones which lie above the brain shall project, he shall be sentenced to 1200 denarii.
4. But if it shall have been between the ribs or in the stomach, so that the wound appears and reaches to the entrails, he shall be sentenced to 1200 denarii.
5. If any one shall have struck a man so that blood falls to the floor, and it be proved on him, he shall be sentenced to 600 denarii.
6. But if a freeman strike a freeman with his fist so that blood does not flow, he shall be sentenced for each blow—up to 3 blows—to 120 denarii.

The law covered other areas related to feuds, particularly insults, so that it was illegal to slander someone by calling them a fox or a hare. It also regulated relations between Franks and Romans, though it made it clear who was running the show. For instance, "Title XIV. Concerning Assault and Robbery" stated:

1. If any one have assaulted and plundered a free man, and it be proved on him, he shall be sentenced to 2500 denarii, which make 63 solidi.
2. If a Roman have plundered a Salian Frank, the above law shall be observed.
3. But if a Frank have plundered a Roman, he shall be sentenced to 35 solidi.

It was obviously worse for Romans to plunder Franks than the other way around. The different treatment of Romans and Franks shows that while the Franks had laws, they did not have "equality before the law"—the notion and the practice that laws applied equally to everybody. This critical aspect of laws under the Shackled Leviathan emerged only slowly as the Red Queen got to work.

The Salic Law didn't resemble Roman law. It was much more like the codification, regulation, and strengthening of existing norms attempted initially by Draco and then Solon in ancient Athens. But in this process, the laws were also bringing the resolution of conflict under the remit of the state. By the late sixth century, legislation was taking a decidedly more Roman turn, incorporating elements of the Theodosian code. The Salic Law was another step in the fusion of Roman state structure with the norms and political institutions of the Franks.

The significance of the way the Salic Law was formulated is evident once we get to the reign of Charlemagne, who reached the apogee of the Roman connection by crowning himself emperor in Rome on Christmas Day 800. All the same, Charlemagne did not act like a Roman emperor when it came to his relations with his people. The same assemblies, customs, and expectations that shackled Clovis's reign constrained Charlemagne too. Two royal edicts issued at Regensburg in 789 indicate that agents of the state were misusing their power and the king received complaints from people that "they do not have their law maintained." The emphasis on "their law" is critical. It was the law of the people, not of the king, and it was the king's job to enforce it. Indeed, "if a count or *missus* or any man has done this, let it be reported to the lord king, for he wishes to set such matters most fully to rights." Here *missus* refers to "sent men," royal agents who linked the provinces with the central court.

What about liberty? Though Clovis and Charlemagne led states that had entered into the corridor, one wouldn't see many signs of flourishing liberty in their empires. These were turbulent times where few would feel any security from violence. Clovis's followers were warriors, and martial norms were powerful among the Franks. This can be seen from the fact that it was the gift of a spear and shield by the assembly that made a young Frank a citizen. The Franks were also still firmly in the cage of norms, with customs, traditions, and practices severely restricting the economic and social actions of all people, not least because there were many religious and cultural taboos as well as a clear social hierarchy in Frankish society. Slavery was still common, and men and women could voluntarily place themselves into servitude, not unlike what we saw in African societies in Chapter 1, but something that had disappeared in Athens after Solon's reforms. Torture was routinely used for extracting a confession in court procedures. Feuding remained endemic too, as our excerpts from the Salic Law indicate. All the same, in getting a foothold in the corridor these societies started on a process that would gradually change all of these things.

Disunited Kingdom

While the Franks were trying to unite Western Europe, across the English Channel stood a very disunited kingdom. The Western Roman Empire collapsed most completely in Britain. Money, writing, and the wheel vanished, and cities were abandoned. York, once a major Roman urban center, reverted to marshland in the fifth century. Archaeological evidence from this period shows the fossils of beetles that would have lived in high grass and reeds, and we find the remains of field mice, water voles, shrews, and froghoppers that had taken over the city. They weren't the only newcomers. Peoples from continental Europe, particularly Germany and southern Scandinavia, identified by the eighth-century historian the Venerable Bede as "Angles, Saxons and Jutes," had also migrated to the isles. By this time these peoples, along with the survivors of Roman Britain and other migrants such as Celts from Ireland and Scotland, had formed an unstable set of competing polities, many of which are today remembered only in the names of current English counties, like Kent. Nevertheless, these polities gradually coalesced. By 796, at the death of King Offa of Mercia, there were just four left: Wessex in the south, East Anglia in the east, Mercia straddling the center of the country, and Northumbria in the north (see Map 9).

In 871 the twenty-two-year-old Alfred succeeded his brother Æthelred as the king of Wessex. This succession was probably agreed to in a *witan*, the assembly of the Anglo-Saxons. In the words of abbot Ælfric of Eynsham:

> No man can make himself king, but the people has the choice to choose
> as king whom they please; but after he is consecrated as king, he then
> has dominion over the people.

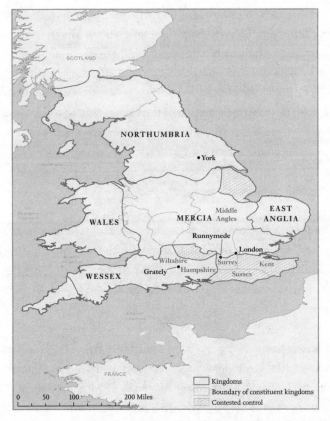

Map 9. Disunited Britain: The Kingdoms During the Ninth Century

The best surviving description of a witan from this period comes from the monk Byrhtferth of Ramsey. He describes the second coronation of King Edgar ("the Peaceful") at Bath in 973:

> At that time it was the holy season when, in accordance with custom, the archbishops and all the other distinguished bishops and the glorious abbots and religious abbesses, and all the ealdormen, reeves and judges . . . were all to assemble. From "the sun's rising in the east, from the west, from the north, and from the sea" went out the king's edict, that all these persons should assemble in his presence. This splendid and glorious army of his realm did not assemble thus in order to depose him, or to take the decision to put him to death or hang him . . . but rather they came for the entirely plausible reason . . . that the venerable bishops should bless, anoint, and consecrate him.

This remarkable account makes it clear that the assembly, composed of people like the ealdormen, high-ranking royal officials usually in charge of a shire, and reeves who were their subordinates, could have deposed Edgar rather than crowned him. Then the king vowed:

> I promise in the first instance that the Church of God and the entire Christian populace shall under my authority keep true peace at all times; I also promise that I shall proscribe theft and all manner of wickedness for persons of all stations; and thirdly, that in all judgements I shall enjoin justice and mercy.

Shortly after this, bishop Dunstan placed a crown on his head.

The crown was a Roman symbol of royal authority, imported to Britain by Germans. But even more important than that, Saxons brought their assemblies, on which the witan was based. In his *Ecclesiastical History of the English People*, Bede reports:

> Old Saxons have no king, but several lords who are set over the nation. Whenever war is imminent, these cast lots impartially, and the one on whom the lot falls is followed and obeyed by all for the duration of the war, but as soon as the war ends, the lords revert to equality of status.

Apart from such direct influences, Anglo-Saxon leaders traveled in Europe and borrowed freely from the institutional models they encountered. Alfred even had a Carolingian adviser, Grimbald of Saint-Bertin. Byrhtferth of Ramsey mentions another assembly held in 965, also attended by "an incalculable number of the populace" in addition to "all the important leading men, and the outstanding ealdormen, and powerful thegns from all the boroughs and towns and cities and territories."

When Alfred ascended to the throne, he had his hands full. Since 865 the British Isles had been occupied by what the *Anglo-Saxon Chronicle*, a collection of annals instituted by Alfred, refers to as the Great Heathen Army. This army was a massive force of Scandinavians, mostly Danes, who had come not simply to raid, but to conquer the island. Alfred had already fought them a number of times as they rampaged around the four kingdoms. Alfred's army then suffered a series of defeats, and it is likely that Alfred had to pay the Danes to retreat. By 878 three of the kingdoms had been conquered, and Wessex, beleaguered, stood alone. By that summer, however, Alfred had reorganized his forces and inflicted a severe defeat on half of the Great Heathen Army commanded by the Danish king Guthrum at the battle of Edlington, in what is now Wiltshire (see Map 9). This victory resulted in a peace treaty with Guthrum, which entailed the Danes retreating into the Danelaw territories (where Danish law held), roughly the former kingdoms of East Anglia and Northumbria along with eastern Mercia. This relative peace allowed Alfred to reorganize his kingdom and rationalize taxation and the military, yet another step in the state-building process. His successors, his son Edward ("the Elder") and three grandsons, Æthelstan, Edmund, and Eadred, gradually conquered the Scandinavian kingdom. Eadred finally expelled the last Scandinavian king of York, Eric Bloodaxe, in 954. England was unified.

From this period we have detailed evidence of the nature and actions of assemblies. We discover that in 992 military expeditions against the Danes and a subsequent treaty were made by "the king and all his councillors (witan)." The Anglo-Saxon Chronicle records how defense measures were discussed after "all the councillors (witan) were summoned to the king." But the witan didn't just discuss defense and military matters. It also legislated. The major legal text from the reign of Æthelstan noted, "All this was established at the great assembly at Grately, at which Archbishop Wulfhelm was present, with all the nobles and councillors who King Æthelstan had assembled." Of the twenty-two law codes that exist from the period between 899 and 1022, nineteen include similar clauses. Byrhtferth's "incalculable number of the populace" notwithstanding, just as in the Frankish kingdom, the number of people who could attend such meetings was relatively small. Nevertheless, as in Francia, the Anglo-Saxons made systematic attempts to consult more broadly and disseminate decisions. During the reign of Edgar, we learn, "many documents are to be written concerning this, and sent both to Ealdorman Ælfhere and Ealdorman Æthelwine, and they are to send them in all directions, so that this measure may be known to both the poor and the rich." These assemblies, together with the law they helped formulate and enact, formed the basis of two critical institutional features of the corridor—the English parliament and the notion that kings were constrained by law.

King Alfred's law code is reminiscent of the surviving fragment of Draco's and Clovis's Salic Law. On the one hand, it represents a transition from a society without a state where conflicts and disputes were resolved via feuding, to centralized state authority. On the other, it is meant to work with and strengthen existing norms, not to repudiate them. So it spends quite a lot of time institutionalizing punishments to stop feuds from breaking out and escalating. It begins,

> I, then, Alfred King of the West Saxons, have shewn these to all my councilors, and they have declared that it met with the approval of all,

again invoking the role of the witan. A central concept in the laws is that of wergeld. The wergeld of a person was the amount of money that his life was valued at if he was killed. Paying wergeld stopped a feud. For example, clause 10 reads, "If anyone lies with the wife of a man whose wergeld is 1200 shillings, he shall pay 120 shillings compensation to the husband; to a husband whose wergeld is 600 shillings, he shall pay 100 shillings compensation; to a commoner he shall pay 40 shillings compensation." Thus higher-status people, like ealdormen, had higher wergeld, and this status influenced how other violations of the laws were dealt with. As in the Albanian *Kanun*, if someone was wronged in a society based on feuding, then his relatives were responsible for retribution, and liability for wrongs was collective. Clause 30 states, "If anyone who has no paternal relatives fights and kills a man, his maternal relatives, if he has any, shall pay one-third of the wergeld and his associates shall pay one-third. In default of payment of the [remaining] third, he shall be held personally responsible."

Other clauses outlined how specific conflicts can be handled without feuds.

> We further declare that a man may fight on behalf of his lord, if his lord is attacked, without becoming liable to vendetta.

And

> A man may fight, without becoming liable for vendetta, if he finds another [man] with his wedded wife, within closed doors or under the same blanket.

The law code also introduced a detailed specification of fines for the loss or wounding of different body parts, fingers, toes, eyes, the jaw, etc.

But the similarities with the *Kanun* are less striking than the differences. Alfred's law code didn't just codify and rationalize existing norms for dispute resolution; it also brought these under the authority of the newly emerging state (recall that the Albanian *Kanun* wasn't written down, and wasn't even recorded until the early twentieth century). This is significant for at least two reasons. First, it underscores the distinction between the feud in an environment without state authority and the beginning of a process of conflict resolution managed by the state. Once the king's law code asserts how various conflicts are to be resolved, the next step is for the state to start doing the resolving, which is exactly what eventually happened after Alfred. Second, the law code reminds us again that Alfred, as a leader shackled by existing institutions and norms, wasn't so much imposing his laws upon society as he was working with society and its assemblies to rationalize existing norms. This is all in evidence in Edgar's coronation oath at Bath, which forms the basis for the modern British coronation ceremony. Edgar promised to judge with justice and mercy. It is also clearly visible in key moments in post-Alfredean England, particularly the reigns of Æthelred ("the Unready"), Cnut, and Edward ("the Confessor"). Æthelred suffered a series of military defeats at the hands of the Danes and took refuge in Normandy in France. He was recalled by "all the councillors (*pa witan ealle*) who were in England," but on terms that were clearly imposed by the witan involving reforms of his laws and behavior.

The British historian Sir Frank Stenton pointed out that it was a moment of "great constitutional interest as the first recorded pact between an English king and his subjects." Yet it was not a rupture with the past, but a continuation of Anglo-Saxon and Germanic political norms. Indeed, the witan made a similar constitutional deal with the Danish king Cnut when they accepted him as king in 1016. And in 1041 when Edward, who had also been in exile, returned to England from Normandy, "the thegns of all England" met him where he landed at Hurst Head on the Hampshire coast and told him they would only accept him to be king if he swore to uphold Cnut's laws.

1066 and All That

In 1066, England was invaded by William "the Conqueror" and his Norman army, which decisively defeated the English forces at the battle of Hastings in Sussex, killing their leader, Harold Godwinson, in the process. William expropriated the Anglo-Saxon aristocracy and implemented the feudal system created by the late Carolingian kings in France. To head off dissent, he claimed to be the legitimate king of England because Edward the Confessor supposedly named him as his heir during Edward's years of exile in Normandy. In the photo insert we include a scene from the Bayeux Tapestry, woven by the women of the Norman court to celebrate 1066, that shows

Edward instructing Harold Godwinson to travel to Normandy and confirm that William is his successor. Hence one of William's first acts was to reconfirm Edward's law codes. But this act also reaffirmed the shackles that existed before the Conqueror had arrived, ensuring continuity between the two regimes.

The feudal order that the Normans had adopted in France and William exported to England was a consequence of the fragmentation of the Frankish state after Charlemagne. The central state weakened in the face of the power of local lords, and a new state structure based on a series of hierarchical relationships emerged. All land, at least in principle, was owned by the king, who granted it as a fief to his vassals in exchange for "council and aid," particularly military aid. At the time of the Domesday Book, the great census that William collected in 1086 to catalogue the assets of his new realm, there were 846 "tenants in chief" in England who were the first-line vassals. These men then engaged in what is called subinfeudation, granting land to lower-level vassals in a cascade of "council and aid." Thus, if William needed aid in the form of military service, or maybe money, he first called on his tenants in chief, who then went to those they had subinfeudated, and so on. This feudal organization strengthened the elites, especially the barons, and weakened the ability of common folk to participate in politics. For example, open opposition to the king, such as that targeted at Edward the Confessor on his return from France, was now impossible as it would have been construed as breaking feudal oaths. Perhaps a step out of the corridor? But in the context of deeply rooted assemblies, society's participation in politics couldn't be easily cast aside.

The influence of assemblies was soon re-created under the requirement to give "council and aid." Like the assembly politics of Germanic tribes, this involved meetings between the king and the leading elites, both lay and religious, and in some contexts much broader segments of society. Moreover, vassals' *obligation* to give counsel turned out to be not so different from the *right* to give counsel, especially since this right had been exercised under the old system of government, ratified when William came to power. There was still the latent right of freemen to be consulted too. By the time of the reign of Henry II, William the Conqueror's great-grandson, who ascended the throne in 1154, a number of factors coalesced to make councils even more powerful in shackling the emerging state, particularly in the way they interacted with the legal system.

The law had been in transition since the early days of William's reign. A notable feature of the laws of Clovis and Alfred is that they specify compensation to the victims, not state punishments, like prison sentences or fines paid to the state. In Alfred's laws, if you struck off someone's ear, you had to pay 30 shillings (you had to pay 60 shillings "if the hearing is stopped"). But this wasn't a fine that you gave to the state; it was compensation to the person whose ear you had struck off. Under William there was a movement toward punishments with fines being payable to the state. The most famous example was the crime of *murdrum*, whereby a whole community (usually a "hundred" or village) was fined if a Norman was killed and the community did not bring forth the perpetrator. A related institution was the tithing. The tithing, a group of ten or twelve men who had to take an oath to keep the law, was responsible for catching and bringing forward any one of its members who committed an offense. If a crime took place in a particular community and nobody was caught, then the whole community could be fined. This system was often called frankpledge and those pledged in effect became the local enforcers of the law.

The idea of collective responsibility and punishment probably comes from feuding codes that identify groups of people, usually extended kin, as being responsible for avenging wrongs. But there is a big difference between kin groups and a geographically based village community being held responsible, especially when it comes to the implications of this for the cage of norms. In fact, William removed the legal right of vengeance and continually attempted to discourage kin groups and clans from dispensing justice themselves and engaging in feud and vendetta. A consequence was the disintegration of kin relations. The French historian of feudalism Marc Bloch pointed out that in this period

> the vast kindreds of not so long before were slowly being replaced by groups much more like our small families of today.

This began to show up in the practice of naming. In the early Norman period people might have a single name, often associated with the name of a broader kin group or clan. But by the twelfth century they began to add a surname of some sort. This was at first an individual decision which seems to have started with the aristocracy and spread through society. Non-aristocrats often took craft surnames, like Smith, Baker, or Cooper, which reflected their occupation. Bloch emphasizes the fundamental role of the state in this process, or as he put it:

> The permanent family name, which today is held in common by men often devoid of any feeling of solidarity, was the creation not of the spirit of kinship, but of the institutions most fundamentally opposed to that spirit—the sovereign state.

The state was reconfiguring the nature of society, and in the process slowly dismantling myriad restrictions on behavior, obligations, and social hierarchies.

The nature of the law took a dramatic new form during Henry II's reign. England had been plagued by succession disputes and civil war during the reign of Henry's predecessor Stephen. Henry needed to rebuild the country and wanted to recover territory that had been lost in Scotland, Wales, and especially France. Furthermore, he wanted to help sustain the Crusader states in the Holy Land. To do all this he needed money, and in 1166 he levied a tax on revenues and moveables. Until then the king had survived on revenues from his own lands, feudal dues, and fees from judicial actions. The new tax was controversial and Henry levied it in a council of the archbishops, bishops, and magnates of his French fiefs "with the counsel and assent of all." For taxes that fell on everyone like this, Henry needed consent from society.

While Henry began to raise taxes, he also implemented a series of legal reforms that greatly increased the power of royal government over the judicial system. The most famous was the creation of the "eyres," instituted sometime around 1176. This was a system of itinerant royal judges who toured the country with broad authority to judge different types of cases. But Henry's reforms also triggered the Red Queen. Society came to participate in conflict resolution in new ways because judges now would have to create a type of court called assizes, and would summon "twelve lawful men" to aid them. This had already been anticipated in the Assize of Clarendon in 1166, a law that stated:

> Inquiry shall be made throughout every county and every hundred, through twelve of the more lawful men of the hundred and through four of the more lawful men of each village upon oath, that they will speak the truth, whether there be in their hundred or village any man accused or notoriously suspect of being a robber or murderer or thief, or any who is a receiver of robbers or murderers or thieves.

This was significant in establishing the jury system, even if it was to a large extent anticipated by the tithing system. It is also noteworthy that it emphasized the collection of evidence as opposed to determining guilt. The assize did not yet give the "jury" the right to pronounce guilt or innocence, just provide information. The right to give verdicts would come later.

The notion of trial by a "jury of your peers" is a key part of the emergence of what came to be known as the "common law" in England. The other major part associated with Henry II's reforms is the idea that judges made laws. When judges ruled on cases, they had to interpret existing laws that were vague and often open-ended. Their rulings set precedents for how laws were to be interpreted and these cases themselves became a basis for new laws. The emerging autonomy of what was to become a legal profession in England, whose rulings accumulated into the common law, was another significant step in the development of a new way of resolving conflicts. It ensured that the ruler could not impose arbitrary laws on society, because the norms working through the power of the legal profession would constrain it. The Red Queen was now in action, with yet more sweeping consequences. For one, in a significant step toward equality before the law, the rising authority of the legal profession also meant that laws could be applied to everybody, and even to the king. For another, it empowered the legal profession to start relaxing the cage of norms, ruling against practices that were most restrictive and most inconsistent with the spirit of the laws that were developing. As we'll see shortly, this power was most significantly manifested in the collapse of the feudal system.

That equality before the law was on people's minds is evident in the writings of Richard FitzNigel, one of Henry's itinerant judges. As he put it in his famous treatise about the exchequer, *The Dialogue Concerning the Exchequer*, published in 1180:

> The forest has its own laws, based, it is said, not on the common law of the realm, but on the arbitrary decree of the king; so that what is accordance with the forest law is not called "just" absolutely, but "just" according to the forest law.

The king could make laws. But these were "arbitrary," not "just"!

Stepping back we can see these measures as playing a defining role in the strengthening of the central state at the expense of society—for example, by taking judicial authority away from local courts controlled by barons. However, this process of centralization was still subject to two major limitations. First, Henry's reforms were constrained by norms, and the common law meant that decisions by the judges in local communities created precedents for future decisions, whether the ruler liked it or not. This ensured that the implementation of laws could not deviate too much from prevailing norms. Second, the ability of courts to impose the state's will on society was highly circumscribed. For example, nearly all legal actions and prosecutions were initiated by ordinary people. The judges who sat in the assizes had no independent investigatory power. They had to wait for people to bring cases so the demand for justice was critical.

That society helped to summon this greater state capacity made it no less real. Underscoring the nature of state building in the corridor, there was a simultaneous increase in the enforcement of laws (often with society playing a critical role in the process), in various public services, and in the bureaucratic capacity of the state. This last point can be seen from the estimates of the increase in the amount of wax used to seal letters by the English chancery, the personal staff of the lord chancellor, one of the king's most important advisers and the "keeper of the king's seal." Between the late 1220s and the late 1260s, the amount of sealing wax increased from 3.6 to 31.9 pounds per week. This ninefold increase reflects a ninefold increase in letters that needed sealing, itself the result of a large expansion of recorded state business. State capacity was growing by leaps and bounds.

The Red Queen Effect in Action: The Magna Carta

The reaction of society to the strengthening of the state continued after Henry II's centralizing reforms and after his son John ascended to the throne in 1199. Antagonized by what they saw as King John's endless demands for taxation and attempts to break free of the constraints imposed by law and norms, a group of barons rebelled and captured London. John met them at Runnymede on the river Thames, just west of London, to negotiate a peace on June 10. The place for the negotiation was significant. The name Runnymede seems to be derived from the Anglo-Saxon words *runieg* ("regular meeting") and *mede* ("meadow"), and indeed Runnymede was one of the places where the witan had met during Alfred's reign. At this assembly the barons started by proposing what came to be known as the Articles of the Barons. Over the next ten days they negotiated the Magna Carta, the Great Charter.

The Magna Carta became the foundation of England's political institutions. It focused on many things: the role of the Church; the hostages held to control the Welsh and Scottish kings; and John's French officers (the charter insisted they should be fired). But its key clauses focused on the issues of taxation without consent and on how to constrain the king by laws and institutions. Critically, though the Magna Carta might have been negotiated by some rebellious barons, it was conceded by the king "to all the free men of our kingdom," and "the whole community of the land" could be called on to enforce it. With respect to the issues of taxation and "illegal" charges levied by John, paragraph 12 read:

> No "scutage" or "aid" may be levied in our kingdom without its general consent.

"Scutage" was a sum of money that a feudal vassal could pay to the king in exchange for exception for military service. "Aid" included other feudal payments that a vassal owed to his lord. But the charter didn't just limit the aid that vassals had to give to the king. Paragraph 15 stipulated, "In future we will allow no one to levy an 'aid' from his free men" unless it is "reasonable." More startling, the charter protected non-free people, that is, serfs or villeins. The next paragraph read:

> No man shall be forced to perform more service for a knight's fee, or other free holding of land, than is due from it.

This meant that villeins were protected from increases in labor services. Moreover, in judicial fines a "villein" would be spared the "implements of his husbandry." Villeins were also directly protected from arbitrary behavior by royal officials since paragraph 28 stated, "No constable or other royal official shall take corn or other movable goods from any man without immediate payment." The words "any man" are significant.

Everywhere the Magna Carta tried to uphold the participation of the people in the implementation of the law and a broadly, even if not perfectly, equal standing in front of the law. Paragraph 20 noted that fines could not be imposed "except by the assessment on oath of reputable men of the neighborhood," and 18 said that

> inquests . . . shall be taken only in their proper county court. We ourselves . . . will send two justices to each county four times a year and these justices, with four knights of the county elected by the county itself, shall hold the assizes in the county court.

Paragraph 38 stated, "In future no official shall place a man on trial upon his own unsupported statement, without producing credible witnesses to the truth of it," while the next one stipulated:

> No free man shall be seized or imprisoned, or stripped of his rights or possessions, or outlawed or exiled, or deprived of his standing in any way . . . except by the lawful judgment of his equals or by the law of the land.

The final remarkable piece of the charter was the mechanism it set up to make sure that the clauses were implemented. It called for the creation of a council of twenty-five barons, and if four of them became aware that the king or his officers were violating any clause, they could "assail us in every possible way . . . by seizing our castles, lands, possessions, or anything else saving our own person." Everyone could get into the action since this clause went on to note, "Any man who so desires may take an oath to obey the commands of the 25 barons for the achievements of these ends."

This monitoring mechanism was never set up, and the barons and John were soon at war. Nevertheless, the power of the Magna Carta as a statement of some critical political principles was continually reaffirmed by subsequent kings and assemblies that came to be called Great Councils. By 1225, taxes at the Great Council were formally conceded by "archbishops, bishops, abbots, priors, earls, barons, knights, free tenants and everyone in our kingdom." It was significant that taxes were agreed not just by the usual elites but also by "knights and freemen." Moreover, the magnates and knights were making decisions "on behalf of themselves and their villeins," suggesting a notion of representation for the wider community. By April 1254 this representation was taken one step further. For the first time two knights were chosen from each shire, initiating a system that would last until the Representation of the People Act of 1918. The word "parliament" seems to have been used for the first time in a legal case from November 1236 when an action was delayed until the next meeting of Parliament in January 1237. During the parliament convened without the king's permission by the rebel Simon de Montfort in 1264, two burgesses were summoned from each urban borough for the first time. Though Montfort was defeated, the structure he initiated became the norm, and the knights and burgesses started to become known as "the Commons," from the same root as "commune," a word we met in the previous chapter.

It was in this period that the knights and burgesses also began to be elected rather than appointed by the king's sheriff. By the middle of the fourteenth century the Commons were meeting separately from the House of Lords, marking the beginning of the bicameral system that came to define English democracy.

The fingerprints of the Red Queen are everywhere in the evolution of the English parliament. Though initially based on the popular assemblies that the Anglo-Saxons had brought to the island, Parliament had now become a more powerful institution. This took place despite the rise of feudalism, which could have increased the despotism of the king and elites greatly, as in other parts of Europe. Even more notably, this was all happening as the capacity of the state was growing, as witnessed by its much greater role in codifying and enforcing laws, in the reorganization of the administrative structure of the realm, and in its increasing bureaucratic footprint, for example, with the usage of sealing wax. Of course, Parliament in the fourteenth century wasn't a democratic institution as we understand it today (even if we leave aside the fact that it was only for men). Even after the 1290s, when members of Parliament began being elected, the franchise was restricted to adult males who were quite well off. Parliament continued to be a body for the more aristocratic and privileged part of society. All the same, society's further mobilization and the institutionalization of its power during this period support our interpretation that England was already in the corridor and traveling toward greater state and societal capacity, albeit with major ups and downs. And this balance of power wasn't simply rooted in Parliament, but rather emerged from how society was structured, how it was playing a critical role in the implementation of laws and provision of public services, and how it was initiating change.

To see one of the most significant changes, note the language of "knights" and "villeins" in the clauses of the Magna Carta we reproduced. Feudal society was a society of relatively rigid and highly hierarchical orders; one either fought, prayed, or worked. Those who worked—the villeins or serfs—were decidedly at the bottom and were trapped into hereditary servitude. Contemporary attitudes toward such people have lingered on in the modern use of the word "villain." In practice this meant they and their descendants were tied to the lands of particular lords and were subject to various types of social and economic restrictions as well as fines. In fourteenth-century England these included "merchet," which meant that a villein could not marry without the lord's permission. Permission was usually granted in exchange for a payment of money. Another, "millsuit," was a charge on the wheat grown by villeins, which had to be ground in the lord's mill. "Tallage" was a more ad hoc charge that was periodically levied on villeins who farmed the lord's land. Landless villeins weren't exempt; they got hit with "chevage." Perhaps most onerous of all, villeins had to provide free labor services all year round on the land of the lord. This nexus of feudal institutions choking the liberty of villeins crumbled away in the second half of the fourteenth century. Their demise happened in the wake of the Black Death, the catastrophic spread of the bubonic plague that wiped out at least one-third of Europe's population between 1347 and 1352. The collapse of population created a severe shortage of labor and a general disorganization of rural society. Villeins started to refuse to undertake labor services and obey the whole gamut of feudal regulations. They refused to grind their corn in the lord's mill. They didn't bother asking permission to marry. Courts of law refused to enforce the old rules. Highlighting the critical role of the state in modifying and shaping norms, villeins could now appeal to the new systems of courts and judges established by Henry II. Lords were forced to offer new types of tenancy and leasing arrangements for land, which by 1400 had replaced most of the old hereditary tenures based on villeinage. The cage of norms of the feudal order was disintegrating bit by bit.

The Grumbling Hive

In 1705 the Anglo-Dutch philosopher and satirist Bernard Mandeville published a poem, "The Grumbling Hive," in which he compared English society to a colony of bees. People lived in "luxury and ease" and there was a balance between the state and society.

> They were not Slaves to Tyranny,
> Nor ruled by wild Democracy;
> But Kings, that could not wrong, because
> Their Power was circumscrib'd by Laws.

But yet the bees were discontented, and while "No bees had better government," it was also true that no bees had "More Fickleness, or less Content." But why was this society "Grumbling"? Let's look at a famous case, the village of Swallowfield in Wiltshire. In December 1596 a number of inhabitants of the village got together to write a little constitution. It was made up of twenty-six different resolutions. Resolution 25 stipulated, "The whole company promesethe to meete once in every monethe," so there were to be regular meetings with clear protocols. The first resolution read:

> ffirst it is agre[e]d, That every man shal be h[e]ard at o[u]r metynge quyetly one after an other, And th[a]t non shall interrupte an other in his speeche, And th[a]t every man shal speake as he is fyrste in accompt, & so in order, th[a]t therby the depthe of every mans Judgment w[i]th reason may be concedered.

People were to be respectful and not interrupt others when they were speaking so that the depth of everyone's judgment could be considered. Resolution 11 required that there was to be proper record keeping of the meetings in a paper book.

What were the substantive resolutions about? They were in effect customary laws for controlling misdemeanors, as resolution 25 put it, "wilffull & vyle synns." These included petty theft, malicious gossip, wood stealing, pride, dissent, and arrogance (resolution 18); insubordination and disturbance of the peace (resolution 15); fornication and illegitimacy (resolutions 8, 13); improvident marriage (resolution 20); harboring inmates (resolution 21); profanation of the Sabbath (resolutions 22, 24); and drunkenness (resolution 23).

It's clear from the resolutions that the residents of Swallowfield thought of their community as self-governing. If they waited long enough, they might get help from the central state in terms of indictment and punishment. But even after Henry II's massive expansion of state capacity, most state activity was voluntarily conceived and implemented by local communities. For example, though there were one or two constables for each "hundred" and usually a petty constable in each village, these had to be jacks of all trades. Petty constables were responsible for controlling any disturbances and for enforcing most types of economic, social, and military regulations and obligations. They had to collect local taxes, maintain roads and bridges, and attend the quarter sessions and twice-yearly assizes. Existing legal records show the extent to which it was left to individuals and the community to catch criminals and bring them to law enforcement officials.

Take the case of George Wenham of Penhurst in Sussex in the early seventeenth century. He woke up one morning to find that a hog had disappeared from the pen next to his house. He started to search the vicinity, and half a mile from his house he found a spot which recently had been used for slaughtering. There was blood on the ground and he found entrails thrown over a hedge along with the prints of a horse's hoofs. Wenham followed the hoof marks and drops of blood, but had to stop when night fell. The tracks were leading in the direction of John Marwick's house. At this point Wenham went to the local petty constable and asked him to search Marwick's house. Although eventually law enforcement officials got involved, it was the victims who had to do the legwork of identifying and often even catching the criminals. If people decided not to enforce a law, the wheels of justice would grind to a halt.

Returning to Swallowfield, who were these people who wrote the resolutions? They were not closely related kin (kin groups had long ceased to play such roles in England). They were not the local elites or the clergy. There were two large landowners in the neighborhood, Samuel Blackhouse and John Phipps, but neither was present. Nor was the local priest. Rather, the drafters of Swallowfield's constitution were what British historians call the "middling sort of person," likely the same people that the Assize of Clarendon referred to as the "more lawful men of each village." None of them had enough income to be among the eleven taxpayers listed in the parliamentary tax return for Swallowfield of 1594. These were the people who ran the local state even in the late sixteenth century. They were the people who served in local administrative positions as jurors, churchwardens, overseers of the poor, and in the new position of local constable.

This bustling civic engagement did not escape the notice of contemporaries such as Sir Thomas Smith, a scholar, diplomat, and member of the English parliament. In 1583, a little before the Swallowfield constitution, Smith published *De Republica Anglorum: The Maner of Governement or Policie of the Realme of England*, which became one of the most famous political analyses of Elizabethan England. He noted, "We in England divide our men commonly into foure sortes, gentlemen, citizens or burgesses, yeoman artificers, and laborers." The fourth sort of person was made up of "day laborers, poore husbandmen, yea merchants or retailers which have no free lande, copiholders, all artificers, as Taylers, Shoomakers, Carpenters, Brickemakers, Bricklayers, Masons etc. . . . And in villages they be commonly made Churchwardens, alecunners, and manie times Constables, which office toucheth more the common wealth." Even laborers played an extensive role in running local government and so did yeomen who "hath his part" in the "administration in judgementes, corrections of defaultes, in election of offices . . . and in making laws." With respect to the popular administration of justice Smith stated, "Every English man is a Sergeant to take the thief."

This example and many others like it show that, just as the Red Queen effect implies, there was a huge amount of participation at the bottom of the English state. Participation and representation didn't just take place in Parliament. They happened at all levels and through many channels. One estimate suggests that in 1700 there might have been 50,000 parish officers at any one time in England, representing around 5 percent of adult males. Since there was frequent rotation of offices, the number of people who had held office must have been considerably larger. In 1800 the figure was probably more like 100,000.

This popular participation in the operation of the state had major consequences. It was very difficult for the central state and the national elites to implement policies that were not consistent with what local people wanted. Indeed, the early modern state couldn't completely ignore existing norms, because its legitimacy originated from its claim to deliver justice and improve social welfare, even if its ability to do either of these things was dependent on the cooperation of ordinary people. Exactly as in Athens we are seeing the multifaceted relationship between laws and norms in the corridor. On the one hand, norms mobilized society, constrained what the state could do and how far state building could go. On the other hand, state centralization and new laws gradually and little by little relaxed some aspects of the cage of norms, especially as the growing clout and presence of the courts and the legal profession weakened the feudal order, its social hierarchy, and its role in conflict resolution.

Finally, local communities didn't just decide whether or not to implement national policy, they also initiated it. Before the early twentieth century, the English social safety net for the destitute and the poor, such as it was, consisted of the Poor Laws. The first of these laws was enacted in 1597. Yet even before this, there were many similar local initiatives: in 1549 in Norwich, 1550 in York, and then in Cambridge, Colchester, and Ipswich in 1556–1557. The Poor Laws were not some inspired policy by Queen Elizabeth or her advisers. They were local initiatives that the state picked up and rolled out nationally. There are many other examples of the central state following the local lead. For instance, a 1555 act stipulated that the parish be responsible for the appointment of surveyors to coordinate the repair of local roads, but such surveyors are documented from at least 1551 in Chester.

Why then were people grumbling? Because, inside the corridor as they were, they wanted more, expected more, and demanded that the state deliver more. At the same time they were competing with the state, competing for authority, contesting its power.

A Profusion of Parliaments

The story we are telling in this chapter is not confined to England; it is a European one as well. England was politically distinctive in a few small senses, for example in the extent of continuity between Anglo-Saxon assemblies and subsequent parliaments, in the territorial way in which parliamentary representation was organized, and in the various events that further strengthened assemblies, such as the critical role they played in legitimizing successions of new kings. But other parts of Europe weren't all that different from it, and also experienced the fusion of Germanic assembly politics with Roman state institutions (even if, as we'll see in Chapter 9, once you look more closely at Europe there is plenty of interesting diversity that our theory can help explain as well).

One way to see this is to return to the Magna Carta. How unique was it? Answer: not at all. Later, in 1356 in Brabant, subsequently partitioned between the Netherlands and Belgium, a parliament extracted from the new duke the "Joyous Entry," a charter that the duke had to swear an oath to obey and implement. The duke agreed that the assembly had to consent to war, taxation, and the minting and debasement of the coinage. One can find similar documents and joyous entries all over Europe, and more or less at the same time as the Magna Carta. These include a charter by Peter I, king of Aragon, given to Catalonia in 1205; the Golden Bull granted by Andrew II of Hungary in 1222; and a charter by Frederick II in Germany in 1220. These entries all focused on many of the same issues, particularly making sure that rulers had to consult citizens and get agreement to raise taxes.

There weren't just "great charters," there were also parliaments everywhere in Europe. They started in Spain, with the Cortes of León in 1188 and then spread to the Crown of Aragon, which was a merger of Aragon, Catalonia, and Valencia, all of which had their own parliaments. Parliament-like assemblies subsequently developed in the Iberian kingdoms of Navarre and Portugal. In France, even if the development of a national assembly, the Estates General, was slower, there was a great proliferation of regional estates. Farther east in Switzerland, the rural cantons had their own assemblies, which then merged into the Swiss Confederation in 1291. To the north, German principalities making up the Holy Roman Empire typically had assemblies, called *Landtage*. In the West in what was to become Belgium and the Netherlands, Flanders, Holland, and Brabant all had vibrant assemblies. Moving north, there were parliaments in Denmark starting in 1282 and in Sweden from the middle of the fifteenth century. Both of these, along with that of

West Friesland in the Netherlands and Tyrol in Austria, also granted representation to peasants. Scotland had a parliament from the thirteenth century, and in Poland there was, and still is today, the Sejm.

Northern Italy of course had its own version of charters and parliaments in the context of the communes as we saw in the previous chapter. These too had their roots in assemblies. In fact, the north of Italy was a perfect mixing ground for the state institutions of the Roman Empire and the tradition of assembly politics brought first by another Germanic tribe, the Lombards, and then later by the Carolingians. This in fact distinguished the north from the south of Italy, which did not have a history of assemblies, and neither developed charters and parliaments nor experienced the same flourishing of liberty.

When we look around the continent in the medieval and early modern periods, we see not just joyous entries and parliaments but also the same vibrant community life administering its own affairs, engaged in sustained attempts to influence and shape the more centralized political institutions. A well-documented example is the German territory of Hesse, where an assembly called a diet was convened by the ruler. The diet comprised nobles and elites but also delegates from towns, and it emerged as a forum to approve demands for taxation. Unlike the English parliament, the Hesse Diet did not have the right to draft legislation, but it had considerable influence through a process of formulating *gravamina* (grievances), which it presented to the ruler of Hesse. This process was related to a more general pan-European approach of "petitioning" rulers, particularly prevalent in the English case. In Hesse, by the end of the sixteenth century, the state was receiving 1,000 petitions a year, and this increased to 4,000 a year by the end of the eighteenth century. It's clear that the gravamina and initiatives of the diet had a large impact on legislation and policy in Hesse. Many prologues of princely edicts acknowledge the role of local initiatives and record that the impetus for a policy came from the diet. In 1731, for example, at least fifteen different initiatives from the diet are mentioned as impulses for government policies. Between 1764 and 1767 these "initiatives from below," as they were actually referred to, influenced tithes, brewing, taxation, urban jurisdiction, and fire insurance, among many other things. They also involved a request for a common law code covering all parts of the Hessian territory, suggestions for the improvements of schooling, in 1731, 1754, and 1764, and measures to promote manufactures in 1731 and 1764. The diet also called for more "open government," including measures such as the publication of all current ordinances, court sentences, and resolutions agreed to in the diet.

The gravamina emerging from the diet did not only address the concerns of urban dwellers and elites. We see complaints about *Kontribution*, the heaviest form of taxation, which fell primarily on peasants, and also complaints about the damage caused by deer and other wild beasts. There were persistent complaints about land laws that interfered with traditional inheritance customs as well. In the end, the ruler relented and revoked the laws. The Hessian experience is not exceptional. One sees similar things in the territories of Lower Austria, Hohenlohe, and Württemburg.

At the root of the remarkable clustering of great charters, parliaments, and popular participation in politics in medieval Europe is the Red Queen, and the impulse she generated both for the emboldening of society and the increase in state capacity. Indeed, the amount of wax use didn't just increase in England; throughout Western Europe states became more bureaucratized and more centralized.

Society didn't just respond by demanding representation, it organized in lots of other ways too, including in the form of communes, as in Italy. Also present were many kinds of "leagues," alliances that asserted their authority against rulers and tried to influence their policies. Some, like the famous Hanseatic League, were groups of city-states that began to coalesce around the shores of the Baltic Sea after the 1240s. Another, the Rhenish League, which formed in 1254, consisted of over one hundred members that included towns, churches, and even princes, all within the bounds of the Holy Roman Empire. In Spain there were various "brotherhoods," such as those in Castile and León and the Hermandad General, which formed in opposition to King Alonso X of Castile in 1282.

But life in the corridor is never tranquil, and it wasn't easy to reach a peaceful balance between the demands of the state and the reaction of society. One consequence in the fourteenth century was a wave of popular revolts driven by the expanding authority of the state. People revolted against tax payments and they revolted against what they perceived to be abuses by their governments. The Flemish revolt of 1323–1328 reacted to the reintroduction of a "transport tax"; the Jacquerie of 1358 in northern France was partly a response to increased taxation in the 1340s and 1350s; so was the Tuchinat, which convulsed Languedoc and southern France in the 1360s and 1380s; and the English Peasants' Revolt of 1381 was a reaction to the imposition of a series of new poll taxes starting in 1377, in addition to attempts by lords to maintain feudal restrictions. Interestingly, these revolts targeted political centers, such as Paris or London, which they were trying to influence. This was because people felt they were part of a political community, even if they didn't like the way this community worked, and they revolted to influence politics and improve the way things functioned.

From Thing to Althing: Europe Outside the Corridor

Do we see the beginnings of the Shackled Leviathan everywhere in Europe? No, for the simple reason that the requisite balance of power between state and society wasn't present everywhere. Some parts, like Iceland, were outside the influence of Roman institutions, making it much more likely for them to remain under an Absent Leviathan.

Iceland was settled by Vikings sailing from Norway sometime in the ninth century and had previously been uninhabited. What we know about this early period comes from the famous Sagas, oral stories, that were passed from generation to generation before being written down in the thirteenth and fourteenth centuries. Archaeological and linguistic research suggests that after the end of the last Ice Age, starting in the third millennium BCE, Scandinavia and northern Germany received waves of migrants speaking Indo-European languages. Out of this emerged the Germanic branch of Indo-European that includes German and all of the Scandinavian languages (except Finnish). It seems likely that the sorts of political institutions described by Tacitus characterized not just the German tribes but also the peoples of Scandinavia. The fact that the lower region of Sweden was called Götaland is suggestive of close cultural connections between the settlers of this area and another one of the major Germanic tribes, the Goths. When Scandinavians, usually in the guise of Vikings or Norsemen, come more into recorded history, their political organization is similar to those of earlier Germanic tribes described by Julius Caesar and Tacitus. They held *things*, which all free men participated in, they were not unified into states, and their chiefs had very limited powers.

The first settlers of Iceland had similar institutions too. To start with, Iceland was divided between possibly fifty or sixty different chiefs, and by 900 CE *things* were meeting regularly. In 930 an assembly for the whole of Iceland, the Althing, was established at Thingvellir, now a national park just east of Reykjavík. Though the chieftains agreed to the establishment of the Althing, they did not agree to the creation of a state. There was no centralization authority, just the office of "law speaker," who had to recite one-third of the laws annually (he had a three-year term), though this became less important after 1117, when the laws were written down. The Althing then took on only legal functions. During the subsequent Icelandic Free State, there was no centralized authority and independent chieftains fought each other and amalgamated, ultimately creating a set of territorial lordships in charge of "realms." Rather than the *things'* evolving and strengthening over time as in England and Western Europe, they weakened and lost their ability to choose their chieftains. Iceland, without a Leviathan of any sort, became famous for endless feuding.

Iceland had the Germanic shackles, but not the Roman bureaucracy and centralizing institutions. Its early history shows that there is nothing straightforward about moving into the corridor; it's certainly not the natural outcome of the deliberations of stateless societies or a direct consequence of the cultures and customs of Germanic tribes, *thing* or no *thing*. It's not enough to have only one blade of the scissors.

The Dollar of the Middle Ages:
The Byzantine Leviathan

Though the Western Roman Empire did fall in the fifth century, the Eastern Roman or Byzantine Empire survived and occasionally thrived for another ten centuries. By the fifth century, Byzantium was already embodying almost all of the Roman institutions, so one of the blades of the European scissors was faithfully represented in this powerful empire. Indeed, our account of late Roman bureaucracy, composed by John Lydus, comes from Byzantium. One indicator of the strength of the state was its ability to maintain a stable and widely circulated coinage. As Cosmas Indicopleustes, a contemporary of Emperor Justinian, put it, the Byzantine gold coin, the nomisma, "is accepted everywhere from end to end of the earth. It is admired by all men and in all kingdoms, because no kingdom has a currency that can be compared to it." The economic historian Robert Lopez dubbed it "the dollar of the Middle Ages."

Byzantium faced more challenges after the collapse of the Western Roman Empire, particularly the Justinian plague of 541–542, which devastated the population, and the loss of half its territory during the Arab conquests of the seventh century. Nevertheless, the Byzantine state maintained its coherence, and Justinian even kept the fiscal system functioning in the teeth of the plague. In the words of the historian Procopius:

When pestilence swept through the whole known world and notably the Roman Empire, wiping out most of the farming community and of necessity leaving a trail of desolation in its wake, Justinian showed no mercy towards the ruined freeholders. Even then he did not refrain from demanding the annual tax, not only the amount at which he assessed each individual but also the amount for which his deceased neighbors were liable.

The Byzantines inherited this fiscal system from Rome, and implemented it much more faithfully than did the Merovingians or the Carolingians; Clovis wasn't able to levy land taxes, but the Byzantine emperors were. They even had a rural cadastre that valued land and was updated every thirty years. The tax rate was set at around one twenty-fourth of the value of land per year. There were other taxes too, including on animals and even bees, and in the 660s a household tax was introduced. There were also various types of labor corvées for the construction of roads, bridges, and fortifications.

The state didn't just tax wealth or production, it was a producer itself. In the eighth century it was the biggest landowner in the empire and marketed the produce. It owned mines, quarries, and workshops for weaving and dyeing, and arms factories. It also regulated the economy. In the eighth century there was a list of "forbidden goods" that nobody was allowed to export. These included cereals, salt, wine, olive oil, fish sauce, precious metals, and strategic commodities like iron, weapons, and high-quality silks. The state provided free food and even tried to regulate profits in Constantinople.

All of this speaks to a state with a great deal of capacity, more than the Merovingian or Carolingian states in the West. Yet what was completely missing in Byzantium was the other blade of the scissors—the participatory politics of German tribes. There were no assemblies, no institutionalized representation, and subsequently no great charters or parliaments.

Byzantium thus provides us with a perfect European exemplar of the evolution of the Despotic Leviathan. Indeed, the concentrated nature of state power allowed Alexios Komnenos to take over the state in 1081 and create dynastic dominance over Byzantium. Komnenos privatized the state to his family, even reorganizing the system of honors and titles so that they applied to his family, rather than more generally. He used the Byzantine state to cow his enemies and took control of the Church hierarchy. It's true that the capacity of the state was already on the decline, and the nomisma was only 30 percent fine gold at this point. As it happened, Komnenos laid the seeds for the final collapse of the state. In 1082 he gave the Venetians their first commercial privileges and in 1095 he tried to use the First Crusade as a way to retake territory that had been lost to the Seljuk Turks in Anatolia. By 1204 the Fourth Crusade had sacked Byzantium, an event from which the empire would never recover.

Moving On in the Corridor

The relationship between state and society we described in Swallowfield in late Tudor England didn't stand still. In fact the Red Queen effect implies that just to stay where it was, Swallowfield would have to keep running, developing greater organizational capacity, trying to keep the fearsome face of the state at arm's length. When the Stuart dynasty in the seventeenth century attempted to assert the "divine right of kings," society did not take it lying down. Conflict came to a head with the English Civil War and the execution of Charles I in 1649 and the overthrow of James II with the Glorious Revolution in 1688.

The seventeenth century was certainly not a time one would associate with liberty. Hobbes, as we have seen, was compelled to turn to an all-powerful Leviathan because of the chaos and carnage created by the English Civil War. But the journey of English society in the corridor during the century ended up securing the preconditions for liberty, and the Red Queen was again in the middle of the action. The Glorious Revolution brought in a host of changes in political institutions, most importantly asserting the sovereignty of Parliament, which now became the unchallenged executive authority, replacing the king. This wasn't the end, because Parliament was mostly constituted of elites who wanted to exert their own control over society. After 1688 they had new tools to do so because they rapidly ramped up the capacity of the English state. Most notably, the excise tax system created a fiscal administration that penetrated into every nook and cranny of English society. Professional state officials such as excisemen, previously a rare sight in the English countryside, were suddenly everywhere, and quite threatening to the locals. To maintain its position, society had to "up the ante." The way it did this was studied by Charles Tilly in his book *Popular Contention in Great Britain, 1758–1834.*

Tilly was interested in the changing nature of what he called "popular contention," the way in which common people organized collectively to try to influence the government. He noted that in the middle of the eighteenth century contention was about "local people and local issues, rather than nationally organized programs and parties." Yet "between 1758 and 1833 a new variety of claim-making had taken shape in Britain . . . Mass popular politics had taken hold on a national scale."

Completely new forms of collective action emerged in this period. Among these he emphasizes the "open meeting," which had become "a kind of demonstration . . . a coordinated way of publicizing support for a particular claim on holders of power. Frequently a special-purpose association, society or club called the meeting. What is more, meetings recurrently concerned national issues, emphatically including issues that the government and Parliament were on their way to deciding." He points out that

> the means by which ordinary people made collective claims . . . underwent a deep transformation: increasingly they involved large-scale, coordinated interaction [and] direct contact between ordinary people and agents of the national state.

What drove all of this was the intensification of the process of state building in Britain, which had begun after the Glorious Revolution. Tilly argued that the "state's size" and "weight" increased, and

> in the process Parliament—critical to every decision concerning government revenue, expenditure, and personnel—occupied ever more space in political decisions. These changes . . . promoted a shift towards collective action that was large in scale and national in scope.

Particularly significant was the way people stopped focusing on parochial issues since "the expansion of the state pushed popular struggles from local arenas and from significant reliance on patronage towards autonomous claim-making in national arenas." The continued expansion of the state's capacity and presence after 1688 had raised the stakes for English people, and Tilly notes:

> The increasing importance of Parliament and national officials . . . for the fates of ordinary people generated threats and opportunities. Those threats and opportunities in turn stimulated interested parties to attempt new sorts of defense and offense: to match association with association, to gain electoral power, to make direct claims on their national government. Through long, strenuous interaction with authorities, enemies,

and allies, those ordinary people fashioned new ways of acting together on their interests and forced their interlocutors to change their own ways of making and responding to claims. Cumulatively, struggles of ordinary people with powerholders wrought great changes in the British structure of power.

The expansion of the state generated a reaction from society and this in turn fed back onto the process of state building, exactly as the Red Queen effect suggests. In response to all this newfound contention, by the end of the eighteenth century the state started to finally root out corruption.

The process set in motion by popular contention picked up speed with a series of major institutional changes in the nineteenth century. The First Reform Act of 1832 extended voting rights from about 8 percent to 16 percent of the adult male population, and reallocated representation away from the countryside and unrepresentative "rotten boroughs" toward industrial cities with much larger populations. This process continued with the Second Reform Act of 1867 and the Third Reform Act of 1884, when the electorate reached about 60 percent of the adult male population. Another set of crucial steps in the corridor was taken in 1918 when all men over the age of twenty-one obtained the right to vote (while political rights for women came later, as we discuss next). All of these major reforms were a response to societal organization and demands. For example, universal suffrage, equal constituencies, annual parliaments, and payments to members of Parliament so that common folk could also serve were central demands of the Chartist movement of the mid-nineteenth century.

Together with this greater institutionalized power of society against elites came greater state capacity, but now very much along the lines of society's demands. The first in a series of reforms was the Saint Helena Act of 1833, which incorporated the East India Company into the administrative structure of the state. The Northcote-Trevelyan Report of 1854 picked up what the Saint Helena Act started and recommended a professional civil service with meritocratic selection. Even though the report faced opposition, its main recommendations were gradually implemented in the next two decades, ultimately leading to the establishment of competitive examinations for selection into the civil service. Simultaneously, the state also moved in the direction of providing a broad range of public services, including mass schooling, which became effectively free of charge in 1891; health insurance; and unemployment insurance and pensions, all financed by redistributive taxes. This process culminated in the Beveridge Report of 1942 and its implementation, which we'll discuss in Chapter 15.

The Next Cage to Be Broken

In the same way that a movement into the corridor doesn't put an end to violence and feuding in one fell swoop, it doesn't break down the cage of norms all at once. The evolution of liberty is a protracted process, especially for groups, such as women, who have been systematically discriminated against and suffer heavy restrictions on their social and economic behavior.

Caroline Sheridan experienced the full reality of this in 1830s England. Born in 1808, she married a lawyer, George Norton, in 1827 and took his name. Caroline Norton was a talented author and poet, but her husband was abusive and violent. In 1836 she finally decided to leave him. However, under English law she had few rights. The income from her writings went to her husband. Her property was his. As a 1632 compilation, *The Lawes Resolutions of Womens Rights*, stated baldly,

> That which the husband hath is his own. That which the wife hath is the husband's.

She had no right to either. William Blackstone, the great British legal scholar, summarized the common law situation in his *Commentaries on the Laws of England*, published in 1765:

> By marriage, the husband and wife are one person in law: that is, the very being or legal existence of the woman is suspended during the marriage.

Everything was under the control of the husband "under whose wing, protection, and cover, she performs everything."

In 1838 Caroline Norton wrote a pamphlet, *The Separation of Mother and Child by the Laws of Custody of Infants Considered*. She pointed out that under English law a father could give his children to a stranger, and the mother could do nothing about it. The dramatic publicity generated by her case helped induce Parliament to pass the Infant and Custody of Infants Act in 1839, which gave mothers some say for children under the age of seven. Caroline Norton wasn't finished there. In 1854 she published *English Laws for Women*, brilliantly outlining the inequity and hypocrisy of the legal status quo. She followed it a year later with *A Letter to the Queen on Lord Chancellor Cranworth's Marriage and Divorce Bill*. She pointed out:

> A married woman in England has *no legal existence:* her being is absorbed in that of her husband. Years of separation [or] desertion cannot alter this position . . . the legal fiction holds her to be *"one"* with her husband, even though she may never see or hear of him.
>
> She has no possessions . . . her property is *his* property . . .
>
> An English wife has no legal right even to her clothes or ornaments; her husband may take them and sell them if he pleases, even though they be the gifts of relatives or friends, or bought before marriage.
>
> An English wife cannot make a will . . .
>
> An English wife cannot legally claim her own earnings. Whether wages for manual labour, or payment for intellectual exertion, whether she weed potatoes, or keep a school, her salary is *the husband's* . . .
>
> An English wife may not leave her husband's house. Not only can he sue her for "restitution of conjugal rights," but he has a right to enter the house of any friend or relation with whom she may take refuge, and who may "harbour her,"—as it is termed,—and carry her away by force, with or without the aid of the police.

In 1857 Parliament passed the Matrimonial Causes Act, establishing grounds for which women could sue for divorce. In 1870 came the Married Women's Property Act.

Norton and others began to bring into focus the fundamentally discriminatory nature of English law, which had been identified clearly in 1792 by Mary Wollstonecraft's *A Vindication of the Rights of Woman*. Wollstonecraft's powerful book argued that women "are treated as a kind of subordinate beings, and not a part of the human species." Much of her book was a call to action for women to assert their individuality and throw off the binds that held them. She continued, "To account for, and excuse the tyranny of man, many ingenious arguments have been brought forward to prove, that the two sexes, in the acquirement of virtue, ought to aim at attaining a very different character . . . How grossly do they insult us who advise us only to render ourselves gentle, domestic brutes."

Wollstonecraft clearly recognized that this discrimination was rooted in norms and customs as well as laws, and pointed out that the dominance wielded by men over women and these norms of "outward obedience, and a scrupulous attention to a puerile kind of propriety" stunted women's development. She powerfully rejected them by stating:

> Gentleness, docility, and a spaniel-like affection are . . . consistently recommended as the cardinal virtues of the sex . . .
>
> I love man as my fellow; but his scepter, real, or usurped, extends not to me, unless the reason of an individual demands my homage; and even then the submission is to reason, and not to man.

The cause of liberty for women subsequently acquired an influential supporter in the British philosopher John Stuart Mill, whose 1869 book, *The Subjection of Women*, was a powerful call for complete equality for women in legal, economic, and political life. Mill, echoing Wollstonecraft, compared the subjection of women to slavery and argued that "in the case of women, each individual of the subject class is in a chronic state of bribery and intimidation combined . . . All women are brought up from the earliest years in the belief that their ideal character is the very opposite to that of men; not self-will, and government by self-control, but submission, and yielding to the control of others." For Mill, too, it was clear that the norms that were at the root of this subjugation had to be broken, especially when he argued that

> human beings are no longer born to their place in life, and chained down by an inexorable bond to the place they are born to, but are free to employ their facilities, and such favourable chances as offer, to achieve the lot which may appear to them most desirable.

He continued:

> We ought . . . not to ordain that to be born a girl instead of a boy, any more than to be born black instead of white, or a commoner instead of a nobleman, shall decide the person's position through all life. . . . The social subordination of women thus stands out an isolated fact in modern social institutions; a solitary breach of what has become their fundamental law.

In short, the oppression of women grossly violated liberty.

Norton's victories and the support of figures such as Mill signaled a fundamental change in norms. But they still left women without the right to vote and political representation. Women still suffered massive economic discrimination. This started to change in 1918, when women over the age of 30 got the vote, and finally in 1928, all adult women were enfranchised. These political fruits came after intense mobilization and protests by the suffragettes as we saw in the Preface. Predictably, norms and economic relations changed more slowly. The Equal Pay Act of 1970 establishing the legal principle of gender equality in the workplace was an important step, but equal economic opportunities and pay for women is still a work in progress in Britain as elsewhere. The photo insert includes a picture of a woman holding out her bra, something that became a symbolic act of emancipation during the 1960s.

The Origins of the Industrial Revolution

The emergence of the Shackled Leviathan starting in the fifth and sixth centuries was a political and social revolution, even if it took place with gradual, sometimes tentative, steps. The Industrial Revolution, which got under way in the middle of the eighteenth century in Britain, was its economic offshoot because, just as in the Italian communes we saw in the previous chapter, it was produced by the liberty, opportunities, and incentives that the Shackled Leviathan made possible. In the course of a few decades, technology and the organization of production were transformed in a number of key industries. Leading the way were textiles, where a series of innovative breakthroughs in spinning, such as the water frame, the spinning jenny, and the mule revolutionized productivity. Similar innovations occurred in weaving, with the introduction of the flying shuttle and various types of power looms. Equally transformative were the novel forms of inanimate power starting with Thomas Newcomen's atmospheric engine and then James Watt's steam engine. The steam engine not only made mining much more productive by enabling the pumping of water out of mines, but also changed transportation and metallurgy. The landscape for transport was reconfigured both because of steam trains in the nineteenth century and because a series of canals and new roads linked up major cities starting in the late seventeenth century. Many other industries, including machine tools and agriculture, were also revolutionized because of cheaper and higher-quality iron, made possible thanks to the replacement of charcoal by coke in iron smelting and the production of pig iron in blast furnaces and then steel with the Bessemer process.

The conditions for the Industrial Revolution were prepared by the progress of British society in the corridor. After the end of the Middle Ages the center of gravity of economic activity in Europe had started moving north toward the Netherlands and England. This was intimately connected with the discovery of the Americas and the impact of the new economic opportunities this created on the race between state and society. Countries that were better poised to take advantage of these opportunities in ways that strengthened state and society were able to move ahead institutionally and then economically. In England, the existing balance of power favored society so that the Tudor state in the sixteenth century was unable to exert monopoly control over access to trade. As a result there was broad-based participation in trade with the Americas, fostering a new class of dynamic and assertive mercantile interests. These new groups didn't look kindly upon the Stuart monarchs' attempts to increase their dominance over the economy and social life, and soon got into a prolonged conflict with the crown. Their demands centered not just on greater access to opportunities that were monopolized by the crown's allies but also on broader institutional changes that would further strengthen them and weaken the elites.

The Glorious Revolution of 1688 was a result of this struggle between the crown and new groups. The sweeping implications of this revolution included the emergence of Parliament as the primary executive body in England and greater economic opportunities and incentives for most in English society, as well as a reenergized Red Queen effect. Society's mobilization deepened and its power became more firmly institutionalized via the legislative process while the state's capacity also increased. Equally critical were the changes in the judicial landscape. The Statute of the Monopolies of 1624 had created the patent system, which made the wave of innovations defining the Industrial Revolution possible. Domestic monopolies were subsequently completely dismantled during the English Civil War of the 1640s, undergirding much more broadly distributed economic opportunities. The Glorious Revolution finally established the independence of the judiciary with the Act of Settlement of 1701, a significant further step toward equality before the law, unbiased enforcement of laws and contracts, and secure property rights. The state did not simply remove impediments to economic activity and start providing crucial public services. It also actively encouraged and aided industry (and in this, it had no problem in impinging on the liberty of others; for example, it supported and benefited from English slave traders, and its Navigation Acts made it illegal for foreign ships to carry goods to England or its colonies, helping English merchants and manufacturers monopolize trade).

All these economic and social changes unleashed a tremendous amount of experimentation and innovative energy. Thousands from all walks of life started pursuing their own ideas and paths to improve technology, solve outstanding problems, start businesses, and make money. Critically, this experimentation was not just decentralized, but it was unrestrained by political authority. So different people could pursue distinct approaches in order to innovate better, succeed where others failed, and perhaps more important in the process, formulate completely new problems and ideas. We see the significance of this type of experimentation in some of the iconic technologies of the Industrial Revolution, such as the steam engine. Innovators and entrepreneurs such as Robert Boyle, Denis Papin, Thomas Savory, Thomas Newcomen, John Smeaton, and James Watt all approached the problem of using steam power differently and experimented in their own ways in a cumulative process that ultimately led to much more efficient and powerful steam engines.

Both the nature of experimentation, with plenty of false starts and a multitude of disparate approaches, and its critical role in innovative breakthroughs are perhaps best illustrated by the quest for a way for ships to tell their longitude at sea. Latitude could be calculated from the stars, but longitude was a bigger challenge. Ships frequently got lost at sea and the problems this caused became all too obvious in October 1707 when four out of a fleet of five British warships returning from Gibraltar miscalculated their longitude and sank on the rocks of the Isles of Scilly. Two thousand sailors drowned. The British government established the Board of Longitude and offered a series of prizes in 1714 to encourage a solution to this problem.

It was known that one solution was to have two clocks on board a ship. One set to, say, Greenwich mean time, and another that could be reset to noon each day by the sun at sea. Then one would know the time in Greenwich, and the time where you were. The difference between these times allowed you to calculate longitude. The trouble was that clocks were inaccurate, based on pendulums which got hopelessly out of whack at sea, or made of metals which expanded or contracted under different climatic conditions. The great physicist Isaac Newton, charged by the government to advise them on ways to calculate longitude, was deeply committed to the idea that this must come through astronomy and star positions. Though he agreed that in principle the clock solution worked, in practice it was dead in the water because by reason of the motion of the ship, the Variation of Heat and Cold, Wet and Dry, and the Difference of Gravity in different Latitudes, such a watch hath not yet been made.

And most probably never would be.

People experimented with all sorts of solutions, some of them very wild. Galileo himself had invented a type of mask, called a celatone, designed to calculate longitude by looking at Jupiter and using the timing of the eclipses of its moons. (A reconstruction of this machine is shown in the photo insert.) Another proposal involved wounded dogs and a mysterious substance called the "powder of sympathy." This powder allegedly had the capacity to heal at a distance if it was sprinkled on something belonging to a wounded person or animal. Critically, this healing involved pain. The idea was to keep a wounded dog on board, and at noon every day in London someone would apply the powder to a bandage that had been used on the dog. The dog would yelp, indicating that it was noontime in London. (Sounds completely nutty until you recall that Newton himself was an alchemist and spent much of his life trying to turn "base metals" into gold.) Another idea involved mooring large numbers of ships in open water with huge cannons being fired at appropriate times so that other ships within earshot could tell the time.

John Harrison, an uneducated carpenter from Barrow upon Humber in the North of England, finally came up with the breakthrough. Harrison successfully tackled all the problems that Newton outlined. He got rid of the pendulum. He eliminated the use of lubricants that expanded or contracted depending on the climate, relying instead on a tropical hardwood, lignum vitae, that emits its own grease. To solve the problem of expanding metals he put strips of brass and steel together so that the expansion of one was counteracted by the other. Harrison didn't get there right away. It took him a series of prototypes and thirty years to arrive at his so-called H-4 in 1761. Along the way he made many profound innovations, for example, using ball bearings for the first time, a technology still used for reducing rotational friction in most machines today. The obsessive search for a solution to longitude and all of the whacky ideas it engendered was was satirized by William Hogarth in a series of paintings called The Rake's Progress. The last in the series depicts the infamous mental asylum in London, Bedlam, filled with those driven mad by the search for a way to calculate longitude.

A consequence of all of this bustling experimentation was greater social mobility. As people from modest backgrounds succeeded in their efforts, they not only made money, but gained greater social recognition. Consider Richard Arkwright, who invented the water frame and set up arguably the world's first modern factory at Cromford, Derbyshire, in 1771. Arkwright was the youngest of seven children whose father was a tailor, poor enough that he was unable to send Richard to school. But Arkwright ended up with a knighthood, ascending to the heights of English society. Or take the case of James Watt, the inventor of the Watt steam engine, who came from a middle-class Scottish family. Within ten years of his death in 1819 James Watt had a statue of himself in Westminster Abbey (and there is also a memorial tablet there for John Harrison). The Abbey houses the tombs of many English kings and queens and famous people, such as William Wilberforce, the man who spearheaded the campaign to abolish the slave trade in the eighteenth and early nineteenth centuries. No cage of norms blocked experimentation or the ability of these men to succeed.

The Industrial Revolution started in Britain for the same reason that Italian communes started underpinning innovation and economic growth in the Middle Ages—the Shackled Leviathan blossomed in the corridor and this brought people greater liberty and economic opportunities. Powered by the Red Queen, the British state became more effective and built greater capacity during this process, but did not throw off its shackles. The expanding capacity of the shackled state then helped rather than hindered the progress of liberty. In this, Britain was ahead of other parts of Europe. But this chapter has also shown that many European societies were moving inside the corridor, albeit each with its own ups and downs and limitations. As the Leviathans of France, Belgium, the Netherlands, and Germany became more shackled and acquired greater capacity, the liberty, economic opportunities, and incentives of their populations also improved and industrialization spread to these areas.

Why in Europe?

The history of Europe is of course rich, complex, and variegated, something to which we cannot do justice in this chapter. Our focus, instead, has been on showing how our conceptual framework provides a different interpretation of this history and the origins of the distinctive set of institutions and political and social practices that emerged in Europe over the last 1,500 years.

Theories that see something distinctive in Europe long before the Middle Ages—its Judeo-Christian culture, its unique geography, its European values, whatever they were—making its subsequent political developments and economic ascendancy inevitable, are plentiful. Our account disagrees sharply with these theories.

There wasn't anything unique in early European history that preordained the rise of the Shackled Leviathan, other than the fortuitous balance of power created by the two blades of the European scissors—state institutions from the Roman Empire and participatory norms and institutions from Germanic tribes. Neither was sufficient by itself to bring forth the Shackled Leviathan. When only the former blade was present, as in Byzantium, a typical Despotic Leviathan emerged. When only the latter blade was present, as in Iceland, there was little political development and no state building. During another epoch with different circumstances, with different contingencies at critical points and perhaps with less skillful political actors than Clovis and Charlemagne attempting to fuse them, even the two blades together might have failed to balance each other in the same way. But during the tumultuous fifth and sixth centuries following the collapse of the Western Roman Empire, together they created a precarious balance, which placed Europe in the narrow corridor and enabled the rise of the Shackled Leviathan.

Placement in the corridor did not immediately create liberty. Violence, murder, and mayhem continued, sometimes very intensively, for more than a millennium. Nevertheless, this placement was the beginning of a process that limited despotism and very gradually led to the development of the preconditions of liberty. Being in the corridor is no guarantee for the rise of the Shackled Leviathan in all its glory either (as we'll see in Chapter 9 when discussing how large shocks can throw a society out of the corridor, and in Chapter 13 when witnessing how the race between state and society can get out of control). But the remarkable point, from the viewpoint of global history, was that a handful of polities did find themselves in the corridor and continued to evolve there, increasing the capacities of their states and societies with the full force of the Red Queen.

The implications of Europe entering the corridor and the Red Queen dynamics that this unleashed have been nothing short of spectacular. It was in Europe that liberty most clearly took the form that we recognize today (even if this was a long, painful, and at times patently violent process). It was also in Europe that this liberty, and the economic and social environment shaped by the Shackled Leviathan, produced broad-based economic opportunities and incentives, supported functioning markets, and created an environment in which experimentation, innovation, and technological breakthroughs could blossom and pave the way for the Industrial Revolution and sustained prosperity.

Our theory underscores that these lessons are applicable beyond Europe. If there was something uniquely European, something manifest in the rise of Europe, then we couldn't derive lessons based on the European experience for societies struggling with the same problems today. But not so with our theory. The Romans' centralized institutions and the norms and popular assemblies of Germanic tribes were of course unique to Europe in the fifth and sixth centuries. But the general principle here—that to move into the corridor a nation needs a balance between powerful, centralizing state institutions and an assertive, mobilized society able to hold its own against the state's power and shackle its political elites—is more broadly applicable. Indeed, we'll see in the rest of the book that the absence of institutions that simultaneously increase the state's capacity and uphold the liberty of its citizens is almost always related to the absence of such a balance of power between state and society. This balance is not a uniquely European affair either and has emerged under different circumstances and in different geographies and cultural milieus, as we saw already in the previous chapter and will see again later.

Chapter 7

MANDATE OF HEAVEN

Capsizing the Boat

Chinese history took a very different path from that of Europe and one that created far less liberty. But it didn't start out that way. To see this let's turn to an era in Chinese history known as the Spring and Autumn period, which began in the eighth century BCE. The Spring and Autumn period gave birth to Confucius, whose philosophy has been a mainstay of Chinese society and state institutions ever since. Confucianism placed great importance on the welfare of the people and argued that this was to be promoted by a virtuous ruler. As Confucius put it:

> One who rules through the power of virtue is analogous to the Pole Star: it simply remains in its place and receives the homage of the myriad lesser stars.

His most famous disciple, Mengzi (often called Mencius), stated, "The people are the most esteemed," and he reproduced an earlier document that argued that "Heaven sees through the people's seeing, Heaven hears through the people's hearing." Such views were common in this period. Confucius himself noted that "a state cannot stand once it has lost the confidence of the people."

Evidence that these ideas were relevant to the period's politics comes from the ancient chronicle of *Zuo Zhuan* (Commentary of Zuo). It quotes Ji Liang, who was employed by the state of Sui. He advised the emperor that "the people are masters of the deities. Therefore, sage kings accomplished the people's affairs first, and then attended to the deities."

Why were the people "masters of the deities" and "the most esteemed"? Most likely this was because society was sufficiently well organized to have some say in politics in this period. Indeed, during this era political power in China was so fragmented that scholars refer to the competing societies as "city states," even comparing them to the Greek city-states. In Athens politics turned around the capital city, and the citizens could make or break political careers and ambitions. The *Zuo Zhuan* documents at least twenty-five instances where the dwellers of capital cities actively influenced internal power struggles, including conflicts over who was to become lord. Just as in Athens, in the state of Zheng the people were meeting to discuss and critique the policies and behavior of the government. A famous prime minister from this era, Zichan, is reported saying:

> The people at morning and dusk retreat and meet together in order to debate the goodness or badness of the power-holder. If I implement whatever they consider good and correct whatever they consider bad— then they are my teachers.

He goes on to note that trying to exclude the people would be "like obstructing the river: when it overwhelms the dam, more people will be hurt." Mengzi agreed with the sentiment, writing:

> There is a way to attain the people: when you attain their hearts, you attain the people. There is a way to attain their hearts: gather them at what they desire, do not do whatever they detest, and that is all.

A later philosophical treatise known as the *Xunzi* summed up the politics of this period:

> The ruler is a boat; people are the water. The water can carry the boat; the water can sink the boat.

In the photo insert we reproduce a version of the original page of the *Xunzi* that includes this saying in Chinese characters.

All-Under-Heaven

The intellectual ferment of the Spring and Autumn period was followed by political consolidation and the emergence of seven large territorial states, and a few smaller ones, locked in incessant warfare (see Map 10). This Warring States period gave rise to a new and highly despotic political philosophy called legalism. This turned into a key pillar of the domination of the Chinese state over society. Shang Yang, also known as Lord Shang, was one of its most influential thinkers and practitioners. Born in 390 BCE, in the middle of the Warring States period, he was acutely aware of the chaos that state weakness could create. Like Hobbes, who almost two millennia later would come up with a similar solution, Lord Shang saw the way out in building up the power of a Leviathan, because "the greatest benefit to the people is order." If society were to be further weakened in the process, all the better, since Shang thought that

> when the people are weak, the state is strong; hence the state . . . strives
> to weaken the people.

He did not just think and write these thoughts, but proceeded to implement them. From his birthplace in the state of Wei, Shang Yang moved to Qin in order to become an adviser to its ruler, Lord Xiao. Under Xiao's auspices Shang Yang proposed a radical series of reforms, which formulated a new legal approach, restructured land relations, started the reform of the administrative structure of the state, and set up more professional state institutions. By the next century, the centralizing reforms had turned Qin into an economic and military powerhouse that went on to conquer all the other states and found the first Chinese empire and recognized dynasty.

That this was already Shang Yang's aim from his early days is evident from the first chapter of *The Book of Lord Shang*, the record of his ideas that has come down to us. The chapter titled "Revising the Laws" sets out a debate between Lord Xiao and three advisers, including Shang Yang. The lord was worried that institutional innovations would lead to the criticism of "All-Under-Heaven." Xiao wasn't just concerned about the opinion of the people in Qin, but All-Under-Heaven, meaning the whole world. The Lord of Qin thought this way because he had appropriated an earlier concept from the previous state of Zhou, whose rulers had developed the notion that they had been given a mandate to rule from Heaven.

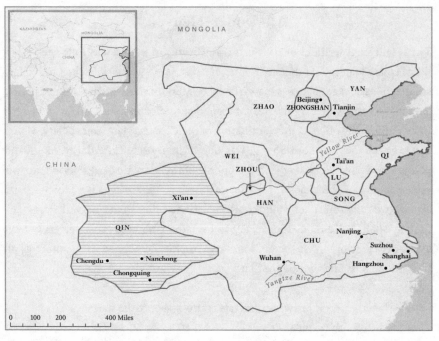

Map 10. China in the Warring States Period, 475–221 BCE

From that point on, emperors of China would claim that they too had received the "Mandate of Heaven." But how can society constrain a ruler whose mandate comes directly from the heavens?

Shang Yang didn't think that such constraints were desirable. His aims were simple: "a rich state and a strong army." Only such a powerful state could bring order and make sure that society did not get any ideas about participating in politics. Without this type of order, discord would result, and that had to be prevented. The *Xunzi* argues in strikingly Hobbesian language:

> Humans are born having desires. When they have desires but do not get the objects of their desires, then they cannot but seek some means of satisfaction. If there is no measure or limit to their seeking, then they cannot help but struggle with each other. If they struggle with each other then there will be chaos, and if there is chaos then they will be impoverished.

It was natural to search for order and the institutions that could achieve it. But how was Qin to do it? The main tool would be the law—but not in the way that law came to develop from society's norms and constrain rulers in the European context as we saw in the previous chapter. In Shang Yang's vision, law and state power had to be used to turn everyone into either farmers or warriors. They would be rewarded for farming or fighting, and punished otherwise.

> The people can be induced to till and fight . . . it all depends on how superiors grant them [ranks and emoluments] . . . Those who do not work but eat, who do not fight but attain glory, who have no rank but are respected, who have no emoluments but are rich, who have no office but lead—these are called "villains."

In other words, the state and only the state gets to decide who and what is valued. Without the recognition of the state you are a villain. The people had to be controlled "as the metalworker controls metal and the potter clay." To ensure that people focused on farming, it was critical to not "let the people shift locations on their own initiative," and to penalize any other sort of economic activity. One way to accomplish this was to structure—or in fact distort—markets to make farming very attractive. Shang Yang proposed:

> If you can cause merchants and peddlers and crafty and tricky people not to prosper, then even if you do not want to enrich the state, you will not but attain that. Hence, it is said: "He who wants the farmers to enrich the state makes food within the borders expensive. He must impose multiple taxes on those who do not farm and heavy levies on profits from the markets."

Those who did not farm were "crafty and tricky people." It was a sentiment that would have profound consequences for China's economic future as legalist thought came to shape both how the state approached business, and how merchants, industrialists, and peasants came to fear the state and withhold their cooperation from it.

In the legalist model, order was the priority and it was to be achieved by an all-powerful ruler crushing society with the weight of the state and its law. Even if the Confucian model disagreed with the heavy-handed approach of legalism and recommended moral precepts and earning "the people's trust," there was agreement between the two approaches on the basic tenet of despotism—that common people would have no say in politics and would certainly not become a counterweight against the power of the state and the emperor. It was only the moral behavior of the ruler that would make him take into account his subjects' well-being. As Confucius put it:

> Commoners do not debate matters of government.

The Rise and Fall, and Rise Again, of the Well-Field System

Shang Yang's achievement was proposing a model of despotic state building that allowed the Qin to overwhelm the other six warring states over the next hundred years, bring an end to that chaotic epoch, and set up the Qin Empire. The details of how the state should be organized changed over the subsequent centuries as successive dynasties experimented with different versions. The reason for this was that while Shang Yang's model was good at eliminating competitors, it didn't provide an effective template for how to govern the new unified territories.

The version that the first Qin emperor, Qin Shi Huang, and his main adviser, Li Si, came up with involved very tight control. The empire was divided into thirty-six, and subsequently forty-two, commanderies, each headed by a governor, a military commander, and a superintendent. Beneath these appointees was an elaborate hierarchy of officials that exercised a suffocating grip over society, just as Shang Yang would have advocated.

The nature of this control is illustrated by administrative documents published by the historian Enno Giele. These show how an overseer of a sub-county unit wrote to the head of the county to approve the appointment of a new village chief and postman in a local hamlet. Four days after the request was filed, he got a negative response. The request was refused because the hamlet had only twenty-seven households and was deemed too small to have such officials. These documents reveal the intricate web of centrally appointed officials and the efficiency with which they dealt with requests, not to mention the extent of their knowledge (the precise twenty-seven households).

The Qin state also imposed a uniform system of weights and measurements, a unified coinage, and a calendar, and it standardized the script in which Chinese would be written. It also constructed an elaborate system of roads emanating from the capital, Xianyang. One of the most important and durable innovations was the "well-field system," named after the Chinese character for a water well, a visual representation of nine equally sized plots of land required for the provisioning of a soldier-warrior. The well-field system emphasized the equal distribution of land along with the fiscal and military burden. It first appears in the writings of Mencius, who argued that

> benevolent government must begin with surveying and allocating lands. When boundaries are not drawn properly, neither the division of land according to the well-field system nor the levy of grain reserved for the ruler's emoluments will be equitable.

At this point a drawback of the Shang Yang model became evident. To support such an intrusive system it was not enough to have a "rich state," it was also necessary to have a heavily taxed society. After all, someone had to provide the resources and the labor commissioned to build the 8,000 life-size terra-cotta warriors that Qin Shi Huang had commissioned for his mausoleum. One consequence of heavy taxation was an upsurge of popular revolts that, shortly after the death of Qin Shi Huang, led to the overthrow of the Qin dynasty after a mere fifteen years of existence and only two emperors. The ultimate winner in the political instability that ensued was a peasant from the conquered state of Chu, Liu Bang, who founded the new Han dynasty under the title of Emperor Gaozu. Gaozu suspended the collection of taxes, eventually reducing them to one-fifteenth of the agricultural crop. He also reduced the extent of compulsory labor services that the Qin state had imposed.

The adjustments made by Gaozu were attempts to move in a more Confucian direction. He built on the legalist precepts and combined them with the ideas of Confucianism. Subsequent Chinese governments and laws, right up to the present, can be interpreted as a fusion of and oscillation between these two philosophies, each falling somewhere between Shang Yang and Confucius. Wherever they happened to be on the spectrum, they agreed on some basic principles. The most critical was the core tenet of the Despotic Leviathan—that of monarchical rule with an omnipotent emperor, providing the people with no role or say in government. The emperor was always above the law. Then came the idea that the state should be staffed and run by people of talent, which was necessary for the emperor to rule society in the way he wished. It also had roots in Confucian philosophy, which maintains that "one who excels in learning should devote himself to official service" and one should "promote those who are worthy and talented." The final key principle was that the emperor should be concerned with the welfare of the people and constrained by moral precepts. This even included the idea that the emperor should promote citizens' economic prosperity or, using a term from later dynasties, that he should "store wealth among the people." These three principles amounted to a sort of social contract that gave the state some legitimacy. If they were violated, then people could rebel.

It took some time for the Chinese emperors to come up with a working institutional model that would satisfy these three principles. The turning point came with the realization that it was difficult to micromanage society in the way that Shang Yang or the Qin emperors envisaged. It was just too expensive. To fund it you had to levy heavy taxes, either in kind or with money or labor services, and that was inconsistent with the last principle. Without any way of allowing people to have a say in the government and how taxes were spent, high rates of taxation caused discontent and ultimately helped foment rebellion. As we'll see, rebellion didn't go away, but subsequent emperors decided to mitigate rebellion and discontent by reducing taxes, even though this also meant less state capacity to provide public services and even stable law enforcement.

Organizing authority to satisfy these three principles was tricky and it never worked perfectly. In fact, there was a constant struggle between the Shang Yang model of micromanagement and coercion, and the more relaxed Confucian strategy of greater withdrawal from society and a reliance on setting an example of good governance. The Han, though they reduced taxes and labor dues, initially kept much of the Qin vision. The Qin had asserted direct control over the most productive assets, which included mines, forests, and even manufacturing processes such as foundries and workshops. So did the Han. However, with fewer tax revenues they were forced to temper their control of society and gradually retreated from the implementation of the Qin model.

Over time the well-field system went into reverse and large landowners appeared in the countryside. But in the absence of any constraints on the power of the omnipotent ruler, these movements could always be reversed. Over the next 2,000 years China was periodically rocked by various attempts to reassert the model of Shang Yang, the most recent being the rise to power of the Communists after 1949 who implemented their own version of the well-field system in the form of collectivized agriculture. The contemporary incarnation of the Confucian model is what we have seen since 1978 under Deng Xiaoping when collectivization went into reverse and Chinese leaders started attacking corruption, since this violated Confucian principles of virtuous rule. To know what's likely to happen in the future in China, it is important to understand this historical oscillation between legalism and Confucianism.

The first attempt to reintroduce strict state control over the economy after the demise of the Qin came from the Han emperor Wu, who ruled for fifty-four years, between 141 and 87 BCE. Wu started a royal monopoly on the production of iron and salt, and asserted control over most industries and commercial activities. The contemporary historian Sima Qian observed that "the wealth of the whole world was exhausted to serve the ruler, and yet he was not satisfied." Wu's reforms did not last.

The next person who tried the same thing was Wang Mang, who became regent to a Han child emperor in 1 BCE and declared himself emperor five years later when the child died. Wang launched a concerted attempt to reassert control over the economy and society which had been gradually slipping away. He decreed that all land belonged to the state, confiscated the estates of many large landowners, and created more state monopolies. In 23 CE a popular insurrection against his policies broke out, culminating in the capture of the imperial palace and Wang's death. Thereafter the well-field model went into reverse once again, and by 30 CE universal military service had been abolished, so society was no longer based on the farmer-solider complex.

The Han dynasty ended in 220, to be replaced by a series of short-lived regimes. In the north these were dominated by nomadic tribesmen from inner Asia, while in the south various offshoots of Han power sprang up. Prior to the reunification of China under the Sui dynasty in 581, there were again attempts to reassert the Shang Yang model, including during the Northern Wei dynasty that lasted from 386 to 524 in northern China. In 485 the Wei came up with their "equal-field system," which was maintained after 581 by the Sui and then by the Tang dynasty when they took over in 618. What sealed the fate of this new version of the well-field system was the An Lushan rebellion, which broke out against the Tang in 755. Though it was finally suppressed in 763 after it sacked the capital, Chang'an, the rebellion cost the lives of hundreds of thousands of people and devastated the Tang state. With the state's ability to control society in tatters, the equal-field system collapsed and private ownership of land became the norm.

In 960 a new dynasty, the Song, replaced the Tang and initiated another restructuring similar to the initial Qin-Han transition. Though there were major continuities, the mode of governance shifted from legalism toward Confucianism. One fruit of this restructuring was the more definitive consolidation of bureaucratic control, with the examination system for entry into the civil service replacing the prior recruitment system based primarily on recommendations. (Another fruit was economic growth, as we'll discuss a little later.) Meritocracy in the civil service, however, was later systematically undermined both by the selling of offices, which took off in the seventeenth century as the state's fiscal resources declined, and by continual government meddling.

In 1127 the northern part of Song China was conquered by the Jurchen people from inner Asia, who formed a new dynasty, the Jin. The Song moved their capital south in response, but then both the Jin and the rump Song Empire were conquered by the Mongols, led by Qubilai Khan, who set up the Yuan dynasty. After Qubilai died in 1294, there were another ten emperors before the Yuan dynasty also collapsed in the midst of mass revolts in the 1350s. In the meantime they had reconfigured the previous organization of the Chinese state, imposing a personalized model based on the hierarchy of their Mongol tribes and organizing the Chinese into hereditary occupational castes. Labor service was introduced as were a plethora of new taxes. Artisans were carted off en masse to the Mongol capital, Dadu, now Beijing, to meet the demand for goods and labor.

The Yuan were overthrown by Zhu Yuanzhang, who founded the Ming dynasty in 1368 after two decades of civil war. Taking the title Emperor Hongwu, he set off the Ming on the Shang Yang end of the spectrum. Hongwu quickly moved to concentrate more power in his hands, for example by abolishing the position of prime minister, which had until then acted as the voice for the civil service. In 1373 he abolished the examination system because he disliked the results, and he heavily and violently purged the civil service several times. Hongwu then attempted to return China to a new version of the well-field system. During his thirty-year reign, Hongwu strove to reverse the marketization of the economy and even went back to collecting taxes in kind rather than in money. In 1374 he banned overseas trade with an edict known as the "sea ban," a prohibition that would last until close to the end of the sixteenth century (only to be reimposed periodically thereafter).

Starting in 1380, Hongwu initiated a massive expropriation of land from large landowners and by the end of his reign perhaps half of the land in the core province of Jiangnan, around the Yangtze delta where his capital, Nanjing, was, had been seized by the state. Despotic state power remained palpable throughout the Ming dynasty. In the 1620s Confucian-inspired criticism of the state emerged with the founding of the Donglin faction around the Donglin Academy in Wuxi County, about 50 miles west of Shanghai. This group even had the effrontery to compose a memorial they called the "Twenty-Four Crimes" (of the state). The response of the Tianqi emperor was to execute twelve of the leaders, while a thirteenth committed suicide. Hundreds more accused of being sympathizers were purged. Their supporters persisted along with other groups inspired by them, such as the Restoration Society (Fushe), only to be ruthlessly repressed by the Qing in the 1660s. Criticism was not allowed.

The Song-Ming transition, taking China back toward legalism, reminds us that an unbridled state doesn't spell liberty for the citizens. On the contrary, it is typically the basis of dominance in the hands of the state, which is what Lord Shang recommended and the Ming quite happily followed.

Cutting the Queue

The intensifying despotism of the Ming state led to a series of uprisings, such as the Red Turban rebellion in the 1620s, underscoring one of the key drawbacks of the legalist model. The dynasty was finally swept away by internal dissent and the opportunism of another expansionary inner Asian people, the Manchus, who formed the Qing dynasty. A firsthand account of the expansion of Manchu power comes from a local history of T'an-ch'eng County, situated close to the coast roughly halfway between Beijing and Shanghai:

> It was on 30 January 1643 that the great army invaded the city, slaughtered the officials, and killed 70 or 80 per cent of the gentry, clerks and common people; inside the city walls and out they killed tens of thousands, in the streets and the courtyards and alleys the people all herded together were massacred or wounded, the remnants trampled each other down, and of those fleeing the majority were injured. Until 21 February 1643 the great army pitched its camps in our county borders . . . They stayed for twenty-two days; over the whole area many were looted and burned, killed and wounded. They also destroyed Ts'ang-shan-pao, killing more than ten thousand men and women there.

By 1644 the Manchus, even if they didn't seem intent on "winning hearts and minds," had taken Beijing and established what would be the last Chinese dynasty. Before they could get there, a bandit leader, Li Zicheng, created another dynasty that lasted six weeks. His improvised regime graded elites, eunuchs, merchants, great landlords, and high officials by income levels and took some 20 to 30 percent of their wealth. Li himself accumulated a fortune of 70 million taels of silver. He even started to talk about the equal-field system, before he was ejected from the throne by a Manchu army.

The Manchus, like the Mongols, were outsiders and had to bring the indigenous Chinese under control. One interesting strategy was the "tonsure decree" which stipulated that all men had to adopt the hairstyle of the Manchus with shaved forehead and a pigtail. The Qing decided that this was a way to force all Chinese to conform to the new dynasty. In March 1647, three years after the Manchus had first occupied Beijing, Chang Shang, the governor of Kansu Province, was on an inspection tour. By March 4 he had reached Yung-ch'ang, a county lying just within the Great Wall. Assembled to greet him was the entire student body of the county school. He noted, "I espied one man who seemed to have retained the hair on the front of his head. After I reached the county yamen [the residence of the local magistrate], I summoned all of the students for academic examination" and "I personally went over to the man in question and removed his cap. Indeed, his hair was totally unshaven." Local officials assured Chang that posters reporting the tonsure decree had been posted and that the culprit, Lü K'o-hsing, had no excuse. Chang had Lü thrown into jail and wrote to the emperor requesting that he be immediately executed "to uphold the laws of the ruling dynasty." The reply quickly came, "Let him be executed on the spot. But what about the local officials, the household head, the local headman, and the neighbors?" The outcome was that Lü's unshaven head was cut from his body and displayed in public to "warn the masses." The patriarch of Lü's household, along with the local headman and neighbors, were all beaten and the county magistrate was fined three months wages.

The Qing dynasty's anxiety about hairstyles persisted throughout their reign. In 1768 a mass scare of "soul stealing" gripped the empire. There was a rash of cutting men's queues, supposedly to steal their souls. A captured soul would allow one to exert power over others. The Chinese government, under the Qianlong emperor, reacted vigorously to accusations of queue cutting. One technique they regularly used to get to the bottom of a case was the *chia-kun*, or "pressing beam," which was applied to extract a confession. This could either be an "ankle-press," a device for slowly crushing the ankles, or an alternate instrument that created multiple fractures of the shinbones.

One accused of soulstealing in 1769 was a monk, Hai-yin. When arrested he was found to be carrying some short lengths of hair, which he claimed he had obtained years before, and indeed he was carrying them on a pole in full sight. He was interrogated and the local authorities decided that torture was required to get to the truth. But the monk was resilient, and after a few days, the local authorities remarked, "If we torture him more just now, he might die, and then we would be unable to uncover anything." "Right," the Qianlong emperor jotted in the vermilion-colored ink he used when annotating official documents. Hai-yin resisted further and the emperor was informed that unfortunately the prisoner "had contracted a prevalent illness of the season" and was also suffering from infected torture wounds. In fact, the situation got so frustrating that the local magistrate decided that it would be "better to publicly execute him in order to dispel the suspicions of the crowd," since rumors had started to fly around after Hai-yin's arrest. Therefore the authorities "had the criminal taken to the public square and beheaded and the head exposed to show the crowd." Another monk, Ming-yuan, was similarly accused. Within a week of being arrested he was dead. "Noted," the Qianlong emperor added in vermilion. So it wasn't just the Franks who were obsessed with hair, even if the Qing showed their obsession in quite a different manner.

Enforcement of the tonsure decree wasn't the only way the Qing signaled to their newly conquered people that they meant business. In May 1645 elites in the Yangtze delta rebelled against the new state and Qing generals massacred about 200,000 men, women, and children. An eyewitness account, *A Record of Ten Days in Yangzhou* by Wang Xiuchu, makes for harrowing reading. After Qing forces had destroyed the city of Yangzhou, the survivors were sent on a forced march:

> Some women came up . . . they were partially naked, and they stood in mud so deep that it reached their calves. One was embracing a girl, whom a soldier lashed and threw into the mud before driving her away. One soldier hoisted a sword and led the way, another leveled his spear and drove us from behind, and a third moved back and forth in the middle to make sure no one got away. Several dozen people were herded together like cattle or goats. Any who lagged behind were flogged or killed outright. The women were bound together at their necks with a heavy rope—strung one to another like pearls. Stumbling with each step, they were covered with mud. Babies lay everywhere on the ground. The organs of those trampled like turf under horses' hooves or people's feet were smeared in the dirt, and the crying of those still alive filled the whole outdoors. Every gutter or pond that we passed was stacked with corpses, pillowing each other's arms and legs. Their blood had flowed into the water, and the combination of the green and red was producing a spectrum of colors. The canals, too, had been filled to level with dead bodies.

Despotism on the Cheap

Being outsiders, the Qing felt their reign was more precarious than their predecessors', and were concerned that taxation would incite opposition against their rule. This was, as we have seen, a familiar theme going back to the founding of the Han dynasty. One scare was the Ma Ch'ao-chu conspiracy of 1752. Ma was a peasant from Hupei who fell under the influence of a monk who convinced him that he had a grand destiny. Ma began to assert connections with the remains of the Ming regime that now inhabited the "Kingdom of the Western Sea" and was ruled by a Ming "Young Lord." The kingdom supposedly contained 36,000 armed warriors as well as the Ming general Wu San-kuei. Ma gathered followers, claiming that he was a general in this kingdom and that magic flying machines would bring the kingdom's army to attack the Yangtze valley at any moment. As Ma's movement gained momentum, officials fortuitously discovered newly forged swords at what turned out to be one of his camps. Ma fled, but some of his relatives were captured. A manhunt was launched which led to the arrest of hundreds of suspects and went on for years even though Ma was never found. Captured disciples related how, upon joining the group and entering one of Ma's bases, people "smeared their mouths with blood and swallowed paper charms. Also they let their hair grow long and didn't shave their foreheads," a clear anti-Qing gesture. Those arrested were "tortured with extreme severity" and their lives were only spared if they confessed. The Qianlong emperor noted in vermilion, "A single spark can start a prairie-fire."

The Qing state was always anxious about rebellion (and for good reason), though this did not mean that they refrained from arbitrary actions. These included the reimposition of the Ming sea ban and Emperor Kangxi's forceful removal in 1661 of essentially all people who lived along the entire southern coast of China to ten miles inland to control trade and piracy.

To deal with the threat of rebellion, the Qing decided in 1713 to take a step toward the Confucian end of the legalist-Confucian axis and freeze the major source of income for the state, land taxes, in nominal terms. From then on everyone paid a fixed sum of money per *mou* (conventionally taken to be approximately 0.15 acres). Since prices rose substantially during the century, the real value of tax revenues available to the state fell dramatically. There wouldn't be much public service provision under the Qing.

Indeed, the few public services that the state provided, such as the granary system of famine relief and large infrastructure projects such as the Grand Canal, withered away. The state could no longer afford to buy the grain needed to stock the granaries, and by 1840 the Canal had fallen into disrepair and was impassable. Between 1824 and 1826 the whole system for controlling the waters of the Yellow River collapsed as a consequence of the lack of maintenance of the locks and dikes, and the absence of dredging necessary to stop silting. Devastating floods followed.

It's worth understanding how the Chinese state was organized at this time, and why it was unable to support commercial and industrial activities or supply many public services. At the top were six ministries or boards—personnel, revenue, rites, war, works, and punishment. The terminology was long-lasting and interesting; not justice, but *hsing pu*, translated as "punishment." In fact, the oldest known legal codes inscribed on bronze vessels were called not law books or legal codes, but "Books of Punishment," very much consistent with how Shang Yang thought about the law. The Tang code of 653 is the oldest surviving complete legal code that we have (only fragments of the Qin code remain). It was modified significantly over the years, and the Qing produced their definitive version in 1740. These codes reaffirm that Chinese laws weren't there to provide justice and certainly not to support liberty, but to administer and regulate society. They were not interested in defendants' rights against the state. Any law could be modified or nullified by the emperor, who was above the law. The treatment of defendants in judicial procedures suggests that the defendant was guilty until proven innocent. Just in case they had forgotten something, statute 386 of the Qing penal code allowed for a severe beating to be administered to someone "doing what ought not to be done."

As we have seen, one of the great claims to fame of the Chinese state was that they chose civil servants through a system of competitive examinations. The aspiration for meritocracy was present even in the days of the Qin, though it only became more systematic with the Song and perhaps reached its zenith with the Qing. There were three layers to the exam. At the lowest level people could attempt to qualify as licentiates. By 1700, some 500,000 people had qualified at this lowest level. Twice every three years several thousands of them were certified to gather in their provincial capital for a test that took three days and two nights. About 95 percent failed. The stakes were very high.

Passing the provincial exam guaranteed permanent elite status and important tax and legal exemptions. Members of officialdom could not be arrested, investigated, or tortured without permission of the emperor, and if found guilty, the usual punishments inflicted on commoners, such as bambooing, exile, or death, were commutable to monetary fines. There was the chance to get an official position as well. There was still one more rung to go, however. In the year after the provincial examination, those who had passed gathered in Beijing for the metropolitan exam. There were only 300 slots to be filled, and 90 percent of the candidates failed. These 300 winners were then personally graded by the emperor with the highest chosen for work in the central ministries and the lowest assigned as subnational officials, such as the magistrates. In the Qing period there were about 1,300 counties, grouped into 180 prefectures, which were in turn combined into eighteen provinces, each with a governor. Each county had a magistrate, the executive arm of the Qing state in the county. Because the population of the empire by the end of the seventeenth century was around 300 million, this meant that on average a magistrate was in charge of around 230,000 people. Large counties could easily have one million people in them. Each magistrate had a staff working for him, but these were not state employees; either the magistrate had to pay them himself out of his own stipend or they had to live off what scholars of China translate into English as "squeeze," what they could extract from ordinary people. When it came to his judicial functions, the magistrate was the detective, prosecutor, judge, and jury all rolled into one. In addition, he was in charge of public works, defense, and policing.

What did these very difficult civil service exams ask? In 1669 the examiners of Shantung asked the aspirants of T'an-ch'eng County to ponder and explain three passages of text. From the *Analects* of Confucius there was, "They who know the truth," and then, "The Master said, 'Man is born for uprightness. If a man lose his uprightness, and yet lives, his escape from death is the effect of mere good fortune.' The Master said 'They who know the truth are not equal to those who love it, and they who love it are not equal to those who delight in it.'" They also had to reflect on the man of sincerity: "Shall this individual have any being or anything beyond himself, on which he depends? Call him man in his ideal, how earnest he is! Call him an abyss, how deep he is! Call him Heaven how vast is he!" There was also a passage from Mencius. All the students failed. In fact not one student from T'an-ch'eng passed the exam between 1646 and 1708.

Though the examination system was competitive, it did not test or encourage any technical knowledge or for that matter any skills that would be relevant for running a bureaucracy or governing the country. Magistrates were supposed to enforce the law without any legal training, and there were no private lawyers or law practitioners. Many nonmeritocratic elements had also crept into the system. As many as one-third of magistrates were appointed at the recommendation of governors. Perhaps most important, the whole system was immensely personalized in the hands of the emperor, who could appoint, promote, and demote people at will. As the Qianlong emperor put it himself, "The evaluation and selection [of high officials] will be daily borne in Our breast."

In response to the lack of tax revenues, starting in the 1680s with the Kangxi emperor, the Qing began selling examination certificates en masse, in effect auctioning off membership to the elite. By 1800 there were an estimated 350,000 holders of purchased degrees. Since the Qing state was unable to pay people properly, there developed an orgy of corruption that reached its peak in the late eighteenth century during the "reign" of Heshen.

Born around 1750, Heshen was a mere palace guard who in 1775 caught the eye of the Qianlong emperor. Supposedly, the emperor saw in him a concubine with whom he had been in love in his youth. He quickly heaped twenty bureaucratic appointments on Heshen, including presidency of the Board of Revenue. Heshen soon built up a massive network of corruption, bringing in appointees who were dependent on his favors. He also developed a veto power over all appointments within the state. He demanded kickbacks for every position and favored people whom he considered loyal to him. In the course of his twenty-year rule over the Chinese civil service, he seems to have systematically undermined the functioning of the Qing state at all levels. As soon as the Qianlong emperor died, his son, the Jiaqing emperor, had Heshen arrested and forced him to commit suicide. He was presented with a list of twenty crimes, including riding a horse and going by sedan chair in the Forbidden City. Most damning, though, was his accumulation of assets and possessions. These included, among others, "Twenty original pavilions and kiosks; Sixteen newly added pavilions; One main residence with thirteen sections and 730 rooms; One eastern residential wing with seven sections and 360 rooms; One western residential wing with seven sections and 360 rooms; One Huizhou-style new residence with seven sections and 620 rooms; One counting house with 730 rooms; One garden with sixty-four pavilions and kiosks; [About 120,000 acres] of farmland." In addition to all this property Heshen was found to have 58,000 ounces of pure gold, 54,600 silver ingots, one and a half million strings of copper cash, huge amounts of jade, ginseng, pearls, and rubies, 380 silver teaspoons, and 108 silver mouthwashing bowls. Heshen became a symbol of the rapid decline of the Qing state. Significantly, however, though Heshen was eliminated, the Jiaqing emperor did not implement a broader purge of the civil service. Nor were there serious reforms to the institution of the Censorate, which was supposed to investigate magistrates and lower-level civil servants. By Qing times it was present only in Beijing and hardly able to police such a huge empire. The lack of state capacity and public services continued.

The discontent bred by the corruption and ineffectiveness of the civil service, and the arbitrary nature of Qing rule, having no other forum for expression, again fed into rebellion. Between 1796 and 1804 the White Lotus sect started a massive uprising, probably organized in response to arbitrary extortion instigated by He-shen's collaborators in the state. In 1850 the empire was rocked by the Taiping Rebellion, possibly started by disgruntled examination holders who were unable to find official positions due to all the corrupt practices. It devastated the country for fourteen years, caused the deaths of millions of people, and bankrupted the state.

A Dependent Society

The defining feature of despotism is its ability to deny a society the means of participating in political decision making. This is exactly what happened in China where any element of popular participation in government was snuffed out by the rise of the Qin state. It never reappeared. Could it be that society had other ways of controlling and shaping the Chinese Leviathan? Rebellion was certainly a live option, one that created a great deal of anxiety for Chinese emperors. Nevertheless, the threat of rebellion was not a constant presence and did not translate into a systematic influence on political decision-making. What about autonomous societal organizations (what is sometimes referred to as "civil society"), capable of articulating demands and making suggestions to the Chinese state? Was there such societal organization in China, even if the popular assemblies and other institutionalized means of societal control over government were absent?

One place where we might expect to see such societal organization and mobilization is the commercial city of Hankou on the Yangtze River, now part of Wuhan. In the late eighteenth and nineteenth centuries, Hankou was a bustling metropolis, active with merchants and artisans. Guilds and other voluntary associations started springing up in the city. The most powerful business interests were the two hundred or so salt merchants who chose their own "head merchant." A charge on salt transactions was put into the "coffer funds" and used for famine relief and militia costs for the protection of the businesses. There were also associations for other merchant groups. This might be viewed as the beginning of an autonomous societal organization.

But appearances can be deceptive. There was little autonomy and little local solidarity in this society. The merchant groups all had their roots in "native-place associations" that came from different parts of China; the salt merchants were from Huizhou, while the tea merchants came from Canton and Ningpo, and they didn't even live in Hankou for most of the year. The tea guild was a branch of the one set up in Shanghai. These associations consisted of groups of families from specific regions or towns, who banded together to share capital or information, and often lived together in separate neighborhoods. Different groups of merchants did not cooperate with each other and had little interest in investing in public services and organizations in Hankou. In fact, a clear sign of a lack of local solidarity was that merchants from different parts of China, rather than working together, engaged in incessant conflict. In 1888 Anhui and Hunan guildsmen got into a conflict over a pier, and when the local magistrate ruled in favor of the former, the latter attacked the Anhui merchants. The annual dragon boat races became so violent, with Cantonese fighting people from Hubei, that they had to be banned. So the nature of mercantile activity in China made it difficult for local society to organize or develop its own identity.

More significant than the local squabbling was the nature of the most important business in the city, salt. This wasn't the sort of endeavor wherein aspiring entrepreneurs competed to expand their business. Salt was a state monopoly, and the power and wealth of the salt merchants was a consequence of the state's grant. The head merchant was typically a rising member of the imperial bureaucracy who had passed the lower levels of the civil service examinations and owed his position to official appointment. This made salt merchants quasi-governmental officials, and their warehouses and salt markets were considered part of the public domain. Even the coffer funds were not under the collective control of the salt merchants, nor were they typically used for providing public services for the city or the merchants. Rather, they were controlled by the head merchant and often used for hiring friends and relatives in the salt administration.

In the nineteenth century, we see the proliferation of new types of business bureaus, including the Official Ferry Bureau, the Telegraph Bureau, and the Lijin Bureau (which was in charge of new taxes). Yet appointments at these bureaus were vetted by provincial officials. Notable in its absence is any description of the activities of bureaus, guilds, or organized merchants trying to influence local officials or the functioning of the state. No doubt this went on behind the scenes, but it was not tolerated publicly, which meant that it did not emerge as a vehicle for popular participation in policy making. After 1863 the salt monopoly was reorganized and about six hundred merchants were allowed to buy tickets to trade in salt. Thereafter, official control of trade became even more intense. Other guilds were active in maintaining streets, opening fire lanes, and building bridges, but these actions were initiated by the state. In 1898 when a Hankou chamber of commerce was set up, it was in response to an imperial edict. None of this looks like Swallowfield, in the previous chapter, where it was the local community that instigated its own organization, initiated new public services, and made demands for more and better governance from the state.

In Europe, at least since the seventeenth century, free media played a critical role in the organization of an active, assertive society. This had no parallel in China either. There seems to have been no widely available newspaper in Hankou until the *Shenbao* in the 1870s. But the *Shenbao* was published in Shanghai by an Englishman, Ernest Major, and though it did carry news about Hankou, it seems unlikely to have provided a tool for a more mobilized society.

So on closer examination, even where we would expect the most autonomous, assertive society to emerge, we see something quite different—a society subservient to and dependent on the state.

Dependent or not, perhaps Chinese society benefited from the state's powerful control as this relaxed the cage of norms and created greater room for social and economic freedoms. We have seen that other state-building efforts, such as those of Mohammed and Shaka in Chapter 4, break stifling norms and disrupt kin-based alliances that stand in their way, loosening the cage of norms a little in the process. But in the Chinese context, kin groups appear to play a major role despite the state's despotism. For example, native place associations were based on lineages. This and other kin relations were in fact encouraged and supported by the state as part of its strategy of managing society.

To see the importance of lineage in China, consider the New Territories, the part of mainland China inland from Hong Kong island. In 1955 this region was still governed by the British, and the commissioner sent out a questionnaire seeking to determine when particular surnames settled in a village and the number of generations since settlement. In the Ping Shan area thirty-four villages were surveyed. Among these, twenty-seven consisted of people who all had the same surname. Of these, one could cite a genealogy stretching back 29 generations, another 28 generations, eight of 27, one of 26, one of 25, two of 23, two of 22, one each of 16, 15, and 14, and so on. But that's not the most amazing thing. Of the eight villages that could cite their ancestry back 27 generations, seven of them had the surname Tang.

Now, it could be that Tangs just like hanging out with other Tangs (even though neither of us has friends called Robinson or Acemoglu or lives anywhere near any of our relatives). But that's not the primary reason for this homogeneity. It comes about because the Tangs owned lineage land collectively and have ancestral halls and temples where they honor the Tang ancestors through rituals and ceremonies. In one county in Guangdong Province, close to the New Territories, lineage groups owned 60 percent of total land before the Communist revolution. In another Guangdong county the proportion was 30 percent. Lineages were not therefore just a group of individuals, they were organized corporatively, and these institutions, their halls and lands, have a deep history in China. Lineages imposed their own rules and tight norms. They dealt with disputes and disagreements. They were in turn fostered and encouraged by the Chinese state because they were deemed to be useful for controlling society and managing disputes, especially given how thin on the ground magistrates were and their limited ability to govern society, resolve conflicts, or provide basic services. From the Song state onward, the Chinese state came up with the idea of delegating these tasks to lineage groups. As early as 1064, the Song passed an edict encouraging the creation of charitable estates, which were the basis of lineage land. Lineages then took on many functions. If you got into a dispute, you were far more likely to encounter the lineage elder than the county magistrate. These elders often didn't arise spontaneously, however; the state legislated them into existence. An order of 1726 stipulated:

> In villages and walled rural communities with lineages with more than one hundred or more, members dwell together . . . A *tsu-cheng* [lineage head] is established in each lineage.

The lineages were thus integrated into the local state. The Ming built on the Song initiatives, which encouraged the construction of ancestral halls and the institutionalization of the family structures. In exchange for providing state-like services, lineages got rights and perquisites, like the opportunity to take part in the salt monopoly. The Tangs were "masters of the market" with the monopoly right to hold a market in their area, and only they had the right to build shops in the vicinity of a market. They also had their own militia.

A Reversal of Chinese Fortune

The history of state despotism we have sketched had clear implications not just for liberty, but also for the Chinese economy. Compared to the Warring States period, the emergence of a centralized state with its ability to maintain order, impose laws, raise taxes, and invest in infrastructure likely had major positive effects on economic activity, securing an era of despotic growth. But the limitations of such growth are obvious. As we have seen, starting with the well-field model of agriculture, there were periodic attempts to closely regulate and control society, whereupon the despotic power of the state erased economic opportunities and incentives for most Chinese. The resulting economic hardships and discontent then triggered movements away from Lord Shang's vision of a tightly controlled economy toward a Confucian approach with a more relaxed grip and lower taxes. Though these relaxations improved private incentives to some degree, they created a state bereft of tax revenues and the capacity to provide law and order or public services necessary for greater private investments. As these different approaches to the economy came and went, Chinese economic fortunes ebbed and flowed. But they never went beyond despotic growth. There was no liberty, no broad-based opportunities, few incentives. So there would be no industrial revolution, no economic takeoff.

The implications of the change from one phase of despotic growth to another are clear from the collapse of the Qin and emergence of the Han. They come into even clearer focus in the later transition between the Tang and Song states. The An Lushan rebellion, itself a clear reaction to the overbearing control of the Tang state, destroyed the equal-field system. The Tang state's onerous compulsory labor services were no longer enforceable, and the decline of other types of servile labor soon followed. The web of market regulations was similarly eroded. Commerce had been restricted to designated markets, and merchants had been actively discriminated against. The state itself undertook all long-distance trade and ran 1,000 state farms. This entire system gradually atrophied.

Out of this undoing came not just a more Confucian organization of society, but also a new and more extensive market economy and a less despotic brand of growth. As the An Lushan rebellion pushed the population to the south, the economy refocused around the Yangtze River floodplain. This was followed by increased investment in land reclamation and the building of dikes, and expanded cultivation of rice as well as tea, which became a common beverage for the first time. We also see during this period the emergence of national markets for luxury goods such as fine silks, lacquer, porcelain, and paper. Other goods, like textiles, were now organized around production for the market. Trade wasn't just within China. Overseas trade with Japan and all over South Asia boomed. The Song introduced the world's first paper money, facilitating the expansion of trade that was already on the rise and created an environment that led to the invention of an array of new and fascinating technologies, including the movable-type printing press, gunpowder, the water clock, the compass, windmills, smelting technology for iron, various astronomical instruments, and an early form of spinning wheel. There was also a significant improvement in agricultural productivity, partly due to extensive irrigation. Nevertheless, these technologies were driven by the state's demand and under its control. The famous water clocks were built by and for government officials. Agricultural innovations and irrigation were state projects, and so were the advances in metallurgy.

Whatever their sources, the increase in agricultural productivity was more than sufficient to support the doubling of the population of Song China, and expanding markets and innovation meant that around 1090, when we have reliable information, China had the highest level of average living standards in the world, about 16 percent above England's. This enormous achievement of the Song dynasty showcases the potential power of despotic growth, particularly in an era when technology was simple by modern standards and could be shepherded by the state. While Europe was staggering in the corridor, with the state and society struggling with each other, China could get ahead, because the despotic state could do things by fiat that nascent Shackled Leviathans could not.

But it didn't last. Despotic growth never does. The Yuan dynasty that followed the Song undermined the meritocratic civil service, introduced a system of hereditary occupations, reversed the expansion of trade and industry, and generally curtailed economic opportunities and incentives. The reversal was completed with the Ming accession to power, which brought their own version of the well-field system, sea bans, and a great deal of insecurity for all private businesses. Commerce and urbanization contracted and incentives to innovate vanished. China started falling behind Europe.

An illuminating example of how the Ming emperors further stifled economic development comes again from the organization of the salt trade. The government began to mortgage the right to have the salt monopoly in exchange for transporting grain to troops in border regions. Someone got the right to produce salt if they shipped the grain for the government. When the grain was delivered, the merchant received a certificate to be redeemed in the capital, Nanjing, for another certificate that allowed him to sell a certain amount of salt. Some merchants started specializing in moving the grain to the frontier and then selling the certificates for having transported grain to others who subsequently sold the salt. The price of these certificates fluctuated since the government also granted the right to sell salt to members of the royal family, palace eunuchs, and senior officials in the bureaucracy. In 1617 the emperor decided to scrap the certificates, making the outstanding ones worthless and effectively expropriating the property rights

of those who had them. He then sold the monopoly to trade in salt to a few different select merchant houses. This initiated a system that came to be known as
"government supervision, merchant management," which in practice meant connected individuals making money because of government grants. In 1832 the
system the Ming had set up was changed once more, this time to attract small
investors. Yet as we saw earlier, in 1863 it was altered again in Hankou, further
tightening the state's grip. Participation in the salt monopoly was a risky business.

The transition between the Ming and Qing created yet more chaos, including
the reimposition of the sea ban in 1662. Even though the international trade ban
was lifted by 1683, trade with Europeans was severely restricted. After 1757 Europeans could trade only in Canton and the right to trade with them was given to a
monopoly called the Cohong. It wasn't just overseas trade; the Yunnan copper
mines were similarly granted to a monopoly.

All the same, the Ming-Qing transition seems to have led to some economic
revival. The Qing allowed trade as long as it was under their control and deemed
to benefit the welfare of rural society. They continued at first to provide some basic
public services, most notably the "ever normal granary system" to counteract famine. The Qing also unwound the leftover hereditary occupation system from the
Ming by 1683 and abolished bonded and servile labor after 1720. This relaxation
led to yet another period of flourishing domestic trade and population expansion.
But this revival was still no more than despotic growth, with all of its limitations.

There were several reasons for this. The most obvious was that the history of
arbitrary state actions in China, for example in the case of the salt monopoly, still
meant fairly insecure property rights and undermined incentives for investment
or innovation. Affirming the absence of any shackles on the powers of the Chinese
Leviathan, there was nothing, short of a wholesale rebellion, that could stop the
imperial state expropriating the fruits of people's labors except Confucian moral
precepts to "store wealth among the people." Yet the history of the Ming or the
early Qing showed that even if the spirit was willing, the flesh was often weak.
Only the very optimistic or the foolhardy could trust these moral guarantees in
Ming-Qing China.

It wasn't just lack of incentives in the form of insecure property rights. A general resistance, starting from the very top, toward mercantile activities, new technologies, and social mobility blocked economic prosperity. Fearing that economic
activity, especially outside the purview of the state, would destabilize the status
quo, all Chinese dynasties, not least the Qing, were suspicious of commerce and
industry. This was one of the main reasons why sea bans were periodically reintro-

duced. It was also the reason why Chinese authorities were lukewarm toward new technologies. In the 1870s the first railway in China, the Wusong line linking the port of Wusong to Shanghai, was built by the British company of Jardine, Matheson and Co. It was bought up by the Qing government and duly destroyed. This suspicious, often hostile attitude to new technology and practices had significant consequences. In contrast, we saw in the previous chapter how the European industrial revolutions and dramatic improvements in living standards from the late eighteenth century onward were based on the embrace of new technologies.

Even more important was the inability or the unwillingness of the Qing state to construct the infrastructure necessary for modern economic institutions and economic activity. The civil component of the Qing legal code was mostly focused on the family and provided no guidelines for commercial contracts. Instead, the Qing let individuals write whatever contracts they liked outside any legal framework, perhaps to be enforced by lineages (again that cage of norms). This created a patchwork of contracts and arrangements, with crucial elements such as limited liability remaining absent until the early twentieth century. The Qing government did not even enforce a uniform system of weights and measures. According to H. B. Morse, a Canadian serving in the Chinese Maritime Customs House between 1874 and 1908, weights and measures varied by locality and even at the same place, and they were different in different trades. The *dou*, for example, was a measure of capacity, but depending on where you were, it varied between 176 and 1,800 cubic inches. Then there was the foot, *chi*, but what this meant depended on whether you were a tailor or a carpenter, and on where you tailored. So according to Morse, a *chi* could be anywhere between 8.6 and 27.8 inches. The common measure of area, a *mou*, showed the same variability. It could be anything between 3,840 and 9,964 square feet. Local guilds and business associations adopted and recognized these different standards, but the state did nothing to systematize them.

More generally, the Qing state, located at the Confucian end of the Lord Shang–Confucius pendulum, collected very little in taxes and was incapable of providing many of the public services necessary for economic activities to flourish. The legal system was so inadequate partly because the state had such a small number of magistrates charged with resolving the disputes and disagreements of 450 million Chinese. With few resources in the hands of the state, not only the administration of justice but also the infrastructure and the famed granary system started withering away.

All of these problems were rooted in the basic political deficiencies of the Chinese system. The Qing state was despotic, even if it chose not to impose high

taxes or follow Lord Shang's imprint. Despotism meant that society and the business community were unable to make demands and influence state policies, for
example, in the form of better contract enforcement, more secure and predictable
property rights, improved infrastructure, or support for investment and innovation.

The contrast with the European experience is once again stark. Most European states around the same time started playing a critical role in standardizing
measures and providing a legal framework to support economic relations. European citizens were also rapidly developing a voice in politics. Britons, for example,
could vote and petition Parliament to pass the laws that they wanted, and they did
so with gusto. In China, all that a businessman could hope for was to get the right
contacts, benefit from state-granted monopolies, and enjoy the security that connections would bring. This was one of the main reasons why the merchant families of the Qing era were so keen on getting a foothold in the civil service.

These pressures and machinations are well illustrated by the history of the
biggest and wealthiest merchant group of the Qing period, a native place association from Anhui. The Anhui merchants, based at Hankou, Suzhou, and Yangzhou, traded salt, textiles, tea, and various other items all along the Yangtze River.
But illustrating a more general pattern among leading merchants, their families
rarely stayed in business, and instead poured their resources into preparing their
children for the civil service examinations. One family that exemplified this pattern was the Ts'ao in the eighteenth and nineteenth centuries. Initially they focused
on the salt trade, but they soon merged business with education and government
office holding. Ts'ao Shih-ch'ang, who started the prosperity of the family, was a
salt merchant. His elder son became a student in the imperial academy, while the
other son, Ching-ch'en, stayed in the salt trade. In the next generation, one son
went into the salt trade, while all other offspring of Ching-ch'en were in the government. By the early nineteenth century only one branch of the whole extended
family was still involved in any type of business. The rest had imperial degrees
and had merged with the gentry and state elites (as the family tree of the Ts'ao in
Map 11 shows). This transition was common. In Hankou, for example, Anhui
merchants created what would become a famous academy for preparing their
children, and those of others, for the imperial examinations. If this academy had
provided education for workers and businessmen, it could have been useful for
economic activity. Yet its focus was not imparting useful knowledge but preparing
scions of privileged families for the arcane civil service examination. It wasn't
unsuccessful; between 1646 and 1802 the large salt merchant families managed
to produce 208 scions who succeeded at the provincial level, and 139 more qualified

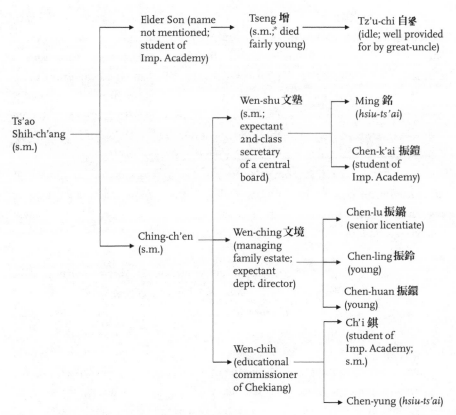

*The abbreviation "s.m." is for "salt merchant."

Map 11. From Salt Merchants to Government Officials: The Ts'ao Family in the Eighteenth Century

at the metropolitan level. Of course, if they couldn't pass the exams, then they could always buy the positions, and during the same period 140 members of these families did so.

Why were salt merchants so keen on leaving the business and moving into the civil service? Salt was as profitable as you would expect from a Chinese state monopoly. Since it was so important to the Qing state as a source of revenue, the merchants who had the monopoly enjoyed their fair share. That makes it even more puzzling that these families were so eager for their children to get out. Could it be because of the prestige of becoming part of the Chinese bureaucracy? The real reason was a little different. Even the salt monopoly wasn't secure, for the state could turn against you at any moment, as we have seen with the Ming emperors. So it was not a bad idea to get out while you could. What's more, having part of the family in the imperial bureaucracy meant greater security. And the imperial bureaucracy itself wasn't a bad business during this period, as a contemporary novel, *The Scholars*, by Wu Jingzi, illustrates. In one passage, he relates how one Fan Jin has unsuccessfully dedicated his life to passing the lowest level of the examination hierarchy. At the age of fifty-four, Fan Jin has failed the exam more than twenty times over a period of thirty-four years. A new commissioner of education takes pity on him and decides to let him pass. Fan Jin is now able to take the next level of the exam at the province levels. The reaction of his relatives, though, is disbelief. Undeterred, Fan Jin decides to take the exam, but when he returns home his family has not eaten for two days and he has to go to the market to sell their only chicken to buy rice. While he's there, mounted heralds arrive at his house to announce he has passed the provincial exam. He is immediately visited by a member of the elite to which he has now been admitted:

> Mr. Zhang alighted from the [sedan] chair and came in. He was wearing an official's gauze cap, sunflower-colored gown, gilt belt and black shoes . . . He took from his servant a packet of silver, and stated "I have brought nothing to show my respect except these fifty taels of silver, which I beg you to accept. Your honorable home is not good enough for you, and it will not be very convenient when you have many callers. I have an empty house on the main street by the east gate, which has three courtyards with three rooms in each . . . Allow me to present it to you."

The gifts to his family keep pouring in:

> Many people came to Fan Jin after that and made him presents of land and shops; while some poor couples came to serve him in return for protection. In two or three months he had menservants and maidservants, to say nothing of money and rice . . . he moved into the new house; and for three days he entertained guests with feasts and operas.

Passing such an exam didn't just make you rich, it made you above the law. This is well illustrated by another Chinese novel of the eighteenth century, *The Dream of the Red Chamber*, written by Cao Xueqin. The book tells the story of a new magistrate dealing with a murder case. But the murderer is a powerful man in the community, his name appearing in *Mandarin's Life Preserver*, the book that lists rich and powerful families in the area. The magistrate has to let him go, because if you were rich or you passed the exam and became established in the community, the laws didn't apply to you. You could get away with murder.

The Mandate of Marx

Today China is no longer an empire. The imperial state collapsed in 1912, and the brief period of Republican rule was followed by the reign of warlords and the autocratic Kuomintang government. The ensuing civil war concluded in 1949 with the triumph of Communists led by Mao Zedong. There would be no more mandate of heaven. Lord Shang's legalism and Confucius's moral precepts were to be supplanted by Communist ideology. A rupture with the past.

Except that it wasn't. The continuities were as strong as the differences. The mandate of heaven was to be replaced by the mandate of Marx. The defining characteristic of the Chinese state since the Qin times had been its overwhelming dominance over society. That did not change. In fact, it got worse under the rule of the Communist Party because of Mao's insistence on securing a greater presence for the party and the state throughout the country. Despite its despotic posturing, the Qing state was absent in much of the country, and particularly in the countryside. Coming to power at the head of a peasant revolution, Mao intended to change that right away. As we saw in Chapter 1, by the time of the Great Leap Forward, party organizations and members were everywhere.

What created continuity with the imperial period was the essence of despotism—the inability of society to organize and influence policy making outside the hierarchy of the state. Mao wanted the only medium for political participation to be the Communist Party, which effectively meant control of the state and the political elite over citizens, with no reciprocal influence. This became painfully clear when during the Cultural Revolution there would be periodic calls for bottom-up criticism, which were then violently stamped out. There would be no voice for society under Communism.

Mao's approach to the economy, too, reveals a lot of continuity with the earlier periods, and especially with Lord Shang's blueprint for tight control and regulation of economic activity. Under a veneer of Marxist ideology, the collectivization of agriculture attempted what the well-field system had tried to do millennia earlier. Its consequences were much worse. Agricultural collectivization, combined with the drive toward industry under the auspices of the Great Leap Forward, led to famines that killed as many as 36 million people.

Nor were the attitudes of Mao and the Communist Party toward private businesses dissimilar to those of Lord Shang, who dubbed them "crafty and tricky." Confucius similarly observed that "the gentleman understands rightness, whereas the petty person understands profit." Merchants and industrialists were treated pretty much the same way as they were under the imperial state, and were only allowed to become members of the party in 2001. It was not until 2007 that a law governing private property rights was passed that made their assets more secure.

Growth Under Moral Leadership

Things changed after Mao's death in 1976. A bitter power struggle at the top of the Communist Party concluded with Deng Xiaoping's dominance over the party and the state in 1978. Deng initiated a radical transformation of the economy, preparing the ground for the subsequent massive boom of the Chinese economy. Should we see a rupture with the past in this transition?

Though there are undoubtedly many new elements in the post-1978 Chinese economy and politics, and it is critical to recognize these, there are remarkable continuities too. There is much in the Mao-Deng transition that resembles the Tang-Song and Ming-Qing transitions, which had previously stimulated economic growth by loosening the grip of the state over the economy and allowing elbow room for the market and private businesses. Just as in the earlier transitions, the economic transformations resulted from a combination of spontaneous eruptions of society that had been buckling under economic hardships and the elite's decision to replace Lord Shang–style control with a more Confucian approach to the economy. We see the former in the first part of China to experience rapid industrial growth in the 1980s, Wenzhou in Zhejiang Province, just south of Shanghai. As early as 1977, before Deng's reforms, the *People's Daily*, the newspaper of the Communist Party, complained that there was "an alarming case of Counterrevolutionary Restoration in Wenzhou." The paper went on:

> Collectivization had been turned into private farming, black market emerged, collective enterprises had collapsed and been replaced by underground factories and underground labor markets.

Indeed, de facto rural reforms had preceded Deng Xiaoping's liberalization of agriculture in 1978. In 1986 Wenzhou was granted the status of an "experimental zone," giving it freedom from "current rules and regulations, and policies of the nation." By that time 41 percent of industrial production was already by the private sector (up from 1 percent in 1980). Alarmed by these developments, the party instructed local cadres to emphasize Communist leadership in economic matters, and news coverage and visits from outside the region were restricted. If the Communist Party could not stop what was going on in Wenzhou, it did not want that being broadcast. And it attempted to stop it. Local cadres actively tried to restrain private sector development, for example in the 1986–1987 "anti-bourgeois liberalism" campaign. It was only in 1988 that the Chinese Communist Party recognized private businesses with more than seven employees. Before then it had maintained the fiction that all nonstate production was by "households." As the Communist Party withdrew from trying to control every aspect of the economy, there was a huge upsurge of entrepreneurship (much of this control had already collapsed during the Cultural Revolution, making some of the later loosening inevitable). In 1990 Wenzhou started its own export processing zone and built its own airport. The real initiative in Wenzhou came from society, not the state.

Nevertheless, the top-down element subsequently came to define the direction of the Chinese economy. Deng's vision was one in which political power would remain in the hands of the Communist Party, which was supposed to be ruled in a more moral manner than under Mao. In fact, there is a striking parallel between the meritocratic Communist Party tapping the best talent to rule the country and the imperial bureaucracy of the earlier empires recruiting the best Chinese minds. Under the tutelage of the party, this system would create enough room for the market economy to flourish. In some ways, it worked brilliantly. China has become the second-largest economy in the world, and its spectacular growth, averaging about 8.5 percent since 1978, is the envy of every leader in the world.

It's also undeniable that economic opportunities and incentives have improved. China has become an entrepreneurial society, and several of the founders and managers of the most successful Chinese corporations, including Jack Ma of Alibaba, come from modest backgrounds in provincial cities (nine of the ten wealthiest Chinese businessmen come from provincial cities, and only one originates from one of the six major cities, Beijing, Shanghai, Guangzhou, Shenzhen, Chongqing, and Chengdu). Indeed, it would have been impossible for China to achieve what it has over the past four decades without such an expansion of opportunities and incentives. This is still despotic growth, however, under the auspices of the state and subject to the whim of the state, and one cannot take for granted that the moral leadership of the Communist Party will always point in the direction of continued economic growth. There is always the potential that unshackled power will be abused for private gain and destroy the potential for economic growth. How the use of despotic power for private gain can undermine incentives is illustrated by the closing down of the Xiushui market in Beijing in 2004. This was a thriving outdoor marketplace that had started spontaneously in 1985 as the government deregulated trade and markets. By 2004 it had become one of the most lively retail outlets in the city, with between 10,000 and 20,000 visitors doing around US$12 million of business per day. In that year local government officials decided to close the market down, relocating it to a new indoor space. The new space was built and controlled by a new entrepreneur with the right political connections who then proceeded to auction off the priviledge to operate in the new market. One bid was as high as US$480,000. In effect, not unlike what the Ming emperors did to salt merchants, the government expropriated the property rights of the old stallholders and transferred them to somebody completely different. It's not too far-fetched to believe that some of the benefits were shared with people in the local government.

Another recent example of political factors blocking economic activity comes from the Township Village Enterprises (TVEs). TVEs were an innovation of the 1980s and were essentially private businesses, but often owned by local governments. The explanation favored by economists as to why this arrangement was so successful is that, with the imperfect institutions of China, forging a coalition with local government officials was a way for entrepreneurs to protect their property rights. Starting in the mid-1990s, however, TVEs started to decline and by the next decade, they had vanished completely. The reason for this appears not to be some natural transition to a more efficient economy, but reflects the fact that national politicians decided to favor large state-owned enterprises that did not want to face competition from the largely rural TVEs. TVEs were ordered to focus on rural areas and were starved of credit. They were squeezed out of existence by political decisions. This is just one facet of a more general problem—property rights are heavily dependent on political favors in China, and there is neither an independent judiciary nor any attempt to apply laws equally to political elites, just as during imperial periods. One has to hope that the moral leadership of the Politburo of the Communist Party, or better, the connections with the right officials, won't disappear too abruptly. So the way for entrepreneurs to maintain their property rights is to enter the state and stay on good terms with it in the same way that businesspeople did in the Qing dynasty. This can help explain the enormous expansion of the Communist Party in the past twenty years. Many leading businessmen, including Jack Ma, are members of the party.

In another parallel with the past, the Communist state continues to be worried about revolt and political instability. In 2005, when rural discontent rocked the countryside, the Communist Party responded by abolishing land taxes—a similar impulse that led the Qing to freeze the nominal value of land taxes in 1713. A major problem for the Qing state was its inability to raise enough taxes to provide public services. So far rapid economic growth has solved this problem and allowed the Chinese state to build massive anounts of new infrastructure. But what happens when economic growth slows down? The Communist Party has defined its legitimacy around continued economic growth and its moral leadership. Its current leader, President Xi, is fond of quoting Confucius and comparing himself to the Pole Star. But things can change, especially if the homage that Xi and the Chinese leadership expect ceases. It is not such a far-fetched possibility that any economic growth and social transformation can come to be perceived as politically destabilizing and the party can turn against economic change because it deems it to be politically threatening. For example, Deng Xiaoping's reform agenda almost went into reverse after the 1989 Tiananmen Square protests as Communist elites blamed economic reforms and the social changes they induced for the pro-democracy movement.

Of course, one could hope that China would ultimately transition toward a society with less anxiety about growth and order, more liberty, and greater security. A famous argument in social science, sometimes referred to as "modernization theory," maintains that as a nation becomes richer, it becomes freer and more democratic. So can we expect such a transformation from China? That's unlikely. Almost two and a half millennia of travel along the despotic path, away from the corridor, means that any change of direction is unlikely to be seamless and any hope of a swift "end of history" in China is likely to remain a fantasy. (Evidence from other countries does not support the optimistic premise of modernization theory either.)

If modernization will not automatically bring liberty, can we hope that the model forged by the Chinese Communist Party will secure vibrant innovation in an economy organized along despotic lines? Can it cultivate innovation without liberty? Can it pour resources into areas such as artificial intelligence in order to gain an innovative advantage? Historical evidence suggests the answer is no, at least so far as diverse and ongoing innovation is concerned. The lack of an autonomous society and broad-based opportunities and incentives doesn't mean no growth; China has achieved rapid growth, even if this has been driven by investment and industrialization based on existing technology. It doesn't mean no innovation and no technological progress, as China's own experience during the Song dynasty and the Soviet Union's early successes attest to. The Soviet Union not only produced some of the world's best mathematicians and physicists, but made important technological breakthroughs in a number of areas, not least in military technology and the space race. Even North Korea today, despite its Shang Yang–style control over the economy and society, has managed to produce advanced weapons. Yet in all of these cases successes came as a solution to well-posed problems in narrow areas and in response to government demands (and not in small part from transferring and copying existing advances from elsewhere). Diverse and ongoing innovation in a range of fields, essential for future growth, depends not on solving existing problems but on dreaming up new ones. That requires autonomy and experimentation. You can provide massive amounts of resources (and data for artificial intelligence applications), you can order individuals to work hard, but you cannot order them to be creative. Creativity is the essential ingredient for sustained innovation and critically depends on a large number of individuals experimenting, thinking in their own different ways, breaking the rules, failing, and sometimes succeeding, which is exactly what we saw in Chapters 5 and 6 among the bustling, unruly, and socially mobile people of Italian city-states and the entrepreneurs of the Industrial Revolution. But how can you replicate that without liberty? What if you got in the way of somebody powerful or ran against ideas sanctioned by the party? What if you broke the rules? Better not to experiment.

Indeed, it was exactly this type of innovation based on experimentation, taking risks, and breaking rules that eluded the Soviet planners for seventy years, and the Chinese economy has not yet cracked it either. One can pour resources into patents, universities, new technologies, and even create huge rewards for success (for some Soviet scientists, the reward was to stay alive). But it's not enough if you cannot replicate the rambunctious, disorderly, and disobedient nature of true experimentation, and no society outside the corridor has so far managed that.

Chinese growth is not likely to peter out in the next few years. But as with other episodes of despotic growth, its existential challenge lies in unleashing large-scale experimentation and innovation. Like all previous instances of despotic growth, it is unlikely to succeed in this.

Liberty with Chinese Characteristics

Liberty doesn't easily germinate under despotism. It is no different in China today. While Hong Kong and Taiwan, so close to China and cut from the same cultural cloth, have created societies that have demonstrated the powerful demand for liberty, China has gone in a different direction. As we write, the Chinese government is piloting its "social credit system." Each Chinese citizen will be monitored and given a social credit score. Monitoring is done of all online activities, but the government is also erecting 200 million face recognition cameras throughout the country, as the image from Tiananmen Square, in the heart of Beijing, in the photo insert illustrates. In his dystopian novel *1984*, George Orwell famously wrote "Big Brother is watching." Technologically this was a dream (or nightmare) in 1949, when the book was published. It isn't anymore. A person with top social credit scores will get special treatment at hotels and airports, easier credit from banks, and preferential access to elite universities and top jobs. As the propaganda has it:

> It will allow the trustworthy to roam freely under heaven while making it hard for the discredited to take a single step.

But how freely? Buy alcohol in the supermarket—bad idea, you lose a few points. Points will also be subtracted if a relative or friend does something the authorities don't like. Whom you date or marry will influence your score as well. If you make decisions the Communist Party doesn't like, you'll be locked out of society, unable to travel, rent a car or apartment, or even get a job. This all sounds like a cage, created not by norms but by the state's watchful eye.

A vivid application of the social credit mentality and what it means for liberty is on view in western China in Xinjiang, home of millions of Muslim Uighur people. The Uighurs have faced constant discrimination, repression, and mass imprisonment, as well as the most intensive use of the state's surveillance techniques. Now they have to tolerate "big brothers and sisters" in their homes, monitoring their every word and deed. The first wave of these social monitors was dispatched in 2014, when about 200,000 Communist Party members were sent to Xinjiang to "Visit the People, Benefit the People, and Bring Together the Hearts of the People," even if they were as welcome by the Uighurs themselves as the city dwellers sent down to the countryside by Mao during the Cultural Revolution. In 2016, a second wave of 110,000 monitors was sent as the vanguard of the United as One Family campaign, which placed them in the homes of Uighurs whose family members had been imprisoned or killed by the police. A third wave of one million cadres was sent out in 2017. In the mornings, brothers and sisters sing together in front of the Chinese Communist Party local headquarters, and they studiously attend information sessions on the "New China" vision of President Xi.

Uighurs are constantly being watched to check their loyalty. Do they speak Chinese well? Any signs of a prayer mat or kneeling toward Mecca? Did I overhear an Islamic greeting (such as *Assalamu alaikum*)? Do they own a copy of the Quran? What happens on Ramadan?

For most, liberty with Chinese characteristics is no liberty at all.

Chapter 8

BROKEN RED QUEEN

A Hate Story

Manoj and Babli made a terrible mistake in 2007: they fell in love. They were from Karoran, a small village in the state of Haryana in northwest India. Manoj had dropped out of school and got a job as an apprentice in an electronics repair shop. Babli attended the local girls' school across the road. They met in the shop, and if it wasn't love at first sight, it was soon afterward. She took in her perfectly functioning cell phone for him to repair, and when he questioned her, she replied, "Of course there was nothing wrong with it. I just wanted to see you again."

Both Manoj and Babli were from the same caste, or *jati*. They were both Banwala Jats. The Jats are what is known as an "Other Backward Class" in India. In itself that wasn't an issue. In fact, in the Indian caste system there are strict rules of caste endogamy, meaning that people have to marry within their caste. But within a caste there are further restrictions and the fatal problem was that Manoj and Babli were from the same *gotra*, or clan. A clan is a kinship group. There was no legal reason why Manoj and Babli could not marry according to Indian law, but some things in India are more powerful than the law.

When they decided to elope and marry, Babli and Manoj violated a rule of the caste system so ancient that it is actually stated in the famous treatise on statecraft, the *Arthashastra*, written by Kautilya sometime around 324 BCE. Kautilya was an adviser to Chandragupta Maurya, the ruler who created the great Mauryan Empire that spanned northern India. In a section outlining the different duties and re-sponsibilities of the distinct castes, Kautilya stipulates that "the duties of a house-holder are: earning his livelihood by pursuing his own profession; marrying a woman from the same varna but not of the same gotra."

By *varna* Kautilya means one of the four great social distinctions that divide the Hindu population: Brahman, Kshatriya, Vaishya, and Shudra. These are four distinct subsets into which most Indians are divided, with the identity being passed on from parents to children. Kautilya was also very clear on what the different varnas were supposed to do:

> The duties of the Brahman are: study, teaching, performing the rituals prescribed for him, officiating at others people's rituals, giving and re-ceiving of gifts.
>
> The duties of a Kshatriya are: study, performing the rituals pre-scribed for him, living by [the profession of] arms and protecting all life.
>
> The duties of a Vaishya are: study, performing the prescribed rituals, agriculture, cattle-rearing and trade.
>
> The duties of a [Shudra] are: service of twice-born [i.e., the three higher varnas] [or] an economic activity [such as agriculture, cattle-rearing and trade] the profession of an artisan [or] entertainer [such as actor or singer].

Only the first three were "twice-born" and entitled to take part in particular religious ceremonies. At the bottom of this hierarchy were the Shudras, who were destined to serve the higher varnas and undertake menial tasks, such as being an entertainer. It is possible that the Shudras were originally composed of peoples who had been conquered by the Indo-Aryans as they migrated into India in the distant past and merged into their society. Top of the heap were the Brahmans, the priestly varna that specialized in education as well as religious ceremonies. Next came the Kshatriyas, who were primarily warriors and soldiers, and after them the Vaishyas, who engaged in commerce, manufacturing, and agriculture. Out-side this system, and at the very bottom of the social hierarchy, were the people known historically as "untouchables" or Dalits, now more formally referred to as being from Scheduled Castes.

Jatis, nested within the varnas, are the groups that are most properly called castes. The Jats are a jati. It is useful to think of the caste system as being com-posed of these jatis, of which there are about 3,000 in India, with each jati embed-ded within one of the varnas. Hence the Banwala Jats to whom Manoj and Babli belonged were members of the Jat jati, who were in turn part of the Shudras, now considered to be part of the more modern Other Backward Classes.

This historical societal organization is not unique to India. As we have seen, Medieval England was also a society of "orders," and historians often make a tripartite distinction between those who prayed, those who fought, and those who worked. These roughly correspond to the Brahmans, the Kshatriyas, and the Vaishyas/Shudras. People also took the name of their job which, as we'll see, is a key part of the Indian caste system. If you were a blacksmith in thirteenth-century England, you were probably called Smith; if you made barrels, you were a Cooper; if you made bread, then a Baker. Likely the son of a Smith was also a blacksmith. The British historian Richard Britnell even used data on last names to develop measures of how economically diverse Medieval England was. He didn't have actual data on the economy, only on people's names from tax records, but that turned out to be the same thing. If you knew people's names, you knew what their economic occupation was, and hence you knew how the economy was organized. These names have persisted over time, but as we saw in Chapter 6, their connection to occupation has been eroded by economic and social change. One of the reasons for the breakdown of name and occupation is that this relationship never got institutionalized in the same way it did in India. In particular, it never got embedded in religion and the nature of the state.

The persistence of caste identities and norms in India is vividly illustrated by the fact that a norm recorded by Kautilya almost 2,500 years ago is still enforced today. Enforced how? Manoj and Babli had to present themselves in court at Kaithal because Babli's family accused Manoj of kidnapping her. They had to attest to the fact that they were legally married and no kidnapping had taken place. To Babli's surprise, her brother Suresh and cousin Gurdev appeared. How did they know that the court hearing was to take place? Two other cousins were there too. Still, Manoj and Babli had anticipated that there could be trouble so, at the suggestion of their lawyer, they had asked the court for police protection. After the court hearing the police took them in a car to the bus to go back to Chandigarh, where they had gotten married and were hiding from their disapproving relatives. They got down from the car at Pehowa bus stand to catch the bus to Chandigarh. The relatives had followed them. The police seemed to recognize the problem. Two were sent with Manoj and Babli on the bus to make sure nothing happened. Two cousins boarded the bus. More were in a car. The bus moved off, but when it reached the town of Pipli, the two policemen declared that this was the boundary of their jurisdiction and that they had to leave. Manoj and Babli were alone. In their desperation they jumped on a bus bound for Delhi; the cousins followed. At a toll plaza shortly before the town of Karnal a silver Mahindra Scorpio SUV swerved in front of the bus and blocked it. Manoj and Babli were forced out of their seats and into the Scorpio. They vanished and were never seen alive again. Their bloated, mutilated bodies, with their feet tied together, were pulled out of the Balsamand Minor canal.

Though you might have thought Manoj and Babli were the victims, the local caste council decided to ostracize Manoj's family. Nobody in the village was allowed to talk to them or sell them anything. If anyone broke this rule, they would be fined 25,000 rupees (about US$350) and ostracized by the rest of the village.

India in the Cage of Norms

In the evolution of Indian state and society, the cage of norms is the big story. While in Athens and Europe the Red Queen not only spawned the development of both state and society but also started relaxing the cage of norms in the process, that didn't happen in India. The consolidation of the caste system and the subservience of the state to its rigid hierarchy fragmented society and made it turn against itself. Society is never a monolithic entity, and its internal conflicts and the inequalities that these engender play a central role in a nation's politics. The Red Queen reshapes these divisions through state-society competition and cooperation, as we saw for instance in late-eighteenth-century Britain, where expanding state capacity induced society to develop new identities, new organizations, and more general demands. In contrast, the fragmentation and divisions that the caste system fomented meant that none of this could take place in India; society couldn't organize and monitor the state and there would be no Red Queen dynamics reshaping society's identities, even though the peninsula, like Europe, has a deep history of popular participation in government. Instead, because political participation was based on caste and the state itself supported and was bulwarked by the caste system, caste-based identities got repeatedly reconfirmed—with abominable consequences for liberty.

The caste system doesn't just explain the lack of liberty in India. It also helps explain the country's poverty. The fact that people are locked into occupations by their inherited status puts a huge impediment in the way of social mobility and innovation. But this is just the visible tip of the massively unequal opportunities and incentives generated by a system based on a rigid social hierarchy and dominance in every nook and cranny of society. Even while India has been a democracy since January 26, 1950, and "liberalized" its economy in the 1990s, the dominance of caste and the gamut of restrictive, divisive, and hierarchical norms have persisted and bred a state devoid of real capacity or much interest in helping its poorest citizens.

To understand all this better, let's begin at the bottom of the caste hierarchy, with the Dalits.

The Broken People

What does "Dalit" mean exactly? The word doesn't appear in Kautilya but has much more recent origins. The Dalits used to be called the "untouchables." The great Indian statesman B. R. Ambedkar, who after independence in 1947 helped draft the first version of the Indian Constitution, coined the term "Dalits." It means literally "broken people." But where does "untouchability" come from?

Untouchability means what is says: you cannot be touched. For a higher-caste person to touch a Dalit causes "pollution" which can only be eradicated by ritual cleansing. As a Dalit worker interviewed by Human Rights Watch in Ahmedabad district, Gujarat, in 1998 put it:

> When we are working, they ask us not to come near them. At tea canteens, they have separate tea tumblers and they make us clean them ourselves and make us put the dishes away ourselves. We cannot enter temples. We cannot use upper-caste water taps. We have to go one kilometer away to get water . . . When we ask for our rights from the government, the municipality officials threaten to fire us. So we don't say anything.

It's not just a matter of physical touching. If a Dalit casts a shadow on a Brahman, that can require ritual cleansing. Dalits should not wear shoes in the presence of the "twice-born." Ambedkar, who was himself a Dalit, didn't like the notion of untouchability and he made sure that the Indian Constitution outlawed it. Article 17, "Abolition of Untouchability," states in no uncertain terms:

> Untouchability is abolished and its practice in any form is forbidden. The enforcement of any disability arising out of Untouchability shall be an offence punishable in accordance with law.

Yet it is estimated that there may be as many as 200 million Dalits in India today. How is that possible?

Ambedkar's most famous statement about untouchability came in a lecture he prepared to give in 1936. He never presented it because when he circulated a draft, it was deemed so outrageous that he was quickly disinvited. He printed it at his own expense and called it "The Annihilation of Caste." Ambedkar knew what he was talking about; as a child he was allowed to go to a school for "touchables," but he had to sit apart from the rest of the children on a sack so as not to pollute the floor for them. He couldn't drink all day because the only tap was for higher castes. Ambedkar starts by outlining what it was like to be an untouchable:

> The Untouchable was not allowed to use the public streets if a Hindu was coming along, lest he should pollute the Hindu by his shadow. The Untouchable was required to have a black thread either on his wrist or around his neck, as a sign or mark to prevent the Hindus from getting themselves polluted by his touch by mistake. In Poona . . . the Untouchable was required to carry, strung from the waist, a broom to sweep away from behind himself the dust he trod on, lest a Hindu walking on the same dust should be polluted. In Poona, the Untouchable was required to carry an earthen pot hung around his neck wherever he went—for holding his spit, lest his spit falling on the earth should pollute a Hindu who might unknowingly happen to tread on it.

But Ambedkar's agenda wasn't just abolishing untouchability. Ambedkar wanted to overthrow the entire caste system because he understood its wide-ranging pernicious effects. He attacked this from an economic point of view. It made no sense to him (and makes no sense to us either) that castes, varnas, and jatis have specific occupations. He of course knew it was based on dominance and was a powerful source of illiberty. But even more important, he understood that caste made society turn against itself and stand divided and disorganized. He wrote that

> the caste system is not merely a division of labor. It is also a division of laborers. Civilized society undoubtedly needs division of labor. But in no civilized society is division of labor accompanied by this unnatural division of laborers into water-tight compartments. The caste system . . . is a hierarchy in which the divisions of laborers are graded one above the other . . . In one of its aspects, it divides men into separate communities.

In its second aspect, it places these communities in a graded order one above the other in social status.

Elsewhere he used a different metaphor, likening the caste system to "a multi-storeyed tower with no staircase and no entrance. Everybody had to die in the story they were born in." The division of labor created by the caste system is economically irrational because "it involves an attempt to appoint tasks to individuals in advance—selected not on the basis of trained original capacities, but on that of the social status of the parent." You couldn't build a modern economy on the "dogma of predestination," and any attempt to do so was like trying to build "a palace on a dung heap."

Ambedkar was very clear, too, on the dreadful consequences of the caste system for liberty and for politics. Not only was a caste society fundamentally illiberal, but Ambedkar stressed that caste created a highly fragmented, disorganized, and prostate society. "Caste has . . . completely disorganized and demoralized the Hindus," he wrote, and this was because "Hindu society as such does not exist. It is only a collection of castes." Except when they might unite against an outside foe, "each caste endeavors to segregate itself and to distinguish itself from other castes . . . the ideal Hindu must be like a rat living in his own hole, refusing to have any contact with others . . . The Hindus, therefore, are not merely an assortment of castes, but are so many warring groups, each living for itself and for its selfish ideal." The overwhelming role of caste in people's identities is why "the Hindu cannot be said to form a society." This is fundamentally because

> a Hindu's . . . responsibility is only to his caste. His loyalty is restricted only to his caste. Virtue has become caste-ridden, and morality has become caste bound . . . There is charity, but it begins with caste and ends with caste. There is sympathy, but not for men of other castes.

What about the illiberal nature of caste society? This is perhaps obvious given the restrictions on occupation, lifestyle, residence, and many other things that go along with caste. But Ambedkar wanted to make a deeper point; the caste system could only be maintained by dominance and the threat of violence. He points out that in the great Hindu epic the Ramayana, King Rama beheads a Shudra he finds meditating. Shudras are not twice-born, they are not meant to meditate. India's oldest law code, the Laws of Manu, is adamant that the king enforce the caste system and specifies very heavy sanctions for breaking with varna. For example, a Shudra who recites or even listens to the Vedas, the ancient holy literature of Hindus, can be punished by having his tongue cut off or having molten lead poured into his ears.

The most menial of tasks were reserved not for Shudras but for Dalits. These include jobs as manual scavengers, tasks such as the removal of dead animal carcasses and human waste (see the photo insert for an illustration of one of these jobs). Among other Dalit occupations are cobblers, leatherworkers, and street sweepers. Dalit children are sold off to upper-caste creditors to pay off debts and Dalit girls are sold to temples in the Devadasi system, in effect a form of institutionalized prostitution. Dalit men, women, and children work in appalling conditions for a pittance as agricultural workers. Human Rights Watch reproduces government statistics suggesting that there are at least one million, and probably far more, Dalits who work as manual scavengers. One of the scavengers interviewed in the state of Andhra Pradesh reported:

> In one toilet there can be as many as 400 seats which all have to be manually cleaned. This is the lowest occupation in the world, and it is done by the community that occupies the lowest status in the caste system.

The demeaning nature of the work they have to do is part of their domination by the upper castes, and it is supported by norms and the threat of violence. Many of the scavengers are told by the community that they have no choice but to do this work. When the Rashtriya Garima Abhiyan, or National Campaign for Dignity, started informing manual scavengers in the state of Madhya Pradesh that they could leave this work if they wanted to, 11,000 of them did so right away. But the pressure and threats on them continued. One scavenger reported that "one of the people I cleaned for warned me, 'Now, if you come to my farm, I'll cut off both of your legs.'"

The nature of the caste system and the cage of norms it creates undermines the ability of Indian society to act collectively. Just as Ambedkar pointed out, society is divided against itself. The Red Queen is broken.

Those Who Dominate

Those who dominate were often the highest varna in the caste hierarchy, the Brahmans. Historically, even in villages with multiple castes, the Brahmans dominated local politics and political institutions such as the local village assembly, the *panchayat*, an institution we'll return to later in the chapter. An autobiography published in 1903 by Thillai Govindan records several meetings of local panchayats to adjudicate legal cases in the village in Tamil Nadu where he lived. In one, of the 25 people who met, 18 were Brahmans. In the course of his fieldwork in the same state in the early 1960s, the anthropologist André Béteille found that the Brahmans, though they made up only one quarter of the village population, had traditionally completely dominated the panchayat.

Yet by the time Béteille started to study the community, things had started to change. This was both because the Brahmans had migrated to urban areas where their better education allowed them access to higher-paid professions and government employment and because democratic politics had empowered the more populous castes. In the village Béteille studied, this caste was the Kallas, a Shudra jati. They emerged as the most powerful group not just because they were the numerically dominant varna in the village. It was also, as Béteille notes, because

> Kallas have a tradition of violence which makes the Adi-Dravidas hesi
> tant in challenging their authority.

The term Adi-Dravidas (meaning literally "Original Dravidians") is used specifically in Tamil Nadu as a label for Dalits. This term came into usage in the early twentieth century as a way of destigmatizing the Paraiyar community, an untouchable group. From the Paraiyars, we get the English word "pariah," which the *Oxford English Dictionary* defines as outcast, persona non grata, reject, outsider, leper. The Dravidians were the first people to populate southern India before the Indo-Aryan migrations, which seem to have originally brought the caste system, so the description Original Dravidians was intended to raise their status.

This antagonism between what the Indian sociologist M. N. Srinivas called the "dominant caste" of a village and the Dalits is common and is often steeped in violence. Human Rights Watch studied this in Tamil Nadu in the context of the conflict between the Dalits and another Shudra jati, the Thevars. As one person they interviewed put it:

> The Thevars are opposed to the Dalits. They themselves are not an ad
> vanced community. They are landlords but not in a big sense. They are
> not advanced in education, but still employed the Dalits as laborers.

So there were economic reasons for keeping the Dalits under control, but Human Rights Watch uncovered a much more pervasive system of hierarchy and dominance. As a Thevar politician told them, without any hint of irony:

> In the past, twenty to thirty years ago, *harijans* [Dalits] enjoyed the practice of "untouchability." In the past, women enjoyed being oppressed by men . . . Most . . . Dalit women enjoy relations with Thevar men. They enjoy Thevar community men having them as concubines. It is not done by force. Anything with Dalits is not done by force. That's why they don't react. They cannot afford to react, they are dependent on us for jobs and protection . . . Without Dalits we cannot live. We want workers in the fields. We are landholders. Without them we cannot cultivate or take care of our cattle. But Dalit women's relations with Thevar men are not out of economic dependency. She wants it from him. He permits it. If he has power, then she has more affection for the landlord.

These dominating relationships not only obliterate liberty for the dominated but also poison the functioning of local political institutions. Supposedly there are seats on the panchayat reserved for Dalits. These reservations challenged the previous hegemony of the dominant castes. In 1996, in the Tamil Nadu village of Melavalavu, the majority caste community, including the Thevars, let it be known that no Dalit should run for the panchayat. A story in the *Times of India* reported that "they were warned that they would lose their jobs as farmhands and not be allowed to graze cattle or draw water from wells located on patta [unutilized] land held by the dominant castes." Elections were scheduled for October, but in the face of this intimidation they had to be canceled because all the Dalit candidates withdrew. In February a Dalit, Murugesan, had the temerity to run. As the dominant castes boycotted the election, he won. Thereafter, however, he needed police protection and he was not able to enter the panchayat buildings because the Thevars prevented him. Murugesan was the target of constant threats, and in June 1997 he was murdered. A firsthand account relates:

> There were nearly forty of them. They were all Thevars. They stabbed Murugesan on the right side of his belly. It was a very long knife. From outside the bus Ramar [the leader] instructed the Thevars to kill all the Pariahs. Among twelve, six were murdered on the spot. They pulled all six out of the bus and stabbed them on the road with bill hooks more

than two feet long . . . Five Thevars joined together, put Murugesan on
the ground outside the bus, and chopped off his head, then threw it in
a well half a kilometer away.

After this massacre, outside intervention allowed five Dalit women to be
elected to the panchayat. In response the Thevars fired Dalit workers and prevented others from hiring them. Dalit children were afraid to go to school. One of
the elected women told Human Rights Watch:

> The office is in the caste Hindu area. I am not allowed in the office. So
> we have to hold our meetings in our TV room here; it is a makeshift
> office. They are still threatening us. They are watching and following
> me . . . If the elected Dalit women go there, the upper caste would do
> some harm. If the women insist on going into the office, they will hit
> them. There is one police guard for me. He has a gun, but he puts it
> inside his bag . . . Everything is paralyzed.

At another Tamil village, a woman called Veludavur told Human Rights
Watch about the endemic sexual violence against Dalit women:

> In the village, the Thevars entered the house and had sexual inter-
> course with the Dalit women. They used force and committed rape. My
> husband died, so if I had stayed then the same things would happen
> to me . . . I left all the lands. This is the regular lot of the dominated
> persons.

The Caged Economy of Caste

Even if Dalits are at the base of a caste system that segregates people socially and
economically, you may be skeptical that this ancient social hierarchy could be so
rigid as to determine people's occupations in recent times. Who would enforce
that? It is certainly not part of Indian law. But we've already seen the power of caste
norms in enforcing caste regulations and even encouraging the murder of people
who violate them. Could these norms have created a durable association between
a person's name and their caste and their occupation?

The first person who systematically investigated this question was a British
colonial administrator, E. A. H. Blunt, who published *The Caste System of Northern*

India in 1931. Using data about caste and occupation from the British colonial censuses, Blunt estimated the extent to which different jatis undertook their traditional occupations. He first sorted the different jatis into twelve broad categories starting with agriculture, laborers and village menials, pastoral occupations, learned professions and going all the way through trade and industry, dealers in food and drink, and even beggars. Within these broad classes were much more specialized occupations. For instance, in agriculture there was the growing of flowers and vegetables, poppy cultivation, and water-nut cultivation. Within learned professions there was astrology, writing, and of course the priesthood, which mapped onto the Brahmans. Within trade and industry Blunt identified thirty-five different specializations that were matched almost one for one to different jatis. For example, the Lohar jati were blacksmiths, the Sonar goldsmiths, and the Pasi toddy drawers (toddy is the sap used to make palm wine). Obviously agriculture was by far the largest occupation, the vocation of 90 percent of all the castes in this category. Yet agriculture was less interesting than the others because it was also a much more general occupation, water-nut cultivation notwithstanding. More astonishing were the results for specific occupations. Blunt found that 75 percent of the sweeper jati followed their profession, and so did 75 percent of goldsmiths (Sonars), 60 percent of confectioners and grain parchers, 60 percent of barbers and washermen, and 50 percent of carpenters, weavers, oil pressers, and potters.

But this segregation doesn't mean that the different castes are autarkic. They are linked by the Jajmani system, which specifies a network of services and favors that different castes have to provide for one another. On the face of it, it is a vast system of in-kind mutual gift giving. Some people's gifts are much more valuable than others', however. The first detailed description of how this worked was made by a missionary, William Wiser, in the 1930s in Karimpur, a village in northern India close to the confluence of the Ganges and Yamuna Rivers in the state of Uttar Pradesh. Wiser, along with his wife, Charlotte, subsequently wrote an ethnography of Karimpur, documenting the intense dominance in the village:

> The leaders of our village are so sure of their power that they make no effort to display it. The casual visitor finds little to distinguish them from other farmers . . . And yet when one of them appears among men of serving caste, the latter express respect and fear in every guarded word and gesture. The serving ones have learned that as long as their subservience is unquestioned the hand which directs them rests lightly.

But let there be any move towards independence or even indifference amongst them, and the paternal touch becomes a strangle-hold . . . in every detail of life have the leaders bound the villagers to themselves. Their favour may bring about a man's prosperity and their disfavour may cause him to fail.

There were 754 people in Karimpur, divided into 161 families. Brahmans made up 41 of the 161 families, and Wiser identified 24 different jatis in total, 2 types of Brahmans, 2 types of Kshatriyas, 12 different Shudra jatis and 8 un- touchable categories. He mapped an intricate system of customary services that different jatis had to do for one another. Let's start with the Brahmans. In prin- ciple Brahmans were priests who tended to the religious needs of the rest of the castes. The most prestigious of the Brahman families acting as priests served only the other Brahman families and received religious services from an even more superior family from outside the village. The next Brahman families in the hier- archy tended to the religious needs of the Kshatriyas and Shudras. Brahmans, who owned most of the land in the village, were owed services by other castes. A car- penter, born into the Barhai jati, had to remove and sharpen his plow blades once or twice a week. When it was harvest season, he had to keep sickles sharp and renew handles as often as required. If a cart was broken, he had to mend it and do other errands that required his skills. Other castes, such as ironworker, barber, water bearer, and potter, had similar fixed tasks that they had to undertake for different people. In exchange there were prespecified payments, normally in kind, which differed according to caste. For example, a Brahman would give the carpenter and ironworker 10.5 pounds of grain each season for every plow owned. Non-Brahmans would give 14 pounds of grain per plow. Such differences were the norm even when monetary payments were involved. The seamster, for example, received from a Brahman half of what non-Brahmans would pay for the same piece of clothing. When a Brahman bought milk it cost 50 percent less than it did for non- Brahmans. Fixed amounts of village land were set aside for the higher castes; Brahmans got the most, but land was also allocated to the carpenter, the sweeper, the oil presser, the seamster, and the washerman. The most onerous service of all occurred in the fields owned by the Brahmans, where lower-caste families were required to work at fixed rates of remuneration.

At the bottom of the social hierarchy, of course, were the untouchables. There were eight families of Chamars, leatherworkers who had a number of fixed tasks such as skinning animals, making leather, and using it to repair shoes, baskets, and bags. The Wisers noted about a Chamar:

> In the village he is regarded not as an individual, but as so-and-so's *chamar*. Outside of the intimate affairs of family life, his time and services and his sons' time and services are in the hands of his master. His wife too must be ready to help in the fields or at the heavier tasks in the house of the patron, whenever sent for. The patron's work and interests come first. If there is any time left over, the *chamar* and his sons spend it on the plot of land granted him as payment for his services. He makes no plans and undertakes nothing that requires time or money without the consent of his patron.

In effect, then, the Jajmani system was an intricate web of services with fixed customary payments that people were obliged to make, based on the hereditary division of labor embodied in the caste system. This might remind you of the Tiv's economy, regulated and constricted by rigid norms, from Chapter 4. But while the Tiv imposed these norms on economic relations in order to preserve equality, especially political equality, the Indian caste system was deliberately anti-egalitarian. Not everyone served everyone else. For instance, thirty-eight of the Brahman families didn't serve anyone, but they received services from others, and the terms of service always favored the higher castes. Exactly as Ambedkar put it, people were trapped into "water-tight compartments," blocking their incentives and opportunities. Talent and ability are widely misallocated, wasted. Not only liberty but economic efficiency was sacrificed at the altar of India's cage of norms. No wonder the country has suffered from endemic poverty and underdevelopment. (And we might add that none of this was made better by 150 years of East India Company and British colonial rule and before that the hegemony of the Mughal Empire, both of which built on and reinforced the caste system.)

But if India is so hierarchical and so riven with divisions, why has it also sustained democratic elections since independence and is it often held up to be the world's largest democracy? Why has this democratic system failed to mobilize anything like the Red Queen? The answer to the first question, as we'll see next, is related to India's history of popular political participation, in many ways similar to those of the Germanic tribes we discussed in Chapter 6. The answer to the second is again related to the factors Ambedkar identified, which shaped the democratic politics of India along the lines of the caste system.

Ancient Republics

Before there was writing, much history was recited orally and passed down from generation to generation of historians. These oral histories were often employed by governments to preserve dynastic traditions, partly to legitimate their power. But they were also preserved by bards and storytellers, as much for pleasure as for legitimation. This is the origin of the great works of Greek literature, the *Iliad* and the *Odyssey*, attributed to Homer, which told the history of the Trojan Wars and their aftermath. These wars occurred around 1200 BCE, but the stories about them were written down at least six hundred years later. In between they were preserved orally.

India too has its versions of the *Iliad* and the *Odyssey*, most notably the Mahabharata and the Ramayana, which were composed sometime between 400 BCE and 400 CE. Even earlier, and more useful for our purposes, are the so-called Vedas. There are four of these, preserved orally by the Brahmans, the priests of the Hindu religion, and first written down as early as 1000 BCE. One of them, the Rig Veda, contains over a thousand hymns and poems. The Vedas are thought to be the literature of Indo-Aryan peoples who migrated into India over a long period of time, probably in many waves. The Rig Veda contains descriptions of society, warfare, and politics. But any interpretation of these requires care, since it is often unclear if they represent history or fiction. What we do get, however, is a pretty clear picture of what political institutions looked like. There were chiefs, called rajas, but they were elected, or at least selected, and their power was heavily circumscribed by assemblies called *vidatha*, *sabha*, and *samiti*, though there is uncertainty about the exact way these institutions worked with one another. The sabha seems to have been smaller, perhaps including only elites, while the samiti was large, perhaps including all free adult male citizens. The importance of the assemblies is illustrated by a passage from another of the Vedas, the Atharva Veda, where a king asserts:

> In concord may Prajapati's two daughters *sabha* and *samiti* protect me. May everyman I meet, respect and aid me. Fair be my words, oh, my fathers, at the meetings.
>
> We know thy name, oh, *sabha*, thy name is interchange of talk. Let all the company who join the *sabha* agree with me.
>
> Of the men seated here, I make the splendor and lore my own. Indra make me conspicuous in all this gathered company.

Prajapati, the creator god, is seen as the source of the assemblies, which are presented as bodies for deliberation and discussion. The passage makes it clear that the king needs their support.

In fact, the rajas look quite a lot like the war leaders of Germanic tribes described by Tacitus. The vidatha, for example, seems to have been an assembly where war booty was divided. "Tribe" is also the word used by Indian historians to describe social organization in this period. The Rig Veda mentions thirty different tribes. Society appears to have been based on kinship and clans.

In the later Vedic period, probably around 600 BCE, we see a divergence between different types of states. In some parts of northern India, chiefs began to evolve into kings and hereditary monarchies sanctioned by religion, and the varna system overseen by Brahmans started to play a pivotal role in legitimizing the authority of a hereditary monarchy. In other parts, assembly politics persisted and even intensified. These latter states are called *gana-sanghas* by historians.

The best documented of the gana-sanghas is the Licchavi state based at Vaisali, now called Basarh, in the state of Bihar, just north of the river Ganges (see Map 12). One contemporary source states, "In that city [Vaisali] there are always 7,707 kings [rajas] to govern the kingdom and a like manner of viceroys, generals and treasurers." Another source reports that there are "the Licchavis of the ruling family to the number of 7,707 and their abode at Vaisali. And all of them given to argument and disputation." Historians interpret these numbers to suggest that the citizen body of Vaisali was probably 4 x 7,707, or 30,828, and perhaps one quarter of these, the "kings," had special political rights and formed the assembly. This was at the heart of the Licchavi state, which might have comprised 200,000 or 300,000 people. As a proportion of the total population, if the total number of citizens was 30,000, then this would be quite similar to the proportion of citizens in ancient Athens or the late Roman Republic. The assembly elected a council of nine, which did most of the routine administrative work, and one of these was elected as the chief king with executive authority. It is possible that this position, once filled, was held for life. The Buddha himself in one text is recorded as saying that the Licchavis "held full and frequent public assemblies" and they came together, debated "in concord," and "rose in concord," Decisions were taken by majority rule and officers who had to undertake specific tasks, like one called the *salaka-gahapaka*, were elected. Five qualities were stipulated for this position. A man had to be "one who does not walk in partiality . . . in malice . . . in folly . . . in fear and one who knows what votes have been taken and what have not been taken." The title *salaka-gahapaka* was derived from *salaka*, meaning a wood chip, which, like our modern ballot papers, was used for recording votes. The Licchavis had other remarkable institutions, including a judicial structure that supposedly had eight layers with a hierarchy of appellate courts that had a great deal of popular participation, just as in ancient Athens. Though our information about the Licchavis is the best, other contemporary states, such as Sakya, where the Buddha was from, appear to have had similar republican and democratic political institutions.

The importance of the gana-sanghas can be judged by the way that Kautilya refers to them in the *Arthashastra*. Kautilya was the closest Indian equivalent of Lord Shang and similarly attempted to compose a manual of statecraft and set of instructions for would-be rulers on how to organize their state. When considering the construction of an ideal state, Kautilya pays no attention to assemblies and has

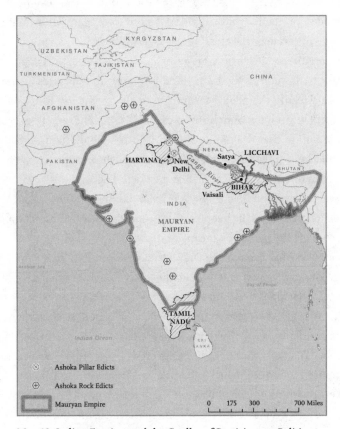

Map 12. Indian Empires and the Cradles of Participatory Politics

in mind a monarchical, highly hierarchical system. Yet in the part of the book that deals with foreign policy, Kautilya explicitly considers gana-sanghas, for which he uses the term *sanghas*. He notes:

> Because sanghas are cohesive entities, enemies cannot break them [easily].
> The chief of a sangha shall endear himself to his people by just behavior, being self-controlled and diligent in pursuing activities which are liked by the people and are of benefit to them.

More remarkable, the gana-sanghas also developed the idea that people collectively agreed to create the institutions of government. This was best articulated in Buddhist writings such as the Digha Nikaya. The Buddha's birthplace, Sakya, was as we noted one of the gana-sanghas, and according to this text there had been a long period of perfection and happiness before rottenness set in. With this rottenness came differences in colors, sexes, and suddenly food, drink, and nourishment were required. Life in heaven gave way to life on earth. People started to create institutions such as the family and property, and disputes and even theft followed. As a result, the people assembled to choose a ruler who was "the best favored, the most attractive and the most capable." Once chosen, the person agreed "to be indignant at that where one should rightly be indignant, to censure that which should be rightly censured, to banish him who deserves to be banished." To compensate him the people agreed to give rice. The Digha Nikaya records that the ruler was elected and held three titles: *mahasammata, khattiya,* and *raja.* The first means "chosen by all the people," the second "lord of the fields," and the third "one who charms the people by means of dharma."

The word *dharma* used in the Digha Nikaya is significant; it comes from the Dharmashastra, a group of texts, the earliest of which date back to between 600 and 300 BCE. Dharma is the proper conduct of a person living in society and the word can be translated as "righteous conduct." The benefit of such moral conduct was the accumulation of spiritual merit that bodes well for one's future lives after reincarnation. Dharma was the Indian version of Chinese Confucian ethical principles, supposed to induce the ruler to rule in a moral way, for the benefit of the people. We saw in the previous chapter that even though Chinese emperors all claimed to be adhering to Confucian principles, these did not always effectively constrain their behavior. The same was true for dharma in India.

When monarchies appeared, they developed a very different rationale to justify the new structure of authority. Critically, this was heavily influenced by the varna system. In many texts, the justification for state power is tied to the need to maintain a social order based on the varnas. This is clear in Kautilya when he notes about the varna system that

> when it is violated, the world will come to an end owing to confusion of castes and duties. Hence the king shall never allow people to swerve from their duties; for whoever upholds his own duty, ever adhering to the customs of the Aryas, and following the rules of caste and divisions of religious life, will surely be happy both here and hereafter.

So the king had to focus on making sure people stuck to their duties according to their varna and caste. In turn the varna system, in the guise of the Brahman rituals, legitimized the state. This is evident from the most famous coronation ritual of the time, the *ratnahavimsi*. The king went to the house of each *ratnin*, or jewel-holder, and made prayers there. Different authors list different numbers of ratnins, between eleven and fifteen, but they all agree on one thing: the Brahman was first. This ceremony signified who held power and to whom the king was responsible for his authority. This relationship between the varnas and the state is another critical reason that the Red Queen was broken in India. The state was supposed to support and honor the varna system, not break it up. The caste system, in turn, preserved hierarchy and prevented society from challenging the state.

The Mauryans, guided by Kautilya, managed to create an empire of a scale previously unknown in India (see Map 12). One way to get a sense of its expanse is from the location of the so-called Rock Edicts of Ashoka, Chandragupta's grandson, the most famous of the Mauryan emperors. Ashoka ruled from 268 to 232 BCE. He had various laws and guiding principles carved onto rocks and stelae throughout his kingdom, presumably so that they were readily available to people. His Major Rock Edicts were carved in Kandahar, all the way in the west in what is now Afghanistan; in Yerragudi, south of Hyderabad in modern Andhra Pradesh; in Dhauli in the east in modern Odisha (Orissa); and far in the north in Shahbazgarhi, Pakistan. This gives a sense of the extent of Ashoka's empire, and the text of the edicts presents us with a window into how he ruled. Though the *Arthashastra* suggests that the Mauryan Empire had a dense bureaucracy which penetrated right down to the village level, modern historians believe this is highly unlikely.

On this point, Kautilya's book was more about what was desirable rather than what actually happened and would have been feasible. To compensate for the absence of such control, Ashoka converted to Buddhism and propagated dharma as a philosophy of rule; the Edicts capture what this was supposed to be about. In Major Rock Edict 6, Ashoka asserts:

> Reporters have to report to me the affairs of the people at any time (and) anywhere, while I am eating, in the harem, in the inner apartment, at the cowpen, in the palanquin, (and) in the park. And everywhere I shall dispose of the affairs of the people.
>
> And also, if in the council (of Mahāmātras) a dispute arises, or an amendment is moved, in connexion with any donation or proclamation which I am ordering verbally, or (in connexion with) an emergent matter which has been delegated to the Mahāmatrās, it must be reported to me immediately, anywhere, (and) at any time.
>
> Thus I have ordered. For I am never content in exerting myself and in dispatching business.

Here Ashoka is projecting the image of a highly accountable ruler concerned with the welfare of his people. The last line of this edict is interesting. Ashoka wryly observes, "But it is difficult to accomplish this without great zeal." Indeed, and great zeal was mostly lacking. The Mauryan Empire collapsed in 187 BCE, less than fifty years after Ashoka's death.

The gana-sanghas survived the rise of the Mauryans and persisted for a long time. Though a series of lesser states waxed and waned in northern India in the thousand years after the collapse of the Mauryan Empire, it was perhaps only with the rise of the Delhi Sultanate in the thirteenth century and subsequently the creation of the Mughal Empire after 1526 that more despotic state institutions were constructed throughout India. Before then we find, for example, the Chauhans—one of the main Rajput clans that ruled Rajasthan prior to the creation of the Delhi Sultanate—having to obtain the agreement of a village assembly to raise new taxes. In the same context we also find the word *panchayat* being used for "assembly"; as we've seen, the word is still used in India for local caste and political assemblies. Even when more despotic institutions started developing, they often did not penetrate local society everywhere, particularly in the south, to which we now turn.

Land of the Tamils

Assemblies and representative systems were not the monopoly of northern India. They were everywhere, probably more so in the south of the peninsula. Here even the Mughals did not consolidate their control and there was a great deal of autonomy up until the British colonial period, which began with the rule of the East India Company (lasting until 1857) and then continued with direct control by the British government until independence in 1947.

Let's examine the Chola state, which illustrates not only the vibrant assemblies in southern India, but also how centralized states emerged from a bottom-up process where autonomous polities voluntarily came together. The Chola state ruled large parts of southeastern India from its base in Tamil Nadu, the "land of the Tamils" (see again Map 12). It likely started in the eighth or ninth century and lasted until the end of the thirteenth century. The early capital was at Thanjavur, southwest of modern Chennai in Tamil Nadu; later capitals included Kanchipuram and Madurai. At the local level their administration was based on village assemblies. In villages dominated by peasants these assemblies were called *ur*, while in villages where Brahmans held power they were called *sabha*, a term we've seen before. The ur seems to have included all adult males of a village, as did the sabha. But there is also some evidence suggesting that the members of the sabha were chosen by lot from the eligible people. A remarkable inscription from a temple in Uttaramerur, a Brahman-controlled village, records a large number of details about how these institutions functioned:

> There shall be thirty wards. In these thirty wards those that live in each ward shall assemble and shall select each person possessing the following qualifications for inclusion for selection by lot:
>
> He must own more than one quarter of the tax-paying land. He must live in a house built on his own site. His age must be below seventy and above thirty-five. He must know the mantras and the Brahmanas [from the Vedic corpus].
>
> Even if he owns only one-eighth of the land, his name shall be included provided he has learned one *Veda* and one of the four *Bhashyas*.

This was followed by a long list of relatives who could not be considered at the same time. A person was also not eligible for the assembly if he was "one who has stolen the property of others. One who has taken forbidden dishes." Also ruled out was anyone who had been on a committee for any of the last three years or who had been on a committee prior to that but had never submitted his accounts.

> Excluding all these, names shall be written on tickets for thirty wards and . . . put into a pot. When the tickets have to be drawn a full meeting of the great assembly including the young and old members shall be convened.

There then came a detailed list of instructions for drawing the tickets that made sure nobody could cheat. By lot, thirty men, one per ward, were chosen. These men sat on various committees, such as the Garden Committee, the Tank Committee, and the Annual Committee. We don't know exactly what the Garden Committee did, but the Tank Committee likely organized water tanks and critical public services for drinking water and irrigation. Irrigation is often mentioned in inscriptions. For example, one records:

> The brahmana assembly . . . makes an agreement with two brothers . . . Because water does not reach the canal flowing to the lake of the brothers' village, the assembly shall desilt their own lake, provide half the labour on a connecting canal, and allow runoff water from their own lake to travel through that canal to the lake of the neighbouring village.

An inscription from a different village discusses "two small canals" where

> a meeting of the local brahmana assembly and the larger nadu assembly determines land boundaries of these canals in relation to surrounding fields, without lowering the water level in canals going to a neighbouring village.

Other villages also had the Fivefold Committee and the Gold Committee.

While in Siena, Italy, assemblies were convened by the tolling of a bell, in one Tamil village it was by the beating of a drum. The ur and the sabha were also in charge of collecting taxes, some of which they kept themselves and some of which they remitted to the Chola state. They also resolved disputes over land and other legal issues.

Here's where it gets really interesting. The urs and sabhas were collected together into a larger unit, called a *nadu*, mentioned above in the inscriptions about canals. The individual urs and sabhas seem to have elected representatives to the nadu, which made collective decisions. One key feature is that the geographical pattern of nadus is very irregular, and some were quite small. For instance, an inscription records that the nadu of Adanur-nadu contained just two villages. Another records that four villages collectively made up the nadu of Vada-Chiruvayil. However, some nadus had as many as eleven or fourteen villages. The historian Y. Subbarayalu used hundreds of inscriptions, mostly on temples, to draw maps of the nadus for the Chola mandalam, the heart of the kingdom around the Kaveri River valley. These show that the shapes and areas of the different nadus varied widely, even in the river valley, which likely had quite uniform population density. This was because, rather than being imposed by some central government on the territory, the Chola state was an amalgam of previously autonomous villages. The state was constructed from the bottom up, a bit like the Swiss state we'll encounter in the next chapter. This inference is confirmed by another inscription from the twelfth century emphasizing that the consent of the nadu had to be obtained to install Rajadhiraja II on the Chola throne.

It is significant too that the region came to be called Tamil Nadu, nowadays translated as "Land of the Tamils," so that the very word for the village groupings, *nadu*, ended up describing the bigger region of the Tamils.

From Gana-Sangha to Lok Sabha

We've now seen that the word *sabha* has deep roots in India. It dates back at least to the assemblies of the gana-sangha states of northern India, over 2,500 years ago. Today the lower house of the Indian parliament is called the Lok Sabha, meaning the Assembly of the People. But how real are these continuities?

The answer: Pretty real. India is a large and heterogeneous country and there is no doubt that there was a lot of variation in the operation of sabhas, even though they appear to have been everywhere. The states of northern India, especially the Mughal Empire, were constructed by outside invasion and were certainly not a bottom-up innovation in the same way that the Chola state was. Nevertheless, the Mughals did not construct the type of state bureaucracy that would have been necessary to replace the sabhas and their village republics. Instead, they were happy to tolerate local autonomy as long as land taxes got paid. The main method for this was a system of tax farming; the Mughals gave an individual known as a zamindar the right to collect taxes in a specified area, and he could keep a share, usually 10 percent. The Mughals did have revenue officials who were able to collect accurate information about local production and productivity, but they did not create a bureaucratic system of tax collection. How did the zamindars collect the taxes? In some situations they were armed pre-Mughal elites who had their own coercive resources, but often they collected the taxes in collaboration with village authorities. In other cases there were no zamindars, and the Mughals dealt directly with village authorities who were collectively responsible for taxes.

There was a lot of continuity in these village institutions too. They were recognized by officials of the British East India Company in the eighteenth century, especially after 1765 when the company was granted the right to collect taxes in Bengal and Bihar by the Mughal emperor. The situation was nicely summarized in the famous *Fifth Report from the Select Committee on the Affairs of the East India Company* presented to the British parliament in 1812. The report focused on the institutional innovations of the company since 1765, particularly with respect to the collection of tax revenues. But it records an interesting evaluation of Indian village life as well.

> A village . . . politically viewed . . . resembles a corporation or township. Its proper establishment of officers and servants consists of the following. The *potail*, or head inhabitant, who has the general superintendence of the affairs of the village, settles the disputes of the inhabitants, attends to the police, and performs the duty . . . of collecting revenues within his village, a duty which his personal influence and minute acquaintance with the situation and concerns of the people renders him best qualified to discharge.

The report then lists a large number of village officials undertaking different tasks, including "the superintendent of tanks and water-courses," and notes, "Under this simple form of municipal government the inhabitants of the country have lived from time immemorial." In the 1830s Sir Charles Metcalfe would write that

> Village Communities are little Republics, having nearly everything that they want within themselves, and almost independent of any foreign relations . . . The union of the Village Communities, each one forming a separate little State in itself, has, I conceive, contributed more than any

other cause to the preservation of the people of India through all revolutions and changes which they have suffered.

The *Fifth Report* does not use the word *panchayat*, but it appears soon after in other contemporary sources and colonial documents. For example, Henry Sumner Maine's *Village Communities in the East and West*, published in 1871, refers to the existence of "village councils" in India with elected functionaries, while B. H. Baden-Powell's *The Origin and Growth of Village Communities in India*, published in 1899, has extensive discussion of panchayats, though he seems to regard them as largely oligarchic. By 1915 John Matthai was observing that "the most characteristic feature of the government of a village community was the *panchayat* or village council," which "might denote either a general meeting of the inhabitants or a select committee chosen from among them." In fact, by 1880 British authorities were already trying to tap into these village institutions. The *Report of the Indian Famine Commission* of that year records:

> In most parts of India some village organization exists which offers a ready and natural . . . machinery . . . for village relief. For the future progress of the country, the encouragement of the principle of local self-government by which business of all kinds should be left more and more to local direction.

In 1892 an act stipulated that panchayats should be elected by the people "in any manner convenient," while an act of 1911 passed in Madras allowed for the election of panchayats and listed a large number of tasks that they should undertake, including the lighting of public roads, cleaning public roads, drains, tanks, and wells, and establishing and maintaining schools and hospitals.

It's no coincidence then that Mahatma Gandhi's vision of an ideal India was based on autarkic villages, what he called Hindu Swaraj, or Indian Home Rule. British colonial authority tried to tap into the same traditions. After independence, these village institutions were strengthened. Clause 243 of the Indian Constitution allows for the creation of a Gram Sabha, a village assembly consisting of adults qualified to vote who would democratically elect a panchayat to govern village affairs. These institutions were further empowered by the Panchayati Raj Act of 1992, which created a hierarchy of three sorts of panchayats and institutionalized them in the Indian political system.

No Honor Among Varnas

So democracy in India has deep roots. But deep-rooted or not, democratic politics doesn't work too well in a society turned against itself, discombobulated by an even deeper hierarchy. This can be seen in the northern state of Bihar (which is also shown on Map 12), where local democracy has created an additional impetus toward divisions in society and in the process undermines rather than builds state capacity, in contrast to what we would have expected from the Red Queen. And this time it wasn't the twice-born ganging up against those below them, but lower castes undermining higher castes, especially between 1990 and 2005, when the chief minister of the state was either Lalu Prasad Yadav or his wife, Rabri Devi.

Bihar is one of the poorest states in India. In 2013 about one-third of its 100 million people lived in poverty. This is one of the highest poverty rates in India. In contrast, only 11 percent of the population of Tamil Nadu is poor, and only 7 percent in Kerala. Bihar also has the lowest rate of adult literacy of any Indian state, 64 percent according to the 2011 census, far below a state like Kerala, at 94 percent. Poverty and illiteracy are pervasive in Bihar because of its crumbling state capacity. The neighboring state of Jharkhand, which was part of Bihar until 2000, when it was split off, shows alarming rates of teacher absenteeism, with 40 percent of teachers who ought to be in school nowhere to be found. The situation in Bihar is similar.

Bihar's local state has so little capacity, in fact, that it cannot collect the payments that the central government is supposed to give it. Indian states receive a large fraction of their revenues from the central government, and to get these, they have to apply for them and complete a number of bureaucratic procedures. This of course requires (a little bit of) capacity. You need to be able to fill in the forms in time, track what's available, make budgets, and approve spending plans. But huge amounts of money earmarked for Bihar never get allocated or spent. Take for instance Sarva Shiksha Abhiyan, a prominent program to improve primary education, something Bihar sorely needs. Between 2001 and 2007, 52 billion rupees were earmarked for Bihar, but only half of this, 26 billion, was actually spent. At the same time, in the period between 2002 and 2006, 40 billion rupees were allocated for the state under a program known as Rashtriya Sam Vikas Yojana. This was money that could be used to fund different sorts of investments in physical and social infrastructure in backward areas. The Bihar state government was able to secure only 10 of the 40 billion and of that, just 62 percent got spent. Even worse was the implementation of the flagship program to boost rural roads, the Gram Sadak Yojana. Here Bihar managed to spend only 25 percent of the money allocated to it.

Meanwhile, half of the 394 projects approved under the national government's Integrated Child Development Scheme were never started. The state systematically claims less than it could from the national government and it massively underspends even what it manages to claim.

This is all due to the inefficient structure of the local state in Bihar. It was centralized in an absurd way; any spending decision that involved more than 2.5 million rupees (US$55,000 in the mid-2000s) had to be approved by the state cabinet. This caused huge delays, and because 60 percent of any initial installment of money from Delhi has to be spent before other installments are released, it was often too late to request or use anything other than the first installment. According to a World Bank report in 2005:

> The existing civil service rules envisage a merit-based system of recruitment, placement, promotion, sanctions and rewards. However, the system operates in an ad hoc, non-transparent and non-meritocratic manner. Problems related to the work environment (including those faced by women employees), infrastructure, and accommodation, local tensions and delayed salaries together affect staff morale. . . . The district magistrates appear to be frustrated by centralization, absence of support and understanding from their superiors, and inaction on reports of malfeasance and inefficiency at subordinate levels.

This assessment suggests a complete failure in the institutions of the state, but there is more to it than that. It was not just that "the system operates in an ad hoc, non-transparent and non-meritocratic manner"; in many cases there was actually nobody there at all to work the system. In the 1990s, there were vast numbers of unfilled vacancies in the government, including an acute shortage of engineers. The main reason for this was not the absence of qualified people, but the fact that the departmental promotion committee did not hold meetings, and even when meetings were held, the committee's recommendations were not approved. The consequence was that the positions of engineer in chief in the two principal engineering departments, the Road Construction Department and the Rural Engineering Organisation, were vacant for long periods of time. All 15 posts of chief engineer in those two departments, as well as 81 out of the 91 superintendent engineer positions, were similarly vacant. Lower down in the bureaucracy, of the 6,393 positions for executive, assistant, and junior engineers, 1,305 were vacant. This failure to appoint people was endemic. A 2006 document published by the government of Bihar itself directly connects the problem of vacancies with the inability to access funds from the national government.

> There has been an acute shortage of technical personnel at all levels in the Road Construction Department and Rural Engineering Organisation. There has not been any significant recruitment at entry levels and promotions have not materialized. The Quality Control Organisation in the Road Construction Department is non-functional for want of equipment, chemicals and personnel. Advance Planning Wing is also non-functional. There has been a total collapse of technical administration. This is a serious constraint not only for implementation of works but also for preparing project proposals for getting more funds from the Central Government or other sources.

Failure to fill vacancies, the underclaiming and underspending of resources, and the general lack of state capacity in Bihar are not just consequences of disorganization. They result from political strategies rooted in the division and fragmentation of society. In fact, the lack of state capacity, though always present in Bihar as in much of India, significantly intensified after 1990, when Lalu Prasad Yadav became the chief minister. The Yadavs are a jati that are part of the Shudra varna and they are the most populous caste in the state. Like most places in India, historically higher castes, particularly Brahmans, had dominated politics in Bihar. But the Shudras displaced the Brahmans and took control of local politics under Lalu Yadav. To gain power, the Yadavs forged a new political coalition with the castes below them as well as the Muslims who were outside the caste system. Their explicit aim was to replace the high castes in power. This is key for understanding all the vacancies. The people who were primarily qualified to be engineers or fill other high-skill jobs were from the upper castes. Lalu Yadav refused to appoint them. Even though the resulting state incapacity meant he lost resources and was unable to provide public services his supporters sorely needed, Lalu Yadav downplayed the impact of "development," claiming that this benefited only high-caste people.

The Broken Red Queen

India is an enigma. A very poor country with endemic state failure and political dysfunctionality, it is at the same time the world's largest democracy, with intense political competition. What explains this puzzling assortment? We have argued that the roots of India's democracy go back to its history of popular participation in politics, resembling the assembly politics of the Germanic tribes we discussed in Chapter 6. But the parallel with the European path stops there. While the Red Queen got to work in Europe and simultaneously expanded state capacity, institutionalized and strengthened society's mobilization, and in the process dissolved the cage of norms in Europe, no such thing happened in India. This is because of the nature and legacy of the caste system. Caste divisions not only manufactured ingrained hierarchies and inequities in society, but they distorted the nature of politics. Society, fragmented and at war with itself, failed to monitor state institutions and singularly lacked the ability to push the state to build further capacity. The Brahmans at the top were too busy dominating the rest and the rest were too preoccupied with their position in the social hierarchy. Everybody was too trapped in the cage of norms. Historically, at least, the state saw it as its duty to enforce and reaffirm the caste system, strengthening the cage of norms at every turn.

When democracy arrived after independence, castes defined the battle lines for political competition and sapped the energy of democratic competition. As the anthropologist Béteille observed, "The weakness of the village panchayat seems to arise from the imposition of a democratic formal structure on a social substratum which is segmented and hierarchical in nature." The same was true of democratic politics at the state and national level. The Red Queen remained broken as caste divisions made it impossible for society to get organized beyond the existing social hierarchy, keep politicians accountable, or induce the state to serve the people. Instead, caste politics often further eroded state capacity, as we have seen in Bihar.

The broken Red Queen had predictable consequences in terms of poverty. But more fundamentally it meant that even if situated in the context of democratic politics, liberty has been absent not just for Dalits but for all Indians, who collectively continue to be dominated by social hierarchy and the cage of caste norms.

Chapter 9

DEVIL IN THE DETAILS

European Diversity

Though as we have seen in Chapter 6 the two blades of the European scissors put much of the continent near or inside the corridor, quite a bit of diversity remained and developed over the next several centuries. England was moving in the corridor toward a much more participatory form of government overseeing the deepening of the state's capacity. The Swiss Confederation, squeezed between France, Italy, southern Germany, and Austria, was likewise already inside the corridor and had created both a "citizen army" to defend itself against the Habsburgs and a powerful assembly controlling politics. In the words of Niccolò Machiavelli in *The Prince*, written in 1513:

> Rome and Sparta for many centuries stood armed and free. The Swiss
> are extremely well armed and are very free.

Indeed, Tom Scott's summary of the consensus among historians is that Swiss peasants were "free of feudal servitude and, as a sign of their liberty, these mountain peasants bore arms and demanded 'honour' even from nobles ... Their medieval clan structures had little to do with our images of democratic forms but these peasants were 'free.'" Farther north, however, Prussia developed a very different type of state, whose despotic character is epitomized by the French philosopher Voltaire's quip that while other states possess an army, Prussia is an army which possesses a state.

A little farther south the situation was completely different in Albania and Montenegro, which lacked any centralized authority and continued to experience uncoordinated violence well into the twentieth century. The Montenegrin writer and intellectual Milovan Djilas described the extent of feuding in the 1950s by writing about his own family history:

> The men of several generations have died at the hands of Montenegrins, men of the same faith and name. My father's grandfather, my own two grandfathers, my father, and my uncle were killed, as though a dread curse lay upon them . . . generation after generation, and the bloody chain was not broken. The inherited fear and hatred of feuding clans was mightier than fear and hatred of the enemy, the Turks. It seems to me that I was born with blood in my eyes. My first sight was of blood. My first words were blood and bathed in blood.

What explains these differences? Why did these European polities diverge so sharply starting from broadly similar conditions?

In this chapter we explain how our conceptual framework is useful for answering these questions and in the process show how it sheds light more broadly on the effects of political, international, economic, and demographic changes, sometimes referred to as "structural factors." The most common way in which social scientists have discussed the implications of different structural factors is by arguing that they create natural affinities for certain types of economic and political development—for example, war and military mobilization are argued to induce greater state capacity, while certain types of crops, such as sugar and cotton, lead to despotism and others, such as wheat, prepare the conditions for democratic politics. Our framework shows why this is not necessarily so. The same structural factor can have very different impacts on a polity's political trajectory depending on the prevailing balance of power between state and society.

The key ideas can be seen in the context of Figure 1 from Chapter 2 summarizing our conceptual framework, which is replicated here as Figure 2. It makes clear that broadly similar conditions in terms of the power of state and society are no guarantee that two different polities will follow very similar trajectories. That depends on whether they are on the same side of the boundaries demarcating the regions of the Despotic, Shackled, and Absent Leviathans. This figure also highlights the fact that the effects of structural factors will be quite distinct depending on the initial positions of different nations. Take an increase in the state's capacity, which in the figure corresponds to a vertical move up as the state's power increases (while society's power remains unchanged). This could be just the shift that puts a polity inside the corridor, as Arrow 1 in the figure indicates. But it could also be the force that moves a society that was lodged in the corridor away from it and toward the Despotic Leviathan, as Arrow 2 illustrates. Or it might be not so consequential at all because it moves a society with the Absent Leviathan a little bit closer to the corridor, but leaves its long-run destination unaltered, as shown with Arrow 3. So when it comes to the effects of structural factors the devil is decidedly in the details.

In the rest of this chapter, we develop these ideas, first focusing on European history and the contrast between Switzerland, Prussia, and Montenegro, and a very specific type of structural factor—the increase in the capacity and power of the state brought forth by military mobilization and war. These ideas and their applications are not confined to European history. We show that they are also useful

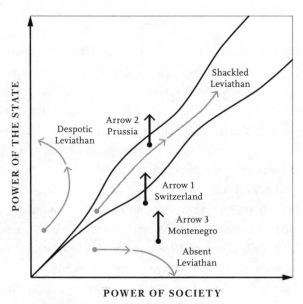

Figure 2. The Divergent Effects of an Increase in the Power of the State

in understanding how more recent big shocks have led to highly diverse responses, for example, in the context of the collapse of the Soviet Union, which opened the way to the birth of all kinds of states in Eastern Europe and Asia. We finally discuss how the first wave of economic globalization in the second half of the nineteenth century differentially impacted individual postcolonial societies, focusing in particular on the divergence between Costa Rica and Guatemala.

War Made the State, and the State Made War

This title is a direct quote from the political sociologist Charles Tilly, who formulated one of the most famous theories about the role of a specific structural factor—increased incidence and threat of interstate warfare—on state building. He applied this idea to Western Europe in the early modern period arguing that the threat of increased warfare following the "military revolution" in the seventeenth century led to the creation of modern states. The military revolution introduced more portable and powerful firearms, new military tactics, and improved fortifications. Standing armies and intensified interstate competition followed. Tilly argued that it revolutionized politics too because it forced states to create much more effective systems for raising taxes and providing infrastructure so they could pay for, equip, and transport larger militaries. In terms of our theory, this corresponds to an induced increase in the state's power in order to deal with the necessities of war. Tilly was right that such a change can fundamentally alter the dynamics of political development, as Arrow 1 in Figure 2 illustrates, but it can have quite different implications as well.

Switzerland provides the perfect illustration of Tilly's argument, even if state building in this case predates the military revolution. Switzerland was historically part of the Holy Roman Empire, the successor institution to the eastern part of Charlemagne's Carolingian Empire. The empire still had an emperor, but it had fragmented into many small and relatively independent polities, and the emperor was actually elected by some of them. We have already seen how in northern Italy, which was quite far from the core of the empire centered on Germany, these polities asserted their independence. Switzerland was also on the periphery of the empire, even if not separated and isolated by the Alps like Italy. The Holy Roman Empire's imperfect control over this area allowed the component Swiss polities, the cantons, to develop their own systems of assemblies. These cantons, some rural, some largely urban, thus came to reflect the broader pattern of assembly politics inherited from Germanic tribes, which had reemerged as the empire had weakened. The Swiss Confederation started in 1291 with the cantons of Uri, Schwyz, and Unterwalden taking oaths and signing the Bundesbrief (Federal Charter) at Rütli, a meadow above Lake Lucerne (see Map 13). The charter was an attempt toward centralization of authority and was particularly concerned with public order and lawlessness. The first substantive clause read:

> Thus, all people of the valley community of Uri, the entirety of the Schwyz valley and the community of people from the lower Unterwalden valley recognize the malice of the times and for their own protection and preservation they have promised to assist each other by every means possible with every counsel and favor, with persons or goods within their valleys and without against any and all who inflict on them or any among them acts of violence or injustice against persons or goods.

It was in effect a pact committing the three cantons to come to one another's aid and providing a framework for resolving disputes, stating that "should disputes arise among any of the people bound by this oath, the most prudent among

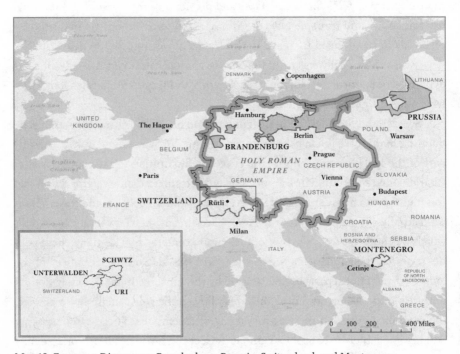

Map 13. European Divergence: Brandenburg-Prussia, Switzerland, and Montenegro

Societal mobilization: The death of suffragette Emily Davison.

Hobbes's *Leviathan*.

Norms controlling hierarchy: The ostracism of Themistocles.

Norms against hierarchy: A Tiv diviner.

The Absent Leviathan: The trash piles up in Lebanon.

The will to power builds a navy in Hawaii.

The Shackled Leviathan: The *Allegory of Good Government.*

The consequences of a Shackled Leviathan: *The Effects of Good Government.*

Another consequence of a Shackled Leviathan: The invention of tortillas.

The Shackled Leviathan's law from below: The Salic Law.

The Bayeux Tapestry.

eaking the cage of norms.

Failed experimentation: Galileo's celatone for calculating longitude.

有天有地而上下有差，明王始立而處國有制。夫兩貴之不能相事，兩賤之不能相使，是天數也。埶位齊，而欲惡同物，物不能澹則必爭，爭則必亂，亂則窮矣。先王惡其亂也，故制禮義以分之，使有貧富貴賤之等，足以相兼臨者，是養天下之本也。書曰「維齊非齊」。此之謂也。

馬駭輿則君子不安輿，庶人駭政則君子不安位。馬駭輿則莫若靜之，庶人駭政則莫若惠之。選賢良，舉篤敬與孝弟，收孤寡，補貧窮。如是，則庶人安政矣。庶人安政，然後君子安位。傳曰「君者舟也庶人者，水也。水則載舟，水則覆舟。」此之謂也。

故君人者，欲安，則莫若平政愛民矣；欲榮，則莫若隆禮敬士矣；欲立功名、

PEOPLE
WATER

WATER
CAN
CARRY
BOAT
WATER
CAN
SINK
BOAT

When the Chinese people were in control: The *Xunzi*.

The Despotic Leviathan is watching: Tiananmen Square.

Trapped in the cage of norms: Dalit manual scavenging.

Redlining in St. Louis.

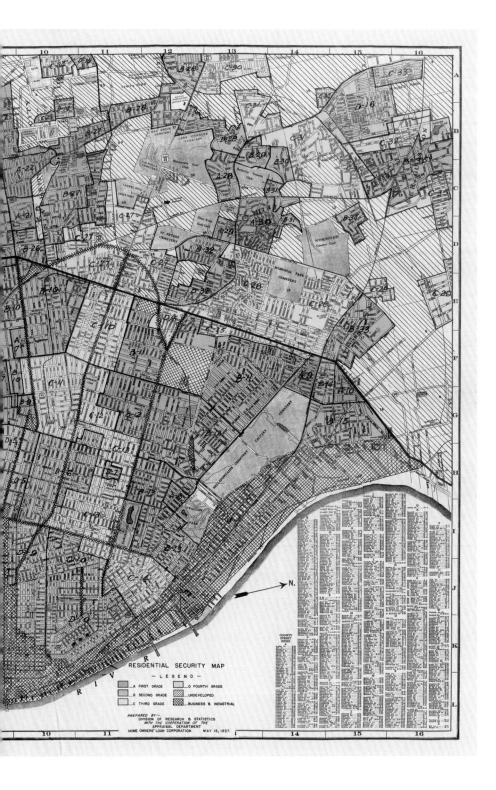

RESIDENTIAL SECURITY MAP

— LEGEND —

A FIRST GRADE   D FOURTH GRADE

B SECOND GRADE   UNDEVELOPED

C THIRD GRADE   BUSINESS & INDUSTRIAL

PREPARED BY:—
DIVISION OF RESEARCH & STATISTICS
WITH THE COOPERATION OF THE
APPRAISAL DEPARTMENT
HOME OWNERS' LOAN CORPORATION   MAY 15, 1937.

The economics of the Despotic Leviathan: Coffee workers in Guatemala.

Latin America's caste system.

The Ikhwan in the Najd.

Saddam Hussein finds religion.

The zero-sum Red Queen: The towers of Bologna.

Moving into the corridor South Africa–style: Mandela giving the Rugby World Cup to Springbok captain Pienaar.

ving into the corridor Lagos-style: Pay your taxes!

Moving into the corridor Bogotá-style: Mockus the supercitizen.

The international state system: Robert Mugabe, the WHO's "goodwill ambassador."

the confederates shall settle the conflict between the parties. All other confeder-ates shall defend this verdict against anyone who rejects it." It didn't specify who the "most prudent" was, but this clause is interpreted as stipulating arbitration by one of the cantons if two others, or the citizens of two others, got into a dispute. Might we have here the roots of the fabled Swiss ability to find compromises?

Uri, Schwyz, and Unterwalden were all part of the Holy Roman Empire. They were supposed to be subservient to the Habsburg Duke of Austria. They had no business signing pacts. The Habsburgs didn't approve of such autonomous orga-nization, and they certainly didn't like the clause that read:

> We have further unanimously vowed and established that we in these
> valleys shall accept no judge who has gained his office for money or for
> any other price and who is not our resident or native.

No Habsburg judges were to be tolerated anymore. In 1315 the first Habsburg army was driven off after the battle of Morgarten. More pacts followed and what came to be known as the Swiss Confederation spread. Lucerne joined in 1332. The League of Zurich of 1351 specifically stipulated that everyone who signed would come to the aid of any other threatened by the Habsburgs. Glarus joined in 1352 and Bern in 1353. Duke Leopold II of Austria finally decided to put a stop to this Swiss recalcitrance, but his army was routed at the battle of Sempach in 1386 by the combined forces of the confederation. Leopold himself was killed along with a lot of the local nobility who had been fighting with him. This didn't exactly free the Swiss from Habsburg dominance. That had to wait until a final war in 1499, followed by the Treaty of Basel, which recognized the confederation's de facto autonomy. Undeterred, the bottom-up construction of the Swiss state continued throughout the fifteenth century. As part of this process, rural people bought themselves out of any residual feudal obligations, and as that happened, what was left of the Swiss nobility slowly withered away. By this time the transformation going on among the Swiss had been noticed throughout the empire and the ex-pression *"schweytzer werden"*—"going Swiss"—was coined. It meant peasants try-ing to become autonomous. After 1415 an assembly made up of delegates from all the cantons in the confederation began to meet regularly. Fribourg and Solothurn were admitted in 1481, Basel and Schaffhausen in 1501, and Appenzell in 1513.

Consistent with Tilly's theory, this all happened in the context of rising mili-tary threats from the Habsburgs, which made it more beneficial for the cantons to come together and increase the Swiss state's capacity. The victory at Sempach had shown the power of Swiss infantry even over armored knights. As early as 1424 Florence asked the Assembly of the confederation for mercenaries, and for the next few centuries the Swiss specialized in providing such troops for warring countries all over Europe. At first the recruitment of these mercenaries was decentralized, organized by private entrepreneurs and various cantonal bodies. But it became apparent that the mercenary activity posed a threat to security and to the state's authority. So the Assembly passed a law in 1503 stipulating that a majority of the body had to approve any recruitment. One reason for this was to avoid the possibility of two Swiss armies facing off against each other, as had happened in Novara in 1500 with one in the employ of France, the other fighting for Milan. The final peace with the Habsburgs didn't stop further threats from France, Milan, and the Dukes of Württemberg, and the military exigencies facing the Swiss state continued, as did the process of state building.

In the Swiss case the threat of warfare, in particular the persistent threat from the Habsburgs to reinstate the overlordship of the Holy Roman Empire, seems to have been an important incentive for the otherwise individualistic cantons and cities to unite into a larger confederation, centralize authority, and increase their state's capacity. Before this centralization, the Swiss cantons were arguably outside the corridor, relying on clan structures rather than laws or state authority for resolving disputes or enforcing laws. But this inheritance also meant that Swiss peasants were free and society already mobilized. The centralization that began in 1291 came in the context of a society that was strong enough to withstand and counterbalance the increasing power of the state, engendering a transition into the corridor and spearheading a process of gradual expansion of the capabilities of both state and society.

The movement of state and society along the corridor created not just the conditions for liberty but also, predictably, incentives and opportunities for economic prosperity. The Swiss became famous first for their watches and subsequently their machine tool industry, and then they took over the world pharmaceutical industry. They used their comparative advantage in cows and milk to become a major producer of chocolates. Switzerland has the highest income per capita of any European country (not counting the small enclaves such as Luxembourg and Monaco).

War made the state in Switzerland, as Tilly would have it, but it also made society. Switzerland went on to build one of the most vibrant democracies in Europe. Yet as Figure 2 emphasizes, such a process is by no means preordained. The threat of war can unleash very different dynamics too.

The Sort of State That War Made

You don't have to look far within Europe to see that if war made the state, it made very different types of states in different circumstances. The prime example is Prussia. Though Prussia was never part of the Holy Roman Empire, in 1618 it merged through marriage with Brandenburg, which was (see Map 13). The ruling family of Brandenburg, the Hohenzollerns, became the ruling family of Brandenburg-Prussia, with the ruler known as the elector. These were difficult times, as the Thirty Years War was afoot and invading armies crisscrossed Central Europe. The elector Georg Wilhelm desperately tried to stay out of the conflict, but had to cave in when told by the king of Sweden, Gustavus Adolphus, that neutrality was not an option. "What can I do? They've all the big guns," was how Georg Wilhelm famously reported the incident. Brandenburg was particularly devastated, losing as much as half of its population.

In 1640 Frederick William I came to the throne as the new elector. He ruled for forty-eight years and charted a new course for Brandenburg-Prussia, and in the process came to be known as the Great Elector. The Prussian experience during the Thirty Years War convinced Frederick William that he too needed "big guns." As he put it:

> I have experienced neutrality before; even under the most favorable circumstances, you are treated badly. I have vowed never to be neutral again as long as I live.

This all meant greater state capacity. With big guns, the state could control more. But to get big guns, it needed more tax revenues. More tax revenues would be easier to raise if Frederick William could increase his power over society, and that's what he did. Previously taxes had to be negotiated with various representative bodies, such as the Estates of Kurmark in Brandenburg. He started out by trying to get permanent grants of taxation, which would free him from the need to endlessly seek the approval of the estates. In 1653 he negotiated the so-called Brandenburg Recess, which gave him 530,000 thalers over a period of six years. Crucially, he, rather than the Estates of Kurmark, got to collect the taxes. In exchange he gave the nobility, which made up a chamber in the estates, tax-exempt status. This was a clever strategy of "divide and rule," which successfully separated the different chambers of the estates and made sure they would not form a unified force against him. He went on to extract similar concessions from the Prussian estates.

Frederick William then overrode the authority of the estates and started to tax without their agreement, something he could do because the 1653 decision allowed him to initiate the building of a tax administration. In 1655 he founded the Kriegskommissariat ("war commissary"), which covered both tax collection and military organization. By 1659 the estates had already atrophied and retreated to just dealing with local issues. Frederick William also transformed the royal council, previously made up of a few aristocrats, into an administration staffed by professional officials. Between 1348 and 1498, 16 universities were founded within central Europe and by 1648 another 18 opened. This meant that there was a large pool of well-qualified graduates trained in Roman law who could be attracted to staff a meritocratic bureaucracy. Governors were appointed to run the various territories under the elector's control. After 1667 he introduced indirect taxes on trade. The administration of the royal estates was also reconfigured and the land was let out to private farmers for money, dramatically increasing government revenues. By 1688, Brandenburg, Prussia, and Kleve-Mark, the largest territories, were paying one million thalers a year in taxes, with about another 600,000 coming in from the other regions under Frederick William's control.

In 1701 Frederick William's son Frederick III changed Brandenburg-Prussia to the Kingdom of Prussia and crowned himself King Frederick I. His son King Frederick William I (not to be confused with the Great Elector of the previous century with the identical name) ruled between 1713 and 1740, and his grandson Frederick II, known as Frederick the Great, ruled from 1740 to 1786. Father and son intensified the project that the Great Elector had started.

In 1723 the bureaucracy was restructured again with the creation of the General Directory, merging the previous war commissary with the administration of the royal estates and putting everything at the service of the military. In 1733 Frederick completely reorganized the basis of military recruitment. He divided the territory into cantons of 5,000 households with a regiment assigned to each for recruitment. At the age of ten every male child was included in the recruitment rolls. Though some occupations and people were exempted, at least a quarter of the male population was included in the rolls. This dramatically increased the potential size of the army. In 1713 the army had about 30,000 soldiers in peacetime. By 1740, when Frederick the Great took over from his father, the figure was 80,000. In the meantime his father had managed to increase tax revenues by almost one half. Frederick the Great had a new strategy for further expanding Prussia's tax base and military machine: he launched an aggressive strategy of territorial expansion.

War might have made the state in Prussia, but it made a famously despotic one. That's certainly how its rulers thought about it. The Great Elector himself observed, "So long as God gives me breath, I shall assert my rule like a despot . . ." Frederick the Great agreed, remarking:

> A well-run government must have a firmly established system . . . in which finance, policy and military all combine to promote the same end, the strengthening of the state and the expansion of its power. Such a system can only derive from one brain.

In the sixteenth century Prussia, like many other parts of the Holy Roman Empire, was inside the corridor with the powerful estates constraining the monarchy. Warfare, by increasing the state's power, pushed it out of the corridor, as Arrow 2 in Figure 2 illustrates—a very different outcome from the one that warfare helped create in Switzerland. Prussia didn't look back and rapidly progressed along the despotic path.

This had predictable consequences for liberty, which far from flourishing as in the Swiss case, was completely snuffed out. In the assessment of the British envoy Hugh Elliot:

> The Prussian monarchy reminds me of a vast prison in the center of which appears the great keeper occupied in the care of his captives.

Freedom on the Heights

The impact of warfare isn't confined to creating Shackled or Despotic Leviathans. Montenegro had a large number of similarities to Switzerland. It too had been part of the Roman Empire, even if more peripherally, and it shared a mountainous ecology and an economy based on herding. The great historian Fernand Braudel emphasized how European terrain created particular types of societies, arguing that "mountains are mountains: that is, primarily an obstacle, and therefore a refuge, a land of the free." Free, like the Swiss. But in some sense people were pretty free in Montenegro and Albania too. Edith Durham, one of the first Western Europeans to systematically study the Balkans, starts her famous book *High Albania* with a line from a poem by Lord Tennyson, "Of old sat freedom on the heights." Yet the connection between freedom and the state is complex. As we've seen, the expansion of the state is often resisted because people want to preserve their freedom from its authority. That's exactly what happened in Montenegro even though it continually experienced the pressure of warfare.

Prior to 1852 Montenegro was in effect a theocracy, but one wherein the ruling bishop, the vladika, could exercise no coercive authority over the clans that dominated society. After a visit to Montenegro in 1807, the French general Marmont observed, "This Vladika is a splendid man, of about fifty-five years of age, with a strong spirit. He conducts himself with nobility and dignity. His positive and legal authority is unrecognized in his country."

The key to understanding why this was so and why no state formed in Montenegro is that it was further from the corridor than Switzerland was. It was made up of kinship groups, clans, and tribes, and lacked the elements of centralization that the Swiss had inherited from the Carolingians. There are many similarities between Montenegro and other societies, such as the Tiv, that have steadfastly refused centralized state authority. As one scholar put it for Montenegro, "Continued attempts to impose centralized government were in conflict with tribal loyalty."

Warfare with the Ottomans did induce the clans to try to coordinate more. Just before a key battle at Krusi in 1796 an assembly of Montenegrin tribal chiefs met at Cetinje and adopted a measure called Stega, or "fastening," which proclaimed the unification of the Montenegrin heartlands. Two years later they met again and agreed to convene a "council" of fifty members, in effect the first time there had been any institutionalized structures of government above the tribe. The first attempt at a legal code in 1796 by Vladika Peter I reflected the fact that order in society was regulated by the institution of blood feuds and included the clauses:

> A man who strikes another with his hand, foot, or chibouk, shall pay him a fine of fifty sequins. If the man struck at once kills his aggressor, he shall not be punished. Nor shall a man be punished for killing a thief caught in the act.

> If a Montenegrin in self-defense kills a man who has insulted him . . . it shall be considered that the killing was involuntary.

This looks more like Clovis's Salic Law or King Alfred's law code than a modern legal system. But there was little of the subsequent state-building effort of Clovis or Alfred in this case. The feud continued with centralized state authority nowhere in sight.

The lack of state authority and dominance of the feud lasted sufficiently long that the anthropologist Christopher Boehm was able to reconstruct it in great detail in the 1960s. Boehm captures the essential difficulty of central authority in Montenegro when he writes, "It was only when their central leader attempted to institutionalize forcible means of controlling feuds that the tribesmen stood firm in their right to follow their ancient traditions. This was because they perceived in such interference a threat to their basic political autonomy." Boehm is referring to the attempts of Vladika Njegoš to establish the state's authority in Montenegro in the 1840s. Djilas analyzed the same situation in the following terms:

> It was a clash between two principles—the state and the clan. The former stood for order and a nation, and against chaos and treason; the latter stood for clan freedoms and against the arbitrary actions of an impersonal central authority—the Senate, the Guard, the captains.

Djilas records that Njegoš's reforms were immediately confronted by the revolt of the Piperi and Crmnica clans because "the imposition of government and a state was putting an end to the independence and internal freedom of the clans." Njegoš was succeeded by his nephew Danilo, who made himself the first secular prince of Montenegro in 1851, but his project to build something resembling a state ran into fierce opposition too. An attempt to raise taxes in 1853 triggered clan revolts with the Piperi, Kuči, and Bjelopavlići declaring themselves independent states. A member of the Bjelopavlići assassinated Danilo in 1860.

War did make states of different sorts in Switzerland and Prussia, but not so in Montenegro or, for that matter, in neighboring Albania, where society remained highly fragmented and suspicious of centralized power. Montenegrins fought the Ottomans not by creating a powerful centralized authority but by using their tribal structures. Any pressure to increase state capacity, just as with Arrow 3 in Figure 2, was not sufficient to bring Montenegro or Albania close to the corridor. They would stay with the Absent Leviathan.

Our theory also highlights the ironic implications of this resistance for liberty. Even though they remained free from state control, and maintained their egalitarian clan structures, Montenegrins were still subject to dominance and insecurity due to endemic feuding. For them this was better than being dominated by the Ottomans or the vladika, but it was still very far from liberty. Society was armed and violent. An interesting question is, Why, in contrast to many other stateless societies, such as the Asante, the Tiv, and the Tonga, whom we have seen in Africa, did Montenegro or Albania not develop norms to control feuds and recurrent violence? One possibility is that this was in fact because of the incessant wars. Violence had to be part of any order in these societies, and this made it difficult to create any type of nonviolent social order.

Differences That Matter

Readers familiar with our earlier book *Why Nations Fail* will see some parallels between our discussion of the divergent implications of structural factors here and the role of small institutional differences during critical junctures in our earlier work. Our discussion in *Why Nations Fail* emphasized how large shocks can lead to very different responses depending on prevailing institutions. Our theory here goes further both because it distinguishes between societies under the control of despotic states and those without any centralized state, and also because it explicitly focuses on the dynamics of the state's capacity and society's ability to control the state and the elites. This enriched framework leads to a more nuanced discussion by clarifying the sources of divergent behavior—changes in various structural factors can move us into different parts of Figure 2. This framework highlights the dynamic implications of such differences in a way that goes considerably beyond our earlier book. For example, Prussia, like Switzerland, was able to build considerable state capacity in the face of increasing threats of interstate warfare, but this ushered in a very different type of evolution of the state.

Indeed, consistent with our theory here, Prussia ultimately ended up with less state capacity than Switzerland. This may at first appear paradoxical. Shouldn't all of that emphasis on controlling society, raising revenues, and fighting wars lead to a huge amount of capacity? The fact that it doesn't is one of the distinctive implications of our theory as already emphasized in Chapter 2. In the absence of the Red Queen effect, the development of state capacity will remain incomplete.

Take one of the most basic public services a state is supposed to provide—dispute resolution and justice. Though Prussia created a despotic state, it did this without the cooperation of society. As a result, state institutions were built on preexisting feudal structures. The new merit systems were merged with an older structure described by one historian as being "sustained by aristocratic patronage, social heredity, amateurism, and, often, proprietary tenure." This tenure was evident in the prominence of several aristocratic families, for example, the Heinitzes, von Redens, von Hardenbergs, von Steins, Dechens, Gerhards, and their kinsmen dominating bureaucratic offices. As they filled the positions at the top, they intensively repressed the serfs at the bottom, who made up 80 percent of the labor force in agriculture. They achieved this through their control of manorial courts, which could administer punishments ranging from small fines for minor misdemeanors to corporal punishments, including whippings and imprisonment. So there was little provision of justice, but instead a systematic use of courts to impose the feudal order. Although it looked impressive, this despotic state had a hard time enforcing most of its policies. An obvious consequence of this lack of capacity, despite all the tax revenues and military expenditures, was the shattering defeat of Prussian armies at Jena in 1806. A big French advantage came from the fact that three different people were nominally in charge of the Prussian army and they had five different battle plans which they couldn't agree on.

The situation in Switzerland was very different. The Swiss confederacy was founded in 1291 on a demand for the objective resolution of disputes, which Habsburg courts did not deliver. Magistrates were elected at the local level and the state was built up from the bottom by a series of oaths, covenants, and pacts that recognized the autonomy and self-governance of local society. Feudal dues lapsed or were negotiated away. Manorial courts were gradually replaced by equality before the law. The Swiss eradicated the type of local despotism that Prussian peasants had to put up with (and did not cooperate with if they could get away with it).

Armed with this general framework, we now revisit several iconic turning points in European history, some of which were discussed in *Why Nations Fail*, but now with additional insights about the dynamics that they imply for European states and societies.

One important turning point in Europe in the fourteenth and fifteenth centuries was the huge collapse of the population following the Black Death. As we saw in Chapter 6, the feudal order, even if it could not completely obliterate the balance between state and society in England, had created a significant edge for elites in their control over peasants and society in many parts of Europe. With declining populations and society getting emboldened as a result of the greater scarcity of labor, feudal elites became less able to control and obtain taxes and servile labor obligations from their serfs. Serfs asked for their obligations to be reduced and, despite feudal restrictions on labor mobility, started leaving manors. In our framework, this change corresponds to an increase in the power of society, and in many parts of Western Europe the result was a further move away from despotic control of the state and elites over society. This was a significant step up in the corridor. But in Eastern Europe, where, by the fourteenth century, landowners and elites were already more dominant, things worked out quite differently. In this case any mobilization of peasants was more limited and insufficient to move these areas closer to the corridor, and there was no lasting damage to the power of the Despotic Leviathan. Then the subsequent act of this confrontation played out with the "second serfdom," significantly increasing the dominance of elites over society. In the context of the declines in the population throughout Europe and growing demand for agricultural produce in the West, the East's powerful landlords were incentivized to increase their demands from the peasants, which they achieved by tightening their grip over them. By the end of the sixteenth century a much more intense exploitation of serfs had emerged in the East. So while England, France, and the Netherlands moved up in the corridor, Poland, Hungary, and other parts of Eastern Europe launched deeper into the lands of the Despotic Leviathan.

Potentially divergent influences on a nation's political development come not only from military threats or demographic shocks but also from major economic opportunities. Such a change reconfiguring European trajectories arrived with the discovery of the Americas by Christopher Columbus and the rounding of the Cape of Good Hope by Bartolomeu Dias. Once again, the different balances between state and society produced divergent responses. In England, as we mentioned in Chapter 6, the tight limits on what the crown and its allies could do in terms of monopolizing overseas trade meant that it was new groups of merchants that benefited most from these economic opportunities. This fueled a rise in the power and assertiveness of society in its protracted struggle against the crown. Merchants who had already profited from trade with the New World were looking to continue doing so and became some of the chief supporters of Parliament in the English Civil War between 1642 and 1651 and then later constituted major segments of the opposition to Charles II and James II in the run-up to the Glorious Revolution. While in England these new economic opportunities tilted the balance between state and society in favor of the latter, they did no such thing in Spain and Portugal, where the monarchies had been able to create overseas monopolies. This difference was largely due to the initial balance of power, which favored the elites in these countries. Roman Iberia had been conquered by a German tribe too, the Visigoths, who left a legacy of assembly, later institutionalized as the Cortes of Castile, León, or Aragon (see Map 8 in Chapter 6). But these survived only in the north of the country after the Arab invasions starting in the eighth century pushed Iberia out of the corridor. The "reconquest" of the penninsula from the Arabs greatly intensified the despotic instincts of the Iberian state. The more despotic Spanish and Portuguese monarchies and their allies could then more successfully control the economy and monopolize Atlantic trading opportunities. As a result, rather than facing emboldened opposition, they themselves got richer, more powerful, and even more despotic, and society became more crippled. There would be no respite from despotism in the Iberian Peninsula.

The next big economic opportunity played out similarly. We have seen in Chapter 6 how the pace of societal transformation in Britain got a lot more intense and the Red Queen effect more fervent after the Industrial Revolution. These changes offered a multitude of new economic possibilities, and in most cases it was people from every nook and cranny of society who took advantage of these. But there would be no such Red Queen effect in parts of Europe that had already diverged quite considerably. In the Habsburg Empire or in Russia, as we recounted in *Why Nations Fail*, the Despotic Leviathan tightened its grip and even resisted the introduction of new industrial technologies and railways, lest this reawaken their submissive societies.

So it is the same pattern we see in all of these examples. The outlines of European history, very much like the history of other parts of the world, are heavily shaped by the impact of big shocks but critically, this happens on a canvas drawn by the balance of power between state and society.

In the Lenin Shipyard

Divergent effects of big shocks have characterized other iconic episodes, including the collapse of the Soviet Union in 1991. The Soviet state was a perfect specimen of the Despotic Leviathan at home in Russia, and acted as the fountainhead of despotic power in Eastern Europe and in the Soviet republics it controlled in Asia. Its collapse in 1991 thus corresponded to a sharp decline in the state's power. As Czech playwright and dissident, and soon-to-be president, Václav Havel put it in his essay *The Power of the Powerless*:

> Not only is the dictatorship everywhere based on the same principles
> and structured in the same way . . . but each country has been com-
> pletely penetrated by a network of manipulatory instruments controlled
> by the superpower center and subordinated to its interests.

But now there was a disintegration of not just the Soviet "manipulatory instruments" and the state's capacity to control society. The newly independent countries were also left without tax systems and many other aspects of modern administrations.

All of this didn't happen at once, of course. When Mikhail Gorbachev came to power in 1985, his plan was to revitalize, not destroy, the Soviet Union. He launched the joint policies of glasnost ("openness") and perestroika ("restructuring"). It was mostly perestroika that Gorbachev was interested in, so that he could reconfigure the institutions and incentives of the stagnating Russian economy. But he feared that hard-liners within the Communist Party would never accept these reforms, so he complemented them with a political opening that was designed to weaken the hard-liners. It's not clear if he foresaw the risks, but his strategy ended up unearthing massive discontent, particularly in regions that resented the centralized control of Moscow. Nowhere was this discontent larger than in Eastern Europe and the Baltic States that had been occupied by the Soviet Union at the end of World War II. Anti-Soviet protests had flared up before, in Hungary in 1956 and in the Prague Spring of 1968, where Havel cut his political teeth, but had been crushed. By January 1990 the Polish Communist Party was voting to disband itself, and by December of the next year Mikhail Gorbachev was forced to declare the Soviet Union extinct. Russia was soon flooded with Western economists and experts to help the new government forge a transition to a market-based liberal democracy. Poland was too, but the two countries ended up on remarkably different paths.

The fall in the state's power brought about by the Soviet collapse had very different effects depending on where a country was relative to the corridor. Though there were many similarities between them, Russia was much deeper into the territory of the Despotic Leviathan. Poland, when Gorbachev rose to power, was under the iron fist of general Wojciech Jaruzelski, but was still closer to the corridor because its state, propped up by Soviet power, had less dominance over society and its civil society was less emasculated than in Russia. In fact, Jaruzelski's rise to power was a response to the reawakening of Polish civil society in 1980–1981. The collapse of the Soviet Union pushed Jaruzelski from office and pushed Poland into the corridor.

There were other, deeper differences too. For one, the mass collectivization of agriculture that Stalin had engineered in Russia and Ukraine never happened in Poland. People were mostly left with their land; there was some respite, some breathing space for civil society to grow under the shadow of the hammer and

sickle. Ironically enough, it was in the Lenin Shipyard in Gdańsk that Polish society really got organized. Led by Lech Wałęsa, an independent trade union, Solidarity, emerged in September 1980. One year later it had mushroomed throughout
Polish society with ten million members, perhaps two-thirds of the labor force.
The government responded with martial law and the appointment of Jaruzelski.
But by this time Solidarity was too big to be easily put down and a stalemate ensued. By January 1989, Jaruzelski had reconciled himself to a power-sharing arrangement. In April 1989, Solidarity signed the Round Table agreement with the
government that allowed for elections to be held in June of that year. But everything was rigged so that the Communists, who had reserved seats, would have
a majority and Jaruzelski would be elected president. He hoped that Solidarity
would be mollified by this vote. This was exactly how the German playwright
Bertolt Brecht characterized the East German state's attitude toward elections in
the 1950s:

> Would it not be easier
> In that case for the government
> To dissolve the people
> And elect another?

But Jaruzelski had miscalculated. The Communist Party lost every single
seat where there was free competition, completely undermining the legitimacy
of the whole agreement. Solidarity pushed for more, and by August had taken over
the government and appointed Tadeusz Mazowiecki prime minister.

Mazowiecki was now faced with the unenviable task of masterminding the
transition from socialism. First in line was economic restructuring and he appointed Leszek Balcerowicz to come up with a plan. The plan turned out to be a
famous instance of what became known as "shock therapy," a dramatic "leap" to
a market economy. Balcerowicz removed price controls, allowed state-owned businesses to go bankrupt, and taxed wages in state-owned enterprises to deliberately
make them noncompetitive with the new private sector. And they did go bust!
National income fell sharply and there were mass layoffs from the state-run industries that were allowed to wither away.

Society reacted and protested. Instead of democracy pacifying the labor movement, it led to an incessant wave of strikes as incomes fell and unemployment
mounted. From 250 strikes in 1990 there were 305 in 1991, then over 6,000 in 1992
and over 7,000 in 1993. Protests, demonstrations, and strikes provided an important

source of pressure on the government to build social consensus around its agenda. After Wałęsa's election as president, Balcerowicz conceded to bringing trade unions into the discussion over wage policies and particularly the contentious tax on wage increases in state-owned enterprises. By the end of 1991, Balcerowicz was fired, but the transition had already mobilized society. By 1992 there were twenty-eight different political parties in the Polish parliament, the Sejm, and of course a lot of disagreement about how to move forward. Despite these divisions the Sejm managed to negotiate the "Little Constitution," which was a mixed system of parliamentarianism and presidentialism set in place until a new constitution was finally introduced in 1997. In the meantime, Wałęsa tried to increase his own power at the expense of the Sejm, but couldn't. The resulting political compromise led to an adjustment in the economic transition of the country. The government started to allocate more resources to the state sector and tried to cushion the pain of shock therapy. A new broad-based personal income tax was introduced. In February 1993, Minister of Labor Jacek Kuroń proposed the formation of a tripartite commission wherein the government, management, and trade unions could discuss economic policy making. Some in the West fulminated at how this was undermining the transition to a market economy, but it provided legitimacy to the reforms and got society at large on board, without which a transition into the corridor had no hope, as we'll now see in Russia.

Moving into the corridor created the conditions for liberty in Poland, which rapidly built a vibrant democracy on the back of its highly mobilized civil society. Its track record on democratic politics and civil rights persuaded the European Union to accept Poland into its club. However, moving into the corridor does not immediately generate liberty, which only emerges after the Red Queen gets into operation. In 2015 the Law and Justice Party came to power in Poland and had to be sanctioned by the European Union for attempting to undermine the independence of the Supreme Court. Liberty is always a work in progress, not least in nations that have suffered decades of despotic rule.

The Un-Taming of the Russian Bear

As General Jaruzelski began negotiating with Solidarity in the spring of 1989, Gorbachev proposed his own carefully crafted version of democratization for the Soviet Union. As part of this process, Boris Yeltsin was elected chairman of the Russian Supreme Soviet in May 1990. By August, Yeltsin was famously announcing to other regional leaders that they should "take as much sovereignty as you can swallow." Soviet hard-liners next attempted a coup to stop the inevitable, arresting Gorbachev. Yeltsin bravely defied the coup by standing on the turret of a tank. He survived and the coup failed. By Christmas the Soviet Union had fallen and in the summer of 1991 Yeltsin was elected to the newly created position of Russian president. His platform, on the basis of which he beat four Communists and a hardcore nationalist, included a radical program of market reform just like the one in Poland. Democracy, economic reforms—it looked like the Russian despotic state was getting tamed.

Yeltsin picked Yegor Gaidar to run the economic reform program, and Gaidar in turn nominated Anatoly Chubais to spearhead the privatization of state-owned industry. Gaidar and Chubais had to come up with a strategy to put the main assets of the Soviet Union into private hands. Starting in the spring of 1992, the government began to sell off small firms such as stores and restaurants. People could take ownership of their own apartments for free, or almost for free. In late 1992 Chubais started on the big firms. Large and medium-sized enterprises were required to sell 29 percent of their shares in "voucher auctions," and in October 1992, each Russian adult was issued vouchers with a nominal value of 10,000 rubles that could be acquired at the local branch of Sberbank for just 25 rubles. By January 1993 almost 98 percent of Russians had claimed their vouchers. These vouchers could be sold or used to bid for the shares of specific companies when they were privatized.

The first auctions were held in December 1992. About 14,000 enterprises held such auctions. Most of the assets from these firms went to their workers and managers, however. A law allowed for workers and managers to buy 51 percent of the voting shares of a firm at a discount and using the firm's own funds. In effect the majority of privatizing firms' assets were handed to insiders at huge discounts. Even shares that had been distributed more widely re-concentrated. In 1994 workers owned 50 percent of the average Russian enterprise; by 1999 this was down to 36 percent. By 2005, 71 percent of medium and large industry and communications enterprises had a single shareholder who owned half the stock.

The most controversial stage of the privatization was the "loans for shares" deal in 1995 in which the most valuable state assets in the energy and resource sector were given to a group of politically connected people who promised to finance Yeltsin's reelection campaign. Here's how the details worked. State shares in twelve highly profitable enterprises concentrated in the energy sector were used as collateral for bank loans. If the loans were not paid off, the banks would have the right to sell the shares. In fact, the government never had any intention of paying off the debts. Between November 1996 and February 1997 the government sold shares of the energy giants Yukos, Sidanko, and Surgutneftegas, and in each case banks themselves bought the shares in auctions where outside bids were ignored or disqualified. After Yeltsin's reelection two of those closely involved in this deal, Vladimir Potanin and Boris Berezovsky, were brought into the government. Berezovsky and another oligarch, Vladimir Gusinsky, dominated the media by controlling two national television stations.

In the meantime Yeltsin had pushed for, and got, a constitution with strong presidential powers. Nobody was able to oppose him, and unlike in Poland, the Russian transition had not involved the mass mobilization of society. Nobody organized en masse against the "loans for shares deal," and people voted Yeltsin back into power with the help of money he raised from his new backers. But the new Russian elite used its power to extract all sorts of concessions from the state. In 1996 the Ministry of the Economy declared that beer was a nonalcoholic beverage so that Russia's largest brewers could avoid a tax hike. But they were living in a system with a lot of potentially despotic power at the top, and after Yeltsin left the scene, they fell prey to Vladimir Putin. Rather than the "liberal democratic" state that Westerners had hoped would emerge in the 1990s, after 2000 a new type of despotism was busy consolidating itself using the playbook of the old Soviet state.

Someone who saw it from the inside was Alexander Litvinenko. Litvinenko was an operative in Russia's FSB (Federal Security Bureau), the successor to the Soviet-era KGB (the Russian abbreviation for "Committee for State Security"). It was even housed in the same building in Lubyanka Square. Litvinenko and the FSB were heavily involved in the war against separatists in Chechnya starting in 1994. In that conflict, as Litvinenko put it, "secret services enjoyed generous operational freedom: they could detain, interrogate and kill without legal constraints"—just like the good old days, and all during Russia's "transition to a market economy." The government decided to start a new top-secret unit with the acronym URPO. The URPO soon got involved in all sorts of "activities," and Litvinenko was assigned to work for them. He explained:

> My unit was ordered to plan the assassination of Boris Berezovsky, the entrepreneur-turned-politician who was close to President Yeltsin. No one told us of the reason, but there was no need to: Berezovsky was the most visible of oligarchs.

It wasn't quite the shock therapy that Western economists had envisioned, but it showcased the new activities of the security services. They didn't stop at proposing to kill the president's friends. They also accumulated vast personal fortunes. This was done via a coalition with drug lords and involved massive extortion rackets. Litvinenko remembered how

> a local shopowner had been visited by a man claiming to be a police officer and demanding protection money. The demands went up and up from $5,000 a month to $9,000 then to $15,000 and more. Next the shopowner received a visit at his home—he was beaten up and threatened.

Litvinenko watched horrified, and took notes. But whom to trust? In July 1998 he thought he had caught a break. Yeltsin appointed a relative outsider to head the FSB, Vladimir Putin, a former lieutenant colonel in the KGB. Litvinenko went to him and put his cards on the table, detailing all of the crime and rackets he had documented. He recalled, "Before our meeting, I spent all night drawing up a chart with names, places, links—everything." Putin listened pensively and the same day opened a "file" on him. Litvinenko was fired from the FSB. A friend told him, "I do not envy you, Alexander. There is common money involved." A mutual acquaintance said, "Putin will squash you . . . and no one can help you." In October 2000, Litvinenko fled the country with his family and was granted political asylum in the United Kingdom. He wrote two books documenting what he had learned about the corruption and violence of the Russian state. But the arm of the FSB is long. On November 1, 2006, Litvinenko fell ill in London after meeting with two former KGB agents. They had put poison in his teacup, and he died three weeks later of polonium-210-induced acute radiation syndrome.

When Putin took over, the oligarchs were finished; they were exiled or jailed, and their assets were expropriated—unless they were Putin's loyal allies. Any modicum of liberty that had emerged since 1989 was next. Today in Russia independent media is suppressed and journalists are murdered. Politicians who dare to oppose Putin, most recently Alexei Navalny, are jailed or banned from politics. Despotism is back, untamed.

Why did the Russian "transition" fail so spectacularly? The most basic reason is that Russia was too far outside the corridor. After the Soviet Union collapsed, though state institutions were reconstructed, there wasn't much of an attempt to reform the security apparatus. Indeed, politicians thought they might be able to use it to their advantage, as in Chechnya. At the root of the problem was lack of popular mobilization or even independent private interests that could stop the unrestrained exercise of power of the state and limit the sort of high-level discretion that Yeltsin enabled. Privatization and economic reform on their own could not create the broad and legitimate distribution of assets that might have formed the economic underpinnings of a Shackled Leviathan. This allowed Putin to reverse the gains of the 1990s and consolidate a new despotism. Indeed, the inequality that resulted from privatization, particularly the "loans for shares" deal, not only re-concentrated the ownership of key assets in Russia, but also completely delegitimized the reform process. This made it very easy for the re-energized KGB, under Putin's leadership, to grab control of the economy and society.

Russia was too distant from the corridor. Though the collapse of the despotic Soviet state pushed it in the right direction, it wasn't enough to tame the Russian state, which just picked up where the Soviet one had left off and reconstituted its despotic control over society.

From Despotism to Disintegration

Even if the decline in the power of the state and Communist Party elites was insufficient to move Russia away from the orbit of the Despotic Leviathan, it was more than enough to completely change the trajectory of a state that had a more precarious hold on society, such as the former Soviet Republic of Tajikistan on the border with Afghanistan and China. As the Soviet Union crumbled, Tajikistan had to decide on its future. First Party Secretary Kakhar Makhkamov initially supported the putschists who briefly imprisoned Gorbachev in August 1991. When the putsch failed, mass demonstrations in the capital, Dushanbe, forced Makhkamov to resign. Tajikistan was independent by the next month and Rakhamon Nabiev was elected president shortly thereafter.

To follow what happened next in Tajikistan you have to understand the *avlod*. In the words of the Tajik sociologist Saodot Olimova, "An *avlod* is a patriarchal community of blood relatives who have a common ancestor and common interests, and in many cases shared property and means of production and consolidated or coordinated household budgets." Sounds a bit like the cage of norms we saw with stateless societies, except that this system survived under the despotic reign of the Russian and then the Soviet state. Tajikistan was conquered by the Russians in the second half of the nineteenth century and then ruled by the Soviets until 1991, but the underlying social structures, the clans, persisted relatively unchanged. In a 1996 nationwide survey 68 percent of Tajiks said they belonged to an avlod. It is useful to think of the clans as regionally based aggregations of these avlods. Political scientist Sergei Gretsky describes how in the 1940s the clans from Khujand were allowed to take over much of the local Soviet state administration:

> When the Khujandis ascended to top party and government positions in Tajikistan . . . they endorsed localism as the corner stone of their policy, and kept regional rivalries boiling, while preserving for themselves the role of arbiter . . . In Tajikistan the popular wisdom put it in the following way: "Leninobod governs, Gharm does business, Kulob guards, Pamir dances, Qurghonteppa ploughs."

Leninobod is the capital of the Khujand region in the northwest of the country. Despotic though its rule was, the Soviet state controlled Tajikistan indirectly via the regional clans. Much of the arbitration was through clan relations and alliances, and outside the formal state institutions.

President-elect Nabiev was from one of the traditional ruling families of the Khujand. He faced immediate opposition from other parts of the country, particularly from the Gharm and Pamir who began to organize demonstrations. In response, Nabiev handed out 2,000 machine guns and formed irregular forces to repress the opposition. His opponents managed to take the capital and the Khujandis withdrew to start a guerrilla war that they eventually won. In the process, the state completely collapsed and Tajikistan was plunged into five years of horrific civil war between the clan-based regional alliances. The death toll is uncertain with estimates ranging from 10,000 to as many as 100,000. More than one-sixth of the population was displaced and national income fell by 50 percent.

The difference between Tajikistan and Poland or Russia is clear: Tajikistan, ruled by the Soviets through regional clans and alliances, started the transition process with a weak state and a society without any institutionalized means of participating in politics. Once the despotic power of the Soviet rule melted down in 1991, the country had no easy way of mediating disputes between the clans, which were now intensified with the prospect of taking control of the assets of the country and the vestiges of the Soviet state. The clans armed themselves and fought while the state disintegrated.

So we see an even richer tapestry of divergence following the collapse of the Soviet Union. The decline in the power of the state wasn't enough to dislodge Russia away from despotism, but just enough to open a door into the corridor for Poland, and more than enough to hurl Tajikistan into a situation wherein the state completely collapsed and civil war and clan conflicts ensued. Figure 3 sketches how in our framework these different responses may come from the same impulse: the collapse of the Soviet Union leading to a decline in the power of the state. Arrow 1 is the hopeful scenario where the reduction in the power of the state moves the country into the corridor, as was the case for Poland. Arrow 2 is the case, as in Russia, where a country starts so far from the corridor that even after the decline in the power of the state, the Despotic Leviathan has commanding control. Finally, Arrow 3 illustrates the possibility that, starting with a sufficiently weak state and society, the same change can cause the state's control to wither completely, moving society toward the Absent Leviathan.

This richness of outcomes underscores that even after decades of the state gaining power at the expense of society, big enough shocks—in this case the col-

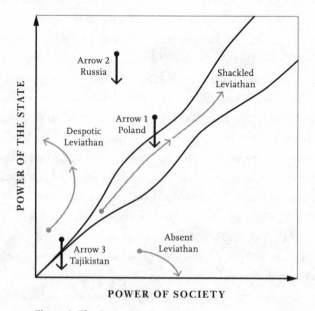

Figure 3. The Soviet Divergence

lapse of the Soviet Union—can completely reconfigure the subsequent trajectories of state and society. The evolution of a Leviathan is always subject to myriad influences and disruptions.

Because We Have To

Economic opportunities created by new technologies haven't just influenced the development path of European nations. They have also shaped the pattern of colonial divergence, as illustrated by the contrasting trajectories of Costa Rica and Guatemala in the nineteenth century.

Institutions of Central American neighbors Costa Rica and Guatemala were initially similar. Both countries were still under the despotic control of the Spanish colonial state until 1821. But in the next hundred years they diverged as sharply as any of the examples we have discussed in this chapter. Costa Rica gradually witnessed the strengthening of society and moved into the corridor over the course of the late nineteenth century. By 1882, Costa Rica was holding regular and peaceful elections, and the role of the military and general repression had started to wane. These changes meant not only much greater security and lower violence for Costa Ricans, but a very different social and economic world. For example, by 1900, 36 percent of adults were literate, and by 1930, two-thirds of all adults could read and write.

Guatemala looked very, very different. A sense of how different and why can be gleaned from the life of Nobel Peace Prize winner Rigoberta Menchú. Menchú is from the Quiché indigenous people of Guatemala, a country made up of "twenty-two indigenous groups . . . twenty-three including the *mestizos, or ladinos.*" The ladinos are those of Spanish descent, or at least mixed Spanish and indigenous descent. Menchú's grandmother

> got work as a servant to the town's only rich people. Her boys did jobs around the house like carrying wood and water and tending animals. But as they got bigger, her employer said she didn't work enough for him to go on feeding such big boys. She had to give away her eldest son, my father, to another man so he wouldn't go hungry. By then he could do heavy work like chopping wood or working in the fields but he wasn't paid anything because he'd been given away. He lived with the *ladinos* for nine years but learned no Spanish because he wasn't allowed in the house . . . They found him repulsive because he had no clothes and was very dirty.

Eventually Menchú's father left and found work on the coffee estates, the *fincas*, along Guatemala's Pacific coast. He brought his mother and "got her away from that family as soon as he could. She'd sort of become her employer's mistress although he had a wife. She'd had to agree because she'd nowhere else to go." The fincas became their life. Menchú was born in 1959. "From when I was very tiny, my mother used to take me down to the *finca*, wrapped in a shawl on her back." Trucks would pick them up from the highlands. Menchú recounts, "I remember the journey by lorry very well. I didn't even know what it was . . . [It] holds about forty people. But in with the people, go the animals (dogs, cats, chickens) which the people from the *Altiplano* take with them when they are in the *finca*." The trip took two nights and a day during which time people soiled the truck and vomited. "By the end of the journey, the smell—the filth of people and animals—was unbearable . . . we were like chickens coming out of a pot . . . we could hardly walk."

From the age of eight Rigoberta worked on the coffee plantation, and then on a cotton plantation; she never went to school. (The photo insert shows a contemporary scene of Guatemalan women and children on a coffee finca.) The workers were given tortillas and beans to eat but the cantina of the finca had other things too, especially alcohol. "Every *finca* in Guatemala has a *cantina*, owned by the landowner, where the workers get drunk . . . and pile up debts. They often spend most of their wages. They drink to get happy and to forget the bitterness." But Rigoberta was taught to be very careful. "My mother used to say: 'Don't touch anything or we'll have to pay for it.' . . . I used to ask my mother, 'Why do we go to the *finca*?' And my mother used to say, 'Because we have to.'"

Rigoberta recalled the first time she saw the landowner. "He was very fat, well dressed and even had a watch. We didn't know about watches then." Rigoberta didn't have shoes, let alone a watch. When the landowner arrived,

> he was accompanied by about fifteen soldiers . . . The overseer said, "Some of you have to dance for the owner" . . . The landowner was speaking, and the overseer started translating what he was saying. They told us we all had to go and make a mark on a piece of paper . . . We all went to make our mark on the paper . . . I remember that the paper had some squares with three or four drawings on it . . . He warned us that anyone who didn't mark the paper would be thrown out of work [and] not paid.
>
> The landowner left, but afterwards . . . I dreamed about him over and over again . . . it must have been the fear, the impression made on me by that man's face . . . All the children there ran away . . . and cried when

they saw that *ladino*, and even more at the soldiers and their weapons. They thought they were going to kill their parents. I thought so, too. I thought they were going to kill everybody.

Finally the "election," Guatemalan-style, took place. "They came to the *finca* and told us that our President had won, the one we had voted for. We didn't even know that they were votes they'd taken away. My parents laughed when they heard them say, 'Our President,' because for us he was the President of the *ladinos*, not ours at all."

The state of Guatemala was distant, alien. It was not even a state for the majority of the population; it was a state for the ladinos. The first time Rigoberta went to the capital, Guatemala City, she had to be careful. Her father had been called to the INTA (the National Institute for Agrarian Transformation) and explained that "there was a prison for the poor people and if you didn't go to that office, that's where they put you . . . My father said the people there didn't let you in unless you showed respect. 'When you go in, keep still, don't speak,' he said."

Back in the countryside the Quiché people had to deal with a hierarchy of government officials, starting with the military commissioner, then the mayor and then the governor, all ladinos. Rather than provide public services, the officials extracted bribes: "To get to see the Military Commissioner, you first have to give him a *mordida*, that's what we call a bribe in Guatemala." A *mordida*, literally "a bite." Rigoberta ruefully concluded, "In Guatemala if it's to do with the Government, there's no way we can defend ourselves." They tried. Rigoberta's father and brother started to organize the local village. On September 9, 1979, her brother was murdered by the army.

> They took him over rough ground where there were stones, fallen tree trunks. He walked about two kilometers being kicked and hit all the time . . . His whole face was disfigured with beating, from striking against stones, the tree trunks; my brother was completely destroyed . . . They tied him up, they tied his testicles . . . they left him in a hole with water and a bit of mud in it, they left him naked there all night. There were a lot of corpses there in the hole with him . . . My brother was tortured for more than sixteen days. They cut off his fingernails, they cut off his fingers, cut off his skin, they burned parts of his skin. Many of the wounds, the first ones, swelled and were infected. He stayed alive. They shaved his head, left just the skin, and also they cut the skin off

his head and pulled it down on either side and cut off the fleshy part of his face. My brother suffered tortures on every part of his body.

Not content with this barbarism, the army then brought the captives back to the village as a lesson to the people. "The captain gave a panoramic description of all the power they had, the capacity they had. We, the people, didn't have the capacity to confront them." The captives, including Rigoberta's brother, were then covered in gasoline and set on fire. This was brutal, violent dominance over society. A world apart from neighboring Costa Rica.

So why this savagery in Guatemala while Costa Rica had already brought violence under control, built a democracy supported by a fairly well-organized society, and created the preconditions for liberty? How did they diverge so completely? The answer is related to coffee.

Grounds for Divergence

The rapid growth of Western Europe and North America in the nineteenth century did more than transform their economies. By creating a huge demand for tropical crops, such as sugar, tobacco, cotton, and coffee, and the technological opportunities for transporting them across the world, this growth also reconfigured postcolonial societies. Steamships came early in the century, and by 1838 the SS *Great Western*, designed by British entrepreneur Isambard Kingdom Brunel, was the first constructed for regular service between Bristol and New York. The *Great Western* was made of wood and used steam-driven side paddle wheels. By 1845 Brunel had launched the *Great Britain*, which had an iron hull and used a steam-powered screw propeller. Iron hulls were cheaper and could be used to build much larger ships, and propellers were far more powerful than sails or paddle wheels.

After these technological changes, it became profitable to export crops like coffee in large quantities to distant parts of the world. Central America was at the epicenter of this trade not only because of its great climate for growing coffee, but also because it was situated close to the booming markets of the United States, where coffee imports doubled between 1830 and 1840 and then increased by another 50 percent by 1850. This was followed by steadily rising prices of coffee in the rest of the century.

To take advantage of this growing demand, some basic public services were needed. Roads and enough infrastructure had to be built to export the crops, and property rights in land had to be sorted out so that people would be willing to undertake the necessary investments to plant coffee (since it takes three to four years after planting before a coffee bush bears fruit). All of this required an expansion of state capacity. It was this demand for increased state power and capacity that underpinned the subsequent developments in Costa Rica and Guatemala.

Costa Rica was part of the Kingdom of Guatemala during the colonial period and both briefly unified with Mexico after gaining independence in 1821 and then joined the Federal Republic of Central America. Costa Rica seceded in 1838 and finally became an independent nation. It had been peripheral throughout colonial times, and it escaped the Bourbon reforms aimed at strengthening colonial states and increasing tax revenues. There were few indigenous peoples left after imported diseases had undermined their population in the sixteenth century, and it had no precious metals or minerals worth mining. At independence it had a population of 60,000 to 70,000 people, most of whom lived in the highland central valley. The colonial economy was largely underdeveloped except for a brief boom in cocoa on the Caribbean coast in the seventeenth century. Guatemala, which controlled the colonial monopoly, had blocked the development of tobacco growing in Costa Rica. Costa Rica therefore lacked both powerful elites and a dominant city or town at independence. The four main population centers, Cartago (the colonial capital and center of conservative groups), San José, Alajuela, and Heredia, were fierce rivals. Each town conducted its own foreign policy and sought alliances with powerful factions in neighboring countries, such as Colombia. As the Argentine politician and intellectual Domingo Sarmiento put it, "the South American republics have all, more or less, passed through the propensity to decompose into small fractions, attracted by anarchical and rash aspirations to ruinous, dark independence . . . Central America had made a sovereign state out of every village."

In 1823 and 1835 this "propensity to decompose" led to civil wars and San José subsequently established itself as the capital city. But while the towns might compete, they could also cooperate. In 1821 as Latin American independence beckoned, the council (*ayuntamiento* or *cabildo*) of Cartago, the colonial capital, invited the councils of the other towns to discuss how they should declare independence. In October of that year the four main towns, along with Ujarrás, Barba, and Bagaces, jointly issued the "act of the ayuntamientos," declaring independence from Spain. By December they had signed the Pacto de la Concordia, which created a governing junta made up of seven popularly elected members. The location of the body would rotate between the four main towns. These towns made heavy use of the *cabildo abierto*, a type of open council meeting that allowed for much broader political participation.

Though Costa Rica was gradually unraveling itself from the Spanish Empire, it remained poor and underdeveloped. The one asset it had was a lot of unexploited land. The first wave of politicians after 1821 understood this very well. Just as the United States had passed the Northwest Ordinances as early as 1787 to govern the expansion of the Union, Costa Ricans did the same thing. By 1821 San José was giving away land for free to anyone who could fence it and grow and export crops. Laws granting title and subsidies to smallholders for coffee were then passed by the central government in 1828, 1832, and 1840. By 1856 all public lands had been sold off. These laws opened up the lands of the central valley that were previously state owned. Individual towns tried to attract labor and migrants by selling them land at low prices and by encouraging coffee production. A measure of 1828 induced settlement and agricultural exploitation outside the four townships by granting up to 110 acres of land for free in underpopulated areas. Costa Rica was in fact the first Central American nation to start exporting coffee, and during the 1840s, after independence, exports increased fivefold to 3,800 tons. At this point, coffee represented 80 percent of Costa Rica's exports. That decade saw the construction of the first road from the central valley to the Pacific port of Puntarenas so that coffee could be shipped by ox carts rather than on the backs of mules.

It was this early dynamic for the distribution of land that was responsible for the absence of a large class of landowners in Costa Rica. Instead, the economic elites of Costa Rica, such as they were, concentrated on the control of finance, purchase, and export of the crop. Thus there was never any coalition in favor of the type of labor coercion that was so prevalent in Guatemala. Even rich families who went into the coffee business were generally well diversified. There certainly were attempts by the Costa Rican elite to reduce the prices at which they bought coffee from smallholders, and they profited from high prices for loans and finance, which they fought to protect. The most famous example of this is the overthrow of President Juan Rafael Mora by the Montealegre family in 1859 because Mora proposed to create a bank to lend directly to smallholders, thus breaking the market power of financiers. But none of this derailed the smallholder coffee economy. The historian Ciro Cardoso summed up the state of the Costa Rican economy as "there was an absolute predominance of small farms, both of numbers and of the total land occupied."

The coffee business required institutional support. For one thing, land had to be surveyed and property rights defined and enforced. After independence,

president Braulio Carrillo began to build a state capable of performing these duties. He promulgated civil and criminal codes and constructed a state bureaucracy
for the first time. He also reorganized the national militia and created a national
police force. Though he considered himself a dictator for life, he made little effort
to create a large military and had an army of no more than 500 soldiers.

The most likely explanation for Carrillo's policies is that, like the Federalists
of the United States, he recognized that without a central authority it would be
difficult to provide the basic public services that the new country needed to take
advantage of the new economic opportunities and maintain order in the face of
the competition between the four main towns. But like the Federalists, he was also
probably wary of the Gilgamesh problem—how to control a very powerful state—
and refrained from building a large military. After Carrillo was deposed in 1842,
the increasing power of coffee elites became evident, since different families and
factions backed separate candidates for president and elections were marred by
military involvement. Some presidents, like Mora, were overthrown in revolts, and
others, like Jesús Jiménez in 1870, were cast aside by coups. At the urging of the
Montealegre family, Jiménez was replaced by Tomás Guardia, the first military
man to serve as president in nineteenth-century Costa Rica. He stayed in power
for twelve years, and in the process professionalized the military with the help of
Prussian advisers and reduced its size so that in 1880 there were a mere 358 professional soldiers (though there was a militia that could be called upon in emergen-
cies). As a result of these reforms, the military remained out of politics. It was after
Guardia's death in 1882 that Costa Rica started holding regular elections, though
it did take until 1948 for electoral fraud to be brought under control. Like Carrillo,
Guardia expanded state capacity, increasing the size of the civil service by close to
40 percent. He also organized the construction of the first railway linking the
central valley to the coast. Instead of the military, Costa Rica invested in education.
A major educational reform of 1888 started increasing literacy.

By this point, Costa Rica was already in the corridor, moving along in it. In
1948 the slow transition toward democracy was finally consolidated after a fraud-
ulent election led to a brief civil war where rebels led by José Figueres were victorious. Figueres led a junta for eighteen months before giving way to the legitimate
winner of the 1948 election. In that period he oversaw some dramatic changes,
not least the abolition of the army. Costa Rica is the largest country in the world
that doesn't have an army (others include Andorra, Liechtenstein, and a group
of small island nations, like Mauritius and Grenada). The junta also created a
constitutional convention and passed a series of laws to develop a meritocratic

bureaucracy, introduce compulsory public education, and enfranchise women and illiterates. Since then Costa Rica has been democratic and peaceful, a rather remarkable achievement in a region where every other country has been a dictatorship at some point since the 1950s, often for long periods of time.

Repression on the Finca

While a smallholder coffee economy, and together with it a type of Shackled Leviathan, developed in Costa Rica, coffee expanded in Guatemala too, but in a very different, repressive direction. The reason why Rigoberta Menchú was witnessing such savagery can be traced to the edifice of labor coercion surrounding coffee cultivation in Guatemala. The logic was that anything that could threaten this machine would have to be stamped out with extreme force.

Guatemala had been the seat of colonial power in Central America, and unlike Costa Rica, it had a strong conservative merchant guild and powerful big landowners. It had a much more developed economy as well. The Indigo Growers Society had been founded as early as 1794. Guatemala also had a dense population of indigenous people. After Guatemala became independent it was ruled by a dictator, Rafael Carrera, who was in power either de facto or de jure for much of the period between 1838 until his death in 1865. As Carrera's biographer Ralph Lee Woodward put it:

> Notwithstanding the importance of Carrera's army as the base of power for the dictator, it was the consolidation of the conservative elite of the capital that gave the regime its character and was important in establishing policies that made Guatemala the "citadel of conservatism" . . . While Carrera always reserved the right to make final decisions . . . he usually allowed a small clique of well-educated and aristocratic advisers to make and execute policy. The consolidation of this conservative elite in Guatemala and its control of the capital's society, economy, and political structure is what so clearly distinguishes the period 1850–1871.

During this period Guatemala maintained colonial-era policies including various types of monopolies. In marked contrast to Costa Rica, little attempt was made to develop agricultural exports. All the same, the growth of markets led to a gradual expansion of coffee production. In 1860 exports had been negligible but they expanded rapidly as the decade went on. By 1871 coffee exports made up half of Guatemala's total exports. In that year the government of Vicente Cerna y Cerna, one of Carrera's conservative successors, was overthrown by a revolution that brought the "Liberals" to power, first Miguel García Granados and soon after the more enduring figure of another military caudillo, Justo Rufino Barrios, who ruled until 1885.

The new regime had the explicit goal of developing the agricultural export economy. To achieve this, it sought to privatize landholdings. Among other things, this involved the expropriation of land from indigenous people. Between 1871 and 1883 nearly one million acres of land were privatized. One of the key problems was that much of the indigenous population was in the highlands, while the prime coffee-growing areas were lower down toward the Pacific coast. Barrios used the coercive power of the state to help large landowners gain access to labor. There was a long tradition of coerced labor in Guatemala, going right back to the early colonial days, when indigenous people had been divided up in grants of *encomienda* and entrusted to Spanish conquistadors. The onset of large-scale coffee production induced the state to recodify and increase the intensity of coercion by reintroducing or reinventing colonial-era institutions such as the *mandamiento* and also through debt peonage, much in evidence in Rigoberta's description of the finca's cantina. *Mandamiento* (literally "commandment" or "order") was a system in which employers could request and receive up to 60 workers for 15 days of wage work. These workers could be forcibly recruited unless they could demonstrate from their personal workbook that such service had recently been performed satisfactorily. Land policies were designed not just to allocate land to politically connected people; they were also intended to facilitate labor coercion by undermining the subsistence economy of the highland indigenous people. Without access to subsistence, they would be easier to incorporate into the wage economy at low pay or by coercion if necessary. The way to do this was to eliminate traditional communal lands and deprive people of the possibility of a subsistence life. To live, you had to go down to the finca.

Nothing much had changed by the time Rigoberta was describing it. This strategy was complemented by other legislation such as laws to "prohibit vagrancy," another pretext for coercing people to work. While the Guatemalan government focused on "land privatization" and other related policies, it failed to provide much in terms of public services. There was a reason why Rigoberta did not attend school. As her memoir documents, child labor was widespread in the 1960s; children's nimble fingers were just too useful not to be put to work picking coffee. The lack of interest in providing any sort of public services shows up in data on education and literacy in Guatemala. In 1900 a mere 12 percent of adults could read and write. As late as 1950 this was only 29 percent, while nearly every adult in Costa Rica could read and write.

The Guatemalan state wasn't content to expropriate people's lands in the nineteenth century. It was still doing it in the 1960s and 1970s when Rigoberta was growing up. One day around 1967 people turned up and started surveying the land that Rigoberta's village farmed in the highlands. She recalled, "The Government says the land belongs to the nation. It owns the land and gives it to us to cultivate . . . we could either stay and work as *peónes* [sic] or leave our land."

Work for whom? The politically connected families. She names the Martínez, García, and Brols families, who had been handing out "big bites" to get the government to allocate the land to them. Though they tried to complain,

> we didn't realize then that going to the Government authorities was the same as going to the landowners . . . They turned us out of our houses, and out of the village. The Garcías' henchmen set to work with ferocity . . . First they went into the houses without permission and got all the people out. Then they went in and threw out all our things. I remember that my mother had her silver necklaces, precious keepsakes from my grandmother, but we never saw them again after that. They stole them all. They threw out our cooking utensils, our earthenware cooking pots . . . they hit the ground and broke into pieces.

They fled.

The staggering divergence that took place in Costa Rica and Guatemala over the past 150 years was not something that was preordained. The two countries had similar histories, similar geographies and cultural inheritance, and were faced with the same economic opportunities in the nineteenth century. But it is once again in line with the implications of our conceptual framework. The same impulse to increase state capacity, brought about by international economic changes, had hugely different consequences because it was coming in the context of different balances between state and society. Compared to Costa Rica, Guatemala had more of a history of militarized labor coercion and a significantly larger indigenous population, and had inherited the despotic state institutions of the Kingdom of Guatemala. The state-building incentives of the coffee boom at the end of the nineteenth century thus created a powerful Despotic Leviathan there. In Costa Rica, the collapse of the Spanish Empire meant that there were no powerful central state institutions at all and four towns vied for control. Coffee helped them to stave off collapse and pushed Costa Rica into the corridor. The Red Queen effect was most evident in the emergence of a smallholder coffee economy bolstered by public services and improved property rights in land. Within a few decades, this process forged the social basis for a functioning democracy.

How History Matters

We have seen several examples of the same impetus for building a stronger state, or in some instances the same forces reducing the despotic control of the state, having very different implications for the subsequent path of states and societies. This is the most important lesson of the current chapter. In contrast to the prevailing emphasis in much of social science, structural factors do not create strong dispositions for one type of economic, political, or social template to emerge. Rather, they generate "conditional effects"—meaning that their consequences are very much dependent on the existing balance of power between state and society.

This point is general and helps us understand certain key turning points in European as well as world history, and it has some very novel implications going beyond the scope of this chapter. Most important, such structural factors, especially those related to the nature of economic relations and the tendencies created by international relations, not only shift the position of a nation in Figures 2 and 3, but can also alter the shapes of the different regions in these figures. Most crucially, the lines demarcating the boundaries of the Despotic, Shackled, and Absent Leviathan change as these factors change. This, as we will see in Chapters 14 and 15, has a lot to tell us about what types of societies are more likely to build and maintain a Shackled Leviathan because they have a wider corridor.

Our discussion in this chapter also clarifies why history matters in our framework. Once a society is in the corridor, it behaves very differently from when it is in the orbit of the Despotic Leviathan or living under the Absent Leviathan, so historical differences tend to persist. It is for this reason that the balance of power between state and society often endures. But of course, this balance in turn depends on certain economic, social, and political relationships and it is in this sense that the structure of the economy or politics in a country not only determines the width of the corridor but also shapes its future path. For example, a history of labor coercion renders the state and elites more powerful against an emaciated society, and this makes labor coercion more likely to persist and intensify, as our discussion of Guatemalan history illustrates; or past collectivization of agriculture makes despotism more likely to endure because it emasculates society, as our discussion of recent Russian history emphasizes. Indeed, it is this persistence that belies any simple tendency for there to be an "end of history," where all nations eventually converge toward the same types of states, societies, or institutions. History does persist and does generate divergences that aren't easy to erase or undo. More interestingly, different historical evolutions of the relationship between state and society can have momentous implications when confronted with changes in structural factors and big shocks like those discussed in this chapter. This is both because, as we have just noted, such things as a history of labor coercion, industrialization, or deep-rooted social hierarchy impact the shape of the corridor, but also because countries with different pasts will find themselves with different balances of power between state and society, laying the groundwork for divergent consequences of the same structural factors.

This discussion highlights as well, and later chapters will underscore, that history isn't destiny. Nations move in and out of the corridor, altering their historical trajectories, even if the likelihood and the manner in which this happens are themselves heavily influenced by their history (where the country is in the figure) and by economic, political, and social conditions that determine the shape of the corridor. This approach then gives us a way of thinking about what social scientists call agency—the ability of key actors to influence the course of their societies, for example by forming new and enduring coalitions; articulating new demands, grievances, and narratives; or coming up with technological, organizational, or ideological innovations (as we saw in Chapter 3). Agency matters in our framework not because it can freely reshape the trajectory of a nation as if it were a blank slate. Instead, agency, as well as sometimes completely insignificant-looking contingencies, can have durable effects by tilting the prevailing balance of state and society and modifying the way that a nation responds to structural factors. We saw with the Federalists in Chapter 2 the role that leaders capable of articulating a new vision and forming new coalitions can play in state building. We see the same in the Costa Rican case too. Though there were structural differences between Costa Rica and Guatemala, the path Costa Rica took was also significantly influenced by individuals such as Braulio Carrillo in the 1830s and 1840s. His decision to separate Costa Rica from the Federal Republic of Central America allowed the country to diverge from the rest of the isthmus. His decisions to build more-effective state institutions allowed for the smallholder coffee economy to develop. Perhaps most interesting of all, his decision to keep the army small paved the way for a relatively muted role of the military in Costa Rican politics and its eventual abolition in 1948. Had Carrillo made different decisions, Costa Rica would likely be much more like Guatemala today. It took another individual, José Figueres, to finally abolish the military and create the constitutional basis for a modern state and functioning democracy. As with the choices of Carrillo, there was nothing predetermined about what Figueres did, bordered as he was by a recently emerged dictatorship under the Somozas in Nicaragua. In all of this, agency influenced how the forces highlighted in Figures 2 and 3 played out, but did not act freely from the prevailing balance of power. Indeed, it would have been impossible for Carrillo or Figueres to build a Shackled Leviathan if Costa Rica had had the same labor-repressive agriculture as Guatemala.

Chapter 10

WHAT'S THE MATTER
WITH FERGUSON?

A Killing at Noon

Shortly after noon on August 9, 2014, Michael Brown, an eighteen-year-old African American, was shot dead by police officer Darren Wilson in Ferguson, Missouri, a city in St. Louis County. Brown had stolen a packet of cigarillos from a store and was with a friend when Wilson, who had learned of the robbery on his radio, asked them to stop. A struggle took place with Wilson still in his car, and two shots were fired. Brown fled and Wilson chased him, eventually hitting him with six bullets. A mere ninety seconds expired between Wilson's encountering Brown and the young man's death.

The tragic killing arose in the context of highly strained relations between Ferguson's predominantly African American population and its almost totally white police force. Brown's killing led to days of prolonged rioting that brought the city to the attention of the world. More rioting followed when a grand jury decided not to indict Officer Wilson. The subsequent Justice Department report on the Ferguson Police Department (FPD) revealed staggering violations of the constitutional rights of the citizens, particularly the black citizens, of Ferguson. According to the report, it was typical for the FPD to harass African Americans. For example,

in the summer of 2012, a 32-year-old African-American man sat in his car cooling off after playing basketball in a Ferguson public park. An officer pulled up behind the man's car, blocking him in, and demanded the man's Social Security number and identification. Without any cause, the officer accused the man of being a pedophile, referring to the presence of children in the park, and ordered the man out of his car for a pat-down, although the officer had no reason to believe the man was armed. The officer also asked to search the man's car. The man objected, citing his constitutional rights. In response, the officer arrested the man, reportedly at gunpoint, charging him with eight violations of Ferguson's municipal code. One charge, Making a False Declaration, was for initially providing the short form of his first name (e.g., "Mike" instead of "Michael"), and an address which, although legitimate, was different from the one on his driver's license. Another charge was for not wearing a seat belt, even though he was seated in a parked car.

The report noted that the Ferguson police's pattern of stops without reasonable suspicion and arrests without probable cause along with their use of excessive force all violated the Fourth Amendment; their infringement of free expression as well as retaliation for protected expression violated the First Amendment. What's worse, "excessive force" was a constant in Ferguson.

In January 2013, a patrol sergeant stopped an African-American man after he saw the man talk to an individual in a truck and then walk away. The sergeant detained the man, although he did not articulate any reasonable suspicion that criminal activity was afoot. When the man declined to answer questions or submit to a frisk—which the sergeant sought to execute despite articulating no reason to believe the man was armed—the sergeant grabbed the man by the belt, drew his ECW [electronic control weapon, usually known as a Taser], and ordered the man to comply. The man crossed his arms and objected that he had not done anything wrong. Video captured by the ECW's built-in camera shows that the man made no aggressive movement toward the officer. The sergeant fired the ECW, applying a five-second cycle of electricity and causing the man to fall to the ground. The sergeant almost immediately applied the ECW again, which he later justified in his report by claiming that the man tried to stand up. The video makes clear, however, that the man never tried to stand—he only writhed in pain on the ground. The video also shows that the sergeant applied the

ECW nearly continuously for 20 seconds, longer than represented in
his report.

What happened in Ferguson is not an isolated incident. Similar violations of
basic rights of African Americans and excessive force have been widespread in
many cities and towns across the country. The consequences of this abuse along
with the violence that is endemic in many U.S. poor urban areas are illustrated by
the torment that lack of effective law enforcement creates among the most vulnerable citizens. Leaving aside the toll of murder and physical violence, a recent study
of an inner-city neighborhood in Atlanta, Georgia, found that fully 46 percent of
people suffered from post-traumatic stress disorder (PTSD). Wasn't this sort of
trauma something that war veterans who witnessed huge levels of violence and
danger while fighting in Afghanistan or Iraq suffered? Yes, but that's not so different from the daily threat inhabitants of poor neighborhoods in many inner
cities experience. In fact, their average rate of PTSD, at 46 percent, exceeds that of
war veterans, which stands at around 11 to 20 percent.

This doesn't look much like liberty. Fear and violence are everywhere in
these neighborhoods. So is dominance. What's going on in Ferguson? In the
United States?

The Collateral Damage of American Exceptionalism

The most common narrative of U.S. history emphasizes its exceptionalism in
building durable republican institutions, starting with the brilliant design of the
Constitution. The reality is more complex. There is indeed much to admire in the
evolution of the American Leviathan, but it has also inflicted collateral damage,
as in Ferguson, along its path. As we recounted in Chapter 2, the American Leviathan was in some sense created by the Federalists. Their project of building a
state was not without anxieties. They were worried that a powerful president could
get out of control and abuse his powers or be captured by some group, or "faction";
hence all the checks and balances and the separation of powers between the executive and the legislature. They were also worried that there would be too much
popular participation; hence the indirect election of senators by state legislatures
and the Electoral College to elect the president. They had to make concessions to
those who worried about the preservation of "states' rights" and the autonomy of
the constituent states; hence the limits on federal power and the understanding
that anything not specifically in the Constitution was the domain of the states.

They also had to make concessions to the mobilized, rebellious, and suspicious common people who worried that this could all spell despotism; hence the Bill of Rights.

The story of this chapter is that this architecture, though it worked to lever the U.S. into the corridor, was a Faustian bargain. One of the major things it protected was the ability of Southern slaveholders to exploit their slaves, making the hands of the state not just tied but also sullied. These sullied shackles meant that the federal state remained impaired in some important dimensions. For one, it obviously didn't protect slaves and later its African American citizens from violence, discrimination, poverty, and dominance. It is emblematic of this pattern too that it was the poor, black citizens of Ferguson who were harassed, fined, imprisoned, and even killed.

For another, the concessions to the states and the various constraints also meant that the federal state would be hobbled when it came to protecting all of its citizens, not just African Americans, from violence and economic hardship.

Another related consequence of the Constitution's architecture, especially the limits on federal taxation, is the state's difficulty in providing broad-based public services. This can be seen in the frequent reliance on public-private partnerships for providing even the most basic public services—from various war efforts to health insurance to law enforcement. Public-private partnerships involve the state providing support, inducement, and sometimes funding, but then counting on the private sector and segments of society to implement policies and also sometimes to influence their directions. This strategy is often praised in popular discussions as a way of tapping into the energy and creativity of the private sector. It has sometimes achieved that, and more important, it has helped keep the U.S. in the corridor despite deep conflicts and myriad new challenges which the state has had to rise up to. The Red Queen then contributed to a steady expansion in the American state's capacity, but its weakness and inability to tackle urgent problems have remained, and as a result many things have fallen by the wayside. Some public services, such as healthcare and infrastructure, not to mention redistribution of income via taxation, are much harder to provide effectively with public-private partnerships—because markets, even with the support of the state, will often not provide the right level of provision or coverage. The public-private partnership model becomes even more problematic when it comes to law enforcement and conflict resolution. We have seen several times already that "society" is not a monolithic entity, and it will be its more mobilized and politically engaged and powerful segments that succeed in turning societal relations and norms to their advantage, just like elders and men in many stateless societies (Chapter 2) or the Brahmans in India (Chapter 8). The same has been true in the United States in general, and even more so when it has come to public-private partnerships. It has been these segments that have taken part in these partnerships and managed to imprint their wishes on conflict resolution, law enforcement, and public services. African Americans and the poor, the less well-organized groups in U.S. society, have often been left out, with detrimental consequences for their liberty.

Like other Shackled Leviathans, the American state has been quite successful in providing economic opportunities and incentives, and the unification of markets over this vast territory and the modicum of coordination of policies between states that followed the Constitution created an environment ripe for economic growth. Americans took advantage of this with gusto. The economy industrialized rapidly in the nineteenth century, and became the world's technological leader in the twentieth. But this prosperity too has borne the stamp of American exceptionalism—with all the constraints on the central state, the enduring power of elites and the states, and the peculiarities of the public-private partnership model, American economic growth has been associated with significant inequality and with certain segments of the population, not just the slaves before the Civil War, being completely left out of its benefits.

From this perspective, it's no surprise that the United States has a homicide rate about five times as high as the Western European average. Or that there are high levels of poverty in many parts of the country and that African Americans have often been excluded from opportunities and public services. Nor should we be surprised that this public-private partnership model hasn't worked well for providing a social safety net to poor Americans. As society became more mobilized and assertive, the American Leviathan has sometimes been induced to step in with programs such as President Johnson's "War on Poverty" to fill this void, but this has often been an incomplete effort.

Perhaps paradoxically, we'll also see that this path of the American Leviathan has had another important unintended consequence: the lack of effective monitoring of state activities in some crucial dimensions. Hemmed in by the straitjacket imposed by the Federalists' compromises and the public-private partnership model, the American state could not deal through legitimate channels with the increasingly complex security challenges posed by the Cold War and the recent rise in international terrorism. Nor could it effectively play its role as the most powerful country, the de facto policeman of the world. So it developed these capacities on the side without much oversight from society. This set the scene for a Leviathan, though subject to myriad constraints and still wearing the imprint of its foundational weakness, in command of an unshackled security service and military. The resulting fearsome face of the American Leviathan was on display when Edward Snowden laid bare the massive surveillance and data-gathering activities of the National Security Agency targeted at U.S. citizens that had been taking place without any checks from society or even other branches of government.

What Bill of Rights?

So why did the FPD harass the city's black citizens so much? The short answer is: Money, no doubt mixed with racism. Ferguson used its police department to raise revenues. Officers were ordered to issue as many tickets as possible in order to boost the city's resources. This meant that any pretext could be used to slap a fine on someone, and a big fine at that. The Department of Justice documented instances in which people were charged $302 for a single Manner of Walking violation, $427 for a single Peace Disturbance violation, $531 for High Grass and Weeds, $777 for Resisting Arrest; and $792 for Failure to Obey and $527 for Failure to Comply, two charges that officers appear to use interchangeably. Once ticketed, if you failed to appear at court, you were issued further tickets. The report recorded an iconic example:

> An African American woman who has a still-pending case stemming from 2007, when, on a single occasion, she parked her car illegally. She received two citations and a $151 fine, plus fees. The woman, who experienced financial difficulties and periods of homelessness over several years, was charged with seven Failure to Appear offenses for missing court dates or fine payments on her parking tickets between 2007 and 2010. For each Failure to Appear, the court issued an arrest warrant and imposed new fines and fees. From 2007 to 2014, the woman was arrested twice, spent six days in jail, and paid $550 to the court for the events stemming from this single instance of illegal parking. Court records show that she twice attempted to make partial payments of $25 and $50, but the court returned those payments, refusing to accept anything less than payment in full . . . As of December 2014, over seven years later, despite initially owing a $151 fine and having already paid $550, she still owed $541.

Since all of this abuse was targeted at them, it led to a serious deterioration in the African American community's trust in and cooperation with state institutions. The FDP didn't dispense justice; it dispensed tickets. The basic function of law enforcement broke down and the police were viewed with suspicion and dread.

But how could the FPD violate the constitutional rights of Ferguson's inhabitants with such impunity? Isn't the Bill of Rights meant to protect them? Well, actually only to a point. The compromise that created the Bill of Rights only applied to the federal government, not the states. The states ended up with something called "police power," granting them immense discretion. Though the actual language of the Bill of Rights didn't spell this out, it was understood at the time. The issue was definitively settled by the Supreme Court in 1833, which ruled that the Bill of Rights applied only to actions that the national legislature could take. For example, the First Amendment states that

> Congress shall make no law respecting an establishment of religion, or prohibiting the free exercise thereof; or abridging the freedom of speech, or of the press; or the right of the people peaceably to assemble, and to petition the Government for a redress of grievances.

The Fourth Amendment asserts:

> The right of the people to be secure in their persons, houses, papers, and effects, against unreasonable searches and seizures, shall not be violated, and no Warrants shall issue, but upon probable cause, supported by Oath or affirmation, and particularly describing the place to be searched, and the persons or things to be seized.

Yet the 1833 ruling made it clear that states could pass laws that abridged the freedom of speech and allowed for unreasonable searches and seizures since they were not covered by the Bill of Rights. Only the national legislature was barred from making such laws. The main aim of this interpretation of the Bill of Rights in Southern states was to ensure that slaves did not have any of the rights that "free citizens" had.

The attempted secession of the U.S. South and its defeat at the end of the Civil War in 1865 should have been the death knell for this view of the Bill of Rights. Indeed, the Fourteenth Amendment, passed in 1868, stated:

No State shall make or enforce any law which shall abridge the privileges or immunities of citizens of the United States; nor shall any State deprive any person of life, liberty, or property, without due process of law; nor deny to any person within its jurisdiction the equal protection of the laws.

Yet the Supreme Court repeatedly decided that this did not override the police power of the states. In 1885 Associate Justice Stephen Field argued that "neither the Fourteenth Amendment, broad and comprehensive as it is, nor any other amendment, was designed to interfere with the power of a state, sometimes termed its police power."

All of this has to be understood in the context of the Redemption period in the South after 1877. The Fourteenth Amendment was one of three amendments aimed at the Reconstruction of the South, meaning institutional reforms aimed at ending slavery and guaranteeing that African Americans had economic opportunities and political rights. Yet in 1877 President Rutherford Hayes doubled down on the original Faustian bargain and gained a majority in the Electoral College by making a deal with Southern politicians to withdraw Northern troops and end Reconstruction. Once Northern troops were gone, the South was "redeemed"—the thrust of Reconstruction was thrown into reverse and many of the old repressive institutions were refashioned in new guises. Particularly notorious were the "Jim Crow" laws which consolidated racial segregation. By the 1890s Southern states were rewriting their constitutions to disenfranchise blacks through poll taxes and literacy tests. Police power was at the heart of the action. The North agreed to leave the South alone and tolerate Jim Crow, and the "interpretation" that the Bill of Rights did not apply to state legislatures was critical to this deal.

It is true that states themselves wrote "bill of rights" amendments to their constitutions. The first thirty-five clauses of the current Constitution of Missouri constitute such a bill of rights. Yet these were not meant to, and did not, have the same bite as the federal Bill of Rights when it came to protecting citizens against state power. The Justice Department report makes it clear that the Ferguson Municipal Code violates the Missouri Bill of Rights. It observes that Section 29-16(1) declares it unlawful to "fail to comply with the lawful order or request of a police officer in the discharge of the officer's official duties where such failure interfered with, obstructed or hindered the officer in the performance of such duties." The report found that many legal cases initiated under this provision began with an officer ordering an individual to stop even though there was no objective indication that the individual was engaged in any wrongdoing. The order to stop is not a "lawful order" under those circumstances because the officer lacks reasonable suspicion that criminal activity is afoot. Yet when people did not stop, they were arrested anyway.

The South that Redemption created persisted right up to the 1960s. A major disruption came with the appointment of Earl Warren to the Supreme Court in 1953 just as the civil rights movement was gathering momentum. Warren decided that the Constitution had to adapt to changing circumstances, and there was a majority of like-minded justices on the court. They decided that many of the police actions being used in Southern states to repress and harass civil rights activists were unconstitutional, police power or no police power.

The Supreme Court's first opportunity to make this point came on May 23, 1957, when police officers muscled their way into the house of Dollree Mapp in Cleveland, Ohio. Mapp worked in the illegal gambling or "numbers" business, and police had received a tip-off that they would find at her house a man named Virgil Ogletree, suspected of bombing a rival numbers boss, Don King (the man who later went on to become boxer Muhammad Ali's manager). The police found Ogletree, though he turned out to be innocent. They also found some betting slips and some pornographic magazines that Mapp claimed had been left by a previous tenant. She was charged and sentenced to seven years in prison for possession of pornographic materials. Mapp took the case to the Supreme Court, claiming that there were no reasonable grounds for suspecting her to have such materials and that the police did not have a search warrant. In its verdict in *Mapp v. Ohio*, the court stated that the Fourth Amendment prohibited states from conducting unreasonable searches, concluding that "all evidence obtained by searches and seizures in violation of the Federal Constitution is inadmissible in a criminal trial in a state court." Note the expression "state court." The Supreme Court then went after a list of other behaviors by states which, while they might have been consistent with individual states' bills of rights and their police power, were not consistent with the Constitution. In *Gideon v. Wainright* (1963), it ruled that anyone charged with a felony had the right to an attorney. In *Malloy v. Hogan* in 1964, the justices decided that the right against self-incrimination, part of the Fifth Amendment (hence the expression "taking the fifth"), applied to state courts. In the famous case of *Miranda v. Arizona* in 1965, they ruled that confessions elicited from people who had not been read their rights were inadmissible in state courts. And in *Parker v. Gladden* (1966) and *Duncan v. Louisiana* (1968), they established that the Sixth Amendment gave people the right to an impartial jury in state courts.

The cumulative effect of these rulings was to push the criminal justice systems of the states to conform to the federal Bill of Rights. The evidence from Ferguson, however, suggests that this is still a work in progress.

This pattern of discrimination against African Americans has deep roots, and paradoxically, it was intertwined with the whole creation of American liberty—for some.

American Slavery, American Freedom

Slavery was central to the debates about the reach of the federal government. Slaves weren't only a huge part of the "assets" of some of the richest people in the original thirteen colonies, but their status was a crucial element in how political power in the new federal state would be distributed. In *American Slavery, American Freedom*, the historian Edmund Morgan asked how it came to be that so many of the leading figures who formulated the Constitution—George Washington, James Madison, and Thomas Jefferson—were slaveholders from Virginia. Jefferson was the main author of the Declaration of Independence, which gloriously states:

> We hold these truths to be self-evident, that all men are created equal,
> that they are endowed by their Creator with certain unalienable Rights,
> that among these are Life, Liberty and the pursuit of Happiness.—That
> to secure these rights, Governments are instituted among Men, deriv-
> ing their just powers from the consent of the governed.

There are many things to note about this assertion, such as the focus on "men" and not people. But even more blatantly, the government that Jefferson, who owned around six hundred slaves, conceived of was obviously not going to be ultimately instituted with their consent or for their "pursuit of Happiness." Rather, it made sure that they had no rights for another eighty-seven years.

Morgan's aim wasn't just to condemn the hypocrisy of these sentiments, but to understand the connections between slavery and freedom. How could they coexist? And did the freedom for white men in some way rest on the fact that there was a great deal of unfreedom for black folk?

Returning to the beginnings of the colonization of Virginia, starting with the foundation of Jamestown by the Virginia Company in 1607, there was no plan to import slaves. The first and most central leg of the initial design was to exploit indigenous peoples. But indigenous people were few on the ground in Virginia.

The second leg was to use indentured English people, who signed themselves up for seven years of service in exchange for room and board and a free passage to the Americas. The option of the indentured laborers was tried, but it turned out that they were difficult to control once on the ground, especially since they could run away to the open frontier. Treating them more harshly wasn't an attractive option either, as this would make it very difficult to induce more to come. In 1618, the Virginia Company switched from a strategy of trying to exploit indigenous people and indentured laborers to one based on incentivizing colonists. They freed them from their labor contracts, gave them land, and made the whole transition credible by granting white men political rights in a newly conceived General Assembly.

Yet the colony was not economically viable. Early on the colonists had tried to cultivate the local tobacco, but the quality was not good. John Rolfe, who famously married the local princess Pocahontas, experimented with different varieties from the West Indies with much better results. In 1614 the first shipment of tobacco was exported from Jamestown. In the fall of 1619 the first group of some twenty slaves was acquired from a visiting Dutch ship in exchange for Virginia provisions. Tobacco, though it was at first strenuously discouraged by the Virginia Company, eventually made the colony prosperous. After the company collapsed in 1624, there was no holding people back. The indentured laborers could be used to work on tobacco, but soon it became clear that buying slaves was cheaper. The colony spread geographically and many colonists became landowners and tobacco planters. As the space began to fill up, they had second thoughts about the nature of the Assembly and in 1670 decided to restrict the franchise, noting that many

> haveing little interest in the country doe oftener make tumults at the election to the disturbance of his majesties peace, then by their discretions in their votes provide for the conservation thereof.

Landowners, on the other hand, could be relied on to behave more responsibly. Just a year previously the Assembly had passed "An act about the casual killing of slaves" which stipulated that "if any slave resist his master . . . and by the extremity of the correction should chance to die, that his death shall not be accompted Felony, but the master . . . be acquit from molestation, since it cannot be presumed that prepensed malice (which alone makes murder Felony) should induce any man to destroy his own estate." Who would hold malice toward his own property, after all?

As the slave economy flourished, some got very rich and accumulated large plantations with numerous slaves. But it wasn't just the large-plantation owners who benefited. Less prosperous citizens acquired land and slaves too, even if in more modest quantities. The wealth that the tobacco-slave complex generated came to be shared more equally among the whites. Between 1704 and 1750, for example, the average size of landholdings in the Tidewater, the area along the navigable waterways that provided prime tobacco land, fell from 417 to 336 acres. At the same time the number of property owners increased by 66 percent. Looking at the Chesapeake Bay area more broadly, evidence from wills shows a steadily more equal distribution of wealth in the eighteenth century. In 1720 some 70 percent of the people who died had estates that were valued at 100 pounds or less. By the 1760s such people made up just over 40 percent of the population, with a corresponding increase in the number of people worth more than 100 pounds. The Virginia Assembly, which had previously changed the franchise to exclude those without property, adopted policies that were friendly toward those same people. It reduced the poll tax and legislated improved terms and conditions for white servants. In any case, the majority of white men were becoming landowners. The slave economy thus created a certain solidarity among white people. Indeed, in Virginia all the slaves were poor and, in effect, all the poor people were slaves. As the English diplomat Sir Augustus John Foster noted in the early nineteenth century, the Virginians "can profess an unbounded love of liberty and of democracy in consequence of the mass of the people, who in other countries might become mobs, being there nearly altogether composed of their own Negro slaves."

This solidarity also helped with the other major objective of the U.S. Constitution—to control the people and their participation in politics. A strong state was useful for keeping order, unifying markets, and providing national defense, but it had to be a state immune from capture by the common people if they got to be excessively interested and involved in politics. So spreading power broadly via the separation of powers and indirect elections wasn't just a solution to the Gilgamesh problem and the anxieties about the federal state acting despotically of its own volition. It was also a way to make sure that state institutions could not be taken over by the common people. The danger of popular political participation terrified both the Federalists and the Southern elites whose wealth was tied up in their slaves and the plantation economy. So an opportunity was born to kill two birds with one stone: by limiting the ability of the common people to exercise political power, the Federalists would both achieve one of their own objectives and make the whole project more palatable to Southern elites who could otherwise resist their state-building project. Moreover, many of the elites of the day, like Jefferson, were confident that even non-elite whites shared this outlook and so could be granted "certain unalienable Rights" and "freedom," without much fear that they would share those privileges with the slaves. So the notion of freedom that came out during the process of American state building was at once glorious (for whites) and fettered (for blacks), with predictable consequences.

The Circuitous Path of American State Building

The U.S. Constitution managed, in one fell swoop, to address the key problems confronting the Federalists. It built a state; it made sure that its powers couldn't be captured by factions or the general population, thus guaranteeing property rights, a particularly important issue for American elites; it preserved the autonomy of the states; and it reluctantly granted people essential rights against potential abuse by the state. Reluctantly, grudgingly, but also with the knowedge that even poorer whites shared many of the interests of the elites—for example in the slave economy, as we have seen.

But spreading power between different bodies and groups ran the risk of creating quite a bit of gridlock. This became particularly apparent later when organized political parties emerged. One party might have a majority in Congress, and a different one might have a majority in the Senate, since it was elected according to different rules. The president, chosen by yet another method, might not be able to gain majority support in either house. Yet this potential for gridlock made it easier to control the federal government, and thus made the Constitution more acceptable to the states. But there was also a clear downside. While the main objective of the Constitution was to create a powerful central state with more capacity, this system generated a fair bit of incapacity as well. This incapacity was particularly damaging for social policies and redistribution of income, since someone could always object and block them. This combination of state strength and weakness, something the Federalists had to put up with to satisfy all of their objectives, and how it has been dealt with over time, is a consequence of American exceptionalism in state building.

In some dimensions American state building worked quite nicely. The weakness of the federal state meant that it could not turn into a Despotic Leviathan, and society knew this. Guarantees such as the police power of states were a crucial element in persuading state elites to ratify the Constitution in the first place and for the most part to refrain from blocking its expansion later on. A powerful Red

Queen effect then followed, strengthening state institutions. At the same time, however, the initial weakness endured and made it difficult for the state to meet the growing demands coming from a society in the grips of rapid economic and social change in the nineteenth and twentieth centuries.

One initial side effect of this weakness was the lack of revenues. With the newly created federal tax system, the government was able to fund George Washington's army that marched off to western Pennsylvania to crush the Whiskey Rebellion. But the Constitution stated that "No Capitation, or other direct, Tax shall be laid, unless in Proportion to the Census or enumeration herein before directed to be taken." So no "direct taxes," specifically income taxes, for the federal government. With one hand the Constitution gave and with the other it took away. How could the federal state achieve its objectives without revenues?

It had to improvise. This improvisation then turned into a strategy of public-private partnership, with the government relying on the private sector for both implementing and setting the direction of many of its important functions, with its own role limited to providing land, inducement, and some subsidies. For example, the government wanted to make sure that the east and west coasts were linked by a railway line, but could not build one itself. For one thing, before the Civil War, Southern politicians had blocked the route that Northerners preferred. For another, the government did not have the money to build the railway. So it decided to incentivize the private sector to do it. In 1862 Abraham Lincoln signed the Pacific Railroad Act. The act gave railway companies not only guaranteed loans backed by the government, but also vast amounts of land along the line of rail. Section 2 of the act granted right of way for two hundred feet on either side of the railways and allowed the railway company to freely take any material needed for the construction of the railway. Section 3 gave the railway companies up to five square miles of land on each side of the line of rail for every mile of track that they laid (the railway companies' take was doubled in 1864). This created huge incentives for the railway companies to get the work done, since once the railroad was built the land would be valuable and they could sell it for considerable profit. We saw in Chapter 1 how the Union Pacific railway, as soon as it constructed the track in Wyoming, founded the city of Cheyenne and began to sell off the land. None of this required new spending, so the federal government did not need to raise taxes.

The public-private partnership strategy to build the transcontinental railway wasn't just about spending as little government money as possible. It also aimed at shackling the budding American Leviathan. It focused on incentivizing the private sector to do work that in other parts of the world might have been done by the government, so that the state did not grow too big or too powerful. It kept the private sector involved too, so that the Leviathan remained tightly monitored.

Working with the private sector to provide basic public services was not new in 1862. One of the most iconic institutions of nineteenth-century America, the U.S. Post Office, was also founded on this model. As early as 1792 the first Congress passed the Post Office Act to create a federal postal service and quickly managed to form a huge web connecting the country. The post office soon became the single most important government employer. In 1816, 69 percent of the federal civilian workforce were postmasters. By 1841 this number had risen to 79 percent, and there were over 9,000 postmasters. *The New York Times* described it in 1852 as the "mighty arm of civil government." Yet the post office was a public-private partnership as well. The mail was carried by private stagecoaches subsidized by the federal government. By 1828 there were over 700 private mail contractors. This partnership enabled the federal state to establish a widespread presence throughout this vast territory. Relative to population, the United States had twice as many post offices as Britain and five times as many as France at this time. The pervasiveness of the postal service was apparent to Tocqueville during his famous travels in 1831. He remarked:

> There is an astonishing circulation of letters and newspapers among these savage woods . . . I do not think that in the most enlightened districts of France there is an intellectual movement either so rapid or on such a scale as in this wilderness.

He also noted how it provided a "great link between minds" and "penetrates" into the "heart of the wilderness." The post office wasn't just indicative of the presence and functionality of the state. It also facilitated the flow of information, and helped ideas spread and spurred new ones. It made many critical economic activities, including patenting and securing intellectual property rights, much easier. Economic historian Zorina Khan notes that "rural inventors in the United States could apply for patents without serious obstacles, because applications could be submitted by mail free of postage. The U.S. Patent and Trademark Office also maintained repositories throughout the country, where inventors could forward their patent models at the expense of the Post Office. As such, it is not surprising that much of the initial surge in patenting during early American industrialization occurred in rural areas." Moreover, already by the 1830s, the Post Office was a modern bureaucratic institution, working and acting quite autonomously.

We see a version of public-private partnership in the federal judiciary as well. The U.S. legal system partially outsourced the business of investigating infringements and bringing lawsuits to private citizens. So when Title VII of the Civil Rights Act of 1964 banned employment discrimination in the private sector based upon race, gender, national origin, or religion, it left the enforcement not to government agencies but to private lawsuits brought under Title VII. This decision significantly contributed to the explosion of private litigation over the past five decades. At about 20,000 cases per year, employment discrimination lawsuits are today the second-largest category of litigation in federal courts after petitions by prisoners asking to be freed. Private civil action in courts was also encouraged by potentially large economic damages and attorney fee awards for winning plaintiffs. Similarly, infringements by corporations in the United States are typically policed by private class-action suits, not by the bureaucracy or the prosecutorial power of the U.S. judicial system. Taking the public-private partnership in legal matters to its extreme, U.S. law also came to depend on private lawsuits to deal with fraud against the government. Building on a provision in English common law called *qui tam* that has long been disused in Britain, U.S. law allows private individuals to bring lawsuits against parties that defraud the government. If a lawsuit succeeds, the plaintiff receives a fraction (ranging between 15 and 25 percent) of the amount the federal government recovers.

This unusual process of judicial evolution has restrained the power of the federal government (with the independent judiciary acting as a barrier against government overreach), developed a legal system rooted in the demands and concerns of (at least some of) its citizens, and made the expanding capacity of the state palatable to powerful segments of society. Like the post office, the judiciary played a key role in knitting the United States together with a common set of rules, which also made westward expansion possible. The first thing that happened while a territory still had less than 5,000 people was the appointment by Congress of a governor and two judges.

Public-private partnerships were complemented with another political compromise: federal-local partnerships. U.S. federalism came to mean not only dividing powers between federal and state and local governments, but also devolving law enforcement and many public services to local authorities. So even though the United States has an education system that relies on public provision of elementary and secondary education, all of this provision is at the local level, carried out and financed by school districts, counties, and states out of their own revenues. The roots of this system go back to the Tenth Amendment, which reserved the power to provide and control education for the states. Even though the power of the federal government to raise revenues was circumscribed, it wasn't so for states and local governments. So, many states passed legislation during the early Republic to allow their school districts to impose taxes in order to finance local education. In the nineteenth century these revenues financed not only schools in urban areas and townships, but also rural "common schools," whose distinguishing feature was their local finance and control. The common schools taught elementary subjects, but in a way that was consistent with the preferences and values of their communities. Consistent with the public-private partnership, the federal state again played the role of inducer and subsidizer. The Land Ordinance of 1785, written by Thomas Jefferson, divided federal lands in what was then the Northwest into townships of thirty-six square miles, and each township into thirty-six sections, and the revenues of one section were set aside to finance schools. The states incorporated later in these lands thus had resources for schooling reserved. The same arrangement continued later, with even more sections set aside to generate revenues for schooling in California and the Southwest.

When malnourishment among schoolchildren first became evident in the nineteenth and early twentieth centuries, it was the cities that started providing free school lunches to children from poor families. The federal government came in only later to subsidize and spread these programs, especially with the National School Lunch Act in 1946. When the extent of discrimination against, and the poor quality of education received by, students with disabilities caught the public's attention, Congress passed the Education for All Handicapped Children Act in 1975, but left the financing for specialized education to school districts and states, which still bear over 90 percent of the cost.

In all of these instances, we are witnessing a highly shackled U.S. Leviathan, forced to develop new and creative methods to expand its capacity in the face of novel and sometimes urgent challenges. Remarkably, in the American version of the Red Queen effect the weakness of the central state has been a source of its strength too. It has encouraged the state to develop new models to work with society and local governments to deal with these problems. It has also constantly reassured actors to cede power to the federal state, safe in the belief that it would remain constrained. So the central state expanded its remit and capacity, while still maintaining its original weaknesses and remaining in the corridor—a brilliant way to create a continually evolving Shackled Leviathan. Yet as we have already anticipated, this success had significant downsides.

We Shall Overcome

The standard narrative of American history is not only deficient in turning a blind eye to the injurious consequences of the compromises and the architecture of the Constitution. It also ignores the critical role that society's mobilization and the Red Queen played at every turn. The Constitution and the Bill of Rights, as we have seen, were not a gift of benevolent elites; they were the result of the tussle between elites and the people, and without this ongoing struggle, they would have been as ineffectual as the creation of Enkidu was for liberty in Uruk.

There is no better way to illustrate this than by the activities and successes of the civil rights movement. Perhaps the two most famous fruits of the movement were the Civil Rights Act of 1964 and the Voting Rights Act of 1965. As the civil rights movement organized and gained adherents in the 1950s, it devised a set of strategies to confront the discriminatory policies of the Southern states, which had until then remained safe in their insulation from the federal Bill of Rights. At first the federal government tried to remain neutral and only intervened when absolutely forced by widespread deteriorations of public order. The civil rights movement then began intensifying its activities to force federal action. One strategy was that of the "freedom riders," mixed-race groups riding interstate buses in violation of Southern segregation laws. In May 1961 mobs attacked freedom riders in various parts of Alabama, creating such havoc that the Justice Department asked a federal district court in Montgomery, the state capital, to intervene. Attorney General Robert Kennedy, brother to the president, ordered six hundred U.S. Marshals to Montgomery to protect the freedom riders. Yet the first impulse of the Kennedy government was to try to avoid intervention, and it sought to undermine the solidarity of civil rights activists. One example was the Voter Education Project, which seems to have been intended to channel activists into actions that Kennedy viewed as less dispruptive. People in the civil rights movement got the message. In 1963 they launched a plan for disrupting segregationist laws in Birmingham, Alabama, intended to induce such a strong reaction that the federal state would have to intervene more systematically. As activist Ralph Abernathy put it:

> The eyes of the world are on Birmingham tonight. Bobby Kennedy is
> looking here at Birmingham, the United States Congress is looking at

Birmingham. The Department of Justice is looking at Birmingham.
Are you ready, are you ready to make the challenge? . . . I am ready to go
to jail, are you?

Most controversial was the "Children's Crusade" of May 2, when six hundred
children were arrested, the youngest being eight years old. President John F. Kennedy
had no choice but to conclude that "the events in Birmingham and elsewhere have
so increased cries for equality that no city or state or legislative body can prudently
choose to ignore them." The next month he proposed what became the 1964 Civil
Rights Act, which was the start of not just reinstating African Americans' political
power but also combating the norms of economic and social discrimination against
them especially prevalent in, but not confined to, the South.

The civil rights movement didn't halt there. Next stop was Selma, Alabama.
Beginning in January 1965 civil rights activists started a sustained campaign to
highlight the violation of the basic rights of blacks, particularly the right to vote.
On March 7 some six hundred activists began a march from Selma to Montgomery. They were attacked by local law enforcement officers: seventeen marchers
were hospitalized and another fifty were treated for lighter injuries. By then John F.
Kennedy had been assassinated and Lyndon B. Johnson had become president.
Johnson intensified federal intervention in the South, and a local federal judge,
Frank Johnson, ruled that "the law is clear that the right to petition one's government for the redress of grievances may be exercised in large groups . . . and these
rights may be exercised by marching, even along public highways."

Just as the Birmingham demonstrations had paved the way for the Civil
Rights Act, the Selma march cleared the way for the 1965 Voting Rights Act, abolishing many of the ruses—specifically literacy tests and poll taxes—that had been
used to disenfranchise African Americans. One week after the Selma march,
President Johnson made his famous "We Shall Overcome" speech. He began:

> I speak tonight for the dignity of man and the destiny of Democracy . . .
> At times, history and fate meet at a single time in a single place to shape
> a turning point in man's unending search for freedom. So it was at
> Lexington and Concord . . . So it was last week in Selma, Alabama.

Johnson compared the civil rights movement to the U.S. War of Independence by "patriots" in Massachusetts. He was right; both were reactions of society against despotism. Johnson's speech drove home that the shackled nature

of the American Leviathan wasn't simply a matter of some clever constitutional architecture; it critically depended on the society's mobilization and growing assertiveness.

Life in the American Corridor

As the nature of challenges changed, the American Leviathan took on more responsibilities, sometimes even temporarily breaking free of the grip of its original weakness. As with the civil rights movement, this was often a response to society's demands.

A turning point, emblematic of the dynamics of the Red Queen effect, was the Progressive era, when the federal state stepped up to respond to new demands, while social and institutional changes simultaneously intensified society's checks over the state. The economic opportunities and the unified national market created by the federal state in the nineteenth century and especially after the Civil War unleashed rapid industrialization and growth. It was an uneven process, often dominated by and benefiting a handful of companies, especially those who knew how to work the system. As a result, the period Mark Twain described as "the Gilded Age," from the 1870s to the early twentieth century, witnessed the emergence of huge companies that came to dominate their sectors or even the entire economy. Led by railway tycoons such as Cornelius Vanderbilt and Jay Gould, industrialists including John D. Rockefeller and Andrew Carnegie, and financiers such as John Pierpont Morgan, these "robber barons" not only invested massively and drove economic expansion, but also built unparalleled fortunes and routinely abused their economic and political power. This was growth, but of a very unequal sort, made worse by the fact that nineteenth-century American institutions were not up to the task of controlling these powerful, unscrupulous men and their "trusts," as their companies were known at the time.

The American Leviathan reacted to the changing economic and political circumstances by augmenting its capacity to regulate such monopolies, starting with the Interstate Commerce Act of 1887, the first step toward national regulation of industry, followed by the Sherman Antitrust Act of 1890, the Hepburn Act of 1906, and the Clayton Antitrust Act of 1914. Three successive activist presidents, Theodore Roosevelt, William H. Taft, and Woodrow Wilson used these laws to break up monopolies. Taft not only prosecuted the trusts but also changed the landscape of the American economy in 1913 by proposing the Sixteenth Amendment, which introduced a federal income tax.

But this wasn't a process in which just the state got stronger. These acts and the election of the activist presidents were consequences of mounting popular mobilization of the Progressive movement, which brought discontented farmers and urban middle classes together to exert a powerful influence on the era's politics. Media, including journalists known as "muckrakers," began playing an even more active role in influencing public policy by exposing the abuses of the robber barons and how they were manipulating politics for their own private gain. Major institutional reforms strengthened society against the state and political elites. The Seventeenth Amendment of 1913 dismantled the election of senators by state legislatures and introduced direct elections. This started to reduce the oversized influence of tycoons over the legislature that had been brilliantly satirized in the series of articles David Graham Phillips published in *Cosmopolitan* magazine in 1906, titled "The Treason of the Senate."

The expansion of the central state's capacity and its role in the economy accelerated during Franklin Delano Roosevelt's presidency. This was once again a response to fresh exigencies created by new economic conditions, this time in the form of the most severe economic downturn of modern times, the Great Depression. FDR's New Deal initiated tighter regulation of banks (with the Emergency Banking Act of 1933, the Securities Act of 1933, and especially the founding of the Federal Deposit Insurance Corporation, which insured small deposits in order to prevent bank runs); a major expansion of government spending on public works with the establishment of the Public Works Administration and the Tennessee Valley Authority; a new program to prop up agricultural prices and farm incomes under the auspices of the newly founded Agricultural Adjustment Administration; and modern Social Security in 1935 and the Food Stamp Plan in 1939, which have remained as the mainstays of U.S. welfare policy. FDR also signed the National Labor Relations Act of 1935 and created an elaborate bureaucracy to enforce this law, investigating whether firms were in compliance and bringing lawsuits against them if they weren't (even though, as we have seen, later legislation such as Title VII of the Civil Rights Act eschewed this approach and went back to the public-private partnership model).

An equally significant expansion of the role of the federal state in the economy was spearheaded by President Johnson's "Great Society" program. Johnson introduced the central tenet of the program, the "War on Poverty," in his 1964 State of the Union address by stating, "This administration today, here and now, declares unconditional war on poverty in America."

The War on Poverty too was a response to social changes, driven by both high rates of poverty that had long existed in many parts of the United States and the growing disparities between whites and blacks who had come to form a majority in many neighborhoods in inner cities. These economic conditions came to be viewed as the primary cause of the growing crime rates. Huge riots in New York City, Rochester, Chicago, Philadelphia, and especially Los Angeles in 1964 and 1965 added significant urgency to these concerns. In addition to expanding and making permanent New Deal programs such as Social Security and food stamps, the Great Society increased disability insurance payments and coverage, initiated job-training programs for disadvantaged youth in the context of the ambitious Economic Opportunities Act of 1964, and founded Community Action Agencies tasked with helping poor citizens. The two continuing pillars of public funding of healthcare in the United States, Medicare for older Americans and Medicaid for welfare recipients, were both created by the Social Security Act of 1965. Most innovative perhaps were the educational programs, which included Head Start, providing preschool education for poor children; the Bilingual Education Act of 1968 for local school districts to assist children from non-English-speaking families; and the huge expansion of federal aid to universities and students from poor backgrounds for attending college.

Though society's mobilization has triggered a spectacular growth in the capacity of the federal state, the architecture of the Constitution continued to influence the way that some of these programs were developed as well as their outcomes (Ronald Reagan quipped about the War on Poverty that "the federal government declared war on poverty, and poverty won"). Consider, for example, FDR's flagship Social Security Act. Until the New Deal the United States had failed to develop any broad-based social insurance policy while Britain had started to move in that direction in 1906 and Germany even earlier in the 1880s. Private pension plans did exist in the United States but they reached less than 10 percent of the workforce. Most people had to rely on their families or what little they could save themselves to provide for old age. The government provided pensions for veterans, and veterans' widows, and these represented 85 percent of people who had pensions in 1928. The centerpiece of the Social Security Act was a mandatory system of old-age pensions. The first section stated:

> For the purpose of enabling each State to furnish financial assistance, as far as practicable under the conditions in such State, to aged needy individuals, there is hereby authorized to be appropriated for the fiscal year ended June 30, 1936, the sum of $49,750,000, and there is hereby

authorized to be appropriated for each fiscal year thereafter a sum sufficient to carry out the purposes of this title.

So the states were in the heart of the action. The act specified how much you would earn upon retirement, which depended on a person's salary prior to retirement, but in no case could be more than $85 per month. This was a modest amount, and around one half of average wages at the time; yet it represented a dramatic commitment to a universal welfare program by the government. Ironically, Social Security made private pensions more attractive for companies because they could target them at their higher-paid and more-skilled workers, for whom government pensions would be inadequate. In fact, prior to the Social Security Act private firms were inhibited from introducing pension plans just for highly paid workers without simultaneously doing something for all the workers. But providing such benefits to all workers would have been expensive for employers. Once the act was passed, low-wage workers had access to pensions, reducing firms' inhibitions in targeting private plans at higher-paid workers. As a spokesman for the National Dairy Producers Corporation noted, "The first thing that came to our attention was that only 1,200 of our total number of employees received over $3,000. Among those 1,200 were practically every employee that had a real influence on how the company went ahead, how it achieved success over its competitors . . . So we decided . . . we will have nothing paid into the plan by either employer or employee on salaries below $3,000, and we will let the social-security tax program take care of the salaries under $3,000."

In effect, firms free-rode on the new policy. In doing so they benefited from the fact that such pension payments were tax deductible for the employer, counting as if they were an expense like wages. These pension benefits for employees, and up to a limit their own contributions, would only be taxed as income when they were drawn on during retirement, shifting tax payments into the future. While the government was introducing universal public pensions, it was simultaneously subsidizing private pensions. Moreover, high-paid workers would earn too much to actually benefit from Social Security. So the basis of a dual system, rather than a universal public pension system that covered everyone, was put in place. Predictably, after the introduction of Social Security, the coverage of private pensions rapidly increased from less than 10 percent of the labor force to 40 percent by the 1970s. Indeed, the coverage of the public system was far from universal to start with, since Southern politicians forced FDR to exclude agricultural and domestic workers so they could avoid giving benefits to African Americans.

If the situation of the United States with respect to pensions diverges from other developed countries, the approach to healthcare, despite Johnson's Great Society, does so more nakedly. Here there is nothing like Social Security. In fact the only universal policies are Medicare for the elderly and Medicaid for some segments of the poor. Otherwise, most Americans receive healthcare through their employers via private health insurance that is heavily subsidized by the government. So the public-private symbiosis is slanted even more toward the private.

The public-private partnerships and the constraints on the state, even as it was getting emboldened, have shaped other dimensions of state actions as well. They explain how the U.S. mobilized for World War II and the way it organized to fight the Cold War. They also account for the controversial role that contractors and companies such as Halliburton and Blackwater played in the Iraq War. It's worth recalling that Edward Snowden, at the time of his explosive revelations about the National Security Agency's secret data collection program, was a private contractor for the Central Intelligence Agency.

Who Gets Their Kicks on Route 66?

The shifting mix of private and public provision was an expedient way for the American state to gain greater capacity over time, but it also meant that it was particularly hamstrung in dealing with several critical problems. Many of the pressing challenges facing the country today, ranging from high levels of poverty and lack of access to healthcare (by the standards of other rich nations) to crime (gargantuan compared to other countries) and lack of protection for citizens (easily visible in Ferguson, Missouri, or in Hyde Park, Chicago, where one of us lives), have their origins in this hamstrung state building.

The killing of Michael Brown must be seen in the context of the lamentable state of relations between the citizens and the police force in Ferguson. This is the complex outcome of many things, but it is common across many poor, minority urban neighborhoods. These areas have the same problems everywhere; they disproportionately house racial minorities; they have fewer jobs and economic opportunities than elsewhere in the nation and poverty rates are far higher than normal; they have a severe undersupply of public services; and they have much higher rates of crime, particularly gun crimes and homicides. This last feature is one of the reasons for the tense relations with the police. In the United States there is more or less a gun for every person—that's over 300 million guns. The country with the next-largest number of guns relative to population is Yemen, though it has only about half a gun per person. Other countries are terribly badly supplied with guns; Britain and China, for instance, have only about one gun per twenty people. There are so many guns in the United States that they get into the capillaries of society, including into the ghettos with their immense social problems. One of the consequences of widespread distribution of guns is that the police are scared and they shoot first and ask questions afterward. They have a right to be scared. The city of St. Louis was the murder capital of the United States in 2015, with Baltimore and Detroit a close second and third. The murder rate in St. Louis in that year was 59 per 100,000 people, meaning that there were 188 homicides. This compares to the U.S. average of 5 per 100,000 for homicides, itself about five times higher than the average in Western Europe.

About two-thirds of all homicides in the United States involve firearms. The extraordinary number of guns in the country and their role in homicide is directly related to the Constitution and the Second Amendment's guarantee of "the right of the people to keep and bear Arms." The right to bear arms, nowadays "firearms," has been endlessly affirmed by the Supreme Court, no matter the extent of carnage inflicted on innocent people. As recently as 2008, in *District of Columbia v. Heller*, the court struck down laws in Washington, D.C., meant to restrict people's access to firearms and to keep legally owned guns unloaded at home. It asserted for the first time that the ownership of arms was not in any way connected to militia membership but was for self-protection. The original wording of the Second Amendment, an attempt to keep the federal state weak, has left a long trail of violence and death in its wake. Remarkably, the Second Amendment's scope got expanded over time, reflecting both the general feeling in the population about the importance of individuals protecting themselves (rather than the central state doing so) and the role of private interest groups and organizations, in this instance the National Rifle Association, which has effectively opposed any type of gun control in the U.S.

Yet the collateral damage in Ferguson from the peculiar path of U.S. state building doesn't begin or end with gun violence. Ferguson has not always been such a hot spot of racial tensions. It used to be a suburban middle-class area, inhabited not by African Americans or other minorities, but by relatively affluent white people in single-family houses. In 1970 less than 1 percent of Ferguson's population was black. In fact until the 1960s it was a "sundown town"—one of the characteristics of the U.S. illiberty, a town from which African Americans were banned once darkness fell. As we noted in Chapter 2, half of the counties through which the famous icon of personal liberty, Route 66, ran on its way between Chicago and Los Angeles had sundown towns. St. Louis, the first stop mentioned in the song made famous by Nat King Cole and Chuck Berry, had many sundown towns. Ferguson blocked off the main road from the neighboring predominantly black suburb of Kinloch with a chain and construction materials. It only kept open another road during the day so (black) housekeepers and domestic workers could get to their jobs in Ferguson. After 1970, however, the city's black population rapidly grew, to 14 percent by 1980, 25 percent by 2000, 52 percent by 2010, and 67 percent today. This rapid change reflected some very common dynamics in the nature of U.S. urban areas, which are critical in understanding who got their kicks and how in Ferguson at the time of Michael Brown's killing.

Let's pick up the story of how Ferguson became a black neighborhood in the 1930s. So far we've seen the New Deal as a period of progressive national policy initiatives such as the Social Security Act, which tried to create universal social welfare policies (even if this was unsuccessful in the face of resistance from Southern states). But the story of dysfunctional policies isn't just a story of the states. The federal state didn't only fail to propose progressive policies; it implemented regressive ones. The most relevant example in Ferguson is the Federal Housing Authority (FHA), created by the National Housing Act of 1934. The FHA had worthy goals, one of which was to insure mortgages so as to encourage banks to issue them. If you received a mortgage from a bank but were unable to pay, the FHA would come in and pay the balance. Obviously there were greater and lesser risks, and to take account of these the FHA incorporated "residential security maps" into their 1936 underwriting handbook. These maps, constructed by the Home Owners' Loan Corporation, divided urban areas into four zones labeled A, B, C, and D. A denoted the most desirable neighborhoods, and D the worst. In the maps, D areas were demarcated with a red pencil, thus initiating the practice of "redlining." (The FHA's redlined map of St. Louis is reproduced in the photo insert.) Redlining has since become a catch-all term for racial discrimination. There was little ambiguity about what zone D was meant to signify. The underwriting handbook contains a telling section on "Protection from Adverse Influences." Section 228 advocates the use of "deed restrictions" to protect against such adverse influences. The next section notes that "natural or artificially established barriers prove effective in protecting a neighborhood . . . from adverse influences" and in particular they prevent the "infiltration" of "inharmonious racial groups." Further, in valuing an area, "the Valuator should investigate areas surrounding the location to determine whether or not incompatible racial . . . groups are present," since naturally they have to assess the "probability of the location being invaded by such groups." As if this weren't all clear enough, the manual then notes, "If a neighborhood is to retain stability it is necessary that properties shall continue to be occupied by the same . . . racial classes."

In practice, of course, D areas were largely black neighborhoods, whose residents thus could not get their houses insured by the FHA. Hence African Americans could not get mortgages. Complementary strategies were also utilized to make sure that African Americans could not buy property in A areas, which were mostly white suburban residential neighborhoods. These strategies included explicit "deed restrictions" forbidding residents from selling their properties to a black person.

The net effect of these measures was to solidify a great deal of residential segregation. The FHA had to tone down the racial language of its manual in 1947, and in 1948 the Supreme Court ruled that racially explicit covenants were unconstitutional. Yet other practices discriminating against blacks continued. A recent Federal Bureau of Investigation report provides evidence consistent with the claim that Donald J. Trump's real estate company discriminated against black applicants for its rental apartments. The report quotes a former doorman repeating his supervisor's instructions as: "If a black person came to 2650 Ocean Parkway [in Brooklyn] and inquired about an apartment for rent, and he, that is [redacted] was not there at the time, . . . I should tell him that the rent was twice as much as it really was, in order that he could not afford the apartment."

It is clear that redlining and other discriminatory practices aimed at minorities left a long shadow, and even today one finds large discontinuities in the racial composition of neighborhoods right at the boundaries of those maps drawn in the 1930s. In 1974, a three-judge panel of the federal Eighth Circuit Court of Appeals concluded that

> segregated housing in the St. Louis metropolitan area was . . . in large measure the result of deliberate racial discrimination in the housing market by the real estate industry and by agencies of the federal, state, and local governments.

As the population of the D areas rose and exceeded the available housing units, a few lucky African Americans managed to get homes in previously all-white areas, even in sundown towns. When they did, this opened the door to a process called "blockbusting," which involved real estate agents scaring white tenants into selling at knockdown prices by warning them that the neighborhood was about to turn black and their property would become worthless. These tactics could quickly "tip" a city from white to black. Ferguson followed this path starting in the 1970s. A collapse in the provision of public services followed, moving the city toward becoming a ghetto. One of the first black people to buy a house in Kirkwood, another white suburb of St. Louis, was Adel Allen. He recalled how when he first moved there,

> we had patrols on the hour. Our streets were swept neatly, monthly. Our trash pickups were regular and handled with dignity. The street lighting was always up to par. All of the services were—the streets were cleaned when there was snow, et cetera.

But as the composition of the neighborhood changed, the services went away.

> We now have the most inadequate lighting in the city. . . . Now we have the people from the other sections of town that now leave their cars parked on our streets when they want to abandon them. . . . What they are making now is a ghetto in the process. The buildings are maintained better than they were when they were white but the city services are much less. Other sections of the city I believe are being forced to take sidewalks, for example. We are begging for sidewalks.

This is pretty much what happened in Ferguson. Take the Normandy school district, where Michael Brown graduated from high school just eight days before his death. The quality of education was so abysmal that in 2013 the state revoked the school district's accreditation.

The hobbled nature of U.S. federal policies, forcing the government into public-private partnerships and a reliance on local authorities even when this isn't warranted, generated other adverse consequences as well. Take healthcare. The United States spends about 50 percent more on healthcare as a proportion of national income than the average of the "rich nations club," the Organisation for Economic Co-operation and Development (OECD). Yet it has the highest proportion of the population who lack access to healthcare. The OECD calculated in 2011 that approximately 85 percent of Americans had "health insurance coverage for a core set of services." Of this figure, about 32 percent came from public insurance and 53 percent from private insurance. Even Mexico did better in terms of the proportion of the population covered. The way to reconcile high levels of spending with poor coverage is to note that the distribution of spending is much more unequal in the United States and cost controls are much weaker than in the rest of the OECD. Both features are a consequence of the peculiar U.S. model based on public-private partnerships. In 1998, before the Obamacare reforms, it was estimated that of the lowest-paid 20 percent of the labor force, only 24 percent were covered by health insurance. The same problems plague the pensions system where the benefits are skewed toward high-paid workers. Again in 1998, of the lowest-paid 20 percent of the labor force, only 16 percent were covered by a private pension, while for the highest-paid 20 percent the coverage rate was 72 percent. When Obamacare attempted to introduce a public option to give people access to low-cost insurance, this was shot down for being too reliant on the public sector. So even when the United States attempted to move toward universal healthcare coverage, this could not deviate much from the public-private partnership model.

This private-public combination ends up shunting the benefits from government subsidies squarely to the wealthiest people as well. The U.S. Treasury Department calculated in 2000 that the total amount of tax subsidies built into the pension and healthcare system added up to $100 billion a year (meaning that if they were removed the government would receive an extra $100 billion in tax revenues). Two-thirds of these subsidies went to the richest one-fifth of Americans. A mere 12 percent went to the bottom 60 percent. At its root, the private-public model is much less equitable than universal programs would be, but the organization of the American state doesn't allow universal programs.

Why Can't We Collect All the Signals All the Time?

In hindsight, it is perhaps understandable that the shackles and compromises imposed on the American Leviathan from its founding have kept it weak and forced it to come up with innovative, sometimes unusual solutions to deal with new problems and expand its capacity. It is more surprising that the same architecture has also made it overly powerful and harder to control in other dimensions. The roots of this paradoxical outcome are that when new security challenges and a growing international role made it necessary for the American state to take on more responsibilities, this couldn't be done easily within the straitjacket that the Constitution had created. The state had to improvise to build these capacities away from the eyes of the public and the control of American institutions—a recipe for unshackling the Leviathan.

The story of the FBI and its director J. Edgar Hoover illustrates this paradoxical development. The Justice Department was founded in 1870 and charged with upholding laws and fighting crimes, including those against the United States. But it had no police force at its disposal. Reflecting the public-private partnership model, American presidents before Theodore Roosevelt and their Justice Departments had to rely on a private company, the Pinkerton National Detective Agency, as their police force and sometimes even spies. Roosevelt, as part of his broader state-building drive, wanted to build a federal police force. His attorney general, Charles J. Bonaparte, went to Congress in 1908 to get permission and money to create such a force. The House of Representatives flatly turned down the request. Representative George E. Waldo, Republican from New York, summarized many lawmakers' fears when he stated that it would be "a great blow to freedom and to free institutions if there should arise in this country any such great central secret-service bureau as there is in Russia."

The typical way that the federal government had dealt with such constraints in other matters was to find an arrangement that would assuage the concerns of those worried about its growing powers. But not this time. Bonaparte ignored Congress's refusal and established a new investigative division using the expense fund of the Justice Department while Congress was in recess. He notified Congress only later and gave it his assurance that the new bureau would not be a secret police force. But the cat was out of the bag. It was never to go back in there once Hoover got to work.

In 1919, Hoover became the chief of the Radical Division of the Justice Department, charged with monitoring "enemies of the state." By this point, the Radical Division had over a hundred agents and informants, and could arrest people accused of subversion. Allied with Attorney General A. Mitchell Palmer, Hoover started drawing up a long list of Communists, anarchists, socialists, and others he viewed as subversives, especially among immigrants. Hundreds were deported because of their political views during the so-called Palmer raids organized by Hoover. Hoover was promoted to head the Bureau of Investigation in 1924, and remained in that post until his death in 1972. During that time he oversaw a massive expansion of the personnel and powers of the bureau, which changed its name to Federal Bureau of Investigation in 1935. Hoover turned the

FBI into a mass surveillance force unaccountable to Congress, courts, or even the president. The FBI under Hoover wiretapped tens of thousands of U.S. citizens and others because of their politics, including Martin Luther King Jr., Malcolm X, and John Lennon; spied directly on the leadership of the Soviet Union and China (something explicitly banned by its charter); and even went so far as to undermine the power and authority of several U.S. presidents. The apogee of the FBI's covert activities was the program COINTELPRO, between 1966 and 1971, which aimed at surveilling, infiltrating, discrediting, and otherwise neutralizing various domestic political groups and organizations, including anti–Vietnam War organizers, activists and leaders in the civil rights movement, various black organizations, and an assortment of other left-wing groups, the vast majority of which were nonviolent. It was under this program's auspices that Martin Luther King was wiretapped, publicly discredited and, by means of an anonymous letter, encouraged to commit suicide.

The Church Committee, which was tasked with investigating abuses by the FBI and other agencies in 1975 and led by Senator Frank Church, concluded that

> the domestic activities of the intelligence community at times violated specific statutory prohibitions and infringed the constitutional rights of American citizens. The legal questions involved in intelligence programs were often not considered. On other occasions, they were intentionally disregarded in the belief that because the program served the "national security" the law did not apply. . . . Many of the techniques used would be intolerable in a democratic society even if all the targets had been involved in violent activity, but COINTELPRO went far beyond that . . . The Bureau conducted a sophisticated vigilante operation aimed squarely at preventing the exercise of First Amendment rights of speech and association.

The creeping increase of the unaccountable power of security agencies did not stop with the FBI. The CIA, which came out of the Office of Strategic Services and the Strategic Services Unit, two agencies tasked with espionage, information gathering and analysis, counterintelligence, and other covert operations during World War II, was officially established in 1947. Its mission and monitoring were poorly defined from the beginning. The CIA has been involved in several coups against foreign governments, typically unknown and uncontrolled by other branches of government. These included successful coups against several democratically elected leaders of foreign governments, such as the prime minister of Iran, Mohammed Mosaddegh, in 1953, Guatemala's president Jacobo Árbenz in 1954, Patrice Lumumba of the Congo, and Chile's president Salvador Allende in 1973, as well as several unsuccessful plots in Syria, Indonesia, the Dominican Republic, Cuba, and Vietnam before the war. Although the CIA is not supposed to operate against American citizens, it has also been engaged in domestic wiretapping and "extraordinary renditions," which involved the extrajudicial transfer of individuals suspected of terrorism to secret prison sites or to countries where they were likely to be subject to torture.

Though the military remains one of the most trusted institutions among the U.S. public, its role and power have expanded as America's involvement in foreign affairs and its engagement in the Cold War and then the war on terror have deepened. All of this has happened almost entirely away from the monitoring of society and the legislature. Even though President Dwight D. Eisenhower himself ordered some of the CIA operations against foreign governments, in his farewell address in January 1961 he expressed concerns about the unchecked power of the U.S. military, especially when allied with companies supplying it with arms and equipment. Eisenhower prophesied that

> we must guard against the acquisition of unwarranted influence, whether sought or unsought, by the military-industrial complex. The potential for the disastrous rise of misplaced power exists and will persist. We must never let the weight of this combination endanger our liberties or democratic processes. We should take nothing for granted. Only an alert and knowledgeable citizenry can compel the proper meshing of the huge industrial and military machinery of defense with our peaceful methods and goals so that security and liberty may prosper together.

Well said. But how can the citizenry do that if it has no idea about what the FBI, the CIA, or the military are up to?

The revelations about the NSA wiretapping programs should thus be seen as a continuation of this trend of expanding military and security powers away from the supervision and monitoring of either other branches of the government or society at large. Information revealed by Edward Snowden indicates that the NSA used several different media, ranging from Internet servers and satellites to underwater fiber-optic cables and phone records in order to collect information about both foreigners, including leaders of American allies such as Germany and Brazil, and millions of Americans. The expansion of the NSA's data collection mission appears to have taken place mostly under the auspices of Keith Alexander, its chairman between 2005 and 2014, whose unhinged approach is summarized by his question "Why can't we collect all the signals all the time?"

The irony of the NSA debacle is that, even though the agency appears to have clearly and massively overstepped its purported boundaries and unconstitutionally collected information against American civilians, it has done so in a distorted version of the public-private partnership; it relied on private contractors and it compelled (or received the cooperation of willing) phone companies such as AT&T and Verizon and tech giants such as Google, Microsoft, Facebook, and Yahoo! to share their customers' data.

The Paradoxical American Leviathan

It is possible, perhaps even compelling, to see the rise of the American Leviathan as a success story—a society committed to liberty, a Constitution enshrining rights and protections, a state born with shackles on and remaining and evolving in the corridor because of the weight of the shackles. A case of the Red Queen gradually empowering the state to increase its reach and capacity without breaking free of the constraints imposed on it by society and its founding constitution. We may even argue that the American story has much to teach other nations about how to balance the power of the state and society. But we have also seen that there are two important elements missing from this optimistic reading of American history. First, the liberty that has been created by the American Leviathan is as much due to society's mobilization as to clever design in the Constitution. Without the mobilized, assertive, and irreverent society, the Constitution's protections wouldn't be worth much more than empty promises. Second, the architecture of the Constitution, to the extent that it has been important, has had a dark side too. The compromises it introduced have made the federal state unable and unwilling to protect its citizens against local despotism, enforce its laws equally on all, or supply the type of high-quality and broadly available public services that other rich nations routinely provide to their peoples. When notable exceptions to this slumber of the federal state came, they were triggered by the mobilization of society and sometimes its more discriminated-against, disadvantaged parts. Paradoxically, however, beyond the weakness and incapacity of the state created by the Constitution, other dimensions of the state have developed out of the purview of society and even of other branches of government, and have become increasingly unshackled. An exceptional American success, but a very mixed one.

In this light, a pressing issue is whether the American state, encumbered as it is by the tight constraints imposed at its founding and the public-private partnership model that developed as a result, is up to the task of dealing with the increasingly complex challenges on the horizon. Can it better protect its citizens and generate more opportunities for its entire population? How can it gain the flexibility to come up with new models to augment its capacity and face new social and economic problems while still remaining shackled by society and institutions? Is U.S. society up to the task of pushing the state to confront these challenges while increasing its own vigilance? We'll return to these questions in the final chapter.

Chapter 11

THE PAPER LEVIATHAN

Patients of the State

It's a spring day in September 2008 in Buenos Aires, the capital of Argentina. Summer is on the way, but it's chilly. Paula is trying to register for a welfare program called Nuestras Familias (Our Families) to receive the welfare payments that poor Argentines are entitled to. "This has been the longest wait," she told the sociologist Javier Auyero. "I've been in this since March. They asked me to come many times; there was always something (a document, a paper) missing." But "you have to be calm, to be patient. Here you have to have patience. This is an aid that the government gives you, so you have to be patient."

Patience is a prime virtue for those hoping to access public services in Argentina. Leticia, another aspirant for Nuestras Familias, "is by herself, standing alone in the back of the waiting room." She has come to the office three times in the last two weeks. "I'm used to waiting, I have to wait everywhere. But the worst thing is that they make you go here and then there . . . I came two weeks ago; they told me to come back in three days. I came back and the office was closed. I returned the next day, and they told me there were no funds in the program." She concludes, "You have to wait, because that's how things are here. You have to come many times because if you don't show up, you don't get anything."

Another of Auyero's testimonies brilliantly characterized the nature of the interaction between the Argentine state and its citizens.

María: They delay attending to you. They don't listen to you, they are there but they don't listen to you.

Interviewer: They don't pay attention to you?

M: I don't know if they are eating breakfast, until 10 they eat breakfast, drink mate, [eat] cookies; they talk a lot among themselves.

I: And how do you get their attention?

M: No, I wait for them to assist me.

I: You just wait for them to pay attention to you?

M: It's that you just have to wait.

I: Of all the times that you have gone, do you remember if there was any time a commotion was made there?

M: One time yes . . . a patient fought shouting . . .

I: What patient, some kind of health patient?

M: No, a patient here, a woman who waited.

Argentines are not citizens with rights, they are patients of the state who may or may not be tended to. Milagros, another "patient," talks about how you are given the "runaround." "You feel despondent here, because [the welfare agents] tell you to come on day X . . . They tell you to come on Monday, and then Wednesday, and then Friday . . . and those are working days." The previous time she came to the office she "left with nothing" feeling "impotent," but she emphasizes, "Here I didn't say anything."

The state is arbitrary, creating uncertainty and frustration, manipulating and disempowering people who are reduced to waiting and begging. There is an absence of routine, there are endless exceptions; when does the office open? What are the procedures? What documents do I need? Nobody is ever really sure. Many Argentines say "they kick us around like balls."

Auyero wrote in his fieldnotes:

September 11. A woman from Paraguay obtains her appointment even when she doesn't have the birth certificate with the apostille (official seal of approval). Today I meet Vicky. She is here for a second time because the first time she came they denied her an appointment because her birth certificate was missing the apostille.

Auyero's research took him not just into the waiting rooms of Nuestras Familias, but also to the office where you apply for a national identity card, a DNI (Documento Nacional de Identidad). In principle the office opens at 6 a.m. and starts giving appointments until 10 a.m., when it closes. It reopens from 6 p.m. to 10 p.m. People start queueing the night before. But the rules and the opening times change all the time. "October 26: I come back . . . after the morning observations expecting a big line outside. It's 2:50 p.m. And it's empty! There's nobody outside. No people, no vendors, nobody! A cop tells me that: "People from the office came out and said they'd close for the day." Alternatively the doors may open and admit people at any time. Or not. "October 24: There's no more waiting outside . . . People wait inside the building in a big waiting room. November 7: People make a line outside the building. They are told that it is forbidden to wait in line outside and that they should come back at 6 p.m. Officials try, unsuccessfully, to dissolve the line. November 9: Officials now let people form a line outside—and they also allow a line in the exterior hall." Auyero continues:

> **October 2, 2008:** A woman asks me if I think Monday will be a holiday. They told her to come back on Monday (October 12 is a holiday in Argentina). I tell her that if they instructed her to come back on Monday it is because it will not be a holiday. I assume that they don't give appointments for impossible days. The woman corrects me and tells me that the last time they gave her a Sunday appointment.

As it turned out, Monday was a holiday.

———

So far we have focused on three sorts of Leviathans: Absent, Despotic, and Shackled. The Argentine state doesn't seem to be any of these. It is not absent; it exists, it has elaborate laws, a large army, a bureaucracy (even if its bureaucrats don't seem to be interested in doing their jobs), and it appears to function to some degree, especially in the capital city, Buenos Aires (though much less in other areas). It's not a Despotic Leviathan either. Certainly, the Argentine bureaucrats we've just encountered seem unaccountable and unresponsive to society (the hallmark of a despotic state) and are quite capable of displaying cruelty toward people. As Argentines witnessed during the "dirty war" of the military dictatorship between 1974 and 1983, when as many as 30,000 people "disappeared" (secretly murdered by the junta), its officers and policemen can turn to murderous violence. But the despotism of the Argentine state is disorganized and erratic. It is far from the sort of authority that the Chinese state uses to control its people. When the civil servants wanted to stop people queueing outside, they were ignored. They are often incapable of regulating the economy or enforcing laws throughout the country. This is obviously not a Shackled Leviathan either; it lacks both the sort of state capacity we have associated with the Shackled Leviathan and society's ability to influence and control the state. What sort of state is the Argentine state?

We'll see in this chapter that it is a sort of state that is common in Latin America, Africa, and other parts of the world. In fact, it has a lot in common with the state in India in being founded on and supported by the weakness and disorganization of society. It combines some of the defining characteristics of the Despotic Leviathan, in being unaccountable to and unchecked by society, with the weaknesses of the Absent Leviathan. It cannot resolve conflicts, enforce laws, or provide public services. It is repressive but not powerful. It is weak itself and it weakens society.

Gnocchi in the Iron Cage

Auyero's study was about bureaucracy. Bureaucracy is vital to state capacity. As we mentioned in Chapter 1, its great theorist was the German sociologist Max Weber. In Weber's theory what distinguished the modern world from the past was "rationalization." This was manifest in modern firms that calculated costs, revenues, profits, and losses. It was there too in governments, rationalizing policy making and imposing impersonal administrative structures. Weber called this "rational-legal authority" and saw bureaucracy as its epitome. He wrote:

> The purest type of exercise of legal authority is that which employs a bureaucratic administrative staff . . . that consists . . . of individual officials who are appointed and function according to the following criteria: (1) They are personally free and subject to authority only with respect to their impersonal official obligations. (2) They are organized in a clearly defined hierarchy of offices. (3) Each office has a clearly defined sphere of competence in the legal sense. . . . (5) Candidates are selected on the basis of technical qualifications . . . They are appointed,

not elected . . . (7) The office is treated as the sole, or at least the primary, occupation of the incumbent . . . (9) The official works entirely separated from ownership of the means of administration and without appropriation of his position. (10) He is subject to strict and systematic discipline and control in the conduct of the office.

So the bureaucracy was run on impersonal lines; bureaucrats were professionals, beholden to nobody except their official obligations; they were selected and promoted on merit; and they would be disciplined if they stepped out of line. In Weber's view the power of bureaucracy could not be resisted. In a section titled "The Technical Superiority of Bureaucratic Organization," he wrote:

The decisive reason for the advance of bureaucratic organization has always been its purely *technical* superiority over any other form of organization. The fully developed bureaucratic apparatus compares with other organizations exactly as does the machine with the non-mechanical modes of production. Precision, speed, unambiguity, knowledge of the files, continuity . . . reduction of friction and of material and personal costs—these are raised to the optimum point in the strictly bureaucratic administration.

For Weber the triumph of rational-legal authority was inevitable. But he also recognized that it could be dehumanizing. He argued that while in the past people may have labored because they chose to, now "we are forced to do so." In the modern world there is an order "bound to the technical and economic conditions of machine production which to-day determine the lives of all the individuals who are born into this mechanism, not only those directly concerned with economic acquisition, with irresistible force." To capture how insidious this force could be, Weber coined the metaphor of the "iron cage" in which we were trapped by this spread of rational-legal authority.

Precision, speed, unambiguity, knowledge of the files . . . It doesn't sound like what Auyero observed in Buenos Aires. The bureaucracy he witnessed was slow, ambiguous, and uncertain, and there was copious ignorance about the files. Where was Argentina's iron cage?

Auyero's evidence shows that the Argentine state was greatly personalized: if you didn't get involved personally, there was no chance of getting services; that was the point of being a "patient"—you had to build a personal relationship with a bureaucrat in order to expect anything. His evidence does not directly speak to other aspects of Weber's ideal notion. Perhaps the bureaucrats that María or Leticia interacted with were recruited on merit as Weber foresaw? Unlikely, since recruitment into the Argentine bureaucracy is dominated by "gnocchi."

Gnocchi are an Italian gastronomic speciality, delicious dumplings that were brought to Argentina by Italian immigrants. In Argentina they are traditionally served on the twenty-ninth of each month. But the word has a double meaning in Argentina; it also means government "ghost workers," people who don't actually ever show up for work but who collect their paychecks. There are a lot of gnocchi in Argentina. When Mauricio Macri became the new president of Argentina in 2015, he fired 20,000 gnocchi who he claimed had been appointed by the previous government of President Cristina Fernández de Kirchner of the Peronist Party (named after its founder, Juan Domingo Perón). However the 20,000 gnocchi got hired, they were certainly not "selected on the basis of technical qualifications." It's also clear that working for the government was not the "sole, or at least the primary, occupation of the incumbent." One might also doubt that they were "subject to strict and systematic discipline and control in the conduct of office." They were typically party workers and supporters of the Peronist Party who got their "jobs" because of their political connections. That insulated them from any disciplinary actions that might have been a threat if they did not do their job, whatever that was supposed to be. The presence of gnocchi probably played a big role in what Auyero observed. Having 20,000 people like this running around in the bureaucracy can have seriously negative impacts on state capacity, even beyond the fact that they are totally useless. These impacts were all too easy to see during the presidency of Cristina Fernández de Kirchner.

As we discussed in Chapter 2, a central function of the government is to collect information on its citizens both to understand society's needs and to control it. You'd think that Hobbes's Leviathan would pay quite a bit of attention to collecting information on its citizens. Yet we also saw that that's not quite how things work in Lebanon, and it's not how they work in Argentina either. In 2011 Argentina was the first country ever censured by the International Monetary Fund for failing to provide accurate price level and national income data. *The Economist* magazine stopped reporting data from Argentina because it deemed the data totally untrustworthy. That's one of the downsides of filling the iron cage with gnocchi.

But we are still left with a puzzle. Weber thought that the iron cage was inevitable and the rationalization of society was unstoppable. He claimed, "The needs of mass administration make it today completely indispensable. The choice is only that between bureaucracy and dilettantism in the field of administration." How do we explain Argentina? Dilettantism?

Failing the Duck Test

Argentina in the 2000s had a modern-looking state, with a bureaucracy, judiciary, ministers, economic and social programs, representatives in all the international bodies such as the United Nations, and a president, Cristina Fernández de Kirchner at the time of Auyero's research, who got the red carpet treatment from other heads of states. The Argentine state had all the trappings of the modern state and looked like a Leviathan. To adapt the "duck test" to our context, if it looks like a state, swims like a state, quacks like a state, then it probably is a state. But is it?

Not really, not in the way we've been describing states so far. Both Despotic and Shackled Leviathans have quite a bit of capacity to get things done. Not so with the Argentine state. The Chinese dictator Mao Zedong used to call the United States a "paper tiger" to imply that its power was illusory. We'll call states such as those in Argentina, Colombia, and several other Latin American and African countries that fail the duck test and, despite appearances, lack anything beyond the most rudimentary state capacity Paper Leviathans. Paper Leviathans have the appearance of a state and are able to exercise some power in some limited domains and in some major cities. But that power is hollow; it is incoherent and disorganized in most domains, and it is almost completely absent when you go to outlying areas of the country they are supposed to be ruling over.

Why is it that Paper Leviathans do not accumulate more power? After all, wouldn't the political elites controlling the state and the state bureaucrats themselves want to have more capacity to get things done? To dominate society? To enrich themselves more, steal more if possible? What happened to the "will to power" that spurred powerful state-building efforts? The answers to these questions tell us a lot about the nature of many states around the world. It's not that there is no will to power in societies that have come to house the Paper Leviathan, but that the dangers to political leaders and elites of pursuing that will to power are too overwhelming. There are two fundamental reasons for this.

The first, paradoxically, relates to the Red Queen effect, which we have seen as powering the simultaneous development of state and society in the corridor. The Red Queen effect originates in society's desire to better control and better protect itself against a more capable state and more assertive political elites. The same impulses are present outside the corridor too; if the state gets more despotic, you'd better find a way of protecting yourself against that. But unless state builders are sure that they can quash any unwanted reaction from society and cling to power against rivals, these impulses would also spell trouble. We are going to refer to these perceived dangers of state building as the "mobilization effect"—in their attempt to build capacity, political leaders may end up mobilizing opposition against them. This is not unrelated to the slippery slope that creating a political hierarchy would set in motion. In the same way that some societies that were powerful enough to severely curtail political inequality were nonetheless afraid of the slippery slope, political elites who are ostensibly unrestrained by society may be concerned about reactions and competition that deepening state capacity would usher in. The mobilization effect was present in some of the iconic examples of state building such as the creation of the Islamic state pioneered by Muhammad or state building in China. But in these cases state builders were either powerful enough to be less worried about such mobilization, for example, because they had an "edge" (as we saw in Chapter 3), or they had no choice given outside threats or competition that they were locked into (the Qin state and Lord Shang had other, more existential things to worry about in the Warring States period, as we discussed in Chapter 7). Yet we'll see that, in other circumstances, the mobilization effect can be a paralyzing force against the building of state capacity.

The second reason why Paper Leviathans are quite common and unwilling to rise up from their slumber is that lack of state capacity is sometimes a powerful tool in the hands of unscrupulous leaders. To start with, exercising political control is much more about persuading others to follow your orders than naked repression. Tools to reward compliance are very useful in this endeavor, and handing out positions in the bureaucracy to friends and supporters, or those you want to turn into supporters, is a very powerful tool indeed. But imagine that you start building state capacity by institutionalizing a meritocratic recruitment and promotion system in the bureaucracy, in the way that Max Weber envisaged. That would mean no more gnocchi, no more opportunities to use these positions as rewards (how would the Peronist Party survive in that case?). This creates a powerful political logic for abandoning meritocracy and the building of state capacity.

It's not all high politics, of course. There are other, more mundane benefits from being able to use the judiciary and bureaucracy at your discretion. Soon after President Macri fired the gnocchi, he had to ban members of the government from hiring their own family members. The labor minister's wife and two of his sisters were out of jobs, as were the interior minister's mother and father.

This is a much more general pattern. Impersonal rules in the judiciary and bureaucracy, which come with state capacity, limit the ability of rulers and politicians to use laws in the way the former Brazilian president Getúlio Vargas purportedly expressed it: "For my friends, everything; for my enemies, the law." Such legal discretion, very different from the way the law evolved in the corridor in Europe, allows the political elite to use state institutions, such as they are, to suppress their opponents while enriching themselves, grabbing land from others, granting monopolies to friends, and directly looting the state. Like the mobilization effect, the ability to benefit from the discretionary use of the law encourages state incapacity and disorganization, not just in Argentina, but in many other Paper Leviathans.

That Paper Leviathans fail to build state capacity is a two-edged sword for their citizens. A less capable state is a state less capable of repressing its citizens. Could this be the basis of some liberty? Alas, this isn't typically the case. Rather, citizens of Paper Leviathans have the worst of both worlds. These states are still pretty despotic—they get very little input from the people and continue to be unresponsive to them, and then don't have many scruples about repressing or murdering them. At the same time, citizens miss out on the role of the state as resolver of disputes, enforcer of laws, and provider of public services. Paper Leviathans make no attempt to create liberty or relax norms inimical to liberty. In fact, as we'll see, Paper Leviathans often tighten the cage of norms rather than relaxing it.

No Place for Roads

What could trigger the mobilization effect in practice? The historian Eugen Weber, in his study of the making of the French state and society, *Peasants into Frenchmen*, proposed several "agencies of change"—factors that he thought had been crucial in the development of modern French society. He led with a chapter called "Roads, Roads, and Still More Roads." In his view basic infrastructure, by creating a national community, can mobilize society, change their demands, and transform the political agenda. In short, it can generate what we've called the mobilization effect.

The Colombian state, another perfect specimen of a Paper Leviathan, has never been interested in building roads. Today quite a few departmental capitals are not connected to the rest of the country except by air, or maybe river. Can you imagine Augusta, Maine, not being connected by road to the rest of the United States?

An interesting example is from the department of Putumayo in southern

Colombia, whose capital is Mocoa (see Map 14). In 1582, Fray Jerónimo de Escobar noted:

> This town is next to the mountains, far away from the road, so that it is a great travail to enter. Said town of Agreda [Mocoa], is not growing . . . it scares people away. There is no way to communicate [with] . . . everyone having a miserable life.

Things hadn't gotten much better by 1850 when a prefect of the then Territorio de Caquetá, just to the north of Putumayo, noted that "the journey from Pasto [capital of the neighboring department of Nariño] to this city [Mocoa] is gruelling, often bumping into horrifying places. Those of thin build travel on the back [of] Indians in a ridiculous, extravagant, and painful position: fastened with bale-rope and tied like pigs."

Map 14. Colombia: Elites, Paramilitaries, and the Trampoline of Death

Putumayo was a scary place for people from the capital, Bogotá. Future president Rafael Reyes wrote in his autobiography of his days prospecting in the region:

> Those virgin and *unknown* forests, those immense spaces, fascinated and attracted me to explore them, to traverse them and . . . to open roads for the progress and welfare of my country; those forests were *absolutely unknown* to the inhabitants of the *cordillera*, and the idea to penetrate them terrified me since the popular imagination populated them with wild beasts and monsters, besides the numerous savage cannibals found there.

Reyes had a solution to this isolation; in 1875 he proposed the construction of a road from Pasto, the capital of the neighboring department of Nariño, to Mocoa (which is also shown in Map 14). By 1906, Reyes was president and he authorized a study of potential routes. An engineer, Miguel Triana, was given the contract with the expectation that he would lay out the road. He did the survey, but the road was not started. Another contract was given to a Victor Triana, but by 1908 the new project was abandoned for lack of funds. In 1909 the national government decided to put the Capuchin friars of the Sibundoy Valley in charge of construction, with the governor of Nariño in charge of the money. With the aid of coerced indigenous labor, the Capuchins managed to finish the 120 kilometer road from Pasto to Mocoa in 1912, but only after an attack by Peruvian soldiers on a Colombian military garrison at La Pedrera on the Caquetá River induced the national government to provide 36,000 pesos. By the end of 1912, however, the road was in a bad state. A local administrator wrote to the minister of government that "regarding to state of the road from Pasto to this place [Mocoa] . . . most of the road has suffered grave damages due to collapsing of slopes and platforms and destruction of palisades in the flat and swampy areas, to the point that the traffic, even for pedestrian travellers, is now extremely difficult." An engineer reported that there were serious problems with the road design and construction; the bridges were "poorly built" and the road width was "inadequate for traffic needs."

The great Irish writer Samuel Beckett had a motto: "Try again, fail again, fail better." It might have been written for Paper Leviathans. In 1915 the national government put out a public tender to repair the road and finish the part to Puerto

Asís on the banks of the Putumayo River. In December 1917 the government canceled the contract because the contractor had not met his obligations. The government put it back in the hands of the Capuchins. A telegram to the Ministry of Public Works from Mocoa in June 1919 read "National road totally abandoned. From here to San Francisco thirty landslides; from here to Umbría, all bridges destroyed." In 1924 the road was taken away from the Capuchins again due to "unsatisfactory execution of works" and a contract given to an engineer in Pasto. A 1925 a law decreed the upgrading of the first 25 kilometers of the road out of Pasto to a motor road. But in 1928 the government removed the funding with 5 kilometers built. In 1931 Law 88 incorporated the road into the national road network, which meant that the portion up to Puerto Asís would have to become a motor road.

In Chapter 9 we discussed Charles Tilly's maxim "War made the state, and the state made war." If it did, in 1932 the Colombians might've caught a break. In that year, a border conflict started with Peru, and the Colombian government labeled the road a "national defense road" and allocated 120,000 pesos to maintain and expand it. An engineer's evaluation concluded that the road was "little less than an eyesore." The gravel road reached Puerto Asís in November 1957, twenty-five years after Peru had won the war and annexed a large slice of Colombian territory. No roads and not much state in the Colombian case, wars or no wars.

Though a road of sorts was open to Puerto Asís, it soon acquired a sinister but descriptive nickname: the Trampoline of Death. In 1991 the national newspaper *El Tiempo* reported: "The entire road to the Putumayo is horrifying. The drivers that cross it daily call it the road of death . . . [and] travelers are constantly threatened by the guerrilla." In 2005, President Álvaro Uribe promoted the Integration of the Regional Infrastructure of South America plan. By 2016 some 15 kilometers of the road had been built, and then the work was suspended because of lack of funds.

What sort of society does the absence of roads in Colombia create? One dispersed into isolated pockets. In 1946 in an address to the Society of Agriculturalists, Alberto Lleras Camargo, who was to become the Colombian president in 1958, observed:

> When we refer to campaigns of rural health, credit or education that are
> going to save the *campesino*, don't we know that most of these programs

reach [only] the villages [*aldeas*] and the upper echelon of Colombian society? . . . Among the 71 percent of our [rural dwelling] fellow citizens and the rest of society, there is no direct communication, there is no contact, there are no roads, there are no channels of direct interchange. Fifteen minutes from Bogotá there are *campesinos* who belong to another age, to another social class and culture, separated from us by centuries.

But that's the way a Paper Leviathan likes it; a very fragmented society focused on parochial issues. In the British case, we saw in Chapter 6 that parochial issues disappeared as society was further mobilized in response to state building. Not so in Colombia. In 2013, the country was convulsed by a series of strikes and protests. In July of that year striking miners overwhelmed Quibdó, the capital of the department of Chocó (also shown in Map 14). The miners insisted that informal miners be recognized, and they wanted "subsidies and preferential credit for miners, as well as technical assistance." In addition they asked the government "to cease the selling of land to multinational mining companies" and "to subsidize fuel for mining purposes." There were no demands in the list other than the immediate ones of the miners. Tellingly, there is no road from Quibdó to the rest of the country. The same was true of the many other strikes that took place in different parts of the country. The Dignidad Cafetera (literally "coffee dignity"), in the coffee-growing region of Colombia, wanted the government to give them price subsidies for coffee; they demanded the democratization of the National Federation of Coffee Growers, and insisted that mining in coffee-growing areas be regulated more stringently. The Dignidad Papera, Lechera y Cebollera ("potato, milk and onion dignity") was an organization that claimed to represent the producers of potatoes, milk, and onions. They also asked for price subsidies, but this time for their crops. They advocated that the rehydration of powdered milk should be banned, and that they should be compensated for the importation of powdered milk and frozen or precooked potatoes. The Dignidad Panelera ("raw sugar dignity"), organized by the producers of raw sugar, wanted the government to introduce higher tariffs on imported substitutes for sugar, and they demanded that the government purchase 3,500 tons of panela (the raw cane sugar that they produced). This is a society with little prospect of mobilization, and that's very convenient for Colombian elites and very easy for the Colombian government to manage. A few subsidies here, and a few purchases of panela there, and the genie is back in the bottle.

The Orangutan in a Tuxedo

It's not just the absence of infrastructure. Like Argentina, Colombia doesn't do bureaucracy, and for similar reasons. In 2013 in some national ministries 60 percent of the employees were "provisional staff," recruited outside the meritocratic rules and hired most likely through patronage. Colombians are less fond of gnocchi than are Argentines, but they still manage to house a fair number of them in the civil service.

The consequences of the lack of rules and bureaucratic procedures were dramatically illustrated by the tenure of Samuel Moreno, elected mayor of the capital city of Bogotá in 2008. Once he was in power, Moreno created a "shadow government" for Bogotá, which he delegated to his brother Iván. Iván constructed what Colombians now call the "contract carousel," which was in charge of allocating all of the contracts for the city. The brothers used this as a way to extract bribes, which were often 50 percent of a contract. To hide all the illegal activities, they frequently met in Miami, traveling by private plane. The brothers developed a slang: their cut in a contract was called a bite—*una mordida*—the same slang we saw in Guatemala in Chapter 9. The jewel in the crown of bites was the contract to run the city's integrated public transport system, which carries millions of people per day. The Morenos' cut was eight pesos per passenger. The brothers did not stop there. They looted everything. Existing hospitals were very lucrative, but building new ones created even better opportunities for stealing, and between 25 and 30 percent of the outlays went to the Morenos. They decided who got the ambulance contract, and then the brothers and their cronies took half of what was allocated. If you didn't pay the bite, you didn't get the contract and were told by the brothers that you were "too cheap." So 45,000 million pesos (US$15 million) were set aside to build a bridge linking Carrera 9 to Calle 94 to address the traffic jams in part of Bogotá. The construction work was never begun and the money vanished. Nobody really knows how much the brothers bit off; one conjecture is that it could be as high as US$500 million.

Samuel Moreno was not an outsider to Colombian politics. His grandfather Gustavo Rojas Pinilla was a military dictator in the 1950s who tried to reinvent himself as a democrat in the 1960s. Like Moreno, Colombian political elites have a habit of looting the state budget. When they have the opportunity, they are happy to loot the land as well.

An extensive amount of rural Colombia is classified legally as *baldío* (wasteland) and owned by the government. Since the nineteenth century the Colombian government has promulgated many laws that have shaped the distribution of this land and the issuing of titles. Law 160, passed in 1994, specified that people who had been settled on baldío for five years or more could petition the agrarian reform institute INCORA (Instituto Colombiano de Reforma Agraria) for the title to the land they occupied. This type of concession applied only to citizens who were landless. Supposedly poor or displaced people got priority, and the amount of land a person could claim was limited to an "Unidad Agrícola Familiar" (Agricultural Family Unit), an amount of land judged by the INCORA to allow a family "to live with dignity." But it turned out that this system could be easily gamed by well-connected elites, especially when they had the help of sophisticated Bogotano law firms, well versed in the art of bending the law. A notorious case involves Riopaila Castilla, a sugar company in Valle del Cauca. The company gamed the system by creating twenty-seven Anonymous Simple Societies in 2010 with the aid of the law firm Brigard Urrutia. They bought 42 parcels of baldío in the eastern department of Vichada (see Map 14), equivalent to 35,000 hectares, all intended for the poor and the displaced but instead destined for Riopaila. Similar strategies allowed Luis Carlos Sarmiento, the wealthiest person in Colombia, to acquire 16,000 hectares of baldío land for himself. When asked by a journalist how a respectable law firm could facilitate such blatant violations of the law, a lawyer from Brigard Urrutia stated:

The law is there to be interpreted. Here they are not white or black.

The fragmented, ineffective nature of the Paper Leviathan has major consequences for liberty, in particular, for the control of violence. Max Weber defined the state as "a human community that (successfully) claims the monopoly of the legitimate use of physical force within a given territory." Because of the way they use power, Paper Leviathans cannot have such a monopoly of physical force, legitimate or otherwise. Colombia also illustrates the devastating consequences of the lack of monopoly of violence by the state.

In his research in Colombia, James Robinson, and his collaborators Maria Angélica Bautista, Juan Diego Restrepo, and Juan Sebastián Galan, documented how in 1977 Ramón Isaza, a former soldier and farmer, started a group he named the Shotgunners. Isaza had a farm in the municipality of Puerto Triunfo in the east of the department of Antioquia (see Map 14). Court documents recorded how in the mid-1970s the Marxist guerrilla group the FARC (Revolutionary Armed

Forces of Colombia) had created a new front in the area and initiated a policy of "taxing" local farmers and expropriating their livestock. In 1977, Isaza purchased ten shotguns, an act that christened the group. They ambushed the FARC, killed them, and stole their guns. By the year 2000 the Shotgunners had changed their name to the Peasant Self-Defense Forces of the Middle Magdalena, received support from landowners, and expanded to six fronts. One front was led by Isaza's son-in-law Luis Eduardo Zuluaga (nicknamed MacGyver, after the U.S. television character). MacGyver commanded the José Luis Zuluaga Front (FJLZ), named after his brother, who had been killed by the guerrillas. The FJLZ controlled an extensive territory whose core covered around 5,000 square kilometers. The front had a written legal system of *estatutos* (statutes), which was 32 pages long, and they tried to enforce it equally even to the extent of applying it to both their members and civilians. The FJLZ also had a bureaucracy and was separated into a military wing made up of about 250 uniformed fighters, a civilian wing of "tax collectors," and a "social team" focused on their political project of combatting the Marxist guerrillas. They regulated trade and social life; they had a mission statement, an ideology, a hymn, a prayer, and a radio station called Integration in Stereo. The front even awarded medals, including the Order of Francisco de Paula Santander and the Grand Cross of Gold. How did they pay their bureaucrats and soldiers? They taxed landowners and businessmen in the area they controlled and also attempted to tax production, specifically of milk and potatoes. The front built tens of kilometers of roads, extended the electric grid, and constructed schools. In La Danta, where they were based, the front built a health clinic, reconstructed an old-people's home, built houses that they allocated by lot to poor people, started an artisan center, and constructed a bullring, though MacGyver claimed, "I don't approve of bullfighting, it is cruel to the animals."

The area was controlled not by the Colombian state but by Isaza and Mac-Gyver. In a statement to the magistrate following the group's demobilization in 2006, Ramón Isaza explained their role in elections in the following way:

> What we did do was in the veredas, such as La Danta, also in San Miguel or Cocorná which didn't have police, that were little towns removed from the main roads and there was no military or police force. There we protected these regions but we didn't tell anybody to vote for a particular person. Rather we looked after—what did we look after?—that maybe elections wouldn't be spoiled, that maybe fights or quarrels occurred.

This we did in this and all the regions where these towns were; we provided security for the elections.

Colombians often excuse their Paper Leviathan by pointing out that the country has high mountains and jungles. In fact, Isaza and his fronts were placed on the main road between the two largest cities, Bogotá and Medellín, right under the nose and in full view of the Colombian state. As another powerful Colombian paramilitary boss, Ernesto Báez, ironically put it to a different judge: "How could a small independent state work inside a lawful state such as ours?" The answer is: quite easily in a Paper Leviathan.

The Colombian state doesn't just neglect and ignore its citizens, it actively victimizes them. One illustration comes from the so-called false-positives scandal. When Álvaro Uribe was elected president in 2002, his mandate was to intensify the fight against left-wing guerrillas. He introduced a series of powerful incentives for the military, such as financial bonuses and holidays, if they produced dead guerrillas. A consequence was that members of the army murdered as many as 3,000 innocent civilians and dressed them up as guerrillas. One Colombian judicial prosecutor even referred to a military unit, the Batallón Pedro Nel Ospina, as a "group of assassins dedicated to creating victims which they then pretended were killed in combat." If the guerrillas and paramilitaries don't get you, the army might.

Another consequence of the Colombian Paper Leviathan was noted almost two hundred years ago by Simón Bolívar, Latin America's "liberator," who led its revolution against Spanish colonial rule, when he stated:

> These Gentlemen think that Colombia is full of simple men they've seen gathered around fireplaces in Bogotá, Tunja, and Pamplona. They've never laid eyes on the Caribs of the Orinoco, the plainsmen of the Apure, the fishermen of Maracaibo, the boatmen of the Magdalena, the bandits of Patia, the ungovernable Pastusos, the Guajibos of Casanare and all the other savage hordes of Africans and Americans that roam like deer throughout the wilderness of Colombia.

Bolívar is claiming that Colombians elites don't really know or understand the country they claim to be governing (and are looting). Indeed, the famous nineteenth-century Colombian president Miguel Antonio Caro, the mastermind of the 1886 Constitution that was in force until 1991, never left Bogotá his entire

life (nor for that matter did one of the subsequent presidents, José Manuel Ma-
rroquín). Who was he writing the constitution for? The gentlemen of "Bogotá,
Tunja, and Pamplona," of course. The periphery of the country was run from
Bogotá and received few resources or public services. Of 18,500 kilometers of roads
in 1945, only 613 kilometers (none paved) were in the peripheral territories that
made up three quarters of Colombia's land area. Political elites in Bogotá made
sure that the periphery stayed peripheral. But before you conclude that this implies
that things were all right in Bogotá, at least when Samuel Moreno wasn't in power,
next time you are there try posting a letter. What would Tocqueville have said?

The Colombian politician Dario Echandía once quipped that Colombian democracy was like "an orangutan in a tuxedo." It's a remark that captures the nature of the Paper Leviathan. The tuxedo is its outward appearance of an orderly
state with a functioning bureaucracy, even if it is sometimes used for looting the
country and is often disorganized. The orangutan is all the things the Paper Leviathan cannot and doesn't wish to control.

Plowing the Sea

None of this was created overnight. To understand how the Colombian state
evolved, let's turn to Bolívar again, now lying ill with tuberculosis in the port city
of Barranquilla. On November 9, 1830, he wrote to his old friend General Juan José
Flores. By 1830 continental Latin America was free from Spanish colonialism and
Spain retained only the islands of Cuba, parts of Hispaniola, and Puerto Rico. Yet
Bolívar was disillusioned. He wrote:

> I have ruled for twenty years, and I have derived from these only a few
> sure conclusions: (1) America is ungovernable, for us; (2) Those who serve
> the revolution plow the sea; (3) The only thing one can do in America is
> emigrate; (4) This country will fall inevitably into the hands of the unre-
> strained multitudes and then into the hands of tyrants so insignificant
> they will almost be imperceptible, of all colors and races; (5) Once we've
> been eaten alive by every crime and extinguished by ferocity, the Europe-
> ans won't even bother to conquer us; (6) If it were possible for any part of
> the world to revert to primitive chaos, it would be America in her last hour.

Why was he so pessimistic? Why did he think that trying to govern "America,"
by which he meant Latin America, was like "plowing the sea," an impossible task?

There were several reasons. Perhaps the most important was that Latin American society had been created on a premise of political hierarchy and inequality. Colonial society was an institutionalized hierarchy with white Spaniards on top and indigenous people and, in many areas black slaves, at the bottom. Over time, the Spanish elites became native to Latin America and were known as Creoles (Bolívar was one of them), and as miscegenation took place, an elaborate system of caste (*casta* in Spanish) was created to identify who was superior to whom. The castas were memorialized in a famous series of paintings in colonial Mexico, one of which we reproduce in the photo insert. Caste mattered, since laws and taxes applied differently to people depending on their social station, and if you were sufficiently powerful, the laws didn't apply to you at all. Without any equality before the law, the law itself was illegitimate in the eyes of most Latin Americans, making them adopt the famous motto of the colonial era, *Obedezco pero no cumplo* (I obey but I do not comply); I recognize your right to issue laws and orders but I maintain my right to ignore them. Even more important, it meant a great degree of hierarchy, dominance, and inequality, as indigenous people and black slaves were systematically exploited. Hierarchy, dominance, and inequality are still on display today.

Their origins can be seen by returning to the road between Pasto and Mocoa, which ran through the Sibundoy Valley. After the conquest of the Americas the indigenous peoples of the valley had been given in a grant of *encomienda*, literally "entrusted," to a Spaniard, known as the *encomendero*. Many indigenous people had died of the infectious diseases the Spanish brought with them from the Old World, but there were still 1,371 people left to exploit. According to the encomienda, a lot of animals, birds, and produce of Indians had to go to the abbey and the *cacique* (the word imported into Latin America from the Caribbean and used to designate an indigenous chief or ruler). Also, it specified "145 Indians to work in the mines for eight months," 10 Indians to work on the land of the encomendero, "8 Indians for the cacique's domestic service," and so on with the coercive labor practices.

This highly unequal society was ultimately held together by force, and Latin Americans knew that it could never survive under the type of democratic institutions that had emerged in the United States. By the nineteenth century there were no encomiendas left, but they had been replaced by a new exploitative system in which Indian "tribute" continued to provide the fiscal basis of the state. The extent of inequality at this point was if anything more intense than ever. The perpetuation of this system, Bolívar and others reasoned, required much stronger autocratic power than any U.S. president was going to get. But that didn't mean it would be easy to maintain such a society. Here the second main factor leading to ungovernability becomes important.

Like many colonies, Spanish America had some state institutions imposed by the colonists (most notably sufficient force to repress the indigenous people), but it was governed "indirectly" by Spain. The encomienda of the Sibundoy Valley gave a lot of the produce, birds, and pigs to the cacique because he was the indirect representative of the Spanish. The Spanish created no bureaucracy and no state administration to run the encomienda; they manipulated the indigenous political hierarchy to do this. At the time of the revolt against the Spanish, leaving aside the military, there were just 800 people working for the Spanish state in the whole of Colombia.

These two factors left a society with enormous inequality and hierarchy, but without an effective state. That meant no state institutions or legal apparatus to control the "Caribs of the Orinoco, the plainsmen of the Apure, the fishermen of Maracaibo, the boatmen of the Magdalena, the bandits of Patia, the ungovernable Pastusos, the Guajibos of Casanare." Creole elites stuck with what they knew. They tried to create an autocratic, centralized society to the extent they could, but just to be sure they backed it up with many of the same strategies that the Spanish had used to rule over their colonial empire. There was no room for a Weberian state. Rather, the government was a tool for controlling power and the law an instrument for stabilizing this unequal status quo.

The difference between Latin American and U.S. concepts of limits on presidential power is perhaps best illustrated by the speech Bolívar gave in 1826 in Lima, Peru, after he had personally written a constitution for the new country of Bolivia, now liberated from the Spanish. It's worth pointing out that the name Bolivia came from Bolívar himself. How many people have countries named after them? One is Christopher Columbus, who had his name given to the country of Colombia. The Saud family have Saudi Arabia named after them, and the Luxembourg family, one of the surviving remnants of the Holy Roman Empire, also have a country named for them. The great entrepreneur of British colonialism in Africa, Cecil Rhodes, had one named after him, Rhodesia, until 1980, when the name was changed to Zimbabwe. It's a small and exclusive club, and you typically don't become a member if you are running a country democratically. Introducing his constitution for Bolivia, Bolívar focused on the role of the president:

> Under our constitution, the president of the republic is like the Sun, immovable at the center of the universe, radiating life. This supreme

authority should be permanent . . . a fixed point around which magistrates and citizens and men and events revolve . . . Give me a fixed point, said an ancient, and I will move the earth. For Bolivia, this point is a president for life.

The Bolivian constitution specified a president for life and made him "the Sun." Initially that person would be chosen by "legislators." Subsequent presidents would be chosen by the existing president for life. The notion of a president choosing who would follow him turned out to have a long half-life in Latin America. As recently as 1988, Mexican presidents were chosen by the *dedazo*. Google Translate hasn't managed to figure out how to translate that word into English yet, but the root of the expression is the Spanish word *dedo*, "finger." A *dedazo* is when you tap someone on the back with your finger, meaning "your turn now." It's hard to translate, but Bolívar knew what it meant; it was a surefire guarantee that the presidency would stay in safe, elite hands. After all, it seemed highly likely that he was going to be chosen as the first president, and indeed he was. On paper, the Bolivian Constitution had some separation of powers and checks and balances, but it also allowed the president for life to personally appoint all military officers and command the army. Mix that with a bit of *Obedezco pero no cumplo* and the rest, as they say, is history.

It's true that just as the U.S. War of Independence against Britain unleashed all sorts of radical energy and movements, so did the Latin American wars of independence. But again and again, Latin American elites were able to construct political institutions to control this energy even if Bolívar himself never managed to really implement his plans. We find that even when Latin American constitutions allowed for the types of checks and balances and even rights for citizens that the U.S. Constitution enshrined, these were always trumped either by strong formal presidential powers or a disregard for the law. Ramón Castilla, the authoritarian president of Peru, clearly explained this logic in 1849:

> The first of my constitutional functions is the preservation of internal order; but the same constitution obliges me to respect the rights of the citizen. . . . the simultaneous fulfillment of both duties would be impossible. The former . . . could not be accomplished . . . without some measures to check the enemies of that order in a manner more stringent than was provided for by the laws. Ought I to have sacrificed the internal peace of the country for the constitutional rights of a few individuals?

If constitutional rights got in the way, then so much the worse for constitutional rights. The mastermind of the Chilean state, Diego Portales, articulated this view even more forcefully:

> With the men of the law one cannot come to an understanding; and if it's that way, what [expletive] purpose do Constitutions . . . serve, if they are incapable of providing a remedy to an evil that is known to exist . . . In Chile, the law doesn't serve for anything but to produce anarchy, the lack of sanctions, licentiousness, eternal law suits . . . Damned law then if it does not allow the Power to proceed freely in the opportune moment.

The view that "the Power" should be able to "proceed freely in the opportune moment" is rather different from how the state is expected to behave in the corridor.

This notion of power is again rooted in Latin America's history. Alexis de Tocqueville identified its origins in his 1835 book, *Democracy in America*, when he argued that in South America the Spanish found territory "inhabited by peoples . . . who had already appropriated the soil by cultivating it. To found their new states they had to destroy or enslave many populations." But, he went on, "North America was inhabited only by wandering tribes who did not think of using the natural riches of the soil. North America was still, properly speaking, an empty continent, a wilderness land, that awaited inhabitants." Tocqueville's claim that North America was an "empty continent" is not correct, but the gist of the argument, that North America could not develop based on the exploitation of sedentary indigenous peoples, is on target. This meant that the type of highly unequal and hierarchical society that emerged in South America could not be reproduced in the North (even though the early English settlers did try). The slave society of the U.S. South looked a lot like Latin America, including low levels of public services, prosperity for the elites, and of course no liberty for the majority. But the U.S. South was embedded in an institutional setting partly created by the very different state-society dynamics of the North, and when it tried to fight in the Civil War to free itself from these dynamics, it lost. That wasn't the end of the despotic and exploitative system of the U.S. South, as we saw in the previous chapter, but it did put the whole of the United States on a different path from Latin America's.

In Latin America, society remained emaciated and unable to shape politics and control the state and the elites, paving the way for the Paper Leviathan, with predictable consequences for liberty.

Mississippi in Africa

Paper Leviathans are hardly restricted to Latin America. They are also the characteristic form of state in sub-Saharan Africa. In fact both mechanisms underpinning the continued weakness and disorganization of the state operate in Africa with a vengeance. Let's take them one at a time: first, the fear of societal mobilization.

One of the best documented examples of this fear comes from Liberia in West Africa. In 1961 the newly created United States Agency for International Development (USAID) sent a team of scholars off to Liberia to study its development. They began with their usual ideas about why poor countries are poor. Yet they soon realized the situation was very different. As one of them, the social anthropologist George Dalton, later put it:

> The economic backwardness of Liberia is not attributable to the lack of resources or to domination by foreign financial or political interests. The underlying difficulty is rather that the traditional Americo-Liberian rulers, who fear losing political control to the tribal people, have not allowed those changes to take place which are necessary to develop the national society and economy.

Who were these "Americo-Liberian rulers"? To understand this, we need to recall that the country of Liberia was started as a colony in 1822 by the American Colonization Society (ACS) as a home for freed and repatriated African slaves from the United States. The descendants of these repatriated slaves became the Americo-Liberians. In 1847 Liberia declared itself independent of the ACS, and in 1877 the True Whig Party (TWP) emerged and dominated politics until they were overthrown by a military coup headed by Samuel Doe in 1980. The TWP was spearheaded by Americo-Liberians, who in the 1960s made up less than 5 percent of the population. As Dalton describes it, "Like the Portuguese in Angola or the Afrikaners in South Africa, the rulers of Liberia are the descendants of an alien minority of colonial settlers. Americo-Liberian families."

Liberia became a two-class society. Different laws, different public services, and differential access to education governed Americo-Liberians and "tribal people." Before 1944 the hinterland had no political representation whatsoever. Dalton observed, "Ironically, it is the ethic of Mississippi that most nearly characterizes

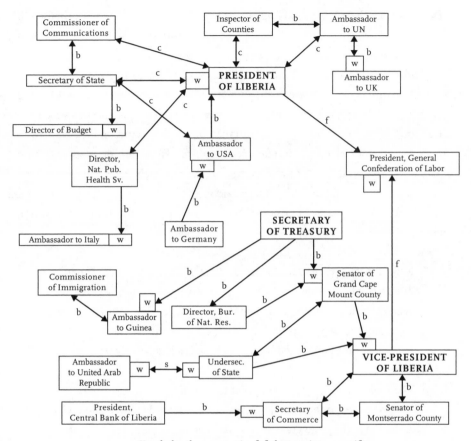

Key: b=brother; c=cousin; f=father; s=sister; w=wife

Map 15. Kinship in Liberia: The Political Appointments of President Tubman in 1960

their outlook: to retain power in traditional fashion and keep the natives in their place." Now you begin to see why the Americo-Liberians feared societal mobilization. Building an effective state might have mobilized the indigenous Liberians who made up the other 95 percent of the nation.

The other fundamental mechanism supporting Paper Leviathans—the usefulness of discretionary power in a nonmeritocratic, disorganized bureaucracy and judiciary—is also clearly visible in Liberia and other African countries. The Liberian state was systematically used to reward followers. For instance, Dalton found in the 1960s that "to understand Liberian politics, knowledge of kinship connections is more useful than knowledge of the Liberian constitution." He presented elaborate data on how political elites filled bureaucratic positions with their immediate family. (Map 15, for example, shows the bewildering family connections of Liberia's political elite in 1960 during President Tubman's rule.)

The nonmeritocratic nature of African states is also highlighted in Tony Killick's seminal book *Development Economics in Action*. Killick worked for the government of Kwame Nkrumah in Ghana in the early 1960s and witnessed the disastrous economic failures of Nkrumah's regime firsthand. Killick wanted to understand what caused them. He recorded the construction of a fruit-canning factory "for the production of mango products, for which there was recognized to be no local market, [and] which was said to exceed by some multiple the total world trade in such items." The government's own report on this factory is worth quoting.

> **Project:** A factory is to be erected at Wenchi, Brong Ahafo, to produce 7,000 tons of mangoes and 5,300 tons of tomatoes per annum. If average yields of crops in that area will be 5 tons per acre per annum for mangoes and 5 tons per acre for tomatoes, there should be 1,400 acres of mangoes and 1,060 acres of tomatoes in the field to supply the factory.

> **The Problem:** The present supply of mangoes in the area is from a few trees scattered in the bush and tomatoes are not grown on commercial scale, and so the production of these crops will have to start from scratch. Mangoes take 5–7 years from planting to start fruiting. How to obtain sufficient planting materials and to organize production of raw materials quickly become the major problems of this project.

Killick wrote, "It is difficult to imagine a more damning commentary on the efficiency of project planning." What was going on? The factory wasn't meant to further economic development. Rather, it created innumerable opportunities to employ political supporters in a region where President Nkrumah wanted support. It made no economic sense to build the factory there, and projects like this undermined the coherence of the civil service and the "efficiency of project planning." But it made good political sense. As Nkrumah told Sir Arthur Lewis, his Nobel Prize–winning economic adviser, "The advice you have given me, sound though it may be, is essentially from an economic point of view, and I have told you, on many occasions, that I cannot always follow this advice as I am a politician and must gamble on the future."

Killick additionally documented that Nkrumah's government also lived in fear of initiating societal mobilization. Standard development economics at the time maintained that it was critical for a developing country to generate a strong "entrepreneurial class" of businesspeople who could lead the transformation toward a more industrialized economy. Yet Killick observed:

> Even had there been the possibility [of creating an indigenous entrepreneurial class] it is doubtful that Nkrumah would have wanted to create such a class, for reasons of ideology and political power. He was very explicit about this saying "we would be hampering our advance to socialism if we were to encourage the growth of Ghanaian private capitalism in our midst." There is evidence that he also feared the threat that a wealthy class of Ghanaian businessmen might pose to his own political power.

In fact E. Ayeh-Kumi, one of Nkrumah's main economic advisers, noted that "[Nkrumah] informed me that if he permitted African business to grow, it will grow to becoming a rival power to his and the party's prestige, and he would do everything to stop it, which he actually did." His solution was to limit the size of Ghanaian businesses. Killick notes, "Given Nkrumah's desire to keep Ghanaian private businesses small, his argument that 'Capital investment must be sought from abroad since there is no bourgeois class amongst us to carry on the necessary investment' was disingenuous." He goes on to add that Nkrumah "had no love of foreign capitalists but he preferred to encourage them rather than local entrepreneurs, whom he wished to restrict." Better foreign capitalists than societal mobilization.

Another seminal book on African economics and politics, Robert Bates's *Markets and States in Tropical Africa*, illustrates how the discretionary use of the law was a powerful political strategy. Bates was trying to explain the dismal economic performance of African nations after independence and particularly why the agricultural sector, which should have been the engine for growth, was performing so badly. The simple answer he gave is that urban-based governments, such as that of Nkrumah in Ghana, were taxing the agricultural sector at punitive rates. Farmers stopped investing and producing because the tax rates were so high. How could the government respond? An obvious way would have been to increase prices, reduce taxes, and restore incentives. But Bates observed, "Were the governments of Africa to confer a price rise on all rural producers, the political benefits would be low; for both supporters and dissidents would secure the benefits of such a measure." Instead, governments kept prices low and used other policy instruments, which they could target in a discretionary way.

> The conferral of benefits in the form of public works projects, such as state farms, on the other hand, has the political advantage of allowing the benefits to be selectively apportioned.

The same was true of subsidized fertilizer given to supporters and withheld from opponents. Bates asked a suffering cocoa farmer in 1978 why he did not try to organize resistance against the government policies.

> He went to his strongbox and produced a packet of documents: licenses for his vehicles, import permits for spare parts, titles to his real property and improvements, and the articles of incorporation that exempted him from a major portion of his income taxes. "If I tried to organize resistance to the government's policies on farm prices," he said while exhibiting these documents, "I would be called an enemy of the state and I would lose all these."

"For my friends, everything; for my enemies, the law," Ghanaian-style.

Postindependence governments in Ghana did not operate in a social vacuum. Recall in Chapter 1 how we introduced the notion of the cage of norms using Robert Rattray's research in Ghana. When the country became independent a mere thirty years after Rattray wrote, the forces he described were still powerfully present. The philosopher Kwame Anthony Appiah recalls being told by his father growing up in Kumasi in the 1960s "that one must never inquire after people's ancestry in public." Appiah's "auntie" was the child of a family slave. As another Asante proverb puts it, "Too much revealing of origins spoils a town." The dense web of norms, mutual obligations, and the remnants of the supporting institutions lived on. This cage of norms heavily shaped how postindependence politics worked and why Nkrumah organized the state the way he did. The networks of reciprocity and kinship and ethnic relations translated into a very non-Weberian state wherein those in power were pushed into using their influence to favor their dependents, as witnessed by the factory in Wenchi. Similarly, the dependents were obliged to help and support their benefactors, for example in elections. The cage of norms created a social environment that perpetuated the Paper Leviathan, blocking society's ability to act collectively while at the same time stunting the state's capacity. The more the Paper Leviathan exploited the network of mutual dependences and ethnic ties, the more it reaffirmed the cage of norms that these created in many African societies.

The Postcolonial World

Paper Leviathans are not restricted to Latin America and Africa; they inhabit many different parts of the world. Several of them, like the ones we discussed in this chapter, have one thing in common—they are products of European colonization. This is true even for Liberia, which wasn't a colony so much as an outpost for later-freed slaves of a European colony, the United States of America. This is because the way that European colonial powers governed and manipulated the institutions of many of their colonies created the conditions for Paper Leviathans to emerge.

What is it about the residues of colonization that created such a state? As we have already seen in the Latin American context, two axes were particularly important. First, colonial powers introduced state institutions, but without any way for society to control them (especially since the colonizers had no interest in Africans controlling the state or its bureaucracy). Second, they tried to do all this on the cheap, propagating "indirect rule" where power was delegated to locals, such as chiefs in Africa, and this meant that no meritocratic bureaucracy or judiciary emerged. Remember how we explained in Chapter 2 that Lugard wanted to rule Nigeria indirectly. To achieve this, he had to establish a political body he could deal with, which in practical terms meant state-like structures. But who would be the bureaucrats, tax collectors, judges, and legislators of this state? Not the British. In 1920 there were just 265 British officials in the whole of Nigeria. There was nobody but the traditional chiefs and this meant that there was no national administrative apparatus to work with at independence.

The lack of capacity and dearth of public services were constants during colonial times. But things only got worse after independence in 1960, when the British up and left Nigeria so that the Nigerians could rule themselves. But with what state? A Leviathan of sorts, but paper-thin in its ability to resolve conflicts, raise taxes, provide public services, and even maintain basic order. The political incentives we have seen in Argentina, Colombia, Liberia, and Ghana then kicked in.

To the legacy of haphazardly imposed state institutions and indirect rule was added a third factor, further weakening both state and society—the arbitrary nature of postcolonial countries. One of the reasons it was so attractive for Nkrumah to use the state as a political tool was that Ghana had no coherence as a nation. There was no national language; there was no common history, no common religion or identity, and no legitimate social contract. Instead, the country had been cobbled together by the English in the late nineteenth century from various African polities with very different levels of centralization and disparate political traditions. In fact Ghana ranged from one of the most highly centralized states in precolonial Africa, the Asante in the south, to completely stateless societies like the Tallensi, in the north. This incoherence meant that there was little societal mobilization, and this made it particularly attractive for leaders such as Nkrumah to make discretionary use of the state and the law to maintain power. In essence Paper Leviathans formed in the terrain left by colonial empires, which created weak states and weak societies and a situation wherein both were likely to perpetuate each other.

A final factor completed the foundations of the Paper Leviathan—the international state system. The postwar world was ostensibly based on independent states following international rules, cooperating in international bodies, and respecting one another's borders. It worked (partly because the West imposed it). It is remarkable that though cobbled from different types of societies and myriad entities with no natural borders and no national unity, African states fought essentially no wars with one another over the last sixty years (even if civil wars have been commonplace in the continent and spilled across national boundaries in some notable cases such as the Great War in the eastern part of the Democratic Republic of the Congo). This system cemented the Paper Leviathans, because it conferred international legitimacy on these states, even if they completely failed the duck test. Once you have the red carpet treatment from the international community, and once you can get most of the looting you want domestically, the fact that your power is really hollow matters less.

We can put all of these threads together using the figure we introduced in Chapter 2, which we replicate here as Figure 4. Our discussion implies that Paper Leviathans are found near the bottom left corner, on the side of the Despotic Leviathan—little societal power, little state power, but still despotic. This provides some more insights into the fear of the mobilization effect—an increase in the power of society can throw a Paper Leviathan into the orbit of the Absent Leviathan or even ultimately push it into the corridor, with detrimental effects on the

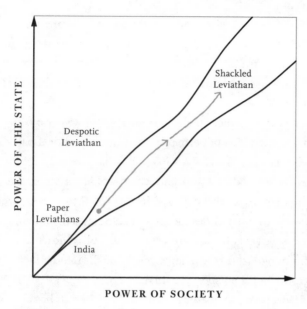

POWER OF SOCIETY

Figure 4. Paper Leviathans

ability of elites to control politics. In this context, it is also useful to contrast the Paper Leviathan with the Indian state. We saw in Chapter 8 that the Indian state is disorganized and feeble too, and this is maintained by the fragmented nature of society, just like the Paper Leviathan. But there are notable differences too. In India, this situation was forged by the history of caste relations and the cage of norms this created, not by the history of colonial rule. This also implies that it was the society's peculiar organization that kept the state weak. This makes India closer to a state impaired and constricted by society, more of a weak state than a despotic one. As such, in terms of our figure, India is on the other side of the line demarcating the division between the Absent and Despotic Leviathans. It isn't the fear of the mobilization effect keeping the state weak and incapable in India; it is the unbearable weight of caste divisions.

The Consequences of Paper Leviathans

The type of state discussed in this chapter, and of many countries of the postcolonial world, is very different from the Despotic, Absent, and Shackled Leviathans we have discussed so far. This Paper Leviathan has some of the worst characteristics of both the Absent and Despotic Leviathans. To the extent that it has any powers, it is despotic, repressive, and arbitrary. It is fundamentally unchecked by society, which it continually tries to keep weak, disorganized, and discombobulated. It provides its citizens little protection from Warre, and doesn't try to free them from the cage of norms (and may in fact get to use the cage for its own purposes). This is all because the Paper Leviathan doesn't care about the welfare of its citizens and certainly not about their liberty. But it is also because it lacks the capacity to do much, except perhaps enriching the political elites in charge. We have argued that the roots of the Paper Leviathan are to be found in the political elites' fear of societal mobilization, which would constrain their ability to benefit from their control of the state and loot society's resources. We have also pointed out how sharp inequalities, unaccountable state structures, and the history of indirect rule left over from colonial times as well as the abrupt and haphazard transition from colonial rule to independence and the international state system prepared the ground for the Paper Leviathan.

The Paper Leviathan has not only been bad for liberty. It has also been disastrous for economic prosperity. We have seen that economic opportunities and incentives need to be based on the law, security, and effective and equitable public services, and that's why economic growth is nonexistent under the Absent Leviathan. The Despotic Leviathan can enforce laws, resolve conflicts (even if often to the advantage of the politically powerful), control looting, and, if it wishes, provide public services. On this basis, it can unleash despotic growth, as most recently illustrated by China's spectacular rise. Not so with the Paper Leviathan. It doesn't have the capacity to do many of these things, and often doesn't wish to control the looting anyway. So the toll of the Paper Leviathan in Latin America and Africa has been not only continued fear, violence, and dominance for most of its citizens, but a corruption-ridden, inefficiently organized economy exhibiting little growth. Prosperity as well as liberty will have to wait.

The Paper Leviathan's incapacity also sets the stage for uncontrolled conflict and civil war, as Liberia illustrates. Between 1989 and 2003 the Liberian state collapsed and the country was ravaged by two civil wars. Estimates of the total number of casualties in the two civil wars go as high as half a million and above. Though there has been some reconstruction and stability since then, the paper-thin nature of the Liberian state persists to this day, with a resulting inability and unwillingness to provide public services, even if the country has become much more popular with the international community since then. In 2013 all 25,000 students who sat the University of Liberia's entrance exam failed. Not one, apparently, was qualified to attend university, an incredible statement about the low quality of Liberian high schools. In 2018 newly printed currency to the tune of US$104 million, about 5 percent of the country's national income, simply vanished from containers in the port of Monrovia. The country has about the same living standards as it had in the 1970s.

Chapter 12

WAHHAB'S CHILDREN

The Tactician's Dream

In the West, the Middle East, especially Saudi Arabia, has come to epitomize lack of liberty, with personal freedom abridged by custom, religion, and despotism. What explains the perfect storm of unchecked despotism and a stifling cage of norms? Such an outcome is surprising given Muhammad's successful state-building drive, which originated in part of Saudi Arabia, and the spectacular civilization that Islamic empires built in the following centuries. What happened? Why did the cage of norms become so fervent and suffocating in the Middle East, when we have seen many other state-building drives relax rather than intensify the cage's restrictions?

As we saw in Chapter 3, Muhammad's state spread rapidly through much of the Middle East and North Africa. But not everywhere. Arabia is divided into several distinct regions (as can be seen in Map 4 in Chapter 3). Medina and Mecca are in the Hijaz, nestled in the Sarawat Mountains, which run along the western side of the peninsula bordering the Red Sea. On the eastern side the mountains end and the great vastness of the Arabian desert interior, the Najd, begins. Field Marshal Erwin Rommel, who headed the German Afrika Korps during World War II, called the desert "a tactician's dream and a quartermaster's nightmare." Such was the Najd.

Rather than taking on this logistical nightmare, the Islamic empires after Muhammad spread up toward Damascus and Baghdad, and then west into Egypt and North Africa, where they could conquer already centralized states. Even later, after the various early caliphates collapsed and the seat of Islamic power shifted to Constantinople and the Ottoman Empire, the Najd resisted integration. The Ottomans controlled the Hijaz and the Muslim holy cities as well as Mesopotamia between the Tigris and Euphrates, but they left the interior of Arabia more or less alone.

Though the Bedouin of the Najd converted to Islam, they avoided political centralization. All great religions are flexible and open to multiple interpretations and implementations (otherwise how could they spread so successfully?). Though Muhammad was intent on building a powerful state and spelled out the nature of centralized authority in the Constitution of Medina, the Quran was less specific on this issue. In fact there are only two surahs (chapters) that directly address constitutional issues. In one, obedience to authority is emphasized. Another calls for consultation, the norm among the Bedouin tribes of the desert. There was plenty of wiggle room there to assuage the Arabs' skepticism of centralized authority. Perhaps most important, there would be no elaborate hierarchical church structure with priests, bishops, and popes in Islam. Instead, each Muslim could connect directly to Allah with no intermediaries (not unlike many Protestant denominations). This made it harder for a centralized authority to imprint its wishes on local communities and made the new religion more palatable to the Bedouin tribes. It also implied that the tribal structure in areas such as the Najd was more likely to persist and fuse with the teachings of Islam.

So the Najd remained divided into competing, autonomous tribes ruled by sheikhs or emirs well into the eighteenth century. Competition sometimes turned violent. At the oasis of al-Diriya, just outside Riyadh, the modern capital of Saudi Arabia, a series of assassinations led to the emergence of a new emir, Muhammad ibn Saud, who assumed power either in 1726 or 1727. It was Saud's descendants who in 1932 were to give their name to the as yet unimagined kingdom of Saudi Arabia. Our earliest existing sources of information about Saud come from early in the nineteenth century and all agree on the centrality of one event to Saud's and his kingdom's destiny—his first meeting with Muhammad ibn Abd al-Wahhab.

Al-Wahhab came from Uyaina, an oasis town about twenty miles north of al-Diriya. His family was deeply steeped in Islamic teaching and his father was a qadi, a judge appointed by the local emir to resolve cases using the Islamic law, Sharia. This law had emerged along with Muhammad and the early Islamic empires. Its most basic elements were the holy book, the Quran, and the hadiths, a large collection of sayings and actions attributed to Muhammad and written down by his followers. During the early Middle Ages various schools of thought, most prominently the Hanafi, Maliki, Shafi'i, Hanbali, and Jafari, had started debating about what constituted Sharia. Though they all agreed on the centrality of the Quran and the hadiths, they disagreed on the extent to which judges could create precedents or make rulings based on analogies. Of these schools, the Hanbalis were the most conservative. They rejected all such evolution of the law, and their interpretation of Sharia dominated the Najd.

Al-Wahhab had memorized the Quran by the age of ten and began traveling in Iraq, Syria, and Iran, returning to the Najd to begin preaching in the early 1730s. In the absence of a religious hierarchy, anyone with knowledge of the Quran and the hadiths could be recognized as an *ulama*, a religious teacher who could issue fatwas, which were rulings articulating particular interpretations of the Islamic scriptures, usually in the context of some contemporary problem or debate. Sometime during his travels, al-Wahhab formulated a distinct interpretation of Islam and what he decided were its failings in Arabia. Following the Hanbali school, he thought that the people had strayed from the real religion by worshipping idols. Remember that prior to Muhammad's revelation in Mecca, the Kaaba had been a shrine of different pre-Islamic gods. Worship of these gods persisted, and people sanctified saints and Muhammad's tomb at Medina. For al-Wahhab this was all idolatry. He preached that holy war, jihad, could be waged against anyone engaged in such idolatry. These interpretations turned out to be very useful for Saud, who was an astute tactician.

But first al-Wahhab had to develop his doctrine and build a following. Two of his ideas turned out to be particularly attractive to rulers: people must obey the authorities and they must pay *zakat*, the obligatory religious tax stipulated in the Quran. Zakat was not popular among the Bedouins of the Najd and seems to have been seldom paid in this period. It was supposed to be used for charity and religious activities, but presumably sheikhs and emirs might get a cut too. The cornerstone of what became Wahhabism, however, was the idea that anyone who didn't pay zakat was an infidel.

Al-Wahhab began to put his new doctrine into action in Uyaina. He cut down a sacred tree with his own hands. There was to be no worship of trees. He destroyed the grave of Zaid ibn al-Kattab, a companion of the Prophet, which had turned into a place of pilgrimage. There was to be no worship of tombs, no pilgrimages except the hadj, the annual pilgrimage to Mecca. When a woman from Uyaina was found guilty of fornication, al-Wahhab applied a strict interpretation of Sharia and ordered her to be stoned to death. This was a step too far, and in the face of opposition from local ulama who disliked his radical new teachings, al-Wahhab was forced to flee from Uyaina to al-Diriya. There he and Saud had a meeting of minds. No firsthand account of the fateful meeting exists, but al-Wahhab wanted military support for the jihad he planned to wage in order to spread his new doctrines. Saud saw the potential for Wahhabism to be a powerful tool of military expansion and social control. Saud asked al-Wahhab to stay in al-Diriya and support his planned military campaign into the Najd. He also demanded that al-Wahhab agree that he could raise regular taxes on local harvests. Al-Wahhab accepted the first, but not the second. He instead granted that Saud could take one-fifth of all the booty from jihad and pointed out that this would be far more money than taxing harvests. The deal was sealed; Saud relied on Wahhabism, and Wahhabism relied on Saud. The marriage was to be fabulously successful. The Sauds expanded out of a little oasis, taking over first the Najd, and by 1803 had captured Mecca and the Hijaz from the Ottoman state. One account records how Saud seized al-Hasa, to the east of the Najd.

> When morning came and Saud went on his way after the prayer, when they [the Wahhabis] rode camels and horses and shot their hand-guns at once, the sky darkened, the earth shuddered, puffs of smoke rose in the air and many pregnant women suffered miscarriages. Then all the people of al-Hasa came to Saud, throwing themselves on his mercy.
>
> He ordered all of them to appear before him and so they did. He stayed there for some months, killing, exiling and jailing everybody he wanted to, confiscating property, destroying houses and erecting fortresses. He demanded 100,000 dirhams from them and received that sum . . . Some people . . . toured the markets and caught those who had led a dissolute life . . . Some people were killed in the oasis, others were taken to the camp and their heads chopped off in front of Saud's tent until they were all destroyed.

For the first time ever the Arabian peninsula was more or less unified under one state, though what is now Yemen and Oman in the south remained independent. None of this would have surprised Ibn Khaldun; the desert people who had asabiyyah were conquering the urban areas under the banner of Islam.

The political system that developed in the Najd after the 1740s and eventually gelled in Saudi Arabia was very different from what existed before. At the time, tribal sheikhs had to consult other notables in councils called *majlis*. The English writer and explorer Charles Dougherty noted that this was still the case in the 1860s and 1870s. The principle was "Let him speak here who will, the voice of the least is heard among them; he is a tribesmen."

In fact, sheikhs were elected and potentially any Bedouin could rise to the position, even if it was typically monopolized by notable families. As the Swiss traveler Johann Ludwig Burckhardt noted earlier in the century:

> The sheikh has no actual authority over the individuals of his tribe.

Just a garden-variety Absent Leviathan. When Muhammad ibn Saud died in 1765, he was succeeded by his son Abd al-Aziz Muhammad ibn Saud, who still needed to gain legitimacy by being elected by the people of al-Diriya. But this balance between state and society was soon toppled. Abd al-Aziz carried on the conquests of his father, using conversion to Wahhabism as a pretext for military expansion and annexing territory in the region. A copy of a letter, which was read out to those about to be conquered, states:

> Abd al-Aziz to the Arabs of the tribe of ***. Hail! Your duty is to believe in the book I send you. Do not be like the idolatrous Turks, who give God a human intermediary. If you are true believers, you shall be saved; otherwise, I shall wage war upon you until death.

When an oasis was conquered, Wahhabi ulama were sent to preach. Saud replaced local emirs and sheikhs with people he handpicked. He appointed Wahhabi qadis to implement their strict version of Sharia. He also appointed an official known as a *muhtasib*. The muhtasib had various administrative roles, such as overseeing commerce and weights and measures, and also ensured that key Islamic practices, such as prayers, were observed. Ibn Saud also built quite an elaborate bureaucracy of tax collectors to raise the zakat, supposedly sending out seventy teams of collectors each year, each consisting of seven collectors. He started to settle tribal disputes too. In 1788 al-Wahhab issued a fatwa declaring that the Sauds were the hereditary emirs and all Wahhabis had to swear allegiance to the ruling Saud. The despotism of the Sauds was fusing with the Wahhabi cage of norms.

The initial triumph of the Sauds and Wahhabis over the Ottomans did not last long. The Ottoman sultan tasked Muhammad Ali, the general of Albanian origin who had made himself de facto independent ruler of Egypt, to confront the

Wahhabi threat. Muhammad Ali and later his son Ibrahim Pasha invaded the Hijaz and destroyed the aspiring Saudi state in 1818. Yet it was difficult to govern the Najd. In 1824 a second Saudi state formed, but with the Ottomans more securely in charge of the Hijaz, it never had the authority or scope of the initial state. It collapsed in 1891, defeated by a rival Najd family, and the Sauds went into exile in Kuwait. But not for long.

Domesticating the Ulama

In 1902 the Sauds were back, led by Abd al-Aziz bin Saud, a great-great-great-grandson of Muhammad ibn Saud. Abd al-Aziz trekked across the desert from Kuwait and captured Riyadh, al-Diriya having been abandoned after being destroyed by Ibrahim Pasha in 1818. Saud had a new version of his ancestor's religious secret weapon—the Ikhwan. The Ikhwan, meaning literally "brothers," was a religious organization started by the qadi of Riyadh, a member of the al-Shaikh family, descendants of al-Wahhab. They formed settlements devoted to a strict version of Islam, shunned foreigners, adopted a rigid code of conduct, and developed strong norms of cooperation and mutual support. They also inherited the Wahhabi habit of declaring jihad on those who did not adhere to their rules. Muhammad ibn Saud had seen the potential of Wahhabism in his state-building efforts and used the Wahhabi fighters to attack his rivals. So did Abd al-Aziz with the Ikhwan.

The first Ikhwan settlement dates back to 1913 at al-Artawiya, to the northwest of Riyadh. Soon Abd al-Aziz was giving them money and seed and helping build mosques and schools. This assistance was followed by guns and ammunition, even if the Ikhwan seemed to have preferred traditional weapons like swords. He encouraged and built more settlements, inducing the ulama of Riyadh to issue a fatwa promoting settled life and agriculture. He managed to get the right to appoint qadis to the settlements, typically from the al-Shaikh family, which bolstered the Saud-Wahhab alliance. The Ikhwan were then subjected to a military draft and became Abd al-Aziz's shock troops. (A surviving photo of the Ikhwan from this period is shown in the photo insert.) They fought for jihad, he for a kingdom. It was an uneasy balance, but for a while these goals coalesced around the despotism–cage of norms axis. As early as 1914, however, he had to induce an ulama to issue another fatwa appealing for tolerance to reign the Ikhwan in.

Things came to a head when the Ottoman Empire, still in control of the Hijaz and the holy cities, entered World War I on the side of Germany. The British, Lawrence of Arabia included, encouraged the emir of Mecca, Hussein, to lead the famous

Arab revolt of 1916 by promising him that after the Ottomans had been defeated they would guarantee the emergence of an Arab state "in the limits and boundaries proposed by the Sherif of Mecca," but excluding "portions of Syria" which lay to the west of "the districts of Damascus, Homs, Hama and Aleppo." By 1918 the Ottoman army had collapsed, and the British took advantage of the ambiguities of the agreement with Hussein to restrict his state to the Hijaz. Together with the French they carved up the rest of the former Ottoman Empire with the exception of part of Turkey. Hussein was livid at this betrayal and refused to sign the Treaty of Versailles in 1919. In the meantime, Abd al-Aziz and the Ikhwan consolidated their dominance over the Najd. At first they had no desire to confront the Ottoman troops. Nor did they wish to fight Hussein, ruling over the Hijaz with the backing of the British. But Hussein's antagonism to Britain's postwar plans, particularly those involving Palestine, led Britain to switch its support to Abd al-Aziz in 1924. Emboldened, he invaded the Hijaz. Mecca fell in October of that year and Medina was captured in December 1925.

Abd al-Aziz became the king of the Najd and Hijaz thanks to the Ikhwan. He had what he wanted, but the Ikhwan didn't. They were on a jihad against apostates, and not just those confined to the Arabian peninsula. They started launching attacks on the British protectorate of Transjordan, only to be beaten back by the British air force. Abd al-Aziz decided that the Ikhwan had done their job and were more of a nuisance than an asset. He turned on them, defeated them at the battle of Sabilla, and rounded up and killed their leaders. In 1932 he unified the Hijaz and Najd into the Kingdom of Saudi Arabia.

The defeat of the Ikhwan was a powerful message that in the coalition of the Sauds and Wahhabism, the Sauds called the shots. But it took some time for the Saudi kings to institutionalize this in its modern form. A pivotal moment came following the death of Abd al-Aziz in 1953. He was succeeded by his son Saud, but there was intense rivalry with other brothers who wanted the throne, particularly his half brother Faisal. Faisal turned out to be politically far more astute. As Saud was struggling with health problems, Faisal gradually took control of many policy portfolios and built a coalition of supporters within the royal family. Finally, confident of his power, Faisal convened the ulama to consider the issue of excluding Saud from the affairs of state. They dutifully issued a fatwa on March 29, 1964, emphasizing two main points: first, "Saud was the country's sovereign and must be respected and revered by all"; second, "As prime minister, Prince Faisal could freely manage the kingdom's internal and external affairs without consulting the king." It was in effect a coup d'état, sanctioned by religious authority. Except that there was no precedent for this decision in the Quran or any relevant scripture; the ulama just recognized where power lay. But even this wasn't enough for Faisal and his supporters. They decided they needed to get rid of Saud completely. In October 1964 Faisal convened the ulama again, now to find a way to justify deposing King Saud. One of those who participated in these negotiations recalled how Faisal's group

> on several occasions contacted Shaykh Muhammad ibn Ibrahim . . . to persuade him to issue a fatwa deposing King Saud . . . Action was necessary in order to preserve the unity of the community and of the Islamic state. The ulama had to support the decision of the royal house. Shaykh Muhammad therefore decided to gather together the ulama at his home . . . After a brief discussion of the country's situation, they concluded that it was necessary to confirm the royal house's choice.

Sheikh Muhammad was the Grand Mufti, the most important ulama in the country. The language here is striking. Though historically al-Wahhab and his descendants probably had a large amount of autonomy from the Sauds, it is clear here that by 1964 the ulama did what they were told by whatever faction of the Sauds was most powerful, and they agreed to depose the king after only a "brief discussion." The fatwa deposing Saud was duly issued on November 1.

Faisal became king. Prior to his reign the relationship between the royal family and the ulama was informal. Faisal started to change this and forged an institutional structure he could control more directly. He announced a series of reforms that included creating "an advisory council consisting of twenty-two members who will be chosen amongst leading jurists and scholars." They were charged to "issue rulings and give advice on questions of interest to members of the Muslim community."

It took until 1971 to finally create this Committee of the Grand Ulama, apparently because of the opposition from the Grand Mufti Sheikh Muhammad. After he died in 1969, Faisal abolished the post of Grand Mufti (it was later reintroduced). The Committee of the Grand Ulama has various subcommittees to consider different types of problems and issue fatwas relating to different areas of Islamic law. But they are only able to hear questions that are authorized by the royal cabinet, which can modify their agendas at will. The committee thus became a tool for the domestication of the ulama.

Perhaps the most striking evidence of this comes in 1990. After Saddam Hussein's army overran Kuwait, the Saudis were terrified that they were next, and invited the U.S. to send troops to protect them. King Fahd, Faisal's brother who acceded to the throne in 1982, was worried that this might be interpreted to be in contradiction with the Sauds' self-proclaimed role as defenders of the holy cities of Mecca and Medina. But the Grand Ulama quickly issued a fatwa to reassure the Saudis. It noted that to defend the nation

> by all possible means . . . the Supreme Council of Ulama supports what was undertaken by the ruler, may God grant him success: the bringing of forces equipped with instruments capable of frightening and terrorizing the one who wanted to commit an aggression against this country. This duty is dictated by necessity in the current circumstances, and made inevitable by the painful reality, and its legal basis and evidence dictates that the man in charge of the affairs of Muslims should seek the assistance of one who has the ability to attain the intended aim. The Quran and the Prophet's Sunna (activities and statements) have indicated the need to be ready and take precautions before it is too late.

The Sunna refers to the set of practices, norms, and beliefs of the Islamic community drawn from the Quran and the hadiths. No doubt it came as a relief to Saudi citizens to learn that the presence of "crusaders," as Osama bin Laden would later call them, on Saudi soil was all perfectly consistent with the Sunna. Phew!

Intensifying the Cage of Norms

The story of Saudi Arabia exemplifies the cage of norms, and its intensification. Norms of societies without centralized authority often evolve to constrain behavior in a multitude of ways, both to regulate conflicts and prevent the destabilization of the status quo. These norms take root in the customs, beliefs, and practices of the people, and they become ingrained in religion and religious practice. So they did with Islam, despite Muhammad's strong drive to build centralized authority in Medina and beyond. With the efforts of the Hanbali legal school and Wahhabism, and their emphasis on tradition and opposition to innovation, these norms powerfully reproduced themselves. Then came the deal with ibn Saud, who exploited the Wahhabis' zeal for military expansion, and he and his successors bought into the mainstream Wahhabi norms and restrictions as part of this quid pro quo. A small price to pay for a kingdom.

But in the hands of ibn Saud and Abd al-Aziz, the Wahhabi ideas and restrictions started having an impact well beyond the oasis of al-Diriya. Other would-be despots in the Middle East began using the same ideas and strategies, similarly stiffening the cage of norms to support despotic power. Three interrelated factors explain the popularity of this strategy in the region. One follows from Islam's institutional structure. As we have noted, in Islam, especially Sunni Islam, there is no church hierarchy, no priests intermediating between an individual and the deity. The ulama, who are learned in religion, can give people guidance on the interpretation of the scriptures and issue fatwas. On the one hand, this means that anybody with sufficient knowledge of the Quran and the hadiths can play this role and interpret Islam and its teachings (a dynamic whose implications we'll discuss in a little bit). On the other hand, this organizational structure opened the door for the takeover of the ulama and the supply of fatwas to shore up the Saudi regime. There was nothing like the hierarchy of the Catholic Church to act as a counterweight to Saudi machinations. Other despotic regimes in the Middle East have done the same.

A second factor is related to the fact that, as noted above, the Quran is not a constitutional document, and is open to interpretation on the degree of power vested in rulers. For example, because the Quran and the Constitution of Medina are silent on who should take part in councils and consult with a ruler, there was a lot of leeway for the Sauds to sideline existing councils, the majlis of Bedouin tribes, and to limit their role to local affairs and completely control who gets to sit in the larger Majlis Ash-Shura, or Shura Council.

A third factor is a Hobbesian view of state-society relations that developed and became ingrained during the reign of the despotic Islamic empires. For example, as the famous tenth-century philosopher al-Ghazali noted:

> The tyranny of a sultan for a hundred years causes less damage than one year's tyranny exercised by the subjects against another . . . Revolt was justified only against a ruler who clearly went against a command of God or His prophet.

Thus Warre was much worse than despotism, and as long as a despot stuck to Sharia, he was to be tolerated.

So this interpretation of Islam provided an alluring set of principles for a potential despot (and as we'll see, the history of the Middle East meant that there were plenty of those around). It seemed easy to manipulate, it held no strong inclination toward democracy or any other type of political accountability, and it preached submission, as long as Sharia was followed. But of course Islam was much more than this, it was a whole system of beliefs about how one should live one's life in accord with God's laws. Many of these principles were encoded in the 620s in Arabia and reflected the norms of the region and the period. Groups like the Hanbalis or Wahhabis emphasized a strict traditionalist interpretation of Sharia and reified a very restrictive cage of norms, quite anomalous in the modern world.

This cage of norms was not simply a powerful tool in the hands of the Sauds. It was also the price they had to pay for their coalition with the Wahhabis. For instance, Abd al-Aziz had founded a commercial court in 1926 with seven magistrates, only one of whom was a religious figure. He was trying to minimally modernize economic relations. In 1955 the ulama persuaded King Saud to abolish the court completely. In 1967 Faisal resuscitated it, creating three commercial courts, one in Riyadh, and one each in the major port cities of Jeddah and Damman. But now one-half of the magistrates had to be ulama. By 1969, two-thirds had to be ulama. Sharia trumped any attempt to introduce modern civil commercial codes.

One might have thought that after the defeat of the Ikhwan and the domestication of the ulama, the Saudi royal family would have the upper hand and start relaxing parts of the cage of norms that did not suit their political or economic interests. However, as King Fahd's fatwa on the defense of the nation illustrates, in a nakedly despotic system without any consultation with society there is often demand for religious authorities to reaffirm Saudi policies and practices. This dynamic got much worse after two events in 1978 and '79. First came the Iranian Islamic Revolution, which threatened the Saudi claim to be the standard-bearer of Islam in the region. Second, more ominously for the Saud family, hundreds of insurgents (nobody knows the exact number) led by a man called Juhayman al-Otaybi stormed the Grand Mosque in Mecca. Al-Otaybi came from a settlement established by King Abd al-Aziz to house the Ikhwan, and his father and many of his relatives were active members of the brotherhood and had been part of the conflict with the king. His and the insurgents' grievances had Wahhabi roots. They argued that the House of Saud had deviated from Muhammad's teachings by becoming westernized, and called for a return to a more traditional interpretation of Islam. They (rightly) noted that the ulama had been captured by the Sauds and had lost their legitimacy. The reaction by the Saudi ruling family, after the long siege was defeated with the help of Pakistani and French special forces and al-Otaybi and his captured followers were beheaded, was to double down on Wahhabism. The interpretation and the teaching of the religion became more strict, especially as a way of indoctrinating Saudi youth in schools. The cage of norms tightened yet again.

The Untouchables of Saudi Arabia

In 1955 King Saud announced that there would be public education for girls. But four years later, in the face of resistance from the ulama, Saudi policy changed and put this education under the supervision of the ulama. The Grand Mufti and ulama maintained this control until 2002. It is not only women's education; every aspect of women's treatment in Saudi society is constricted by the cage of norms forged by the Saud-Wahhab pact.

A key enforcer of the cage in Saudi Arabia is the Committee for the Promotion of Virtue and the Prevention of Vice, members of whom are known as the *mutaween*, typically translated to English as the religious police. The mutaween are charged with compelling people to adhere to Sharia and Islamic norms, such as the strict dress code for women. They take this seriously, very seriously—so seriously that in March 2002 when a fire broke out in a girls' school in Mecca, they tried to stop girls who were inappropriately dressed—without headscarves and abayas (the black robes required by the Kingdom's traditional interpretation of Islam)—from leaving the burning building. Fifteen girls died. A rescue worker was quoted as saying:

> Whenever the girls got out through the main gate, these people forced
> them to return via another. Instead of extending a helping hand for the
> rescue work, they were using their hands to beat us.

You might think that the Committee for the Promotion of Virtue and the Prevention of Vice was an ancient Islamic institution, but it isn't. It's true, as we saw, that as the Saudi state expanded, it appointed muhtasibs to capture oases, whose duties included enforcing religious norms and laws, and the roots of this office extend back to the Abbasid Caliphate in the early Middle Ages. But "the Committee" was a new institution, whose progenitor, "the Company" for the Promotion of Virtue and the Prevention of Vice, was created by Abd al-Aziz in 1926 after he had completed his conquest of the Hijaz. The company turned into the committee in 1928. As the Saudi state consolidated its power, the cage of norms tightened. This was partly because of the concessions to the Wahhabi ulama. But it was also because it was quite useful for shoring up despotism. The cage helped keep people under control even as the economy and life modernized; hence the creation of the committee.

The brunt of the cage of norms in Saudi Arabia is borne by women. In 2014 a female student at King Saud University in Riyadh died because male paramedics were not permitted to treat her. Men who are not close relatives are not allowed to touch women, not even to politely shake hands, let alone give essential medical care. In Saudi Arabia, women are the untouchables.

The dress code, the no-touching stipulation, and the web of regulations placing women under the control of men come from particular interpretations of the Quran. Surah 4, verse 34 says that "men are the protectors and maintainers of women, because God has given the one more [strength] than the other, and because they support them from their means." This is interpreted in Saudi Arabia to mean that women are under the control of men, like children, and this reading is thought to be consistent with the one clause, number 41, of Muhammad's Constitution of Medina, formulated in 622, that mentions women and says, "A woman shall only be given protection with the consent of her family."

So women are under the control of their family (read "men"). In Saudi Arabia the dominance of men over women is institutionalized via the guardianship system. Every woman must have a male guardian from whom she needs to get permission to do many things, like travel. The guardian can be her father, her husband, or even her son. If a woman travels without a guardian, she must carry a yellow card that documents the number of trips and for how many days her guardian has approved travel for. Permission is also needed to open a bank account, rent an apartment, start a business, or apply for a passport. The government's electronic portal stipulates that a male guardian has to fill out the application for a woman's passport. A woman even needs a man's permission to get out of prison when her sentence is over!

Until recently, permission was required to get a job too. Though this has changed, Saudi law requires segregated workplaces with separate areas for men and women which significantly disincentivizes hiring women. If a woman wants to study abroad, she must be accompanied by a male relative. Women cannot eat at a restaurant that doesn't have a separate walled off "family" section and a separate entrance for women. A fatwa from the Grand Council states that "a woman should not leave her house, except with her husband's permission."

Of course, there is no equality before the law. In legal cases the testimony of women is worth one half of men's. Similarly, under Sharia, women inherit half the amount that men inherit. Women have trouble filing a case or being heard in court without a legal guardian intervening. Courts, presided over by male judges, generally refuse to accept the testimony of a woman as a witness in criminal cases. Two women told Human Rights Watch researchers that judges had refused to allow them to speak in the courtroom because they deemed their voices to be "shameful." Judges allowed their guardian to speak on their behalf. But what happens when women are abused by their guardians or husbands?

One ranking of gender parity by the World Economic Forum puts Saudi Arabia 141 out of 149 countries (the United Arab Emirates, despite its gender equality awards we saw in the Preface, ranks only a little above Saudi Arabia, 121). This ranking combines many things; one is labor force participation, which stands at just 22 percent in Saudi Arabia compared to 56 percent in the United States.

The guardianship system and systematic discrimination against women have been consistently upheld by religious authorities. In the 1990s when the Grand Ulama was asked to make a ruling about the appropriateness of a woman's delaying marriage to finish her university education, it issued a fatwa decreeing that

> for a woman to progress through university education, which is something we have no need for, is an issue that needs examination. What I see [to be correct] is that if a woman finishes elementary school and is able to read and write, and so she is able to benefit by reading the Book of God, its commentaries, and Prophetic hadith, that is sufficient for her.

When asked about women's employment, it ruled:

> God Almighty . . . commended women to remain in their homes. Their presence in the public is the main contributing factor to the spread of fitna [strife]. Yes, the Shari'ah permits women to leave their home only when necessary, provided that they wear hijab and avoid all suspicious situations. However, the general rule is that they should remain at home.

And definitely no touching. No leading either. Another fatwa by the same body stated that women could not fill positions of leadership over men due to their "deficient reasoning and rationality, in addition to their passion that prevails over their thinking." The typical defense of these rules by officials of the Saudi government is that Saudi Arabia is a conservative society and the rules reflect the way the people think.

But this claim receives no support from the available evidence. A recent study by Leonardo Bursztyn, Alessandra González, and David Yanagizawa-Drott asked men in Riyadh whether or not they agreed with the simple statement "In my opinion, women should be allowed to work outside of the home." Eighty-seven percent agreed with this statement. But reaffirming the cage of norms, many men still were not comfortable for their wives to be working outside the home because of how they thought others would react. In particular, they reasoned that others would be less favorable toward outside work by women and only 63 percent of them thought that other men from their neighborhood would agree with the same statement. So in the cage of norms, everybody is afraid of what others would say about the most basic empowerment of women. Women's work becomes stigmatized and the cage of norms is reinforced.

Though scholars can cite the Quran and hadiths in support of the control of women by men, everything is subject to political imperatives. As recently as 1996 the Grand Ulama issued a fatwa that categorically stated that women were not allowed to drive according to Sharia law.

> There is no doubt that such [driving] is not allowed. Women driving lead
> to many evils and negative consequences. Included among these is her
> mixing with men without her being on her guard. It also leads to the
> evil sins due to which such an action is forbidden.

There were obviously no cars during Muhammad's lifetime. A fatwa like this is no more than a speculative interpretation of what basic Islamic principles would imply for women driving, had there been cars in the 620s. But the fact that women were not allowed to drive in Saudi Arabia became a more and more embarrassing facet of the regime, remorselessly referred to in international media. In 2017 it was announced that this would be changed under the reform agenda of Crown Prince Mohammad bin Salman. But hang on, in 1996 the Grand Council had announced that it was definitely against Sharia to allow women to drive. No problem; the Sauds just got them to issue a new fatwa declaring that it was perfectly Islamic after all.

Nebuchadnezzar Rides Again

Even if Saudi Arabia is the poster child for the intensification of the cage of norms, other despotic regimes in the region have followed the same playbook. Take the government of Saddam Hussein in Iraq. Iraq emerged as a British mandate out of the same shady plan that Emir Hussein of Mecca felt had cheated the Arabs of their true rewards for fighting the Ottoman Empire. To sweeten the pill, the British made one of Hussein's sons, Faisal, king of Iraq. Iraq was a colonial creation, an amalgamation of three Ottoman provinces, Mosul, Baghdad, and Basra. Putting Faisal in charge of it was a bizarre piece of colonial politics; when he was crowned, the band played the British national anthem, "God Save the King," because Iraq didn't have its own yet. The monarchy didn't last. Iraq became independent in 1931 and the first coup happened in 1936, followed by two decades of intense political instability until members of the Free Officers, a group led by Brigadier Abd al-Karim Qasim, finally overthrew the monarchy in 1958. In the first hours of the coup, Qasim's men summarily executed the king and his family.

Qasim imposed state control over the ulama and tried to secularize the state. But his attempts were short lived. He was himself murdered in 1963 by the military putschists who sympathized with the Baath Party. Founded in 1947 in Syria, the Baath Party had an ideology rooted in pan-Arabism, anticolonialism, and socialism. Even though the Baathists were secular, they had no problem using Islam to subjugate society and intensify the cage of norms. This process started in 1968, when the Baathists definitively took control in another coup, and escalated after 1979 when Saddam Hussein grabbed personal power. Saddam was not a military man, but had ruthlessly worked his way up through the party. He took his chance when it came. To consolidate his hold on power, Saddam held family members of one-third of the members of the Revolutionary Command Council hostage. Then he really got going. He orchestrated and filmed a confession from Muhyi Abdel-Hussein, the secretary of the Revolutionary Command Council (Saddam was vice chairman), which was shown to party members from all over the country. According to a version recorded by a historian:

> A grief-stricken Saddam addressed the meeting with tears running down his cheeks. He filled in the gaps in [Abdel-Hussein's] testimony and dramatically fingered his former colleagues. Guards dragged people out of the proceedings and then Saddam called upon the country's top ministers and party leaders to themselves form the actual firing squads.
>
> It seems that some five hundred high-ranking Baathists were executed by August 1, 1979.

Saddam was now in full control. He made the ulama salaried employees of the state and subservient to him. He constructed an elaborate ideology to legitimize his rule, claiming a line of descent from the great Babylonian king Nebuchadnezzar from the fifth century BCE. Nebuchadnezzar was not a Muslim, of course, but as the rule of Saddam became more and more precarious and less and less legitimate, he tried to shore up his power not just by extensive appeals to Islam but by any means he could think of. The year after taking power Saddam invaded Iran, launching the disastrous Iran-Iraq War. He had hoped to exploit the weakness of the Iranian regime after the overthrow of the shah in 1979 and grab their oilfields. Instead, there was a bloody stalemate that lasted eight years.

By 1982 Saddam had completely cast aside his secularist roots. He was talking of jihad and finishing his speeches with religious phrases such as "God will defend and protect you and lead you on the road to victory." In a 1984 celebration of the Prophet's birthday, Saddam was lauded along with "our historical, ingenious, Jihad-launching leadership, fighting for the future of our Iraqi people and elevating our monotheistic Islamic religion, guided by the Message of Eternal Islam." By the time he invaded Kuwait six years later, Saddam was claiming "it was God that showed us [read: me] the path . . . God has blessed us." His picture kneeling down for prayer began adorning public spaces, as shown in our photo insert. After the complete defeat at the hands of the (mostly) U.S. military in Operation Desert Storm in January 1991, Saddam intensified his appeals to Islam. He initiated a massive program of Islamic education, doubling or even tripling the amount of time spent studying the Quran and the hadiths in school. Adults, even cabinet ministers, were forced to take classes on the Quran, and he started the Saddam Center for the Reading of the Quran and the Saddam University for Islamic Studies. Teachers' knowledge of the scriptures was tested and prisoners could have their sentences reduced if they managed to successfully memorize key passages of religious texts. In 1992 Saddam insisted that the words *Allahu Akbar* (God is Great) be added to the Iraqi flag and he announced in public that the flag had become

the banner of jihad and faith . . . against the infidel horde.

Saddam was now styling himself "the Commander of the Congregation of the Believers" and burnishing his religious bona fides by doubling down on the cage of norms. In 1994, Decree No. 59 brought the first of a host of Sharia-inspired laws that would transform the Iraqi legal code. For robbery and car theft, punishment would be amputation of the hand at the wrist. For a second offense, the left foot would be amputated at the ankle. Soon unauthorized money changers got the same punishments, as did "profiteering bankers." These measures had been preceded in 1990 by laws that introduced "tribal customs" into the penal codes, for instance making it legal for relatives of an adulterous woman to kill her.

Saddam continued to intensify the cage of norms, decreeing measures similar to Saudi Arabia's male guardianship system. Women were not allowed to travel abroad unless they were in the company of a male relative. He announced that women should give up employment and stay at home, but did not enforce this decree, apparently deeming that it would be too unpopular. It was left to the new U.S.-installed government in 2003 to fire all women judges in Iraq on the basis that their employment was un-Islamic.

———————

The Saudi strategy of marrying unchecked despotism with an intense (and intensifying) cage of norms was attractive not just for Saddam but for many other regimes in the Middle East. The region was fertile ground for this unholy alliance for several reasons. The first enticement was the history of despotic rule. The Islamic empires evolved into a rigidly despotic direction for the reasons Ibn Khaldun identified. This despotic evolution was continued and if anything aggravated by Ottoman rule. There were few pathways for society to have a say in political decision making or any type of accountability for rulers save for rebellion. After World War I, European colonial powers replaced the Ottomans. Aspirations for self-governance and independence that had built up over the last several decades were quashed and a patchwork of artificial client states was soon created. They had little in common with existing political structures and boundaries, except for their penchant for despotism. Then came oil, which would be the biggest export for the region, even if quite unequally distributed across the countries of the region. Natural resources that create great rewards for those who control political power tend to give a boost to despotism, and the Middle East's recent history hasn't been an exception. Then came the founding of the state of Israel and the incessant Arab-Israeli conflicts that followed. The scene was set for the exploitation of religion and the cage of norms to create and re-create despotism throughout the region.

The Seeds of 9/11

We've seen that it is not a coincidence that despotic states in the Middle East are associated with an intensified cages of norms. There's no doubt that Saudi Arabia is the most extreme case; there is no other Muslim country that features such aggressive separation of men and women in the workplace, for example. But all of these states have played the same game of exploiting the decentralized structure of Islam to bolster their political authority. In Egypt a fatwa was issued in 1962 by Al-Azhar University, the most authoritative voice of Sunni Islam, declaring peace with Israel to be anti-Islamic. Yet when President Anwar Sadat signed the Camp David Accords with Israel's prime minister Menachem Begin in 1979, the sheikh of Al-Azhar issued a fatwa citing the Quran and the treaties that Muhammad had made to show that peace with Israel was indeed consistent with Islamic principles. When the Egyptian military wanted to make peace with Israel, they could count on the ulama to come to the rescue.

The economist Jean-Philippe Platteau has pointed out one more implication of this symbiotic relationship between the ulama, or at least part of it, and Middle Eastern despotic states. Recall that when al-Wahhab became an ulama nobody appointed him, he just started teaching and became recognized by the people as a religious authority and learned man. He made rulings, and people started to listen. So while the Saudi state can have their Great Council of Ulama and tell them what fatwas to issue, they can't really prevent someone else from setting himself up as an ulama and issuing contradictory fatwas. That's exactly what Osama bin Laden did. In 1996 he issued his first fatwa bemoaning the terrible state of the Middle East, and particularly Saudi Arabia, where the people

> believe that this situation is a curse put on them by Allah for not object-
> ing to the oppressive and illegitimate behavior and measures of the rul-
> ing regime: Ignoring the divine Sharia law; depriving people of their
> legitimate rights; allowing the American to occupy the land of the two
> Holy Places; imprisonment, unjustly, of the sincere scholars. The honor-
> able Ulama and scholars as well as merchants, economists and eminent
> people of the country were all alerted by this disastrous situation.

Much of bin Laden's fatwa is an anti-American tirade, but he was also high-lighting his view of the real problem in Saudi Arabia, "the ruling regime," and was calling for a jihad against it.

The political strategy of Middle Eastern states not only extinguishes liberty by tightening the cage of norms. It also sows the seeds of violence, instability, and terrorism. Every society's cage restricts freedoms by regulating both behavior and discourse—what people talk about and how they talk about it. The Middle Eastern cage of norms makes it very difficult to develop a discourse that criticizes the despot, because the despot claims to represent religion. Criticize him and you are criticizing Islam. This generates a natural tendency to couch and develop criticisms by pointing out that the despot is not sufficiently religious and you are more devoted to the faith. In Platteau's words:

> When despots use religion to legitimize themselves in a highly contested environment they may provoke a counter-move in the form of religious backlash in which the ruler and his opponents compete to demonstrate their superior fidelity to the faith.

This is exactly what bin Laden was doing. His fatwa went on to note the "Suspension of the Islamic Sharia law and exchanging it with statutory laws and embarking upon bloody confrontation with devoted scholars and righteous youths." The Sauds may have captured most of the ulama, but there remained the "devoted scholars," like bin Laden. Indeed, though the Sauds tried, bin Laden couldn't be captured. He forged a social movement and a radical, violent agenda, not just around his hatred of the West and the United States, but also around his hatred and contempt for the Sauds and "the oppressive and illegitimate behavior and measures of the ruling regime."

The fact that the strategy of manipulating the ulama for the goals of the Despotic Leviathan has been used most intensively and successfully in Saudi Arabia helps explain how Osama bin Laden was forged in the Saudi crucible and why fifteen of the nineteen hijackers who crashed planes into buildings in the United States on September 11, 2001, were Saudi citizens. The concoction of Despotic Leviathans and the institutional structure of Islam doesn't just intensify the cage of norms, it creates terrorism, violence, and instability.

Chapter 13

RED QUEEN OUT OF CONTROL

A Revolution of Destruction

On March 23, 1933, the German parliament convened in the Kroll Opera House in Berlin. The unusual location was necessary because the parliament building, the Reichstag, had been burned down the previous month. It was the turn of Otto Wels, the leader of the Social Democratic Party, to address parliament. Wels was the only person who spoke that day, except for the recently appointed chancellor and leader of the Nazi Party, Adolf Hitler. Wels forcefully argued against Hitler's Enabling Act. The act, the next step in what the German politician Hermann Rauschning called "the revolution of destruction," effectively abolished parliament and gave all power to Hitler for a period of four years. Wels didn't think his speech was going to change anything, and fully expected to be beaten up, arrested, or worse, and had come prepared with a cyanide capsule in his pocket. From what he'd seen so far, he had decided it was better to kill himself than fall into the hands of the Nazis and their paramilitary units such as the Storm Detachment (also known as Brownshirts or the SA) and the Protection Squadron (the SS). Wels knew that the first concentration camp, at Dachau, had been opened just the day before and two hundred political prisoners had already been moved there. He knew because the Nazis had been only too happy to publicize what was going to happen to their enemies. Hitler had talked about such camps as early as 1921, and the head of the SS, Heinrich Himmler, had given a press conference on March 20 to announce the opening of Dachau. Wels spoke in an environment of intense intimidation and latent violence. The opera house was hung with Nazi flags and swastikas, and members of the SA and the SS thronged the corridors and exits.

Wels acknowledged that the act was going to pass, but argued forcefully against it, stating:

> In this historic hour, we German Social Democrats solemnly profess our allegiance to the basic principles of humanity and justice, freedom and socialism. No Enabling Law can give you the power to destroy ideas which are eternal and indestructible . . . From new persecutions Social Democracy can once again gather new strength. We salute the persecuted and oppressed . . . our friends throughout the country. Their constancy and loyalty . . . the courage of their convictions, their unbroken confidence, promise a brighter future.

Alas, the passing of the act was a foregone conclusion. The Nazis had, by hook or crook, secured the support of all delegates that could attend except the Social Democrats.

What was so unexpected was that things had come to such a critical point for Weimar democracy, with Hitler as chancellor and parliament about to disband itself. The National Socialist German Workers' (Nazi) Party was a fringe movement that had received only 2.6 percent of the vote in the 1928 election. The Great Depression, which destroyed as much as half of the German economy's output; mounting discontent; and a string of ineffective governments had caused a huge shift of votes toward the Nazis in the first election after the beginning of the Depression in 1930, followed by a further increase in the Nazi vote share in the elections of 1932. In the last free election Germany held, in November 1932, the Nazis received about 33 percent of the vote. The next election, in March 1933, following Hitler's accession to chancellorship two months earlier, took place under a reign of terror and repression by Brownshirts and the police controlled by the Nazis. The Nazis now had almost 44 percent of the vote. Under Weimar's proportional representation system, this translated into 288 out of the 647 deputies. To pass the Enabling Act the Nazis needed a quorum of at least two-thirds of elected members to be present and a two-thirds majority of those present to support it. They were far short, particularly if everyone showed up. First they barred the 81 elected Communist members of parliament from attending, and by not counting them at all, they managed to reduce the quorum from 432 to 378. Of the 120 Social

Democratic members, only 94 were present; the others were in prison, ill, or simply too terrified to show up. All 94 voted against the act, but this wasn't enough, since every other party supported it. A democratically elected legislature had voted itself out of existence.

That this was going to happen wasn't a secret, even if the Nazis were certainly at times ambiguous about their aims. Their 1930 election manifesto had stated:

> Through its victory the National Socialist Movement will overcome the old class and estate mentality. It will allow the reconstitution of a people out of the estate madness and class nonsense. It will educate the people to iron decisiveness. It will overcome democracy and enhance the authority of the personality.

But what did "overcome democracy" mean, exactly? Hitler had also talked about needing only four years, hence the initial duration of the Enambling Act (it was renewed in 1937 and then again in 1939 and eventually made permanent in 1943). In a speech on February 10, 1933, in the Berlin Sports Palace, he asserted: "Give us four years, and I swear to you, just as we, just as I have taken this office, so I shall leave it. I have done it neither for salary nor for wages; I have done it for your sake." Yet the day after this speech, when Hitler secretly met with industrialists to raise money for the Nazis' election campaign, Hermann Göring stated that the forthcoming election would be the last not just for four years but for one hundred. In a public address the previous year, on October 17, 1932, Hitler had already declared, "If we do one day achieve power we will hold onto it, so help us God. We will not allow them to take it away from us again." On the day Hitler became chancellor, his future propaganda minister Joseph Goebbels announced, "Prepare the election campaign. The last."

How did it ever come to this? Germany's Weimar Republic had built a vibrant democracy and had a highly educated, politically active population. Why was it succumbing to the revolution of destruction by a band of thugs?

To answer these questions, we have to retrace the steps of the Weimar Republic. As Germany surrendered in October 1918, its naval admirals planned a reckless last-ditch attack on Britain and the Dutch coast. In response, their sailors mutinied. These events escalated into a full-scale revolution by November, leading to the flourishing of Soldiers and Workers Councils all over Germany and the creation of the Council of the People's Deputies. On November 9, Kaiser Wilhelm II abdicated and went into exile, and the Weimar Republic was founded with the

Social Democrat Friedrich Ebert as its first chancellor. Ebert tried to contain the revolutionary mobilization by creating, among other things, a parallel structure called the Executive Council of Workers' and Soldiers' Councils. By December Ebert was moving loyal troops into Berlin and disbanding the Council of the People's Deputies. He armed nationalistic paramilitaries recruited from the ranks of former soldiers, known as the Free Corps, and when the Communist revolt broke out in January 1919 in Berlin, he went along with the murder of its leaders, Rosa Luxemburg and Karl Liebknecht. Declarations of socialist republics in Bavaria and Bremen were also met with swift repression by loyal military units and the Free Corps.

All of this violence and instability notwithstanding, Germany appeared to be moving in the corridor and the Red Queen was in full force. Germany had a legislative house with adult male suffrage after 1848, but on the whole it was still dominated by the Prussian elite, both because of the presence of an elite-controlled upper house, and because of Prussian control of state institutions and the bureaucracy. Despite these obstacles, the Social Democratic Party had already become a major player before the war. After the kaiser's abdication, the Weimar Constitution introduced universal adult suffrage and removed the upper house's control over politics. But this was only one step in the Red Queen dynamics that would play out in the aftermath of the war. The collapse of German armies intensified the discontent that many Germans felt with the country's institutions and brought about a surge in societal mobilization. Citizens demanded more power, greater rights, and effective political representation. Unions flourished and managed to get employers to acquiesce to the eight-hour day, the subject of long and fruitless negotiation before the war.

A major part of this social mobilization was what some called the *Vereinsmeierei* ("associational mania"). Associations, clubs, and civil society organizations were flourishing in record numbers. It appeared that if three or more Germans got together, they were likely to start a club. Or write a constitution. As the historian Peter Fritzsche put it:

> More voluntary associations attracted more members and did so in a
> more active fashion . . . than ever before. Just as retailers, bakers, and
> commercial employees had organized into economic-interest groups, so
> also did gymnasts, folklorists, singers, and churchgoers gather into clubs,
> rally new members, schedule meetings, and plan a full assortment of
> conferences and tournaments.

This was not only an era of social mobilization. The cage of norms was crumbling, too, particularly for women, who had won the right to vote under Weimar in 1919. Elsa Herrmann's 1929 book *This Is the New Woman* celebrated women's new freedom and identity. She decried traditional stereotypes of the role of women in society, noting that "the woman of yesterday lived exclusively for and geared her actions toward the future. Already as a half-grown child, she toiled and stocked her hope chest for her future dowry. In the first years of marriage she did as much of the household work as possible herself to save on expenses . . . she helped her husband in his business or professional activities." But things were changing:

> The new woman has set herself the goal of proving in her work and deeds that the representatives of the female sex are not second-class persons existing only in dependence and obedience.

Women's suffrage was not the only innovation in German political institutions after the country's defeat in the First World War. The constitution, written in the city of Weimar following elections in January 1919, made Germany a republic with an elected president rather than a hereditary monarchy. It granted equality before the law and all sorts of individual rights as well. You were now free to express your opinions, to assemble, and to participate in politics. Article 124 read:

> All Germans have the right to form societies or associations for purposes not prohibited by the criminal code. This right may not be limited by preventive regulations. The same provision applies to religious societies and associations.
>
> Every association has the right to incorporate according to the provisions of the civil code. Such right may not be denied to an association on the ground that its purpose is political, social, or religious.

Together with unparalleled social mobilization during the Weimar era came a great deal of cultural change and creativity. The Bauhaus art school, founded in 1919 under the visionary directorship of Walter Gropius and Ludwig Mies van der Rohe, forged a new synthesis of art and design. The Blue Four group of painters, including Wassily Kandinsky and Paul Klee, emerged out of the earlier Blue Rider group. Both Kandinsky and Klee taught at the Bauhaus. Modernist composers like Arnold Schönberg and Paul Hindemith revolutionized orchestral music. Fritz Lang and Robert Wiene created Expressionist cinema.

But as is typical of the unruly dynamics of the Red Queen, as society became stronger, the elite reacted. Even though the Social Democratic Party remained in power for much of the period, the elite were still heavily represented in the bureaucracy and could count on the loyalty of much of the army. When they couldn't, they turned to the Free Corps. They repressed social mobilization and the Council of the People's Deputies. This elite reaction deepened the polarization in interwar Germany.

The flourishing of German civil society also set in motion other responses, with important institutional consequences. Ebert had used the army to repress more radical forces in late 1918 and early 1919. But this strategy could unleash other forces at his, and Weimar's, expense. There were also institutional peculiarities that would have important implications in the years to follow. Right from the start, the Weimar Republic was hamstrung by the fact that as many as half of the elected representatives did not believe in its institutions. Roughly a fifth on the left were Communists who favored a Russian-style revolution. To them the Weimar democratic state was "bourgeois" or even "fascist." About 30 percent of the representatives on the right, just like the majority of the traditional elites allied with them, wanted to return to the pre-1914 conservative-dominated status quo and restore the monarchy, and some, like the Nazis, completely rejected the legitimacy of the republic's institutions. Nothing is perhaps more telling than the scenes in parliament after the 1930 elections when the Nazis first became a significant presence. One hundred and seven Nazis, uniformed in their brown shirts, colluded with the seventy-seven Communist members to disrupt the proceedings. Both right and left shouted and obstructed parliamentary business, and abused the rules, endlessly raising points of order. Right and left had no respect for the institution to which they had been elected.

Indeed, reflecting the widespread lack of trust in state institutions, it was not just the Nazis who had paramilitary groups. We have already seen the critical role that the paramilitary Free Corps played in fighting Communists in Munich and elsewhere. The Free Corps were only an arm's-length distance from the SA, which had started out in 1920 as the Nazis' "Gymnastics and Sports Section" and absorbed Free Corps veterans en masse, including Ernst Röhm, who became the SA's commander. The Social Democrats had their paramilitary group too, called the Reichsbanner, and the Communists had theirs, the Red-Front Fighters' League. Ominously, despite Prussia's history of strong state institutions, the Weimar state never possessed a monopoly of violence.

These uncompromising positions and the electoral system based on proportional representation made it very hard for Weimar democracy to work. By 1928 fifteen different political parties were represented in the Reichstag, including the Saxon Peasants party and the German Farmers' Party. Another twenty-six parties had run candidates unsuccessfully, diluting the votes of the main parties. No single party ever had a majority in any Weimar election, so every government was a coalition. For half of this period the government did not even have a majority in parliament, which meant that they had to build a new coalition for every piece of legislation. Between 1919 and 1933 there were twenty different cabinets, each one lasting an average of only 239 days. The resulting frustration and stasis led governments to increasingly rely on the prerogatives of the president to get things done. Extensive emergency powers granted to the president by Article 48 of the Weimar Constitution facilitated this presidential activism. Though these powers could in principle be overturned by a parliamentary vote, the president could dissolve the parliament, enabling him to use Article 48 as he wished. The first president, Friedrich Ebert, invoked Article 48 on 136 different occasions, even though it was supposed to be an emergency clause.

A Rainbow Coalition of the Discontented

Into this highly mobilized society with its fragmented party system came the Nazis. The Nazi Party evolved out of the German Workers' Party, which had been founded in Munich in 1919. Adolf Hitler, then still a corporal in the army, was an early recruit and he quickly distinguished himself with his compelling oratory and was made head of propaganda. The name change in 1920 was designed to broaden the appeal of the party by adding "socialist" to the title. By 1921 Hitler's ruthlessness and charisma had allowed him to take over the leadership of the party with complete authority over objectives and strategy. In November 1923 he made a mistake. He decided that the Nazis would be able to get local military units in Munich to support them in the so-called Beer Hall Putsch. It was a fiasco. The party was banned and Hitler was arrested.

That the putsch took place in Munich was not a coincidence. The Nazi party had been banned nearly everywhere in Germany after June 1922 when Foreign Minister Walther Rathenau had been assassinated by right-wing nationalists. But in Bavaria the party was still legal and flourished under the government of the right-winger Gustav Ritter von Kahr, who had supported paramilitary groups in 1918–1919 and maintained his own independent group, known as the Denizens' Defense Force. The position of many conservatives was that the Nazis were criminals and thugs, but useful criminals and thugs; their energy could be harnessed to restore the pre-Weimar regime. The Beer Hall Putsch was a step too far, however. Kahr repudiated the putsch and the military held firm.

Nevertheless, Hitler's subsequent trial shows that the local authorities were sympathetic to him. They made sure the trial was held in Munich and that Georg Neithardt, an avowed nationalist, was appointed as judge. Neithardt gave Hitler a platform to address the court for hours, turning the whole thing into what one journalist at the time referred to as a "political carnival." After Hitler's opening remarks, one of the judges declared, "What a tremendous chap, this Hitler!"

Hitler was sentenced to five years' imprisonment, but was released early in December 1924, just thirteen months after his initial arrest. During his comfortable prison sojourn Hitler wrote his famous book *Mein Kampf.* He also learned a critical lesson—instead of the putsch, the Nazi party had to take the democratic path to power.

Yet as late as the 1928 election the Nazis were no more than a marginal party, polling at less than 3 percent. That all changed with the Wall Street Crash of 1929 and the start of the worldwide Great Depression. Though the full brunt of this was not to hit Germany until 1930, already 1929 saw a collapse of investment. In 1930 national income fell by 8 percent. By 1931 it had fallen by one-quarter, by 1932 by almost 40 percent. Many Germans saw their earnings drop precipitously, but the greatest burden fell on those losing their jobs as the unemployment rate rocketed to 44 percent, the highest rate recorded in an advanced economy. For comparison, U.S. unemployment in 1932 was 24 percent while in Britain it was 22 percent.

Yet the unemployed themselves did not vote predominantly for the Nazis. They tended to support left-wing parties, as did those who were members of trade unions. Rather, it was the massive economic insecurity of the times that led the Protestant middle classes, shopkeepers, and farmers as well as the discontented urban youth to be attracted by the Nazis' vague promises of national renewal. The Nazis became a catchall party for those disillusioned with the existing party system and the politics of Weimar, making the historian Richard Evans describe them as "a rainbow coalition of the discontented."

In March 1930 the president, Paul von Hindenburg, appointed a new government with Heinrich Brüning of the Center Party as chancellor. The Center Party was only the third-biggest party behind the Social Democrats and the conservative German National People's Party, and had 61 out of 491 seats. The appointment of Brüning by Hindenburg heralded the waning of parliamentary rule, as it was done without consultation with the parliament, and most of the new cabinet ministers had no affiliation with any of the parties. Brüning's government was unable to pass a budget. In response Hindenburg dissolved the parliament. According to the constitution, new elections had to be held within sixty days. They saw the vote share of the Nazi party surge to 18.25 percent, giving them 107 seats in the new parliament. Hindenburg again named Brüning as chancellor and Brüning struggled on in the face of the mounting economic crisis until he was replaced by Franz von Papen in June 1932. The Communists, in cahoots with the Nazis, immediately tried to organize a no-confidence vote, but before they could manage it Hindenburg again dissolved the parliament. New elections were held after sixty days in July 1932, but in this period Hindenburg, and effectively Papen, could rule without parliamentary opposition. They took advantage of this opportunity on July 20 to issue an emergency decree, declaring Papen Reichskommissar (Reich Commissioner) for Prussia, giving him direct control over the Prussian government. This type of emergency decree would later be put to nefarious use by the Nazis, dismissing the democratically elected government of the state of Prussia and taking control of its massive security force. Papen himself didn't seem to have any reservations about the overthrow of the democratically elected government in Prussia. In his memoirs he stated that his goal upon coming to power was to restore the imperial system and monarchy, and it appears that a plan to abolish elections later in 1932 was shelved only because of the threatened no-confidence vote. At this point, repeating the mistakes of other traditional elites, Papen hatched a strategy of using the popularity of the Nazis as a way to revert the political institutions to the status quo ante Weimar. This turned out to be a terrible miscalculation.

In the election of July 31, 1932, the Nazi vote share shot up to over 37 percent, giving them 230 seats in the Reichstag. After fruitless negotiations over a new government, Hindenburg again dissolved parliament and ruled unopposed through Papen. The next election in November saw the Nazis reduced to 33.1 percent of the vote with 196 seats. It was still a stalemate. Papen was replaced on December 3 by the Reich minister of defense, Kurt von Schleicher, a former general yearning to engineer a coup to set up a conservative authoritarian government with the support of the military but, crucially, without the Nazis. But this scheme came to nothing. Parliament's disintegration was clear. In 1930 parliamentarians sat for 94 days and passed 98 laws, and President Hindenburg issued only 5 emergency decrees. By 1932 they sat for a puny 13 days and managed to enact just 5 laws. Hindenburg, on the other hand, was much busier, passing 66 emergency decrees. In a vain attempt to create a government that could function, Hindenburg agreed, at Papen's urging, to appoint Hitler as chancellor, on January 30, 1933. Hitler convinced Hindenburg to dissolve the parliament. Until new elections were held on March 5, 1933, Hitler was in charge of the state.

On February 27 a Dutch Communist, Marinus van der Lubbe, possibly in collaboration with others, burned down the Reichstag. This gave Hitler the excuse he needed to declare that the act was the start of a Communist coup. He induced Hindenburg to use Article 48 to pass the Reichstag Fire Decree, which suspended most civil liberties in Germany, including habeas corpus, freedom of expression, freedom of the press, the right of free association and public assembly, and the secrecy of the post and telephone. With this decree in hand, Hitler was able to use all of the paramilitary and organizational might of the Nazi Party to intimidate and cow into submission any opposition before the March election. In this he was aided by Franz von Papen's previous takeover of the Prussian government because Hitler got Göring appointed Prussian minister of the interior, effectively putting him charge of the police in half of Germany.

The next step was the Kroll Opera House, the Enabling Act, and the end of Weimar democracy.

The Zero-Sum Red Queen

However shocking, the collapse of Weimar democracy was not just a consequence of unforeseen events and Adolf Hitler's force of personality. The Weimar Republic had deep fault lines that made the Red Queen effect potentially unstable, more pregnant with danger, more likely to get out of control. In this chapter, we study why this was the case in Germany and clarify the circumstances under which the dynamic contest between state and society can topple a nation out of the corridor.

The first of Weimar's fault lines relates to the nature of the competition between state and society. The Red Queen effect in ancient Athens (Chapter 2) or in the U.S. case (Chapters 2 and 10) involved each side building up their capacity to have the upper edge, but this didn't mean the state repressing and attempting to emasculate society. Nor did it involve societal mobilization aimed at completely destroying the elites. (For instance, even when an elite was ostracized from Athens, his property was not confiscated.) Indeed, Solon and Cleisthenes and U.S. founding fathers such as George Washington and James Madison emerged as arbiters acceptable to both elites and non-elites; they institutionalized the power of society as they were simultaneously contributing to the expansion of state capacity. This created a political environment in which state capacity developed with better regulation, institutions for provision of public services, and the ability to resolve conflicts—an example of "positive sum" Red Queen, where both sides ultimately strengthen as a result of their competition. The situation in Germany was different, more polarized. By polarization we mean that there appeared to be little room for compromise between the elites and the segment of society most mobilized and intent on leaving its mark on German politics (in particular, the workers' movement and its most important organization, the Social Democratic Party). Consequently, rather than supporting state-society cooperation and broad-based state building, German Red Queen dynamics turned out to be much more "zero-sum," with each side intent on destroying the other in order to be able to survive itself.

This zero-sum Red Queen in Germany was mostly but not entirely due to the attitudes of German elites. Elites in the army, the bureaucracy, the judiciary, academia, and the business world did not accept Weimar democracy and wanted to engineer a return to the more authoritarian, elite-controlled society of the famous nineteenth-century chancellor Otto von Bismarck. The army, dominated by the Prussian elite, associated the new democracy with the defeat in the war and the onerous terms of the Versailles peace treaty they had to accept. The business elite felt threatened by the Social Democratic Party and the mobilization generated by mass politics. These attitudes not only supported repression rather than compromise at critical points, they also created an environment conducive to the rise of various fringe, right-wing organizations, such as the Nazi Party.

This is most visible in the tacit support that the Nazis received from the German elite. It wasn't only after the failed Beer Hall Putsch that Hitler and his allies received favorable treatment from the establishment. The police and judiciary often sided with the Brownshirts who beat up, and at times killed, Communists and Social Democrats, emboldening their campaign of terror. The statistician Emil Julius Gumbel put together data from 1919 to 1922 showing that 22 political murders committed by left-wingers led to 38 convictions and 10 executions, while the 354 political murders by right-wingers, mostly Nazis, led to only 24 convictions and no executions.

German universities too were siding with the right against the left. In the words of Richard Evans, "Where political allegiance of the young to the far right was at its most obvious was in Germany's universities, many of them famous centres of learning, with traditions going back to the Middle Ages . . . The vast majority of professors . . . were also strongly nationalist." In consequence, the universities were among the first institutions to embrace the Nazi ideology in the

1920s, with a huge number of university students joining the party. As we have seen, all of this came to a head after support for the Nazis began expanding, and large parts of the bureaucracy and the army, and most ominously the president, Hindenburg, took no action to stem their surge; they preferred the Nazis, whom they thought they could control, not just to the Communists but to the Social Democrats as well.

But why were German elites, officers, and bureaucrats so opposed to the Weimar experiment? Part of the reason is related to structural factors determining the nature of life in the corridor; they were mostly cut from the same cloth, rooted in the Prussian landed aristocracy. Landed interests have often viewed the strengthening of society and the beginnings of democracy in zero-sum terms, and for good reason. Industrialists and professionals can flourish in the corridor both economically and politically, because they have assets (in the form of their expertise, knowledge, and skills) that remain valuable even as the economy transforms, and because their urban existence gives them new opportunities to organize and remain politically relevant in the midst of the Red Queen dynamics. Not so for landowners, who fear losing their lands, which are much more easily taken away from them than the factories of industrialists and the skills of professionals. Indeed, societal mobilization often comes with demands for loss of economic, political, and social privileges for landowners, and the situation in the Weimar Republic was no different (even if such attempts were stymied by President Hindenburg, who was himself from the Prussian landed aristocracy and sympathetic to their concerns). Landowners also feared, again rightly, becoming marginalized as the political center of gravity shifted away from them as a result of democratic politics. All of this made them skeptical of the burgeoning Shackled Leviathan.

The role of landowning elites in interwar Germany illustrates a broader point. We have so far emphasized the different nature of politics inside and outside the corridor, and in this chapter, we are seeing how the struggle between state and society may take a nation out of the narrow corridor. But clearly, the narrower the corridor, the easier it is for a society to spin out of it. Consider Figure 5, for instance. On the left panel, we see a corridor that is very narrow, while the one on the right is wider. In the next chapter, we'll discuss the various factors that shape the corridor and how this determines the feasibility not just of staying in it, but also of getting into it. For now, we can note that the importance of the power and wealth of landowners, as in Weimar Germany, is one of the factors that makes the corridor narrower—because landowners' fear of losing their lands and political power makes them unwilling to compromise and coexist with a mobilized society, while

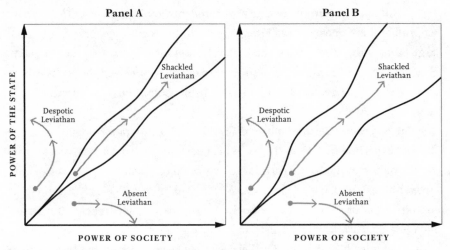

Figure 5. The Shape of the Corridor

their intransigence helps radicalize society. So the situation in Germany looked much more like Panel A of Figure 5 and hence more fraught with instability.

Even if the attitudes of the Prussian landowners and the structural difficulties that they posed for life in the corridor were not uncommon, the Prussian landed elites were better able to form a coalition to resist societal mobilization. To start with, many of the top officers, judges, and bureaucrats originated from this social class and shared their outlook. The Prussian elite had remained relatively coherent and politically dominant during the second half of the nineteenth century, even as social change was ongoing. This convinced them that they could control German politics, and if necessary dial back the clock to the days of Otto von Bismarck.

It wasn't just the elite who showed little commitment to Weimar democracy. The votes of German workers were divided between many parties, but most importantly between the Communists and the Social Democrats. The Communists dreamed of engineering a Russian-style revolution and worked to undermine Weimar democracy and parliament, even sometimes in coalition with their mortal enemy, the Nazis. Though Social Democrats became the party most associated with the Weimar Republic, and had many pragmatic or even opportunistic leaders like Ebert, their commitment to democratic politics was also at times tenuous. They had their roots in Marxist politics and had only recently split with the Communists, not so much because they disagreed with the ultimate objective of setting up a socialist society, but on the issue of support for the German war effort. Compared to some other social democratic parties in Europe, German Social

Democrats had a stronger Marxist pedigree, making them much more threatening to business elites and contributing to polarization.

The polarization that resulted from the lack of compromise and the adversarial approach of all sides was both a cause and a consequence of the nature of civil society organizations in the Weimar years. Had he witnessed it, Tocqueville would have been even more impressed by the bustling associational life of interwar Germany than he was with the mid-nineteenth century United States. And yet, all of this was along sectarian lines. Even in small towns, associations were divided between those of Catholics, nationalists, Communists, and Social Democrats. A youth with nationalist sympathies would belong to nationalist clubs, attend a nationalist church, and probably socialize and marry entirely within these nationalist circles. The same was true for Catholics, Social Democrats, and Communists. This polarized societal mobilization contributed further to a zero-sum Red Queen effect, which involved each side investing to undercut the other. There were no Solons or James Madisons to address both state and society in Weimar Germany.

All of this paved the way for the second fault line of Weimar democracy. Red Queen dynamics often increase tensions in society, so the capacity of institutions to resolve and contain these conflicts becomes particularly important to channel them in the direction of capacity-building competition rather than instability. The fact that the courts neither increased their capability to deal with myriad new disputes in Germany nor accepted the legitimacy of societal mobilization, especially from the left, meant that there were no impartial arbiters in these conflicts, and partly as a result, the conflicts intensified and society became more polarized. The fractured, gridlocked nature of parliament further empowered extremist parties and precluded democratic compromises that could have managed these conflicts. In a sense, the institutions could not run as fast as state and society, making the Red Queen much more likely to get out of control.

It isn't only structural factors that influence how the struggle between state and society works out in practice. As we pointed out in Chapter 9, the leadership of certain groups or individuals can sometimes play a defining role, for better or for worse. The charismatic, albeit largely deranged, single-mindedness and vitality that Adolf Hitler brought to the fringe right-wing movements of interwar Germany no doubt contributed to the swift fall of the Weimar Republic and to the character of the murderous regime that replaced it.

With these fault lines and Hitler's oratory and charismatic leadership, the ride of Weimar democracy was destined to be a bumpy one. But all of this might still have been long forgotten today had it not been for the third structural factor—the huge shock of the Great Depression, which intensified conflict and polarization in society and delegitimized the democratic institutions of the era, especially when the fractured parliament was unable to deal with the economic crisis. Weimar was now teetering on the edge of the corridor.

Despotism from Below

The problem with the Red Queen is that the same energy that fuels the building of the capacity of both state and society can also get out of control and destabilize life in the corridor. Yet ultimately, what doomed the burgeoning German Shackled Leviathan wasn't a coup by Prussian elites or the army, which is what many among the traditional elites, like Kurt von Schleicher, were hoping to organize, as we have seen. Rather, it was a bottom-up societal movement that brought this episode to an end. Though there were some industrialists and elite bureaucrats, judges, and university professors who supported the Nazis early on, the party was mostly a movement of discontented middle classes and youth. Until well into the 1930s, the Nazi movement was little more than its Brownshirts wreaking havoc, getting into street brawls, and beating up and sometimes murdering Communists, Social Democrats, and Jews. As late as July 1932, Joseph Goebbels would use a campaign speech to urge, "Now, people, rise up, and let the storm break loose!" If the Nazi party was the agent coming from the bottom of society and taking Germany out of the corridor, shouldn't this have led to a collapse of the state's capacity and control over society? Shouldn't we expect the post-Nazi society to look a little bit like Tajikistan after the fall of the Soviet Union or perhaps Lebanon?

Obviously, that's not what happened. Though the Nazi movement came from below, it did not weaken the state's despotism and dominance over society; on the contrary, it strengthened them. There were domains in which Nazi control did reduce state capacity, most notably in the police, the judiciary, and the bureaucracy, with the arrival of ideologically committed or opportunistic Nazis who were unqualified for the job and uninterested in impartially carrying out their duties. But in most respects, the German state got more despotic and powerful under the Nazis, with the army growing in size and responsibility, the bureaucracy organizing mass deportations and exterminating Jews, and the security forces acquiring sweeping powers, as exemplified by the Gestapo. The Nazi program was one of increasing repression, weakening independent societal mobilization and associations, and intensifying the state's supremacy over society. In this, the Nazis were similar to Italian fascists, who had been their role model. Hitler's Beer Hall Putsch was inspired by Mussolini's successful March on Rome. Mussolini captured the spirit of fascism and Nazism when he stated:

> For the Fascist, everything is in the State, and nothing human or spiritual exists, much less has value, outside the State. In this sense Fascism is totalitarian, and the Fascist State, the synthesis and unity of all values, interprets, develops and gives strength to the whole life of the people.

The historian of fascism Herman Finer summed up the philosophy of the fascist state as "There are no citizens . . . There are only subjects." This philosophy owed much to fascism's and Nazism's militaristic origins and their refusal of any checks on the power of their leaders or the state once they took control. It was also rooted in the way in which these movements were reactions to the socialist and Communist societal mobilization, and thus viewed reestablishing the state's despotic control over the left as their natural objective.

But more fundamentally, even absent these ideological leanings, it would not have been feasible for a nation like Weimar Germany to evolve in the same way as Lebanon today, given its history of strong state institutions. Once these institutions—the army, the police, the judiciary, and the bureaucracy—were there for the taking, any group that gained the political upper hand would take them and use them, whether or not it came from the bottom up or advocated thuggery. Thus even if the German Red Queen got out of control and passed the reins to a group originating in grassroots mobilization, once the nation was out of the corridor, the odds were always in favor of the state institutions' being refashioned and used for the benefit of the new dominant group over others, especially after democratic and other constraints on state power were lifted. So as the Nazis destroyed the budding Shackled Leviathan and took power, they swiftly reestablished and intensified the state's despotic dominance over society.

How the Red Queen Gets out of Control

The problem with the corridor is that you can leave it. We have seen one way this happens with the Weimar Republic as well as some of the reasons why this was likely to happen in Germany.

The three factors that put interwar Germany in a precarious position—polarization between state and society, making compromise unlikely and the Red

Queen effect much more of a zero-sum affair; the inability of institutions to contain and resolve conflicts; and shocks destabilizing institutions and deepening the discontent—appear in one form or another in many other examples where the Red Queen gets out of control. But this doesn't mean that there will always be a bottom-up movement undercutting the Shackled Leviathan, as in Germany. It could be the elites who reestablish the Despotic Leviathan as they emerge the stronger party out of the competition with society, or feel able or compelled to use whatever power they have to reassert their control, perhaps because they are themselves threatened by polarization. This, we'll see, is what happened in Chile when Augusto Pinochet led a violent coup to overthrow democracy in 1973.

Or it may be certain segments of society that put an end to life in the corridor because they become convinced they can no longer control it, which is what brought down most of the Italian communes we studied in Chapter 5, and what we can see playing out in many parts of the world today.

How Much Land Does an *Inquilino* Need?

We have seen that Shackled Leviathans aren't created overnight. They are the result of a long struggle between state and society. In 1958 Chile was experiencing the latest phase of such a struggle which had already led to the political emancipation of a large fraction of the rural labor force, known as *inquilinos*. *Inquilino* means "tenant," but the connotation in rural Chile was a bit more sinister. While they were not slaves or serfs, in practice inquilinos were tied to farms, so much so that when people sold their farms, they also sold the inquilinos with them. Inquilinos worked on the farms and provided other "services" too. Particularly important among these services was their contribution to the political power of the landlords, since they were forced to vote the way their landlords told them to. When an election came around, landowners bused the inquilinos to the polling station, where they were given ballots and told whom to vote for. Their votes were not secret, and the landlords could observe the whole process. Anyone going against the landlords' wishes ran the risk of being fired and dispossessed.

How could Chile have been in the corridor in 1958 with this sort of thing going on? Remember that being in the corridor is a process. The corridor can start when both state and society have modest but balanced capacities. In this Chile was no different from other places. Secret ballots only arrived in British elections in 1872. As late as 1841, conservative politician and three-time prime minister Lord Stanley could observe, "When any man attempted to estimate the probable result of a county election in England, it was ascertained by calculating the number of the great landed proprietors in the county and weighing the number of occupiers under them." Indeed, in rural England, big landowners controlled a sufficiently large fraction of the voting population that their control determined the outcome of an election. As in 1950s Chile, if an "occupier" went against his landlord, there was going to be trouble. The great British economist David Ricardo recognized this in 1824, writing, "It is the most cruel mockery to tell a man he may vote for A or B, when you know that he is so much under the influence of A, or the friends of A, that his voting for B would be attended with the destruction of him. It is not he who has the vote, really and substantially, but his landlord, for it is for his benefit and interest that it is exercised in the present system."

Lord Stanley's logic applied in Chile too. During the debate in the Senate on the introduction of the secret ballot, socialist senator Martones argued in favor of introducing the secret ballot because

> if that law [the old electoral law without a secret ballot] did not exist, instead of there being 9 Socialist senators there would be 18, and you [the Conservatives] would be reduced to 2 or 3 . . . [laughter] you laugh, but the truth is that there would be not 2 Conservative senators from O'Higgins and Colchagua, which corresponds exactly to the number of inquilinos in the fundos which belong to the Conservative hacendados in that region. Conservatives would have only one or perhaps none.

The secret ballot, enacted in 1958, had dramatic effects on elections in Chile. For one, it transformed the political prospects of Salvador Allende. Allende had run as the presidential candidate for the Socialist Party in 1952, getting a mere 5.4 percent of the vote. In 1958 he was the candidate for a coalition the socialists had built, known as the FRAP (Popular Action Front), and did a lot better, winning 28.8 percent of the vote, just 3 percent behind the winner, Jorge Alessandri.

Allende was a great example of the adage "If at first you don't succeed, try again." He did in 1964, and lost for a third time. But it was fourth time lucky in 1970. Though he only got 36.6 percent of the vote, just 1.5 percent more than his longtime opponent Alessandri, Congress elected him president with the support of the Christian Democratic Party, which had come third in the race for president. In 1970 Allende headed a new left-wing coalition called, somewhat ironically as it turned out, Popular Unity (U.P.). He was intent on transforming Chile into a socialist country.

There was no consensus for this in Chilean society, but Allende had ridden a wave unleashed by the secret ballot and other political and social changes that were playing out along Red Queen lines. For example, 1958 also saw the legalization of the Communist Party, which formed part of the FRAP and then the U.P. In addition, voter registration became compulsory and failure to register could even be punished by a prison term. This led to a large increase in the electorate, from 1.25 million people in 1960 to 2.84 million in 1971, when illiterates were finally enfranchised. The Christian Democratic government of Eduardo Frei in the 1960s, brought to power in part in response to these changes, spearheaded not just a range of reforms, including land redistribution, but also a general strengthening of society. Finally, 1961 also saw the launch of President John F. Kennedy's Alliance for Progress. On March 13 of that year Kennedy declared:

> We propose to complete the revolution of the Americas, to build a hemisphere where all men can hope for a suitable standard of living and all can live out their lives in dignity and in freedom. To achieve this goal political freedom must accompany material progress . . . Let us once again transform the American Continent into a vast crucible of revolutionary ideas and efforts, a tribute to the power of the creative energies of free men and women, an example to all the world that liberty and progress walk hand in hand. Let us once again awaken our American revolution until it guides the struggles of people everywhere.

The frequent use of the word "revolution" is ironic, because the Alliance for Progress was partly a plan to stave off socialist revolution spreading throughout the continent. It was one of the policy responses of the U.S. government to the Cuban Revolution. (Another response was launched a month after Kennedy's speech, in the Bay of Pigs, Cuba.) The Alliance argued that land reform would transform Latin America. As Kennedy put it, the Alliance planned "to satisfy the basic needs of the American people for homes, work and land, health and schools— techo, trabajo y tierra, salud y escuela."

Unsurprisingly, *tierra* (land) was on the minds of a lot of newly politically enfranchised inquilinos. This, plus the fact it was now promoted by the U.S., put land reform on the policy agenda in 1964. In 1967 Frei launched an agrarian reform program aimed at redistributing land and expropriating all farms that were over the equivalent of 80 hectares in the Maipo Valley. (This meant that farms could be larger in places where land was of lower quality.) In anticipation of the land reform, some 200 rural unions, which were then illegal, had organized. They were legalized by the same piece of legislation. By 1970 there were close to 500 such unions. There was a surge in labor strikes, which went from 88,000 in 1960 to 275,000 in the year 1969.

Illustrating once again the Red Queen in action, in response to this societal mobilization Frei didn't just initiate land reform; he also increased the state's capacity. In particular, Frei attempted to reduce the ability of politicians to use clientelistic policies to buy support without doing much for the population they were supposed to serve. He did this in various ways, for example, using a line-item veto to eliminate "pork barrel" expenditures from bills, and also by reducing the ability of congresspeople to influence public works projects and salaries. The jurisdiction of Congress and the Senate with respect to the budget was also curtailed.

There were significant obstacles to Allende's agenda. For example, he did not have a majority in Congress. Even his presidency had been due to the Christian Democrats who had only voted for him after he agreed to amend the constitution with a "statute of guarantees." These introduced a gamut of new individual rights into the 1925 constitution. The amendments clearly show what the Christian Democrats and others were concerned about. One clause states, "It cannot be constitutive of crime or abuse to sustain and spread any political idea." Others deal with a fear that the education system might be taken over as a tool of propaganda, for example, stating, "The education that is imparted through the national system will be democratic and pluralistic and will not have official party orientation. Its modification will also be carried out democratically, after free discussion in the competent bodies of pluralist composition." Other clauses indicate a concern about paramilitary groups. One asserted, "The public force is constituted solely and exclusively by the Armed Forces and the Carabineros, essentially professional, hierarchical, disciplined, obedient and non-deliberative institutions." They were right to be concerned.

Once in power Allende started to implement his plan. This involved intensifying land reform and expropriation, and creating worker cooperatives. He also had plans to massively nationalize industry. Other aspects of his economic policy involved granting workers huge pay raises. Some of these policies, such as pay hikes for government workers, could be implemented by presidential decree. But others required the agreement of Congress. What would Allende do when this was not forthcoming? Operate outside the constitution? This is what the statute was supposed to prevent, but who was going to enforce the statute?

In March 1971, Allende gave an interview to the French Marxist philosopher Régis Debray. At one point Debray pointed out, "You . . . have the Executive Power. But not the Legislative, the Judicial, or the repressive apparatus. The legality, the institutions, these were not made by the proletariat; the Constitution was made by the bourgeoisie for its own purposes." Allende responded:

> Evidently, you're right, but listen to me a little, we're going to get there. What did we say in the election campaign? We said that if it was difficult to win the election and not impossible, the stage between victory and the takeover of the government was going to be very difficult and it was even harder to build, because we were making a new path, a Chilean road for Chile, the Chileans for our country. And we have said that we will take advantage of those aspects of the current Constitution to make way for the new Constitution, the People's Constitution. Why? Because in Chile we can do it. We present a project and the Congress rejects it; we will organize a plebiscite.

So Allende was advancing his belief that socialism could be implemented in Chile via constitutional means. Even though he lacked a legislative majority, he could move the project ahead via direct appeal to the people, via a plebiscite. Quite how that was going to work was not clear. After all, Allende had won only 36.6 percent of the vote. When Debray pushed him, Allende noted:

> We win within their rules of the game. Our tactic was correct, theirs was wrong. But I told the people: Between September 3 and November 4, Chile is going to shake more than a soccer ball kicked by Pele.

While Allende may have believed that he could move Chile to socialism via constitutional means, many in his own coalition didn't, and Allende couldn't control them. Groups of workers occupied farms and factories, ignoring the legal processes, and the government moved in to ratify the occupations. Land reform and nationalization became chaotic. As the newspaper *El Mercurio* pointed out in an editorial in 1972, "Neither the President of the Republic, Salvador Allende, nor the parties of the U.P. . . . believe, even remotely, that repressive measures can be taken against groups of workers, farmers, and students who violate the law." Such groups understood this and took advantage of it. These actions were increasingly justified by the notion that the political institutions were creations of U.P.'s opponents and therefore were designed to defend the status quo—a status quo that the U.P. was dedicated to uprooting. This was again a zero-sum Red Queen effect, very different from what we witnessed in ancient Greece or the United States. As it played out, Chilean politics became even more polarized. The auditor general decried the polarization of politics, arguing at a news conference that an institution such as his was neither "revolutionary or reactionary." Compromise was necessary, but there was an unwillingness to compromise. Senator Carlos Altamirano of the Socialist Party argued:

> There are those who pretend to urge "democratic dialogues" with Christian Democracy. As Socialists we say that a dialogue is possible with all those forces who clearly define themselves as against exploiters and against imperialism. We foster and will develop dialogue at the level of the masses, with all the workers, whether they are our militants or not, but we reject dialogues with reactionary and counter-revolutionary leaderships and parties.

When members of the Christian Democrats reached a tentative compromise with the government, it was sunk by their own conservative faction, who warned of the "communist threat." The die was cast. Violence erupted on all sides.

When questioned by Debray on how he would deal with opposition violence, Allende had said, "We are going to contain it, first, with the force of its own law. In addition, to the reactionary violence we are going to answer with revolutionary violence, because we know that they are going to break the rules of the game." Allende was right that the other side would break the rules of the game, but quite wrong on how he could counter it with revolutionary violence.

He was brought down by a coup on September 11, 1973. There had been a failed attempt earlier in the year, and Allende's opponents were pushing the army to try again. *El Mercurio* published an article in June that stated, "In order to accomplish this task of political salvation, we have to renounce all political parties, the masquerade of elections, the poisoned and deceitful propaganda, and turn over to a few select military men the task of putting an end to political anarchy."

The process of social mobilization and the strengthening of society that took place in Chile in the 1960s was matched by the strengthening of the state, but this only led to more radical demands after 1970. These radical demands stoked fear among the Chilean elites who worried about mass expropriation of land and businesses. The elite's reaction threw Chile out of the corridor.

This fire was being fueled by the U.S. government's policy even as Kennedy was heralding a "revolution" of political freedom for Latin America. The CIA was pouring money and effort into Chile to destabilize Allende's government. The Senate Select Committee on Intelligence Activities report on "Covert Actions in Chile, 1963–1973," declassified in 2010, observes that the CIA tried to intervene in all areas of Chilean life to alter the political realities. It gave over $2 million to the Christian Democratic Party to help fund its 1964 election campaign. Another $4 million was provided to anti-Allende parties after 1970. It poured $1.5 million into *El Mercurio*, which was judged to be the most influential anti-Allende newspaper. It financed "democratic trade unions" against the Communist-led union confederation. President Nixon directly ordered that the CIA try to stop Allende taking power after his election. The Senate report notes:

> After Allende finished first in the election . . . President Nixon met with Richard Helms, the Director of Central Intelligence, Henry Kissinger and John Mitchell. Helms was directed to prevent Allende from taking power . . . It quickly became apparent that a military coup was the only way to prevent Allende's accession to power. The CIA established contact with several groups of military plotters and eventually passed weapons to one group.

The coup was supposed to start with the kidnapping of the head of the military, General René Schneider. Schneider was shot and killed and the coup collapsed in a fiasco. The extent to which the CIA helped precipitate the 1973 coup is controversial, with some relevant U.S. documents still classified. The Senate report concludes that while "there is no hard evidence of direct U.S. assistance to the coup," nevertheless "the United States—by its previous actions, its existing posture and the nature of its contacts with the Chilean military—conveyed the signal that it would not look with disfavor on a military coup."

The coup, on which the U.S. did not "look with disfavor," unleashed a torrent of violence and murder on the Chilean people. Around 3,500 people were killed for their political beliefs and activities; tens of thousands were imprisoned, beaten, and tortured. Tens of thousands were fired from their jobs because of their political affiliation. Unions were banned, collective action became impossible, and Congress was duly closed. What had started with the usual race between state and society in the corridor and an intensification of society's mobilization in the 1960s got out of control and ended up with Chile spinning out of the corridor and into a seventeen-year period of despotism.

———

So in the Chilean case, we are again seeing the zero-sum Red Queen, leading to polarization and attempts by the two sides to undercut each other rather than finding a middle ground or compromise. The structural factors that made the corridor particularly narrow and the Red Queen fraught with danger for the Weimar Republic had many parallels in the Chilean case. It started with the landed elites, terrified of land reform and the eclipse of their political power, which fueled a broader unwillingness by the elite to accept societal mobilization and redistribution. Mounting polarization, resulting from the intransigence of the elite and from the radical Marxist ideology of Allende's government, was a defining factor as well. So was the inability of Chilean institutions, including Congress and the courts, to mediate the conflict. Both groups thus came to the conclusion that the conflicts would be resolved by force. There was no external shock like the Great Depression destabilizing Chile, underscoring that a country can easily leave the corridor without an external rupture. All the same, Allende's policies and the elites' uncompromising opposition created a severe recession of their own making, adding to the turmoil.

Chile, like Germany, left the corridor. In this case, it wasn't the Brownshirts, but an elite-supported military coup that ended the prospects of the Chilean Shackled Leviathan (at least for a while).

For Whom the Bells Toll

In 1264 a solemn meeting took place in the city of Ferrara in northern Italy. It was chaired by the Podestà, who, as we saw in Chapter 5, was an external executive brought in to run the government of the republican Italian communes. The record of the meeting states:

> We Pierconte of Carrara, podestà of Ferrara, in a full assembly of all
> the people of the city of Ferrara in the piazza of the city, gathered in
> the usual way by the tolling of bells, by the wish, consent and order of the
> whole commune and population gathered in this assembly . . . have
> decreed as follows . . . The magnificent and illustrious Lord Obizzo,

grandson and heir of the late magnificent Lord Azzo of happy memory . . . is to be Governor and Ruler and General and permanent Lord of the City of Ferrara and its districts at his own will. He is to possess jurisdiction, power and rule in the City and outside it and to have the right to increase, do, order, provide and dispose as he shall wish and as shall seem useful to him. And in general he is to have powers and rights as permanent Lord of the City of Ferrara and its district to do and arrange all things in accordance with his wishes and orders.

Perhaps we need to run that by you again. The "whole commune and population," gathered in an assembly, had created a "permanent Lord." Things then got even weirder because this wasn't just about Lord Obizzo, since the statement continued, "We wish all the above to apply in perpetutity not only to the Lord Obizzo . . . but after his death we wish his heir to be Governor and Ruler and general Lord of the City." It wasn't just a permanent personal lordship, it was hereditary; it was the creation of dynastic rule consummated by the "whole commune and population" meeting "in a full assembly of all the people." The republican commune had voted itself out of existence.

To understand what happened in Ferrara, and in much of the rest of communal Italy, we need to back up a little. We have already seen how the communes emerged in the early Middle Ages from the roots of Lombard and Carolingian participatory political institutions, and how they created elaborate systems of republican government supporting Shackled Leviathans. The communes were also helped by the legacy of Rome, where elites were urban and consequently easier to control by society, which was also organized in urban areas. But the elites did not disappear after the communes took over power. They often maintained landed estates and feudal ties in the countryside, which enabled them to preserve their wealth and political influence. Communes tried to fight against this, and passed laws attempting to restrict feudal relations, stating things like "No man is to become the vassal of any other or swear fealty to him." In the commune of Perugia this was taken to the extreme, and anyone involved in an oath of vassalage, including any notary who recorded it, could be subject to capital punishment. One of the concerns was that vassals could be easily armed and threaten to destabilize the communes, and they were.

In line with the logic of the Red Queen, and to paraphrase William Shakespeare, "the course of true competition never did run smooth." This was certainly true for competition between elites and the communes. Elites didn't take the creation of the communes lying down. They began to organize. Indeed, while the communes emerged, elites started to form a type of association, called a consortium (*consorzeria*). These were alliances whereby elites agreed to come to each other's aid, especially in their struggle against the communes. A consortium agreement of 1196 records: "We swear to help each other without fraud and in good faith . . . with our tower and common house and swear that none of us will act against the others directly or through a third party."

The reference to a tower is significant. Throughout Italy, elites began to build towers. Communes were soon promulgating laws limiting the height of these towers, which still dot the skyline in modern Bologna and Pavia. (A photo of some of the remaining towers of Bologna is included in the photo insert.) In effect these towers were fortifications. The traveler Benjamin of Tudela observed in the 1160s that in Genoa "each householder has a tower to his house and at times of strife they fight each other from the tops of the towers." He noted something similar in Pisa. In 1194 a Genoese citizen recorded fighting in the city of Pistoia between two groups, called the Blacks and the Whites.

> The Blacks had fortified the tower of messer Iacopo's sons and from there they did much harm to messer Ranieri's sons. And the Whites had fortified messer de Lazzari's house . . . That house did much harm to the Blacks with crossbow fire and stones, so that they could not fight from the street. When the Blacks saw that they were being opposed by servants inside the house, Vanne Fucci and some of his companions went up to it, attacked it frontally with crossbow fire and then won it by setting fire to one side of the house and entering it by the other side. Those who were inside began to run away and they pursued them, wounding and killing and plundering the house.

Something was clearly going wrong with conflict resolution in many of the communes. The Blacks and the Whites were competing elite consortia, and they were feuding incessantly. This type of feuding between elite Italian families was enshrined in literature by William Shakespeare's Capulets and Montagues in his play *Romeo and Juliet*. In Reggio an actual feud, between the Da Sesso and Da Fogliano families, went on for fifty years and claimed possibly 2,000 lives. At one point the Da Fogliano family laid siege to the Da Sessos, who, rather than surrender, reportedly discussed drawing lots to eat one another. Apparently a less bad end than capture!

Members of the elite didn't just fight one another, they also threatened the whole edifice of republican rule. Many communes had been unable to remove all elite privileges and feudal relations. As late as 1300 in many places, including Milan, Genoa, Pisa, Mantua, Modena, and Ravenna, elites still controlled various customs, taxes, and the right to issue coins and determine weights and measures. Some, like the Visconti family in Milan, actively exercised these rights. Properties of citizens in several communes were restricted by various types of fiefs, and contracts were signed on the basis of feudal laws and customs.

In opposition to this elite activity and continued privilege, the citizens mobilized in the guise of the Popolo, the people. In Chapter 5 we briefly mentioned an executive office called the Capitano del Popolo, which was in charge of organizing the people. The Popolo was a countermobilization against the elite. In Bergamo every member of the Popolo had to swear the oath:

> I shall do the best that is in my power to see that the council . . . and all the offices and honours of the commune of Bergamo should be chosen in the interest of the community and not by reason of any party or parties. . . .
>
> If any party or alliance in the city of Bergamo or any gathering takes up arms or begins to fight and if they intend to act against the honour and good estate of the podestà . . . or against the commune or this corporation (the Popolo) . . . I shall defend and aid and maintain the . . . podestà . . . and the commune in every way of which I am capable.

The existence of the Popolo is in itself an indication that all wasn't well in the communes. Society needed to organize to defend the communes from the elites. But couldn't the commune and its legal institutions have dealt with fighting elites? Why did the people have to take things into their own hands? The Popolo justified itself in Bologna by arguing that it was needed so that "rapacious wolves and meek lambs should be able to walk with equal steps." The rapacious wolves were the elites, the ordinary people the lambs. The roots of the Popolo differed in different cities. Some came from guilds, some from area associations, and many had military elements. They modeled themselves on the communes, hence the key role of the Capitano, the first of whom seems to have appeared in Parma in 1244. They stipulated fixed representation for their members on the boards of the commune. In Vicenza, as early as 1222, half of the positions in the commune were allocated to the Popolo. At the same time, they demanded that elites should have only limited representation in such offices. They even demanded greater legal rights than the elites. In Parma "the oath of any member of the *Popolo* is to be full proof against any magnate or powerful man," while the same wasn't true in reverse. By the 1280s in Florence and Bologna the Popolo was drawing up lists of elite families and demanding that they make payments as guarantees for their future good behavior.

To make things worse, the cleavage between elites and the Popolo was not the only division that rocked Italy. The communes, you will recall, were nominally part of the Holy Roman Empire, the successor state to the eastern part of Charlemagne's Carolingian Empire, which he had divided between his sons. Though the communes had gained their de facto independence, there were still those who supported the empire, and those who opposed it. The former became known as Ghibellines, a name supposedly derived from the castle of Waiblingen, a property of the Hohenstaufens, the ruling dynasty of the empire for most of the twelfth century and the family of its most dominant ruler, Frederick Barbarossa. The latter were called the Guelfs, derived from the German Welf, the family name of one of Frederick Barbarossa's main challengers, Otto IV. The conflict between the Ghibellines and the Guelfs was just as acrimonious as that between elites and the Popolo. When the Guelfs took control of the government of Florence in 1268, they immediately drew up a list of the Ghibellines, 1,050 people in all, 400 of whom were sent into exile.

By now we have some sense of what went on in Ferrara. The creation of the communes had induced a reaction from feudal elites. This is turn led to a reaction by the citizens in the form of the Popolo. The Popolo started tilting the legal system in its favor, banning elites from representation in the commune and fixing its own representation in undemocratic ways. Elites in turn tried not just to subvert the system but also to overthrow it. Often they did this in the name of a "party" like the Guelfs, who in Florence and Lucca named the king of Sicily, Charles of Anjou, as Podestà for a term of six years, in effect delegating to him the task of choosing who would run the cities. When Guelfs took over Florence and Bologna, all public positions, including military ones, were reserved for party members. Often parties took the names of individual elite families and provided a vehicle for the overthrow of the commune. In Milan there were the Visconti and Della Torre parties; in Como the Rusconi and Vittani; in Bologna the Lambertazzi and Geremei; and in Orvieto the Monaldeschi and Filippeschi parties. The elites were at first successful in increasing their control over republican regimes. In Ivrea, outside Turin, the city promised loyalty and even "vassalage" to the Marquis of Montferrat, promising him half of the city's revenues and allowing him to name the Podestà. In other instances, as in Venice, until then one of the most successful Italian city-states, the elites simply changed the rules to exclude others from political power. Military muscle also helped consolidate the rule of the Bonacolsi family in Mantua in 1272, the Polentas in Ravenna after 1275, the Da Caminos in Treviso in 1283, and the Malatestas in Rimini after 1295. By 1300 at least half of the cities that previously had communes were under despotic rule. The consequences were soon obvious. In Ferrara, where we began, popular participation in councils was severely restricted and guilds and confraternities were suspended. The new lords had started calling the shots.

Against this creeping elite power, the Popolo reacted, but not just by fighting against the elite. If political power was likely to completely revert to the elite, then it was better to overthrow the whole system. It started in Piacenza in 1250 when, spearheaded by the Popolo, Uberto de Iniquitate was elected as Podestà and an official of the Popolo for one year. But soon the position was extended to five years with the stipulation that if he died his son would assume the office. Such events were common. Buoso da Dovara initially received the position of Podestà in Cremona for ten years in 1248. By 1255 he had a lifetime Podestà-ship in Soncino. Uberto Pallavicino received lifetime positions as Podestà in Vercelli, Piacenza, Pavia, and Cremona. In Perugia the Popolo helped to catapult Ermanno Monaldeschi into power. After he left office, one of Monaldeschi's supporters proposed that the constitution be suspended and a commission of twelve people formed to reshape the city's institutions. The commission decided to endow Monaldeschi with almost absolute power and the title of *gonfaloniere* (standard-bearer) for life.

In effect the communes were doomed because of the conflicts they could not contain. They could not eliminate the threat of elites, which triggered the countermobilization of the people. The conflict between the two groups could not be contained by the institutions either, and indeed both groups were happy to work outside them and even overthrow them. The resulting instability led to the communes' demise. In Ferrara, Lord Obizzo and his family looked like a safer bet than continual conflict and violence or, worse, elite takeover.

The Allure of Autocrats

The way Italian communes dismantled their participatory institutions and disbanded themselves in the process is puzzling at first. Wouldn't society want to defend its existence in the corridor?

We have argued that the answer is yes, but only if people think they can stay in the corridor despite the power and opposition of the elite. If they become pessimistic that the Red Queen dynamics will increasingly advantage the elite and thus lead to the elites' despotism, then they may opt for passing the power to an unaccountable autocrat who, they hope, will be more favorable to their interests than an elite-dominated regime would. Though this is often just wishful thinking, it hasn't stopped societies from destroying their own Shackled Leviathan to get the upper hand in their struggle with the elite.

A common factor in the history of the demise of Italian communes and the overthrow of the Weimar and Chilean democracies is the power and opposition of landed interests, which made the corridor narrower and led to an increasingly polarized society. The Red Queen effect, in turn, became much more of a zero-sum, existential fight rather than a race between state and society that advanced the capacities of both. This is visible in the Italian case from the fact that the elites started fighting not just to increase their standing against the communes but to destroy them, and the communes came to view coexistence with the elites as impossible, preferring autocracy to the elites' creeping influence.

Machiavelli summed this up well in *The Prince* when he observed that

> the people do not wish to be commanded or oppressed by the nobles, while the nobles do desire to command and to oppress the people. From these two opposed appetites, there arises in cities one of three effects: a principality, liberty, or licence. A principality is brought about either by the common people or by the nobility, depending on which of the two parties has the opportunity. When the nobles see that they cannot resist the populace, they begin to support someone from among themselves, and make him prince in order to be able to satisfy their appetites under his protection. The common people as well, seeing that they cannot resist the nobility, give their support to one man so as to be defended by his authority.

Machiavelli is in fact identifying a force propelling many modern-day movements sometimes labeled "populist." Though the term originates with the late nineteenth-century U.S. Populist movement, exemplified by the People's Party, its recent specimens, even if diverse, disparate, and lacking a generally agreed definition, do have some common hallmarks. They include a rhetoric that pits the "people" against a scheming elite, an emphasis on the need to overhaul the system and its institutions (because they are not working for the people), a trust in a leader who (supposedly) represents the people's true wishes and interests, and a repudiation of all sorts of constraints and attempts to compromise because they will stand in the way of the movement and its leader. Contemporary populist movements, including the National Front in France, the Freedom Party in the Netherlands, the Partido Socialista Unido de Venezuela (United Socialist Party of Venezuela) started by Hugo Chávez, and the Republican Party refashioned by Donald J. Trump in the United States, all have these features, as did the earlier fascist movements (though they augmented them with a stronger militarism and fanatical anticommunism). As in the case of the Italian communes, the elite may in fact be scheming and against the common people, but the claim that a populist movement and its all-powerful leader will protect the people's interests is just a ruse.

Our framework helps clarify what drives these populist movements and why they threaten the stability of a society in the corridor. Red Queen dynamics are never tidy and orderly. If they work within the corridor, they can increase the capacities of both state and society. But as we have seen, they can become polarized and zero-sum. Even worse, when the institutions are not up to the task of containing and resolving these conflicts and when the competition between the elite and the non-elites seems not to generate gains and real power for non-elites, trust in the very institutions that make up the corridor may fall apart. This is part of what transpired during the Weimar Republic: democratic institutions became gridlocked, the judiciary and security forces could not adjudicate the conflicts in society, and the economy collapsed—with dire consequences for many Germans. The same process happened in the Italian communes as people in many cities lost hope that they would be able to contain the increasing dominance of the elites. In both cases, the people's trust that the institutions could work for them and protect their interests collapsed, making it more attractive to turn to an authoritarian leader and a movement claiming to look after the people's interests—if only they were brought to power and all of the constraints on their autocratic power were lifted.

From this perspective there are certain parallels between these events and what is going on around the world today. The fact that there have been very limited economic gains for many citizens of industrialized nations over the last three decades (as we discuss in greater detail in Chapter 15) even as technological change and globalization have enriched others, is all too real and is a significant source of discontent. That the political system has not been responsive to their plight is largely accurate as well. These legitimate concerns then became more explosive as it became clear that the West's much-cherished institutions couldn't deal with the economic fallout from the global financial crisis of 2008 and from the reality that politically powerful financial interests came to dominate and benefit from the responses to the crisis. The scene was set for a precipitous drop in people's trust in institutions, paving the way for the rise of populist movements.

The ascendancy of populism in turn corrodes politics in the corridor. The Red Queen is more likely to get out of control when the competition between state and society (and between different segments of society) becomes more polarized, more zero-sum. The rhetoric of populist movements, painting everyone outside the movement as enemies and part of the scheming elites holding down the people, contributes to such polarization. As trust in institutions declines, it becomes harder for them to broker compromise.

Our analysis also highlights why, even if defined by important bottom-up elements and even if claiming to represent the people, populist movements will ultimately lead to despotism when they come to power. This is exactly for the same reasons we emphasized in our discussion of the rise of the Nazi regime—the populist claim that checks on their power will help the scheming elite, and their focus on taking control of the state makes it difficult for shackles on state power to remain effective after a populist takeover.

Does this mean that any political movement claiming to speak for the people and opposed to an all-powerful elite is populist and likely to destabilize life in the corridor? Certainly not. Movements committed to working with the institutions of the corridor, which are today almost always democratic institutions, can contribute to the flourishing of the Red Queen, rather than turning it into a destabilizing force. They can also significantly help the more disadvantaged members of society. Recall from Chapter 10 how the American civil rights movement, though it recognized the adversarial attitudes of many elites, attempted to use the courts and federal government to further its agenda, rather than rejecting them outright. The defining characteristic of populist movements that makes them contribute to a zero-sum Red Queen is their refusal to accept constraints and compromise, and it is this feature that makes them ultimately unlikely to redress imbalances in society. They are about creating new dominances, not ending them.

Who Likes Checks and Balances?

One telling set of examples illustrating the forces shaping modern-day populism and its implications comes from the experiences of several Latin American countries, including Peru, Venezuela, and Ecuador. Many of these countries hold regular elections and have some of the trappings of democratic institutions, even if they are far from having a Shackled Leviathan. Part of the reason why these nations were in the orbit of the Despotic Leviathan was that, elections or no elections, traditional elites, often rooted in the countryside and in large agricultural estates, managed to control politics. In the polarized environment this created, populist support often swung behind the dismantlement of checks and balances on presidents and suspension of democratic institutions for the same reasons that the people lent their support to autocrats in Italian communes.

Take Peru. In 1992 President Alberto Fujimori, keen on relaxing the democratic checks on the office of the president, issued Decree 25418, unconstitutionally suspending the legislature and launching new elections. The people should have been up in arms. But Fujimori presented his power grab as a reaction to traditional elites, both from the right in the guise of the political party started by Mario Vargas Llosa, and from the left in the shape of APRA (the American Popular Revolutionary Alliance). Elite dominance in Peru was, of course, not a fabrication, even if ending it wasn't Fujimori's primary motivation. All the same, his propaganda worked. His supporters gained a majority in the new legislature. They proceeded to rewrite the constitution, abolishing one of the two chambers of the legislature and bolstering presidential powers. These changes were endorsed by a plebiscite. Peru was now in the grips of Fujimori's authoritarian dictatorship.

Hugo Chávez's rise to power in Venezuela had similar roots. As soon as he came to power in 1998, Chávez organized a constitutional assembly that introduced a unicameral legislature and moved significant powers to the president. Seventy-two percent of the people who voted in a referendum supported the new constitution. As if this weren't enough, in 2000 Chávez was given the right to rule by decree for a year without needing to get the legislature's agreement. This power was renewed and extended to eighteen months in 2007. It was further extended in December 2010 for another eighteen months. How did Chávez pull this off? The same way as Fujimori did—he presented himself as a revolutionary looking after the interests of the Venezuelan people against the traditional elites who had long controlled politics and the economy in Venezuela. Like Fujimori, he was right about the elites' control and scheming, and about the playing field being heavily tilted against Venezuela's poor and indigenous communities, but his commitment to furthering people's power and welfare was at best weak. The Venezuelan economy collapsed under Chávez and his successor, Nicolás Maduro, and Venezuelan institutions have been decimated. The opposition and regular Venezuelans are repressed, silenced, and now, increasingly, killed by security forces loyal to the regime. The country is on the brink of civil war as we are writing.

The situation in Ecuador, which brought President Rafael Correa to power, is similar. In 2007, Correa articulated his populist agenda perhaps even better than Fujimori and Chávez. He argued that despite his explicit aim to dismantle checks and balances and participatory institutions in Ecuador, he was the man of the people:

> We said we were going to transform the fatherland in the citizen's revolution, democratic, constitutional . . . but revolutionary, without getting entangled in the old structures, without falling into the hands of those with the traditional power, without accepting that the fatherland has particular owners. The fatherland is for everyone without lies with absolute transparency.

As Machiavelli foresaw, if desperate, "the common people . . . give their support to one man so as to be defended by his authority." Correa was that man and on September 28, 2008, 64 percent of Ecuadorian voters ratified a new constitution with a unicameral legislature and increased the powers for president Correa. Correa no longer had to contend with an independent judiciary or central bank, and he had the power to suspend the legislature. He was also allowed to run for two more terms.

Back into the Corridor?

In May 1949, a short (or if you actually lived through it, a painfully long) sixteen years after the Nazis' takeover in 1933, Germany adopted its new constitution, the Basic Law of the Federal Republic of Germany, which enshrined all sorts of checks on the powers of the state and elites and guaranteed the rights and freedoms of individuals. In August that year, the country held democratic elections for parliament, followed a month later by elections for president. Germany, or more correctly the part of it not under the Soviet yoke, was back in the corridor. It has never looked back.

Chile also quickly returned to the corridor, with a peaceful transition to democracy seventeen years after General Augusto Pinochet's brutal coup. The landed and industrial elites' power in Chile has not waned completely (far from it), but the country has developed a vibrant democracy and has experienced a resurgence of the power of society, which has led to a range of reforms reducing the elites' privileges, reversing constitutional changes introduced by the military, and improving education and economic opportunities for the less well-off.

How was this possible? Both the Nazis and Pinochet's dictatorship dismantled constraints on the power of the police and the army; imprisoned, exiled, or
killed their adversaries; viciously repressed all societal organizations; and generally wreaked havoc. How come less than two decades later, they were back to bal-
ancing the powers of state and society?

However bloody and intent on subjugating society the German and Chilean
dictatorships might have been, both countries started inside the corridor. Even
after they spun out of the corridor, many of the factors that had made their societies active and mobilized remained in place. These factors included norms of
societal mobilization and belief that elite and state institutions can be made accountable. They included memories of times when common people were organized and
empowered, laws applied to everybody, and the Leviathan was shackled by society.
They included, too, blueprints for building responsive and constrained bureaucratic
institutions. Take Germany. Although elements of despotic control were important during the period of absolutism after 1648 and during Bismarck's chancellorship, even in these periods Germany had institutional characteristics capable
of shackling the Leviathan. For one, most of Germany, if not Prussia, had deep
Carolingian roots. The state and representative institutions inherited from this
history were never abolished completely, even in the midst of Prussian absolutism.
They bounced back in the nineteenth century, particularly after the 1848 revolutions. These legacies were important in allowing the Social Democrats to become
the largest party in the pre–World War I Reichstag. Though the Reichstag's powers
were restricted by the Kaiser and the Prussian elite dominated the upper house,
these still provided the basis for an institutional architecture inside the corridor.
These historical elements were reinforced and further developed by the Weimar
Republic. As a result, even after almost two decades of moving away from the corridor, Germany was still close to it. Compare this to China, which has been in the
orbit of the Despotic Leviathan for so long that the corridor is not even on the
horizon and the country looks very unlikely to move within range anytime soon.

This perspective thus suggests that, disastrous though it is to have the Red
Queen out of control, if the balance between state and society can be rebuilt before
too long, moving back into the corridor is a possibility.

But this doesn't imply that getting back into the corridor is easy or automatic.
Had it not been for Germany's complete defeat in World War II and the subsequent
efforts by the Americans and (some of) the European powers to build democracy
in Germany, we don't know how things might have played out (in fact, we suspect,
Germany wouldn't be the democratic, peace-loving, freedom-respecting country it

is today). The transition to democracy in Chile was also partly a response to international factors, which persuaded the generals to have a soft, controlled landing rather than risk mounting pressure. Without these external influences, the military dictatorship in Chile might have lasted much longer.

The history of the Italian communes shows us that there is nothing automatic about moving back into the corridor. And of course, the prospects for anything like a move into the corridor for Venezuela, which is experiencing not just a zero-sum conflict but the complete meltdown of institutions, are not good. So the rebound of Germany and Chile should not be read as a tale of predestined democracy or the inevitability of the Shackled Leviathan. Rather, they should be viewed as examples of successful, even if fortuitous, reconfigurations of the balance of power between state and society before it could entirely disappear.

Danger on the Horizon

A population failing to benefit from economic changes, feeling that the elites are getting the upper hand, and losing its trust in institutions. A struggle between different parties becoming increasingly polarized and zero-sum. Institutions failing to resolve and mediate conflicts. An economic crisis further destabilizing institutions and eviscerating trust in them. A strongman claiming to stand for the people against the elites, and asking for the institutional checks to be relaxed so that he can serve the people better. Sound familiar?

The problem is that this describes not just one but many countries. It could be Turkey, where the strongman is Recep Tayyip Erdoğan, pitting himself against Turkey's secular elite and asking the conservative middle classes and rural voters to keep on supporting him as he peels away all institutional checks. It could be Hungary, where Viktor Orbán is doing the same, with an added dose of anti-immigrant rhetoric and action (even if the country is still constrained by the European Union's institutions). It could be the Philippines, where the strongman is Rodrigo Duterte, running murder squads against real and suspected drug dealers and users as he demonizes his opponents. It could be Marine Le Pen, who came close to an upset victory in the French presidential elections of 2017 with her masterful reframing of the conflict of the twenty-first century not as between left and right but between globalists and patriots.

Or it could be Donald J. Trump.

But it couldn't happen in the United States, could it? A country with a wonderful constitution that balances elite and non-elite power and creates layers of checks against overeager politicians. A political system that epitomizes the separation of powers. A society with a tradition of political mobilization and suspicion of autocrats. A cherished legal tradition, highly protective of the country's democracy and individual freedoms. A history of successfully overcoming previous challenges from the legacy of slavery to the domination of robber barons to the widespread discrimination against African Americans. A nation firmly lodged in the corridor that has been empowered by the Red Queen so many times.

And then again, it couldn't have happened in the Weimar Republic either, could it?

Chapter 14

INTO THE CORRIDOR

Black Man's Burden

Awakening on Friday morning, June 20, 1913, the South African Native
found himself, not actually a slave, but a pariah in the land of his birth.

So begins Sol Plaatje's book *Native Life in South Africa*. Plaatje was a black journalist, writer, and political activist, one of the founders in 1912 of the South African Native National Congress (SANNC), a social movement that turned into the African National Congress (ANC) a decade later. The SANNC formed in reaction to the 1910 Union of South Africa, which brought together the former British colonies of the Cape and Natal with the Dutch-speaking Boer (Afrikaner) Republics of the Orange Free State and Transvaal after the conclusion of the Boer Wars. In the Cape, political rights were determined on the basis of wealth or property, not race. But the Boer Republics had a white-only franchise. The Union had been precipitated by the triumph of the British Empire in the Second Boer War which lasted from 1899 to 1902. During the war the British had criticized the Afrikaners' harsh treatment of black Africans, creating hope that the postwar order might give black Africans more rights. So there was a window of opportunity for institutional change at war's end. Yet the newly formed Union of South Africa ended up adopting the harshest common denominator. The more liberal franchise of the Cape was not extended elsewhere, and was gradually eroded. Representation was eventually denied to all blacks.

The lack of political power had dire consequences. It allowed for the passage of the Native Land Act in 1913, which paved the way for blacks, or "natives," in Plaatje's words, to become "pariahs" in their own country. Plaatje used another striking phrase, "black man's burden," when he observed:

> "The black man's burden" includes the faithful performance of all the unskilled and least paying labour in South Africa, the payment of direct taxation to the various Municipalities . . . to develop and beautify the white quarters of the towns while the black quarters remain unattended . . . [and] taxes . . . for the maintenance of Government Schools from which native children are excluded.

But that's not how whites saw it. During the debate in the parliament of the Union of South Africa on the law, Mr. van der Werwe, member from Vredefort in the Orange Free State, noted approvingly that the "native would only be tolerated among the whites as a laborer," while Mr. Keyter from nearby Ficksburg argued that the Free State "had always treated the coloured people with the greatest consideration and the utmost justice" and the Native Land Act was a "just law" that "told the colored people plainly that the Orange Free State was a white man's country, and that they intended to keep it so." At this point the record of the proceedings reports "hear, hear" as members voiced their support for Mr. Keyter's interpretation of justice. To ensure the Free State remained white, the native was "not going to be able to buy land there or to hire land there, and that if he wanted to be there he must be in service." In support of the law another member, Mr. Grobler, chimed in arguing that "it was impossible to delay the solution of the Native problem." Plaatje remarks in a note reproduced in his book, "By a 'solution to the Native Problem,' 'Free' State farmers generally mean the re-establishment of slavery."

Plaatje traveled the country witnessing the implementation of the act and how it forced black landowners and tenants off their lands in 87 percent of South Africa, the portion that made up the "white man's country." The experience of Kgobadi, a black farmer who had previously been making an income of 100 pounds a year, is typical. On June 30, 1913, he was given a letter ordering him to "betake himself from the farm of the undersigned by sunset of the same day, failing which his stock would be seized and impounded, and himself handed over the authorities for trespassing on the farm." He was offered a position paying 30 shillings a month to avoid eviction. So the white farmer could use "the services of himself, his wife and his oxen" at a fraction of what he had earned. Kgobadi refused and was evicted, left to wander the roads with his family and dying stock, nowhere to go except to take another desultory offer or somehow find a way to one of the designated black "homelands," the areas to which the white government had confined Africans to live.

Why did the majority of whites want to disposses black Africans? Taking their land and stock was one reason. But they also wanted to secure an abundant supply of cheap black labor for white-operated farms and mines, if necessary by coercion, and preventing them from earning a living in agriculture was an essential step in this process. The Holloway Commission of 1932 acknowledged the situation at the beginning of the century, describing it thus:

> In the past difficulty was experienced in obtaining a sufficient supply of
> labour for the industries of the country . . . Not accustomed to anything
> more than his simple wants of tribal life [the black native] had really no
> incentive for work for more. The European Governments, wanting labour
> for their industries, decided to bring pressure to bear on the Native to
> force him to come out to work, and did this by imposing taxation.

Convened in 1909, just before the founding of the Union of South Africa, the Select Committee of Native Affairs of the Cape Colony underscored this intention in its deliberations, which include the following passage:

> **A. H. B. Stanford, Chief Magistrate of Transkei:** [Population pressure and competition for land are acute] and we are getting to the end of our tether in some parts . . .
>
> **W. P. Schreiner, member of Select Committee:** Of course, the natural economic result would be . . . that the surplus population would turn to handiwork and labor throughout South Africa; they would go abroad, so to speak?
>
> **Stanford:** They will have to develop other avocations besides agriculture.
>
> **Schreiner:** And make their living by honest toil somewhere?
>
> **Stanford:** That seems to me to be the only solution.
>
> **Schreiner:** And a very good solution too, is it not?

But this "very good solution" could only be implemented if the majority of the population were completely disenfranchised so that they could not object. That's what the Union of South Africa proceeded to do. The political disenfranchisement was followed by various legislations, like the Native Land Act, that forcefully created a low-wage labor force for white-owned businesses. Other measures included the "color bar" banning black South Africans from pretty much all skilled and professional occupations. Almost all educational expenditure was directed to whites as well, while, as Plaatje noted, blacks had to pay the taxes. Practically landless, stuck on the homelands, without education and without an opportunity to work in anything other than agriculture or mining, black labor was going to be abundant, easy to coerce, and cheap for white farmers and mine owners. The repression and overt discrimination against blacks only deepened as the National Party, dominated by Afrikaner interests, gained power and from 1948 onward institutionalized and extended what came to be known as apartheid.

South Africa was outside the corridor with the type of extractive institutions common to Despotic Leviathans. How can such a society move into the corridor? A serious challenge or an existential crisis is typically necessary for a change in the path of such a nation. But even such circumstances are not sufficient for a transition into the corridor. In this chapter we highlight three critical factors affecting whether and how a nation can make such a transition. These are the ability to form coalitions that support such a transition; the location of the current balance of power between state and society relative to the corridor; and the shape of the corridor, which affects how these two factors play out.

The Rainbow Coalition

In 1994 the apartheid regime collapsed and South Africa peacefully transitioned to democracy and moved into the corridor. This historic change was spearheaded by a massive mobilization of black South Africans, undeterred by systemic repression and led by the ANC. It was also founded on a new coalition, between the ANC, the black middle classes, and the white industrialists.

Agricultural and mining elites were the main beneficiaries of the political and economic arrangements keeping black wages low. White workers also benefited handsomely because arrangements such as the color bar and the desolate conditions of the educational system for blacks meant that whites could receive high wages in skilled and semiskilled occupations, anywhere between 5.5 and 11 times as much as blacks, who were practically barred from competing against them. The apartheid regime was never as good a deal for industrialists, however. While the color bar benefited white farmers, mine owners, and workers, it increased labor costs for industrialists, who could not employ the very cheap black labor in anything other than the most menial, unskilled occupations. Industrialists were also less worried than mine owners and farmers about their assets' being expropriated if the black majority gained political power, because taking over and operating a modern factory is much harder than grabbing farms or mines. There were social differences between elites of Afrikaner and British descent too. Apartheid as a social philosophy was a creation of Afrikaners, while industrialists were often English-speaking and less wedded to apartheid. Hence, they were the weak link in the apartheid coalition and a good target for a new coalition that could bring down the regime.

Coalitions seldom form by themselves. They need to be cemented by relationships, guarantees, and trust. It was no different for the coalition underpinning the transition to democracy in South Africa. A key instrument in forging a relationship between industrialists and ANC leaders (and black middle classes) was the program of Black Economic Empowerment (BEE). Although the notion was formulated in the government's 1994 Reconstruction and Development Programme, it was in fact the private sector that initiated the first wave of BEE projects. These involved the transfer of equity from a white company to a black person or black-run company. As early as 1993 the financial services company Sanlam sold 10 percent of its stake in Metropolitan Life to a black-owned consortium led by Nthato Motlana, a former secretary of the ANC's Youth League and one-time doctor to the ANC's leader and future president Nelson Mandela and Archbishop Desmond Tutu. After 1994 the number of such BEE deals began to grow rapidly, reaching 281 by 1998. By this time some estimates suggest that as much as 10 percent of the Johannesburg Stock Exchange (JSE) was owned by black businesses. The problem was that the black people who wanted to buy shares often could not afford to. Solution: the companies lent them the money to buy their own shares at massive discounts, usually 15 to 40 percent below market value.

In 1997 the ANC government appointed a BEE commission headed by Cyril Ramaphosa (who later became post-apartheid South Africa's fourth president). Beginning with the report of the BEE commission in 2001, the government moved to institutionalize asset transfers and also to greatly broaden the nature of BEE to encompass "elements of human resource development, employment equity, enterprise development, preferential procurement, as well as investment, ownership and control of enterprises and economic assets." The commission included a series of specific objectives that the South African economy should achieve within ten years. Among the most important goals were transferring at least 30 percent of productive land to blacks and collective organizations, increasing the black equity participation in the economy to 25 percent, and achieving 25 percent black ownership of JSE-listed shares. In addition, the commission specified a target of 40 percent of black nonexecutive and executive directors in JSE-listed companies, 50 percent of government procurements directed to black-owned companies, 30 percent of private sector procurements for black-owned companies, and 40 percent of black executives in the private sector. Guidelines also specified that 50 percent of the borrowers from public financial institutions should be black-owned companies, 30 percent of contracts and concessions made by the government should involve black companies, and 40 percent of government incentives to the private sector should go to black-owned companies.

The wake of the BEE commission's report also brought a series of industry charters in anticipation of forthcoming legislation. The first of these, the mining charter issued at the start of 2002, caused a huge stir. When a draft version of the charter committing the industry to 51 percent black ownership within ten years was leaked to the press, share prices on the JSE plummeted. The next six months saw a capital outflow of 1.5 billion rand (about US$250 million). The subsequent negotiations led to a charter wherein companies in the sector would be 15 percent black-owned in five years and 26 percent black-owned in ten years. The mining industry also agreed to raise 100 billion rand to finance these transfers. The culmination of the BEE process was the Broad-Based Black Economic Empowerment Act, signed into law by President Mbeki in January 2004. The act empowered the minister of trade and industry to issue codes of good practice with respect to BEE and enforce them. In essence, if a company wants to bid for a government contract or renew a license, it has to prove that it is BEE compliant. This gives the government huge leverage in some sectors, such as mining.

The South African social scientist Moeletsi Mbeki, brother of President Thabo Mbeki, described BEE as an unholy alliance:

> The South African political elite is being encouraged to pursue BEE by elements of the super rich who seek political favors from the state in order to (1) Externalize their assets by moving the primary listing of their corporations from the Johannesburg Stock Exchange to the London

Stock Exchange, (2) get the first bite of government contracts, and (3) buy seats at the high table of economic policy decisionmaking.

Unholy or not, this alliance was essential to secure South Africa's move into the corridor. It not only initiated close relationships between industrialists and segments of society previously left out of political power, it also provided guarantees to businesses that ANC leadership and the black middle classes, who now had a stake in the economy, would be much less interested in expropriating white-owned assets and wealth. The interim constitution adopted in 1993 reassured white South Africans by enshrining a bill of rights as well as various other checks that made it harder for the ANC to repress the white minority. Also important was the Truth and Reconciliation Commission, set up in 1995, which granted a broad amnesty to those guilty of crimes, including human rights abuses, in return for truthful testimonies and evidence that the acts were politically motivated. This was a signal that the re-empowered black majority under the ANC's leadership would not seek revenge against whites.

But relationships and guarantees are not enough unless there is trust between the partners in the coalition, and here symbolic gestures of compromise matter greatly. This is where Nelson Mandela's inspiring leadership played a critical role. One episode epitomizing Mandela's efforts took place on June 24, 1995, on the day of the first Rugby World Cup final in South Africa. The country's national team, the Springboks, was allowed to compete for the first time, after the end of the international boycott against the apartheid regime, and was facing the odds-on favorite, the New Zealand All Blacks. The Springbok rugby team was closely identified with apartheid, and its jersey was an Afrikaner symbol, much hated by the black population. How would the president of the new, post-apartheid South Africa perform his duties as head of state on this day? Brilliantly, as it turned out. Nelson Mandela added to his year-long efforts to remove the bitterness and distrust between the black majority and the white minority by turning up wearing the Springbok jersey with the number 6 of the captain, François Pienaar. The 63,000-strong audience, about 62,000 of them white, and mostly Afrikaners, were stunned. The Springboks, perhaps galvanized by Mandela's magnanimous gesture, beat the All Blacks against all odds with a drop goal in extra time. Pienaar, when asked what it felt like to have the strong support of 63,000 people, replied, "We didn't have the support of 63,000 South Africans today. We had the support of 42 million." When handing the cup to Pienaar (as shown in the photo insert), Mandela told him:

Thank you very much for what you have done for our country.

Pienaar replied, without missing a beat,

Mr. President, it's nothing compared to what you have done for our country.

Doorways into the Corridor

We have seen the role of the ANC-backed coalition in South Africa's transition into the corridor. The second critical factor is the position of a country relative to the corridor.

The only way of achieving durable liberty is to move into the corridor and forge the balance necessary for building a Shackled Leviathan. True liberty can flourish neither without a state nor under the yoke of a Despotic Leviathan. But there is no universal way of building a Shackled Leviathan, and no single doorway into the corridor. Every country's prospects are molded by its unique history, the types of coalitions and compromises that are possible, and the exact balance of power between state and society. For instance, feasible paths into the corridor are very different starting with an Absent, Despotic, or Paper Leviathan. Figure 6 illustrates this point.

Nations with a Despotic Leviathan can most easily enter the corridor by strengthening their societies (or fostering new ways of checking and weakening the power of their states), as the arrow labeled Path 1 in the figure indicates. This was the situation in South Africa, dominated by a powerful white economic elite and one of the most effective state institutions on the continent. So the problem in South Africa was one of mobilizing society and its ability to contest power, which the ANC and the black labor movement achieved.

This is not the problem confronting a society starting with an Absent Leviathan; strengthening society further and weakening the state would backfire. Instead, Path 2 in the figure traces one possible way of entering the corridor in this case, with an increase in the state's power.

Finally, countries and peoples near the very bottom left, which include many Paper Leviathans and those like the Tiv that have very limited state capacity and no institutionalized ways for society to exercise power, face an even taller order. They cannot enter the corridor by increasing the power of either the state or society separately, since there is no corridor nearby. To enter the corridor they must simultaneously increase the capacity of their states and societies as in Path 3. One

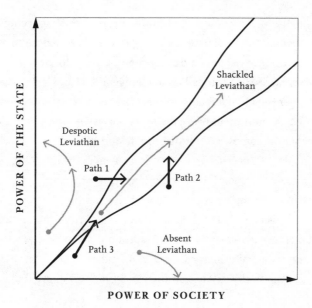

Figure 6. Doorways into the Corridor

way to do this, as we'll discuss below, is by exploiting the mobilization effect introduced in Chapter 11—by allowing society to get stronger in response to growing
state capacity, and vice versa.

We now discuss how these different paths work, what types of coalitions and
compromises are necessary to support a move into the corridor, and how doorways
to the corridor close when such coalitions cannot be formed.

Building on the Iron Cage

South Africa is an example of Path 1, where the main conflict was between society,
represented by the black majority of the country, and the white elite controlling
state institutions. The composition of the elite and the nature of their power can
be very different in other Despotic Leviathans, with major implications for the
type of coalition that needs to be constructed along Path 1. In early-twentieth-
century Japan, as in many other societies, the most powerful elements in the elite
were high-level bureaucrats and military officers, even if big business was a willing fellow traveler. Japan had taken a turn toward greater despotism, building its
own version of the "iron cage" during the early twentieth century, based on the
growing clout of the military, whose upper echelons were staunchly opposed to any
move away from elite-dominated politics. The control of the military, together with

the emperor and the bureaucratic cadres around him, over politics centering on the philosophy of *kokutai*, the "Japanese national essence," elevated these groups over society. This dominance deepened during the war years following the Japanese invasion of Manchuria. But things had to change after Japan's decisive defeat in World War II, after the United States dropped the atom bombs on Hiroshima and Nagasaki in 1945. Would there be a Japanese doorway into the corridor with the military-bureaucratic complex relinquishing its dominance?

There was a lot of uncertainty about this as General Douglas MacArthur, the supreme commander for the Allied powers, landed at the Atsugi Naval Air Base on August 30, 1945. MacArthur was optimistic that he could somehow transform Japan into a pro-U.S. democracy. By the time he arrived, MacArthur and his advisers had formed a vision of how to reform Japanese institutions and politics. In 1944 MacArthur's right-hand man and military secretary, Brigadier General Bonner F. Fellers, had written a document titled "Answer to Japan," which anticipated that

> only through complete military disaster and the resultant chaos can the Japanese people be disillusioned from their fanatical indoctrination that they are the superior people, destined to be the overlords of Asia. . . .
>
> To the masses will come the realization that the gangster militarists have betrayed their sacred Emperor. They have led the Son of Heaven, Divine Ruler of the Empire, to the very precipice of destruction. Those who deceive the Emperor cannot exist in Japan. When this moment of realization arrives, the conservative, tolerant element of Japan which has long been driven underground possibly may come into its own.
>
> An independent Japanese army responsible only to the Emperor is a permanent menace to peace.

So there was a need not just for Japan's complete defeat but also its total demilitarization. This is what the United States proceeded to implement. MacArthur personally convened a team of Americans to draft a constitution for Japan. Its Article 9 disbanded the Japanese military, declaring:

> War, as a sovereign right of the nation, and threat of use of force, is forever renounced as a means of settling disputes with other nations.
>
> The maintenance of land, sea, and air forces, as well as other war potential, will never be authorized. The right of belligerency of the state will not be recognized.

The next target was *kokutai*, viewed as the fountainhead of Japan's international aggression. But MacArthur and Fellers had decided that the Japanese could not govern themselves and needed an emperor. So they refrained from accusing Emperor Hirohito of war crimes. Nor did they attempt to dethrone him, instead simply demanding that the emperor renounce his claims to divinity. The emperor accepted. In his New Year's statement, issued on January 1, 1946, he included the following passage:

> The ties between me and my people have always been formed by mutual trust and affection. They do not depend upon mere legends or myths. Nor are they predicated on the false conception that the Emperor is divine, and that the Japanese are superior to other races and destined to rule the world.

Again rooted in the belief articulated in Fellers's "Answer to Japan" that the Japanese needed strong leaders, the United States was willing to work with high-ranking members of the military and the bureaucracy, including those who had leading roles in the Japanese war cabinet.

The career of Nobusuke Kishi, who more than anybody else was the architect of the postwar Japanese political system, is telling. Kishi rose as a bright bureaucrat with strong political views in the interwar years; he praised top-down economic management, including Taylorist methods of worker control, and maintained that the political and economic policies of Nazi Germany were the best path for Japan. He later allied himself even more strongly with high-ranking members of the military, calling for a "total war" to increase Japan's dominance in the region. Kishi's rise to prominence came with the Japanese invasion of Manchuria and the installation of the puppet regime of Manchukuo. The Manchukuo regime intended to ruthlessly exploit Manchuria's resources and jump-start a military-led industrialization there, and Kishi became its architect. He was involved in expropriating from private shareholders of the largest corporation in Asia at the time, the South Manchuria Railway, transferring their shares to the military occupying the area. In 1935, he was appointed deputy minister of industrial development of Manchukuo and organized its state-led economy, which heavily relied on the systematic coercion and exploitation of Chinese labor.

His star rose even higher in 1940 when he was appointed a minister in the Japanese government and allied himself with General, later Prime Minister, Hideki Tojo. He supported the war against Britain and the United States, and was one of the architects of the slave labor program to man Japanese factories and mines with Korean and Chinese workers during the war. After the Japanese defeat, he was arrested as a Class A war criminal, and spent three years in prison, but unlike Tojo and other fellow leaders of the Japanese war effort, he was not tried in the war crimes tribunal. (Tojo and several others were tried, convicted, and hanged.)

Kishi was released on Christmas Eve 1948 and jumped back into politics right away. He repeatedly undermined from the right the postwar prime minister of Japan, Shigeru Yoshida, himself no liberal. In part to get the upper hand over Yoshida, he formed the Liberal Democratic Party in 1955, which has since dominated Japanese politics. Kishi himself served as prime minister twice between 1957 and 1960. Many of his handpicked protégés, including Hayato Ikeda, played leading roles in Japanese politics and the economy, in particular in the industrial policies of Japan formulated in the Ministry of International Trade and Industry. Ikeda, for example, became the key architect of postwar Japanese industrialization and prime minister after Kishi. Kishi's influence on Japanese politics is felt not just through the continued dominance of the Liberal Democratic Party. His grandson Shinzo Abe is Japan's current prime minister.

Kishi, sometimes called "America's favorite war criminal," epitomizes the strategy that MacArthur and Fellers came up with to influence the path of Japanese institutions: co-opt the old bureaucratic elite. It worked. They firmed up a coalition consisting of the more liberal-minded parts of Japanese society and many of the captains of the older despotic Japanese state that acquiesced to a greater role for society and democratic politics (and to a more limited role for the military-bureaucratic complex). At times, this coalition undercut the power of trade unions and left-wing parties, but it did manage to move Japan into the corridor and keep it there for the next seventy years.

In the Japanese experience we see another path to a coalition, this time built on the same iron cage that supported the previous despotic regime, which nonetheless allows for greater societal mobilization in politics and makes a move into the corridor possible. Though in many cases morally ambiguous, this process helps create a balance and keeps the transition process sufficiently gradual to prevent it from spinning out of control. But of course it's neither easy to ensure (could it have happened in Japan without its complete defeat in the war?) nor a guarantee that a Shackled Leviathan will emerge, as we discuss next.

Black Turk, White Turk

In the early 2000s, Turkey had its own window of opportunity for moving into the corridor. It too started with a Despotic Leviathan dominated by the military and the bureaucracy. Turkey benefited from both the economy's strong rebound from its financial crisis in 2000–2001 following a series of major economic reforms and the impetus for political reform from the European Union (EU) accession process. For a while it looked like Turkey might be moving into the corridor. But the coalitions and compromises necessary for such a transition did not materialize.

The Republic of Turkey, though founded by repudiating much of the institutional inheritance of the Ottoman Empire, shows a lot of continuities from the earlier era. The roots of the Republic are in the reform efforts that began in the nineteenth century, first with sweeping fiscal and political reforms promulgated in the Rose Garden Edict of 1839 and later by the "Young Turks" and the powerful organization of (mostly) junior military officers, the Committee of Union and Progress (CUP). These reform movements, especially CUP, did not intend to fundamentally change the direction of the despotic Ottoman Leviathan. Their aim was to build up the capacity of the state in order to stop its decline. The reforms and the modernization that they brought were distinctly top-down. For example, when CUP officers catapulted to power in 1908 at the head of a parliament, now sharing power with the Ottoman monarch Sultan Abdülhamit II, they combined their modernization drive with robust repression against protesters, trade unions, and the nascent civil society that had emerged after 1839. Six years later CUP engineered the Ottoman Empire's entry into World War I via a secret treaty with Germany that two of their leaders negotiated the day after Russia's declaration of war against Germany.

The Turkish Republic, founded in 1923 after the victory of the forces led by Mustafa Kemal, later named Atatürk, "Father of Turks," followed CUP's playbook in many ways (and its leaders, including Atatürk, were former CUP members). The path was open for efforts to further reforms and state building, but always of the despotic sort, led by members of the military and the bureaucracy (business owners and others were only added as peripheral elements to the coalition). The seat of power was now Atatürk's Republican People's Party, known by its Turkish abbreviation, CHP. The CHP modernized the economy and society, but also built unchecked power and economic riches for its leaders and their allies. Even though some reforms it implemented, such as liberating and empowering women, modernizing the bureaucracy, and encouraging industrialization, were crucial steps in both building state capacity and introducing a modicum of liberty for many segments of society that had enjoyed none before, they were not meant to move Turkey into the corridor. Many of the reforms, including the Latin alphabet, the Western dress code, and the restructuring of religious institutions, were imposed forcefully on society without any consultation, and those resisting the reforms, for example insisting on wearing the fez rather than Western-style hats, were prosecuted and in some cases executed.

Although in the decades that followed, the CHP's monopoly of power, initially institutionalized by Atatürk in the one-party system, collapsed, the military and the bureaucracy remained disproportionately powerful. When the military perceived its grip loosening or society mobilizing, it intervened via coups in 1960, 1971, 1980, and 1997. The military and civilian governments, though often secular, were quite willing to use religion for societal control too, and did move in and out of coalitions with religious groups. In the aftermath of the 1980 military coup, the military junta and the subsequent center-right governments strengthened the role of religion in daily life and in schools as a counterweight to left-wing forces.

Emboldened by these social changes, the more conservative, religious, and poorer segments living in provincial cities or in less-well-off neighborhoods of major cities such as Istanbul started to feel disempowered and demanded greater recognition from the military and bureaucratic elites, whom they viewed as westernized and unrepresentative of their concerns. This situation formed the background for the rise of the Justice and Development Party, known by its Turkish abbreviation, AKP, led by Recep Tayyip Erdoğan. The AKP was next in a string of religious, conservative parties gaining popularity. It came to power in the elections of 2002 with a plurality (though far from a majority) of the vote. At the time of the party's victory at the polls, Erdoğan was barred from taking part in politics because, while mayor of Istanbul, he had recited a religious poem. He captured, and to some degree exploited, the mood among the party's base by stating in a rally:

> In this country there is a segregation of Black Turks and White Turks.
> Your brother Tayyip belongs to the Black Turks.

The "white Turks" were the Turkish elite, representing the military and bureaucratic cadres and the westernized big business allied with them, pitted against society. Though exaggerated and more than a little self-serving, this quote captured the perceived competition between bureaucratic and military elites and a significant portion of society. The rise of the AKP could thus have been an opportunity for power to shift away from the military and the bureaucracy, as it did in Japan after World War II, toward less represented, poorer segments of society. In the first few years of the 2000s, a move into the corridor looked possible as civil society flourished and Turkish democracy deepened with a series of political and economic reforms.

Then it all capsized. Several things that needed to go right for such a move into the corridor all went wrong. In Japan, U.S. tutelage and the repudiation of the old militarist regime made it easier for members of the powerful political elite to willingly join the new coalition and support a move into the corridor. Not so in Turkey. Though some of the liberal and leftist intelligentsia initially supported the AKP and its reforms, the military and bureaucratic establishment was hostile, so much so that in April 2007 the military threatened a coup against the AKP with a memorandum on its website, and the powerful Constitutional Court filed papers to close the party (the trigger was that the wife of the AKP's candidate for president wore a headscarf!). This almost exactly paralleled what happened to the previous religious party in power in 1997, when it was forced to resign by a military memorandum and then closed by the Constitutional Court. Though the AKP survived, this event was a watershed in the increasingly polarized, zero-sum relations between the party and the military-bureaucratic establishment.

Another important factor was the ambition of the AKP itself. In Japan, society was badly organized and far from mobilized in the years following World War II. The main threat that the business community and conservative elites feared was from the left of the political spectrum, but this was easily controlled by consolidating the right under the auspices of the Liberal Democratic Party. In Turkey, the AKP was already powerful enough to win the election in 2002 and kept getting stronger. The collapse of two other center-right parties, implicated in the mismanagement and endemic corruption of the 1990s, suddenly made the AKP dominant at the polls, granting it much greater political power than even its founders could have dreamed of. So the cards swiftly became stacked against a balance of power in Turkey.

The shepherding role that General MacArthur and American forces played in Japan was at first partially filled by the EU accession process, motivating reforms to improve human and civil rights, including Kurdish rights, and constitutional reforms to rein in the overweening power of the military in civilian affairs. Initially, the prodding of the EU was greatly welcomed by the AKP leadership because it was pushing for reduced military tutelage in politics and was arguably one of the reasons why the 2007 military memorandum failed to bring down the government. But the EU accession process soon slowed down and then totally collapsed, removing a powerful anchor tying the AKP to the process of institutional reform.

Turkey went from one phase of despotic state control to another. After 2007, the AKP hardened its stance and began to take complete control of different levers of power in the country. Critical in this process was the alliance between the AKP leadership and the clandestine organization of the Muslim cleric Fethullah Gülen, which had taken root in Turkey's security forces, bureaucracy, judiciary, and educational system. Early on, the AKP, suspicious of bureaucrats with secularist sympathies, wanted to appoint people more in line with its own conservative preferences and priorities, but did not have access to cadres with enough expertise. It turned to the Gülen movement, which, thanks to its organization in many high schools and universities, had more qualified members. With the Gülen movement thus empowered, its covert expansion in state institutions intensified. After 2007, the AKP and Gülenists started a systematic purge of people they viewed as hostile to the party, employing sham trials based on manufactured evidence. During this time, the government started cracking down on various critical media outlets and independent societal organizations that had began to flourish thanks to the greater freedoms of the 2000s.

By 2011, Turkey topped the list of countries locking up journalists. In May 2013, protests erupted in Gezi Park, near Istanbul's Taksim Square, first in reaction to plans to build a new shopping mall in one of the few remaining green areas of the metropolis. Soon the protests came to focus on issues of freedom of belief, expression, and the media, the erosion of secularism in Turkish society, and corruption. They quickly spread to all major cities. The government's response was to crack down on protesters. The peace process that the AKP had initiated with Kurdish insurgents in the southeast of the country was reversed and freedoms were further curbed. In the meantime, Erdoğan and Gülen, erstwhile allies when sidelining secularists and leftists, turned against each other, probably as part of a power struggle. This process culminated in an unsuccessful coup attempt in July 2016 that appears to have been masterminded by officers in the military secretly aligned with Gülen. After this failed coup attempt, Erdoğan and his allies declared martial law and started purging Gülenists from the security forces, judiciary, and bureaucracy. More than 130,000 people have been fired from the public sector and more than 50,000 have been arrested, in many cases with only circumstantial evidence. In several cases, campaigners for Kurdish rights, critics of the government, and leftists, including some who spent their careers exposing the Gülen movement's machinations, have been arrested as Gülenists. Limits on the media and free speech hardened during this process. Erdoğan proceeded to introduce an executive presidency with few checks. This narrowly became law through a 2017 referendum under martial law while no mainstream media outlets could campaign against the constitutional change. Turkey still tops the list of countries jailing the highest number of journalists, but now also holds in jail several elected politicians, including the co-heads of the pro-Kurdish party in parliament.

Turkey missed its opportunity to move into the corridor.

Turkey's missed opportunity is telling about what we should expect from China, another celebrated example of despotic state control led by a bureaucratic elite in the form of its Communist Party. Our discussion of Japan underscores the importance of forming a coalition including elements of this bureaucratic elite in order to secure a move into the corridor. In the Chinese case, the strong imbalance between state and society is not the only factor making such a transition very difficult; the absence of any group within the Chinese Communist elite willing to join a coalition moving away from the Despotic Leviathan further stacks the cards against it. In fact, the unity of the Communist Party makes it unlikely for individuals who join such a coalition to remain powerful, as Zhao Ziyang, the general secretary of the Communist Party in 1989, discovered when he lent his support to the Tiananmen Square protests. He was swiftly stripped of power and put under house arrest, where he remained until his death, and witnessed his entire public record being expunged. Starting under the yoke of a Despotic Leviathan, coalitions to move into the corridor are not easy to build.

The situation is different under Absent and Paper Leviathans. Because the state is weak, it cannot completely clamp down on society's developing new organizations and capabilities, even if this is no simple matter under a weak state doing its best to avoid the mobilization effect. Conversely, the mobilization effect also creates room for such Leviathans to gain capacity, even as society is getting stronger and more assertive. So the path to the corridor is not completely closed.

What's more, society and various civil organizations, including local governments, can sometimes build both state capacity and societal mobilization at the local level. This is potentially transformative for citizens because many of the public services and law enforcement functions under the auspices of an Absent or Paper Leviathan are dependent on what's being done at the local level (since not much is provided by the national government). Local societal engagement may also be less threatening to national political elites, and might create a window of opportunity for an improvised balance of power between state and society. In addition, there may be room for local experimentation, meaning the possibility of trying different approaches to increasing state capacity and improving the quality of public services. But even more important than this type of experimentation that is sometimes emphasized in public discussions may be political experimentation, which would involve attempts to build new coalitions in support of expanding state capacity while at the same time involving society at the local level. Successful local political experiments may even provide blueprints for subsequent national changes. We next illustrate these dynamics with two successful episodes of local state building, one approximating Path 2 and the other Path 3 in Figure 6.

A Viagra Spring

We saw in Chapter 1 how Robert Kaplan epitomized his bleak predictions for the coming anarchy around the world with the complete breakdown of law and order in Lagos. Wole Soyinka's journey in 1994 seemed to confirm Kaplan's worst fears. But a mere twenty years later Lagos looks completely different. It took Path 2 toward the corridor, even if it still has a long way to go. How?

The 1990s were a tough time for autocrats in Africa. With the Cold War over, to hang on to power you had to reinvent yourself as a democrat (or at least as a faux democrat), hold elections, wear a suit, and not be quite so obvious about repressing your opponents. Nigerian military dictator General Sani Abacha, whom we encountered in Chapter 1, died on June 7, 1998, possibly of an overdose of Viagra consumed in anticipation of a sexual liaison with two Indian prostitutes. Soon his wife was attempting to flee the country. When stopped at Kano International Airport, she was found to have slightly exceeded her baggage allowance; she had checked in thirty-eight suitcases, all of which turned out to be packed with cash. The Nigerian military decided they didn't have it in them anymore. In 1999 they gave up power and Olusegun Obasanjo was democratically elected president. It was a Viagra spring.

Back in Lagos there was an election too, and a man called Bola Ahmed Tinubu was elected governor of Lagos state. On assuming office, he did something unexpected: instead of appointing political allies to important positions, he gave the jobs to qualified people. A respected law professor became the attorney general, while a Citibank executive was given the job of commissioner for economic planning and budget. Lagos faced a lot of problems, not just the mounting piles of trash. For one thing it was broke, and its meager share of resources from the national oil money were unreliably distributed by the federal government. Tinubu inherited a tax authority with 1,400 personnel, but only thirteen who were professional accountants and six who were chartered tax practitioners. Most of the others were political appointees. Even if Nigerians prefer cassava or yam to gnocchi, the hiring process was similar to how "gnocchi" swarmed into Argentina's bureaucracy. In 1976, during a previous military government in Nigeria, a new constitution had to be drafted. The drafting committee had to grapple with how to define "power." In the end it decided that power was

> the opportunity to acquire riches and prestige, to be in a position to hand out benefits in the form of jobs, contracts, gifts of money etc. to relations and political allies.

In other words, even the drafting committee of the Nigerian Constitution attested that power is all about the ability to create gnocchi!

Tinubu had a different idea of what to do in Lagos. He wanted to deal with the trash and many of the other problems of the city, but he faced a classic catch-22. He couldn't do anything without tax revenues, and the nature of the state he had inherited made it impossible to collect taxes. His solution was to introduce electronic tax payment. People had to pay taxes electronically rather than in cash to tax collectors. He thought this would reduce the scope for corruption. Then he put a private company in charge of the tax payment system. In exchange for developing a database of potential taxpayers and collecting the taxes, they got to keep a share. This outsourcing strategy was used in other fields too. In 2001 the state hired private auditors to audit companies in exchange for a commission on liabilities. It also encouraged citizens to pay their taxes (as shown by the banner depicted in the photo insert).

The result was an increase in much-needed tax revenues. With these in hand, Tinubu and his chief of staff, Babatunde Raji Fashola, who became governor after him, began to rebuild the bureaucracy. In 2003 they started a semiautonomous revenue agency, Lagos State Internal Revenue Service (LIRS), that hired competent, well-trained people. State tax revenues, mostly from personal income taxes, rocketed from around US$190 million in 1999, raised from just 500,000 taxpayers, to US$1.2 billion in 2011, levied on nearly 4 million taxpayers.

The expansion of the fiscal resource base began to fund all sorts of things, one of which was an effort to register all residents through the Lagos State Residents Registration Agency. Another was a sustained attack on the trash, with thousands of new trash collectors. The number of refuse transport vehicles went from 63 in 2005 to 763 in 2009 and then to over 1,000 in 2012. Lagos became a clean city. It also became a lot safer, especially under Fashola when the area boys, who had been terrorizing and robbing the city's inhabitants, were largely eliminated. Every aspect of society became better regulated. Motorcycle taxis, which were involved in almost half of all traffic accidents, were banned from large parts of the city and Lagos state. In 1999 there were 529 fatal motor traffic accidents and 1,543 serious ones. By 2012, despite a significant increase in the number of vehicles in the city, these had fallen to 116 and 240, respectively. New infrastructure sprang up everywhere, including a light railway to ease commuting. In 1999 there were no new streetlights installed. Maybe there wasn't much point when there was no electricity to operate them. By 2012 the city had electricity and 1,217 new lights.

Improved public services and lower crime had dramatic effects on economic livelihoods. Between 2004 and 2010, the fraction of the population in poverty fell from 57 percent to 23 percent (at the same time poverty levels increased in almost half of Nigeria's 36 states).

So Tinubu transformed Lagos by expanding the capacity of the local state. But this would not have been possible without society's cooperation. Tinubu's mother was the head of the Lagos market traders' association. After she died in 2013, she was replaced by Tinubu's daughter. Since Lagos had a massive informal sector, the market traders association was a valuable political resource. It was also a huge political constraint because its opposition could have sunk the entire project. Cooperation and contestation with the association is evident in tax policy. The traders were one of the key potential revenue bases, but they were very hard to monitor. Lagos state negotiated tax rates with the association, which then took on the job of providing information on which traders used which markets and recording who had paid. In exchange the state promised public services and security for the markets. Organizations of informal bus drivers, artisans, and others entered into similar agreements. The formal sector has also been active in making demands within the institutional structure. In 2000 the Manufacturers Association and the Eko Hotel sued the Tinubu government over the introduction of a sales tax, and in 2003 the government had to cut the rate of property taxes due to opposition. More broadly, the contestation of power by society meant that Tinubu and Fashola had to refashion a social contract based on the notion that if people paid taxes and obeyed the rules and regulations, they could expect the state to perform. This contract was cemented by many channels of information, complaints, and accountability. Fashola even gave out his personal telephone number, encouraging people to send him SMS messages. Lagos solved the Gilgamesh problem and enabled greater state capacity, not via some complex institutional architecture, but through an active society monitoring the state.

Lagos shows why Robert Kaplan's prediction of coming anarchy isn't right everywhere. Obviously it is not heading toward a digital dictatorship. History hasn't ended in Lagos either. All the same, the city shows that even starting from desperate situations a move toward the corridor is possible. The Roman soldier and scholar Pliny the Elder remarked, "There is always something new out of Africa." He was right. Today there is much local experimentation out of Africa, for people are finding a way to improve their crumbling state capacity and liberty. A huge mass of people still live in poverty in Lagos, and compared to those of us residing in the United States, their lives are short. However, they are a lot less short than they were in 1999 and there are far fewer poor people. Life for most of them is also quite a bit less brutish and nasty than it was in 1999. Governors Tinubu and Fashola started to build a Lagos-style local Shackled Leviathan, with many of the benefits we would expect.

Taking the Orangutan out of the Tuxedo

Lagos had a hard time in the 1980s and 1990s, and so did Bogotá, the capital of Colombia. We already saw the interlocking mechanisms that sustain the Colombian Paper Leviathan in Chapter 11. Virgilio Barco, who was mayor of Bogotá in the 1960s and became Colombia's president in 1986, bemoaned that "of that booming city that I governed, today all that is left is an urbanized anarchy, tremendous chaos, immense disorder, a colossal mess." Barco had become mayor during Colombia's "National Front" agreement, which divided power for sixteen years between the Liberal and Conservative parties. There were elections, but the results were decided in advance. Parties even took turns at the presidency. In many ways Barco epitomized the "organutan in the tuxedo." In the words of another former president, Alberto Lleras, "In Bogotá he was a technocrat, but in Cúcuta he was a manzanillo." *Manzanillo* is another word Google doesn't translate. An apt translation would be a person who hands out wine at the bullfight. Free wine wins votes, all part of what the orangutan does. Barco had studied at MIT and knew how to wear a tuxedo. But out in the provinces, in Cúcuta, he knew how to be a manzanillo.

In the 1980s, as Marxist guerrillas and drug cartels flourished, Colombia gained a reputation as the world's kidnapping and homicide capital. Political elites became a little edgy and society mobilized and got involved in politics. A little democracy came out of this process, and in 1988 mayors were popularly elected for the first time. Bogotanos chose Andrés Pastrana, a traditional politician from the Conservative Party, later Colombia's president. But the elections didn't immediately solve Bogotá's mess, because all the vested interests benefiting from the mess remained powerful. The abuse of state employment and contracts was particularly common in Bogotá's legislative council. The council had joint executive authority with the mayor, so councillors could directly hand out contracts to their friends and supporters. Councillors even sat on the boards of publicly owned companies, which meant more gnocchi and more corruption. The deplorable state of the bureaucracy and its attitude toward the public wasn't much different from the one in Argentina. In Bogotá, the main administrative building was known colloquially as "the humiliator."

In 1989 and 1990 things in Colombia got even worse. Three presidential candidates were assassinated. The incoming president, César Gaviria, under pressure to do something, backed a far more radical reconfiguration of Colombian institutions by promoting a constitutional convention. Almost a third of the convention was made up of members of the demobilized guerrilla group M-19. The new constitution, which was adopted in 1991, had several innovations, but one was particularly important for Bogotá. One of the delegates, Jaime Castro, persuaded the convention to include a clause that required the next mayor of Bogotá, soon to be Castro himself, to draft a law restructuring the city's administration. Critically, once written, the law could be implemented by presidential decree, without the city legislature having a veto over it. Castro was elected in 1992 and the new law turned the mayor into the supreme executive officer of the city. Councillors couldn't hand out jobs and contracts anymore, and they couldn't sit on the boards of public companies. They were weakened by a decentralization of the city's administration to twenty "localities" with elected "local mayors." Castro thus managed to circumvent the traditional political machines. The law also closed tax loopholes. The immediate effect was to turn Bogotá's finances around. Tax revenues increased by 77 percent between 1993 and 1994.

Castro worked from the top, but his reforms generated the mobilization effect and a version of Path 3 in Figure 6 as society reacted and organized. A complete political outsider, Antanas Mockus, was elected mayor in 1994. Mockus was a mathematics and philosophy professor from the National University of Colombia. He reached the critical realization that it was possible to simultaneously build state capacity and get society involved in politics—the mobilization effect again!

This meant changing how people thought about the rules, the law, and the state so that they could get involved and push for greater state capacity and its deployment in a way that would be useful for them. Liliana Caballero, his chief of staff, described their philosophy as

> to not have the citizens go around the state asking for a favor, asking for their rights, but rather the administration going around the citizen that should be at the center.

Mockus's focus on changing people's attitude led to many creative measures. He wore a superman outfit and called himself "Supercitizen" (as we show in the photo insert). He pinned a toad made of fabric on his lapel to encourage people to be *sapos*, or toads. A common expression in Colombia is *No sea sapo*, don't be a toad. This powerful norm means "Mind your own business, if you see something wrong happening, stay out of it." Mockus instead said it was people's duty as citizens to be sapos. He hired first 20 and then an additional 400 mime artists to walk the streets of Bogotá and make fun of people who crossed the street on a red light, threw litter on the floor, or broke the rules. He handed out 350,000 thumbs-up and thumbs-down cards for people to approve or disapprove others' behavior on the street. Traffic fatalities fell from 1,300 to 600 a year during his time in office. He used all sorts of strategies to help people recover public spaces. One of his initiatives was "Night for Women," in which he asked men to stay home for four hours so that only women were on the street, watched over by 1,500 women police officers. It was a huge success in empowering women.

In all of this, Mockus's idea was to harness the mobilization effect—mobilize society to make the state work better, deliver more, deliver right. The average time required to pay a bill declined from an hour and a half to five minutes. The "humiliator" was no more. When there were too many gnocchi to deal with, Mockus privatized public companies. However, when he privatized the electricity company, he kept 49 percent of the shares for the city. When a private company returned it to profitability, the city started acquiring resources to spend on public services. Tax revenues tripled during his administration. Between 1993 and 2003 the fraction of households with piped drinking water rose from 79 to 100 percent. The proportion with access to sewage went from 71 to 95 percent. Not surprisingly, Bogotanos were most worried about violence. That also fell. People started reclaiming the streets, and the homicide rate went down from 80 per 100,000 to 22 per 100,000 by the time Mockus's tenure was over.

Mockus still had to fight against the councillors who wanted jobs and contracts, but he had a strategy. He later recalled that if someone started asking for special favors, he would look at the person "as if he had vomited . . . I used just body language [as if] I was wondering how to collect back his vomit from the carpet." When a senator wrote to him on his personal letterhead asking for favors, Mockus penned a reply: "Senator, someone has been using your personal letterhead."

There is still a long way to go in Bogotá; as we saw in Chapter 11, all the benefits that Castro and Mockus created didn't stop Samuel Moreno from looting the city (in part because society's mobilization in Bogotá was only partial and because Moreno was able to exploit the trust in local institutions that Mockus had built). But Mockus experimented with something new and managed to forge a coalition directly with the citizens, ushering in a potent mobilization effect. He called this Cultura Ciudadana, "civic culture," a strategy for prying the orangutan out of the tuxedo. As in Lagos it started at the local level.

We have now seen how the different doorways into the corridor depend on the initial balance of power between state and society. Starting with a Despotic Leviathan, we need an increase in society's power (and loosening of the grip of the economic elite or the military-bureaucratic complex). Starting with the Absent Leviathan, we need the capacity of the state to increase. Starting with a Paper Leviathan or a situation where the corridor is absent, we need the state and society to simultaneously increase their powers.

We have stressed that regardless of where doorways are located, it is not easy to move into the corridor. It requires a broad coalition, often a new coalition, to support such a move, and it necessitates a balance of power within that coalition, lest one group sideline the others to establish its own despotic control. It depends on compromise so that the contests for power do not become completely polarized and zero-sum. It depends too on the shape of the corridor, in particular, on how wide or narrow it is. We next discuss factors affecting the shape of the corridor and what these imply for the future of Shackled Leviathans and democracy.

The Shape of the Corridor

In South Africa, just as important as Nelson Mandela's charismatic and farsighted leadership was the fact that economic conditions and thus the shape of the corridor were very different in the 1990s from how they were at the beginning of the century. In the previous chapter, we saw how the width of the corridor affects the likelihood that a country in the corridor will stay there. It's no different for a country trying to move into the corridor. Comparing the two panels of Figure 5 from the previous chapter underscores how the same increase in society's power (say, because the ANC has improved the organization of the black majority) may fall short of moving a country into the corridor when the corridor is narrow (in Panel A), but take it right into the corridor when it is wider (in Panel B). South Africa's corridor was wider in the 1990s, improving its prospects for a transition into it.

Many factors impact the shape of the corridor. One that is related to our discussion of powerful landed interests in the previous chapter is labor coercion. Coercive labor relations impact the width of the corridor because they affect how the political power of the state and elites can be used; because they alter the benefits of this type of despotic power; and also because they influence how society is organized. Let us take each one of these three interrelated effects in turn.

First, labor coercion, whether it takes the form of slavery or serfdom or economic coercion via redistribution of land, regulations, or employer threats as in South Africa, creates a deeper hierarchy in society where the elites doing the coercing are significantly empowered at the expense of the coerced. This hierarchy means that, for any given configuration of the powers of state and society, securing an enduring balance between them is harder. As a result, the same combination of the powers of state and society that is safely in the corridor without labor coercion may be outside when labor is coerced and the might of the state is targeted at repressing and forcing the majority into low-wage economic activities. The consequence is a narrower corridor.

Second, economic activities that rely on labor coercion encourage the elites to act in unison and use the power of the state to defend and cement the existing economic system at all cost. If their dominance over society can be increased, this will allow them to intensify labor coercion as they did in South Africa after 1910. This too corresponds to a narrower corridor in our framework—starting from the same configuration of power of state and society, the presence of labor coercion weighs the scales in favor of the despotic dominance of the state and the elites, and thus makes it harder to support a Shackled Leviathan.

While these two mechanisms strengthen the reach of despotism, a third channel alters how society organizes and contests power. Labor coercion erodes society's ability to organize and solve its collective action problems. Coercion erodes both because it prevents collective action and because it blocks organizations such as trade unions from formulating effective political and economic demands. With a poorly organized society, despotism becomes harder to resist and the corridor narrows on the other, Absent Leviathan, side as well. Recall that entry into the corridor starting with a weak or absent state crucially depends on society's ability to institutionalize its power so that it can organize and continue to exert control over the state and elites after the process of state building begins. But under the yoke of labor coercion, such institutionalization becomes harder because different segments of society are not able to organize and act collectively. As a result, just as in our discussion of the Tiv in Chapter 1, the slippery slope is more acutely felt, and it becomes harder to get the process of state building off the ground and the corridor becomes narrower on both sides, making it harder for polities to move into it and stay in it once they are there.

We see all of these factors in South Africa's early and recent history. The co-ercion of black labor was particularly widespread in South African agriculture and mining, which had become vitally important after the discovery of gold in Trans-vaal in 1886. The desire of white farmers and mine owners to have access to, and coercively employ, cheap black labor was a critical factor in their embrace of insti-tutional changes completely disenfranchising blacks, expropriating their lands, and establishing the repressive apartheid regime. Any attempt during the early history of the Union of South Africa to expand the land allocated to blacks or ease the color bar was strenuously resisted by white farmers and mine owners intent on benefiting from cheap black labor, whatever the social consequences and human toll. In part as a result of coercive employment relations in agriculture and mining, blacks lacked the organization to resist these despotic institutional changes, even if uprisings erupted from time to time.

The situation in the 1980s and 1990s was rather different. By the 1990s, though gold and diamonds still played an important role, South Africa had an industrial economy. Many industrialists were happy to see the end of the color bar, and they also believed that their assets would be secure under a more representative, democratic regime, especially if they could bring powerful black leaders to their side (which Black Economic Empowerment managed to do). South Africa in the 1990s was very different from the country that labor coercion had created during the early history of the Union. And of course, the toll that international sanctions imposed on the apart-heid regime was an additional inducement to South African business to shed its overtly repressive and discriminatory institutions. Industrialists were now ready to splinter from the apartheid coalition, which is what the ANC managed to achieve.

Equally important for the widening of the South African corridor were the more assertive and organized demands of its black citizens, many of whom were now employed in manufacturing and had organized into trade unions. Even before black unions were formally recognized, they played a vital role in conjunction with the ANC in organizing black workers and formulating economic and political demands. After the Soweto uprising in 1976, which was a response to the imposition of Afrikaans language education in schools, black trade unions were formally recognized and began exerting pressure on the apartheid regime.

The impact of labor coercion on the shape of the corridor helps us understand not just the South African experience, but also the divergent trajectories of Costa Rica and Guatemala discussed in Chapter 9. The absence of coercion in smallholder coffee production in Costa Rica, compared to the heavy labor coercion in large coffee fincas in Guatemala, likely widened Costa Rica's corridor and facilitated the subsequent evolution of its Shackled Leviathan, while making it even less likely for Guatemala to later move to its narrowed corridor.

Labor coercion and its implications for the shape of the corridor also explain the different trajectories of South Africa and Zimbabwe, formerly Rhodesia, another exploitative white-minority regime. There are many parallels between Rhodesia and South Africa, not least the massive misallocation of land for the benefit of the white minority and how blacks were forced to supply their unskilled labor to white-owned farms and mines for a pittance. Both countries had powerful armed organizations trying to undermine their repressive regimes and hard-liners on the regime side unwilling to compromise. But South Africa had the industrialists as well as the mine owners and farmers, whereas Rhodesia for the most part had only mines and farms. There were few cracks in Rhodesia's white minority, and the end of the regime came only after a protracted and violent struggle. When the regime finally collapsed, there was little to sustain the balance of power necessary to create a movement into the corridor. The Rhodesian regime headed by one of the leaders of the independence struggle, Robert Mugabe, and his cronies in the Zimbabwe African National Union-Patriotic Front (ZANU PF) became despotic, unchecked, and unbalanced. The consequences, predictably, were disastrous for the people and economy of the newly formed country of Zimbabwe.

In Zimbabwe, there was no Mandela and no BEE to cement the coalition that enabled what Archbishop Desmond Tutu dubbed the "rainbow nation." This was partly because Zimbabwe, with its narrower corridor, did not possess the economic foundations of the rainbow nation.

Shackled Leviathans are just much harder to create in some conditions. When the conditions for their emergence are ripe, then the type of coalition forged by Mandela's leadership and of the BEE becomes critical. This was clearly recognized by South African industrialists. The executive director of the South African Petroleum Association, a white business group, pointed out:

> To avoid following Zimbabwe down the slippery slope to economic ruin, all South Africans and business people in particular, must take black economic empowerment seriously.

And so they did.

A Different World?

Although the end of history is not near and all nations will not converge to the same type of state-society relations, the last four decades have witnessed some notable changes in political institutions around the world. Take one reasonably well-measured aspect of institutions, whether a country has an electoral democracy where candidates are free to compete and campaign and citizens are free to vote. By one measure, the number of countries that are electoral democracies has increased from a handful at the end of the nineteenth century, to 40 in the 1970s, to 120 in 2010 (even if the 2010s have not been a good decade for democracy). Although electoral democracies are not necessarily in the corridor (as our discussion of India and Latin America underscores) and many nations that historically entered the corridor, such as many in Europe during the Middle Ages, were far from being democratic, there is an elective affinity between democratic regimes and Shackled Leviathans. So this trend signals the presence of many more countries entering or attempting to enter the corridor. Why?

Our framework suggests that changes in the shape of the corridor are a major factor. In commenting on Stanley Engerman and Robert Fogel's influential book *Time on the Cross*, about American slavery, often called by nineteenth-century American historians the "peculiar institution," the famous historian of the ancient world Moses Finley quipped:

> In the context of universal history, free labor, wage labor is the peculiar institution.

From the massive slave economies of ancient Egypt to serfdom in Europe, to modern slavery in the New World and various types of forced labor in other colonies, including those in Africa, labor coercion has played a fundamental role in most civilizations. Coercive practices directed at workers were not uncommon in the early stages of industrialization, and disappeared in Britain only after the 1889 repeal of various Masters and Servants Acts. But large-scale labor coercion has gradually withered away in most economies over the last half century except in a few dystopian corners of the world, such as North Korea and, until recently, Uzbekistan and Nepal. A major driver of this trend, as in South Africa, has been the expansion of industry, where labor coercion has always been less widespread than in agriculture and mining. This is largely because, as we have already emphasized, manufacturing makes coercion less profitable and feasible, both because the more complex production structure reduces the returns from relying on coercion and because the greater opportunities for workers to organize collectively in factories make coercion more costly to maintain. (Another cause of the decline of labor coercion is the Red Queen effect, once society enters the corridor; we saw, for example, in Chapter 6 that coercive feudal labor relations disappeared, albeit slowly, as several European nations moved along in the corridor.) The result is a wider corridor, creating greater room for transitions into the corridor, democracy, and liberty.

The decline of labor coercion is not the only factor transforming the corridor. Another important economic trend, but with more complex, multifaceted implications for liberty, is globalization.

The Corridor Globalization Makes

The economic logic of globalization leads to specialization. As international connections deepen, some countries will increase their manufacturing output and exports, while others will specialize in agriculture and mining. What does that imply about the shape of the corridor?

For countries specializing in agriculture, the corridor may get narrower. Even if landowners in the twenty-first century are not overtly repressive, agriculture will be less favorable toward societal mobilization for the reasons we have already discussed. Workers will be less well organized and thus less capable of contesting power in a heavily agricultural economy. Collective action may be harder to organize in agriculture for other reasons too. For example, coordinating civil society organizations, protests, and even political parties is easier in urban areas.

Conversely, specialization in manufacturing, as well as services and high-tech activities, will make the corridor wider and improve the prospects for a Shackled Leviathan. One case that illustrates this possibility is South Korea. The country started as a market-friendly but increasingly autocratic regime under the presidency of Syngman Rhee after its separation from North Korea along the 38th parallel in 1948. The existential threat from the Communist North and U.S. support led to a series of reforms, particularly radical land redistribution, and subsequently to a powerful drive toward industrialization. The focus on industrialization intensified after General Park Chung-hee came to power, initially in a coup in 1961 and subsequently in elections until 1972, when he declared martial law. International trade and manufacturing exports played a pivotal role in South Korea's economic development during this period. Growth was driven mainly by government planning in cooperation with large industrial conglomerates called *chaebol*, which include some famous names like Samsung and Hyundai, and there were also significant investments in education, partly to meet the demands of Korean industry. But this development took place in a context where, in spite of systematic repression, the civil society that had flourished in the 1950s was still active and trade unions had already become organized in the course of the industrialization process. These changes prepared the grounds for mass protests against the military regime in the 1970s. Opposition culminated in the withdrawal of the military regime, and democratic elections in 1987. The loss of support that the military government suffered both at home and abroad when it violently cracked down on student protesters and trade unions was critical for this transition. The whole process was encouraged because repression is much more disruptive and costly in an industrializing economy than one relying on agriculture or natural resources. Thus, in the South Korean case, specialization in manufacturing, brought about by economic globalization, made the corridor wider and drove the country into it.

Critically, however, the effects of economic specialization depend on the existing balance between state and society. This is evident when we compare South Korea to China, which has experienced even more rapid industrialization fueled by globalization. Nevertheless, given its much weaker society and more despotic government, these changes have not generated any durable movement toward the corridor. Even if the corridor becomes wider, countries too far from it will not easily move into it.

So we see that economic globalization is a mixed bag. Some countries will tend to specialize in natural resources or agricultural products where various coercive practices are still feasible and social mobilization is harder; this will tend to make the corridor narrower. Counteracting this, globalization will also induce other countries to specialize in manufacturing, in services, and even in some cases in high-tech activities, which can facilitate a movement into the corridor. Globalization and the economic and social changes it brings can also facilitate the exchange of ideas, sometimes fueling further social mobilization and new aspirations. When it comes to the effects of economic globalization, the devil is in the details too.

―――――――

Economic globalization is not the only factor changing the patterns of specialization. Most countries move people out of agriculture into manufacturing and services once they manage to achieve some degree of economic growth (partly because demand for manufacturing and services expands more rapidly than demand for agricultural produce as consumers become richer). In addition, new and more efficient technologies introduced in more-developed economies spread to the rest of the world and generate another boost to manufacturing. These secular trends, even if slow and uneven across countries, tend to shift the balance away from agricultural production and natural resources and help widen the corridor, with or without globalization.

The shape of the corridor doesn't just depend on economic factors. International relations also impact the corridor and the prospects for liberty. But like globalization, they have mixed effects, on the one hand pushing toward a wider corridor, and on the other, helping despots. We end this chapter with a discussion of these international factors.

We Are All Hobbesians Now

King Leopold II of Belgium emerged as the real winner from the Berlin Conference of 1884, where the African continent was partitioned among European powers. Leopold convinced the participants in the conference, and other heads of state including U.S. president Chester Arthur, that he was going to control the huge area of the Congo basin under the auspices of the independent "Congo Free State" for humanitarian and philanthropic work. In reality this state was anything but free, and certainly had nothing to do with humanitarian objectives. Leopold ran the state as his personal property and ruthlessly exploited its resources, mainly natural rubber, which was in great demand before synthetic rubber started replacing it in the 1930s. Leopold's private army, the Force Publique, imposed demanding rubber quotas on coerced native workers, and enforced these quotas with savage violence, including whippings, burning of villages, mutilation of the arms of workers who failed to realize their quotas, and mass killings. Estimates put the loss of population during Leopold's rule as high as 10 million out of a base population of 20 million.

Out of this huge human tragedy came the beginnings of the international human rights movement, which built on the abolitionist movement's earlier campaign to end slavery. In the early 1890s an American journalist traveling in the Congo, George Washington Williams, was the first to expose the extreme ill treatment of the population in the Congo, even if the international response to these revelations was tepid. In 1899 Joseph Conrad's *Heart of Darkness*, based on his experience as a captain on a steamer on the river Congo, was published and began to draw international attention to the atrocities in the colony. Two other pioneers of the international human rights movement, Edmund Morel and Roger Casement, adopted the plight of the Congo Free State's population as their cause, founding the Congo Reform Association with the explicit aim of ending Leopold's control over the Congo.

Morel came to understand the depth of human tragedy and exploitation wrought by King Leopold's regime while working as a clerk at the Liverpool shipping firm Elder Dempster, shipping goods to and from the Congo Free State. His revelations on the abuses in the Congo led to a resolution in the British House of Commons to investigate these allegations, which was carried out by the then British consul, Irishman Roger Casement (who was later executed by the British authorities because of his involvement in the Irish struggle for independence). Casement discovered much of what we know about the situation in the colony. His diary gives a sense of the atrocities he observed. The entries between June 5 and September 9 read:

June 5: The country a desert, no natives left.

July 25: I walked into villages and saw the nearest one—population dreadfully decreased—only 93 people left out of many hundreds.

July 26: Poor frail folk . . . —dust to dust ashes to ashes—where then are the kindly heart, the pitiful thought—together vanished.

August 6: Took copious notes from natives . . . They are cruelly flogged for being late with their baskets.

August 13: A. came to say 5 people from Bikoro side with hands cut off had come as far as Myanga intending to show me.

August 22: Bolongo quite dead. I remember it well in 1887, Nov, full of people then; now 14 adults all told. I should say people wretched, complained bitterly of rubber tax . . . 6:30 passed deserted side of Bokuta . . . Mouzede says the people were all taken away by force to Mampoko. Poor unhappy souls.

August 29: Bongandanga . . . saw rubber "Market," nothing but guns—about 20 armed men . . . The popln 242 men with rubber all guarded like convicts. To call this "trade" is the height of lying.

August 30: 16 men women and children tied up from a village Mboye close to the town. Infamous. The men were put in the prison, children let go at my intervention. Infamous. Infamous, shameful system.

September 2: Saw 16 women seized by Peeters's sentries and taken off to Prison.

September 9: 11:10 passed Bolongo again. The poor people put off in canoe to implore my help.

The Casement Report was published in 1904 and vividly documented the staggering abuses in the Congo based on eyewitness accounts. It was particularly detailed on the mutilations Leopold's men exacted on natives for missing their rubber quotas. For example:

Two cases (of mutilation) came to my actual notice while I was in the Lake District. One, a young man, both of whose hands had been beaten off with the butt ends of rifles against a tree; the other a young lad of 11 or 12 years of age, whose right hand was cut off at the wrist . . . In both these cases the Government soldiers had been accompanied by white officers whose names were given to me. Of six natives (one a girl, three little boys, one youth, and one old woman) who had been mutilated in this way during the rubber régime, all except one were dead at the date of my visit.

The overall verdict of the report was damning:

By the mid-1890s the Congo Basin and its products became a source of great wealth to Leopold who used his riches to beautify his Belgian capital Brussels while using his agents in Africa to establish a brutal exploitative regime for the extraction of rubber in the interior forest regions of the Free State.

The report transformed international public opinion, and thanks to it, the Congo Reform Association's cause started receiving support from celebrities on both sides of the Atlantic, including Sir Arthur Conan Doyle, Mark Twain, Booker T. Washington, and Bertrand Russell as well as Joseph Conrad. It eventually led to the end of Leopold's rule over the colony.

The international human rights movement matured and gained greater international influence after World War II. The Universal Declaration of Human Rights of 1948, which we'll discuss in the next chapter, was pivotal. An equally important step was the United Nations' Convention on the Prevention and Punishment of the Crime of Genocide in 1948, and not just because it took on the notorious genocides of the first half of the century. In contrast to earlier treatments and declarations such as the Hague Conventions of 1899 and 1907 and the Geneva Convention dating back to 1864, which recognized states as sovereigns and sought to regulate their interrelations and the treatment of combatants and civilians during wartime, this convention enshrined the notion that states were not free to treat their citizens however they wanted. The convention stated:

> Persons committing genocide or any of the other acts enumerated in article III shall be punished, whether they are constitutionally responsible rulers, public officials or private individuals.

The message was clear. Leviathan or no Leviathan, atrocities against people would not be allowed. At first this was just a statement of intent, without real teeth. But the international pressure and scrutiny on sovereign states intensified with the activities of several organizations such as Amnesty International and Human Rights Watch, which are working to expose and prevent violations of human and civil rights within countries, and the International Criminal Court, founded in 2002, which has jurisdiction to prosecute individuals and even heads of state for genocide, crimes against humanity, and war crimes.

Of course, the effects of these conventions and organizations shouldn't be exaggerated, and there are scores of instances in the post–World War II era of human rights abuses and even genocides, including in Cambodia in the 1970s, Rwanda in 1994, and Sudan in the 2000s. Nevertheless, the international human rights movement has had two fundamental effects on state-society relations around the world. It has made extreme oppression much more visible, increasing the cost to states and elites of repressing society; and it has provided a common set of criteria and common language for societal organizations to rally around in countering despotism. The roles of both of these influences can be seen in many of the "color revolutions," where mobilization was partly triggered by the clear documentation of systematic human and civil rights abuses by dictatorial regimes. In terms of our framework, this international reaction makes the corridor wider at the expense of the Despotic Leviathan—the same power of the state that would have otherwise led to despotic dynamics can now be contained with the help of international human rights groups and the societal mobilization that they help generate.

The international human rights movement also expands the corridor on the other side, in particular by encouraging state capacity to be organized and used against discrimination and abuses directed toward disadvantaged subgroups. One example comes from the role that Amnesty International has played in campaigns against domestic violence and female genital mutilation. In 2012 the United Nations finally passed a resolution against female genital mutilation, and Amnesty International's campaign was crucial in this process. The resulting expansion of the use of state capacity to protect the discriminated against corresponds to the widening of the corridor on the side of the Absent Leviathan.

With these forces in play, one might think that international relations have become a powerful force toward a wider corridor, facilitating the rise of Shackled Leviathans. The reality, however, is more nuanced. A more pervasive facet of international relations renders the corridor narrower and bolsters Despotic and Paper Leviathans.

———————

In October 2017, the World Health Organization (WHO) appointed Zimbabwe's then president Robert Mugabe its "goodwill ambassador" for noncommunicable diseases, declaring that he could use this position "to influence his peers in his region." (President Mugabe is depicted addressing the UN in our photo insert.) What influence? This goodwill ambassador is the same Robert Mugabe who repressed his population, massacred thousands of civilians in Matabeleland, expropriated and redistributed land to himself, his family, and his party supporters, oversaw a huge collapse of an otherwise productive economy, and regularly stole elections. But perhaps Zimbabwe has done well in terms of health and healthcare? Not so. The general health of Zimbabweans has been declining together with the country's economic fortunes. As much as 8 percent of the population might be infected by HIV, and life expectancy has fallen, perhaps to as low as fifty-nine years at birth for men. The shattering of the country's healthcare system contributed to a massive cholera epidemic in 2008–2009, with estimates of the consequences of the disease running up to 4,000 deaths from 100,000 cases. The best testament to the state of Zimbabwe's healthcare system is that before being deposed, Mugabe kept flying to Singapore for medical care rather than trusting his health to Zimbabwe's doctors. The cost of his health tourism in 2016 was estimated at $53 million, one-sixth of the country's entire healthcare budget.

The appointment doesn't make sense until you look at the broader international state system. International organizations, including the United Nations, which at times has played an important role in the international human rights movement, exist to work with heads of state of sovereign nations. Their charter is to be Hobbesian—if a state exists, it represents its country and deserves international respectability. This implies recognizing presidents, prime ministers, military dictators, and kings even as they are engaged in robust repression against their populations, including human and civil rights abuses. It's not only international respectability but financial resources that flow to whoever represents the state in a given territory. These financial resources can amount to as much as 40 percent of the government's budget for some African countries, such as Somalia. There are good reasons for this international state system. Not recognizing states as legitimate partners would make international cooperation much harder and potentially destabilize regimes. In one sense, the international state system has worked well. It has, for example, prevented wars in Africa and Latin America, despite ripe conditions for border disputes and conflicts.

But from the vantage point of our conceptual framework, an unintended consequence of this international system that enshrines the most suspect part of Hobbes's theory—that the sovereign is always legitimate and might does make right—is to narrow the corridor. International legitimacy translates into domestic legitimacy, and provides a cover for repressing and suppressing dissent at home. It provides access to resources and cements hierarchy with the current elites on top. This tilting of the balance in favor of the state has pernicious effects for state-society relations. For one, it makes it much harder for society to counteract the despotic power of the state. It also makes it harder for society to institutionalize its power. We already saw these effects in Chapter 11—the international state system props up Paper Leviathans. Even though Paper Leviathans' roots can be seen in colonial rule, their continued existence relies on the international state system that treats them as true, respectable Leviathans. But Paper Leviathans are too concerned with the mobilization effect and the reaction of society to be able to build any type of state capacity, and in the process they undermine any prospect for institutionalizing society's power. The consequence is a potent force pushing in the opposite direction to the international human rights movement and making the corridor narrower.

———————

So with all of these forces, and many others we haven't discussed, at play, should we expect the corridor to become wider and prospects for liberty to improve in the coming decades? The answer is unclear, but we are optimists and even in the current juncture, when support for autocrats is soaring in many countries and some in the corridor are looking shakier than ever, we see grounds for thinking that the corridor is getting a little wider for most. But the main message from Chapter 1 remains—there is no natural tendency for all nations to move toward a uniform set of state institutions and state-society relations. Despotic, Paper, and Absent Leviathans are no less robust than the Shackled kind. Another message from this chapter is no less important. Regardless of the shape of the corridor, countries failing to form new, broad coalitions and support compromise will fail to get a toehold in the corridor.

Chapter 15

LIVING WITH THE LEVIATHAN

Hayek's Mistake

In the middle of World War II, the director of the London School of Economics (LSE), William Beveridge, led a team of civil servants to produce a government report titled *Social Insurance and Allied Services*. This document, now known as the Beveridge Report, became the foundation of the expansion of the welfare state in the UK. Its key recommendations included a significant expansion of National Insurance, the program that provides unemployment benefits, sick pay, and pensions, creating universal free healthcare in the guise of the National Health Service and implementing a minimum wage. The report was hugely popular among the British public. The postwar Labour minister of national insurance, James Griffiths, wrote in his memoirs, "In one of the darkest hours of the war [the report] fell like manna from heaven."

Some of the report's recommendations were implemented during the war, with an expansion of infant, child, and maternity services, a program providing fuel and subsidized milk to mothers and families with children under the age of five, and free school meals for children. In 1945, the Labour Party swept to power based on its promise to implement the Beveridge Report, and proceeded to enact a number of iconic legislations making the report's plans a reality. These included the Family Allowances Act of 1945, the National Insurance Act of 1946, the National Assistance Act of 1948, and the National Health Service Act of 1946.

A brilliant émigré from Vienna, then teaching at the LSE, was alarmed. Friedrich von Hayek's main concern was the rise of the totalitarian state, and he saw Nazism, from which he had fled several years earlier, as one extreme form of this totalitarian state. Hayek was particularly concerned about "socialist" state planning and administrative regulation of the economy morphing into a type of totalitarianism. He first expressed his ideas about the dangers of growing state administration in the economy in a memo written to William Beveridge. This memo grew into a magazine article, and then into a book, *The Road to Serfdom*, that has since become one of the most influential works of social science of the twentieth century. Hayek was not against all government intervention or social insurance. He wrote, "Probably nothing has done so much harm to the liberal cause as the wooden insistence of some liberals on certain rough rules of thumb, above all the principle of laissez faire," and added "there can be no doubt that some minimum of food, shelter, and clothing, sufficient to preserve health and the capacity to work, can be assured to everybody." But he was worried about the state playing a defining role in influencing wages and the allocation of resources. This, he thought, might be the direction that many countries were moving toward, partly because of the influence of socialist ideas, and his book was meant to be a corrective. In the foreword to the 1956 U.S. edition, Hayek, having seen the Labour government's policies, wrote:

> That hodgepodge of ill-assembled and often inconsistent ideals which under the name of the Welfare State has largely replaced socialism as the goal of the reformers needs very careful sorting-out if its results are not to be very similar to those of full-fledged socialism. This is not to say that some of its aims are not both practicable and laudable. But there are many ways in which we can work toward the same goal, and in the present state of opinion there is some danger that our impatience for quick results may lead us to choose instruments which, though perhaps more efficient for achieving the particular ends, are not compatible with the preservation of a free society.

He continued:

> Of course, six years of socialist government in England have not produced anything resembling a totalitarian state. But those who argue that this has disproved the thesis of *The Road to Serfdom* have really missed

one of its main points: that the most important change which extensive government control produces is a psychological change, an alteration in the character of the people. This is necessarily a slow affair, a process which extends not over a few years but perhaps over one or two generations. The important point is that the political ideals of the people and its attitude toward authority are as much the effect as the cause of the political institutions under which it lives. This means, among other things, that even a strong tradition of political liberty is no safeguard if the danger is precisely that new institutions and policies will gradually undermine and destroy that spirit.

Hayek's "psychological change" here is similar to what we have called the dominance of the state over society. Viewed from this perspective, Hayek's concern was that the increased power of the British state would emasculate society and pave the road to despotism. As Hayek himself argued elsewhere and even in the quote above, some of the goals may be "practicable and laudable." But that wasn't enough, because the character of state-society relations might be endangered by this increased power of the state. That's what he was afraid of. In fact, the defense Hayek envisaged against this potential problem is in line with our thesis. He wrote: "The consequences can of course be averted if that spirit reasserts itself in time and the people not only throw out the party which has been leading them further and further in the dangerous direction but also recognize the nature of the danger and resolutely change their course."

In other words, Hayek recognized that the only way to prevent the Despotic Leviathan from emerging is for society to reassert itself against the state's power and dominance. So far so good. But Hayek's astute analysis misses a vital force—the Red Queen effect. The only option of society against expanding state capacity is not to rein it back completely. It can alternatively increase its own capacity, its own checks over the state. That is what happened in Britain and in most of Europe in the decades following World War II. And as we saw in Chapter 10, some of these dynamics played out in the United States as well.

In fact, a lot of human progress depends on the state's role and capacity advancing to meet new challenges while society also becomes more powerful and vigilant. Nipping greater state capacity in the bud would preclude such human progress. It is particularly important for the state to expand its remit during moments of economic or social crisis. In Britain the Beveridge report was a response to such a crisis.

So Hayek's mistake was twofold. First, he did not foresee the power of the Red Queen and recognize that it could keep the Shackled Leviathan inside the corridor. Second, perhaps unsurprisingly, he did not see what is now much more evident—the need for the state to play a role in redistribution, creating a social safety net and regulating the increasingly complex economy that had already emerged in the first half of the twentieth century.

———

Staying in the corridor is not automatic, especially in the face of new challenges. We saw in Chapter 13 how countries fall out of the corridor when the Red Queen turns zero-sum. Hayek was concerned about an even more basic challenge to liberty—the increasing power of the administrative state ushering in a new type of "serfdom." But the Red Queen effect, provided that it doesn't turn zero-sum, can also be a powerful force helping a society stay in the corridor while developing new capabilities and institutional arrangements for keeping in check an expanding state. There is perhaps no better example than the founding of the Swedish welfare state in the midst of the Great Depression to illustrate how the Red Queen can play this role and how her mobilization often necessitates new coalitions.

The Cow Trade

The Great Depression created a crisis for state and society everywhere in the West. The economic crisis begot a political crisis, but one that played out very differently in different countries. While Germany succumbed to Nazism and swiftly left the corridor, and the United States scrambled to deal with these problems within its own constraints, Sweden embarked upon what has become an iconic example of the simultaneous expansion of the state's and society's capacities powered by the Red Queen effect. In the interwar years Sweden introduced universal male suffrage, a more competitive electoral landscape emerged, and new coalitions not only kept Sweden inside the corridor but significantly increased the state's capacity to regulate the labor market and influence the distribution of income. Several factors prepared the ground for these changes.

The Swedish economy was largely rural at the turn of the century, with as much as half of the population still working in agriculture. Sweden had a long history of parliamentary representation, including for peasants, as we saw in Chapter 6, and by the nineteenth century the landed aristocracy had lost much of its wealth and power. Nevertheless, the extent of the franchise was limited and its second, aristocratic chamber still exercised considerable influence over politics. Universal male suffrage was introduced in 1909 for the Second Chamber and in 1918 for all elections, and the power of the monarchy was curtailed in 1918, paving the way for parliamentary democracy with competitive elections. The Swedish Workers Party (SAP) played a defining role in these institutional changes.

In contrast to many other European socialist parties, the SAP had shed its Marxist roots quite thoroughly before it started contesting power. One of the architects of this transformation was its influential early-twentieth-century leader Hjalmar Branting. While other socialist parties on the continent were holding out for a revolution led by the proletariat and undermining their electoral prospects with bitter ideological quarrels, Branting was busy looking for coalition partners to turn the SAP into a veritable electoral force. He argued in 1886, "In a backward land like Sweden we cannot close our eyes to the fact that the middle class increasingly plays a very important role. The working class needs the help it can get from this direction just like the middle class for its part needs the workers behind it . . ."

This quest was helped by the fact that a major objective of the SAP at the beginning of the century was to secure universal male suffrage for both chambers of parliament, which meant a program committed to a strategy of empowering all those who did not have representation, including farmers and peasants.

When the Great Depression hit, Sweden was not spared. As in many other countries, the government tried to defend the value of its currency, the krona, and the resulting policies led to deflation and a deeper crisis as unemployment soared. Even though Sweden partially reversed course and abandoned the gold standard after the British devalued in 1931, conditions did not improve. It was in this context that the SAP's search for coalition partners began transforming Swedish politics. The SAP at this point turned from the middle class to farmers and peasants as coalition partners. It was an uphill struggle. The SAP was allied with trade unions, whose main priorities were to preserve unemployment compensation, maintain high wage levels, and create jobs in the industrial sector using public works and government spending. They stood against any policy that would increase food prices for workers. Farmers, on the other hand, were opposed to high wages for workers and instead sought price supports via marketing boards and other methods to prop up agricultural prices.

But this did not stop the SAP's quest. In advance of the 1932 elections, its leader, Per Albin Hansson, presented the SAP as the "people's home," open to all Swedes. He explained that its

most important task [is] working with all energy to help all groups suffering from unprovoked effects of the economic crisis . . . The party does
not aim to support and help [one] working class at the expense of the
others. It does not differentiate in its work for the future between the
industrial working class and the agricultural class or between workers
of the hand and workers of the brain.

The leaders of the SAP presented this strategy as a response to the dire conditions created by the economic crisis, and the party's main selling point for the
electorate was its willingness to experiment with activism to counter the adverse
effects of the Depression. Its manifesto in the 1932 election made this clear, stating that the country was engulfed by

a crisis developing which claims victims in all sectors of society . . . [the
party] strives for measures for lasting improvement of the situation
[and] devotes its efforts towards inducing the state to bring effective help
to the innocent victims of the crisis.

It worked. The party massively increased its vote share compared to the 1928
election, capturing 41.7 percent of the total vote, an historic success, even if not
enough for a majority. It was at this point that Hansson's efforts to court farmers
bore fruit and the SAP arranged the "cow trade," entering into an alliance with the
Agrarian Party to form a government. The SAP accepted protectionist measures
to increase agricultural prices, and in return received a mandate to implement a
crisis package aimed at increasing government spending and wages in the industrial sector.

This package was initially opposed by powerful banking interests such as the
Wallenbergs and the largest and most assertive segment of the business community, which was producing for the export market and was thus concerned about
higher labor costs eroding its competitiveness. But this changed after the 1936
election, which witnessed the electorate lining up behind the SAP in greater numbers. This broad support led to a meeting between representatives of business
interests, trade unions, and farmers as well as the government, in the small resort
town of Saltsjöbaden in 1938. The meeting resulted in an expansion of the "social
democratic" coalition to include businesses, which acquiesced to the new government programs, the welfare state, and the resulting high wages in return for more
cooperative labor relations and reduced strike activity.

This model was further developed after World War II. The social consensus came to form around the idea that the Swedish state should support both equity and growth. Out of this consensus emerged the corporatist model, wherein the state provided generous benefits to workers while also encouraging moderation in wage setting and facilitating greater fluidity in the labor market via active labor market policies (for example, helping workers find jobs by retraining them). In line with the agreement at Saltsjöbaden, this strategy benefited businesses as well. A bulwark of the system was the Rehn-Meidner model of centralized wage setting in which a social bargain would fix industry-level wages for all firms. This not only created a more equal distribution of earnings among workers via "wage compression" (all workers doing the same job being paid the same amount) but also implied that the more productive firms would not have to pay higher wages. This was a huge profit opportunity for high-productivity firms that would pay the same wage as the rest of the industry. By the same logic, the system encouraged firms to invest, innovate, and reorganize to increase their productivity, since they could get to keep all of the increase in productivity as additional profits.

Meanwhile, the Swedish welfare state continued to expand and develop. Sweden not only established more generous social benefits, but also provided them at similar levels to all citizens following the universal template of the Beveridge Report. Generous unemployment benefits and health insurance were followed by pioneering maternity and child benefits and an egalitarian high-quality education system, which came out of an effort to "democratize the Swedish school system." These programs enabled the country to be at the forefront of reducing poverty, a huge achievement during the Great Depression when sky-high poverty rates not only created an environment of fear and uncertainty but also threatened the democratic political system, as in Germany.

From the viewpoint of our framework, the crucial point isn't just the major expansion of the role and capacity of the Swedish state, but the way this took place together with a deepening of democracy and societal control; society's capacity increased at the same time as the state's. There were several facets to this process. First, a primary concern with any expansion in the role of the state is the possibility of "elite capture," turning state involvement into a tool for a few businesses or some narrow interests to benefit at society's expense. The fact that this was all happening under the leadership of the SAP and the pivotal role that trade unions came to play as partners in this process and in monitoring and administrating the system was a major obstacle to this type of hijacking of state institutions. The universal nature of the Swedish welfare programs precluded the possibility that these could become tools of patronage in the hands of the elite, and further helped create social cohesion and a sense of ownership in the population, contributing to society's mobilization to support them.

Second, a major danger related to Hayek's worries was that the greater role of the state in the economy could come at the expense of business in general, for example, with nationalizations and expropriation of capital. Sweden contained this possibility by engaging the business community in the social democratic coalition after Saltsjöbaden. It is telling in this context that the SAP had consistently refused to partner with Communists and stayed away from nationalization or overt expropriation of profits or capital. At times, trade unions attempted to push for policies that would further increase wages, but the SAP typically resisted them. One exception, which affirms the extent of societal control, was the reaction against a movement in the trade unions and the SAP in the 1970s to change the terms of the Rehn-Meidner model of centralized wage setting by creating "wage-earner funds" to claw back the "excess profits" accruing to high-productivity firms still paying industry-level wages. As it became clear that the implementation of these funds threatened the very coalition that undergirded Swedish social democracy, opposition to them grew. This forced the SAP to back down and ultimately lose power for the first time in 1976.

Third, the expansion of the state coincided with a deepening of democracy. As the major parties in Sweden all came to accept the basic tenets of social democracy, the electorate started having a choice between different parties that would implement versions of the social democratic approach, and also if necessary pull back from more extreme policies such as the wage-earner funds proposed by the trade unions and the SAP in the 1970s.

Finally, the Swedish bureaucracy and judiciary developed in tandem with these changes, especially in the course of administering and overseeing these programs together with the trade unions. In the process, they gained the competence to implement the social programs and restrain abuses of the system.

In sum, the new necessities and conditions of crisis created by the economic downturn were met by the Swedish state expanding both its role and its capacity. In contrast to Hayek's fears, this did not pave the way to totalitarianism. On the contrary, because state expansion was carried out by a coalition of workers, farmers, and business interests and because the Red Queen effect triggered societal mobilization to keep the state in check, Swedish democracy, far from weakening, got stronger in the process.

Though the details of the Swedish experience are unique, its broad outlines parallel what transpired in several other countries. Denmark and Norway built similar welfare states, even if the way in which their coalitions came together differed. Germany too developed a welfare state supported by a high level of state capacity and societal controls after World War II.

Equally interesting is the American experience. FDR confronted the same economic and social upheaval that the SAP encountered but also had to grapple with a society that was sharply divided along racial and regional lines and more suspicious of government action. Nevertheless, his early policy initiatives, which included the National Industrial Recovery Act (NIRA) in 1933 and the founding of the Agricultural Adjustment Administration, went in the same direction and expanded the capacity of the state to bolster the safety net and help the economy recover. This program sought to bring both workers and farmers on board as well. Title I of NIRA, for example, had a very similar remit to the industrial policies that the SAP adopted, while support for farmers in the form of higher prices was at the center of the administration's agricultural policies. In both cases, FDR's initial plans involved administrative controls and implementation, just as in Sweden. The U.S. conditions were different from those in Sweden, however; the NIRA faced fierce opposition from businesses and courts, and many of its provisions had to be abandoned or were implemented differently. But even if FDR's plans were partly watered down and fell into line with the U.S. public-private partnership model, they achieved some of the same objectives as Sweden's cow trade, and in the process fundamentally transformed the regulation and administration of the U.S. economy.

The Leviathan vs. the Market

A crucial debate in economics and social science concerns the balance between the state and the market. How much should the state intervene in the economy? What is the right scope and extent of regulation? Which activities should be left to markets and which others should be the purview of the state? The textbook economic answer is that the state should intervene only under clearly delineated circumstances. These include the presence of "externalities," which arise when actions by individual actors have major consequences for others that are not mediated via markets, paving the way for excessive levels of some activities such as pollution; the provision of "public goods," which are goods from which everybody benefits, such as infrastructure or national defense; and situations in which there is pervasive "asymmetric information," meaning that some market participants will not be able to accurately judge the quality of the products and services they are trading. They include as well the presence of monopolies that need to be regulated to prevent them from charging excessively high prices or engaging in predatory activities to drive out their competitors. Critically, government intervention is also needed for social insurance or redistribution to limit inequality. An important tenet of the textbook approach is that when working to influence the distribution of income in the economy, the state should minimize its impact on market prices and instead rely on taxes and transfers to achieve its objectives.

This is consistent with *The Road to Serfdom*, where Hayek advocated limits on the scope of the state in the economy because markets are more efficient at allocating resources. But critically, Hayek went further and also argued that the increase in the power and involvement of the state can have adverse political implications. Even if some of Hayek's conclusions were neither fully compelling nor have been borne out by the political developments of the intervening decades, the way he approached the problem broke considerable new ground. Perhaps Hayek's most brilliant insight is that the balance between the state and the market isn't just about economics; it is about politics (and we are not saying this just because it is one of the main implications of our conceptual framework as well). The vital challenge is to make sure that the state can increase its capacity to meet society's needs but still remain shackled. That necessitates new ways in which society is empowered to monitor and control the state and elites. So the diagnosis of beneficial state interventions is not just about economic trade-offs, but also about the interventions' political implications. It's not just about state capacity, but about who controls and monitors that capacity and how it will be used.

In this light, the real institutional innovation in Sweden, and subsequently in other Scandinavian nations, was not just creating a more interventionist, redistributive state but doing so under the auspices of a coalition including businesses and the great majority of workers organized in politically active trade unions, which imposed tight shackles on the state. On the one hand, as we have noted already, the involvement of businesses, including the biggest corporations in Sweden, meant that the Swedish welfare state never went in the direction of wholesale nationalization of industries or abrogation of markets. On the other hand, the pivotal role that trade unions played in this process enabled much greater popular participation in politics, stacking the cards against the hijacking of the now more powerful state institutions by elite interests. This coalition and the Red Queen effect enabled the Swedish political system to reorient itself when some of the regulations went too far in the 1970s and then again in the 1990s.

There are three other vital lessons from the Swedish experience for understanding the balance between the state and the market. The first is a corollary of what we have already argued. When conditions necessitate new responsibilities for the state, this expansion must be accompanied by new ways for society to participate in politics, monitor the state and bureaucrats, and pull the carpet from under the new programs if necessary. This means that a lot of the debate about the proper scope of markets and governments fails to grapple with the most defining question—even though Hayek long ago identified the critical importance of this question. Can we keep the Leviathan under control even with its new responsibilities and newly acquired powers? Do the costs of introducing new checks on the Leviathan, especially when these will not be automatically forthcoming due to the Red Queen effect, outweigh the benefits from the additional state intervention?

From this perspective, the reason why the government should not regulate the prices of most goods isn't because these prices are set perfectly by markets (or, in the terminology of economics, because there are no externalities, public goods, asymmetric information, or distributional concerns), but because the political costs of the state widening its remit would be too high, either because of the additional precautions this requires or because of the heightened risk of spinning out of the corridor. This line of reasoning implies that the state should intervene only when the benefits from intervention are larger than the political costs of intervention. More important, it also shows that interventions and activities that set in motion powerful (positive-sum) Red Queen effects are much more likely to be socially beneficial. So it is preferable for the state to provide social insurance and broad-based services and coordinate bargaining between employers and employees while getting both trade unions and businesses involved (which is likely to empower the Red Queen, as in the Swedish case) than to engage in specific, often opaque government regulations and corrective actions in narrow areas like sugar or steel tariffs (in the way that Paper Leviathans dealt with social demands, as we saw in Chapter 11).

The second lesson is that some apparently inefficient aspects of the economy might have a useful social role after all. One such aspect is trade unions themselves, which are often viewed with great suspicion, because one of their main objectives is to push for higher wages for their members even if this makes it harder for non-members to find jobs. Indeed, we have seen that even in the Swedish context, trade unions have at times pushed for excessively high wages. This suspicious attitude is more than shared by many policy makers in the United States, who have sought to undermine the power of unions. Partly as a result of these policy attitudes (and partly because of the decline of manufacturing employment), today union membership is much lower in the U.S. economy, especially in the private sector, than it was in the heyday of labor unions in midcentury, after the rights of workers to organize in unions, engage in collective bargaining, and go on strike were recognized with the National Labor Relations (Wagner) Act of 1935. Similar declines in the power of labor unions have been ongoing in other advanced economies. Whether the opposition to trade unions makes sense on purely economic grounds is debatable. But an essential role of trade unions is political; they are central for maintaining a partial balance of power between well-organized business interests and labor. The decline in the power of unions over the past several decades may thus have been one of the factors tilting the balance of power in U.S. society in favor of large corporations. The more important point for our framework is that, in evaluating the role of various policies and institutions, we must take into account the supporting arrangements that seek to create a balance and thus help keep the Leviathan and the elites shackled.

The third important lesson is about the form of government intervention. Here we diverge more sharply from Hayek and the textbook answer in economics. They maintain that it is always better to refrain from meddling with market prices, and if the government wishes to create a more equitable division of income, then it should let the market work and use redistributive taxation to move toward the desired distribution. But this way of thinking incorrectly separates economics from politics. For the Leviathan to take market prices and the distribution of income as given and just rely on fiscal redistribution to achieve its objectives might translate into very high levels of taxes and redistribution. Wouldn't it be better, especially from the viewpoint of controlling the Leviathan, if market prices could be altered so as to achieve some of these objectives without as much fiscal redistribution? This is exactly what the Swedish welfare state did. The social democratic coalition was built on the corporatist model wherein trade unions and state bureaucracy directly regulated the labor market. This generated higher wages for workers and meant that there was less need for redistribution from the owners of capital and corporations to labor. It also generated wage compression so that the distribution of income among laborers was more equal. As a result, there was less need for redistributive taxation, even if quite a bit of that also took place in the Swedish economy to finance the generous welfare state. Much of this was not designed or planned in advance. Nevertheless, our framework highlights one reason things came to be organized this way; by ensuring that wages were higher and more compressed, and thus departing from what an unfettered market outcome might have been, the state avoided the need for even greater fiscal redistribution and taxation. With the fiscal role of the state diminished, keeping the state in check became a more feasible objective.

Unshared Prosperity

Many Western nations, not least the United States, are facing fundamental economic exigencies today. The political response so far has been closer to the zero-sum Red Queen than the type of dynamic we saw in the Swedish cow trade, which involved the development of novel coalitions and institutional architectures to deal with new challenges. But the latter path is open to most countries in the corridor, and the first step in supporting it is to understand what these new challenges are. These challenges are the focus of the next three sections.

Two of the most powerful engines of economic prosperity over the last several decades have been economic globalization and the rapid introduction of automation technologies. Economic globalization has increased the volume of trade, and outsourcing and offshoring have enabled the production process to be distributed around the world to take advantage of lower cost of production for certain tasks and goods. Both developing and developed nations have benefited from this globalization process. The spectacular growth of economies such as South Korea and Taiwan in the 1970s, '80s, and '90s and of China in the 1990s and 2000s would not have been possible without globalization. Nor would we have enjoyed the lower prices of hundreds of products ranging from textiles and toys to electronics and computers. We saw in the previous chapter that globalization impacts how narrow the corridor is and the prospects for some of the nations outside the corridor to move into it. But its effects on the economics and politics of developed nations have been more complicated because of how the gains from globalization have been shared, or more to the point, have failed to be. Though much economic policy advice emphasizes how everybody benefits from economic globalization, the reality has been different both in the United States and in Europe, where corporations and the already well-off have seen their incomes rise, while workers have experienced much more limited gains and in some cases lower wages and job losses. This is in fact what economic theory predicts: globalization creates winners and losers, and when it takes the form of integration of an advanced country

with a less advanced economy abundant in low-skill, low-wage labor, workers—
and especially less skilled workers in the advanced economy—lose out.

The other powerful engine of economic prosperity, technological change, has
had similar effects. Technological progress increases productivity and expands
the range of products available to consumers, and has historically been at the root
of sustained economic growth. At times, it has also been the tide that has lifted all
(or most) boats. From the 1940s to the mid-1970s in the U.S. economy, there was
rapid productivity growth along with growth of earnings of all education groups,
all the way from workers with less than high school education to those with postgraduate degrees. But the bewildering array of new technologies that have transformed workplaces over the past thirty years appears to have had quite different
effects. Many of these technologies, including much more powerful computers,
numerically controlled and then computerized machines, industrial robots, and
more recently artificial intelligence, have automated the production process, allowing machines to take over tasks that were previously performed by workers.
By its nature, automation favors capital, which is now used more extensively in
the form of the new machines. It also tends to favor skilled workers relative to the
less skilled, whose tasks are being taken over by machines. Not surprisingly,
therefore, new automation technologies have had sweeping distributional consequences.

The combined effects of globalization and automation have led to divergent
fortunes. In the United States, the pattern of broad-based wage increases ceased
after the late 1970s and was replaced by a widening gap between the workers at
the bottom of the earnings distribution and those at the top. For example, while
the (inflation-adjusted) earnings of men with postgraduate education increased
by almost 60 percent since 1980, those of men with high school education or less
declined by more than 20 percent. In the course of the last three and a half decades, the real take-home pay of less skilled workers has fallen precipitously.

The same period has also witnessed declining job creation in the American
economy. U.S. manufacturing employment fell by about 25 percent from the mid-
1990s, while the overall employment-to-population ratio has declined significantly since 2000. Similar trends are visible in several other advanced economies,
even if the staggering decline in the real earnings of less educated workers is
unique to the U.S. labor market.

There is general agreement that both automation and globalization have been
major contributors to these trends. Employment and earnings losses are concentrated in areas, industries, and occupations that used to specialize in activities that

either have been automated or have witnessed a rapid expansion of imports from developing economies, particularly China. Estimates in the literature suggest that imports from China alone may have reduced employment in the U.S. economy by over two million jobs, and the adoption of industrial robots, one salient example of new automation technologies, may have led to the loss of as many as 400,000 jobs. In both cases the majority of the effects were felt by workers at the lower end of the skill distribution.

Wall Street Unhinged

Economic globalization and automation are not the only trends contributing to high levels of inequality. The rapid deregulation of several industries in the United States, accompanied by more modest changes in other developed economies, has been a major contributor to inequality as well. Particularly important in this process was financial deregulation.

The financial industry in much of the world was highly regulated during the several decades following World War II, so much so that in the United States banking occupations came to be viewed as typical white-collar jobs, and their pay reflected this, typically hovering around the same level that workers would receive in other sectors. The bedrock of the postwar financial system in the United States was "Regulation Q," which restricted interest rates on savings accounts, limiting competition between different financial institutions, as well as interstate branching restrictions that prevented banks from competing for deposits in multiple states. These restrictions were augmented by the Glass-Steagall Act, which was enacted in 1933 and separated retail banking (mainly deposit taking and lending) from the riskier business of investment banking (which focused on such things as underwriting, mergers and acquisitions, financial derivatives, and trading). In this regulated environment, the bureaucratized and comfortable jobs in banking came to be described by the "3-6-3 rule"—take deposits at 3 percent interest rate, lend them at 6 percent interest rate, and hit the golf course by 3 p.m. This started to change in the 1970s, particularly after Regulation Q was abolished in 1986, paving the way to a significant rise in concentration in banking. Together with greater concentration came a huge shift toward riskier activities, such as financial derivatives including interest rate swaps (where one party to the financial contract makes payments to the other depending on whether a benchmark interest rate is below or above a threshold) or credit default swaps (where payments are made depending on whether a debtor defaults). Even though the financial sector was branching into riskier activities, the rising political power of banks blocked any new regulations and in fact pushed for further deregulation. With greater concentration, fewer regulations, and more aggressive risk-taking came greater revenues and profits. Between 1980 and 2006, the financial sector grew from 4.9 percent of gross domestic product in the United States to 8.3 percent, and its profits rose 800 percent in real terms, more than three times the growth of profits in the nonfinancial sector.

In a powerful feedback cycle, greater size and profits led to increased political power. By 2006, the financial sector was contributing $260 million to political campaigns, up from about $61 million in 1990. The consequence of this was continued and bolder financial deregulation. Other important pillars of post–Great Depression financial regulations were dismantled, beginning with the 1994 Riegle-Neal Interstate Banking and Branching Efficiency Act which relaxed interstate banking regulations and opened the way to a series of mergers leading to the formation of gargantuan banking corporations such as JPMorgan Chase, Citicorp, and Bank of America. In 1999, the Gramm-Leach-Bliley Act demolished most of the remaining barriers between commercial and investment banking. During the same period, even as complex financial derivatives were spreading, bankers strenuously opposed new regulations. As a result, the huge growth in collateralized debt obligations based on mortgage-backed securities (which created synthetic securities of different risk profiles from large pools of mortgages) and credit default swaps took place almost entirely outside any regulatory framework. This was one of the reasons why an insurance company, the American Insurance Group (AIG), could sell massive amounts of credit default swaps and take on a vast amount of risk. With this wave of deregulation in place, the cycle continued, and profits in finance grew.

Deregulation in finance contributed to inequality. Megaprofits on Wall Street not only added to the more unequal distribution of income between owners of major financial institutions, including hedge funds specializing in risky investments for wealthy clients, but boosted overall inequality because high-level managers and traders in the financial industry started receiving huge pay packages and bonus payments. The earnings of workers and executives in finance, which had tracked those of their counterparts in other sectors until 1990, started diverging sharply thereafter. By 2006, workers in finance were receiving 50 percent more than their counterparts, while executives in the financial industry were receiving a staggering 250 percent more than executives with similar qualifications employed in other industries.

An indicator of this aspect of inequality is the share of national income accruing to those in the top 1 percent and top 0.1 percent of the income distribution, which respectively represent the very rich and the very very rich, among whom owners and executives of financial corporations are heavily overrepresented. The top 1 percent of Americans received around 9 percent of national income in the 1970s. By 2015 this number had increased to 22 percent. The increase has been even more striking for the share of the top 0.1 percent, which went up from around 2.5 percent in the 1970s to almost 11 percent of national income in 2015.

The second challenge is related to the allocation of resources. Finance, by transferring funds from savers to those with new ideas and investment opportunities, plays a vital role in improving the efficiency of economic activity. But when it becomes concentrated, specialized in risk-taking, and protected by its political power, it can conversely become a source of widespread inefficiencies. By the time of the 2007–2008 crisis, the financial industry had moved far in this direction. Excessive risk-taking was rooted in the unregulated competition in finance that was encouraging many institutions to lend recklessly and take risks in their own trading divisions in order to raise the rates of return they could promise to investors. It was also fueled by the belief of many in the leading financial institutions that the government and the Federal Reserve Bank would not let them go under even if their investments failed abysmally (and they weren't proven wrong). It was ultimately the collapse of such risky investments that spurred the financial crisis, which then morphed into a global economic downturn. Though the Dodd-Frank Act of 2010 and tighter regulations by the Federal Reserve System have attempted to limit the extent of such risk-taking and the negative consequences of financial losses on the economy, this has been at best a partial success. The financial industry, relying on its powerful lobbying, has resisted and prevented the full implementation of these regulations and often has sought to dial them back. Meanwhile, the sector has in fact become more concentrated. The share of the five largest banks in the U.S. financial system, which increased from 20 percent in 1990 to 28 percent in 2000, stands above 46 percent in 2019.

Supersized Firms

Greater concentration has not been confined to finance. Together with general deregulation and new technologies has come a huge increase in economic concentration in many sectors, and especially in online services, communications, and social media. The size of the largest companies relative to the rest of the economy is at an all-time high. The tech giants Alphabet (Google), Amazon, Apple, Facebook, and Microsoft have a combined market value (as measured by their stock market valuations) equivalent to over 17 percent of U.S. gross domestic product. The same number for the five largest companies in 1900, when policy makers and society became alarmed about the power of large corporations, was less than 6 percent. This huge increase in concentration appears to have several causes. The most important is the nature of the technology of these new companies, which creates what economists call "winner take all" dynamics. Take Google, for instance. Founded in 1998, when there were already several successful search engines for the Internet, Google quickly distinguished itself because of its superior search algorithm. While its competitors, such as Yahoo! and AltaVista, ranked websites by the number of times they included the term being searched for, the founders of Google, Sergei Brin and Larry Page, came up with a much better approach when they were graduate students at Stanford University. This approach, which came to be called the PageRank algorithm, ranked a web page according to its relevance estimated from how many other pages also mentioning the search term linked to this website. Because this algorithm was much better at suggesting relevant websites to users, Google's market share of Internet searches grew quickly. Once it had a large market share, Google could use more data from user searches to refine its algorithm, making it even better and more dominant. These dynamics got stronger once data from Internet searches started being used for artificial intelligence applications, for example, for translation and pattern recognition. Early success also brought more resources to invest in research and development and acquire companies that were developing technology that would be useful to Google's further expansion.

Winner-take-all effects were also at the root of the meteoric rise of Amazon, whose early growth as an online retailer and platform made it more attractive to sellers and users, and of Facebook, whose popularity as a social media platform critically depends on the users' expectations that their friends are joining as well. Though the nature of the winner-take-all considerations are somewhat different for Apple and Microsoft, they are no less important, because once again the value of their products depends on their overall popularity and widespread adoption in the population.

Even if the nature of the technology of the Internet age has been a defining factor in the rise in economic concentration, the inaction of regulatory agencies, particularly in the United States, has been a major factor too. This contrasts with what we have seen in U.S. history at similar junctures. When several companies reached similarly dominant positions at the turn of the twentieth century, administrations influenced by the progressive agenda came to power and started taking action to break them up, as we saw in Chapter 10. Today there are no similar institutional or policy proposals on the agenda. It is of course true that many of these companies have grown rapidly because they have offered new, better, and cheaper products. This does not obviate the concerns over increased concentration, especially with the prospect that companies that dominate markets will at some point exercise their monopoly power, charge higher prices, and start choking off innovation. The rise in economic concentration has been a major factor in the increase in inequality, too, not just because the owners and major shareholders of these corporations have become very rich but also because their employees have seen their wages increase relative to those working in other industries.

———

The economic trends we have briefly described—economic globalization and automation, the growth of finance, and the rise of supersized firms—pose urgent challenges for the United States and several other advanced economies for at least three reasons. The first is their inequality implications, which we have already emphasized. The second is economic efficiency. Some see our epoch as the golden age of technology, and yet income and productivity growth for at least the last two decades have been disappointing despite the spectacular rise of globalization and fascinating new technologies. The causes of this disappointing productivity growth are not well understood. They may well be related to the trends we have outlined. Globalization and rapid automation bring benefits, but their recent rise may have been at the expense of other technological advances that would have contributed to productivity and prosperity even more. Excessive growth in the financial sector and inefficient risk-taking have probably been quite costly because they have created instability in the economy (think of the financial crisis) and diverted resources that should have gone into other sectors and innovation toward finance (think of the smartest graduates going to hedge funds and investment banking instead of innovation, science, or public service). The huge increase in economic concentration has also likely undermined efficiency by both hamstringing competition and distorting the new technologies being adopted and developed.

The third challenge is related to trust in institutions. The Shackled Leviathan doesn't just need a balance of power between state and society. It also needs society to trust institutions. Without trust, citizens won't protect these institutions from the state and the elite, and the Red Queen becomes much more zero-sum.

Without trust, institutions will not be able to mediate conflicts in society (as in interwar Germany). Rising inequality, sluggish employment growth, the enormous profits in finance, and huge firms that remain unregulated all contribute to the feeling that the economy is rigged and the political system is complicit in this process. This feeling was certainly strengthened by the financial crisis and its aftermath, which witnessed government bailouts of banks partly responsible for the crisis while poor households facing bankruptcy received little help. Worse, as in our discussion of Weimar Germany, segments of society that are falling behind economically and losing trust in institutions are prime targets for movements that seek to destabilize the political system and tear down the balance of power between state and society that underpins life in the corridor. Such movements have been, predictably, in the ascendancy of late.

Inequality, unemployment, low productivity and income growth, and loss of trust in institutions were among the factors that made the period of the Great Depression such a fertile ground for political instability. Though the crisis engulfing advanced economies today is not as extreme as the Great Depression, given the parallels we cannot afford complacency.

Avoiding the Zero-Sum Red Queen

We have seen two diametrically opposed responses to the Great Depression. The first, the collapse of the Weimar Republic in Germany, was an example of a zero-sum Red Queen, where each side competed to undercut the other without any compromise. The second, illustrated by the Swedish response, entailed greater involvement and empowerment of the state, while society also became more capable and better organized to control the state. This societal mobilization was bulwarked by a new coalition supporting the new institutional architecture. The response of many Western nations today is closer to Weimar Germany's than Sweden's, with the elites fighting to defend their advantages and those in the most precarious positions succumbing to the allure of autocrats, and polarization and intransigence becoming the order of the day. Are we doomed to repeat the mistakes of interwar Germany? Or can we prevent the Red Queen from turning completely zero-sum? Can we also heed Hayek's warnings and avoid "serfdom"?

Let's start with the good news. As we emphasized in Chapter 13, the Red Queen is more likely to get out of control when the corridor is narrower. Here the United States and many other Western nations are in a better situation because their diversified economies built on manufacturing and services, very limited role of coercion (recall Chapter 14), lack of dominant groups diametrically opposed to democracy (like the Prussian landed elites), and their recent history of uninterrupted democratic politics translate into a wider corridor. But neither the width of the corridor nor stability in the corridor can be taken for granted. The width of the corridor is bolstered by democratic, participatory institutions. If these institutions lose people's trust, the corridor narrows and the ability of society to handle conflicts is diminished. And the Red Queen can get out of control even in a wide corridor if it turns resolutely zero-sum.

Let's revisit the Swedish experience during the Great Depression to see how to avoid such a zero-sum response. Three pillars of the Swedish response were critical. The first pillar was that the whole project was built on a broad coalition composed of workers, farmers, and businesses. The workers' movement, represented by the trade unions and the SAP, far from undercutting other interests, attempted to strike a compromise with them.

The second pillar was a range of economic responses, both short-term and institutional. These responses involved taking measures to stimulate the economy as well as a series of reforms to redistribute income toward those who were suffering unemployment, loss of earnings, and poverty. They proceeded to institutionalize these measures by developing a social democratic model in which the state would mediate the negotiations between employers and workers in order to ensure industrial peace. They also founded a generous welfare state for making prosperity more equally shared.

The third pillar was political. Deepening state capacity was embedded in a political system in which there were powerful societal controls on both the state's activities and the relationship between the political and economic elites. These controls were helped by the universal nature of the programs, which strengthened the social democratic coalition, by the fact that the administrative capacity of the state developed rapidly in the process of managing the welfare state, and by the direct involvement of the trade unions in the operation of key programs. All of this was in turn undergirded by the earlier political reforms that had significantly democratized Swedish politics.

The first lesson from Sweden is obvious: Engineer compromise and find ways of building a broad coalition to support the Shackled Leviathan and the new policies. This of course may be much harder once politics becomes highly polarized, as we have witnessed in the German case. The hope is to find some common ground before it's too late. In this context it's important that both the right and the left in the United States and many Western nations today agree that the trends we have highlighted here—rising inequality, disappearing jobs, the dominance of Wall Street, and economic concentration—are problems. The challenge is that there is less agreement about solutions. But this is not unusual. New coalitions often necessitate new ideas, perspectives, and institutional innovations. We now discuss where these might come from, focusing on the U.S. case for specificity.

Let's start with coalition building. The challenge is similar to the one that the Federalists faced. The compromises they came up with, even if costly in some dimensions, as we emphasized in Chapter 10, may be useful again. One leg of this compromise was to transfer significant powers to the states (so that local communities would have some say in the process). Given the differences in the economic and political problems and tolerance for government involvement across states, the same compromise may be necessary today too. Another leg was the public-private partnership. This had the virtue of getting the private sector involved and reassured as the state's capacity expanded. Though a similar compromise is necessary in the current U.S. context, there may be need for the institutional architecture to move beyond the current version of the public-private partnership model, as we'll discuss momentarily. Finally, incorporating Hayek's concerns from the beginning would help. This would mean that any social compact entailing greater state involvement and a stronger social safety net should reaffirm a significant increase in the ability of society to monitor the state. Even though Swedish society was less suspicious of state interventions, this is exactly what happened in Sweden in the 1930s.

On the economic front, the nature of the challenges makes it evident that a multipronged expansion in the responsibilities and the capacity of the state is necessary. The responsibilities that the state, especially the American state, must begin shouldering include designing and operating a more generous and comprehensive social safety net, which will protect individuals who are not benefiting from the major economic changes. Policies aimed at improving the social safety net need to be complemented by others that improve job creation and the earnings of workers and help them transition into new jobs. One example of this is the U.S. earned income tax credit, which effectively subsidizes low-wage workers by making their earnings less heavily taxed. It will have to involve a rethink of the U.S. educational system, which has become outmoded not only because it has not kept up with the needs of the changing economic landscape, but also because it has come to reflect the inequities in society, failing to provide a level playing field for most Americans. It will need to develop tighter, bolder, and more comprehensive regulations for many businesses, including the financial industry and the tech sector. To top it off, the recent U.S. experience highlights the fact that excessive reliance on the public-private partnership model is a drawback when building a modern welfare state. The successful operation of welfare and social insurance programs necessitates a deepening of the administrative capacity of the state. This doesn't mean no role for the private sector, but it requires a more autonomous, capable, and authoritative civil service.

Another lesson from the Swedish experience (confirmed by the Danish, Norwegian, and British cases) is to move welfare programs in a more universal direction, encouraging society at large to embrace them and be involved in their monitoring. Subsidies to specific industries or specific types of workers do not typically achieve this objective. Times of major economic and social change offer an especially fertile ground for the introduction of universal benefits, because they require broad-based programs, which can then forge a popular coalition in their support. Possible reforms to deal with the adverse effects of economic globalization, automation, and other economic changes, as well as investments in education to enable more effective and equitable use of these opportunities, must be similarly broad-based and could be designed to furnish their own powerful coalitions.

Once again building on the Swedish experience, we can argue that it would be a mistake to rely just on the tax policy and direct redistribution to pursue these objectives. Rather, it would be preferable to design labor market institutions that directly move the economy toward a more equally shared distribution of the gains from economic growth, such as better opportunities for workers to engage in collective agreements, minimum-wage legislation, and other policies to increase pay. Such policies would both reduce the burden on the state (and thus make it easier to control it) and also contribute to a broader coalition in favor of maintaining these programs.

The same factors suggest that it may be necessary to redirect the path of technological change. Technology's path and impact on the economy are not predetermined. The anemic rate of productivity growth today signals that all may not be well on this front. One problem is the declining support of the U.S. government for fundamental research and corporate R&D since the end of the Cold War. Reversing this decline would certainly be an important step in encouraging faster productivity growth. Moreover, the emphasis over the last several decades has been on rapid cost-saving, which has encouraged greater automation. It's not far-fetched to think that this focus on automation has not generated sufficient productivity growth. A social consensus on making the gains from economic growth more equally shared may motivate investments in technologies that will not simply automate existing tasks but also generate new opportunities for workers with different skills to contribute to production. If this can be achieved, the result will not only be a more equitable distribution of income and jobs and less need for fiscal redistribution, but also higher productivity as human skills are better utilized.

In politics, the challenges are no less formidable. Beyond securing a coalition around the economic reforms and institutions, it is imperative to rein in the excessive influence of private interests via campaign contributions and lobbying, which have reached astronomical proportions over the past two decades. Hence the concern that a larger state will do the bidding of economic elites is not a distant threat for the U.S. political system; it is already here. Yet the enormity of this problem means that both the left and the right in the United States agree that such capture is a problem (even if their favorite solutions differ). Our short list of political reforms to counter these threats include the following. The first is to curtail campaign contributions and limit the impact of lobbying. Specific measures to bring greater transparency to the relationship between firms, lobbyists, and politicians may be particularly important, since accounts of how politicians become faithful servants of certain industries or interests often involve meetings hidden from the public eye and poorly monitored revolving-door arrangements in which regulators and politicians are later hired by the private sector at very attractive salaries.

A second reform is to increase the autonomy of the civil service. Ending the cozy relationship between lobbyists and the state is an obvious first step. But more important, more fundamental reforms reducing the ability of new administrations to make political appointments for all high positions in government agencies would increase the autonomy of the civil service and help prevent its political capture.

Other necessary reforms include actions to reverse several trends that have reduced the representativeness of the U.S. political system, in particular via redistricting, which since the early 2000s has created scores of electoral districts that are safe for one of the two major parties.

Even more important than specific policy reforms is a general increase in the mobilization of society, and here too there is fairly broad agreement in the United States. One of the features of nineteenth-century American society that most fascinated Tocqueville was people's willingness to organize and form associations outside the government. This not only enabled them to solve specific societal problems but also created popular pressure on political decision making. The decline of these types of associations has been much emphasized in recent years. Though the extent and exact causes of this decline are debated and not all organizations have an important political role, a new vigor in the type of associations that are capable of keeping the state and powerful elites in check is essential. This is even more the case because labor organizations, which often counteract the influence of economic elites, have become much weaker over the last several decades. This decline highlights the need for alternate forms of organizations that can enable new pathways into politics for both industrial workers and other citizens. An open question is whether (and how) such organizations can effectively shoulder the role that trade unions played in the past. We return to this question at the end of the chapter.

Learning from the Swedish success in building a diverse coalition to support and monitor the expansion of the state's capacity should not be read as a recommendation that the United States or other Western countries blindly emulate and copy the details of what Sweden started doing more than eighty years ago. To start with, the coalitions that can undergird positive Red Queen dynamics in the United States will have to be very different from the coalitions of workers and peasants in the Swedish cow trade. They will have to involve different regions, different ideological groups, and different ethnic groups. Because the United States is still the world's most innovative country in a range of leading industries, such as software, artificial intelligence, biotechnology, and high-tech engineering, it must pursue a different organization from what Sweden pursued in the 1930s. But securing opportunities and incentives for business dynamism and innovation does not contradict creating a better safety net and welfare state. It does not contradict helping mobilize society to keep the state in check. It certainly does not contradict developing a capable state either, especially since the involvement of the American state in science and research has been a mainstay of the innovative energy of the American economy. This can be seen from the activities of the U.S. government as a major purchaser of high-tech equipment and also as the primary financier of research via organizations such as the National Science Foundation and with generous tax credits for research expenditures. The question then is how the United States and other Western nations can redirect economic activity toward creating a more equitable division of resources, while keeping the state shackled. Some clues about an answer are provided by considering the problem of monitoring the state when it is dealing with security threats.

Leviathan's War on Terror

The template of how the state can expand its capacity to deal with new problems while remaining shackled also applies to non-economic challenges. Some of the most critical demands that citizens make of their states are about security. Indeed one powerful incentive to engage in state building is the search for a centralized authority to enforce laws, resolve conflicts, and guarantee security. But as the world changes, so does the nature of security challenges.

That became abundantly clear to most Westerners on the morning of September 11, 2001, when nineteen hijackers from the terrorist organization Al-Qaeda took control of four U.S. commercial flights and crashed two of them into the towers of the World Trade Center in New York, while another one was flown into the Pentagon building in Washington, D.C., and the final one was brought down in a field in Pennsylvania as passengers fought the hijackers. The overall death toll was 2,996, with over 6,000 people injured. Though of course the world had seen its fair share of murderous terrorist attacks and hijackings before September 11 and Western states had dealt with the various security challenges of the Cold War for some decades, the scale and audacity of these attacks shocked the public. Most citizens and government agencies interpreted this as the beginning of a new world of security threats that had to be confronted, with great urgency. Even if further large-scale attacks have been averted in the intervening eighteen years, this diagnosis has largely been proven right, as there have been many smaller-scale attacks and several foiled attempts engineered by similar organizations, most notably the so-called Islamic State. We thus have a clear example of society calling for an increase in state capacity and activism to confront new challenges.

These calls have been answered, and U.S. security agencies have grown massively and expanded their responsibilities. But as we already pointed out in Chapter 10, this hasn't happened under the control of society, as became painfully clear in June 2013 when the media began to report some of the secret documents released by Edward Snowden revealing the existence and functions of the classified surveillance programs of the federal government. The first program to be revealed was PRISM, which allowed for direct access to Americans' Google, Yahoo!, Microsoft, Facebook, YouTube, and Skype accounts. We also learned about a secret court order requiring Verizon to hand over millions of Americans' phone records to the National Security Agency (NSA); about Boundless Informant, a data-mining program collecting metadata information on billions of e-mails and phone calls; and about XKeyscore, a computer system that allows for collection of "almost anything done on the internet." Snowden revealed that the NSA was harvesting millions of e-mail and instant-messaging contact lists, searching e-mail content, tracking and mapping the location of cell phones, and undermining attempts at encryption. As Snowden put it, "I, sitting at my desk [could] wiretap anyone, from you or your accountant, to a federal judge or even the president, if I had a personal e-mail." After Snowden's revelations, Daniel Ellsberg, famous for leaking the Pentagon Papers, argued:

> Snowden's disclosures are a true constitutional moment . . . Edward Snowden has done more for our Constitution in terms of the Fourth and First Amendment than anyone else I know.

Perhaps all of this is a tempest in a teacup. Maybe it's unavoidable that in fighting serious terrorist threats security agencies must act secretly, collect massive amounts of data, and ignore privacy concerns, and let some in the media complain loudly. Maybe.

Let's turn to the Danish experience to gain a perspective. In 2006 the European Union issued a Data Retention Directive concerning "the retention of data generated or processed in connection with the provision of publicly available electronic communications services or of public communications networks." The Danish government decided to expand on the directive and published a law going far beyond what was slated, including an obligation for "session logging" which required providers to store information on users' source and destination IP addresses, port numbers, session type, and time stamp. In response, Privacy International, a nonprofit organization that monitors and defends privacy around the world, downgraded the country to a score of 2.0 (extensive surveillance societies) from its previous level of 2.5 (systemic failure to uphold safeguards). This places Denmark 34th among the 45 countries included in the study. Most Danes don't seem bothered, however. They trust that the Danish government will not use their IP addresses, port numbers, session types, and time stamps to snoop on them, suppress their freedom of speech, or imprison them because of their political views. In April 2015 the European Court of Justice concluded that Danish data retention practices were "a particularly serious interference with fundamental rights," but the Danish public was not up in arms and did not demand the cessation of the data retention practices.

The difference between the Danish and U.S. responses is not that the Danish government did not aggressively deal with similar security threats. It was that it did this while maintaining the trust of Danish society. This turned on two critical factors. First, while the U.S. program was secret and kept expanding without oversight, the Danish data retention policies were clearly announced to the public and were not subject to mission creep. Second, the Danes started with basic trust in their institutions and believed that their government would not use the information against them or for extraordinary rendition and torture, like the CIA did in the aftermath of September 11. Both of these factors suggest that the Danes believe, for good reason, that the data collected by their government would not threaten the shackled nature of their state. Not so with the American public, precisely because the CIA, the FBI, and the NSA have a habit of acting in unchecked, sometimes unscrupulous ways.

There is therefore a strong parallel between how the Shackled Leviathan might have to deal with new security threats while remaining shackled and how it may have to respond to new economic challenges. This parallel is rooted in the critical importance of institutional and other restraints keeping the Leviathan in the corridor. Society's trust in the state is a reflection of these restraints. From this perspective what was problematic in the response by the NSA and the CIA to new security threats wasn't their expanding responsibilities and activities, but the secret and unmonitored ways in which they went about organizing them. The programs revealed by Snowden were supposed to be monitored by the Foreign Intelligence Surveillance Courts, but the courts functioned secretly as well and were often no more than a rubber stamp. Not the right way to keep the shackles on or build trust.

———

We started in Chapter 1 with some famous predictions about how most countries will move toward liberal democracy, anarchy, or dictatorships. Yuval Noah Harari's warning that digital dictatorship was on the horizon for much of humanity was perhaps the most ominous, and the Chinese "social credit" system and the NSA's aggressive surveillance programs add credence to Harari's predictions. But as we have argued, there is no reason to expect that all or most countries will inexorably move toward the same type of political or economic system. It will be the prevailing balance between state and society that determines their paths. The Danish alternative to the same security threats underscores this point. When security threats are met with expanding and unmonitored powers of the state, abuses are much more likely to occur and the danger of a digital dictatorship increases. When the same actions are taken in plain sight and society can monitor whether these powers are being misused, the balance of power underpinning the corridor is reaffirmed. This reaffirmation encourages the use of new technologies in a way that is much more consistent with the principles of the Shackled Leviathan, even if these technologies could compromise privacy. The way new technologies will be deployed and whether they will disrupt the balance of power is not preordained. It is our choice.

Rights in Action: The Niemöller Principle

It is not just difficult to create a Shackled Leviathan. It also takes hard work to live with it. We have suggested a few specific ways in which society can be strengthened in the presence of a growing Leviathan. The most critical idea is to leverage society's mobilization. But how do you achieve that in practice? Are there organizational avenues to help society expand its capabilities and control over the state and elites? We believe the answer is yes. It relates to the ideas from the previous chapter—to build on the protection for the rights of citizens against all threats, including those from the state, the elites, and other citizens.

Rights are intimately connected to our notion of liberty as protection of individuals from fear, violence, and dominance. Though fear and violence have been the main drivers of people fleeing their homes, dominance—the inability of individuals to make choices and pursue their lives according to their own values—is often as stifling. Rights are fundamentally ways for society to encode in its laws and norms the capacity of all individuals to make such choices in their lives.

The emphasis on rights extends back at least to John Locke as well as to Thomas Jefferson's statement concerning "rights inherent and inalienable, among which are the preservation of life, and liberty, and the pursuit of happiness" in the Declaration of Independence, and the French Declaration of the Rights of Man and of the Citizen of 1789. Our modern conception is shaped by the Universal Declaration of Rights of the United Nations adopted in 1948. William Beveridge anticipated these ideas in a 1945 pamphlet, *Why I Am a Liberal*, in which he wrote:

> Liberty means more than freedom from the arbitrary power of Governments. It means freedom from economic servitude to Want and Squalor and other social evils; it means freedom from arbitrary power in any form. A starving man is not free.

The Universal Declaration similarly asserts:

> Whereas disregard and contempt for human rights have resulted in bar-
> barous acts which have outraged the conscience of mankind, and the
> advent of a world in which human beings shall enjoy freedom of speech
> and belief and freedom from fear and want has been proclaimed as the
> highest aspiration of the common people.

Article 23 proceeds:

> 1. Everyone has the right to work, to free choice of employment, to just and
>   favorable conditions of work and to protection against unemployment.
> 2. Everyone, without any discrimination, has the right to equal pay for equal
>   work.
> 3. Everyone who works has the right to just and favorable remuneration ensur-
>   ing for himself and his family an existence worthy of human dignity, and
>   supplemented, if necessary, by other means of social protection.
> 4. Everyone has the right to form and to join trade unions for the protection of
>   his interests.

FDR was also articulating similar notions. In 1940 and 1941, he emphasized
"four essential freedoms": freedom of speech, freedom of religion, freedom from
want, and freedom from fear. In his State of the Union address of 1944 he went
further and stated:

> We have come to a clear realization of the fact that true individual free-
> dom cannot exist without economic security and independence. "Neces-
> sitous men are not free men." People who are hungry and out of a job
> are the stuff of which dictatorships are made.

He then listed the essential rights as "the right to a useful and renumerative
job"; "the right to earn enough to provide adequate food and clothing and recre-
ation"; "the right of every businessman, large and small, to trade in an atmosphere
of freedom from unfair competition and domination by monopolies at home or
abroad"; "the right of every family to a decent home"; "the right to adequate protection from the economic fears of old age, sickness, accident, and unemployment";

and "the right to a good education." FDR had in the past been willing to abridge some of these rights and freedoms, for example, with the internment of Japanese citizens from 1942 to 1945, and he had worked with Jim Crow laws in the South. (One African American's reaction to FDR's four freedoms is telling: "White folks talking about the Four Freedoms, and we ain't got none.") His conversion to the importance of rights signals how the mood was changing on both sides of the Atlantic.

What is remarkable in these statements are two tenets of the conception of rights: they are universal and general (and in this they go far beyond the Declaration of Independence, which did not cover slaves and was unclear on women), and they recognize the importance of individuals being able to realize their choices. Thus threats of violence and restrictions on freedom of thought or speech against any group are violations of rights, and so is preventing people from exercising their religious activities (or lack thereof) or sexual preferences. But equally important, taking away the means of earning a decent living is a violation as well, because this too will create a form of dominance. This latter dominance is rooted not just in the fact that abject poverty would make it impossible for people to pursue a meaningful life, but also in the realization that under such circumstances, employers can demand work in unpleasant, demeaning, or highly disempowering conditions (remember the Dalit manual scavengers in Chapter 8).

This conception of rights is crucial for the liberty not just of men and the majority; but of women; of religious, ethnic, and sexual minorities; and of people with disabilities and impairments. Enshrining these rights creates clear limits on what the state and powerful elites in society can and cannot do. Taking away the ability of people to organize, argue their case, or pursue their way of life is beyond the limits of what anybody can do when these rights are clearly protected. So is creating conditions that force people to be economically subservient and dominated.

Herein lie the beginnings of a transformative power for society. If clearly delineated boundaries on what the state cannot do are recognized universally, encroachments of these boundaries can create the spark for a broad-based societal mobilization to stop the state's creeping overreach. Recognizing minority rights as universal is crucial, because without such recognition, only the specific minorities whose rights are currently being violated will complain and protest—with no mobilization or response, as in the disorganized, fragmented societies in India (Chapter 8) and Latin America and Africa (Chapter 11). Universal recognition of rights creates the basis for broad coalitions.

The importance of this idea was anticipated by the German Lutheran pastor Martin Niemöller, who in a poem composed in the 1950s pithily captured why it was so easy for the Nazi state to quickly dominate German society. The most well-known version of the poem, engraved at many of the Holocaust memorial museums and often recited at remembrance events, reads:

> First they came for the Socialists, and I did not speak out
>> because I was not a Socialist.
> Then they came for the trade unionists, and I did not speak out
>> because I was not a trade unionist.
> Then they came for the Jews, and I did not speak out
>> because I was not a Jew.
> Then they came for me
>> and there was no one left to speak for me.

So in Niemöller's account it was the lack of universal recognition of very basic rights that was at the root of the inability of German society to rise up to the Nazis, who could deal with and eliminate each group separately, without mobilizing a broad coalition within German society to stand up to them. This turned out to be a particularly bad way of defending the corridor.

These ideas too were to some degree anticipated by FDR, who in the same State of the Union address of 1944 emphasized the importance of a diverse set of rights for everybody, and for good measure quoted Benjamin Franklin's statement from 1776, "We must all hang together, or assuredly we shall all hang separately."

Turning this logic on its head, to the extent that society can make a broad set of (reasonable) rights more universal, it will be better placed to organize and match the state's expanding power. It is noteworthy that these rights as expressed by the Universal Declaration include access to gainful employment, because this creates room and incentives for different parts of society, motivated by economic considerations and grievances, to come together in a broad coalition and organize to resist despotism. These challenges may be particularly vital in the future as the labor movement may never regain its previous influence, as we have already discussed. A (civil) society organized around rights is one alternative.

———

Many of us living in democratic countries with assertive societies and high-capacity states are immensely fortunate compared to those suffering under the yoke of a Despotic Leviathan or surviving under fear, violence, and dominance without any state institutions to protect them. Nevertheless, living with the (shackled) Leviathan is a work in progress. Our argument has been that the key to making this more stable and less likely to spin out of the corridor is to seek to create and re-create the balance of power between state and society, between those who are powerful and those who are not. The Red Queen effect is there to help us, but ultimately society's power is about society's organization and mobilization.

————————

In October 2017, women started speaking up about the sexual harassment and assault they had been subjected to by men with power over them. It began with the allegations against the towering movie mogul Harvey Weinstein. On October 5, actress Ashley Judd added to the accusations. On October 17, actress Alyssa Milano adopted a term coined by activist Tarana Burke in 2006 and tweeted, "If you've been sexually harassed or assaulted, write 'me too' as a reply to this tweet." An avalanche of tweets followed and a social movement was born. Even if we are nowhere near full equality and protection for women around the world, because people have rallied against the violations of these most basic rights, it has become quite a bit more difficult for the powerful to harass, demean, and assault women in government, companies, and schools. Laws started to change in response, for example, with New York State's new sexual harassment prevention law.

Human progress depends on the expansion of the state's capacity to meet new challenges and combat all dominances, old and new, but that won't happen unless society demands it and mobilizes to defend everybody's rights. There is nothing easy or automatic about that, but it can and does happen.

ACKNOWLEDGMENTS

We have accumulated a large number of intellectual debts in writing this book. The most important ones are those to our coauthors who have worked with us on various aspects of the research we build on in this book. We thank Maria Angélica Bautista, Jeanet Bentzen, Davide Cantoni, Isaías Chaves, Ali Cheema, Jonathan Conning, Giuseppe De Feo, Giacomo De Luca, Melissa Dell, Georgy Egorov, Leopoldo Fergusson, Juan Sebastián Galan, Francisco Gallego, Camilo García-Jimeno, Jacob Hariri, Tarek Hassan, Leander Heldring, Matthew Jackson, Simon Johnson, Asim Khwaja, Sara Lowes, Sebastián Mazzuca, Jacob Moscona, Suresh Naidu, Jeffrey Nugent, Nathan Nunn, Philip Osafo-Kwaako, Steve Pincus, Tristan Reed, Juan Diego Restrepo, Pascual Restrepo, Dario Romero, Pablo Querubín, Rafael Santos-Villagran, Ahmed Tahoun, Davide Ticchi, Konstantin Sonin, Ragnar Torvik, Juan F. Vargas, Thierry Verdier, Andrea Vindigni, Sebastian Vollmer, Jon Weigel, Alex Wolitzky, and Pierre Yared for their creativity, hard work, and patience.

We would particularly like to thank Joel Mokyr, who organized a two-day book conference at the Center for Economic History at Northwestern University in March 2018. For over twenty years Joel has been an intellectual inspiration, academic role model, and source of immense professional support, and it's hard to imagine what our careers would have been like without him. At the conference we received penetrating feedback from all of the participants: Karen Alter, Sandeep Baliga, Chris Blattman, Peter Boettke, Federica Carugati, Daniel Diermeier,

Georgy Egorov, Tim Feddersen, Gary Feinman, Gillian Hadfield, Noel Johnson, Lynne Kiesling, Mark Koyama, Linda Nicholas, Debin Ma, Melanie Meng Xue, Suresh Naidu, John Nye, Pablo Querubín, Jared Rubin, Ken Shepsle, Konstantin Sonin, David Stasavage, John Wallis, and Bart Wilson. We are grateful to Bram van Besouw and Matti Mitrunen for taking notes at this conference and helping us keep track of the freewheeling discussion.

This is probably the moment to also mention the scholars who have influenced the trajectory of our research over the past two decades, particularly Lee Alston, Jean-Marie Baland, Robert Bates, Tim Besley, Jared Diamond, Robert Dixon, Richard Easterlin, Stanley Engerman, Jeffry Frieden, Steven Haber, Joe Henrich, Ian Morris, Douglass North, Josh Ober, Neil Parsons, Torsten Persson, Jean-Philippe Platteau, Kenneth Sokoloff, Guido Tabellini, Jan Vansina, Barry Weingast, and Fabrizio Zilibotti.

We received very useful comments on various chapters from Siwan Anderson, David Autor, Peter Diamond, Jon Gruber, Simon Johnson, Lakshmi Iyer, Ramzy Mardini, Mark Pryzyk, Gautam Rao, Cory Smith, David Yang, and Anand Swamy, and we are grateful for their time and erudition. Chris Ackerman and Cihat Tokgöz read the entire manuscript and provided extensive comments, suggestions, and advice.

We have presented versions of the ideas here in many different seminar settings over the past few years, including the Nemmers Lecture at Northwestern, the Munich Lectures, the Kuznets Lecture at Yale, the Richard Stone Lecture at Cambridge, the Sun Chen Lecture in Taipei, the Jean-Jacques Laffont Lecture at Toulouse, the Guillermo O' Donnell Memorial Lecture at Notre Dame, the Linowes Lecture at the University of Illinois (Urbana–Champaign), the Oxford Development Studies Annual Lecture, the ABCDE Keynote Address at the World Bank, and the Annual Social Ontology Conference at Tufts. We received many useful comments and suggestions and would like particularly to thank Toke Aidt, Gabriel Leon, and Min-Jeng Lin.

Superb research assistance was provided by Tom Hao, Matt Lowe, Carlos Molina, Jacob Moscona, Frederick Papazyan, and Jose Ignacio Velarde Morales. Toby Greenberg has been invaluable as our photo editor. Alex Carr, Lauren Fahey, and Shelby Jamerson provided invaluable editorial suggestions and corrections.

We are also eternally grateful to our partners, Asu Ozdaglar and Maria Angélica Bautista, for their support, encouragement, and patience.

Last but not least, we are deeply grateful to our agent, Max Brockman, and our editors, Scott Moyers and Daniel Crewe, and the assistant editor at Penguin Press, Mia Council, for their commitment to this project and very useful suggestions. All remaining errors are of course ours.

BIBLIOGRAPHIC ESSAY

The main arguments in this book are related to many areas of research, and we cannot do justice to all these ideas in this brief essay. We thus focus on some of the most related research here and refer the reader to Acemoglu and Robinson (2016, 2019) for a discussion of the broader literature and our connections to and differences from it.

Most centrally, we build on our previous work on the importance of balance between state and society in Acemoglu (2005) and Acemoglu and Robinson (2016, 2017). We also build on a large literature on the role of institutions (Acemoglu, Johnson, and Robinson, 2001, 2002, 2005a, 2005b; Acemoglu, Gallego, and Robinson, 2014; North, Wallis, and Weingast, 2011; Besley and Pearson, 2011; Acemoglu and Robinson, 2012).

Our book is centrally about the development of state capacity, which has been studied by many social scientists. We sharply differ from the modal emphasis in this literature, which is on the importance of the state setting up its control over society and over violence as a precursor to the development of democratic institutions, civil society, and political rights (e.g., Huntington, 1968; Tilly, 1992; Fukuyama, 2011, 2014; and also Besley and Persson, 2011). Rather, we argue and document that society's mobilization and contestation of power is critical for the development of democratic and participatory institutions and in fact a capable state. This perspective in turn builds on Acemoglu and Robinson (2000, 2006) as well as Therborn (1977) and Rueschemeyer, Stephens, and Stephens (1992). But our argument here is much broader because it brings in the organization of society and associations (inspired by Tocqueville, 2002, and Dahl, 1970); because it stresses the role of norms in this power struggle (partly borrowing from the anthropological literature, such as Bohannan, 1958, as well as Scott, 2010); because, inspired by Migdal (1988, 2001), it recognizes that "weak states" will result when these norms are too strong and prevent the emergence of political hierarchy and autonomous state institutions; and because it also incorporates how the agenda over which political contestation takes place changes, potentially strengthening society, as state institutions develop (as proposed by Tilly, 1995, and Acemoglu, Robinson, and Torvik, 2016).

Finally, our overall approach is also inspired by several important academic works. These include: Mann's (1986) definition of the despotic power of the state (similar to ours as the state not being accountable to society); Moore's (1966) approach to linking the origins of different political regimes and types of state-society relations to historical economic and political circumstances, such as presence or absence of labor coercion, and the resulting social coalition; North and Thomas's (1973) thesis about the "rise of the West"; Engerman and Sokoloff's (2011) work on the historical roots of comparative development in the Americas; Pincus's (2011) analysis of the Glorious Revolution; Bates's (1981) theory of the comparative political economy in Africa; Flannery and Marcus's (2014) synthesis of archaeological and ethnographic evidence and their account of the emergence of complex society; and Brenner's (1976) emphasis on the role of power relations between landowners and peasants in the transition from feudalism to capitalism.

PREFACE

The quotations from John Locke can be found in Locke (2003, 101–2, 124).

The testimonies from Syria are all from Pearlman (2017, 175, 178, 213).

The excerpts from Gilgamesh are taken from Mitchell (2004, 69–70, 72–74).

The 2018 UAE Gender Equality Awards, https://www.theguardian.com/sport/2019/jan/28/uae-mocked -for-gender-equality-awards-won-entirely-by-men.

See Holton (2003) for the women's suffrage movement in Britain and the empowerment of women and the facts we use.

CHAPTER 1. HOW DOES HISTORY END?

The contrasting arguments made by Francis Fukuyama, Robert Kaplan, and Yuval Noah Harari are presented in Fukuyama (1989), Kaplan (1994), and Harari (2018). We quote from Fukuyama (1989, 3), and Kaplan (1994, 46).

The text of the 2005 Constitution of the DRC can be found at http://www.parliament.am/library /sahmanadrutyunner/kongo.pdf.

A useful overview of the rebel groups of the Eastern DRC is provided by the BBC: http://www.bbc.com /news/world-africa-20586792.

On Congo as rape capital of the world, see http://news.bbc.co.uk/2/hi/africa/8650112.stm.

Kaplan's description of Lagos is from Kaplan (1994, 52).

The quotes from Wole Soyinka are from Soyinka (2006, 348, 351–54, 356–57).

The description of bodies under the bridge is from Cunliffe-Jones (2010, 23).

For Lagos disappearing under rubbish, see http://news.bbc.co.uk/2/hi/africa/281895.stm.

The quotes from Philip Pettit come from Pettit (1999, 4–5), and see also the development of his ideas in Pettit (2014).

The seminal paper on the violence of hunter-gatherer societies is Ember (1978); we refer here to the work of Keeley (1996) and Pinker (2011); see specifically the data in Pinker's Figure 2-3 (53). On the homicide rates of the Gebusi, see Knauft (1987).

All quotes from Hobbes are directly from Hobbes (1996, Chapters 13, 17–19: "continual feare," 89; "from hence it comes to passe," 87; "In such condition," 89; "men live without" and "to submit their Wills," 120).

On Eichmann we quote from Arendt (1976, 44–45).

Heidegger is quoted from Pattison (2000, 33–34).

The stories about the Great Leap Forward come from Jisheng (2012, 4–5, 18, 21, 24–25). For the story of Luo Hongshan, see Chinese Human Rights Defenders (2009); we quote from p. 5. Freedom House (2015) reports on the "black jails" and the "community corrections system." The "Four Clean-ups" is discussed at http://cmp.hku.hk/2013/10/17/34310/.

Cruickshank from Cruickshank (1853, 31); Bonnat from Wilks (1975, 667).

Rattray is quoted from Rattray (1929, 33). The stories of Goi and Bwanikwa are from Campbell (1933, Chapters 18 and 19). Spilsbury is quoted from Howard (2003, 272). Miers and Kopytoff, eds. (1977), is an important collection on the nature of "freedom" in precolonial Africa.

Ginsburg (2011) provides an introduction and analysis of the Pashtunwali from a legal point of view. Our quote is taken from the translated Pashtunwali at http://khyber.org/.

Facts about the early history of Wyoming are from Larson (1990); we quote from pp. 42–47, 233, 275. A good treatment of the Johnson County Range War is Johnson (2008).

CHAPTER 2. THE RED QUEEN

There are many superb treatments of classical Greek history and the development of Athenian institutions that are relevant for this chapter. We build particularly on Ober (2015a), Morris (2010), Hall (2013), Osborne (2009), Powell (2016), and Rhodes (2011). On political institutions, see in particular the essays in Brock and Hodkinson, eds. (2001), and in Robinson (2011).

See Finley (1954) for a characterization of Dark Age Greek society. Plutarch (1914), "Theseus" and "Solon," is the source for the life of Theseus and Solon; our quotes come from the relevant chapters. The constitutions of Athens are listed and analyzed in Aristotle (1996), and this book is an invaluable source for the whole chapter, for example, on the nature of the state built by Cleisthenes. All our Aristotle quotes are from it. On what remains of Solon's laws, see Leão and Rhodes (2016), Draco's homicide law is reproduced on p. 20. Hall (2013) is excellent on the bureaucratized nature of Solon's reforms. See Osborne (2009) on Solon's land reforms. Important essays on Athenian political development are Morris (1996) and Ober (2005). Forsdyke (2005, 2012) analyzes Greek norms and their institutionalization. On the fiscal institutions developed by Cleisthenes, see Ober (2015b), Van Wees (2013), and Fawcett (2016). On how laws were enforced in Athens, see Lanni (2016) and Gottesman (2014).

Gjeçov (1989) collected the Kanun. We quote from pp. 162 and 172 of this book.

The U.S. Bill of Rights is online at https://www.archives.gov/founding-docs/bill-of-rights/what-does -it-say.

The Federalist Papers are all available on the Internet at https://www.congress.gov/resources/display /content/The+Federalist+Papers.

Madison is quoted from Federalist no. 51. Our discussion of the Constitution follows Holton (2008), Breen (2011), and Meier (2011). Madison's "divide and rule" letter is quoted from Holton (2008, 207). Jefferson is quoted from Jefferson (1904, 360–62). Tocqueville is quoted from Tocqueville (2002, Vol. 1, Part 2, Chapter 4, and Vol. 2, Part 2, Chapter 5).

On the U.S. Civil War, see McPherson (2003). On the development of the economy and politics of the U.S. South after the Civil War, see Woodward (1955) and Wright (1986).

Alice's race against the Red Queen is from Carroll (1871, 28–30).

The classic ethnographic survey of the Tiv is Bohannan and Bohannan (1953). See Lugard (1922) for the most famous statement of his philosophy of indirect rule, and see Perham (1960) for a comprehensive biography. See Curtin (1995) on the incidence of stateless societies in West Africa at the time of European colonial conquest and Osafo-Kwaako and Robinson (2013) for some basic correlates. The Lugard quote is from Afigbo (1967, 694), and Afigbo (1972) is the seminal study of the warrant chiefs. Quotes from Bohannan are from Bohannan (1958, 3, 11). Akiga's observation is from Akiga (1939, 264).

The concept of illegibility is from Scott (2010). A good overview of communalism in Lebanon is Cammett (2014). On the communal affiliations of Beirut football teams, see Reiche (2011). For prize tweets on the Lebanese parliament, see https://www.beirut.com/l/49413.

On the frequency of parliamentary meetings, see https://www.yahoo.com/news/lebanons-political -system-sinks-nation-debt-070626499--finance.html, which also quotes Ghassan Moukheiber. The Facebook post from the YouStink movement can be found at https://www.facebook.com /tol3etre7etkom/posts/1631214497140665?fref=nf&pnref=story. On the YouStink movement, see https://foreignpolicy.com/2015/08/25/theres-something-rotten-in-lebanon-trash-you-stink.

On Route 66 and sundown towns, see Candacy Taylor (2016), "The Roots of Route 66," at https://www .theatlantic.com/politics/archive/2016/11/the-roots-of-route-66/506255/.

On Tiananmen Square, see Lim (2014). On Liu Xiabo's life, see Jie (2015). On the Weiquan movement, see Pils (2014). The story of Zhao Hua is from Dan Levin (2012), "A Chinese Education, for a Price," https://www.nytimes.com/2012/11/22/world/asia/in-china-schools-a-culture-of-bribery-spreads .html.

Pei (2016) contains detailed information about the sale of offices.

On uncertainty and possible exaggeration about Chinese GDP growth, see https://www.cnbc.com /2016/01/19/what-is-chinas-actual-gdp-experts-weigh-in.html, and also https://www.stlouisfed.org /publications/regional-economist/second-quarter-2017/chinas-economic-data-an-accurate -reflection-or-just-smoke-and-mirrors for an overview. For a survey of business economists on the accuracy of China's GDP statistics, see https://www.wsj.com/articles/wsj-survey-chinas-growth -statements-make-u-s-economists-skeptical-1441980001. On Li Keqiang's statement on unreliability of Chinese GDP statistics, see https://www.reuters.com/article/us-china-economy-wikileaks/chinas -gdp-is-man-made-unreliable-top-leader-idUSTRE6B527D20101206.

CHAPTER 3. WILL TO POWER

There is a vast scholarly literature about the life of Muhammad and Islam. Our treatment of his life follows Watt (1953, 1956), published together in an abridged version in Watt (1961). There are many very good treatments of this period of history, for example Hourani (2010), Lapidus (2014), and Kennedy (2015). The Constitution of Medina is quoted from Watt (1961, 94).

On the notion of an "edge," see Flannery (1999). See Flannery and Marcus (2014) for a development of the idea.

Our description of the battle of Isandlwana comes from Smith-Dorrien (1925, Chapter 1, "The Zulu War"). On the rise of the Zulu state see Eldredge (2014), Wright and Hamilton (1989), and Morris (1998). We quote from Eldredge (2014, 7, 77). Henry Flynn is quoted from Flynn (1986, 71). A seminal analysis of the Zulu state is due to Gluckman (1940, 1960). Ritter (1985) records the scene of Shaka with the witch doctors in Chapter 10.

The study of state formation in the Hawaiian Islands starts with the seminal work of Kirch (2010, 2012), which influenced our discussion. Kamakau (1992) is essential, and see in particular his discussion of Liholiho's abolition of the eating taboo. Our quote from David Malo is from his book (1987, 60–61). Breaking of taboos is discussed in Kamakau (1992). Handy, "in its fundamental," is quoted from Kuykendall (1965, 8); Handy ("Mana was exhibited") and Kepelino are quoted from Kirch (2010, 38, 40–41). Kuykendall (1965, 68) is the source for the contemporary description of Liholiho breaking taboo.

On Georgian history and political economy, see Wheatley (2005) and Christopher (2004). Our approach to the rise of Shevardnadze follows Driscoll (2015).

CHAPTER 4. ECONOMICS OUTSIDE THE CORRIDOR

Colson is quoted from Colson (1974, Chapter 3). On the clan system of the Plateau Tonga, see Colson (1962).

Turner (2007) provides an overview of the conflict in the Congo, and the description of the attack on Nyabiondo comes from pp. 135–38 of his book.

On begging and poverty among the Tonga, see Colson (1967). Our quote comes from pp. 53–56.

Bohannan and Bohannan (1968) is the seminal treatment of how the Tiv organized their economy; we quote from Chapter 16. Akiga's story is published as Akiga (1939).

The sources cited in the previous chapter give a good overview of the basic political history after the rise of the Islamic state. We cite from Ibn Khaldun (2015) and Al-Muqaddasi (1994). See Watson (1983) on innovation in agriculture. On trade in the Islamic empires, see Shatzmiller (2009) and Michalopoulos, Naghavi, and Prarolo (2018). On the economy of the Middle East, see Rodinson (2007), Kuran (2012), Blaydes and Chaney (2013), Pamuk (2014), Özmucur and Pamuk (2002), and Pamuk (2006). Pamuk (2006) presents historical data on real wages illustrating that by the late medieval period real living standards were already significantly lower in the Middle East than in Western Europe.

The 1978 constitutional clause that refers to the splintered paddle is available here: http://lrbhawaii .org/con/conart9.html.

Our discussion of despotic growth in Hawaii uses the same sources as in the previous chapter, especially again the work of Patrick Kirch, who also uses the metaphor of a "shark going inland." Fornander is quoted from Kirch (2010, 41). See Kamakau (1992) on Kamehameha's state building. See Kirch and Sahlins (1992) on the sandalwood trade, and the contemporary visitor; Mathison and Ely are quoted from Kirch and Sahlins (1992, Chapters 3 and 4).

"The Land of Zululand" is from Eldredge (2014, 233). The quote from Gluckman is from Gluckman (1960), cited in the previous chapter.

The analysis of economic growth in Georgia is based on the same sources as in the previous chapter.

CHAPTER 5. ALLEGORY OF GOOD GOVERNMENT

There is a large scholarly literature on the Sienese frescoes and their political meaning and the Italian communes more generally. Rubinstein (1958) and Skinner (1986, 1999) are seminal analyses of the frescoes. Wickham (2015) provides a lucid recent introduction to the communes and their origins. Our discussion of Milanese political names is drawn from his book. Waley and Dean (2013) is a very useful introduction to the Italian communes, as is the more demanding Jones (1997). Bowsky (1981) and Waley (1991) provide detailed discussions of Sienese institutions.

Bishop Otto is quoted from Geary, ed. (2015, 537).

The oath of the Nine is from Waley (1991, Chapter 3).

Benjamin of Tudela is quoted from Waley and Dean (2013, 11).

The discussion of Milanese names comes from Wickham (2015, Chapter 2).

For the life of Saint Francis of Assisi, see Thompson (2012). On the Champagne fairs, see Edwards and Ogilvie (2012).

On the medieval commercial revolution, see Lopez (1976) and Epstein (2009). Mokyr (1990) and Gies and Gies (1994) are excellent overviews of the development of medieval technology. Our data on the populations of the thirty largest cities are from DeLong and Shleifer (1993). See Acemoglu, Johnson, and Robinson (2002) for a defense and use of historical urbanization data as a proxy for economic development. The data on urbanization come from Bosker, Buringh, and van Zanden (2013), and see Buringh and van Zanden (2009) on book production and literacy. See Goldthwaite (2009) for data on Florence, and Fratianni and Spinelli (2006) and Pezzlo (2014) for broader economic and financial trends. Mueller (1997) has a detailed discussion of the nature of bills of exchange.

The life of Francesco di Marco Datini is recorded in Origo (1957), from which we quoted the story of how Datini got rich in the Canary Islands (3–4). The significance of the life of Saint Godric as a representative story of the social origins of merchants was emphasized by Pirenne (1952); here we quote from the biography of Godric written by his contemporary Reginald of Durham (1918).

Our interpretation of the Zapotec state draws heavily from the research of Richard Blanton, Gary Feinman, and Linda Nicholas; see in particular Blanton, Feinman, Kowalewski, and Nicholas (1999) and Blanton, Kowalewski, Feinman, and Finsten (1993). Blanton and Fargher (2008) extend the arguments about the bottom-up construction of many premodern polities. The story about tortillas is from Flannery and Marcus (1996), who present a slightly different and less consensual account of the formation of the Zapotec state.

CHAPTER 6. THE EUROPEAN SCISSORS

Our view of the history of Europe has been influenced by Crone (2003) and by Hirst's (2009) brilliant book, which emphasizes the unique confluence of different factors in the early Middle Ages. We also heavily rely on Wickham's (2016) analysis of the role of assembly politics. See also Reuter (2001), Barnwell and Mostert, eds. (2003), Pantos and Semple, eds. (2004), and especially Wickham (2009, 2017). On the "communal revolution," see Kümin (2013) for an overview and the influential writings of Blickel (1989, 1998).

Gregory of Tours (1974) is the basic source for the early Franks, and from it we draw the description of Clovis's coronation and the scene of the threatened hair cutting (123, 140, 154, 180–81). Murray (1983) and Todd (2004) discuss what we know of the organization of early German society. Wood (1994) provides an overview of Merovingian history. Hincmar of Reims's relevant writings are reproduced in Hincmar of Reims (1980). We quote his description of an assembly (222, 226). Tacitus's description of German assemblies is from Tacitus (1970, 107–112).

Eich (2015) provides an overview of the development of the Roman bureaucracy. See also Jones (1964) and Kelly (2005), who discusses the writing of John Lydus; see Chapter 1.

The Salic Law is quoted from Yale's Avalon Project, http://avalon.law.yale.edu/medieval/salic.asp. See also Drew (1991, 59, 79–80, 82–83). Costambeys, Innes, and MacLean (2011) is a comprehensive overview of Carolingian history; see also Nelson (2003). There is a great deal of academic controversy about the exact nature of the relationship between the Roman and Frankish state; see Wallace-Hadrill (1971, 1982), Geary (1988), James (1988), Murray (1988), Wolfram (2005), and Wickham (2009, 2016).

The collapse of Roman York is described in Fleming (2010). See also her description of post-Roman York on p. 28. On the role of assembly politics in Anglo-Saxon Britain, see Roach (2013, 2017) and Maddicott (2012), whose book profoundly influenced our interpretation of English political history. Byrhtferth of Ramsey's observations are reproduced in Byrhtferth of Ramsey (2009); we quote from pp. 73, 105, and 107. Bede (1991) is quoted from p. 281. There are many fine overviews of Anglo-Saxon history; our account rests on Stafford (1989) and Williams (1999). Ælfric of Eynsham is quoted from William (2003, 17).

Early English legal codes are translated and reprinted in Attenborough, ed. (1922), and its sequel Robertson, ed. (1925). We quote from Attenborough (1922, 62–93). Hudson (2018) is very good on early English law, and his book also importantly influenced our interpretation.

There are many excellent books on 1066 and the Norman invasion; see, for example, Barlow (1999). On English feudalism, see Crick and van Houts, eds. (2011), and in particular the chapter of Stephen Baxter.

We quote from Bloch (1964, 141, and Chapters 9 and 10).

For the Assize of Clarendon, see http://avalon.law.yale.edu/medieval/assizecl.asp.

Richard FitzNigel is quoted from Hudson (2018, 202).

The text of the Magna Carta is reproduced by Yale's Avalon Project, http://avalon.law.yale.edu/medieval /magframe.asp. See also Holt (2015).

Our interpretation and evidence on state formation in early modern England heavily builds on Braddick (2000), Hindle (2000), and Pincus (2011). See also Blockmans, Holenstein, and Mathieu, eds. (2009). Davison, Hitchcock, Keirn, and Shoemaker, eds. (1992), discuss the imagery of the grumbling hive. The quote is from Mandeville (1989), whose poem is readily available on the Internet: https://en.wikipedia.org/wiki/The_Fable_of_the_Bees#The_poem.

See Hindle (1999) on Swallowfield. He reproduces the resolutions in full. The legal cases we reproduce are from Herrup (1989, 75–76; see Chapter 4). Goldie (2001) emphasizes the importance of the number of officeholders in eighteenth-century Britain; our numbers come from his article.

On the origins of European parliaments, see Bisson (2009) as well as Bisson (1964) for Languedoc, and his edited volume of readings (1973). See also Marongiu (1968), Myers (1975), and Graves (2001) for overviews of the history of European parliamentary institutions and the chapters in Helle (2008) on Scandinavia. See Kümin and Würgler (1997) for the analyses of Hesse. See also Guenée (1985) and Watts (2009).

Our discussion of Icelandic history draws on Karlson (2000) and the chapters of Helle (2008); see Miller (1997) on the persistence of the feud.

Angold (1997) and Treadgold (1997) provide overviews of the relevant Byzantine political history. Procopius is quoted from Procopius (2007). Lopez (1951) is the source for the "dollar of the Middle Ages." Laiou and Morrisson (2007) provide a very useful overview of relevant economic history.

Our discussion of the Red Queen effect in eighteenth-century Britain follows Tilly (1995), and all quotes are from Chapter 1. Brewer (1989) is the seminal study of the British state in the eighteenth century.

Lawes quoted from Edgar (2005). Blackstone quoted from Montgomery (2006, 13).

Caroline Norton's "The Separation of Mother and Child by the Law of 'Custody of Infants,' Considered," is at https://catalog.hathitrust.org/Record/008723154. Her letter to the Queen is from http://digital.library.upenn.edu/women/norton/alttq/alttq.html. We also quote from Wollstonecraft (2009, 103, 107) and Mill (1869, Chapter 1).

The material on the British Industrial Revolution draws from Acemoglu, Johnson, and Robinson (2005) and Acemoglu and Robinson (2012). Mokyr (1990) provides an excellent overview of the technological breakthroughs during the Industrial Revolution. On longitude all our quotes come from Sobel (2007, Chapters 3, 5, 7).

CHAPTER 7. MANDATE OF HEAVEN

There are many excellent surveys of Chinese history in English; the most definitive is the multivolume *Cambridge History of China*, and also very useful is the six-volume Harvard University Press history. Spence (2012) is superb for the early modern and modern periods. Dardess (2010) is a nice terse overview of much political history. See Mote (2000) for an exhaustive study of the imperial state. Von Glahn (2016) is a unique recent overview of the economic history of China up until the collapse of the imperial state and also includes much of the relevant political and social history.

Quotes from Confucius come from Confucius (2003, 8, 193). Mengzi is quoted from Mengzi (2008). The *Xunzi* is quoted from *Xunzi* (2016).

Ji Liang is quoted from Pines (2009, 191). Zichan is quoted from Pines (2009, 195).

Our interpretation of early Chinese state building and its long legacy follows Pines (2009, 2012); see also his translation of the book of Lord Shang (Shang Yang, 2017); we quote from pp. 79, 178, 218, 229–30, 233. Our interpretation is also influenced by Lewis's trilogy (2011, 2012a, 2012b). See Lewis (2000) for the comparison between Greek city-states and the Chinese polities of the Spring and Autumn periods. Bodde and Morris (1967) is an important volume on Chinese law that emphasizes the fusion of legalist and Confucian elements and the absence of the rule of law, and see also Huang (1998) for seminal work on how the Qing legal system functioned and its legacy today in

China. Perry (2008) is a very interesting interpretation of the Chinese "social contract" and its endurance over time, even into the Communist period. Von Glahn (2016) tracks the successive attempts to reimpose the well-field system. On T'an-ch'eng County during the Ming, see Spence (1978, 6–7). On the Ming sea ban, see Dreyer (2006). The Ming-Qing transition is analyzed by Farmer (1995) and Wakeman (1986). See Kuhn (1990) on measures against people who refused to adopt the Manchu hairstyle and the Chinese state's reaction to the "soul stealers."

The passage from Wang Xiuchu is from Struve (1998, 28–48); see also the discussion in Rowe (2009). Extracts of Wu Jingzi's novel *The Scholars* are reproduced in Chen, Cheng, Lestz, and Spence (2014, 54–63), which also reproduces the crimes and wealth of Heshen. Zelin (1984), von Glahn (2016), and Rowe (2009) emphasize how the fiscal deterioration of the Qing state undermined its ability to provide public goods such as infrastructure. Rowe (2009, Chapter 6) details the crimes of Heshen.

Our discussion of Hankou comes from Rowe (1984, 1989), heavily influenced by the critique of Wakeman (1993); see also Wakeman (1998).

The seminal work on Chinese lineages is Freedman (1966, 1971), and we quote from 1966 (Chapter 3, and see pp. 80–82). See also Beattie (2009) and Faure (2007) on the lineages of southern China, and Watson (1982).

The facts about the comparative economic growth of China are not in dispute among economic historians. The notion of the "reversal of fortune" comes from Acemoglu, Johnson, and Robinson (2002). Though Wong (1997) and Pomeranz (2001) argued that in fact China, or at least the most developed parts of it such as the Yangtze River valley, had standards of living in the eighteenth century similar to the most developed parts of Western Europe, subsequent research has not supported their claims. Broadberry, Guan, and Li (2017) provide a synthesis of work on historical measures of average living standards suggesting that while Song China had the highest levels of income per capita in the world in the medieval period, they subsequently stagnated, with fluctuations, for example, falls during the Ming and late Qing. In their data, income per capita in China was about one-third of that in the Netherlands in 1800 and only 30 percent of the British figure. Even the focus on the Yangtze as the relative comparison doesn't change the big picture, with Bozhong and van Zanden (2012) finding average living standards there to be about half of the contemporary Dutch level in the 1820s. Other evidence corroborates these facts, for example Allen, Bassino, Ma, Moll-Murata, and van Zanden (2011) show real wages were significantly lower in urban China. These facts make Wong and Pomeranz's broader arguments less compelling because they proposed that what created the economic divergence between Western Europe and China was the favorable location of coal in Europe and the accessibility of land in European colonies. But the evidence does not support the presence of the Malthusian trap in China. For example, there were large increases in population during the Tang-Song transition. These arguments are problematical in many other ways. Early industrialization in Britain, for example, used waterpower, not coal power. Also the mechanisms linking abundant colonial land to economic growth are not clear.

Our interpretation of the slow growth of China after the Song dynasty is partly conventional (e.g., on the antidevelopmental policies of the Ming, or the early Qing, see Liu, 2015, and von Glahn, 2016), and is similar to the work of Faure (2006) and Brandt, Ma, and Rawski (2014). See Morse (1920) for the facts we cite about the weakness of public good provision. These works recognize the presence and importance of markets in early modern China but also present copious evidence for politically motivated impediments to economic growth. We also draw on material from Hamilton (2006), and see also Brenner and Isett (2002). This work follows in the tradition of earlier scholars such as Wright (1957). Our example of the reluctance to build railways comes from Wang (2015). The academic literature of the long-run development of China started with the work of Max Weber, who focused on the cultural differences with Europe, and that of Karl Marx, who developed the notion of an "Asiatic mode of production" (see Brook, ed., 1989, for perspectives on this idea). Subsequently China was characterized as "despotic," e.g., by Wittfogel (1957), a term that historians had no problem using to describe the imperial state even recently (e.g., Mote, 2000; Liu, 2015).

A lot of work on the absence of capitalism in China focuses on the salt merchants. Our examples of how they transitioned into government service come from Ho (1954), and see also Hung (2016) for the Pan family. Other work on the salt merchants is Zelin (2005).

The Wenzhou model is discussed by Liu (1992), and the quote "Collectivization had been turned" is from p. 698.

Huang (2008) gives the examples of the Township Village Enterprises and the Xiushui market in Beijing. For evidence about rural discontent and the land tax, see O'Brien and Li (2006), and O'Brien (2008). On the reluctance of the Communist Party to admit capitalists, see Nee and Opper (2012).

On modernization theory, see Lipset (1959). On the contrary evidence to this, showing that countries that become richer or "modernized" are not automatically becoming democratic, see Acemoglu, Johnson, Robinson, and Yared (2008, 2009).

"Leave no dark corner" is from Carney (2018). See Human Rights Watch (2018) on the repression of the Uighurs.

CHAPTER 8. BROKEN RED QUEEN

The story of Manoj and Babli comes from Dogra (2013). There is a large literature discussing the meaning, history, and importance of caste in India. Seminal general works include Hutton (1961), Dumont (1980), and Smith (1994). Very useful are the large number of ethnographic village studies that give a feel for how caste works in reality, for example Lewis (1965), Srinivas (1976), Parry (1979), and Béteille (2012), and how it influences politics. The modern academic literature tends to stress the large impact that colonialism had on the caste system (e.g., Bayly, 2001, Dirks, 2001, and Chatterjee, 2004). Though this is plausible, the system is indisputably ancient, and it is this feature that is more important for our analysis. There is a small economics literature examining the economic effects of caste that is divided between arguing that in an otherwise imperfect world with many market failures and problems, caste identity can provide useful benefits, such as facilitating insurance and contract enforcement (e.g., Munshi, 2017), and arguing instead that caste is a potent source of inefficiency in economic relations (e.g., Hoff, 2016). Our view is much closer to the latter; see for instance the work of Edmonds and Sharma (2006), Anderson (2011), Hoff, Kshetramade, and Fehr (2011), and Anderson, Francois, and Kotwal (2015), but goes beyond these interpretations in emphasizing the implications of caste for politics and the inability of society to make the state accountable and responsive.

Kautilya is quoted from Kautilya (1987, Chapter I, section ii). On the three orders of European society, see Duby (1982), and Britnell's analysis is presented in Britnell (1992).

Ambedkar's quote "a multi-storyed tower" is from Roy (2014). Ambedkar's other quotes are from Ambedkar (2014). The Dalit worker interviewed by Human Rights Watch in Ahmedabad is quoted from Human Rights Watch (1999, 1).

All the quotes from Béteille (2012) are from Chapter 5. See Srinivas (1994) for his essays on the notion of "dominant castes." On Thillai Govindan, see Matthai (1915, 35–37), Human Rights Watch (1999, 31–32); other quotes come from the same Human Rights Watch report (88, 93, 98, 114).

Gorringe (2005, 2017) is an excellent overview and analysis of the contemporary attempts by Dalits to exercise political power in Tamil Nadu. For Blunt's analysis, see Blunt (1931). The data are from Chapter 12; see in particular the Appendix, pp. 247–52. On the persistence of caste and occupation to today, see Deshpande (2011), who makes a strong argument for the enduring economic relevance of caste. See Shah, Mander, Thorat, Deshpande, and Baviskar (2006) on the persistence of untouchability.

The description of the Jajmani system in Karimpur is from Wiser (1936) and the two quotes from Wiser and Wiser (2000) are from pp. 18–19 and 53. Dumont (1980, 97–102) gives a nice overview of the Jajmani system, including a useful summary of Wiser's book.

There are many good general overviews and narratives of ancient and medieval Indian history and we have relied on Thapar (2002) and Singh (2009). There is nevertheless quite a bit of disagreement among scholars over how to interpret many of the ancient institutions. For example, see the controversy over what happened at the assembly known as the vidatha (see Singh, 2009, 188). On the ancient republics, see Sharma (1968) and in particular Sharma (2005). The Atharva Veda is quoted from Sharma (2005, 110). For different wergeld amounts and the legal system more generally, see Sharma (2005, 245). The discussion of the Licchavi state comes from Sharma (1968, 85–135), and see also Jah (1970), who differs in some interpretations. For instance, Jah argues that Licchavis had universal male suffrage; on this we follow Sharma, whose views seem to be closer to the scholarly consensus. See Kautilya on gana-sanghas (1987). The Digha Nikaya is quoted from Sharma (2005, 64–65). Kautilya on the origins of kings is from Kautilya (1987). Important works on the origins of states and monarchies in northern Indian are Thapar (1999) and Roy (1994), who particularly emphasizes the connection to the varna system, as does Sharma (2005).

Asoka's sixth Rock Edict is quoted from Hultzsch (1925, 34–35). The discussion of the Chauhans is from Thapar (2002, 451).

Basic works on southern Indian society and the political system in the medieval and early modern period are Subbarayalu (1974, 2012), Stein (1980, 1990), Veluhat (1993), Heitzman (1997), and Shastri (1997). Stein proposed the notion of a "segmentary state" as a model for state-society relations in the south of India and his ideas and evidence have heavily influenced our own interpretation of the relevant history. The description of the election and local political institutions comes from Thapar (2002, 375–77) but is widely quoted. The two inscriptions concerning the activities of assemblies in canal building are quoted from Heitzman (1997, 52). Subbarayalu (1974) provides an exhaustive analysis of nadus based on inscriptions and cites the composition of all the nadus in the Chola Mandalam.

There is a large, older literature about the extent to which village assemblies predominated in India historically. Nobody doubts the evidence about the gana-sanghas, or Tamil Nadu, especially in the Chola era. Elsewhere there is a lot of debate. Some scholars have argued that village assemblies and many of the institutions were prevalent everywhere in India, e.g., Mookerji (1920), Majumdar (1922), and Malaviya (1956). Others, like Altekar (1927) argue that they were really restricted to the south, though he includes Karnataka as well as Tamil Nadu (see Dikshit, 1964, for corroborating evidence from Karnataka). He argues that elsewhere in western India, such assemblies were less institutionalized and much more informal. Wade (1988) is useful on the enormous heterogeneity on the extent of participation at the local level in India. Mathur (2013) is an accessible overview of panchayats with an emphasis on their postindependence functioning.

A useful introduction to the organization of the Mughal Empire is Richards (1993); Chapters 3 and 4 of that book provide a good introduction to the bureaucratic organization of the state and its interaction with rural society. Habib (1999) is authoritative on the organization of the rural economy in the Mughal period; see Chapter 4 on village communities and Chapter 5 on zamindars.

The Fifth Report from the Select Committee is quoted from the original (1812, 85). Metcalfe is quoted from Dutt (1916, 267–68). The quotes from Matthai's book (1915) come from pp. 18, 20, with the *Report of the Indian Famine Commission* also quoted there, p. 77.

Our analysis of the politics of state capacity in Bihar has been heavily influenced by the study of Mathew and Moore (2011). Our facts about underspending, vacancies, and Bihar politics come from their paper. The World Bank is quoted from World Bank (2005). The government of Bihar is quoted from Mathew and Moore (2011, 17). There are several useful biographies of Lalu Yadav, see particularly Thakur (2006). Witsoe (2013) is a superb analysis of the antidevelopmental politics of Lalu Yadav. See Kremer, Chaudhury, Rogers, Muralidharan, and Hammer (2005) for the data on teacher absenteeism. The notion that state and society in India coexist without really interacting is implicit in much literature, e.g., Thapar (2002), and Mookerji (1920) makes a clear statement of this thesis.

CHAPTER 9. DEVIL IN THE DETAILS

This chapter is based on the theoretical ideas developed in Acemoglu and Robinson (2017).

Machiavelli is quoted from *The Prince* (2005, 43). The Voltaire quote about Prussia is often used, but its original source is unclear. Montenegro quotes are from Djilas (1958, 3–4).

The most famous statement of Tilly's ideas on the relation between warfare and the state is Tilly (1992). See also the essays in Tilly, ed. (1975). The notion that interstate warfare drove state formation originally comes from Hintze (1975), and Roberts (1956) developed the notion of the military revolution. This idea is extensively discussed in the recent work of economists Besley and Persson (2011) and Gennaioli and Voth (2015). See Pincus and Robinson (2012, 2016) for a different view on the British case.

On Swiss history, see Church and Head (2013) and Steinberg (2016). Sablonier (2015) is also an excellent relevant overview. More specific academic works focused on the origins of Swiss political institutions include Blickell (1992), Marchal (2006), and Morerod and Favrod (2014). The Federal Charter of 1291 in English can be found at https://www.admin.ch/gov/en/start/federal-council /history-of-the-federal-council/federal-charter-of-1291.html. See Clark (2009) for an overview of relevant Prussian history, and Ertman (1997) is very useful on Prussian state building. Rosenberg (1958) is the classic treatment in English. Carsten (1959) and Asch (1988) focus on how the development of the state undermined the power of representative institutions in Germany. See Blanning (2016) for a recent superb biography of Frederick the Great; our quotes from Georg Wilhelm and Frederick William I are taken from there, as is the quote from Elliot.

Roberts (2007) provides an overview of the relevant history of Montenegro. The books of Djilas (1958, 1966) are essential reading, and we quote from these works. Boehm's main study of feuding is in his 1986 book; see also his 1982 book. We quote from 1986, p. 182. Peter I's legal code is quoted from Durham (1928, 78–88), and "Of old sat freedom" is from Durham (1909, 1). Braudel is quoted from Braudel (1996, 39). Marmont is quoted from Roberts (2007, 174).

"Continued attempts" is quoted from Simić (1967, 87). "It was a clash" and "The imposition" are from Djilas (1966, 107, 115).

Havel's quote is from Havel (1985, 11).

Our treatment of the post-Soviet divergence is influenced by Easter (2012). Kitschelt (2003) provides a very interesting interpretation. Castle and Taras (2002) and Ost (2006) are excellent on the politics of the Polish transition, as is Treisman (2011) on the recent history of Russia. Urban, Igrunov, and Mitrokhin (1997) discuss the failure of a popular politics to emerge in Russia. See Freeland (2000) and Hoffman (2002) for overviews and for the rise of the Russian oligarchs. Notable criticism of Russia's privatization came from Black, Kraakman, and Tarassova (2000) and Goldman (2003). The quotation from Bertolt Brecht is from his 1953 poem "The Solution," https://mronline.org /2006/08/14/brecht140806-html/.

Alexander Litvinenko's letter, from which we quote, is available here: http://www.mailonsunday.co.uk /news/article-418652/Why-I-believe-Putin-wanted-dead-.html.

See Driscoll (2015) on the Tajik civil war. See also Collins (2006) for the importance of clans in understanding the politics of Central Asia. Saodot Olimova is quoted from her book. We also quote from Gretsky (1995).

We quote extensively from Menchú's (1984) harrowing book.

Good overviews of the relevant history of Central America are Dunkerly (1988), Woodward (1991), and Gudmundson and Lindo-Fuentes (1995). Wortman (1982) is good on the transition from colonial rule. Williams, (1994), Paige (1997), Yashar (1997), Mahoney (2001), and Holden (2004) all give excellent political economy histories of the relevant period, and our numbers of army size and of teachers in Costa Rica are from the latter book. Gudmundson (1986, 1997) first documented that coffee smallholding was a consequence of nineteenth-century policy, rather than a colonial legacy. Cardoso (1977) is an influential essay on the Costa Rican coffee economy. Sarmiento is quoted from Dym (2006), who emphasizes the importance of towns as political players in Central America. See Karnes (1961) on the political economy of this diversity. Data on coffee prices, exports, and trade volumes are from Clarence-Smith, Gervase, and Topik, eds. (2006). McCreery (1994) is the definitive work on labor coercion in Guatemala in the context of the coffee economy. See Pascali (2017) for econometric evidence consistent with our hypothesis of the divergence between Guatemala and Costa Rica.

Sarmiento is quoted from Dym (2006, xviii).

Woodward on Carrera is from Woodward (2008, 254).

CHAPTER 10. WHAT'S THE MATTER WITH FERGUSON?

Details of the behavior of the Ferguson Police Department are from the Department of Justice (2015) report. BBC (2017) reports the findings on post-traumatic stress disorder in Atlanta. Our treatment of the inapplicability of the Bill of Rights to the states follows the seminal study of Gerstle (2015), from which we took the quote from Associate Justice Field (p. 78). Ansolabehere and Snyder (2008) is an important book about the political consequences of the Warren Court decision. Amar (2000) is good on the Bill of Rights more generally, and see McDonald (2000) on states' rights. There is a great deal of important research by historians, sociologists, and political scientists on the historical nature of the American state. A good place to start is Novak (2008) and the contributions of his commentators, particularly Gerstle (2008). See also King and Lieberman (2009). Much of this literature debunks earlier notions that the American state was "weak," and it has shown in many ways that the state developed a great deal of infrastructural power in many dimensions even in the nineteenth century. Orren and Skowronek (2004) is an excellent overview of the work by political scientists, and important works are by Skowronek (1982), Bensel (1991), Skocpol (1995), Carpenter (2001), and Balogh (2009). Baldwin (2005) is an interesting discussion of the simultaneous existence of state strength and weakness. The notion of a "state out of sight" (Balogh, 2009), or a "submerged state" (Mettler, 2011) that is invisible is a salient idea in this literature as is the idea that the state had to work by finding a balance and synthesis with the private sector (see also Stanger, 2011).

On the U.S. Constitution, see the references and discussion in the bibliographic essay for Chapter 1. The idea that state "incapacity" was used as a way to make sure that the state would not violate people's rights is advanced by Levinson (2014). See also Novak and Pincus (2017) on the origins of the strong American state.

The *Mapp v. Ohio* judgment is at http://caselaw.findlaw.com/us-supreme-court/367/643.html.

We quote from Morgan (1975): "having little interest" (238), and "if any slave resist" (312).

See John (1995, 1997) on the importance of the post office, and see Larson (2001) on infrastructure more broadly and Duran (2012) for the economic impact of the transcontinental railway. Acemoglu, Moscona, and Robinson (2016) provide econometric evidence that the creation of post offices and appointment of postmasters stimulated patenting and thus innovation in the nineteenth-century United States. The quote from Zorina Khan is from that paper, and also see Khan (2009).

"There is an astonishing" is from Tocqueville (2002, 283).

Abernathy is quoted from Eskew (1997, Chapter 7). Robert Kennedy and Judge Frank Johnson are quoted from McAdam (1999, Chapter 7). Lyndon Johnson's speech is available at http://www.historyplace.com/speeches/johnson.htm.

Hacker (2002) is an important analysis of the way the American state combines public with private provision and he also advances important arguments about why this creates, in our language, a "dark side." The quote from a spokesman for the National Dairy Producers Corporation is from his book. He does not relate this, however, to the architecture of the state in the way we do. Balogh's (2015) notion of an "associational state" is closely related. Alston and Ferrie (1993, 1999) is an important analysis of how southern politicians blocked New Deal legislation that threatened their economic interests and autonomy. See also Novak (2017) on the New Deal state. Friedberg (2000) analyzes how the public-private model of the American state had important implications for the way the Cold War was fought; see also Stuart (2008). Our example of how the federal government uses the legal system to implement policy is drawn from Farhang (2010), and see Novak (1996) on the importance of the legal system in the early construction of the capacity of the American state.

Hinton (2016) provides the background to Johnson's Great Society program.

Rothstein (2014) is a brilliant analysis of how Ferguson got to be Ferguson, and he discusses the history of racist federal policies; see also the broader argument in Rothstein (2017). Gordon (2009) presents a detailed history of segregation and urban decline in St. Louis. Loewen (2006) is an important history of "sundown towns," and Aaronson, Hartley, and Mazumder (2017) provide econometric evidence of the long-run negative impact of redlining.

The quotations are from Rothstein (2014).

For the *District of Columbia v. Heller* judgment, see https://supreme.justia.com/cases/federal/us/554/570/opinion.html. On explicit racial terminology in the FHA underwriting handbook, see https://www.huduser.gov/portal/sites/default/files/pdf/Federal-Housing-Administration-Underwriting-Manual.pdf.

Data on poverty rates can be found at https://data.oecd.org/inequality/poverty-rate.htm. For data on healthcare coverage, see http://www.oecd-library.org/docserver/download/8113171ec026.pdf ?expires=1514934796&id=id&accname=guest&checksum=565E13BC154117F36688F63351E843F1. For data on proportion of national income spent on healthcare, see https://data.worldbank.org /indicator/SH.XPD.TOTL.ZS.

Weiner (2012) provides an excellent history of the FBI, on which our discussion draws. See Weiner (2008) on the CIA, and Edgar (2017) on the NSA and the Snowden revelations. The Church Committee report of 1975 can be found at https://www.senate.gov/artandhistory/history/common /investigations/ChurchCommittee.htm.

On Keith Alexander's "Why can't we collect all the signals all the time?," see https://www.theguardian .com/uk/2013/jun/21/gchq-cables-secret-world-communications-nsa.

President Eisenhower's farewell address can be found at http://avalon.law.yale.edu/20th_century /eisenhower001.asp.

CHAPTER 11. THE PAPER LEVIATHAN

The notion of "patients of the state" comes from Auyero (2001), and all the evidence from our first section is from his important book. We quote from pp. 10, 20, 71–72, 83, 85, 99, 109, 120. For Weber's notion of the "iron cage," see Weber (2001). All his observations about bureaucracy are from Weber (1978); we quote from pp. 220–21 and 214. Useful introductions to his writings on these topics are Camic, Gorski, and Trubek, eds. (2005), and Kim (2017). For the concept of gnocchi in Argentina, see BBC (2018a), and for President Macri's measures against nepotism, BBC (2018b). The IMF's censure and its lifting are discussed in International Monetary Fund (2016); on the decision by *The Economist* to stop reporting the Argentine data, see *The Economist* (2012). Auyero (2001) is a seminal study of "clientelistic politics," which is closely related to the issues we discuss here.

The discussion of the Paper Leviathan draws on the synthesis of the political economy of Colombia in Robinson (2007, 2013, 2016). This in turn is based on the studies of Acemoglu, Bautista, Querubín, and Robinson (2008), Mazzuca and Robinson (2009), Acemoglu, Robinson, and Santos (2013), Acemoglu, García-Jimeno, and Robinson (2012, 2015), Chaves, Fergusson, and Robinson (2015), and Fergusson, Torvik, Robinson, and Vargas (2016). See Acemoglu, Fergusson, Robinson, Romero, and Vargas (2016) for "false positives." Weber's definition of the state is in his essay "Politics as a Vocation," reproduced in Weber (1946).

The history of the road to Mocoa is from Uribe (2017), and we quote from pp. 29, 33, 45, 124–25, 128–30, 163.

For Moreno, see Robinson (2016); for the paramilitaries of the Magdalena Medio, see Robinson (2013, 2016); the latter quotes Isaza (18–19). For rioting miners (30), Brigard Urrutia (29), Batallón Pedro Nel Ospina (21). See also Bautista, Galan, Restrepo, and Robinson (2019).

Bolívar's "These gentlemen" is quoted from Simon (2017, 108).

Bolívar's letter to General Flores is reproduced in Bolívar (2003), which also contains his address to legislators at the time of the presentation of his constitutions for Bolivia and the constitution itself. Gargarella (2013, 2014) are fundamental interpretations of Latin American constitutionalism in the nineteenth century and how (and why) it diverged from the U.S. case. Simon (2017) is a very stimulating comparative analysis. In particular he emphasizes what he calls the conservative-liberal fusion that created constitutions that were more centralized and allowed greater presidential powers than in the United States. These constitutional differences were part of a path-dependent equilibrium rooted in Latin America's colonial past. The quote from Castilla is taken from Werlich (1978, 80); that of Portales is from Safford (1985). See Engerman and Sokoloff (2011) for a seminal argument about the divergent development between North and South America. See also Acemoglu, Johnson, and Robinson (2001, 2002) and Acemoglu and Robinson (2012) on this divergence.

Dalton (1965) is the seminal study of the political economy of Liberia; we quote from pp. 581, 584, and 589 of his paper. See Killick (1976) on Ghana, pp. 37, 40, 60, 231, and 233. Bates (1981) is the seminal study of how politics mitigates against the provision of public services. He was the first to propose some of the mechanisms that we develop here. We quote pp. 114 and 117 of his book. Appiah is quoted from Appiah (2007).

See Mamdani (1996) on indirect rule in Africa. See Acemoglu, Reed, and Robinson (2014) for empirical evidence on the local development effects of indirect rule. More broadly, see Acemoglu, Chaves, Osafo-Kwaako, and Robinson (2015) and Heldring and Robinson (2015) for arguments about the intensity within which indirect rule has persisted in Africa, and Acemoglu and Robinson (2010) for how indirect rule fits into a broader account of African underdevelopment.

BBC (2013) reports the complete failure of students in the context of the University of Liberia's entrance exam.

CHAPTER 12. WAHHAB'S CHILDREN

Our interpretation of Middle Eastern history and the relationship between state and society there has been heavily influenced by Jean-Philippe Platteau's seminal book (2017). There are many good books presenting overviews of the history we discuss. Our analysis of Saudi Arabia and the relationship between Saud and al-Wahhab is based on Corancez (1995), Commins (2009), and Vassiliev (2013), but there are many other good analyses, e.g., Steinberg (2005), Zyoob and Kosebalaban, eds. (2009), and the classic Philby (1928). Mouline (2014) is particularly good on the contemporary situation.

Rommel is quoted from Liddell Hart (1995, 328). "When morning came" is quoted from Vassiliev (2013). "Let him speak here" is quoted from Doughty (1888), and Burckhardt from Buckhardt (1830, 116–17). "Abd al-Aziz to the Arabs of the tribe of ***" is quoted from Corancez (1995, 9).

The decision to overthrow King Saud is quoted from Mouline (2014, 123).

Al-Ghazali is quoted from Kepel (2005, 238). On pro-U.S. fatwas, see Kurzman (2003), from which we cite the 1990 Saudi fatwa issued after the invasion of Kuwait.

For the fire in the Mecca girls' school, see http://news.bbc.co.uk/2/hi/middle_east/1874471.stm. Male paramedics: http://english.alarabiya.net/en/News/middle-east/2014/02/06/Death-of-Saudi-female-student-raises-uproar.html. A nice summary of restrictions on women in Saudi Arabia is on CNN: https://www.cnn.com/2017/09/27/middleeast/saudi-women-still-cant-do-this/index.html. "For a woman," "God Almighty," and "deficient reasoning and rationality" from Human Rights Watch (2016); see also Human Rights Watch (2008). Bursztyn, González, and Yanagizawa-Drott (2018) on men's attitudes to female labor force participation in Saudi Arabia. On the issue of women driving, see https://www.nytimes.com/2017/09/26/world/middleeast/saudi-arabia-women-drive.html.

"A grief-stricken Saddam" quoted from Mortimer (1990). Saddam "the banner of jihad and faith" quoted from Baram (2014, 207–208). Platteau (2017) has an incisive analysis of the relationship between Saddam and religion; see also Baram (2014), Helfont (2014), and Dawisha (2009). An English translation of Osama bin Laden's 1996 fatwa can be read at https://is.muni.cz/el/1423/jaro2010/MVZ203/OBL___AQ__Fatwa_1996.pdf. Platteau (2011, 245).

CHAPTER 13. RED QUEEN OUT OF CONTROL

There is a vast scholarly literature on the collapse of the Weimar Republic. Our account is based on Kershaw (2000) and Evans (2005), but we have also used Shirer (1960), Bracher (1970), Lepsius (1978), and Winkler (2006). Myerson (2004) provides an analysis of the faults of Weimar political institutions. See Mühlberger (2003) and King, Rosen, Tanner, and Wagner (2008) for analyses of voting data to identify who voted for the Nazi party. Still powerful are the contemporary testimonies of Germans who supported Hitler collected by Abel (1938). Tooze (2015) is an excellent overview of the political fallout from World War I. Berman (2001) is a useful overview and interpretation of the pre-Weimar imperial political system in Germany.

Wels is quoted from Edinger (1953, 347–348). The 1930 Nazi election manifesto is quoted from Moeller (2010, 44), and Elsa Herrmann from Moeller (2010, 33–34). An English translation of the Weimar Constitution is available at http://www.zum.de/psm/weimar/weimar_vve.php. Berman

(1997) pointed out that the rise of the Nazis tapped into the dense civil society of Weimar Germany, and Satyanath, Voigtländer, and Voth (2017) showed that this correlation was quite general.

For Hitler's Berlin Sports Palace speech, see Evans (2005, 324). Hitler's public address of October 17, 1932, is quoted from Evans (2005, 323). Goebbels's announcement is quoted from Evans (2005, 312). Ferdinand Hermans is quoted from Lepsius (1978, 44). On Hitler's trial after the Beer Hall Putsch and related quotes, see Kershaw (2000, 216). Evans's "a rainbow coalition of the discontented" is quoted from Evans (2005, 294).

Fritzsche is quoted from Fritzsche (1990, 76).

Mussolini is quoted from his "Doctrine of Fascism" speech, which can be found at http://www.history guide.org/europe/duce.html. Herman Finer's quote is from his *Mussolini's Italy*, which can be found at https://archive.org/stream/mussolinisitaly005773mbp/mussolinisitaly005773mbp_djvu.txt.

Our analysis of the overthrow of Chilean democracy follows the seminal study of Valenzuela (1978). His book formed part of a comparative project in political science on the collapse of democracy edited by Linz and Stepan. The conclusions are summarized in Linz (1978).

Angell (1991) is a good overview of the history of the era we focus on and Constable and Valenzuela (1993) provide an excellent treatment of the military dictatorship that followed the coup of 1973. Baland and Robinson (2008) present empirical analyses of the political impact of the introduction of the secret ballot in 1958. Senator Martones is quoted from Baland and Robinson (2008, 1738–39). Brian Loveman is quoted from Loveman (1976, 219). For an analysis of state building under the Frei administration, see Valenzuela and Wilde (1979). They and Valenzuela (1978) tend to interpret the Frei program as disastrous, since the attack on clientelism undermined the ability to make deals when Allende came to power. Our interpretation sees it as a natural part of the Red Queen effect.

Lord Stanley is quoted from Kitson-Clark (1951, 112), and David Ricardo is quoted from Ricardo ([1824], 1951–1973, 506).

Kennedy's speech launching the Alliance for Progress can be found at https://sourcebooks.fordham .edu/mod/1961kennedy-afp1.asp.

The text of Allende's Statute of Guarantees can be found at http://www.papelesdesociedad.info/IMG /pdf/estatuto_de_garantias_democraticas.pdf.

The interview of Salvador Allende by Régis Debray can be found at https://www.marxists.org/espanol /allende/1971/marzo16.htm. The 1972 speech by the secretary general of the Communist Party is quoted from Valenzuela (1978, 68). The editorial from *El Mercurio* is quoted from Valenzuela (1978, 69). A second quotation from *El Mercurio* is quoted from Valenzuela (1978, 93).

Carlos Altamirano is quoted from Valenzuela (1978, 94). The Senate committee report on covert action in Chile can be downloaded at https://www.archives.gov/files/declassification/iscap/pdf/2010-009-doc17.pdf. The quotations are from pp. II.10–11 and IV.31.

Good analyses of the collapse of the Italian republics are Dean (1999), Waley and Dean (2013), and Jones (1997). The proceedings of the 1264 meeting in Ferrara are from Waley and Dean (2013, 180–81); see also Dean (1987) for a deeper analysis of politics in Ferrara. There is some disagreement among scholars over whether this really was a free election. Jones (1997, 624) reports one chronicler as writing that "the whole proceeding was a charade, engineered by a cabal of Este party notables . . . who packed the city and public square with armed followers and outsiders."

The declarations of the consortia in Perugia are quoted from Waley and Dean (2013, 132–33). For Benjamin of Tudela's observations about Genoa, Pisa, and Lucca, see Benjamin of Tudela (1907, 17). For the Blacks and the Whites in Pistoia, see Waley and Dean (2013, 137–38). See Jones (1997, Chapter 4) on the continued power and privileges of feudal elites after the rise of the commune. For the oath of the Capitano del Popolo in Bergamo, see Waley and Dean (2013, 142–43). For the legal powers of the Popolo in Parma: Waley and Dean (2013, 152). On Buoso da Dovara and Uberto Pallavicino, see Jones (1997, 622).

Machiavelli is quoted from *The Prince* (2005, 35).

The discussion of how there is popular support for the dismantling of checks and balances draws on Acemoglu, Robinson, and Torvik (2013); Rafael Correa is quoted from p. 868 of that paper.

CHAPTER 14. INTO THE CORRIDOR

Plaatje (1916) is quoted from Chapters 1 and 2.

On the general history of South Africa, see Thompson (2014). On the Native Land Act, see Bundy (1979), and on the color bar and wages, see Feinstein (2005).

See Feinstein (2005, p. 55) for the Holloway commission. The Select Committee of Native Affairs is quoted from Bundy (1979, 109).

Moeletsi Mbeki is quoted from https://dawodu.com/mbeki.pdf. On Black Economic Empowerment, see Southall (2005), Cargill (2010), and Santos-Villagran (2016). On the 1995 Rugby World Cup Final and the exchange between Mandela and Pienaar, see https://www.theguardian.com/sport /2007/jan/07/rugbyunion.features1.

Our discussion of the rise of Japanese militarism and its postwar political system draws on Dower (1999), Buruma (2003), and Samuels (2003). The details of Kishi's role in pre- and postwar Japan draw on Kurzman (1960), Schaller (1995), and Driscoll (2010).

Bonner Fellers is quoted from Dower (1999, 282). Article 9 of the Japanese constitution and Hirohito's New Year's statement are from the same source, pp. 394 and 314.

Zürcher (1984) and Zürcher (2004) are the best sources on the transition from the Ottoman Empire to the Turkish Republic. For overviews of recent Turkish history, see Pope and Pope (2011) and Çağaptay (2017). For a discussion of recent economic and political changes and their economic implications, see Acemoglu and Üçer (2015). For the "Black Turks, White Turks" quotation from Erdoğan, see https://www.thecairoreview.com/essays/erdo%C4%9Fans-decade.

On Erdoğan's speech, see http://www.diken.com.tr/bir-alman-kac-turke-bedel/.

On journalists jailed in Turkey, see https://cpj.org/reports/2017/12/journalists-prison-jail-record -number-turkey-china-egypt.php.

On the number of people purged after the failed coup attempt, see https://www.nytimes.com/2017 /04/12/world/europe/turkey-erdogan-purge.html and https://www.politico.eu/article/long-arm-of -turkeys-anti-gulenist-purge/.

The best analysis of the developments in Lagos since 1999 is de Gramont (2014). See Williams and Turner (1978, 133) on the 1976 Nigerian constitution drafting committee.

On Bogotá, see the essays in Tognato (2018). Devlin (2009) and Devlin and Chaskel (2009) provide a good overview of the improvements in Bogotá. Caballero is quoted from Devlin (2009). Mockus's "as if he had vomited" is quoted from Devlin and Chaskel (2009).

On the history of Rhodesia and Zimbabwe, see Simpson and Hawkins (2018). The quote "To avoid following Zimbabwe" is from http://www.researchchannel.co.za/print-version/oil-industry -empowerment-crucial-sapia-2002-10-21.

The quote from Moses Finley is from Finley (1976).

An overview of South Korea's industrialization and transition to democracy can be found in Cummings (2005).

For an excellent history of the Congo Free State and the reactions to it, see Hochschild (1999), where our quotation of Casement's diary comes from. The full Casement Report can be found at https:// ia801006.us.archive.org/14/items/CasementReport/CasementReportSmall.pdf. On the international human rights movement, see Neier (2012).

On the role of Amnesty International in the UN resolution against female genital mutilation, see https://www.amnesty.org/en/latest/news/2012/11/fight-against-female-genital-mutilation -wins-un-backing/.

On Robert Mugabe's appointment as WHO's "goodwill ambassador," see https://www.theguardian. com/world/2017/oct/22/robert-mugabe-removed-as-who-goodwill-ambassador-after-outcry, and http://theconversation.com/robert-mugabe-as-who-goodwill-ambassador-what-went-wrong -86244.

CHAPTER 15. LIVING WITH THE LEVIATHAN

Hayek's introduction to the U.S. edition, the quotations therein, and an excellent discussion by Bruce Caldwell can be found in Hayek (2007). The quotations are from pp. 71, 148, 44, and 48. On the Beveridge Report, see Beveridge (1944) and also Baldwin (1990, 116), where we quote James Griffiths.

On the "cow trade" and the rise of Swedish social democracy, see Baldwin (1990), Berman (2006), Esping-Andersen (1985), and Gourevitch (1986). The quotations come from Berman (2006) and Esping-Andersen (1985). See also the chapters on education and housing policies in Misgeld, Molin, and Amark (1988), and we quote from p. 325 of this book. Moene and Wallerstein (1997) develop a model of the connection between wage compression and innovation. See Swenson (2002) for an analysis of the preferences of capitalists with respect to the welfare state.

Our discussion of the role of coalitions is related to the seminal study of democratization by O'Donnell and Schmitter (1986).

On the effects of automation on wages and inequality, see Acemoglu and Restrepo (2018). On the implications of globalization, see Autor, Dorn, and Hanson (2013). The numbers on wage growth by different education groups and inequality in the U.S. labor market come from Acemoglu and Autor (2011) and Autor (2014). The numbers on the share of the top 1 percent and top 0.1 percent in U.S. national income are based on Piketty and Saez (2003), and the updated numbers are obtained from https://eml.berkeley.edu/~saez/ (and refer to numbers that include capital income). Acemoglu, Autor, Dorn, Hanson, and Price (2015) and Acemoglu and Restrepo (2017) discuss estimates of the effects of trade with China and robots on U.S. employment.

Our discussion of reforms in the U.S. financial system is from Johnson and Kwak (2010). On the relative earnings of workers and executives in the finance industry, see Phillippon and Reshef (2012). The share of six largest banks in the sector are computed from the Global Financial website.

Autor, Dorn, Katz, Patterson, and Van Reenen (2017) provide evidence that large firms have contributed significantly to the increase in the share of capital income in GDP, while Song, Price, Güvenen, Bloom, and von Wachter (2015) show that the contribution to inequality of high-productivity firms paying higher wages to their workers has increased over time, especially at the top of the earnings distribution. The market value of the five largest firms relative to GDP in 1990 and today is computed from Global Financial.

On how the institutional structure of one country cannot be directly copied by another one, see Acemoglu, Robinson, and Verdier (2017).

For Snowden's revelations, see Edgar (2017), and for the Danish government's "session logging," see https://privacyinternational.org/location/denmark.

Beveridge's quote is from Beveridge (1994, 9).

For Roosevelt's 1944 State of the Union address see http://www.fdrlibrary.marist.edu/archives /address_text.html. For the comment on Roosevelt's "four freedoms," see https://books.openedition .org/pufr/4204?lang=en. The quote on African Americans' lack of freedoms related to Roosevelt's speech is from Litwack (2009, 50). For the Universal Declaration of Rights of the United Nations, see http://www.ohchr.org/EN/UDHR/Documents/UDHR_Translations/eng.pdf.

SOURCES FOR MAPS

GENERAL SOURCES

Location of cities from Geonames, https://www.geonames.org/.

Recent administrative divisions from GADM (Database of Global Administrative Areas), https://gadm.org/data.html.

Rivers from Natural Earth, http://www.naturalearthdata.com/downloads/10m-physical-vectors/10m-rivers-lake-centerlines.

Map 1: Asante Kingdom from Wilks (1975). Yorubaland and Tivland from Murdock (1959).

Map 2: Athenian demes from Osborne (2009). Borders of the Trittyes from Christopoulos (1970).

Map 3: Bureau Topographique des Troupes Françaises du Levant (1935) and Central Intelligence Agency (2017).

Map 4: Sarawat Mountains from Shuttle Radar Topographic Mission / Consortium for Spatial Information (CGIAR-CSI), http://srtm.csi.cgiar.org.

Map 5: Tongaland and Zululand from Murdock (1959). Provinces of South Africa in 1910 from Beinart (2001).

Map 6: Puna Coast from Evergreen Data Library, https://evergreen.data.socrata.com/Maps-Statistics/Coastlines-split-4326/rcht-xhew.

Map 7: GADM, https://gadm.org/data.html.

Map 8: Shepard (1911).

Map 9: Falkus and Gillingham (1987).

Map 10: Feng (2013).

Map 11: Ho (1954).

Map 12: Mauryan Empire from Keay (2000). Ashoka Pillar and Rock Edicts from Geonames, https://www.geonames.org/.

Map 13: Holy Roman Empire from Shepard (1911). Brandenburg and Prussia from EarthWorks, Stanford Libraries, https://earthworks.stanford.edu/catalog/harvard-ghgis1834core.

Map 14: Trampoline of Death from Humanitarian OpenStreetMap Team, https://www.hotosm.org. Middle Magdalena and Sibundoy Valley from Instituto Geográfico Agustín Codazzi, https://www.igac.gov.co.

Map 15: Clower, Dalton, Harwitz, and Walters (1966).

REFERENCES

Aaronson, Daniel, Daniel Hartley, and Bhash Mazumder (2017). "The Effects of the 1930s HOLC 'Redlining' Maps." Federal Reserve Bank of Chicago Working Paper No. 2017-12. https://www .chicagofed.org/publications/working-papers/2017/wp2017-12.

Abel, Theodore (1938). *Why Hitler Came into Power: An Answer Based on the Original Life Stories of 600 of His Followers*. New York: Prentice-Hall.

Acemoglu, Daron (2005). "Politics and Economics in Weak and Strong States." *Journal of Monetary Economics* 52: 1199–1226.

Acemoglu, Daron, and David Autor (2011). "Skills, Tasks and Technologies: Implications for Employment and Earnings." In *Handbook of Labor Economics*, vol. 4: 1043–1171. Amsterdam: Elsevier-North.

Acemoglu, Daron, David Autor, David Dorn, Gordon H. Hanson, and Brendan Price (2015). "Import Competition in the Great U.S. Employment Sag of the 2000s." *Journal of Labor Economics* 34: S141–98.

Acemoglu, Daron, María Angélica Bautista, Pablo Querubín, and James A. Robinson (2008). "Economic and Political Inequality in Development: The Case of Cundinamarca, Colombia." In *Institutions and Economic Performance*, edited by Elhanan Helpman. Cambridge, MA: Harvard University Press.

Acemoglu, Daron, Isaías N. Chaves, Philip Osafo-Kwaako, and James A. Robinson (2015). "Indirect Rule and State Weakness in Africa: Sierra Leone in Comparative Perspective." In *African Successes: Sustainable Growth*, edited by Sebastian Edwards, Simon Johnson, and David Weil. Chicago: University of Chicago Press.

Acemoglu, Daron, Leopoldo Fergusson, James A. Robinson, Dario Romero, and Juan F. Vargas (2016). "The Perils of High-Powered Incentives: Evidence from Colombia's False Positives." NBER Working Paper No. 22617. http://www.nber.org/papers/w22617.

Acemoglu, Daron, Francisco A. Gallego, and James A. Robinson (2014). "Institutions, Human Capital and Development." *Annual Review of Economics* 6: 875–912.

Acemoglu, Daron, Camilo García-Jimeno, and James A. Robinson (2012). "Finding El Dorado: The Long-Run Consequences of Slavery in Colombia." *Journal of Comparative Economics* 40, no. 4: 534–64.

———— (2015). "State Capacity and Development: A Network Approach." *American Economic Review* 105, no. 8: 2364–2409.

Acemoglu, Daron, Simon Johnson, and James A. Robinson (2001). "The Colonial Origins of Comparative Development: An Empirical Investigation." *American Economic Review* 91: 1369–1401.

———— (2002). "Reversal of Fortune: Geography and Institutions in the Making of the Modern World Income Distribution." *Quarterly Journal of Economics* 118: 1231–1294.

———— (2005a). "The Rise of Europe: Atlantic Trade, Institutional Change and Economic Growth." *American Economic Review* 95: 546–79.

———— (2005b). "Institutions as Fundamental Determinants of Long-Run Growth." In *Handbook of Economic Growth*, edited by Philippe Aghion and Steven Durlauf, vol. 1A, 385–472. Amsterdam: North-Holland.

Acemoglu, Daron, Simon Johnson, James A. Robinson, and Pierre Yared (2008). "Income and Democracy." *American Economic Review* 98, no. 3: 808–42.

———— (2009). "Reevaluating the Modernization Hypothesis." *Journal of Monetary Economics* 56: 1043–58.

Acemoglu, Daron, Jacob Moscona, and James A. Robinson (2016). "State Capacity and American Technology: Evidence from the 19th Century." *American Economic Review* 106, no. 5: 61–67.

Acemoglu, Daron, Tristan Reed, and James A. Robinson (2014). "Chiefs: Elite Control of Civil Society and Development in Sierra Leone." *Journal of Political Economy* 122, no. 2: 319–68.

Acemoglu, Daron, and Pascual Restrepo (2017). "Robots and Jobs: Evidence from U.S. Labor Markets." NBER Working Paper No. 23285. https://www.nber.org/papers/w23285.

———— (2018). "The Race Between Machine and Man: Implications of Technology for Growth, Factor Shares and Employment." *American Economic Review* 108, no. 6: 1488–1542.

Acemoglu, Daron, and James A. Robinson (2000). "Why Did the West Extend the Franchise? Growth, Inequality and Democracy in Historical Perspective." *Quarterly Journal of Economics* 115: 1167–99.

———— (2006). *Economic Origins of Dictatorship and Democracy.* New York: Cambridge University Press.

———— (2010). "Why Is Africa Poor?" *Economic History of Developing Regions* 25, no. 1: 21–50.

———— (2012). *Why Nations Fail.* New York: Crown.

———— (2016). "Paths to Inclusive Political Institutions." In *Economic History of Warfare and State Formation*, edited by Jari Eloranta, Eric Golson, Andrei Markevich, and Nikolaus Wolf. Berlin: Springer.

———— (2017). "The Emergence of Weak, Despotic and Inclusive States." NBER Working Paper No. 23657. http://www.nber.org/papers/w23657.

———— (2019). "The Narrow Corridor: The Academic Debate." https://voices.uchicago.edu/jamesrobinson and https://economics.mit.edu/faculty/acemoglu.

Acemoglu, Daron, James A. Robinson, and Rafael Santos-Villagran (2013). "The Monopoly of Violence: Theory and Evidence from Colombia." *Journal of the European Economics Association* 11, no. 1: 5–44.

Acemoglu, Daron, James A. Robinson, and Ragnar Torvik (2013). "Why Vote to Dismantle Checks and Balances?" *Review of Economic Studies* 80, no. 3: 845–75.

———— (2016). "The Political Agenda Effect and State Centralization." NBER Working Paper No. 22250. https://www.nber.org/papers/w22250.

Acemoglu, Daron, James A. Robinson, and Thierry Verdier (2017). "Asymmetric Growth and Institutions in an Interdependent World." *Journal of Political Economy* 125: 1245–1303.

Acemoglu, Daron, and Murat Üçer (2015). "The Ups and Downs of Turkish Growth: Political Dynamics, the European Union and the Institutional Slide." NBER Working Paper No. 21608. https://www.nber.org/papers/w21608.

Afigbo, A. E. (1967). "The Warrant Chief System in Eastern Nigeria: Direct or Indirect Rule?" *Journal of the Historical Society of Nigeria* 3, no. 4: 683–700.

———— (1972). *Warrant Chiefs Indirect Rule in Southeastern Nigeria, 1891–1929.* London: Longman.

Akiga Sai (1939). *Akiga's Story: The Tiv Tribe as Seen by One of Its Members.* Translated by Rupert East. Oxford: Oxford University Press.

Allen, Robert C., Jean-Pascal Bassino, Debin Ma, Christine Moll-Murata, and Jan Luiten van Zanden (2011). "Wages, Prices, and Living Standards in China, 1738–1925: In Comparison with Europe, Japan, and India." *Economic History Review* 64: 8–38.

Al-Muqaddasi (1994). *The Best Divisions for Knowledge of the Regions.* Translation of *Ahsan al-Taqasim fi ma'rifat al-Aqalim*, by B. A. Collins. Reading: Garnet.

Alston, Lee J., and Joseph P. Ferrie (1993). "Paternalism in Agricultural Labor Contracts in the U.S. South: Implications for the Growth of the Welfare State." *American Economic Review* 83, no. 4: 852–76.

———— (1999). *Southern Paternalism and the American Welfare State: Economics, Politics, and Institutions in the South, 1865–1965.* New York: Cambridge University Press.

Altekar, A. S. (1927). *A History of Village Communities in Western India.* Bombay: Oxford University Press.

Amar, Akhil Reed (2000). *The Bill of Rights: Creation and Reconstruction.* New Haven: Yale University Press.

Ambedkar, B. R. (2014). *Annihilation of Caste: The Annotated Critical Edition.* London: Verso.

Anderson, Siwan (2011). "Caste as an Impediment to Trade." *American Economic Journal: Applied Economics* 3, no. 1: 239–63.

Anderson, Siwan, Patrick Francois, and Ashok Kotwal (2015). "Clientelism in Indian Villages." *American Economic Review* 105, no. 6: 1780–1816.

Angell, Alan (1991). "Chile Since 1958." In *The Cambridge History of Latin America*, edited by Leslie Bethell, vol. 8, *Latin America Since 1930: Spanish South America*, 311–82. New York: Cambridge University Press.

Angold, Michael (1997). *The Byzantine Empire 1025–1204: A Political History.* 2nd edition. New York: Longman.

Ansolabehere, Stephen, and James M. Snyder Jr. (2008). *The End of Inequality: One Person, One Vote and the Transformation of American Politics.* New York: W. W. Norton.

Appiah, Anthony (2007) "A Slow Emancipation." *New York Times Magazine.* https://www.nytimes.com/2007/03/18/magazine/18WWLNlede.t.html.

Arendt, Hannah (1976). *Eichmann in Jerusalem: A Report on the Banality of Evil.* New York: Viking Press.

Aristotle (1996). *The Politics and the Constitution of Athens.* New York: Cambridge University Press.

Asch, Ronald G. (1988). "Estates and Princes After 1648: The Consequences of the Thirty Years War." *German History* 6, no. 2: 113–32.

Attenborough, F. L., ed. (1922). *The Laws of the Earliest English Kings.* Cambridge: Cambridge University Press.

Autor, David (2014). "Skills, Education, and the Rise of Earnings Inequality Among the Other 99 Percent." *Science* 344: 843–51.

Autor, David H., David Dorn, and Gordon H. Hanson (2013). "The China Syndrome: Local Labor Market Effects of Import Competition in the United States." *American Economic Review* 103: 2121–68.

Autor, David H., David Dorn, Lawrence F. Katz, Christina Patterson, and John Van Reenen (2017). "The Fall of the Labor Share in the Rise of Superstar Firms." NBER Working Paper No. 23396. https://www.nber.org/papers/w23396.

Auyero, Javier (2001). *Poor People's Politics.* Durham, NC: Duke University Press.

———— (2012). *Patients of the State: The Politics of Waiting in Argentina.* Durham, NC: Duke University Press.

Baland, Jean-Marie, and James A. Robinson (2008). "Land and Power." *American Economic Review* 98: 1737–1765.

Baldwin, Peter (1990). *The Politics of Social Solidarity: Class Basis of the European Welfare State 1875–1975.* New York: Cambridge University Press.

———— (2005). "Beyond Weak and Strong: Rethinking the State in Comparative Policy History." *Journal of Policy History* 17, no. 1: 12–33.

Balogh, Brian (2009). *A Government out of Sight: The Mystery of National Authority in Nineteenth-Century America.* New York: Cambridge University Press.

———— (2015). *The Associational State: American Governance in the Twentieth Century.* Philadelphia: University of Pennsylvania Press.

Baram, Amatzia (2014). *Saddam Hussein and Islam, 1968–2003.* Baltimore: Johns Hopkins University Press.

Barlow, Frank (1999). *The Feudal Kingdom of England, 1042–1216.* 5th edition. London and New York: Routledge.

Barnwell, P. S., and Marco Mostert, eds. (2003). *Political Assemblies in the Earlier Middle Ages.* Turnhout, Belgium: Brepols.

Bautista, Maria Angélica, Juan Sebastián Galan, Juan Diego Restrepo, and James A. Robinson (2019) "Acting like a State: The Peasant Self-Defense Forces of the Middle Magdalena in Colombia." Unpublished.

Bates, Robert H. (1981). *Markets and States in Tropical Africa.* Berkeley: University of California Press.

Bayly, Susan (2001). *Caste, Society and Politics in India from the Eighteenth Century to the Modern Age.* Revised edition. New York: Cambridge University Press.

BBC (2002). "Saudi Police 'Stopped' Fire Rescue." http://news.bbc.co.uk/2/hi/middle_east/1874471.stm.

BBC (2013). "Liberia Students All Fail University Admission Exam." http://www.bbc.com/news/world-africa-23843578.

BBC (2017). "US Inner-City Children Suffer 'War Zone' Trauma." http://www.bbc.com/news/av/world-us-canada-42229205/us-inner-city-children-suffer-war-zone-trauma.

BBC (2018a). "Argentina's Parliament Sacks 'Gnocchi' Phantom Workers." http://www.bbc.com/news/blogs-news-from-elsewhere-42551997.

BBC (2018b). "Argentine President Bans Family Members in Government." http://www.bbc.com/news/world-latin-america-42868439.

Beattie, Hilary J. (2009). *Land and Lineage in China: A Study of T'ung-Ch'eng County, Anhwei, in the Ming and Ch'ing Dynasties.* New York: Cambridge University Press.

Bede (1991). *Ecclesiastical History of the English People.* New York: Penguin.

Beinart, William (2001). *Twentieth-Century South Africa.* Oxford: Oxford University Press.

Benjamin of Tudela (1907). *The Itinerary of Benjamin of Tudela.* Edited by Marcus N. Adler. New York: Philipp Feldheim.

Bensel, Richard F. (1991). *Yankee Leviathan: The Origins of Central State Authority in America, 1859–1877.* New York: Cambridge University Press.

Berman, Sheri (1997). "Civil Society and the Collapse of the Weimar Republic." *World Politics* 49, no. 3.

———— (2001). "Modernization in Historical Perspective: The Case of Imperial Germany." *World Politics* 53, no. 3.

———— (2006). *The Primacy of Politics: Social Democracy in the Making of Europe's 20th Century.* New York: Cambridge University Press.

Besley, Timothy, and Torsten Persson (2011). *The Pillars of Prosperity.* Princeton, NJ: Princeton University Press.

Béteille, André (2012). *Caste, Class and Power: Changing Patterns of Stratification in a Tanjore Village.* 3rd edition. New York: Oxford University Press.

Beveridge, William H. (1944). *Full Employment in a Free Society: A Report.* London: Routledge.

Bisson, Thomas N. (1964). *Assemblies and Representation in Languedoc in the Thirteenth Century.* Princeton, NJ: Princeton University Press.

Bisson, Thomas N., ed. (1973). *Medieval Representative Institutions: Their Origins and Nature.* Hinsdale: The Dryden Press.

Bisson, Thomas N. (2009). *The Crisis of the Twelfth Century: Power, Lordship and the Origins of European Government.* Princeton, NJ: Princeton University Press.

Black, Bernard, Reinier Kraakman, and Anna Tarassova (2000). "Russian Privatization and Corporate Governance: What Went Wrong?" *Stanford Law Review* 52, 1731–1808.

Blanning, Tim (2016). *Frederick the Great: King of Prussia.* New York: Random House.

Blanton, Richard E., and Lane Fargher (2008). *Collective Action in the Formation of Pre-Modern States.* New York: Springer.

Blanton, Richard E., Gary M. Feinman, Stephen A. Kowalewski, and Linda M. Nicholas (1999). *Ancient Oaxaca*. New York: Cambridge University Press.

Blanton, Richard E., Stephen A. Kowalewski, Gary M. Feinman, and Laura M. Finsten (1993). *Ancient Mesoamerica: A Comparison of Change in Three Regions*. New York: Cambridge University Press.

Blaydes, Lisa, and Eric Chaney (2013). "The Feudal Revolution and Europe's Rise: Political Divergence of the Christian West and the Muslim World Before 1500 CE." *American Political Science Review* 107, no. 1: 16–34.

Blickel, Peter, ed. (1989). *Resistance, Representation and Community*. Oxford: Clarendon Press.

Blickel, Peter (1992). "Das Gesetz der Eidgenossen: Überlegungen zur Entstehung der Schweiz, 1200–1400." *Historische Zeitschrift* 255, no. 13: 561–86.

—— (1998). *From the Communal Reformation to the Revolution of the Common Man*. Leiden: Brill.

Bloch, Marc (1964). *Feudal Society*. 2 vols. Chicago: University of Chicago Press.

Blockmans, Wim, André Holenstein, and Jon Mathieu, eds. (2009). *Empowering Interactions: Political Cultures and the Emergence of the State in Europe 1300–1900*. Burlington, VT: Ashgate.

Blunt, E. A. H. (1931). *Caste System of Northern India*. Oxford: Oxford University Press.

Bodde, Derk, and Clarence Morris (1967). *Law in Imperial China*. Cambridge, MA: Harvard University Press.

Boehm, Christopher (1982). *Montenegrin Social Organization and Values: Political Ethnography of a Refuge Area Tribal Adaptation*. New York: AMS Press.

—— (1986). *Blood Revenge: The Enactment and Management of Conflict in Montenegro and Other Tribal Societies*. Philadelphia: University of Pennsylvania Press.

Bohannan, Paul (1958). "Extra-Processual Events in Tiv Political Institutions." *American Anthropologist* 60: 1–12.

Bohannan, Paul, and Laura Bohannan (1953). *The Tiv of Central Nigeria*. London: International African Institute.

—— (1968). *Tiv Economy*. Evanston, IL: Northwestern University Press.

Bolívar, Simón (2003). *El Libertador: The Writings of Simón Bolívar*. Edited by David Bushnell. New York: Oxford University Press.

Bosker, Maarten, Eltjo Buringh, and Jan Luiten van Zanden (2013). "From Baghdad to London: Unraveling Urban Development in Europe, the Middle East, and North Africa, 800–1800." *Review of Economics and Statistics* 95, no. 4: 1418–37.

Bowsky, William M. (1981). *A Medieval Italian Commune: Siena Under the Nine, 1287–1355*. Berkeley: University of California Press.

Bozhong, Li, and Jan Luiten van Zanden (2012). "Before the Great Divergence? Comparing the Yangzi Delta and the Netherlands at the Beginning of the Nineteenth Century." *Journal of Economic History* 72, no. 4: 956–89.

Bracher, Karl Dietrich (1970). *German Dictatorship: The Origins, Structure, and Effects of National Socialism*. New York: Praeger.

Braddick, Michael J. (2000). *State Formation in Early Modern England, c.1550–1700*. New York: Cambridge University Press.

Brandt, Loren, Debin Ma, and Thomas G. Rawski (2014). "From Divergence to Convergence: Reevaluating the History Behind China's Economic Boom." *Journal of Economic Literature* 52, no. 1: 45–123.

Braudel, Fernand (1996). *The Mediterranean and the Mediterranean World in the Age of Philip II*. Vol. 1. Berkeley: University of California Press.

Breen, T. H. (2011). *American Insurgents, American Patriots: The Revolution of the People*. New York: Hill and Wang.

Brenner, Robert (1976). "Agrarian Class Structure and Economic Development in Pre-Industrial Europe." *Past and Present* no. 70 (February 1976): 30–75.

Brenner, Robert, and Christopher Isett (2002). "England's Divergence from China's Yangzi Delta: Property Relations, Microeconomics, and Patterns of Development." *Journal of Asian Studies* 61, no. 2: 609–62.

Brewer, John (1989). *The Sinews of Power*. Cambridge, MA: Harvard University Press.

Britnell, Richard H. (1992). *The Commercialisation of English Society 1000–1500*. New York: Cambridge University Press.

Broadberry, Stephen, Hanhui Guan, and David Daokui Li (2017). "China, Europe and the Great Divergence: A Study in Historical National Accounting, 980–1850." https://www.economics.ox.ac.uk/materials/working_papers/2839/155aprilbroadberry.pdf.

Brock, Roger, and Stephen Hodkinson, eds. (2001). *Alternatives to Athens: Varieties of Political Organization and Community in Ancient Greece*. New York: Oxford University Press.

Brook, Timothy, ed. (1989). *The Asiatic Mode of Production in China*. New York: Routledge.

Bundy, Colin (1979). *The Rise and Fall of South African Peasantry*. Berkeley: University of California Press.

Burckhardt, John Lewis [Johann Ludwig] (1830). *Notes on the Bedouins and Wahábys, Collected During His Travels in the East*. London: Henry Colburn and Richard Bentley.

Bureau Topographique des Troupes Françaises du Levant (1935). Carte des Communautés Religieuses et Ethniques en Syrie et au Liban (Map of Religious Communities and Ethnic Groups). Institut Français du Proche-Orient. https://ifpo.hypotheses.org/2753.

Buringh, Eltjo, and Jan Luiten van Zanden (2009). "Charting the 'Rise of the West': Manuscripts and Printed Books in Europe, A Long-Term Perspective from the Sixth Through Eighteenth Centuries." *Journal of Economic History* 69, no. 2: 409–45.

Buruma, Ian (2003). *Inventing Japan: 1853–1964*. New York: Modern Library.

Bursztyn, Leonardo, Alessandra González, and David Yanagizawa-Drott (2018). "Misperceived Social Norms: Female Labor Force Participation in Saudi Arabia." http://home.uchicago.edu/bursztyn/Misperceived_Norms_2018_06_20.pdf.

Byrhtferth of Ramsey (2009). "Vita S. Oswaldi." In *Byrhtferth of Ramsey: The Lives of St. Oswald and St. Ecgwine*, edited by Michael Lapidge. New York: Oxford University Press.

Çağaptay, Soner (2017). *The New Sultan: Erdoğan and the Crisis of Modern Turkey*. New York: I.B. Tauris.

Camic, Charles, Philip S. Gorski, and David M. Trubek, eds. (2005). *Max Weber's Economy and Society: A Critical Companion*. Stanford, CA: Stanford University Press.

Cammett, Melani (2014). *Compassionate Communalism: Welfare and Sectarianism in Lebanon*. Ithaca, NY: Cornell University Press.

Campbell, Dugald (1933). *Blazing Trails in Bantuland*. London: Pickering & Inglis.

Cardoso, Ciro F. S. (1977). "The Formation of the Coffee Estate in Nineteenth Century Costa Rica." In *Land and Labour in Latin America*, edited by K. Duncan and I. Rutledge. Cambridge: Cambridge University Press.

Cargill, Jenny (2010). *Trick or Treat: Rethinking Black Economic Empowerment*. Johannesburg: Jacana Media.

Carney, Matthew (2018). "Leave No Dark Corner." ABC (Australian Broadcasting Corporation) News. https://www.abc.net.au/news/2018-09-18/china-social-credit-a-model-citizen-in-a-digital-dictatorship/10200278?section=world.

Carpenter, Daniel (2001). *The Forging of Bureaucratic Autonomy: Reputations, Networks, and Policy Innovation in Executive Agencies, 1862–1928*. Princeton, NJ: Princeton University Press.

Carroll, Lewis (1871). *Through the Looking-Glass, and What Alice Found There*. London: Macmillan.

Carsten, F. L. (1959). *Princes and Parliaments in Germany: From the Fifteenth to the Eighteenth Century*. Oxford: Clarendon Press.

Castle, Marjorie, and Raymond Taras (2002). *Democracy in Poland*. 2nd edition. New York: Routledge.

Central Intelligence Agency (2017). *The CIA World Factbook*. New York: Skyhorse Publishing.

Chatterjee, Partha (2004). *The Politics of the Governed: Reflections on Popular Politics in Most of the World*. New York: Columbia University Press.

Chaves, Isaías N., Leopoldo Fergusson, and James A. Robinson (2015). "He Who Counts Wins: Determinants of Fraud in the 1922 Colombian Presidential Elections." *Economics and Politics* 27, no. 1: 124–59.

Chen, Janet; Pei-Kai Cheng, Michael Lestz, and Jonathan D. Spence (2014). *The Search for Modern China: A Documentary Collection*. New York: W. W. Norton.

Chinese Human Rights Defenders (2009). "Re-education Through Labor Abuses Continue Unabated: Overhaul Long Overdue." https://www.nchrd.org/2009/02/research-reports-article-2/.

Christopher, Barbara (2004). "Understanding Georgian Politics." DEMSTAR Research Report No. 22.

Christopoulos, Georgios, ed. (1970). *Istoria tou Ellinikou Ethnous: Archaikos Ellinismos 1100–479*. Athens: Ekdotike Athinon.

Church, Clive H., and Randolph C. Head (2013). *A Concise History of Switzerland*. New York: Cambridge University Press.

Clarence-Smith, William Gervase, and Steven C. Topik, eds. (2006). *The Global Coffee Economy in Africa, Asia, and Latin America, 1500–1989*. New York: Cambridge University Press.

Clark, Christopher (2009). *Iron Kingdom: The Rise and Downfall of Prussia, 1600–1947*. Cambridge, MA: Belknap Press.

Clower, Robert W., George Dalton, Mitchell Harwitz, and A. A. Walters (1966). *Growth Without Development: An Economic Survey of Liberia*. Evanston, IL: Northwestern University Press.

Collins, Kathleen (2006). *Clan Politics and Regime Transition in Central Asia*. New York: Cambridge University Press.

Colson, Elizabeth (1962). *The Plateau Tonga of Northern Rhodesia*. Manchester: University of Manchester Press.

——— (1967). *Social Organization of the Gwembe Tonga*. Manchester: University of Manchester Press.

——— (1974). *Tradition and Contract: The Problem of Social Order*. Piscataway, NJ: Transactions.

Commins, David (2009). *The Wahhabi Mission and Saudi Arabia*. London: I.B. Tauris.

Confucius (2003). *Analects: With Selections from Traditional Commentaries*. Indianapolis: Hackett.

Constable, Pamela, and Arturo Valenzuela (1993). *A Nation of Enemies: Chile Under Pinochet*. New York: W. W. Norton.

Corancez, Louis A. O. de (1995). *The History of the Wahhabis*. Reading, UK: Garnet.

Costambeys, Marios, Matthew Innes, and Simon MacLean (2011). *The Carolingian World*. New York: Cambridge University Press.

Crick, Julia, and Elisabeth van Houts, eds. (2011). *A Social History of England, 900–1200*. New York: Cambridge University Press.

Crone, Patricia (2003). *Pre-Industrial Societies: Anatomy of the Pre-Modern World*. London: Oneworld.

Cruickshank, Brodie (1853). *Eighteen Years on the Gold Coast*. Vol. 2. London: Hurst and Blackett.

Cummings, Bruce (2005). *Korea's Place in the Sun: A Modern History*. Updated edition. New York: W. W. Norton.

Cunliffe-Jones, Peter (2010). *My Nigeria: Five Decades of Independence*. New York: St. Martin's Press.

Curtin, Philip (1995). "The European Conquest." In Philip Curtin, Steven Feierman, Leonard Thompson, and Jan Vansina, *African History: From Earliest Times to Independence*. New York: Pearson.

Dahl, Robert A. (1970). *Polyarchy*. New Haven: Yale University Press.

Dalton, George H. (1965). "History, Politics and Economic Development in Liberia," *Journal of Economic History* 25, no. 4: 569–91.

Dardess, John W. (2010). *Governing China, 150–1850*. Indianapolis: Hackett.

Davison, Lee, Tim Hitchcock, Tim Keirn, and Robert B. Shoemaker, eds. (1992). *Stilling the Grumbling Hive: Response to Social and Economic Problems in England, 1689–1750*. New York: Palgrave Macmillan.

Dawisha, Adeed (2009). *Iraq: A Political History*. Princeton, NJ: Princeton University Press.

de Gramont, Diane (2014). "Constructing the Megacity—The Dynamics of State-Building in Lagos, Nigeria, 1999–2013." Unpublished MPhil dissertation in government, University of Oxford.

Dean, Trevor (1987). *Land and Power: Ferrara Under the Este, 1350–1450*. New York: Cambridge University Press.

——— (1999). "The Rise of the Signori." In *The New Cambridge Medieval History*, edited by David Abulafia, vol. 5, *1198–1300*. New York: Cambridge University Press.

DeLong, J. Bradford, and Andrei Shleifer (1993). "Princes and Merchants: European City Growth Before the Industrial Revolution." *Journal of Law and Economics* 36, no. 2: 671–702.

Department of Justice (2015). "Investigation of the Ferguson Police Department." https://www.justice.gov/sites/default/files/opa/press-releases/attachments/2015/03/04/ferguson_police_department_report.pdf.

Deshpande, Ashwini (2011). *The Grammar of Caste: Economic Discrimination in Contemporary India.* Oxford: Oxford University Press.

Devlin, Matthew (2009). "Interview with Liliana Caballero." https://successfulsocieties.princeton .edu/interviews/liliana-caballero.

Devlin, Matthew, and Sebastian Chaskel (2009). "Conjuring and Consolidating a Turnaround: Governance in Bogotá, 1992–2003." https://successfulsocieties.princeton.edu/publications/conjuring-and -consolidating-turnaround-governance-bogot%C3%A1-1992-2003-disponible-en.

Dikshit, G. S. (1964). *Local Self-Government in Mediaeval Karnataka.* Dharwar: Karnatak University.

Dirks, Nicholas B. (2001). *Castes of Mind: Colonialism and the Making of Modern India.* Princeton, NJ: Princeton University Press.

Djilas, Milovan (1958). *Land Without Justice.* New York: Harcourt Brace Jovanovich.

——— (1966). *Njegoš.* New York: Harcourt, Brace and World.

Dogra, Chander Suta (2013). *Manoj and Babli: A Hate Story.* New York: Penguin.

Doughty, Charles M. (1888). *Travels in Arabia Deserta.* Cambridge: Cambridge University Press.

Dower, John W. (1999). *Embracing Defeat: Japan in the Wake of World War II.* New York: W. W. Norton.

Drew, Katherine Fischer (1991). *The Laws of the Salian Franks.* Philadelphia: University of Pennsylvania Press.

Dreyer, Edward L. (2006). *Zheng He: China and the Oceans in the Early Ming Dynasty, 1405–1433.* New York: Pearson.

Driscoll, Jesse (2015). *Warlords and Coalition Politics in Post-Soviet States.* New York: Cambridge University Press.

Driscoll, Mark (2010). *Absolute Erotic, Absolute Grotesque: The Living, Dead, and Undead in Japan's Imperialism, 1895–1945.* Durham, NC, and London: Duke University Press.

Duby, Georges (1982). *The Three Orders: Feudal Society Imagined.* Chicago: University of Chicago Press.

Dumont, Louis (1980). *Homo Hierarchicus: The Caste System and Its Implications.* 2nd revised edition. Chicago: University of Chicago Press.

Dunkerly, James (1988). *Power in the Isthmus: A Political History of Modern Central America.* London: Verso.

Duran, Xavier (2012). "The First US Transcontinental Railroad: Expected Profits and Government Intervention." *Journal of Economic History* 73, no. 1: 177–200.

Durham, M. Edith (1909). *High Albania.* London: Edward Arnold.

——— (1928). *Some Tribal Origins, Laws and Customs of the Balkans.* London: George Allen and Unwin.

Dutt, Romesh C. (1916). *The Economic History of India Under Early British Rule, from the Rise of the British Power in 1757 to the Accession of Queen Victoria in 1837.* London: K. Paul, Trench, Trübner.

Dym, Jordana (2006). *From Sovereign Villages to National States: City, State, and Federation in Central America, 1759–1839.* Albuquerque: University of New Mexico Press.

Easter, Gerald M. (2012). *Capital, Coercion and Postcommunist States.* Ithaca, NY: Cornell University Press.

The Economist (2012). "Don't Lie to Me, Argentina." http://www.economist.com/node/21548242.

Edgar, H. Timothy (2017). *Beyond Snowden: Privacy, Mass Surveillance, and the Struggle to Reform the NSA.* Washington, DC: Brookings Institution Press.

Edgar, Thomas (2005). *The Lawes Resolutions of Womens Rights: Or The Lawes Provision for Woemen.* London: Lawbook Exchange.

Edinger, Lewis J. (1953). "German Social Democracy and Hitler's 'National Revolution' of 1933: A Study in Democratic Leadership." *World Politics* 5, no. 3: 330–67.

Edmonds, Eric V., and Salil Sharma (2006). "Institutional Influences on Human Capital Accumulation: Micro Evidence from Children Vulnerable to Bondage." https://www.dartmouth.edu/~eedmonds /kamaiya.pdf.

Edwards, Jeremy, and Sheilagh Ogilvie (2012). "What Lessons for Economic Development Can We Draw from the Champagne Fairs?" *Explorations in Economic History* 49: 131–48.

Eich, Peter (2015). "The Common Denominator: Late Roman Bureaucracy from a Comparative Perspective." In *State Power in Ancient China and Rome,* edited by Walter Scheidel. New York: Oxford University Press.

Eldredge, Elizabeth A. (2014). *The Creation of the Zulu Kingdom, 1815–1828: War, Shaka, and the Consolidation of Power*. New York: Cambridge University Press.

Elton, Geoffrey R. (1952). *The Tudor Revolution in Government: Administrative Changes in the Reign of Henry VIII*. New York: Cambridge University Press.

Elvin, Mark (1973). *The Pattern of the Chinese Past*. Stanford, CA: Stanford University Press.

Ember, Carol (1978). "Myths About Hunter-Gatherers." *Ethnology* 17: 439–48.

Engerman, Stanley L., and Kenneth L. Sokoloff (2011). *Economic Development in the Americas Since 1500: Endowments and Institutions*. New York: Cambridge University Press.

Epstein, Stephen A. (2009). *An Economic and Social History of Later Medieval Europe, 1000–1500*. New York: Cambridge University Press.

Ertman, Thomas (1997). *Birth of the Leviathan: Building States and Regimes in Medieval and Early Modern Europe*. New York: Cambridge University Press.

Eskew, Glenn T. (1997). *But for Birmingham: The Local and National Movements in the Civil Rights Struggle*. Chapel Hill: University of North Carolina Press.

Esping-Andersen, Gosta (1985). *Politics Against Markets: The Social Democratic Road to Power*. Princeton, NJ: Princeton University Press

Evans, Richard J. (2005). *The Coming of the Third Reich*. New York: Penguin.

Evans-Pritchard, E. E., and Meyer Fortes, eds. (1940). *African Political Systems*. New York: Oxford University Press.

Falkus, Malcolm E., and John B. Gillingham (1987). *Historical Atlas of Britain*. London: Kingfisher.

Farhang, Sean (2010). *The Litigation State: Public Regulation and Private Lawsuits in the U.S.* Princeton, NJ: Princeton University Press.

Farmer, Edward (1995). *Zhu Yuanzhang and Early Ming Legislation: The Reordering of Chinese Society Following the Era of Mongol Rule*. Leiden: Brill.

Faure, David (2006). *China and Capitalism: A History of Business Enterprise in Modern China*. Hong Kong: Hong Kong University Press.

——— (2007). *Emperor and Ancestor: State and Lineage in South China*. Stanford, CA: Stanford University Press.

Fawcett, Peter (2016). "'When I Squeeze You with Eisphorai': Taxes and Tax Policy in Classical Athens." *Hesperia: The Journal of the American School of Classical Studies at Athens* 85, no. 1: 153–99.

Feinstein, Charles H. (2005). *An Economic History of South Africa: Conquest, Discrimination and Development*. New York: Cambridge University Press.

Feng, Li (2013). *Early China: A Social and Cultural History*. New York: Cambridge University Press.

Fergusson, Leopoldo, Ragnar Torvik, James A. Robinson, and Juan F. Vargas (2016). "The Need for Enemies." *Economic Journal* 126, no. 593: 1018–54.

The Fifth Report from the Select Committee on the Affairs of the East India Company (1812). New York: A. M. Kelley.

Finley, Moses I. (1954). *The World of Odysseus*. New York: Chatto & Windus.

——— (1976). "A Peculiar Institution." *Times Literary Supplement* 3887.

Flannery, Kent V. (1999). "Process and Agency in Early State Formation." *Cambridge Archaeological Journal* 9, no. 1: 3–21.

Flannery, Kent V., and Joyce Marcus (1996). *Zapotec Civilization: How Urban Society Evolved in Mexico's Oaxaca Valley*. London: Thames and Hudson.

——— (2014). *The Creation of Inequality: How Our Prehistoric Ancestors Set the Stage for Monarchy, Slavery, and Empire*. Cambridge, MA: Harvard University Press.

Fleming, Robin (2010). *Britain After Rome: The Fall and Rise, 400 to 1070*. London: Penguin.

Flynn, Henry F. (1986). *The Diary of Henry Francis Flynn*, edited by James Stuart and D. McK. Malcolm. Pietermaritzburg: Shuter and Shooter.

Fornander, Abraham (2005). *Fornander's Ancient History of the Hawaiian People to the Times of Kamehameha I*. Honolulu: Mutual Publishing.

Forsdyke, Sara (2005). *Exile, Ostracism and Democracy: The Politics of Expulsion in Ancient Greece*. Princeton, NJ: Princeton University Press.

———— (2012). *Slaves Tell Tales: And Other Episodes in the Politics of Popular Culture in Ancient Greece.* Princeton, NJ: Princeton University Press.

Fratianni, Michele, and Franco Spinelli (2006). "Italian City-States and Financial Evolution." *European Review of Economic History* 10, no. 3: 257–78.

Freedman, Maurice (1966). *Lineage Organization in Southeastern China.* London: Athlone.

———— (1971). *Chinese Lineage and Society: Fukien and Kwantung.* London: Berg.

Freedom House (2015). "The Politburo's Predicament." https://freedomhouse.org/china-2015-politiburo-predicament#.V2gYbpMrIU0.

Freeland, Chrystia (2000). *Sale of the Century: Russia's Wild Rise from Communism to Capitalism.* New York: Crown Business.

Friedberg, Aaron L. (2000). *In the Shadow of the Garrison State.* Princeton, NJ: Princeton University Press.

Fritzsche, Peter (1990). *Rehearsals for Faseism: Populism and Mobilization in Weimar Germany.* New York: Oxford University Press.

Fukuyama, Francis (1989). "The End of History?" *The National Interest* 16: 3–18.

———— (2011). *The Origins of Political Order: From Prehuman Times to the French Revolution.* New York: Farrar, Straus and Giroux.

———— (2014). *Political Order and Political Decay: From the Industrial Revolution to the Globalization of Democracy.* New York: Farrar, Straus and Giroux.

Gargarella, Roberto (2013). *Latin American Constitutionalism, 1810–2010: The Engine Room of the Constitution.* New York: Oxford University Press.

———— (2014). *The Legal Foundations of Inequality: Constitutionalism in the Americas, 1776–1860.* New York: Cambridge University Press.

Geary, Patrick J. (1988). *Before France and Germany: The Creation and Transformation of the Merovingian World.* New York: Oxford University Press.

Geary, Patrick, ed. (2015). *Readings in Medieval History.* 5th edition. Toronto: University of Toronto Press. Excerpt from Otto of Freising, *The Deeds of Frederick Barbarossa.*

Gennaioli, Nicola, and Hans-Joachim Voth (2015). "State Capacity and Military Conflict." *Review of Economic Studies* 82: 1409–48.

Gerstle, Gary (2008). "A State Both Strong and Weak." *American Historical Review* 113, no. 3: 779–85.

———— (2015). *Liberty and Coercion: The Paradox of American Government from the Founding to the Present.* Princeton, NJ: Princeton University Press.

Gies, Joseph, and Frances Gies (1994). *Cathedral, Forge and Waterwheel: Technology and Invention in the Middle Ages.* New York: HarperCollins.

Ginsburg, Tom (2011). "An Economic Analysis of the Pashtunwali." University of Chicago Legal Forum 89. https://chicagounbound.uchicago.edu/cgi/viewcontent.cgi?referer=https://www.google.com/&httpsredir=1&article=2432&context=journal_articles.

Gjeçov, Shtjefën (1989). *The Code of Lekë Dukagjini.* Translated by Leonard Fox. New York: Gjonlekaj.

Gluckman, Max (1940). "The Kingdom of the Zulu of South Africa." In *African Political Systems,* edited by Meyer Fortes and Edward E. Evans-Pritchard. London: Oxford University Press.

———— (1960). "The Rise of a Zulu Empire." *Scientific American* 202: 157–68.

Goldie, Mark (2001). "The Unacknowledged Republic: Officeholding in Early Modern England." In *The Politics of the Excluded, c. 1500–1850,* edited by Tim Harris. Basingstoke, UK: Palgrave.

Goldman, Marshall I. (2003). *The Privatization of Russia: Russian Reform Goes Awry.* New York: Routledge.

Goldthwaite, Richard A. (2009). *The Economy of Renaissance Florence.* Baltimore: Johns Hopkins University Press.

Gordon, Colin (2009). *Mapping Decline: St. Louis and the Fate of the American City.* Philadelphia: University of Pennsylvania Press.

Gorringe, Hugo (2005). *Untouchable Citizens: Dalit Movements and Democratization in Tamil Nadu.* London: Sage.

———— (2017). *Panthers in Parliament: Dalits, Caste, and Political Power in South India.* Delhi: Oxford University Press.

Gottesman, Alex (2014). *Politics and the Street in Democratic Athens.* New York: Cambridge University Press.

Gourevitch, Peter (1986). *Politics in Hard Times: Comparative Responses to International Economic Crises.* Ithaca, NY: Cornell University Press.

Graves, M. A. R. (2001). *Parliaments of Early Modern Europe: 1400–1700.* New York: Routledge.

Gregory of Tours (1974). *A History of the Franks.* New York: Penguin.

Gretsky, Sergei (1995). "Civil War in Tajikistan: Causes, Development, and Prospects for Peace." In *Central Asia: Conflict, Resolution and Change,* edited by Roald Sagdeev and Susan Eisenhower. Washington, DC: Eisenhower Institute.

Gudmundson, Lowell (1986). *Costa Rica Before Coffee: Society and Economy on the Eve of the Export Boom.* Baton Rouge: Louisiana State University Press.

—— (1997). "Lord and Peasant in the Making of Modern Central America." In *Agrarian Structures and Political Power in Latin America,* edited by A. E. Huber and F. Safford. Pittsburgh: University of Pittsburgh Press.

Gudmundson, Lowell, and Hector Lindo-Fuentes (1995). *Central America, 1821–1871: Liberalism Before Liberal Reform.* Tuscaloosa: University of Alabama Press.

Guenée, Bernard (1985). *States and Rulers in Later Medieval Europe.* Oxford: Basil Blackwell.

Habib, Irfan (1999). *The Agrarian System of Mughal India, 1556–1707.* 2nd revised edition. Delhi: Oxford University Press.

Hacker, Jacob S. (2002). *The Divided Welfare State: The Battle over Public and Private Social Benefits in the United States.* New York: Cambridge University Press.

Hall, Jonathan M. (2013). *A History of the Archaic Greek World ca. 1200–479 BCE.* 2nd edition. Malden, MA, and Oxford: Wiley Blackwell.

Hamilton, Gary G. (2006). "Why No Capitalism in China?" In *Commerce and Capitalism in Chinese Societies.* New York: Routledge.

Harari, Yuval Noah (2018). "Why Technology Favors Tyranny." *The Atlantic.* https://www.theatlantic.com/magazine/archive/2018/10/yuval-noah-harari-technology-tyranny/568330/.

Havel, Václav (1985). "The Power of the Powerless." In Václav Havel et al., *The Power of the Powerless: Citizens Against the State in Central-Eastern Europe.* London: Routledge.

Hayek, Friedrich A. (2007) *The Road to Serfdom, Text and Documents, the Definitive Edition,* edited by Bruce Caldwell. Chicago: University of Chicago Press.

Heitzman, James (1997). *Gifts of Power: Lordship in an Early Indian State.* Delhi: Oxford University Press.

Heldring, Leander, and James A. Robinson (2018). "Colonialism and Economic Development in Africa." In *The Oxford Handbook on the Politics of Development,* edited by Carol Lancaster and Nicolas van de Walle. New York: Oxford University Press.

Helfont, Samuel (2014). "Saddam and the Islamists: The Ba'thist Regime's Instrumentalization of Religion in Foreign Affairs." *Middle East Journal* 68, no. 3: 352–66.

Helle, Kurt, ed. (2008). *The Cambridge History of Scandinavia.* Vol. 1, *Prehistory to 1520.* New York: Cambridge University Press.

Herrup, Cynthia B. (1989). *The Common Peace: Participation and the Criminal Law in Seventeenth-Century England.* New York: Cambridge University Press.

Hincmar of Reims (1980). "On the Governance of the Palace." In *The History of Feudalism,* edited by David Herlihy. London: Macmillan. All quotations from 222–27.

Hindle, Steve (1999). "Hierarchy and Community in the Elizabethan Parish: The Swallowfield Articles of 1596." *The Historical Journal* 42, no. 3: 835–51.

—— (2000). *The State and Social Change in Early Modern England, 1550–1640.* New York: Palgrave Macmillan.

Hinton, Elizabeth (2016). *From the War on Poverty to the War on Crime: The Making of Mass Incarceration in America.* Cambridge, MA: Harvard University Press.

Hintze, Otto (1975). *Historical Essays of Otto Hintze.* Edited by F. Gilbert. New York: Oxford University Press.

Hirst, John B. (2009). *The Shortest History of Europe.* Melbourne: Black, Inc.

Ho, Ping-ti (1954). "The Salt Merchants of Yang-Chou: A Study of Commercial Capitalism in Eighteenth-Century China." *Harvard Journal of Asiatic Studies* 17, no. 1–2: 130–68.

Hobbes, Thomas (1996). *Leviathan: The Matter, Form, and Power of a Commonwealth, Ecclesiastical or Civil.* New York: Cambridge University Press.

Hochschild, Adam (1999). *King Leopold's Ghost: A History of Greed, Terror, and Heroism in Colonial Africa.* Boston and New York: Mariner.

Hoff, Karla (2016). "Caste System." http://documents.worldbank.org/curated/en/452461482847661084 /Caste-system.

Hoff, Karla, Mayuresh Kshetramade, and Ernst Fehr (2011). "Caste and Punishment: the Legacy of Caste Culture in Norm Enforcement." *Economic Journal* 121, no. 556: F449–F475.

Hoffman, David (2002). *The Oligarchs.* New York: Public Affairs.

Holden, Robert H. (2004). *Armies Without Nations: Public Violence and State Formation in Central America, 1821–1960.* New York: Oxford University Press.

Holt, J. C. (2015). *Magna Carta.* 3rd edition. New York: Cambridge University Press.

Holton, Sandra S. (2003). *Feminism and Democracy: Women's Suffrage and Reform Politics in Britain, 1900–1918.* New York: Cambridge University Press.

Holton, Woody (2008). *Unruly Americans and the Origins of the Constitution.* New York: Hill and Wang.

Hourani, Albert (2010). *A History of the Arab Peoples.* Cambridge, MA: Belknap Press.

Howard, Allen M. (2003). "Pawning in Coastal Northwest Sierra Leone, 1870–1910." In *Pawnship, Slavery, and Colonialism in Africa,* edited by Paul E. Lovejoy and Toyin Falola. Trenton, NJ: Africa World Press.

Huang, Philip C. C. (1998). *Civil Justice in China: Representation and Practice in the Qing.* Stanford, CA: Stanford University Press.

Huang, Yasheng (2008). *Capitalism with Chinese Characteristics.* New York: Cambridge University Press.

Hudson, John (2018). *The Formation of the English Common Law: Law and Society in England from King Alfred to the Magna Carta.* 2nd edition. New York: Routledge.

Hultzsch, Eugen (1925). *Inscriptions of Asoka.* Oxford: Clarendon Press.

Human Rights Watch (1999). "Broken People: Caste Violence Against India's Untouchables." https:// www.hrw.org/report/1999/03/01/broken-people/caste-violence-against-indias-untouchables.

———— (2008). "Perpetual Minors: Human Rights Abuses Stemming from Male Guardianship and Sex Segregation in Saudi Arabia." https://www.hrw.org/report/2008/04/19/perpetual-minors /human-rights-abuses-stemming-male-guardianship-and-sex.

———— (2016). "Boxed In: Women and Saudi Arabia's Male Guardianship System." https://www.hrw .org/report/2016/07/16/boxed/women-and-saudi-arabias-male-guardianship-system.

———— (2018). "Eradicating Ideological Viruses: China's Campaign of Repression Against Xinjiang's Muslims." https://www.hrw.org/report/2018/09/09/eradicating-ideological-viruses/chinas-campaign -repression-against-xinjiangs.

Hung, Ho-fung (2016). *The China Boom: Why China Will Not Rule the World.* New York: Columbia University Press.

Huntington, Samuel (1968). *Political Order in Changing Societies.* New Haven: Yale University Press.

Hutton, J. H. (1961). *Caste in India.* 3rd edition. New York: Oxford University Press.

Ibn Khaldun (2015). *The Muqaddimah: An Introduction to History.* Translated by Franz Rosenthal. The Olive Press.

International Monetary Fund (2016). "IMF Executive Board Removes Declaration of Censure on Argentina." https://www.imf.org/en/News/Articles/2016/11/09/PR16497-Argentina-IMF-Executive -Board-Removes-Declaration-of-Censure.

James, Edward (1988). *The Franks.* Oxford: Basil Blackwell.

Jefferson, Thomas (1904). *The Works of Thomas Jefferson.* Vol. 5. London: G. P. Putnam's Sons.

Jha, Hit Narayan (1970). *The Licchavis of Vaisali.* Varanasi: Chowkhamba Sanskrit Series Office.

Jie, Yu (2015). *Steel Gate to Freedom: The Life of Liu Xiabo.* Translated by H. C. Hsu. Lanham, MD: Rowman and Littlefield.

Jisheng, Yang (2012). *Tombstone: The Great Chinese Famine, 1958–1962*. New York: Farrar, Straus and Giroux.

John, Richard R. (1995). *Spreading the News: The American Postal System from Franklin to Morse*. Cambridge: Harvard University Press.

——— (1997). "Governmental Institutions as Agents of Change: Rethinking American Political Development in the Early Republic, 1787–1835." *Studies in American Political Development* 11, no. 2: 347–80.

Johnson, Marilynn S. (2008). *Violence in the West: The Johnson County Range War and Ludlow Massacre: A Brief History with Documents*. New York: Bedford/St. Martin's.

Johnson, Simon, and James Kwak (2010). *13 Bankers: The Wall Street Takeover and the Next Financial Meltdown*. New York: Pantheon.

Jones, A. H. M. (1964). *The Later Roman Empire, 284–602: A Social, Economic and Administrative Survey*. Oxford: Basil Blackwell.

Jones, Philip (1997). *The Italian City State*. Oxford: Clarendon Press.

Kamakau, Samuel M. (1992). *Ruling Chiefs of Hawaii*. Revised edition. Honolulu: Kamehameha Schools Press.

Kaplan, Robert D. (1994). *The Coming Anarchy: Shattering the Dreams of the Post Cold War*. New York: Vintage.

Karlson, Gunnar (2000). *The History of Iceland*. Minneapolis: University of Minnesota Press.

Karnes, Thomas L. (1961). *Failure of Union*. Chapel Hill: University of North Carolina Press.

Kautilya (1987). *The Arthashastra*. Translated by L. N. Rangarajan. New York: Penguin Books.

Keay, John (2000). *India: A History*. New York: HarperCollins.

Keeley, Lawrence H. (1996). *War Before Civilization: The Myth of the Peaceful Savage*. New York: Oxford University Press.

Kelly, Christopher (2005). *Ruling the Later Roman Empire*. Cambridge, MA: Belknap Press.

Kennedy, Hugh (2015). *The Prophet and the Age of the Caliphates: The Islamic Near East from the Sixth to the Eleventh Century*. 3rd edition. New York: Cambridge University Press.

Kepel, Gilles (2005). *The Roots of Radical Islam*. London: Saqi Books.

Kershaw, Ian (2000). *Hitler: 1889–1936: Hubris*. New York: W. W. Norton.

al-Khalil, Samir (1989). *Republic of Fear: The Politics of Modern Iraq*. Berkeley: University of California Press.

Khan, B. Zorina (2009). *The Democratization of Invention: Patents and Copyrights in American Economic Development, 1790–1920*. Chicago: University of Chicago Press.

Killick, Tony (1976). *Development Economics in Action*. London: Heinemann.

Kim, Sung Ho (2017). "Max Weber." *The Stanford Encyclopedia of Philosophy* (Winter 2017 edition), edited by Edward N. Zalta. https://plato.stanford.edu/archives/win2017/entries/weber/.

King, Desmond, and Robert C. Lieberman (2009). "Ironies of State Building: A Comparative Perspective on the American State." *World Politics* 61, no. 3: 547–88.

King, Gary, Ori Rosen, Martin Tanner, and Alexander Wagner (2008). "Ordinary Economic Voting Behavior in the Extraordinary Election of Adolf Hitler." *Journal of Economic History* 68, no. 4: 951–96.

Kirch, Patrick V. (2010). *How Chiefs Became Kings: Divine Kingship and the Rise of Archaic States in Ancient Hawai'i*. Berkeley: University of California Press.

——— (2012). *A Shark Going Inland Is My Chief: The Island Civilization of Ancient Hawai'i*. Berkeley: University of California Press.

Kirch, Patrick V., and Marshall D. Sahlins (1992). *Anahulu: The Anthropology of History in the Kingdom of Hawaii*. Vol. 1, *Historical Ethnography*. Chicago: University of Chicago Press.

Kitschelt, Herbert P. (2003). "Accounting for Postcommunist Regime Diversity: What Counts as a Good Cause?" In *Capitalism and Democracy in Central and East Europe: Assessing the Legacy of Communist Rule*, edited by Grzegorz Ekiert and Stephen E. Hanson. Cambridge: Cambridge University Press.

Kitson-Clark, G. S. R. (1951). "The Electorate and the Repeal of the Corn Laws." *Transactions of the Royal Historical Society* 1:109–26.

Knauft, Bruce (1987). "Reconsidering Violence in Simple Human Societies." *Current Anthropology* 28, no. 4: 457–500.

Kremer, Michael, Nazmul Chaudhury, F. Halsey Rogers, Karthik Muralidharan, and Jeffrey Hammer (2005). "Teacher Absence in India: A Snapshot." *Journal of the European Economic Association* 3, no. 2–3: 658–67.

Kuhn, Philip A. (1990). *Soulstealers: The Chinese Sorcery Scare of 1768*. Cambridge, MA: Harvard University Press.

Kümin, Beat (2013). *The Communal Age in Western Europe, 1100–1800*. New York: Palgrave Macmillan.

Kümin, Beat, and Andreas Würgler (1997). "Petitions, *Gravamina* and the Early Modern State: Local Influence on Central Legislation in England and Germany (Hesse)." *Parliaments, Estates and Representation* 17: 39–60.

Kuran, Timur (2012). *The Long Divergence: How Islamic Law Held Back the Middle East*. Princeton, NJ: Princeton University Press.

Kurzman, Charles (2003). "Pro-U.S. Fatwas." *Middle East Policy* 10, no. 3: 155–66. https://www.mepc.org/pro-us-fatwas.

Kurzman, Dan. (1960) *Kishi and Japan: The Search for the Sun*. New York: Ivan Obolensky.

Kuykendall, Ralph S. (1965). *The Hawaiian Kingdom, 1778–1854, Foundation and Transformation*. Honolulu, University of Hawai'i Press.

Laiou, Angeliki E., and Cécile Morrisson (2007). *The Byzantine Economy*. New York: Cambridge University Press.

Lanni, Adriaan (2016). *Law and Order in Ancient Athens*. New York: Cambridge University Press.

Lapidus, Ira M. (2014). *A History of Islamic Societies*. 3rd edition. New York: Cambridge University Press.

Larson, John Lauritz (2001). *Internal Improvement: National Public Works and the Promise of Popular Government in the Early United States*. Chapel Hill: University of North Carolina Press.

Larson, T. A. (1990). *History of Wyoming*. 2nd edition. Lincoln: University of Nebraska Press.

Leão, Delfim F., and Peter J. Rhodes (2016). *The Laws of Solon*. New York: I.B. Tauris.

Lepsius, M. Rainer (1978). "From Fragmented Party Democracy to Government by Emergency Decree and National Socialist Takeover: Germany." In *The Breakdown of Democratic Regimes: Europe*, edited by Juan J. Linz and Alfred Stepan. Baltimore: Johns Hopkins University Press.

Levinson, Daryl J. (2014). "Incapacitating the State." *William and Mary Law Review* 56, no. 1: 181–226.

Lewis, Mark Edward (2000). "The City-State in Spring-and-Autumn China." In *A Comparative Study of Thirty City-State Cultures*, edited by Mogens Herman Hansen. Historisk-filosofiske Skrifter 21. Copenhagen: Royal Danish Academy of Sciences and Letters.

——— (2011). *The Early Chinese Empires: Qin and Han*. Cambridge, MA: Harvard University Press.

——— (2012a). *China between Empires: The Northern and Southern Dynasties*. Cambridge, MA: Harvard University Press.

——— (2012b). *China's Cosmopolitan Empire: The Tang Dynasty*. Cambridge, MA: Harvard University Press.

Lewis, Oscar (1965). *Village Life in Northern India*. New York: Vintage Books.

Liddell Hart, Basil, ed. (1953). *The Rommel Papers*. New York: Harcourt, Brace.

Lim, Luisa (2014). *The People's Republic of Amnesia: Tiananmen Revisited*. New York: Oxford University Press.

Linz, Juan J. (1978). *The Breakdown of Democratic Regimes: Crisis, Breakdown and Reequilibration*. Baltimore: Johns Hopkins University Press.

Lipset, Seymour Martin (1959). "Some Social Requisites of Democracy: Economic Development and Political Legitimacy." *American Political Science Review* 53, no. 1: 69–105.

Litwack, Leon F. (2009). *How Free Is Free? The Long Death of Jim Crow*. Cambridge, MA: Harvard University Press.

Liu, Alan P. L. (1992). "The 'Wenzhou Model' of Development and China's Modernization." *Asian Survey* 32, no. 8: 696–711.

Liu, William Guanglin (2015). *The Chinese Market Economy, 1000–1500*. Albany: State University of New York Press.

Locke, John (2003). *Two Treatises of Government*. Edited by Ian Shapiro. New Haven: Yale University Press.

Loewen, James W. (2006). *Sundown Towns: A Hidden Dimension of American Racism.* New York: Touchstone.

Lopez, Robert S. (1951). "The Dollar of the Middle Ages." *Journal of Economic History* 11, no. 3: 209–34.

——— (1976). *The Commercial Revolution of the Middle Ages, 950–1350.* New York: Cambridge University Press.

Lovejoy, Paul E., and Toyin Falola, eds. (2003). *Pawnship, Slavery, and Colonialism in Africa.* Trenton, NJ: Africa World Press.

Loveman, Brian (1976). *Struggle in the Countryside: Politics and Rural Labor in Chile, 1919–1973.* Bloomington: University of Indiana Press.

Lugard, Frederick (1922). *The Dual Mandate in Tropical Africa.* London: Frank Cass.

Machiavelli, Niccolò (2005). *The Prince.* New York: Oxford University Press.

Maddicott, J. R. (2012). *The Origins of the English Parliament, 924–1327.* New York: Oxford University Press.

Mahoney, James L. (2001). *The Legacies of Liberalism: Path Dependence and Political Regimes in Central America.* Baltimore: Johns Hopkins University Press.

Majumdar, Ramesh C. (1922). *Corporate Life in Ancient India.* Poona: Oriental Book Agency.

Malaviya, H. D. (1956). *Village Panchayats in India.* New Delhi: All India Congress Committee.

Malo, David (1987). *Hawaiian Antiquities.* Honolulu: Bishop Museum Press.

Mamdani, Mahmood (1996). *Citizen and Subject: Contemporary Africa and the Legacy of Late Colonialism.* Princeton, NJ: Princeton University Press.

Mandeville, Bernard (1989). *The Fable of the Bees: Or Private Vices, Publick Benefits.* New York: Penguin.

Mann, Michael (1986). *The Sources of Social Power.* Vol. 1, *A History of Power from the Beginning to* AD *1760.* New York: Cambridge University Press.

Marchal, Guy (2006). "Die 'alpine Gesellschaft.'" In *Geschichte der Schweiz und der Schweizer.* Zurich: Schwabe.

Marongiu, Antonio (1968). *Mediaeval Parliaments: Comparative Study.* London: Eyre & Spottiswoode.

Mathew, Santhosh, and Mick Moore (2011). "State Incapacity by Design: Understanding the Bihar Story." http://www.ids.ac.uk/files/dmfile/Wp366.pdf.

Mathur, Kuldeep (2013). *Panchayati Raj: Oxford India Short Introductions.* Delhi: Oxford University Press.

Matthai, John (1915). *Village Government in British India.* London: T. Fisher Unwin.

Mazzuca, Sebastián L., and James A. Robinson (2009). "Political Conflict and Power-Sharing in the Origins of Modern Colombia." *Hispanic American Historical Review* 89: 285–321.

McAdam, Doug (1999). *Political Process and the Development of Black Insurgency, 1930–1970.* 2nd edition. Chicago: University of Chicago Press.

McCreery, David J. (1994). *Rural Guatemala, 1760–1940.* Stanford, CA: Stanford University Press.

McDonald, Forrest (2000). *States' Rights and the Union: Imperium in Imperio, 1776–1876.* Lawrence: University Press of Kansas.

McPherson, James M. (2003). *Battle Cry of Freedom: The Civil War Era.* New York: Oxford University Press.

Meier, Pauline (2011). *Ratification: The People Debate the Constitution, 1787–1788.* New York: Simon & Schuster.

Menchú, Rigoberta (1984). *I, Rigoberta Menchú.* London: Verso.

Mengzi (2008). *Mengzi: With Selections from Traditional Commentaries.* Indianapolis: Hackett.

Mettler, Suzanne (2011). *The Submerged State: How Invisible Government Policies Undermine American Democracy.* Chicago: University of Chicago Press.

Michalopoulos, Stelios, Alireza Naghavi, and Giovanni Prarolo (2018). "Trade and Geography in the Spread of Islam." *Economic Journal* 128, no. 616: 3210–41.

Miers, Suzanne, and Igor Kopytoff, eds. (1977). *Slavery in Africa: Historical and Anthropological Perspectives.* Madison: University of Wisconsin Press.

Migdal, Joel (1988). *Strong Societies and Weak States: State-Society Relations and State Capabilities in the Third World.* Princeton, NJ: Princeton University Press.

——— (2001). *State-in-Society: Studying How States and Societies Transform and Constitute One Another.* New York: Cambridge University Press.

Mill, John Stuart (1869). *The Subjection of Women*. London: Longmans, Green, Reader and Dyer.

Miller, William Ian (1997). *Bloodtaking and Peacemaking: Feud, Law, and Society in Saga Iceland*. Chicago: University of Chicago Press.

Misgeld, Klaus, Karl Molin, and Klas Amark (1988). *Creating Social Democracy: A Century of the Social Democratic Labor Party in Sweden*. University Park: Pennsylvania State University Press.

Mitchell, Stephen (2004). *Gilgamesh: A New English Version*. New York: Free Press.

Moeller, Robert G. (2010). *The Nazi State and German Society: A Brief History with Documents*. New York: Bedford/St. Martin's.

Moene, Karl-Ove, and Michael Wallerstein (1997). "Pay Inequality." *Journal of Labor Economics* 15, no. 3: 403–30.

Mokyr, Joel (1990). *The Lever of Riches*. New York: Oxford University Press.

——— (2009). *The Enlightened Economy*. New Haven: Yale University Press.

Montgomery, Fiona A. (2006). *Women's Rights: Struggles and Feminism in Britain c. 1770–1970*. Manchester: University of Manchester Press.

Mookerji, Radhakumud (1920). *Local Government in Ancient India*. Oxford: Clarendon Press.

Moore, Barrington (1966). *The Social Origins of Dictatorship and Democracy*. Boston: Beacon Press.

Morerod, Jean-Daniel, and Justin Favrod (2014). "Entstehung eines sozialen Raumes (5.–13. Jahrhundert)." In *Die Geschichte der Schweiz*, edited by Georg Kreis. Basel: Schwabe.

Morgan, Edmund S. (1975). *American Slavery, American Freedom*. New York: W. W. Norton.

Morris, Donald R. (1998). *The Washing of the Spears: The Rise and Fall of the Zulu Nation*. Boston: Da Capo Press.

Morris, Ian (1996). "The Strong Principle of Equality and the Archaic Origins of Greek Democracy." In *Demokratia: A Conversation on Democracies, Ancient and Modern*, edited by Joshua Ober and Charles Hedrick. Princeton, NJ: Princeton University Press.

——— (2010). "The Greater Athenian State." In *The Dynamics of Ancient Empires: State Power from Assyria to Byzantium*, edited by Ian Morris and Walter Scheidel. New York: Oxford University Press.

Morse, H. B. (1920). *The Trade and Administration of China*. 3rd edition. London: Longmans, Green.

Mortimer, Edward (1990). "The Thief of Baghdad." *The New York Review of Books* 37, no. 14. https://web.archive.org/web/20031014004305/http://www.nybooks.com/articles/3519.

Mote, Frederick W. (2000). *Imperial China 900–1800*. Cambridge, MA: Harvard University Press.

Mouline, Nabil (2014). *The Clerics of Islam: Religious Authority and Political Power in Saudi Arabia*. New Haven: Yale University Press.

Mueller, Reinhold C. (1997) *The Venetian Money Market: Banks, Panics, and the Public Debt, 1200–1500*. Baltimore: Johns Hopkins University Press.

Mühlberger, Detlef (2003). *The Social Bases of Nazism, 1919–1933*. New York: Cambridge University Press.

Munshi, Kaivan (2017). "Caste and the Indian Economy." http://www.histecon.magd.cam.ac.uk/km/Munshi_JEL2.pdf.

Murdock, George P. (1959). *Africa: Its Peoples and Their Culture History*. New York: McGraw-Hill.

Murray, Alexander C. (1983). *Germanic Kinship Structure*. Toronto: Pontifical Institute of Mediaeval Studies.

——— (1988). "From Roman to Frankish Gaul." *Traditio* 44: 59–100.

Myers, A. R. (1975). *Parliaments and Estates in Europe to 1789*. San Diego: Harcourt Brace Jovanovich.

Myerson, Roger B. (2004). "Political Economics and the Weimar Disaster." http://home.uchicago.edu/rmyerson/research/weimar.pdf.

Nee, Victor, and Sonja Opper (2012). *Capitalism from Below: Markets and Institutional Change in China*. New York: Cambridge University Press.

Neier, Aryeh (2012). *International Human Rights Movement: A History*. Princeton, NJ: Princeton University Press.

Nelson, Janet L. (2003). *The Frankish World, 750–900*. London: Bloomsbury Academic.

North, Douglass C., and Robert Paul Thomas (1973). *The Rise of the Western World: A New Economic History*. New York: Cambridge University Press.

North, Douglass C., John Wallis, and Barry R. Weingast (2009). *Violence and Social Orders: A Conceptual Framework for Interpreting Recorded Human History*. New York: Cambridge University Press.

Novak, William J. (1996). *The People's Welfare: Law and Regulation in Nineteenth-Century America.* Chapel Hill: University of North Carolina Press.

—— (2008). "The Myth of the 'Weak' American State." *American Historical Review* 113, no. 3: 752–72.

—— (2017). "The Myth of the New Deal State." In *Liberal Orders: The Political Economy of the New Deal and Its Opponents,* edited by N. Lichtenstein, J.-C. Vinel, and R. Huret. Forthcoming.

Novak, William J., and Steven C. A. Pincus (2017). "Revolutionary State Foundation: The Origins of the Strong American State." In *State Formations: Histories and Cultures of Statehood,* edited by J. L. Brooke, J. C. Strauss, and G. Anderson. Cambridge: Cambridge University Press.

Ober, Josiah (2005). *Athenian Legacies: Essays in the Politics of Going On Together.* Princeton, NJ: Princeton University Press.

—— (2015a). *The Rise and Fall of Classical Greece.* New York: Penguin.

—— (2015b). "Classical Athens [fiscal policy]." In *Fiscal Regimes and Political Economy of Early States,* edited by Walter Scheidel and Andrew Monson. New York: Cambridge University Press.

O'Brien, Kevin J., ed. (2008). *Popular Protest in China.* Cambridge, MA: Harvard University Press.

O'Brien, Kevin J., and Lianjiang Li (2006). *Rightful Resistance in Rural China.* New York: Cambridge University Press.

O'Donnell, Guillermo, and Philippe C. Schmitter (1986). *Transitions from Authoritarian Rule.* Baltimore: Johns Hopkins University Press.

Origo, Iris (1957). *The Merchant of Prato.* New York: Alfred A. Knopf.

Orren, Karen, and Stephen Skowronek (2004). *The Search for American Political Development.* New York: Cambridge University Press.

Osafo-Kwaako, Philip, and James A Robinson (2013). "Political Centralization in Pre-Colonial Africa." *Journal of Comparative Economics* 41, no. 1: 534–64.

Osborne, Robin (2009). *Greece in the Making 1200–479 BC.* New York: Routledge.

Ost, David (2006). *Defeat of Solidarity: Anger and Politics in Postcommunist Europe.* Ithaca, NY: Cornell University Press.

Özmucur, Süleyman, and Şevket Pamuk. (2002) "Real Wages and Standards of Living in the Ottoman Empire, 1489–1914."*Journal of Economic History* 62, no. 2: 293–321.

Paige, Jeffrey M. (1997). *Coffee and Power: Revolution and the Rise of Democracy in Central America.* Cambridge, MA: Harvard University Press.

Pamuk, Şevket (2006). "Urban Real Wages around the Eastern Mediterranean in Comparative Perspective, 1100–2000." In *Research in Economic History,* vol. 23, edited by Alexander Field, Gregory Clark, and William A. Sundstrom, 209–28. Bingley, UK: Emerald House.

—— (2014). "Institutional Change and Economic Development in the Middle East, 700–1800." In *The Cambridge History of Capitalism,* edited by Larry Neal and Jeffrey G. Williamson, vol. 1, *The Rise of Capitalism: From Ancient Origins to 1848.* New York: Cambridge University Press.

Pantos, Aliki, and Sarah Semple, eds. (2004). *Assembly Places and Practices in Medieval Europe.* Dublin: Four Courts Press.

Parry, Jonathan P. (1979). *Caste and Kinship in Kangra.* New York: Routledge.

Pascali, Luigi (2017). "The Wind of Change: Maritime Technology, Trade, and Economic Development." *American Economic Review* 107, no. 9: 2821–54.

Pattison, George. (2000). *Routledge Philosophy Guidebook to the Later Heidegger.* London: Routledge.

Pearlman, Wendy (2017). *We Crossed a Bridge and It Trembled: Voices from Syria.* New York: Custom House.

Pei, Minxin (2016). *China's Crony Capitalism: The Dynamics of Regime Decay.* Cambridge, MA: Harvard University Press.

Perham, Margery (1960). *Lugard: The Years of Adventure, 1858–1945* and *Lugard: The Years of Authority, 1898–1945.* 2 vols. London: Collins.

Perry, Elizabeth J. (2008). "Chinese Conceptions of 'Rights': from Mencius to Mao—and Now." *Perspectives on Politics* 6, no. 1: 37–50.

Pettit, Philip (1999). *Republicanism: A Theory of Freedom and Government.* New York: Oxford University Press.

—— (2014). *Just Freedom: A Moral Compass for a Complex World.* New York: W. W. Norton.

Pezzolo, Luciano (2014). "The Via Italiana to Capitalism." In *The Cambridge History of Capitalism*, edited by Larry Neal and Jeffrey G. Williamson, vol. 1, *The Rise of Capitalism: From Ancient Origins to 1848*. New York: Cambridge University Press.

Philby, Harry St. John B. (1928). *Arabia of the Wahhabis*. London: Constable.

Phillippon, Thomas, and Ariell Reshef (2012). "Wages in Human Capital in the U.S. Finance Industry: 1909–2006." *Quarterly Journal of Economics* 127:1551–1609.

Piketty, Thomas, and Emmanuel Saez (2003). "Income Inequality in the United States, 1913–1998." *Quarterly Journal of Economics* 118, no. 1: 1–41.

Pils, Eva (2014). *China's Human Right Lawyers: Advocacy and Resistance*. London: Routledge.

Pincus, Steven C. A. (2011). *1688: The First Modern Revolution*. New Haven: Yale University Press.

Pincus, Steven C. A., and James A. Robinson (2012). "What Really Happened During the Glorious Revolution?" In *Institutions, Property Rights and Economic Growth: The Legacy of Douglass North*, edited by Sebastián Galiani and Itai Sened. New York: Cambridge University Press.

—— (2016). "Wars and State-Making Reconsidered: The Rise of the Developmental State." *Annales, Histoire et Sciences Sociales* 71, no. 1: 7–35.

Pines, Yuri (2009). *Envisioning Eternal Empire: Chinese Political Thought of the Warring States Era*. Honolulu: University of Hawai'i Press.

—— (2012). *The Everlasting Empire: The Political Culture of Ancient China and Its Imperial Legacy*. Princeton, NJ: Princeton University Press.

Pinker, Steven (2011). *The Better Angels of Our Nature: Why Violence Has Declined*. New York: Penguin Books.

Pirenne, Henri (1952). *Medieval Cities: Their Origins and the Revival of Trade*. Princeton, NJ: Princeton University Press.

Plaatje, Sol (1916). *Native Life in South Africa*. London: P. S. King and Son.

Platteau, Jean-Philippe (2011). "Political Instrumentalization of Islam and the Risk of Obscurantist Deadlock." *World Development* 39, no. 2: 243–60.

—— (2017). *Islam Instrumentalized: Religion and Politics in Historical Perspective*. New York: Cambridge University Press.

Plutarch (1914). *Lives*. Vol. 1, *Theseus and Romulus. Lycurgus and Numa. Solon and Publicola*. Translated by Bernadotte Perrin. Cambridge, MA: Harvard University Press.

Pomeranz, Kenneth (2001). *China, Europe, and the Making of the Modern World Economy*. Princeton, NJ: Princeton University Press.

Pope, Nicole, and Hugh Pope (2011). *Turkey Unveiled: A History of Modern Turkey*. New York: Overlook Press.

Powell, Anton (2016). *Athens and Sparta: Constructing Greek Political and Social History from 478 BC*. 3rd edition. New York: Routledge.

Procopius (2007). *The Secret History*. New York: Penguin.

Putnam, Robert D., Robert Leonardi, and Raffaella Y. Nanetti (1994). *Making Democracy Work: Civic Traditions in Modern Italy*. Princeton, NJ: Princeton University Press.

Rattray, Robert S. (1929). *Ashanti Law and Constitution*. Oxford: Clarendon Press.

Reginald of Durham (1918). "Life of St. Godric." In *Social Life in Britain from the Conquest to the Reformation*, edited by G. G. Coulton, 415–20. Cambridge: Cambridge University Press.

Reiche, Danyel (2011). "War Minus the Shooting." *Third World Quarterly* 32, no. 2: 261–77.

Reuter, Timothy (2001). "Assembly Politics in Western Europe from the Eighth Century to the Twelfth." In *The Medieval World*, edited by Peter Linehan and Janet L. Nelson. London and New York: Routledge.

Rhodes, Peter J. (2011). *A History of the Classical Greek World: 478–323 BC*. Oxford: Wiley-Blackwell.

Ricardo, David ([1824] 1951–1973). "Defense of the Plan of Voting by Ballot." In *The Works and Correspondence of David Ricardo*, edited by Maurice H. Dobb and Piero Sraffa, vol. 5. Cambridge: Cambridge University Press.

Richards, John F. (1993). *The Mughal Empire*. New York: Cambridge University Press.

Ritter, E. A. (1985). *Shaka Zulu: The Biography of the Founder of the Zulu Nation*. London: Penguin.

Roach, Levi (2013). *Kingship and Consent in Anglo-Saxon England, 871–978: Assemblies and the State in the Early Middle Ages*. New York: Cambridge University Press.

―――― (2017). Æthelred: The Unready. New Haven: Yale University Press.

Roberts, Elizabeth (2007). Realm of the Black Mountain: A History of Montenegro. Ithaca, NY: Cornell University Press.

Roberts, Michael (1956). "The Military Revolution, 1560–1660." Reprinted with some amendments in Roberts, Essays in Swedish History. London: Weidenfeld and Nicholson.

Robertson, A. J., ed. (1925). The Laws of the Kings of England from Edmund to Henry I. Cambridge: Cambridge University Press.

Robinson, Eric W. (2011). Democracy Beyond Athens. New York: Cambridge University Press.

Robinson, James A. (2007). "Un Típico País Latinoamericano? Una Perspectiva sobre el Desarrollo." In Economía Colombiana del Siglo XX: Un Análisis Cuantitativo, edited by James A. Robinson and Miguel Urrutia Montoya. Bogotá: Fondo de Cultura Económica.

―――― (2013). "Colombia: Another 100 Years of Solitude?" Current History 112 (751), 43–48.

―――― (2016). "La Miseria en Colombia." Desarollo y Sociedad 76, no. 1: 1–70.

Rodinson, Maxime (2007). Islam and Capitalism. London: Saqi Books.

Rosenberg, Hans (1958). Bureaucracy, Aristocracy and Autocracy: The Prussian Experience. Cambridge, MA: Beacon Press.

Rothstein, Richard (2014). "The Making of Ferguson." http://www.epi.org/files/2014/making-of -ferguson-final.pdf.

―――― (2017). The Color of Law: A Forgotten History of How Our Government Segregated America. New York: Liveright.

Rowe, William T. (1984). Hankow: Commerce and Society in a Chinese City, 1796–1889. Stanford, CA: Stanford University Press.

―――― (1989). Hankow: Conflict and Community in a Chinese City, 1796–1895. Stanford, CA: Stanford University Press.

―――― (2009). China's Last Empire: The Great Qing. Cambridge, MA: Harvard University Press.

Roy, Arundhati (2014). "The Doctor and the Saint." In B. R. Ambedkar, Annihilation of Caste: The An-notated Critical Edition. London: Verso.

Roy, Kumkum (1994). The Emergence of Monarchy in North India, Eighth to Fourth Centuries B.C. Delhi: Oxford University Press.

Rubinstein, Nicolai (1958). "Political Ideas in Sienese Art: The Frescoes by Ambrogio Lorenzetti and Taddeo di Bartolo in the Palazzo Pubblico." Journal of the Warburg and Courtauld Institutes 21, no. 3–4: 179–207.

Rueschemeyer, Dietrich, Evelyn H. Stephens, and John D. Stephens (1992). Capitalist Development and Democracy. Chicago: University of Chicago Press.

Sablonier, Roger (2015). "The Swiss Confederation." In The New Cambridge Medieval History, edited by Christopher Allmand, vol. 7. New York: Cambridge University Press.

Safford, Frank (1985). "Politics, Ideology and Society in Post-Independence Spanish America." In The Cambridge History of Latin America, edited by Leslie Bethell, vol. 3, From Independence to c. 1870, 347–421. New York: Cambridge University Press.

Samuels, Richard (2003). Machiavelli's Children: Leaders and Their Legacies in Italy and Japan. Ithaca, NY: Cornell University Press.

Santos-Villagran, Rafael (2016). "Share Is to Keep: Ownership Transfer to Politicians and Property Rights in Post-Apartheid South Africa." https://sites.google.com/site/rjsantosvillagran/research.

Satyanath, Shanker, Nico Voigtländer, and Hans-Joachim Voth (2017). "Bowling for Fascism: Social Capital and the Rise of the Nazi Party." Journal of Political Economy 125, no. 2: 478–526.

Schaller, Michael (1995). "America's Favorite War Criminal: Kishi Nobusuke And the Transformation of US Japan Relations." Japan Policy Research Institute, http://www.jpri.org/publications /workingpapers/wp11.html.

Scott, James C. (2010). The Art of Not Being Governed. New Haven: Yale University Press.

Shah, Ghanshyam, Harsh Mander, Sukhadeo Thorat, Satish Deshpande, and Amita Baviskar (2006). Untouchability in Rural India. Delhi: Sage.

Shang Yang (2017). The Book of Lord Shang. Translated and edited by Yuri Pines. New York: Columbia University Press.

Sharma, J. P. (1968). *Republics in Ancient India: c. 1500 B.C.–500 B.C.* Leiden: Brill.

Sharma, Ram Sharan (2005). *Aspects of Political Ideas and Institutions in Ancient India.* 5th edition. Delhi: Motilal Banarasidass.

Shastri, K. A. Nilakanta (1997). *A History of South India: From Prehistoric Times to the Fall of Vijayanagar.* 4th edition. Delhi: Oxford University Press.

Shatzmiller, Maya (2009). "Transcontinental Trade and Economic Growth in the Early Islamic Empire: The Red Sea Corridor in the 8th–10th centuries." In *Connected Hinterlands*, edited by Lucy Blue, Ross Thomas, John Cooper, and Julian Whitewright. Oxford: Society for Arabian Studies.

Shepard, William R. (1911). *Historical Atlas.* New York: Henry Holt. (Viewed at https://archive.org /details/bub_gb_6Zc9AAAAYAAJ.)

Shirer, William L. (1960). *The Rise and Fall of the Third Reich: A History of Nazi Germany.* New York: Simon & Schuster.

Simić, Andrei (1967). "The Blood Feud in Montenegro." University of California at Berkeley, Kroeber Anthropological Society Special Publications 1.

Simon, Joshua (2017). *The Ideology of Creole Revolution.* New York: Cambridge University Press.

Simpson, Mark, and Tony Hawkins (2018). *The Primacy of Regime Survival: State Fragility and Economic Destruction in Zimbabwe.* London: Palgrave Macmillan.

Singh, Upinder (2009). *History of Ancient and Early Medieval India: From the Stone Age to the 12th Century.* Upper Saddle River, NJ: Pearson Education.

Skinner, Quentin (1986). "Ambrogio Lorenzetti: The Artist as Political Philosopher." *Proceedings of the British Academy* 72: 1–56.

——— (1999). "Ambrogio Lorenzetti's Buon Governo Frescoes: Two Old Questions, Two New Answers." *Journal of the Warburg and Courtauld Institutes* 62: 1–28.

Skocpol, Theda (1995). *Protecting Mothers and Soldiers: The Political Origins of Social Policy in the United States.* Cambridge, MA: Belknap Press.

Skowronek, Stephen (1982). *Building a New American State: The Expansion of National Administrative Capacities, 1877–1920.* New York: Cambridge University Press.

Smith, Brian K. (1994). *Classifying the Universe: The Ancient Indian Varna System and the Origins of Caste.* New York: Oxford University Press.

Smith-Dorrien, Horace (1925). *Memories of Forty-Eight Years' Service.* London: John Murray.

Sobel, Dava (2007). *Longitude.* New York: Bloomsbury.

Song, Jae, David J. Price, Fatih Güvenen, Nicholas Bloom, and Till von Wachter (2015). "Firming Up Inequality." NBER Working Paper No. 21199.

Southall, Roger (2005). "Black Empowerment and Corporate Capital." In *The State of the Nation: South Africa 2004–2005*, edited by John Daniel, Roger Southall, and Jessica Lutchman. Johannesburg. HSRC Press.

Soyinka, Wole (2006). *You Must Set Forth at Dawn.* New York: Random House.

Spence, Jonathan D. (1978). *The Death of Woman Wang.* New York: Viking Press.

——— (2012). *The Search for Modern China.* 3rd edition. New York: W. W. Norton.

——— (2014). *The Search for Modern China: A Documentary Collection.* New York: W. W. Norton.

Srinivas, M. N. (1976). *The Village Remembered.* Berkeley: University of California Press.

——— (1994). *The Dominant Caste and Other Essays.* Revised and expanded edition. Delhi: Oxford University Press.

Stafford, Pauline (1989). *Unification and Conquest: A Political and Social History of England in the Tenth and Eleventh Centuries.* New York: Hodder Arnold.

Stanger, Allison (2011). *One Nation Under Contract: The Outsourcing of American Power and the Future of Foreign Policy.* New Haven: Yale University Press.

Stein, Burton (1980). *Peasant State and Society in Medieval South India.* Delhi: Oxford University Press.

——— (1990). *Vijayanagara.* New York: Cambridge University Press.

Steinberg, Jonathan (2016). *Why Switzerland?* New York: Cambridge University Press.

Steinberg, Guido (2005). "The Wahhabi Ulama and the Saudi State: 1745 to the Present." In *Saudi Arabia in the Balance: Political Economy, Society, Foreign Affairs*, edited by Paul Aarts and Gerd Nonneman. London: Hurst.

Struve, Lynn A., ed. (1998). *Voices from the Ming-Qing Cataclysm: China in Tigers' Jaws*. New Haven: Yale University Press.

Stuart, Douglas T. (2008). *Creating the National Security State*. Princeton, NJ: Princeton University Press.

Subbarayalu, Y. (1974). *Political Geography of Chola Country*. Madras: Government of Tamil Nadu.

―――― (2012). *South India Under the Cholas*. Delhi: Oxford University Press.

Swenson, Peter A. (2002). *Capitalists Against Markets: The Making of Labor Markets and Welfare States in the United States and Sweden*. New York: Oxford University Press.

Tacitus (1970). *The Agricola and the Germania*. Translated by Harold Mattingly. London: Penguin Books. All quotations from pp. 107–12.

Thakur, Sankharshan (2006). *Subaltern Saheb: Bihar and the Making of Laloo Yadav*. New Delhi: Picador India.

Thapar, Romila (1999). *From Lineage to State: Social Formations in the Mid-First Millennium B.C. in the Ganga Valley*. New York: Oxford University Press.

―――― (2002). *Early India: From the Origins to AD 1300*. Berkeley: University of California Press.

Therborn, Goran (1977). "The Rule of Capital and the Rise of Democracy." *New Left Review* 103: 3–41.

Thompson, Augustine (2012). *Francis of Assisi: A New Biography*. Ithaca, NY: Cornell University Press.

Thompson, Leonard (2014). *A History of South Africa*. 4th edition. New Haven: Yale University Press.

Tilly, Charles, ed. (1975). *The Formation of National States in Western Europe*. Princeton, NJ: Princeton University Press.

Tilly, Charles (1992). *Coercion, Capital and European States*. Oxford: Basil Blackwell.

―――― (1995). *Popular Contention in Great Britain, 1758 to 1834*. London: Paradigm.

Tocqueville, Alexis de (2002). *Democracy in America*. Translated and edited by Harvey C. Mansfield and Delba Winthrop. Chicago: University of Chicago Press.

Todd, Malcolm (2004). *The Early Germans*. 2nd edition. Oxford: Wiley-Blackwell.

Tognato, Carlos, ed. (2018). *Cultural Agents RELOADED: The Legacy of Antanas Mockus*. Cambridge, MA: Harvard University Press.

Tooze, Adam (2015). *The Deluge: The Great War, America and the Remaking of the Global Order, 1916–1931*. New York: Penguin.

Treadgold, Warren (1997). *A History of the Byzantine State and Society*. Stanford, CA: Stanford University Press.

Treisman, Daniel (2011). *The Return: Russia's Journey from Gorbachev to Medvedev*. New York: Free Press.

Turner, Frederick Jackson (1921). *The Frontier in American History*. New York: Holt.

Turner, Thomas (2007). *The Congo Wars: Conflict, Myth and Reality*. London: Zed Books.

Uberoi, J. P. Singh (1962). *Politics of the Kula Ring: An Analysis of the Findings of Bronislaw Malinowski*. Manchester: University of Manchester Press.

Urban, Michael, Vyacheslav Igrunov, and Sergei Mitrokhin (1997). *The Rebirth of Politics in Russia*. New York: Cambridge University Press.

Uribe, Simón (2017). *Frontier Road: Power, History, and the Everyday State in the Colombian Amazon*. New York: Wiley.

Valenzuela, Arturo (1978). *The Breakdown of Democratic Regimes: Chile*. Baltimore: Johns Hopkins University Press.

Valenzuela, Arturo, and Alexander Wilde (1979). "Presidential Politics and the Decline of the Chilean Congress." In *Legislatures in Development: Dynamics of Change in New and Old States*, edited by Joel Smith and Lloyd D. Musolf. Durham, NC: Duke University Press.

van Wees, Hans (2013). *Ships and Silver, Taxes and Tribute: A Fiscal History of Archaic Athens*. New York: I.B. Tauris.

Vassiliev, Alexei (2013). *The History of Saudi Arabia*. London: Saqi Books.

Veluhat, Kesavan (1993). *The Political Structure of Early Medieval South India*. Delhi: Orient Blackswan.

von Glahn, Richard (2016). *The Economic History of China: From Antiquity to the Nineteenth Century*. New York: Cambridge University Press.

Wade, Robert H. (1988). *Village Republics: Economic Conditions for Collective Action in South India*. New York: Cambridge University Press.

Wakeman, Frederic, Jr. (1986). *The Great Enterprise: The Manchu Reconstruction of Imperial Order in Seventeenth-Century China*. 2 vols. Berkeley: University of California Press.

—— (1993). "The Civil Society and Public Sphere Debate: Western Reflections on Chinese Political Culture." *Modern China* 19, no. 2: 108–38.

—— (1998). "Boundaries of the Public Sphere in Ming and Qing China." *Daedalus* 127, no. 3: 167–89.

Waley, Daniel (1991). *Siena and the Sienese in the Thirteenth Century*. New York: Cambridge University Press.

Waley, Daniel, and Trevor Dean (2013). *The Italian City-Republics*. 4th edition. New York: Routledge.

Wallace-Hadrill, J. M. (1971). *Early Germanic Kingship in England and on the Continent*. New York: Oxford University Press.

—— (1982). *The Long-haired Kings and Other Studies in Frankish History*. Toronto: University of Toronto Press.

Wang, Hsien-Chun (2015). "Mandarins, Merchants, and the Railway: Institutional Failure and the Wusong Railway, 1874–1877." *International Journal of Asian Studies* 12, no. 1: 31–53.

Watson, Andrew M. (1983). *Agricultural Innovation in the Early Islamic World*. New York: Cambridge University Press.

Watson, James L. (1982). "Chinese Kinship Reconsidered: Anthropological Perspectives on Historical Research." *The China Quarterly* 92 (December 1982): 589–622.

Watt, W. Montgomery (1953). *Muhammad at Mecca*. Oxford: Clarendon Press.

—— (1956). *Muhammad at Medina*. Oxford: Clarendon Press.

—— (1961). *Muhammad: Prophet and Statesman*. New York: Oxford University Press.

Watts, John (2009). *The Making of Polities: Europe, 1300–1500*. New York: Cambridge University Press.

Weber, Eugen (1976). *Peasants into Frenchmen*. Stanford, CA: Stanford University Press.

Weber, Max (1946). *From Max Weber: Essays in Sociology*. Edited by Hans H. Gerth and C. Wright Mills. New York: Oxford University Press.

—— (1978). *Economy and Society: An Outline of Interpretive Sociology*. 2 vols. Edited by Guenther Roth and Claus Wittich. Berkeley: University of California Press.

—— (2001). *The Protestant Ethic and the Spirit of Capitalism*. Translated by Talcott Parsons. New York: Routledge.

Weiner, Tim (2008). *Legacy of Ashes: The History of the CIA*. New York: Random House.

—— (2012). *Enemies: A History of the FBI*. New York: Random House.

Werlich, David P. (1978). *Peru: A Short History*. Carbondale: Southern Illinois University Press.

Wheatley, Jonathan (2005). *Georgia from National Awakening to Rose Revolution: Delayed Transition in the Former Soviet Union*. New York: Routledge.

Wickham, Christopher (2009). *The Inheritance of Rome*. New York: Penguin.

—— (2015). *Sleepwalking into a New World: The Emergence of Italian City Communes in the Twelfth Century*. Princeton, NJ: Princeton University Press.

—— (2016). *Medieval Europe*. New Haven: Yale University Press.

—— (2017). "Consensus and Assemblies in the Romano-Germanic Kingdoms." *Vorträge und Forschungen* 82: 389–426.

Wilks, Ivor (1975). *Asante in the Nineteenth Century: The Structure and Evolution of a Political Order*. New York: Cambridge University Press.

Williams, Ann (1999). *Kingship and Government in Pre-Conquest England c. 500–1066*. London: Palgrave.

—— (2003). *Athelred the Unready: The Ill-Counselled King*. New York: St. Martin's Press.

Williams, Gavin, and Terisa Turner (1978). "Nigeria." In *West Africa States: Failure and Promise*, edited by John Dunn. New York: Cambridge University Press.

Williams, Robert G. (1994). *States and Social Evolution: Coffee and the Rise of National Governments in Central America*. Chapel Hill: University of North Carolina Press.

Winkler, H. A. (2006). *Germany: The Long Road West*. Vol. 1, *1789–1933*. New York: Oxford University Press.

Wiser, William H. (1936). *The Hindu Jajmani System*. Delhi: Munshiram Manoharlal.

Wiser, William H., and Charlotte Wiser (2000). *Behind Mud Walls: Seventy-five Years in a North Indian Village*. Berkeley: University of California Press.

Witsoe, Jeffrey (2013). *Democracy Against Development*. Chicago: University of Chicago Press.

Wittfogel, Karl (1957). *Oriental Despotism: A Comparative Study of Total Power*. New Haven: Yale University Press.

Wolfram, Herwig (2005). *The Roman Empire and Its Germanic Peoples*. Berkeley: University of California Press.

Wollstonecraft, Mary (2009). *A Vindication of the Rights of Woman and A Vindication of the Rights of Men*. New York: Oxford University Press.

Wong, R. Bin (1997). *China Transformed: Historical Change and the Limits of European Experience*. Ithaca, NY: Cornell University Press.

Wood, Ian (1990). "Administration, Law and Culture in Merovingian Gaul." In *The Uses of Literacy in Early Mediaeval Europe*, edited by Rosamond McKitterick. Cambridge: Cambridge University Press.

——— (1994). *The Merovingian Kingdoms, 450–751*. Harlow, UK: Pearson Education.

Woodward, C. Vann (1955). *The Strange Career of Jim Crow*. New York: Oxford University Press.

Woodward, Ralph L., Jr. (1965). "Economic and Social Origins of Guatemalan Political Parties (1773–1823)." *Hispanic American Historical Review* 45, no. 4: 544–66.

——— (1991). "The Aftermath of Independence, 1821–1870." In *Central America Since Independence*, edited by Leslie Bethell, 1–36. New York: Cambridge University Press.

——— (2008). *Rafael Carrera and the Emergence of the Republic of Guatemala, 1821–1871*. Athens: University of Georgia Press.

World Bank (2005). *Bihar: Towards a Development Strategy*. New Delhi: World Bank.

Wortman, Miles L. (1982). *Government and Society in Central America, 1680–1840*. New York: Columbia University Press.

Wright, Gavin (1986). *Old South, New South: Revolutions in the Southern Economy Since the Civil War*. New York: Basic Books.

Wright, John, and Carolyn Hamilton (1989). "Traditions and Transformations: The Phongolo-Mzimkhulu Region in the late Eighteenth and Early Nineteenth Centuries." In *Natal and Zululand: From Earliest Times to 1910: A New History*, edited by Andrew Duminy and Bill Guest. Durban: University of Natal Press.

Wright, Mary C. (1957). *The Last Stand of Chinese Conservatism*. Stanford, CA: Stanford University Press.

Xiao, Jianhua (2007). "Review on the Inefficiency and Disorganization of Judicial Power: Consideration on the Development of Civil Proceedings." *Frontiers of Law in China* 2, no. 4: 538–62.

Xunzi (2016). *Xunzi: The Complete Text*. Princeton, NJ: Princeton University Press.

Yashar, Deborah J. (1997). *Demanding Democracy: Reform and Reaction in Costa Rica and Guatemala, 1870s–1950s*. Stanford, CA: Stanford University Press.

Zelin, Madeleine (1984). *The Magistrate's Tael: Rationalizing Fiscal Reform in Eighteen Century Ch'ing China*. Berkeley: University of California Press.

——— (2005). *The Merchants of Zigong: Industrial Entrepreneurship in Early Modern China*. New York: Columbia University Press.

Zürcher, Erik Jan (1984). *The Unionist Factor. The Role of the Community of Union and Progress in the Turkish National Movement, 1905–1926*. Leiden: Brill.

——— (2004). *Modern Turkey: A History*. London: I.B. Tauris.

Zyoob, Mohammed, and Hasan Kosebalaban, eds. (2009). *Religion and Politics in Saudi Arabia: Wahhabism and the State*. Boulder, CO: Lynne Rienner.

PHOTO INSERT CREDITS

page 1: AGIP - Rue des Archives / Granger, NYC—All Rights Reserved.

page 2: Holmes Collection, Rare Book and Special Collection Division, Library of Congress

page 3, top: Album / Art Resource, NY; *bottom:* Paul Bohannan, from *The Tiv: An African People 1949–1953* by Paul Bohannan and Gary Seaman (Ethnographics Press, 2000)

page 4, top: AP Photo/Hassan Ammar; *bottom:* Dixson Galleries, State Library of New South Wales / Bridgeman Images

page 5, top: Palazzo Pubblico, Siena, Italy / De Agostini Picture Library / A. De Gregorio / Bridgeman Images; *bottom:* Palazzo Pubblico, Siena, Italy / De Agostini Picture Library / G. Dagli Orti / Bridgeman Images

page 6, top: Photo courtesy Linda Nicholas; *bottom:* Historic Images / Alamy Stock Photo

page 7, top: Detail of the Bayeux Tapestry—11th Century, with special permission from the City of Bayeux; *bottom:* Bettmann/Getty Images

page 8, top: David Bliss Photography; *bottom: Xunzi jian shi* 荀子柬釋 [*Xunzi*, with selected notes], edited by Qixiong Liang 梁啓雄 (Shanghai: The Commercial Press 商務印書館, 1936), page 100

page 9, top: Ed Jones / AFP / Getty Images; *bottom:* RAJAT GUPTA/EPA-EFE/Shutterstock

pages 10–11: Courtesy Mapping Inequality

page 12: © James Rodriguez/Panos Pictures

page 13, top: Schalkwijk / Art Resource, NY; *bottom:* CPA Media—Pictures from History / GRANGER—All rights reserved.

page 14, top: AP Photo/Ali Haider; *bottom:* robertharding / Alamy Stock Photo

page 15, top: David Rogers / Getty Images Sport Classic / Getty Images; *bottom:* Akintunde Akinleye/REUTERS

page 16, top: All rights reserved. Copyright CASA EDITORIAL EL TIEMPO S.A.; *bottom:* UN Photo/Cia Pak

INDEX